COLLECTED WORKS OF ERASMUS

VOLUME 31

COLLECTED WORKS OF
ERASMUS

ADAGES

Ii1 TO Iv100

translated by Margaret Mann Phillips

annotated by R.A.B. Mynors

University of Toronto Press

Toronto / Buffalo / London

The research and publication costs of the
Collected Works of Erasmus are supported by the
Social Sciences and Humanities Research Council of Canada
(and previously by the Canada Council).
The publication costs are also assisted by
University of Toronto Press.

Canadian Cataloguing in Publication Data
Erasmus, Desiderius, ca. 1466–1536.
Collected works of Erasmus
Contents: v.31. Adages I i 1 TO I v 100
ISBN 0-8020-2373-8 (v. 31)
1. Erasmus, Desiderius, ca. 1466–1536.
I. Phillips, Margaret Mann.
II. Mynors, R.A.B., Sir: 1903–
PA8500 1974   876'.04   C74-6326-X

Collected Works of Erasmus

The aim of the Collected Works of Erasmus
is to make available an accurate, readable English text
of Erasmus' correspondence and his
other principal writings. The edition is planned
and directed by an Editorial Board, an Executive Committee,
and an Advisory Committee.

Contents

Annotator's Foreword

The purpose of the notes is to identify the sources on which Erasmus drew, and to show how his collections increased and fresh comments suggested themselves from the *Adagiorum Collectanea* of his Paris days (1500) into the Aldine Chiliades of 1508 and its successive revisions published in Basel in 1515, 1517/8, 1520, 1523, 1528, 1530, 1533 and 1536. To pursue the use made of individual adages in the vernacular literatures and in the graphic arts would have been the task of a lifetime; it is the aim of this version to serve as a tool to workers in those larger fields.

This first volume should not be judged in isolation. It is the intention of the Editorial Board to conclude the *Adagia* with an introductory volume (CWE 30), in which it is hoped to trace the progress of the work in its compiler's hands, to relate it to the printed sources available to him (which might well constitute a survey of the appearance in print of all classical literature), and to say something of the printed editions and summaries of the *Adagia* and of its relation to similar collections made by others. There will also be the necessary indexes. And that will be the place to acknowledge the immense debt which these notes must owe, not only to living scholars, but to the army of textual editors and compilers of commentaries, dictionaries, and concordances, without whom they could never have been put together.

The collecting of material for the notes of the whole work was greatly assisted by the tenure of a Longman Visiting Fellowship in the University of Leeds.

The Editorial Board and University of Toronto Press are pleased for the opportunity to express once again their gratitude to the patron of the Collected Works of Erasmus, the Social Sciences and Humanities Research Council of Canada, for its generous support of the research and publication costs of the edition.

RABM

Translator's Foreword

The Latin of the first five hundred of the *Adagia* is for the most part clear and presents few unusual difficulties of interpretation. Apart from the intrinsic challenge of the Erasmian style, the problems that confront the translator are those which result from the development and design of the book: its history over nearly forty years of Erasmus' life, and its primary intention of familiarizing the reader, particularly the Greekless reader, with the great authors of antiquity.

The first *Collectanea* of 1500 (818 adages) contained only the germ of the subsequent developments, though it was important as one of the first books issued by the Paris presses to print some words of Greek. The *Adagiorum Chiliades* of 1508 was virtually a new book, containing 3260 adages with long comments and a large proportion of Greek passages. The Froben edition of 1515, envisaging a wider public, added both new adages and long commentaries and offered Latin translation of all the Greek. The process of enrichment was continued in the 1517/18 edition and each of the six editions up to 1536 brought its quota of additions and insertions, until at Erasmus' death the number of adages was 4151.[1]

The text used for this translation is the longest form of the work as left by Erasmus in 1536 and published in the *Opera omnia* of 1540, reproduced in the Leclerc edition of 1704, but with correction of errors in these editions. To avoid breaking the flow of the text, a record of the continuous growth of the work is given in the Annotator's notes: these display the vigilant care taken by Erasmus in correcting his work as edition succeeded edition, showing how he expanded it by adding new quotations or paragraphs, clarified his meaning (sometimes by the change of a single word) verified his references and added more precise ones, and achieved the final form of the work which it is the principal purpose of this translation to present. His attention to the

* * * * *

1 On the history of the *Adagia*, see Margaret Mann Phillips *The 'Adages' of Erasmus* (Cambridge: Cambridge University Press 1964).

task increased rather than lessened: many of the insertions and corrections appear in the last two editions of his life.

This translation should be considered as the work of a team. Accuracy was saved time and again by Sir Roger Mynors, and Erika Rummel was a vigilant reader. Ruth Harvey worked on a collation of the ten editions. Special thanks are due to Virginia Callahan, who translated the Greek passages. The *Adagia* being, among other things, an anthology, the translator is faced with a special problem: are the Greek passages to be translated from the originals or from the Latin versions supplied by Erasmus? His decision to render the Greek verse into Latin verse necessarily implied some modification, and this has on occasion been respected. In the Latin authors some modern versions have been adopted with grateful recognition.

But the *Adagia* is much more than an anthology: it is a collection of essays on topics ranging through textual criticism, archaeological discussion, social comment and personal reminiscence. An ideal translation would attempt to reproduce his own style, its variety, its casual conversational tone and occasional raciness, changing at times into serious eloquence and deeply-felt statement of belief. It would have to take account of the individualism and freedom of his pen, his play with diminutives and puns, his concealed humour, his confidence in the reader. But to capture all this would be a counsel of perfection. What Erasmus means is never in doubt; the art of saying it is a secret of his own.

MMP

ADAGES

Ii1 TO Iv100

[Introduction]

i / What a proverb is

A proverb, according to Donatus, is 'a saying which is fitted to things and times.' Diomedes however defines it as follows: 'A proverb is the taking over of a popular saying, fitted to things and times, when the words say one thing and mean another.' Among Greek authors various definitions are to be found. Some describe it in this way: 'A proverb is a saying useful in the conduct of life, with a certain degree of obscurity but of great value in itself.' Others define it like this: 'A proverb is a manner of speaking which wraps up in obscurity an obvious truth.' I am quite aware that several other definitions of the word proverb exist in both Latin and Greek, but I have not thought it worth while to list them all here, first because I propose as far as possible, in this work especially, to follow the advice of Horace about the brevity required of a teacher; secondly because they all tell the same tale and come back to the same point; but above all because among all these definitions there is not one to be found which covers the character and force of proverbs so as to contain nothing unnecessary and leave nothing diminished in importance.

Setting aside other things for the present, it seems that Donatus and

* * * * *

i
2 A proverb] In these definitions 'proverb' represents the Greek *paroemia* in Latin dress (which is much used in this introduction), and 'saying' is the Latin *proverbium*, which Erasmus uses normally in the *Adagia* when he does not use *adagium*. They come from two well-known sources, the *Ars grammatica* of Donatus 3.6 (*Grammatici latini* ed H. Keil, 4, Leipzig 1864, 402) and of Diomedes 2 (ibid 1, 1857, 462).
5 Greek authors] These definitions are close to those offered by the *Etymologicum magnum* 654.15 (ed Venice 1499) and Suidas II 733, but are not quite the same.
12 Horace] *Ars poetica* 335–6 'Whate'er you teach, be terse; what's brief and plain, / Your readers may learn fast, and long retain.'

Diomedes regard it as essential for any proverb to have some kind of
envelope; in fact they make it into a sort of allegory. They also expect it to   20
contain something *gnomic*, didactic, since they add 'fitted to things and
times.' The Greeks too, in all their definitions, introduce either helpfulness
in the conduct of life, or the outer covering of metaphor, and sometimes they
join the two together. Yet you will find many observations quoted as
proverbs by writers of unshakeable authority which are not hidden in   25
metaphor, and not a few which have no bearing at all on instruction in
living, and are diametrically (as they say) opposed to the nature of a
sententia or aphorism. Two examples out of many will suffice. *Ne quid nimis*,
Nothing to excess [1 vi 96], is accepted by everybody as an adage, but it
is not in the least disguised. And *Quis aberret a foribus?*, Who could miss the   30
gate? [1 vi 36], is given the name of proverb by Aristotle, but I cannot see how
it can be useful for the conduct of life. Again, not every proverb is clothed in
allegory, as Quintilian makes clear when he says in the fifth book of his
Institutions: 'Allied to this is that type of proverb which is like a short form of
fable.' This indicates clearly that there are other kinds of proverb, which do   35
not come close to allegory. I would not deny however that the majority of
adages have some kind of metaphorical disguise. I think the best of them are
those which equally give pleasure by their figurative colouring and profit by
the value of their ideas.

But it is one thing to praise the proverb and show which kind is best,   40
and quite another to define exactly what it is. I myself think (*pace* the
grammarians) that a complete definition and one suitable to our present
purpose may be reached by saying: 'A proverb is a saying in popular use,
remarkable for some shrewd and novel turn.' The logicians agree that there
are three parts to a definition, and here we have them: the word 'saying'   45
indicates the genus, 'in popular use' the *differentia* or species, and 'remarkable for some shrewd and novel turn' the particular characteristic.

ii / What is the special quality of a proverb, and its limits

There are then two things which are peculiar to the character of a proverb,
common usage and novelty. This means that it must be well known and in
popular currency; for this is the origin of the word *paroimia* in Greek (from
oimos, a road, as though well polished in use and circulating), that which   5
travels everywhere on the lips of men, and of *adagium* in Latin, as if you

* * * * *

31 Aristotle] *Metaphysics* 1A.1 (993b5)
33 Quintilian] *Institutio oratoria* 5.11.21; Erasmus returns to this in II ix 84.

should say 'something passed round,' following Varro. And then it must be shrewd, so as to have some mark, as it were, to distinguish it from ordinary talk. But we cannot immediately rank in this category everything which has passed into popular speech, or contains an unusual image; it must be 10 recommended by its antiquity and erudition alike, for that is what I call shrewd. What confers originality on adages I intend to explain soon; at present I shall say a few words about the many ways in which a proverb can achieve a popular circulation.

Proverbs get into popular speech, either from the oracles of the gods, 15 like 'Neither the third nor the fourth' [II i 79], or from the sayings of sages, which indeed circulated in Antiquity as if they were oracles, such as 'Good things are difficult' [II i 12]. Or else they come from some very ancient poet, as for instance Homer's 'When a thing is done, a fool can see it' [I i 30], or Pindar's 'To kick against the goad' [I iii 46], or from Sappho 'No bees, no 20 honey' [I vi 62]; for at a time when tongues were as yet uncorrupted, the verses of the poets were also sung at feasts. Or they may come from the stage, that is, from tragedies and comedies, like this from Euripides: 'Upwards flow the streams' [I iii 15], or this from Aristophanes: 'Off with you to the crows!' [II i 96]. It is comedy especially which by a mutual give-and-take 25 adopts many of the expressions in constant use among the common people, and in turn gives birth to others which are passed on to them for constant use. Some are derived from the subjects of legend, such as the great jar that cannot be filled from the story of the daughters of Danaus [I iv 60], or the helmet of Orcus from the tale of Perseus [II x 74]. Some arise from fables, 30 among which we find 'But we see not what is in the wallet behind' [I vi 90]. Occasionally they are born from an actual occurrence: 'Leucon carries some things, his ass carries others' [II ii 86]. Several are borrowed from history: 'Rome wins by sitting still' [I x 29]. Others come from *apophthegms*, that is from quick witty replies, like that remark 'Who does not own himself would 35 Samos own' [I vii 83]. There are some which are snatched from a word rashly spoken, such as 'Hippocleides doesn't care' [I x 12]. In a word, the behaviour, the natural qualities of any race or individual, or even of an animal, or lastly any power belonging even to a thing, if remarkable and commonly known –

* * * * *

ii
7 Varro] In his *De lingua latina* 7.31 the greatest antiquarian of republican Rome, without a shadow of probability, had connected *adagio* (a form of the word which Erasmus sometimes uses) with an invented word *ambagio*, from *ambi*, an old Italian word meaning 'around,' because an adage 'gets around,' and is not confined to a single application. Erasmus exchanges *ambi* for the more familiar *circum*, and produces *circumagium*, 'something passed round.'

all these have given occasion for an adage. Examples of this are 'Syrians   40
against Phoenicians' [I viii 56], *accissare* [II ii 99] which means to refuse coyly
what you mean to accept, 'A fox takes no bribes' [I x 18], 'Twice-served
cabbage is death' [I v 38], and 'The Egyptian clematis' [I i 22].

iii / What produces novelty in a proverb

I have already mentioned novelty, and this is by no means a simple matter.
For sometimes this is produced by the thing itself, as in 'Crocodile tears'
[II iv 60]; sometimes the metaphor provides it, since the adage may adopt all
kinds of figurative variations, which need not be followed up one by one. I   5
will touch only on those which it most frequently assumes. Metaphor is
nearly always present, but it embraces many forms. Allegory is no less
frequent, though to some people this also is a kind of metaphor. An example
of the first is 'Everything is in shallow water' [I i 45], of the second 'The wolf's
jaws are gaping' [II iii 58]. Hyperbole is not infrequent, as in 'As bare as a   10
snake's sloughed skin' [I i 26]. Sometimes it goes as far as a riddle which,
according to Quintilian, is nothing but a more obscure allegory, as in 'The
half is more than the whole' [I ix 95]. Sometimes an allusion gives the
proverb its attraction, as in 'Keep it up' [II iv 28]; and 'Two heads together'
[III i 51]; and 'The good or ill that's wrought in our own halls' [I vi 85].   15
Occasionally the dialect or idiom itself, the particular significance of a word,
gives it a resemblance to a proverb, for instance 'An Ogygian disaster' [II ix
50] for an immense one. It happens sometimes that sheer ambiguity gives
grace to a proverb: of this sort are 'An ox on the tongue' [I vii 18] and 'Like
Mys in Pisa' [II iii 67–8]. The point of this is that 'ox' means both an animal   20
and a coin, and in the same way Mys, the Greek for 'mouse,' is the name of
an animal and also of an athlete, and Pisa, the name of a town, needs only
one letter added to give *pissa*, the Greek for 'pitch.' Sometimes the very
novelty of an expression is what makes it into a proverb, like 'Wine speaks

* * * * *

iii
12 Quintilian] 8.6.52
13 an allusion] The three examples given are all intended to evoke in the reader's
   mind a scene from Homer.
19 An ox on the tongue] A man is silent, either because he feels suppressed by
   some great weight (of influence, anxiety, etc), heavy as an ox, or because he
   has been bribed (and the ox or bull is an early coin-type).
20 Mys in Pisa] With very little alteration in the Greek, this can mean either a
   mouse stuck in some pitch, or the athlete Mys, competing at Pisa where the
   Olympic games were held.
24 Wine speaks the truth] Literally, In wine is truth.

the truth' [I vii 17], for if you say 'Men speak their minds when drunk,' it will   25
not look like a proverb. Similarly, if you say 'Desire fails without food and
drink,' this has not the look of an adage; but say 'Without Ceres and Bacchus
Venus grows cold' [II iii 97], and everyone will recognize the adage-form.
But of course this kind of novelty, like every other, comes from the
metaphor. Age sometimes lends attractions too, as in 'Stand surety, and   30
ruin is at hand' [I vi 97]. Once again, in proverbs you will find humour in all
its forms. But to follow out these points in detail might seem to be industry
misapplied. However, I shall say rather more later on about proverbial
metaphors.

iv / How the proverb differs from those forms that
seem to approach it closely

There are however some near neighbours to the proverb, for instance
gnômai, which are called by us *sententiae* or aphorisms, and *ainoi*, which
among us are called fables; with the addition of *apophthegmata*, which may be   5
translated as quick witty sayings, as well as *skômmata* or facetious remarks,
and in a word anything which shelters behind a kind of mask of allegory or
any other figure of speech associated with proverbs. It is not difficult to
distinguish these from the proverb itself, if one knows how to test them
against our definition as against a measure or rule; but in order to satisfy the   10
inexperienced as well, I am quite willing to explain more crudely and 'with
crass mother-wit' as the saying goes, so as to make it quite clear what my
purpose has been in this work. In the first place, the relationship between
the aphorism and the proverb is of such a nature that each can be joined to
the other or again each can be separated from the other, in the same way as   15
with 'whiteness' and 'man.' Whiteness is not ipso facto man, nor man
inevitably whiteness; but there is nothing to prevent what constitutes a man
being also white. Thus it not infrequently happens that an aphorism in-
cludes a proverb, but a proverb need not automatically become an aphorism
or vice versa. For instance 'The miser lacks what he has as well as what he   20

* * * * *

30 Age] Because the adage chosen is one of the three said to have been per-
manently written up in the sanctuary at Delphi from early times.

iv
12 saying] I i 37
20 For instance] The examples given are Publilius Syrus (compiler of moral
maxims, each occupying a single iambic line, of uncertain date) T 3, cited by
Quintilian 8.5.6; and Ovid *Amores* 1.15.39, which comes again in II vii 11 and
III x 96.

has not' and 'Ill-will feeds on the living but is quiet after death' are aphorisms, but not for that reason adages. On the other hand, 'I navigate in harbour' [I i 46] is a proverb but not an aphorism. Again, 'Put not a sword into the hand of a child' [II v 18] partakes of the nature of both proverb and aphorism, and of allegory as well. There were those, especially among the Greeks, who 25 willingly undertook the task of making *gnomologies*, collections of aphorisms, notably Johannes Stobaeus. I would rather praise their work than imitate it.

Now to consider the rest. Aphthonius in the *Progymnasmata* calls the *ainos* simply *mythos*, a fable. It has, as he says, various secondary names, 30 taken from the inventors: Sybarite, Cilician, Cyprian, Aesopic. Quintilian says that the Greeks call it a *logos mythikos* or apologue, 'and some Latin authors an apologation, a name which has not gained general currency.' He agrees that the fable is close to the proverb, but says that they are to be distinguished by the fact that the *ainos* is a whole story, and the proverb is 35 shorter 'like a fable in miniature.' As an example he gives 'Not my burden: pack-saddle on the ox' [II ix 84]. Hesiod used it in this way: 'Now will I tell the princes a fable, though they know it well: the hawk thus addressed the tuneful nightingale.' Archilochus and Callimachus use it in the same way, although Theocritus in the *Cyniscae* seems to have used 'tale' for a proverb: 40 'In truth a certain tale is told: the bull went off into the wood' [I i 43].

As for apophthegms, they are differentiated from proverbs in the same way as aphorisms. Just as the phrase 'Who does not own himself would Samos own' [I vii 83] is at the same time both an adage and an apophthegm,

* * * * *

27 Joannes Stobaeus] Compiler of a valuable florilegium, about the year 500 AD, which Erasmus uses in the *Adagia*, but never saw in print. From *1520* onwards his first name was given as Nicolaus.

29 Aphthonius] A technical writer on rhetoric, of the fourth/fifth centuries AD; *Progymnasmata* 1 (21). This was printed in the Aldine *Rhetores graeci* of 1508. His 'secondary names' are expounded in the preface to the proverb-collection ascribed to Diogenianus.

31 Quintilian] *Institutio oratoria* 5.11.20. The manuscripts of Quintilian give the adage which he quotes in the form *vos clitellas*; both here and in II ix 84 Erasmus gives this in *1508*, and in *1515* changes *vos* to *bos*. Editors of Quintilian attribute this emendation to Paris and Lyons texts of 1531.

37 Hesiod] *Works and Days* 202–3

39 Archilochus] A poet of the seventh century BC; frag 174 West, and Callimachus (scholar and poet of the third century BC) frag 194.6–8 Pfeiffer; both passages are quoted in the preface to the proverb-collection called Diogenianus. Erasmus adds Theocritus 14.43, where the word *ainos* is again used of a beast-fable; this he will use again in I i 43.

so that remark of Simonides to someone who was silent at a banquet 'if you   45
are a fool you are doing a wise thing, but if you are wise a foolish one,' and
that well-known saying 'Caesar's wife must not only be innocent, she must
be above suspicion' are apophthegms but not also proverbs. Also 'You are
used to sitting on two stools' [I vii 2] is both a proverb and an insult.
Conversely 'My mother never, my father constantly.' That phrase of Turo-   50
nius, 'They are at the mills,' is a savage jest, but not also an adage. But there
are some of this sort so aptly put that they can easily be ranked as adages,
like 'I'm your friend as far as the altar' [III ii 10]. Here we have brevity,
aphorism and metaphor all together. I have emphasized this at somewhat
too great length, so that no one may expect to find in this book anything but   55
what falls into the category of proverbs, and to prevent anyone from thinking that an omission is the result of negligence, when I have left it on one
side deliberately and on purpose, as not pertaining to the subject.

v / Proverbs are to be respected for their value

Now in case anyone should impatiently thrust aside this aspect of learning
as too humble, perfectly easy and almost childish, I will explain in a few
words how much respect was earned by these apparent trivialities among
the Ancients; and then I will show what a sound contribution they can   5
make, if cleverly used in appropriate places, and finally how it is by no means
everyone who can make the right use of proverbs. To start with, that an

* * * * *

45 Simonides] Of Ceos, the eminent lyric poet, who flourished c500 BC, had a
   reputation in later centuries for winged remarks, many of them no doubt
   apocryphal; this one is from Plutarch *Moralia* 644F.
47 Caesar's wife] The source of this is also Plutarch: *Caesar* 10.6; *Moralia* 206B, and
   elsewhere.
49 an insult] Cicero had complained of close seating in the theatre; the retort
   suggested, not only that he was used to having more space but that he had a
   habit of temporizing politically between two parties.
50 Conversely] Erasmus illustrates his point with two replies made to the Emperor
   Augustus, recorded by Macrobius (see I i 12n) *Saturnalia* 2.4.20 and 28 to
   illustrate the emperor's tolerance of such retorts. A visitor to Rome from the
   provinces resembled him so closely that it was thought he must be Augustus'
   blood-relation. 'Tell me, young man,' said the emperor: 'was your mother ever
   in Rome?' And the man deftly threw back the imputation on his mother's
   chastity by replying: 'My mother never, my father constantly.' Turonius was
   the owner of a band of slave musicians, whose performance pleased Augustus,
   but was rewarded in kind, with a gift of bread-corn, instead of in cash as usual.
   When he commanded another performance, the impresario replied: 'I'm sorry,
   sire; they're all busy grinding.'

acquaintance with adages was held to be not unimportant by the greatest
men is sufficiently proved, I think, by the fact that authors of the first
distinction have thought them a worthy subject for a number of volumes   10
diligently compiled. The first of these is Aristotle, so great a philosopher of
course that he alone may stand for many others. Laertius tells us that he
left one volume of *Paroimiai*. Chrysippus also compiled two volumes on
proverbs, addressed to Zenodotus. Cleanthes wrote on the same subject. If
the works of these men were still extant, it would not have been necessary   15
for me to fish up some things with such labour out of these insignificant
writers, who were both careless and textually most corrupt. Some collections of proverbs are to be found under the name of Plutarch, but they are
few in number and almost bare of comment. Often cited among compilers of
proverbs, by Athenaeus in his *Deipnologia* among others, are Clearchus of   20
Soli, a pupil of Aristotle, and Aristides, and after them Zenodotus, who

* * * * *

v
10 number of volumes] More will be said on the Greek proverb-collectors in the
   introductory volume of this version of the *Adagia* (CWE 30).
11 Aristotle] A reference to the list of his works in Diogenes Laertius 5.26
13 Chrysippus] Of Soli, the eminent Stoic (second half of third century BC)
   compiled several books *On Proverbs*, of which eight fragments are collected by
   H. von Arnim *Stoicorum veterum fragmenta*, Leipzig 1903–5, 3.202. Erasmus
   incorporates six of these.
14 Cleanthes] Another Stoic; von Arnim 1.103–39
18 Plutarch] His name is found attached to more than one of the smaller
   collections, and one was published under his name by Otto Crusius in two
   Tübingen programmes of 1887 and 1895 (reprinted Hildesheim 1961); but it is
   not thought that any of them are his. Erasmus gives his name to nearly fifty,
   most of them in the third Chiliad.
20 Athenaeus] His *Deipnosophistae* ('Doctors at Dinner') was a major source for the
   Adagia, and Erasmus' own copy of the first edition, Aldus 1514, which survives
   at Oxford in the Bodleian Library, is heavily annotated. The title given to it
   here, which is quite unorthodox, is taken from Athenaeus 1.4e, where it
   belongs to a poem on gastronomy, or from Suidas A731. For the minor collectors
   mentioned by him, of whom little is known, see the relevant section of our
   introductory volume (CWE 30).
21 a pupil of Aristotle, and Aristides] These words, and the sentence on the
   proverbs of Theophrastus which follows, were inserted in *1517/8* and *1515*
   respectively.
21 Zenodotus] Zenobius seems to be the right name; Erasmus never closed his
   mind to the question, and recurs to it in *Adagia* III vi 88; see our introductory
   volume. While awaiting a new edition of the Greek proverb collections,
   without which all is dark, we use the name Zenobius, and refer by it to the
   major text published by F.G. Schneidewin in the first volume of the *Corpus*

reduced to a compendium the proverbs of Didymus and Tarrhaeus. In the brief scholia on Demosthenes proverbs of Theophrastus are also quoted. This makes it clear that these writers too left collections on this subject. I am aware that this work is in circulation under the name of Zenobius. But as I find that in the scholiast on Aristophanes there are some things attributed to that very Zenodotus who summarized Didymus and Tarrhaeus which are to be found word for word in this man's collections, I hope I shall not be blamed if in this work I adduce him, whatever his name was (for what does it matter?), under the name of Zenodotus. This writer refers among others to a certain Milo as a collector of proverbs. One Daemon is also quoted, by many others and particularly by the person who explained a number of words and phrases in the speeches of Demosthenes; he appears to have composed many books of proverbs, since book 40 is quoted. There are also extant the collections of Diogenianus. Hesychius states in his preface that he has given a fuller explanation of the proverbs which had been briefly enumerated by Diogenianus; but the work itself seems to conflict with the prologue, since the earlier writer claims to give a list of the authors and the subjects of the proverbs, while the later is so brief that nothing shorter could be imagined. From this I conjecture that this work was produced in a fuller form by the

* * * * *

Paroemiographorum (Göttingen 1839). The reference to Didymus and Tarrhaeus is taken by Erasmus from the Zenobius-text published by Aldus in his Aesop of 1505.

31 Daemon] The mention of him was added to twice: 'by many others ... Demosthenes' and 'of proverbs' were inserted in 1517/8, and 'he appears ... is quoted' had been added in 1515.

35 Diogenianus] This means the form of the collection that passed under this name which is printed by Schneidewin in the volume already referred to. It was the source of almost all the Greek in the Collectanea; therefore Erasmus had access to it while he was still in Paris, and we can identify the text he used with a copy (Oxford, Bodleian Library MS Grabe 30) which belonged to Georgius Hermonymus, from whom Erasmus had Greek lessons in Paris, or with a transcript of it (more likely the latter, as the Grabe text is in a very crabbed hand). Hermonymus made a transcript of his Diogenianus for Guillaume Budé, which is also in the Bodleian, MS Laud gr 7.

35 Hesychius] Of Alexandria (fifth century AD) compiled a lexicon of rare words, which survives in a single late manuscript, Venice Marcianus gr 522, which was used by Marcus Musurus as printer's copy for the Aldine edition of 1514. Here 'Hesychius ... another hand' was inserted in 1517/8. Kurt Latte discusses Erasmus' problem on pp lx–lxi of the first volume of his new edition (Copenhagen 1953–), and decides that Hesychius' copy of Diogenianus had an abbreviated text.

author, and contracted into a summary by another hand. Suidas, who must himself be placed in this category, mentions a certain Theaetetus as having written a work on proverbs. But why should I be talking of these people, when the Hebrew sages themselves did not hesitate to bring out more than one book with this title, and to enclose the venerable mysteries of the   45
unsearchable deity in proverbs which the intellects of so many and such great theologians have struggled to elucidate, as they are struggling to this day?

It is no light argument too that among good authors it was the most learned and eloquent who sprinkled their books most freely with adages. To   50
begin with the Greeks, who is a greater master of proverbs, so to call it, than the great, not to say the divine, Plato? Aristotle, otherwise a grave philosopher, is always ready to interweave frequent proverbs, like jewels, into his discussions. As in other things, so in this, Theophrastus imitates him. As for Plutarch, a serious, religious-minded writer, not to say austere, how he   55
scatters proverbs plentifully everywhere! Nor was he averse to bringing forward and discussing certain proverbs among his 'Problems,' and in this he was following the example of Aristotle. To turn to Latin, setting aside grammarians and poets in both kinds (unless it is thought that among these we should count Varro, who gave proverbial titles to his *Menippean Satires*,   60
so that there is general agreement that he borrowed the subjects of his fables from no other source than proverbs), the rulers of Rome did not think it was demeaning the imperial majesty to reply in proverbs when they were consulted on great topics, as can be found even now in the *Digest*: 'Not everything, nor everywhere, nor from everybody' [II iv 16].   65

* * * * *

41 Suidas] This should properly be 'the *Suda*' (it may mean 'treasure-house'), but Erasmus, in common with all scholars down to very recent times, treated Suidas as the personal name of the compiler, and we have thought it would be unhistorical not to do as he did. It is an immense alphabetical compilation of the tenth century AD, published in Milan in 1499 and by the Aldine press in February 1514. One of the sources was a collection of proverbs, and Erasmus makes much use of it. It mentions Theaetetus' work at o 806.

60 Varro] Marcus Terentius Varro (116–27 BC), whom we have already met as author of the *De lingua latina* (see ii 7n), wrote as part of a voluminous output a series of *Menippean Satires* (taking their name from the third-century Cynic philosopher Menippus), of which we know little more than the titles. Many of these were adapted from proverbs, and it is not surprising that Erasmus should refer to the *Satires* in the *Adagia* over thirty times. The fragments, most of them from the lexicographer Nonius, are collected by F. Buecheler in his *Petronii saturae* (Berlin 1922) 177–250.

64 Digest] The compilation of the opinions of Roman jurists, published on the orders of the emperor Justinian in AD 533. Erasmus, who had read parts of it, at

Then who would dare to despise this mode of speech, when he saw that some of the oracles of the holy prophets are made of proverbs? One example of this is 'The fathers have eaten sour grapes, and the children's teeth are set on edge.' Who would not revere them as an almost holy thing, fit to express the mysteries of religion, since Christ Himself, whom we ought   70 to imitate in all things, seems to have taken a particular delight in this way of speaking? An adage is current in Greek: 'I judge the tree by its fruit' [I ix 39]. In Luke we read the same thing: 'A good tree bringeth not forth corrupt fruit, neither doth a corrupt tree bring forth good fruit.' In Greek, Pittacus the philosopher sent an enquirer to watch boys playing with tops, so as to   75 learn proverbial wisdom from them about taking a wife, and heard: 'Stick to your own' [I viii 1]. Christ cites a proverb from children playing in the market-place: 'We have piped to you and you have not danced; we have mourned to you, and you have not wept.' This is very like that saying in Theognis, if one may compare sacred with profane: 'For Jove himself may   80 not content us all, / Whether he holds rain back or lets it fall' [II vii 55].

If a motive is to be found in reverence for antiquity, there appears to be no form of teaching which is older than the proverb. In these symbols, as it were, almost all the philosophy of the Ancients was contained. What were the oracles of those wise old Sages but proverbs? They were so deeply   85 respected in old time, that they seemed to have fallen from heaven rather than to have come from men. 'And *Know thyself* descended from the sky' [I vi 95] says Juvenal. And so they were written on the doors of temples, as worthy of the gods; they were everywhere to be seen carved on columns and marble tablets as worthy of immortal memory. If the adage seems a tiny   90 thing, we must remember that it has to be estimated not by its size but by its value. What man of sane mind would not prefer gems, however small, to

* * * * *

least, with care, usually calls it *Pandects*, the title in Greek, and gives the name of the lawyer (Ulpian more often than any) whose view he is quoting. Ulpian here (*Digest* 1.16.6.3) cites an imperial rescript on the question how far, if at all, an official is allowed to receive gifts.

68 The fathers] Jeremiah 31:29; Ezekiel 18:2

73 Luke] 6:43

74 Pittacus] One of the Seven Sages. The boys, as they whipped their tops, called to each other to get out of the way; the man who was looking for a wife heard this as advice to stick to his own station in life.

77 proverb] Luke 7:32

80 Theognis] 25–6; a sixth-century BC moralist (in elegiac couplets) referred to in the *Adagia* fifty times. Aldus published the first edition in 1495/6.

88 Juvenal] 11.27; in *1508* he was merely referred to as 'the satyrist,' but the quotation was given more fully and ascribed to him in *1523*.

immense rocks? And, as Pliny says, the miracle of nature is greater in the most minute creatures, in the spider or the gnat, than in the elephant, if only one looks closely; and so, in the domain of literature, it is sometimes the   95
smallest things which have the greatest intellectual value.

vi / The many uses of a knowledge of proverbs

It remains for me to show briefly how proverbs have an intrinsic usefulness no less than the respect in which they were formerly held. A knowledge of proverbs contributes to a number of things, but to four especially: philosophy, persuasiveness, grace and charm in speaking, and the understanding   5
of the best authors.

To begin with, it may seem surprising that I should have said that proverbs belong to the science of philosophy; but Aristotle, according to Synesius, thinks that proverbs were simply the vestiges of that earliest philosophy which was destroyed by the calamities of human history. They   10
were preserved, he thinks, partly because of their brevity and conciseness, partly owing to their good humour and gaiety; and for that reason are to be looked into, not in sluggish or careless fashion, but closely and deeply: for underlying them there are what one might call sparks of that ancient philosophy, which was much clearer-sighted in its investigation of truth than   15
were the philosophers who came after. Plutarch too in the essay which he called 'On How to Study Poetry' thinks the adages of the Ancients very similar to the rites of religion, in which things which are most important and even divine are often expressed in ceremonies of a trivial and seemingly almost ridiculous nature. He suggests that these sayings, brief as they are,   20
give a hint in their concealed way of those very things which were pro-
pounded in so many volumes by the princes of philosophy. For instance, that proverb in Hesiod 'The half is more than the whole' [I ix 95] is exactly what Plato in the *Gorgias* and in his books *On the State* tries to expound by so many arguments: it is preferable to receive an injury than to inflict one. What   25
doctrine was ever produced by the philosophers more salutary as a principle of life or closer to the Christian religion? But here is a principle clearly of the

* * * * *

93 Pliny] *Naturalis historia* 11.2–4

vi
8 Aristotle] Frag 13 Rose, cited by Synesius (fourth-century bishop of Ptolemais) *Calvitiae encomium* 22 (*PG* 66.1204B)
16 Plutarch] *Moralia* 35F–36A, from memory; the passages of Plato referred to are *Gorgias* 473 and *Republic* in several places.

greatest importance enclosed in a minute proverb, 'The half is more than the whole.' For to take away the whole is to defraud the man to whom nothing is left; on the other hand, to accept the half only is to be in a sense defrauded   30 oneself. But it is preferable to be defrauded than to defraud. Again, anyone who deeply and diligently considers that remark of Pythagoras 'Between friends all is common' [I i 1] will certainly find the whole of human happiness included in this brief saying. What other purpose has Plato in so many volumes except to urge a community of living, and the factor which creates   35 it, namely friendship? If only he could persuade mortals of these things, war, envy and fraud would at once vanish from our midst; in short a whole regiment of woes would depart from life once and for all. What other purpose had Christ, the prince of our religion? One precept and one alone He gave to the world, and that was love; on that alone, He taught, hang all   40 the law and the prophets. Or what else does love teach us, except that all things should be common to all? In fact that united in friendship with Christ, glued to Him by the same binding force that holds Him fast to the Father, imitating so far as we may that complete communion by which He and the Father are one, we should also be one with Him, and, as Paul says, should   45 become one spirit and one flesh with God, so that by the laws of friendship all that is His is shared with us and all that is ours is shared with Him; and then that, linked one to another in the same bonds of friendship, as members of one Head and like one and the same body we may be filled with the same spirit, and weep and rejoice at the same things together. This is   50 signified to us by the mystic bread, brought together out of many grains into one flour, and the draught of wine fused into one liquid from many clusters of grapes. Finally, love teaches how, as the sum of all created things is in God and God is in all things, the universal all is in fact one. You see what an ocean of philosophy, or rather of theology, is opened up to us by this tiny   55 proverb.

vii / Proverbs as a means to persuasion

If it is not enough to understand something oneself, but one wishes to persuade others, to be furnished with proverbs is by no means unhelpful, as Aristotle himself makes sufficiently clear by classifying proverbs as evidence

* * * * *

40 He taught] Matthew 22:40
45 Paul] Ephesians 4:4

vii
4 Aristotle] *Rhetoric* 1.15 (1376a1)

more than once in his principles of rhetoric: 'for instance,' he says, 'if one 5
wishes to persuade someone not to make close friends with an old man, he
will use as evidence the proverb that one should never do an old man a
kindness' [1 x 52], and again, if one were to argue that he who has killed the
father should slay the children also, he will find this proverb useful: 'He's a
fool who kills the father and leaves the children' [1 x 53]. How much weight 10
is added to the power of persuasion by supporting evidence is common
knowledge. Aphorisms too are of no small use; but under evidence Aristotle
also classes proverbs. Quintilian too in his *Institutions* also mentions
proverbs in several places as conducive to good speaking in more ways than
one. For in book 5 he joins proverbs with examples and allots them equal 15
force; and he rates the force of examples very high. Again in the same book
he classes proverbs under the type of argument called in Greek *kriseis*,
authoritative assertions, which are very frequently used and of no mean
power to persuade and move. It may be better to quote Quintilian's actual
words: 'Popular sayings which command general assent will also be found 20
not without value as supporting material. In a way they carry even more
weight because they have not been adapted to particular cases but have been
said and done by minds exempt from hatred or partiality for no reason
except their evident connection with honour or truth.' And a little further
on: 'Those things too which command general assent seem to be, as it were, 25
common property from the very fact that they have no certain author.
Examples are "Where there are friends, there is wealth" [1 iii 24] and "Conscience is a thousand witnesses" [1 x 91] and in Cicero "Like readily comes
together with like as the old proverb has it" [1 ii 20]; for these would not have
lived for ever if they did not seem true to everyone.' Thus far I have retailed 30
the words of Quintilian. The same author, a little later, makes the oracles of
the gods follow proverbs as though they were closely related. And what of
Cicero? Does he not use a proverb in the *Pro Flacco* to destroy the credibility
of witnesses? The proverb in question is 'Risk it on a Carian' [1 vi 14]. Does he
not in the same speech explode the integrity in the witness-box of the whole 35
race of Greeks with this one proverb: 'Lend me your evidence' [1 vii 95]?
Need I mention the fact that even philosophers in person are always supporting their arguments with proverbs? No wonder then if historians often
seek to support the truth of their narrative by means of some adage. So true
is it that what vanishes from written sources, what could not be preserved 40

* * * * *

13 Quintilian] *Institutio oratoria* 5.11.37 and 41
33 Cicero] *Pro L. Flacco* 27.65 and 4.9. 'Support me now, and in return I will give
   evidence for you when required, true or false.'

by inscriptions, colossal statues and marble tablets, is preserved intact in a proverb, if I may note by the way this fresh reason to praise adages.

And then St Jerome shows no reluctance in confirming a Gospel maxim with the help of a common proverb: 'A rich man is either wicked himself or the heir of a wicked man' [I ix 47]. Even Paul himself does not   45 scorn to use proverbs as evidence in some passages, and not without cause. For if τὸ πιθανόν, the power to carry conviction, holds the first place in the achievement of persuasion, what could be more convincing, I ask you, than what is said by everyone? What is more likely to be true than what has been approved by the consensus, the unanimous vote as it were, of so many   50 epochs and so many peoples? There is, and I say it again, in these proverbs some native authentic power of truth. Otherwise how could it happen that we should frequently find the same thought spread abroad among a hundred peoples, transposed into a hundred languages, a thought which has not perished or grown old even with the passing of so many centuries,   55 which pyramids themselves have not withstood? So that we see the justice of that saying, 'Nothing is solider than truth.' Besides, it happens (how, I cannot tell) that an idea launched like a javelin in proverbial form strikes with sharper point on the hearer's mind and leaves implanted barbs for meditation. It will make far less impression on the mind if you say 'Fleeting   60 and brief is the life of man' than if you quote the proverb 'Man is but a bubble' [II iii 48]. Lastly, what Quintilian writes about laughter, when he says that the greatest difficulties in pleading a case, which cannot be solved by any arguments, can be evaded by a jest, is particularly applicable to the proverb.   65

viii / Decorative value of the proverb

It hardly needs explaining at length, I think, how much authority or beauty is added to style by the timely use of proverbs. In the first place who does not see what dignity they confer on style by their antiquity alone? And then, if there is any figure of speech that can confer breadth and sublimity on   5 language, any again that contributes to grace of expression, if finally there is any reason for humour, a proverb, being able normally to adapt itself to all kinds of rhetorical figures and all aspects of humour and wit, will of course contribute whatever they are wont to contribute and on top of that will add its own intrinsic and peculiar charm. And so to interweave adages deftly and   10 appropriately is to make the language as a whole glitter with sparkles from

* * * * *

62 Quintilian] 6.3.8–9

Antiquity, please us with the colours of the art of rhetoric, gleam with jewel-like words of wisdom, and charm us with titbits of wit and humour. In a word, it will wake interest by its novelty, bring delight by its concision, convince by its decisive power. 15

ix / The proverb as an aid to understanding literature

Even if there were no other use for proverbs, at the very least they are not only helpful but necessary for the understanding of the best authors, that is, the oldest. Most of these are textually corrupt, and in this respect they are particularly so, especially as proverbs have a touch of the enigmatic, so that 5 they are not understood even by readers of some learning; and then they are often inserted disconnectedly, sometimes even in a mutilated state, like 'Upwards flow the streams' [I iii 15]. Occasionally they are alluded to in one word, as in Cicero in his *Letters to Atticus*: 'Help me, I beg you; "prevention," you know,' where he refers to the proverb 'Prevention is better than cure' 10 [I ii 40]. Thus a great darkness is cast by these if they are not known, and again they throw a great deal of light, once they are understood. This is the cause of those monstrous mistakes in both Greek and Latin texts; hence the abominable errors of translators from Greek into Latin; hence the absurd delusions of some writers, even learned ones, in their interpretation of 15 authors, mere ravings in fact. Indeed, I would mention some of these here and now, if I did not think it more peaceable and more suited to my purpose to leave everyone to draw his own conclusions, after reading my notes, as to the extent to which writers of great reputation have sometimes fallen into wild error. And then it sometimes happens that an author makes a con- 20 cealed allusion to a proverb; and if it escapes us, even though the meaning will seem clear, yet ignorance of the proverb will take away a great part of our pleasure. That remark in Horace is of this type: 'A horse to carry me, a king to feed me' [I vii 20]. And in Virgil: 'And Camarina shows up far away, / Ne'er to be moved; so have the fates decreed' [I i 64]. In one of these is the 25 proverb 'A horse carries me, a king feeds me,' in the other 'Move not Camarina.'

* * * * *

viii
15 convince ... power] These words were added in *1517/8*.

ix
9 Cicero] *Ad Atticum* 10.10.3
25 In one of these ... Camarina] This sentence was added in *1515*.

x / The difficulty of proverbs calls for respect

If according to the proverb 'Good things are difficult' [II i 12], and the things
which seem easy are scorned and held cheap by the popular mind, let no
one imagine it is so simple a task either to understand proverbs or to
interweave them into discourse, not to mention myself and how much   5
sweat this work has cost me. Just as it requires no mean skill to set a jewel
deftly in a ring or weave gold thread into the purple cloth, so (believe me) it
is not everyone who can aptly and fittingly insert a proverb into what he has
to say. You might say of the proverb with justice what Quintilian said of
laughter, that it is a very risky thing to aim for. For in this kind of thing, as in   10
music, unless you put on a consummate performance, you would be ridiculous, and you must either win the highest praise or be a laughingstock.

xi / How far the use of adages is advisable

In the light of all this I will point out to what extent and in which ways adages
should be used. In the first place, it is worth remembering that we should
observe the same rule in making use of our adages as Aristotle elegantly
recommended in his work on rhetoric with regard to the choice of epithets: 5
that is to say, we should treat them not as food but as condiments, not to
sufficiency but for delight. Then we must not insert them just where we like;
there are some places where it would be ridiculous to put jewels, and it is
equally absurd to apply an adage in the wrong place. Indeed, what Quintilian teaches in the eighth book of his *Institutions* about the use of aphorisms   10
can be applied in almost exactly the same terms to proverbs. First, as has
been said, we must not use them too often. Overcrowding prevents them
from letting their light shine, just as no picture catches the eye in which
nothing is clear in profile, and so artists too, when they bring several figures
together in one picture, space them out so that the shadow of one body does   15
not fall on another. For every proverb stands by itself, and for that reason
must anyway be followed by a new beginning. This often causes the writing
to be disconnected, and because it is put together from bits and pieces, not
articulated, it lacks structure. And then it is like a purple stripe, which gives

* * * * *

x
9 Quintilian] Perhaps a reminiscence of 6.3.6–7

xi
4 Aristotle] *Rhetoric* 3.3.3. (1406a19)
9 Quintilian] *Institutio oratoria* 8.5.7

an effect of brilliance in the right place; but a garment with many stripes in   20
the weave would suit nobody. There is also another disadvantage, that the
man who sets out to use proverbs frequently is bound to bring in some that
are stale or forced; choice is not possible when the aim is numbers. Finally,
when anything is exaggerated or out of place, charm is lost. In letters to
one's friends, however, it will be permissible to amuse oneself in this way a   25
little more freely; in serious writing they should be used both more sparingly
and with more thought.

xii / The varied use of proverbs

Here I think it is not beside the point to indicate shortly the ways in which
the use of proverbs can vary, so that you can put forward the same adage
now in one shape and now in another. To begin with, there is no reason why
you should not occasionally fit the same wording with different meanings,   5
as for instance 'A great jar with holes' [1 x 33] can be applied to forgetfulness,
extravagance, miserliness, futility or ingratitude: whatever you have told to
a forgetful person slips from the mind, with the spendthrift nothing lasts, a
miser's greed is insatiable, a silly chatterer can keep nothing to himself, a gift
to an ungrateful man is lost. Sometimes a saying can be turned ironically to   10
mean the opposite: if you are speaking of an arrant liar, you can say Listen to
the oracle 'straight from the tripod' [1 vii 90]. Occasionally it happens that the
change of one small word may make the proverb fit several meanings: for
instance 'Gifts of enemies are no gifts' [i iii 35] can be shifted to fit gifts from
the poor, from flatterers, from poets; for presents from an enemy are   15
believed to bring ruin, and when poor people, sycophants or poets give
anything away, they are fortune-hunting rather than giving. In a word, you
may freely arrange this comparison in any way which it will fit. This method
applies to almost every instance where a transference is made from a person
to a thing or vice versa. Here is an example, applied to a person. 'The   20
proverb says Not even Hercules can take on two [1 v 39]; but I am Thersites
rather than Hercules; how can I answer both?' It can be twisted to refer to a
thing in this way: 'Not even Hercules can take on two; how can I stand up to
both illness and poverty?' Or the proverb can be turned the other way, as in
'It is said Not even Hercules can take on two; and do you dare to stand up   25
against two Herculeses?' Or in this way: 'It is the opposite of the familiar

* * * * *

xii
7 ingratitude] The reference to the ungrateful man here and at the end of the
sentence was added in 1517/8.

Greek proverb [I ix 30]: I expected coals and I have found treasure.' And: 'I have exchanged, not gold for bronze but, quite simply, bronze for gold' [I ii 1]. Sometimes the adage is explained and held up for comparison, sometimes it is an allegory pure and simple which is related. Occasionally even a truncated form is offered, as when you might say to a person whose answer was quite off the point 'Sickles I asked for' [II ii 49], and in Cicero 'Make the best of it' [IV ii 43]. At times it is enough to make an allusion with a single word, as when Aristotle says that 'all such men are potters to one another' [I ii 25]. There are other methods of varying the use of proverbs; but if anyone wishes to follow them out more closely, he may get what he wants from my compilation *De duplici copia*.

xiii / On proverbial metaphors

It remains to set to work on the task of making a catalogue of proverbs, but after first pointing out some proverbial metaphors. For there are some sayings which do not much resemble proverbs at first sight, and some take a proverbial shape, so that they can easily be added to the category of proverbs. Generally speaking, every aphorism approaches the genus proverb, and in addition metaphor and in particular allegory, and among these especially such as are taken from important fields which are generally familiar, such as seafaring and war. Examples of these are: to sail with a following wind, to be shipwrecked, to turn one's sails about, to hold the tiller, to bale out the bilge-water, to spread one's sails to the wind and to take in sail. And these: to give the signal to attack, to fight at the sword's point, to sound the retreat, to fight at long range or hand to hand, to set to, to join battle, and hundreds of others of the same kind, which only need to be drawn out a little to assume the form of a proverb. In the same way there are those which are taken from well-known things and exceedingly familiar in everyday experience, as for instance whenever there is a transference from the physical to the mental, as to turn the thumb down (to show support), to wrinkle one's brow (to take offence), to snarl (to be displeased), to clear one's brow (to grow cheerful). And there are those which come from the bodily senses: to smell out (to get to know), to taste (to investigate). They normally have the look of a proverb about them, whenever expressions peculiar to the arts are used in another sense, as 'the double diapason' from music, 'diametrically' from geometry (another instance is 'words half a yard long'), 'to put it back on the anvil' from blacksmiths, 'by rule' from stone-masons, 'I haven't done a stroke' from painters, 'to add a last act' from the stage. Sometimes without metaphor a tacit allusion contributes something of a proverbial nature. Such an allusion will be most successful when it

concerns an author or fact very famous and known to everybody, Homer for
instance in Greek and Virgil in Latin. An example of this is that phrase in   30
Plutarch: 'Since many good men and true are here to support Plato.' The
allusion is to a liturgical custom: at a sacrifice the priest would say 'Who's
here?' and the assembled company would reply 'Many good men and true.'
Then there is that phrase in Cicero's *Letters to Atticus*: 'Two heads together'
and in Lucian 'the sons of physic' used for physicians.   35

There is also a resemblance to proverbs in those expressions often
met with in pastoral poetry, the impossible, the inevitable, the absurd,
likenesses and contraries. The impossible is like this: 'But it were equal
labour to measure the waves on the seashore,' and in Virgil: 'Ere this the
light-foot stag shall feed in air, / And naked fish be beach-strewn by the sea.' 40
The inevitable like this: 'While boars love mountain-crests and fish the
streams,' and in Seneca: 'While turn the lucid stars of this old world.' An
example of the absurd: 'Let him yoke foxes too and milk he-goats.' An
instance of contraries: 'E'en the green lizards shelter in the brakes; / But I – I
burn with love,' and so in Theocritus: 'The waves are silent, silent are the   45
gales, / But in my breast nothing will silence care.' Of likeness: 'Wolf chases
goat, and in his turn is chased / By the fierce lioness,' and in Theocritus: 'The
goat pursues the clover, and the wolf pursues the goat.'

There are two other formulae very close to the proverb type, formed
either by repetition of the same or a similar word, or by the putting together   50
of opposite words. Examples of this are: To bring a bad man to a bad end, an
ill crow lays an ill egg, and A wise child has a wise father. This is almost
normal in Greek drama, both comedy and tragedy. Further, The deserving
get their deserts; Friend to friend; Evil to the evil, good to the good; Each
dear to each; To every queen her king is fair. Also: Hand rubs hand; Jackdaw   55
sits by jackdaw. The type of opposites goes like this: Just and unjust; Rightly
or wrongly, in Aristophanes; Will he nill he, in Plato; and again, Neither

* * * * *

xiii
31 Plutarch] *Moralia* 698F; see *Adagia* I vi 31.
34 Cicero] *Ad Atticum* 9.6.6; see III i 51.
35 Lucian] *Quomodo historia conscribenda sit* 7
38 like this] Theocritus 16.60, used again in I iv 45
39 Virgil] *Eclogues* 1.59–60, followed by 5.76
42 Seneca] *Oedipus* 503
43 absurd] *Eclogues* 3.91, followed by 2.9 and 68 run together
45 Theocritus] 2.38–9
46 likeness] *Eclogues* 2.63
47 Theocritus] 10.30

word nor deed. So too in our own poets: 'With right and wrong confounded' and 'She truth and falsehood spread.' (This figure was used by Valerius Maximus without keeping to its true sense, merely as a means of emphasis: 60 'protesting' he says 'that against all right and wrong, when he held high command, he was butchered by you, a Roman knight.' For how can it make sense to say that a nefarious outrage was committed 'against all wrong'?) With what justice and what injustice; To do and suffer anything; Worthy and unworthy; What did he say or not say?; At home and at the war; Publicly   65 and privately; What you know, you don't know; Openly and in secret; In jest and in earnest; With hands and feet; Night and day; What you put first or last; Neither great nor small; Young and old; To the applause of gods and men.

To this type belong all those phrases found everywhere in the poets: A   70 maid and no maid, A bride and no bride, A wedding and no wedding, A city and no city, Paris ill-Paris, Happiness unhappy, Gifts that are no gifts, Fear unfearsome, War that is no war, Adorned when unadorned, Thankless thanks, Wealth that is no wealth. This opposition sometimes happens in compound words, like *morosophos*, foolishly wise, and *glukupikros*, bitter-   75 sweet. So lovers, as Plutarch assures us, call their passion, which is a mixture of pleasure and pain, such that they willingly pine. To this belongs that riddling type of contradiction, for example: I carry and carry not, I have and have not; 'A man no man that sees and sees not / With stone that's no

* * * * *

58 our own poets] Virgil *Georgics* 1.505 and *Aeneid* 4.190
59 Valerius Maximus] *Facta et dicta memorabilia* 6.2.8. This is a manual of historical anecdotes for the use of speakers compiled in the early first century AD, cited in the *Adagia* twenty-seven times. These two sentences in parentheses were added here in 1533.
64 With what justice] There is some overlap between this list and II i 24.
73 Adorned ... thanks] This was added (with the Latin versions of those that preceded) in 1515; 'Wealth that is no wealth' in 1528.
75 *glukupikros*] This, and the following sentence referring to Plutarch *Moralia* 681B, were added in 1515.
79 A man no man] The most famous of Greek riddles, ascribed to Panarces, of whom nothing is known, by Clearchus, an early collector of proverbs quoted by Athenaeus 10.452c (frag 95 in F. Wehrli *Die Schule des Aristoteles* 3, 1969). It is mentioned by Plato *Republic* 5.479c, and recorded in the *De tropis*, a late rhetorical treatise ascribed to Tryphon (*Rhetores graeci* ed L. Spengel, Leipzig 1853–6, 3.194.16) and in Suidas AI 230; see *Iambi et elegi graeci* ed M.L. West, Oxford 1972, 2.91. Erasmus' text seems closest to that given by Tryphon. The answer is: A one-eyed eunuch throws a lump of pumice-stone at a bat hanging on a tall reed, and misses it. ('Hits' has to represent two senses of the Greek *ballein*, which normally means 'to hit,' but can carry a colour of 'to throw at with the intention of hitting.')

stone hits and hits not / A bird no bird that on a sapling / That is no sapling   80
sits and sits not.' This riddle is recorded both by Athenaeus, citing Clearchus, and by Tryphon, and is also mentioned by Plato. Others of this type
are: tongue-tied chatterer, vulnerable invulnerable, hairy smooth, son that
was no son. Many things of the kind are put forward and expounded by
Athenaeus in his tenth book. The nature of adages does not rule out a   85
riddling obscurity, which is otherwise not recommended; on the contrary,
the obscurity is welcome, as though there was some family relationship. An
example of this would be to tell a man who was talking nonsense 'to set sail
for Anticyra' or 'to sacrifice a pig' or 'to pluck squills from the tombs'; the
first of these is in Horace, the second in Plautus and the third in Theocritus.   90
So too many oracular responses have been naturalized as proverbs, and the
precepts of Pythagoras [1 i 2] clearly belong naturally among the proverbs.

    One thing specially appropriate to adages as a class is hyperbole, as in
'With his arms affrights the sky' and 'Cracks rocks with his clamour' and 'I
dissolve in laughter,' especially if there is an admixture of any kind of   95
metaphor. This can be done in various ways, either by using a proper name
or with a comparison or with an epithet. Examples are: A second Aristarchus
[1 v 57], This Phalaris of ours [1 x 86], As noisy as Stentor [11 iii 37], Like a
lioness on a sword-hilt [11 ix 82], A Stentorian voice [11 iii 37], Eloquence like
Nestor's [1 ii 56]. And I am quite prepared to point out some of the springs,   100
so to say, from which this kind of figure can be drawn.

    1 / *From the thing itself.* The figure is sometimes taken from the thing
itself, whenever we call a very wicked person wickedness personified, or an
infamous person infamy, a pernicious one a pest, a glutton a sink, a swindler
shady, a morally vile man a blot, a dirty fellow filth, a despicable man trash,   105
an unclean one a dung-heap, a monstrous one a monster, a trouble-maker
an ulcer, a man who ought to be in prison a jail-bird. Every one of these
almost can be also expressed by a comparison: for instance, Golden as gold

    * * * * *

82 Others ... tenth book] Added in *1517/8*
89 Anticyra] Proverbial as the source of hellebore, a drug used in the treatment of
    insanity. These are three ways of dealing with madness, offered in *Adagia* I viii
    52, I viii 55 and II iii 42.
93 hyperbole] The first example given is from Virgil *Aeneid* 11.351 (*Adagia* II iv 6);
    for the third there is a parallel in Apuleius *Metamorphoses* 3.7 (cf IV i 86).
100 I am quite prepared] The reservoir of examples from which this cataract of
    phrases flows was tapped also for the *De copia* (LB 1.34–6), and we have taken
    advantage of Betty I. Knott's version and notes in CWE 24.385–95, where more
    references will be found. Only, as we are concerned with proverbs in English
    and not with the art of writing Latin, we have adopted the English form of the
    proverbs; for English says 'As deaf as a post' where Erasmus writing Latin
    would be bound to put 'Deafer than a post.'

itself, Wicked as wickedness, Blind as blindness, Garrulous as garrulity, Ugly as ugliness, Thirsty as thirst itself, Poor as poverty, As unlucky as 110 ill-luck personified, As infantile as infancy. To this category belong phrases like Father of all famines and Fount of all eloquence and More than entirely speechless and Worse than abandoned.

2 / *From similar things.* Nearest to these are phrases derived from similar things, such as: Sweet as honey, Black as pitch, White as snow, Smooth as 115 oil [I vii 35], Soft as the ear-lobe [I vii 36], Pure as gold [IV i 58], Dull as lead, Stupid as a stump, Unresponsive as the sea-shore [I iv 84], Stormy as the Adriatic [IV vi 89], Deaf as the Ocean, Bibulous as a sponge, Thirsty as the sands, Parched as pumice-stone [I iv 75], Noisy as the bronze of Dodona [I i 7], Fragile as glass, Unstable as a ball, Accommodating as a buskin 120 [I i 94], Thin as Egyptian clematis [I i 22], Tall as an alder, Hard as a whetstone [I i 20], Bright as the sun, Fair as a star, Pale as boxwood, Bitter as Sardonic herbs [III v 1], Despised as seaweed, Seething as Etna, Tasteless as beetroot [II iv 72], As just as a pair of scales [II v 82], As crooked as a thorn, As empty as a bladder, Light as a feather, Changeable as the wind, Hateful 125 as death, Capacious as the abyss [III vii 41], Twisted as the labyrinth [II x 51], Worthless as blue pimpernel [I vii 21], Light as cork [II iv 7], Leaky as a great jar full of holes [I x 33], Transparent as a lantern, Dripping like a water-clock, Pure as a crystal spring, Inconstant as the Euripus [I ix 62], Dear as a man's own eyes, Beloved as the light, Precious as life itself, Inflexible as a dry 130 bramble [II i 100], Revolting as warmed-up cabbage [I v 38], Bright as a purple stripe, Licentious as the carnival of Flora.

3 / *From living creatures.* Similarly from living creatures: Talkative as a woman [IV i 97], Salacious as a sparrow, Lecherous as a billy-goat, Long-lived as a stag, Ancient as an old crow [I vi 64], Noisy as a jackdaw [I vii 22], 135

* * * * *

112 Father of all famines] Catullus 21.1
123 Despised as seaweed] This phrase comes, with the Sardonic herbs, from Virgil *Eclogues* 7.41–2, and they stood together in the *Collectanea* no 741 with 'rougher than butcher's broom.' It can hardly be other than accidental that the third of these should not appear in the *Chiliades* at all and the second only here, while the Sardonic herbs rate a long article (III v 1) on their own. Exact completeness for its own sake is not part of Erasmus' programme.
125 a bladder] The Latin word *ampulla* properly means a bottle, especially an oil-flask; but there is no reason why an oil-flask should be proverbially empty, which seems to be the meaning here, and Erasmus knew that the word was used metaphorically for 'bombast' in writing. It seems likely therefore that he had in mind a bladder filled with wind.
128 lantern] In *1508* Erasmus wrote 'Punic lantern' as in his source, which is Plautus *Aulularia* 566 (possibly meaning glass, traditionally invented by the Phoenicians, *Poeni*); but the epithet was cut out in *1528*; see III vi 59A.

Melodious as a nightingale, Poisonous as a cobra, Venomous as a viper, Sly
as a fox [I ii 28], Prickly as a hedgehog [II iv 81], Tender as an Acarnanian
sucking-pig [II iii 59], Slippery as an eel [I iv 95], Timid as a hare [II i 80], Slow
as a snail, Sound as a fish [IV iv 93], Dumb as a fish [I v 29], Playful as a
dolphin, Rare as a phoenix [II vii 10], Prolific as a white sow, Rare as a black   140
swan [II i 21], Changeable as a hydra [I i 95], Rare as a white crow [IV vii 35],
Greedy as a vulture [I vii 14], Grim as scorpions, Slow as a tortoise [I viii 84],
Sleepy as a dormouse, Ignorant as a pig, Stupid as an ass, Cruel as water-
snakes, Fearful as a hind, Thirsty as a leech, Quarrelsome as a dog, Shaggy
as a bear, Light as a water-beetle. Lucian too collects some things of the kind: 145
'While they are as irritable as puppies, as timid as hares, as fawning as
monkeys, as lustful as donkeys, as thievish as cats, as quarrelsome as
fighting-cocks.' Plutarch in his essay 'On Running into Debt' has 'As untrustworthy as a jackdaw, as silent as a partridge, as lowborn and servile as a
dog.'   150

    4 / *From the characters of the gods.* These arise from the characters of the
gods: Chaste as Diana, Elegant as the very Graces, Lecherous as Priapus,
Lovely as Venus, Eloquent as Mercury, Mordant as Momus [I v 74], Inconstant as Vertumnus [II ii 74], Mutable as Proteus [II ii 74], Changeable as
Empusa [II ii 74].   155

    5 / *From characters of legend.* From legendary characters: Thirsty as
Tantalus [II vi 14], Cruel as Atreus [II vii 92], Savage as a Cyclops [I iv 5], Mad
as Orestes, Crafty as Ulysses [II viii 79], Eloquent as Nestor [I ii 56], Foolish
as Glaucus [I ii 1], Destitute as Irus [I vi 76], Chaste as Penelope [I iv 42],
Handsome as Nireus, Long-lived as Tithonus [I vi 65], Hungry as Erysich-   160
thon, Prolific as Niobe [III iii 33], Loud as Stentor [II ii 37], Blind as Teiresias
[I iii 57], Ill-famed as Busiris, Enigmatic as the Sphinx [II iii 9], Intricate as the
Labyrinth [II x 51], Inventive as Daedalus [II iii 62, III i 65], Daring as Icarus,

* * * * *

145 Lucian] *Piscator* 34
148 Plutarch] Moralia 830C; but these are genuine comparisons, drawn to suit the
    context, not proverbial expressions in comparative form.
158 Orestes] He murdered his mother Clytemnestra, after she and her lover
    Aegisthus had killed his father Agamemnon, and was driven mad by the
    Furies. Erasmus himself uses the phrase (eg in Allen Ep 1342.768), but gave
    Orestes no place of his own in the *Adagia*.
160 Nireus] By tradition, handsomest of all the Greeks who went to the Trojan War.
160 Erysichthon] He offended the goddess Ceres, and was punished with a *bulimy*
    (I ix 67), an inextinguishable hunger.
162 Busiris] A mythical king in Egypt, who sacrificed all foreign visitors
163 Icarus] The son of Daedalus (III i 65), who perished through the failure of a pair
    of wings invented by his father

Overweening as the Giants [III x 93], Stupid as Gryllus, Sharp-eyed as
Lynceus [II i 54], Unremitting as the Hydra [I x 9].   165

    6 / From characters in comedy. From characters in comedy come: Boastful
as Thraso in Terence, Quarrelsome as Demea, Good-natured as Micio,
Fawning as Gnatho, Confident as Phormio, Wily as Davus, Charming as
Thais, Miserly as Euclio.

    7 / From characters in history. From historical characters come: Envious   170
as Zoilus [II v 8], Strict as Cato [I vii 89], Inhuman as Timon, Cruel as Phalaris
[I x 86], Lucky as Timotheus [I v 82], Despicable as Sardanapalus [III vii 27],
Religious as Numa, Just as Phocion, Incorruptible as Aristides, Rich as
Croesus [I vi 74], Wealthy as Crassus [I vi 74], Poor as Codrus [I vi 76],
Debauched as Aesop, Ambitious as Herostratus, Cautious as Fabius [I x 29],   175
Patient as Socrates, Muscular as Milo [I ii 57], Acute as Chrysippus, With as
fine a voice as Trachalus, Forgetful as Curio, The Aristarchus of our time
[I v 57], The Christian Epicurus, A Cato out of season [I viii 89].

    8 / From names of peoples. From peoples: Treacherous as a Carthaginian
[I viii 28], Rough as a Scythian [II iii 35], Inhospitable as the Scythotaurians,   180

    * * * * *

164 Gryllus] One of the shipmates of Ulysses who were turned into animals by
    Circe the sorceress in the tenth book of the *Odyssey*. Gryllus became a pig, and
    defends his situation in Plutarch's *Gryllus* ('Beasts are Rational').
165 the Hydra] Of Lerna (I x 9). The word used, *excetra*, is thought to mean
    'serpent,' but it is the Hydra in Plautus *Persa* 3, and the Hydra was indeed
    'unremitting' and grew a new head for every one that Hercules cut off.
166 characters in comedy] These are all from three plays of Terence (*Adelphoe*,
    Eunuchus, Phormio), except Euclio; he is an old man in the *Aulularia* of Plautus,
    and was added in 1517/8.
171 Timon] The misanthrope; see for instance the *Timon* of Lucian.
173 Numa] Numa Pompilius, the mythical early king of Rome, to whom the Romans
    attributed many of their religious ideas and practices
173 Phocion] Athenian general of the fourth century BC
173 Aristides] Athenian statesman of the fifth century BC. He and the two
    preceding each have a life to themselves in Plutarch's *Lives*.
175 Aesop] Not the writer of Aesop's *Fables*, but a notorious spendthrift of the last
    century BC; Horace *Satires* 2.3.239
175 Herostratus] The man who in order to secure immortality burnt down the great
    temple of Diana at Ephesus in 356 BC – and was regrettably successful.
176 Chrysippus] The eminent Stoic philosopher
177 Trachalus] An orator in Rome particularly praised for his voice by Quintilian
    10.1.119, 12.5.5. One wonders how many of Erasmus' contemporaries would
    have caught the allusion.
177 Curio] A Roman orator who died in 53 BC; Cicero illustrates the badness of his
    memory in the *Brutus* 60.216–8.
180 Scythotaurians] Inhabitants of the Crimea, the 'Tauric Chersonese,' who put
    all strangers to death

Mendacious as a Cretan [I ii 29], Fugitive as the Parthians [I i 5], Vain as the
Greeks, Drunken as Thracians [II iii 17], Untrustworthy as a Thessalian
[I iii 10], Contemptible as a Carian [I vi 14], Haughty as a Sybarite [II ii 65],
Effeminate as the Milesians [I iv 8], Wealthy as the Arabs [I vi 74], Short as a
Pygmy [IV i 90], Stupid as an Arcadian [III iii 27].   185

9 / *From occupations.* From occupations come: Perjured as a brothel-
keeper, Soft as a catamite, Boastful as a soldier, Severe as an Areopagite
[I ix 41], Violent as a tyrant, Brutal as a hangman.

xiv / Of the need for careful introduction of a proverb

This may seem a tiny and negligible thing, but since I have taken on the role
of a teacher, I shall not hesitate to issue a warning for the inexperienced. In
making use of adages we must remember what Quintilian recommends in
the use of newly-coined phrases or daring metaphors: that one should, as   5
Greek most eloquently expresses it, προεπιπλήττειν τῇ ὑπερβολῇ, make an
advance correction of what seems excessive. Similarly we should 'make an
advance correction' of our proverb and, as it were, go halfway to meet it, if it
is likely to prove obscure, or to jar in some other way. For this class of
phrase, as I have pointed out just now, admits metaphors of any degree of   10
boldness, and unlimited innovation in the use of words and unashamed
hyperbole and allegory pushed to enigmatic lengths. Greek makes this
'advance correction' in ways like these: As the proverb runs, As they say (in
several forms), As the old saying goes, To put it in a proverb, As they say in
jest, It has been well said. And almost exactly the same methods are in use in 15
Latin: As they say, As the old proverb runs, As is commonly said, To use an
old phrase, As the adage has it, As they truly say.

* * * * *

181 Parthians] The *Adagia*-text gives 'As vain as the Parthians,' and does not
mention the Greeks. But the Parthian cavalry were as famous for their tactics
of appearing to run away and then turning round to shoot with deadly aim as
the Greeks were (in Rome) for unreliability. We think Erasmus intended, and
we have translated, *Parthis [fugacior Graecis] vanior.* So it is in the *De copia.* 'As
big a liar as a Parthian' appears in I ii 31, but not till 1533.

xiv
4 Quintilian] 8.3.37

1   **Amicorum communia omnia**
    Between friends all is common

Τὰ τῶν φίλων κοινά, Between friends all is common. Since there is nothing
more wholesome or more generally accepted than this proverb, it seemed
good to place it as a favourable omen at the head of this collection of adages.   5
If only it were so fixed in men's minds as it is frequent on everybody's lips,
most of the evils of our lives would promptly be removed. From this proverb
Socrates deduced that all things belong to all good men, just as they do to the
gods. For to the gods, said he, belong all things; good men are friends of the
gods; and among friends all possessions are in common. Therefore good   10
men own everything. It is quoted by Euripides in his *Orestes*: 'Shared in
common are the possessions of friends,' and again in the *Phoenissae*: 'All
grief of friends is shared.' Again in the *Andromache*: 'True friends have
nothing of their own, but with them all is common.' Terence says in the
Adelphoe 'For there is an old proverb, that between friends all is common.' It   15
is said that this was also in Menander, in a play of the same name. Cicero in
the first book of the *De officiis* says 'As the Greek proverb has it, all things are
in common between friends,' and it is quoted by Aristotle in the eighth book
of his *Ethics* and by Plato in the *Laws*, book 5. Plato is trying to show that the
happiest condition of a society consists in the community of all possessions: 20
'So the first kind of city and polity and the best laws are found where the old
saying is maintained as much as possible throughout the whole city; and the

* * * * *

1 In the *Adagiorum collectanea* of 1500 this was no 94, taken from Terence with the
   Greek added probably from Diogenianus 5.76 (it is also in Zenobius 4.79); here
   it has been entirely rewritten. Otto 87; Tilley F 729 Among friends all things are
   common. According to Clearchus (above, xiii line 79n) frag 72, the original
   source of this saying was the Delphic oracle.

8 Socrates] Perhaps a slip of memory; in Diogenes Laertius 6.37 a similar remark is
   ascribed to the Cynic philosopher Diogenes. Laertius' *Lives of Eminent
   Philosophers* (perhaps early third century AD) were not printed complete in
   Greek until 1533, and Erasmus' many references are normally in Latin. He was
   presumably using the version of Ambrogio Traversari, which had been in print
   since 1475; but now and again he shows knowledge of the Greek original.

11 Euripides] *Orestes* 735; *Phoenissae* 243; *Andromache* 376–7

14 Terence] *Adelphoe* 803–4

16 Menander] Frag 10, cited by Suidas κ 2549

16 Cicero] *De officiis* 1.16.51

18 Aristotle] *Ethica Nicomachea* 8.9.1 (1159b31)

19 Plato] *Laws* 5.739b–c. In the *Collectanea* Erasmus had written 'This aphorism is
   cited in Plato under the name of Euripides.' Maria Cytowska in 'Erasme de
   Rotterdam et Marsile Ficin son maître' *Eos* 63 (1975) 165–79 has shown how at
   the outset he depended on the Latin version of Plato made by Marsilio Ficino.

saying is that friends really have all things in common.' Plato also says that a state would be happy and blessed in which these words 'mine' and 'not mine' were never to be heard. But it is extraordinary how Christians dislike   25
this common ownership of Plato's, how in fact they cast stones at it, although nothing was ever said by a pagan philosopher which comes closer to the mind of Christ. Aristotle in book 2 of the *Politics* moderates the opinion of Plato by saying that possession and legal ownership should be vested in certain definite persons, but otherwise all should be in common   30
according to the proverb, for the sake of convenience, virtuous living and social harmony. Martial in book 2 pokes fun at a certain Candidus, who was always quoting this adage, but otherwise gave nothing to his friends: 'O Candidus, what's mine is yours, you say; / Grandly you chant this maxim night and day,' and the epigram ends thus: '"What's mine is yours," yet   35
naught you give away.' An elegant remark of Theophrastus is quoted in Plutarch, in the little essay entitled 'On Brotherly Love': 'If friends' possessions are in common, then friends' friends still more should be in common too.' Cicero in the first book of the *De legibus* seems to attribute this adage to Pythagoras, when he says: 'Hence that word of Pythagoras "Between   40
friends things are in common, and friendship is equality."' In Diogenes Laertius also Timaeus reports that this saying first began with Pythagoras. Aulus Gellius in his *Attic Nights*, book 1 chapter 9, bears witness that not only was Pythagoras the author of this saying, but he also instituted a kind of sharing of life and property in this way, the very thing Christ wants to   45
happen among Christians. For all those who were admitted by Pythagoras into that well-known band who followed his instruction would give to the common fund whatever money and family property they possessed. This is called in Latin, in a word which expresses the facts, *coenobium*, clearly from community of life and fortunes.   50

* * * * *

23 Plato] This sentence was inserted in *1515*.
28 Aristotle] *Politics* 2.1 (1261a2), added in *1526*
32 Martial] 2.43.1–2 and 16
36 Theophrastus] See I i 44 note; frag 75, cited by Plutarch *Moralia* 490E
39 Cicero] *De legibus* 1.12.34
42 Laertius] 8.10, citing the lost historian Timaeus of Tauromenium (fourth/third century BC), *FGrHist* 566F13b. The ascription to Pythagoras is found also in Jerome *Adversus Rufinum* 3.39 (*PL* 23.485B).
43 Gellius] 1.9.12, added in *1515*; but the word *coenobium*, which attracted Erasmus with its suggestion of a cenobitic or communal life, is a mistaken correction, found in early printed texts, of an old legal formula *ercto non cito*, which puzzled Gellius' first editors. His *Noctes Atticae*, a valuable literary and antiquarian miscellany of the mid second century AD, is quoted in the *Adagia* about a hundred and twenty times.

2 Amicitia aequalitas. Amicus alter ipse
Friendship is equality. A friend is another self

These also are ascribed to Pythagoras as their author, containing as they do
the same opinion, that friendship is equality and having one soul, and that a
friend is a second self. For there is nothing not shared where there is equality   5
of fortune; nor is there any dissension where the mind is one and the same,
nor any separation where two are joined in one. Aristotle in the *Magna
Moralia*, book 2: 'Whenever we wish to say emphatically "friend" we say
"My soul and his are one." ' Again, in the same book: 'for a friend, as we say,
is a second self.' Plato in book 6 of the *Laws* quotes it as an old saying and   10
accepted as a proverb: 'There is a saying old and true and finely phrased,
that equality is the maker of friendship.' However, Plato did not think that
everything should be offered equally to young and old, learned and un-
learned, stupid and wise, strong and weak, but that distribution should be
made to each according to his worth. Otherwise, as he says in the same   15
passage, 'to unequal people equal things will be unequal;' and just as
extreme right turns into extreme wrong, so equality pushed to extremes
becomes extreme inequality. Pliny observed wittily that in counting votes
there is nothing to be found more unequal than equality. Some think
however that this also came out of Homer, where one sometimes finds the   20
expression 'as much as my own life.' The law of the Hebrews does not differ
from this, when it commands us to love our neighbour as ourselves. And
Aristotle quotes all this as proverbial in his *Ethics*, book 9.

THE PRECEPTS OF PYTHAGORAS
But since I have happened to mention Pythagoras, I will not hesitate to set   25
down the rest of his precepts, which circulated among the Ancients with the

* * * * *

2 This appeared, in brief, as *Collectanea* no 95, in a series of Pythagorean maxims
   (see below). Otto 111; Tilley F 761 Perfect friendship cannot be without
   equality, and F 696 A friend is one's second self.
3 Pythagoras] A common attribution, eg Cicero *De officiis* 1.17.56; Diogenes
   Laertius 8.10.
7 Aristotle] *Magna moralia* 2.11 (1211a32) and 2, 15 (1213a23), added in 1523
10 Plato] *Laws* 6.757a
17 extreme wrong] *Adagia* I x 25
18 Pliny] the Younger *Letters* 9.5.3
20 Homer] *Iliad* 18.82
21 Hebrews] Leviticus 19:18, cited in Matthew 5:43 and often
23 Aristotle] *Ethica Nicomachea* 9.4.5 (1166a31), added in 1515
24 Precepts of Pythagoras] This sixth-century, but sometimes almost legendary,
   philosopher from the island of Samos enjoyed continuing fame as a source of

force of oracles – such at least as I have been able to find in Greek authors at the time of writing. Although at first blush, as they say, some of these injunctions may seem superstitious and laughable, yet if one pulls out the allegory one will see that they are nothing else but precepts for the good life.   30 There is no need to imitate the superstition of the Etruscans, who obeyed them literally, as Plutarch testifies in his 'Table-talk.' He also states in his life of Numa that some of Numa's precepts of this kind agreed with those of Pythagoras.

Ne gustaris quibus nigra est cauda   35
Μὴ γεύεσθαι τῶν μελανούρων, Taste not of anything with a black tail. Plutarch interprets this in his essay 'On the Education of Children' as meaning Do not have anything to do with wicked people and those whose character is black and disreputable. The grammarian Tryphon, discussing this also among his examples of riddling phrases, interprets it as follows: 'Do   40 not tell a lie. For a lie grows blacker in the end, and brings darkness with it.' Some think this is a reference to the cuttle-fish, which hides itself in the ink

* * * * *

wisdom (cf *Adagia* III x 1). The *Collectanea* of 1500, nos 93–107, provided thirteen of his celebrated sayings in Latin and two paragraphs of comment, the source being Jerome *Adversus Rufinum* 3.39 (*PL* 23.481), with a few words of Greek added in the revision of 1506. Our first two were nos 94 and 95; no 96 was *Duorum temporum maxime habenda est ratio mane et vesperi*, Bethink you specially of two times of day, morning and evening, which found no place here, possibly through an oversight. In the *Chiliades* we find not 13 but 36, given of course in Greek. The first ten of these stand in the same order in Plutarch's essay 'On the Education of Children' (*Moralia* 12E–F), and that is no doubt their source. Then follows one from Plutarch's life of Numa, inserted in 1526. Then thirteen (but really twelve, for one of the two beginning *Adversus solem* is a duplicate, caused by a variant reading in the Greek) from Diogenes Laertius' life of Pythagoras (8.17), and four from a later passage (8.34–5). Then one perhaps from the *Protrepticus* of Iamblichus; four from Plutarch's life of Numa, with comments added in 1526; another perhaps from Iamblichus; and lastly a familiar one for which several sources were available. S. K. Heninger jr in *Renaissance Quarterly* 21 (1968) 162–5 has not much to add.

28 as they say] *Adagia* I ix 88
32 Plutarch] *Moralia* 727C; Numa 8.4, the latter added in 1526
36 black tail] Cf Diog. Laert. 8.19; Tilley T 197 Taste not of things that have black tails. The blacktail, *melanurus*, is a small fish, in Latin *oculata*, according to D'Arcy W. Thompson *A Glossary of Greek Fishes* (Oxford 1947) 159. Who identified it with *sepia*, the cuttle-fish, we do not know.
37 Plutarch] *Moralia* 12E
39 Tryphon] A Greek grammarian of the first century BC in his *De tropis; Rhetores graeci* ed L. Spengel 3 (1856) 194

it carries in its tail. But Pliny, in the last chapter of book 32, lists among
the fishes a black-tail, *melanurus*, though he has discussed the cuttle-fish
lengthily in previous books, so that it appears that the *melanurus* and the   45
cuttle-fish are not the same. Theodorus Gaza translates *melanurus* by
oculata, eye-fish, a kind he mentions only in the place I have just indicated.

Stateram ne transgrediaris
Μὴ ζυγὸν ὑπερβαίνειν, Exceed not the balance, that is, You shall not do
anything which is not just and right. For the balance was commonly held in   50
old days to be a symbol of equity, as is shown by that Doric proverb: As fair
as a pair of scales. Demetrius of Byzantium gives the same interpretation in
book 10 of Athenaeus' *Doctors at Dinner*.

Choenici ne insideas
Χοίνικι μὴ ἐπικάθισαι, Do not sit on the grain-measure. St Jerome says this   55
means Do not worry about food for the morrow. The *choenix* was a slave's
ration, the daily allowance, as in Homer, *Odyssey* 19: 'Not idle shall I allow
him to remain who has had a daily portion from me,' a *choinix*. Laertius and
Suidas give the same explanation. It was the custom in old time to distribute
the day's ration to the slaves by this measure, and they in turn were to   60
furnish a day's work; so the Pythian Apollo calls the Corinthians choenix-
measurers, because they possessed forty-six thousand slaves. The source of
this information is Athenaeus, book 6. Plutarch however takes it quite
differently, as follows: it is not right to indulge in leisure, but one must work
diligently for one's living, so as not to be in want later. The same author   65
recalls this precept in his 'Table-talk,' in these words: 'Together with Pythagoras' grain-measure on which he forbade us to sit, teaching us to leave some
of what we have for the future, and every day to think of the day to come.'
But he also sees in it a reference to our ancestors, who had a religious scruple

* * * * *
43 Pliny] *Naturalis historia* 32.149, inserted in *1528*
46 Gaza] The well-known fifteenth-century Byzantine scholar, whose Latin version of Aristotle's *Historia animalium* was reprinted by Aldus in 1503/4 and
   1513. This sentence was added in *1528*.
48 *Stateram*] Diog. Laert. 8.17
51 Doric proverb] *Adagia* II v 82
53 Athenaeus] 10.452d, added in *1517/8*
54 *Choenici*] Diog. Laert. 8.17
55 Jerome] *Adversus Rufinum* 3.39
57 Homer] *Odyssey* 19.27–8
58 Laertius] Diog. Laert. 8.18
59 Suidas] Π 3124
63 Athenaeus] 6.272c, added in *1517/8*
63–70 Plutarch] *Moralia* 12E; 703E; 279E, used in *Adagia* I ix 43

against taking away the tables empty. Demetrius of Byzantium in Athe-   70
naeus interprets this as meaning that we should not look only at the present
but always take thought for the future; in this he almost agrees with
Plutarch.

For my part at least, since when one is dealing with this kind of precept
it is not only allowable but necessary to make a guess, I should say that this   75
Pythagorean riddle is taken from the passage I have just quoted in Homer;
and that it means that we should not idly seek leisure and sustenance from
others, but acquire through our own industry the means to sustain life
decently. For it is parasitical and dishonourable 'to live on the crumbs from
another man's table,' and have no skills whereby one can pay for the food in   80
one's own home. Homer blames this in Irus, when he says in *Odyssey* 18:

> Known for his idle belly,
> To eat and drink unceasingly. In him
> Was neither strength nor might.

The remark of the Apostle Paul concurs with this, and it too is in common   85
circulation: 'If any will not work, neither shall he eat.'

As I was preparing the sixth edition (if I am not mistaken) of my *Adagia*,
that is, in the year of grace 1517, a book saw the light just at that moment, the
Antiquae lectiones of Ludovicus Caelius Rhodiginus. There is no need to give
an opinion now as to the book in general. However a first taste of it (for I   90
have only taken a sip) at once indicated that the author was a man who
flitted round among writers of every kind with an insatiable desire to read,
and delighted in taking to pieces the garlands of other people to plait them
into new wreaths. The fact that he nowhere, so far as I could find out,

* * * * *

70 Athenaeus] 10.452e, added in *1517/8*
79 the crumbs from another man's table] Juvenal 5.2 (tr J. D. Duff)
81 Homer] *Odyssey* 18.2–4 (cf *Adagia* I vi 76).
85 Paul] 2 Thessalonians 3:10
89 Caelius] Lodovico Ricchieri (1453–1525) of Rovigo (Allen II p 348n), whose
   Antiquae lectiones, a folio of 862 pages, was published by Aldus in February
   1516. Erasmus added this comment in *1517/8*, beginning the third sentence
   'Although when I knew him as a young man years ago in Ferrara, where we
   lodged together, he seemed to me a person of respectable learning and very
   great promise, and the first taste' etc. A conciliatory reply from Milan (Ep 949 of
   22 April 1519) did not mollify him, and in *1520* after 'Ferrara' he inserted 'if this
   is really the same Celio,' and also the clause 'even if when he is writing' etc, as
   well as side-shots in I viii 56 and II iv 42. In *1523* came another acidulated
   reference, in *Adagia* II i 45. But in *1526*, after hearing of Celio's death, he cut out
   the allusion to their meeting in Ferrara as it had stood since *1520*, and added
   four charitable sentences at the end of the paragraph.

mentioned the name of Giorgio Valla of Volterra, or my name: (although it is   95
probable that he was helped to a certain extent by our collections) I know to
have been the result of discretion and not malice; even if, when he is writing
about this very precept he asserts that he does not wish to put anything
forward which bubbles up in anyone else's work (this is how he talks), and
at the same time he produces a good many things which I find in my own   100
Chiliades. I do not think it any concern of mine that he should also beget
proverbs of his own, though of a kind with which one could fill out hundreds of *Chiliades*, if one had a mind to it. When I have a little more time, I
shall not hesitate to take a more careful look and see if there is anything in
this book which belongs to this project of mine – not wishing to defraud the   105
man of his due credit if he has made a contribution. As far as concerns the
interpretation of this riddle, I am aware of his guesses about the grain-
measure and the rolled-up blankets, but at present I neither accept nor reject
his discovery. Personally, I do not feel free to make guesses in this way, if
there is any help to be had in other ways from reliable authors. As soon as   110
this protection fails me, I shall perhaps do some guessing too, but without
putting too much serious work into such things. What is the point of
anxiously searching out the meaning of an author who has taken great care
not to be understood?

When I was writing this, I learnt through letters from scholars that   115
Rhodiginus had breathed his last – a great grief to all who love learning, and
a loss to learning itself. Those who knew him in his private life say that he
was a man of true Christian character, untiring in his studious labours
though he reached extreme old age. In the face of such virtues, I cannot hold
it against him if he was not quite fair to me. The value of learning to the   120
public is more important to me than the matter of my own reputation.

Ne cuivis dextram inieceris
Μὴ παντὶ ἐμβάλλειν δεξιὰν, Do not hold out your right hand to all and
sundry; that is, do not rashly admit to your friendship no matter whom, but
choose whom you cherish. This is quoted and explained by Plutarch in his   125
'On Having Many Friends.' It agrees with that remark of Solon, which
Diogenes Laertius records out of Apollodorus: 'Do not make friends quickly;
but when made, do not reject them.'

* * * * *

95 Valla] Giorgio Valla, generally described as a native of Piacenza, died in
January 1500 as a professor in Venice. His *De expetendis et fugiendis rebus* was
published by Aldus in two folio volumes in December 1501.
122 *Ne cuivis*] Diog. Laert. 8.17; Tilley H 68 Give not your right hand to every man.
125 Plutarch] *Moralia* 96A; 'and explained' was inserted in *1515*.
127 Diogenes Laertius] 1.60

Arctum anulum ne gestato

Μὴ φορεῖν στενὸν δακτύλιον, Do not wear a tight-fitting ring. According to St   130
Jerome this means: Do not live in anxiety, and do not plunge yourself into
slavery or into a manner of life from which you cannot extricate yourself. For
whoever wears a tight-fitting ring puts himself, as it were, in fetters.

Ignem ne gladio fodito

Πῦρ σιδήρῳ μὴ σκαλεύειν, Stir not the fire with a sword, that is, Do not   135
provoke a man who is already in a rage. It is wiser to give way, and soothe
the fuming spirit with gentle words. So says St Jerome, and Demetrius of
Byzantium in Athenaeus. Diogenes Laertius explains that the wrath of the
mighty and the fierce should not be stirred up by recriminations, because a
flame grows stronger and stronger the more it is stirred up. Plutarch does   140
not disagree with this interpretation. But Plato in the sixth book of the *Laws*
used it in such a way as to make it seem to refer normally to those people
who vainly attempt something which can by no means be done; he explains
that it was a kind of game 'to cut fire with a sword.' St Basil in the letter to his
nephews gave it much the same meaning, so that to cut the fire with a sword   145
has the same effect as to draw water in a sieve. Certainly Lucian was
alluding to this in book 2 of his *True Stories*, when on leaving the Fortunate
Isles he imagines himself warned by Rhadamanthus to observe three rules
when he should return to this world of ours: 'not to stir the fire with a sword,
not to eat lupins, and not to become attached to a boy over eighteen years of   150
age.' If he were mindful of these things, he might someday return to that

* * * * *

129 *Arctum anulum*] Tilley R 129 Do not wear a tight ring.
131 Jerome] *Adversus Rufinum* 3.39
134 *Ignem*] Diog. Laert. 8.17. Otto 845
137 Jerome] *Adv, Rufinum* 3.39
138 Athenaeus] 10.452d, added in *1517/8*
138 Diogenes Laertius] 8.18
140 Plutarch] *Moralia* 12E
141 Plato] *Laws* 6.780c, repeated in *1533* in III v 84. But Plato in that passage is using
     a different proverbial expression, Εἰς τὸ πῦρ ξαίνειν, To card wool into the
     fire, as a type of labour wasted, for which see I iv 55. Erasmus' version 'to cut
     fire to pieces with a sword,' as distinct from poking or stirring it, is simply an
     error caused by ignorance of the verb, though it gave rise to Tilley F 250 Cut not
     the fire with a sword.
144 Basil] Bishop of Caesarea (d 1 January 379), *Ad adulescentes* or *De legendis
     gentilium libris* 9 (PG 31.582B; p 55 in the edition by F. Boulenger, Paris 1935).
     'To draw water in a sieve' is I iv 60.
146 Lucian] *Verae historiae* 2.28

island. Horace seems to apply this saying to cruelty joined with insanity; for love is in itself madness, and if it breaks out in fighting and slaughter, the fire is pierced with a sword. In the third satire of book 2: 'To these add bloodshed, and poke the fire with a sword.'   155

Cor ne edito

Μὴ ἐσθίειν τὴν καρδίαν, Do not eat your heart out, that is, Do not torture your own soul with cares (in Athenaeus, Demetrius of Byzantium interprets it in this way) or Do not shorten your life by worry. Aristotle in his *On the Parts of Animals*, book 3, says the heart is the source of all the senses, and of   160 life and blood. Aristophanes in the *Clouds*: 'Nevertheless biting my heart I said.' Theognis too: 'Something bites my heart; my spirit is divided.' It seems to have been taken from Homer, who writes in *Iliad* 6: 'Alone he wandered in the empty plains, / Eating his heart out with cares, shunning the path of men.' And in book 24: 'You are eating your heart out.' So in the   165 *Odyssey*, book 9: 'There two whole nights and two whole days we lay / Eating our hearts with weariness and pain.' And in the *Iliad*, book 1: 'You tear your inmost heart.'

A fabis abstineto

Κυάμων ἀπέχεσθαι, Abstain from beans. There are various interpretations   170 of this riddle. Plutarch in his essay 'On the Education of Children' explains it in this way; one must abstain from holding public office, because in Antiquity, when magistrates were to be elected, the votes were taken by beans instead of pebbles. However in his 'Problems' he gives a different reason, that all leguminous plants affect the body with wind and tainted humours,   175 and accordingly arouse sexual passion. Cicero seems to have been of the same opinion, as he writes thus in the *On Divination*, book 1: 'Therefore Plato prescribes that one should seek sleep in such a disposition of body that nothing can confuse or disturb the mind. It is thought that this is why the Pythagoreans are forbidden to eat beans, a thing highly conducive to wind.   180

* * * * *

152 Horace] *Satires* 2.3.275–6, probably quoted from memory; added in *1533*
156 *Cor ne edito*] Diog. Laert. 8.17; Tilley H 330 Do not eat your heart out.
158 Athenaeus] 10.452d, added in *1517/8*
159 Aristotle] *De partibus animalium* 3.4 (666a11)
161 Aristophanes] *Clouds* 1369
162 Theognis] 910 (see I i 62n).
163 Homer] *Iliad* 6.201–2; 24.129; *Odyssey* 9.74–5; *Iliad* 1.243
169 *A fabis*] Cf Diog. Laert. 8.24; Tilley B 119 Abstain from beans.
171 Plutarch] *Moralia* 12F; 286E
176 Cicero] *De divinatione* 1.30.62

That kind of food, according to him, is unfavourable to those who seek tranquility of mind.' But Aristoxenus in Aulus Gellius, book 4 chapter 11, rejects this opinion, affirming that there was no leguminous vegetable more frequently used by Pythagoras than beans, because that food gently purges and soothes the bowels. Gellius thinks that 'the cause of this mistake as to   185
habitual abstention from eating the *cyamus* was a line found in a poem by Empedocles, a follower of Pythagoras: "Ah! wretched, wretched men! Draw back your hands; / Touch not that *cyamus*." Most people believe that *cyamus* was a common term for a leguminous plant. But those who have considered the poems of Empedocles with more care and intelligence' (I will quote the   190
words of Gellius) 'think that in this passage *kuamoi* signifies testicles; and that in the Pythagorean fashion they were called *kuamoi* figuratively and symbolically, as if they were efficacious' in helping the womb to conceive or 'in causing conception, and were favourable to human procreation. Thus that line of Empedocles is not intended, according to them, to deter people   195
from eating beans but from excessive sexual indulgence.' Laertius quotes the following from Aristotle about the reason for forbidding beans: 'Aristotle says in his book on beans that he [Pythagoras] ordained abstention from beans because they resembled the privy parts or the gates of Hades, for this vegetable alone is devoid of generative power; or because it has injurious   200
properties, or because it resembles the nature of the universe, or belongs to an oligarchical system because beans are used in electing men to office.' This last point mentioned by Aristotle coincides with the opinion of certain authors, who believe Pythagoras to have used this riddle to deter people from seeking public office. For myself, I prefer the explanation added by the   205
writer who collected the incidents referred to by Gregory of Nazianzus: that those who 'eat beans' are men corrupted by bribery in the casting of their votes. In Gellius again Plutarch bears witness that Aristotle left on record how Pythagoras 'abstained from eating the matrix, the heart, the sea-anemone and some other things of this sort.' Theon the grammarian tells in   210
Plutarch's 'Table-talk' that among the Egyptians there were such strong

* * * * *

182 Aristoxenus] (Fourth century BC) frag 25 Wehrli, cited by Aulus Gellius 4.11.4
185 Gellius] 4.11.9, citing Empedocles frag 31B141 Diels-Kranz (see I i 72n).
194 conception] There is a play on words between *kuamos*, bean (given by Gellius in Greek) and *kuein*, to conceive.
196 Laertius] Diog. Laert. 8.54, citing Aristotle frag 195 Rose
203 certain authors] Eg Plutarch *Moralia* 12F, already cited. This reference and the next were added in *1517/8*.
205 the writer] Nonnus the abbot (so-called) on Gregory of Nazianzus, first *Oratio contra Julianum* 17 (*PG* 36.994D)
208 Plutarch] Frag 122, cited by Gellius 4.11.12; *Moralia* 729A, citing Herodotus 2.37

religious feelings against beans that they neither sowed nor ate them, nor
was it permissible even to look at them – so says Herodotus.

In Rome moreover beans were thought to be one of the things that
denoted death, and in fact it was forbidden for the priest of Jove to touch   215
them 'or name them, because they were thought to belong to the dead. For
they were scattered before ghosts and spectres and used in sacrifices at the
Parentalia, and on their flowers there seem to appear letters that indicate
mourning,' as Festus Pompeius testifies. Pliny thinks that beans were con-
demned by Pythagoras because they dull the senses and cause dreams, or   220
because the spirits of the dead are in them; hence their use at the Parentalia
too. Hence Plutarch asserts that pulse-foods are most powerful in the
evocation of spirits. Varro records that the reason why the priest did not eat
them was the presence of the sinister letters found on the flowers. In any
case, when Plutarch relates among other things in his 'Antiquarian Prob-   225
lems' that beans were forbidden because they were synonymous with Lethe
and Erebus, I did not quite understand the meaning of this; but finally on
consulting the Greek manuscripts I gathered that there had been an error,
either of copyist or translator. The Greek text runs thus: 'Did they, like the
Pythagoreans, abominate beans for the reasons which are commonly given,   230
but vetch and chick-pea because they take their names *lathyrus* and
erebinthus from Lethe and Erebus?' I have given Plutarch's actual words. He
was thinking of *lathyrus* and *erebinthus*, which are kinds of chick-pea; Lethe
means forgetfulness in Greek and Erebus takes its name from darkness –
and both are ill-omened words to the student of wisdom. This mistake had   235
its uses, in allowing me to show up a fault in the Latin text and so prevent
anyone from stumbling over the same stone.

* * * * *

215 priest of Jove] The *flamen dialis,* a senior priest in Rome whose office subjected
    him to special taboos
219 Festus] P 77 (see I i 28n), added in 1515. The Parentalia was a festival held in
    February in honour of dead members of the family. For the use of beans in
    ridding the house of ghosts, see for example Ovid *Fasti* 5.435–40.
219 Pliny] *Naturalis historia* 18.118, added in 1515
222 Plutarch] *Moralia* 286E, added in 1526
223 Varro] Cited by Pliny *Naturalis historia* 18.119; added in 1515
224 sinister letters] This looks like a variant of the ancient belief that a flower,
    generally supposed to be the wild gladiolus but unidentifiable, had markings
    on its petals that could be read as AI, the Greek for 'Alas' or the first syllable of
    the name of the hero Ajax who came to a bad end.
225 Plutarch] *Moralia* 286D–E, added in 1528. Lethe and Erebus, as names
    connected with the Underworld, are sinister, but they have no connection with
    the two words for beans which have a superficial resemblance to them.
237 stumbling over the same stone] *Adagia* I v 8

Cibum in matellam ne immittas

Σιτίον εἰς ἀμίδα μὴ ἐμβάλλειν, Do not put food in a chamber-pot. Plutarch
interprets this saying as meaning that one should not pour courteous words   240
into the mind of a bad man; for speech is the food of the mind, and it decays
and goes rotten if it falls into a mind that is impure. This means, as Epictetus
warns us in Gellius, that we must look with great care to see what kind of
mind we are making the recipient of our words. For if we put them into an
impure container, he says, they will turn to vinegar or urine. Horace refers   245
to this with his 'A dirty bottle sours all you pour in.'

Ad finem ubi perveneris, ne velis reverti

Μὴ ἐπιστρέφεσθαι ἐπὶ τοὺς ὅρους ἐλθόντα, Do not turn back when you have
come to the final stage: that is, according to Plutarch, when the day selected
by fate has come and 'you see the end of life approaching, you are to bear it   250
with serenity, and not lose heart' through a shameful desire for life. In his
life of Numa he writes rather differently: 'Those who have set out on a
journey should not turn back.' Jerome speaks otherwise: 'After death, thou
shalt not wish for this life,' in the way we so often hear people repeating
those words of Virgil: 'O my lost years, if Jove would bring them back!'   255

Superis impari numero, inferis pari sacrificandum

Τοῖς μὲν οὐρανίοις περισσὰ θύειν, ἄρτια δὲ τοῖς χθονίοις, Sacrificing must be
by odd numbers to the gods above, but by even numbers to the gods below.
This he only quotes as a riddle of Pythagoras, and does not explain. However, in his 'Problems of Roman Antiquity' he tells us the first month was   260
sacred to the gods of heaven and the second to the gods of the underworld,
and in the latter month it was customary to undergo certain purification
ceremonies, and they offered sacrifices for departed members of the family.
Moreover they wished to mark three days of a complete month as important

* * * * *

238 *Cibum in matellam*] Tilley M 834 Put not thy meat in an unclean dish.
239 Plutarch] *Moralia* 12F
242 Epictetus] See I iv 4 note; frag 10, cited by Gellius 17.19.3.
245 Horace] *Epistles* 1.2.54. This stood as an independent adage, with the Epictetus
    fragment, in *Collectanea* no 591; Otto 1849.
247 *Ad finem*] Diog. Laert. 8.17
249 Plutarch] *Moralia* 12F; *Numa* 14.3, the latter added in 1526
253 Jerome] *Adversus Rufinum* 3.39
255 Virgil] *Aeneid* 8.560
256 *Superis impari numero*] The maxim is from Plutarch *Numa* 14.5, the comment
    from his *Moralia* 270A. Erasmus added the whole paragraph in 1526, and ap-
    parently did not notice that he had not given Plutarch's name.

and influential, the calends, nones, and ides, which they kept as festivals   265
and holy days, as though sacred to the gods of heaven; the following days,
that is the day after the calends, the nones, and the ides, they gave to the
spirits of the underworld, and hence they regarded these days as evil and
unlucky. In the same way too among the Greeks the third bowl of wine was
dedicated to Jove the saviour, the second to demigods and daemons. The   270
beginning of all number is the monad, one, and the dyad, two, is in
opposition to it, first among even numbers, having no end and no completion, while three is absolute. You will find much about the mysteries of
number in Plato and the Pythagoreans, and even something in the early
theological writers. As to the interpretation of this precept, I think it means   275
that God, being Mind in its singleness and perfect in itself, takes delight
above all in the endowments of the spirit. For what belongs to Body is
composite, and can be propagated by multiplication to infinity; while Spirit
is simple, immortal, and desiring nothing but itself.

Per publicam viam ne ambules   280
Λεωφόρου μὴ βαδίζειν, Walk not in the public highway. St Jerome's explanation is: Do not follow common errors. For human affairs have never gone so
well that the best pleases the majority. Hence some express it like this:
'Refuse the king's highway and take the byroads.' This piece of advice
agrees with the teaching of the Gospel, which recommends us to avoid the   285
broad road where most people walk, and take the narrow way, trodden by
few but leading to immortality.

Tollenti onus auxiliare, deponenti nequaquam
Φορτίον συγκαθαιρεῖν, μὴ δὲ συνεπιτιθέναι, St Jerome cites it in this form:
'To the burdened another burden must be added; no help should be given to   290

* * * * *

280 *Per publicam viam*] The Greek of this and the twelve that follow comes from
    Diogenes Laertius 8.17.
281 Jerome] *Adversus Rufinum* 3.39. Of Athenaeus 10.452e, citing Demetrius of
    Byzantium.
285 Gospel] Matthew 7.13–4.
288 *Tollenti onus*] Does this precept recommend moral discipline, or kindness to
    those in trouble? In Jerome *Adversus Rufinum* (already quoted in *Collectanea*
    no 106), in Diogenes Laertius and in Plutarch *Moralia* 728c (not cited here) it is
    discipline: Increase a man's burden, or at best help him to lift it; do not help him
    to lay it down. But in Clement of Alexandria *Stromateis* 5.5 (*PG* 9.45–55) and in
    Iamblichus' *Life of Pythagoras* 18.84 the negative is in a different place: Help a
    man to set down his burden, do not add to it. Erasmus gives the first sense in
    his Latin: Help him who takes up his burden, not him who lays it down, and the
    second in his Greek: Help a man to lay down his burden, do not help to lay

those who lay their burden down.' He thinks the meaning is that those who
strive towards virtue should be given an increasing burden of instructions,
while those who give themselves up to idleness must be left alone. So the
proverb is to be quoted in this form: Φορτίον συγκαθαιρεῖν, μὴ δὲ
συναποτιθέναι. I thought it necessary to point this out, because in some   295
printed books this precept is corrupt.

Ollae vestigium in cinere turbato
Χύτρας ἴχνος συγχεῖν ἐν τῇ τέφρᾳ, Obliterate the trace of the pot in the ashes.
Plutarch in his 'Table-talk' interprets this to mean that no evident trace of
anger should be left, but as soon as resentment has cooled down and   300
subsided, every recollection of past injuries must be wiped out.

Unguium criniumque praesegmina ne commingito
Ἀπονυχίσμασι καὶ κουραῖς μὴ ἐπουρεῖν μὴ δὲ ἐφίστασθαι, Do not make
water on clippings from nails or hair nor tread on them. So far I have found
no explanation of this. But I conjecture the meaning to be: if we have   305
relatives or kindred who are lowly and unprofitable, we should not constantly pour scorn on them nor cover them with reproaches.

Extra publicam viam ne deflectas
Εκτὸς λεωφόρου μὴ βαδίζειν, Do not walk outside the public highway. This
also is quoted by Diogenes Laertius as a Pythagorean precept, although it is 310
the opposite of the one cited above. We need not be surprised at this
contradiction since, as has been rightly laid down, one should speak like the
many but think like the few, and yet at the same time there are matters in
which it is the part of a skilful man to agree with the multitude, and others in
which a good man must entirely differ from it. Horace well says: 'At times   315
even the common herd sees right, / At times 'tis wrong.'

* * * * *

burdens on him – a straightforward contradiction between Greek and Latin.
But he seems to have complicated this by taking the first of the two Greek verbs
to mean its opposite: Help the man to lift it; and he quotes the Greek a second
time with the second verb altered by conjecture to mean Do not help him to lay
it down. He seems to have thought that the revised Greek now meant the same
as the Latin, whereas it really means Help to take off a man's burden, do not
help to remove it.
297 *Ollae vestigium*] Diog. Laert. 8.17, like its neighbours
299 Plutarch] *Moralia* 728B
308 *Extra publicam viam*] Tilley M 281 A man must not leave the king's highway for a
path.
310 Diogenes Laertius] 8.17
315 Horace] *Epistles* 2.1.63, added in 1526

Quae uncis sunt unguibus ne nutrias

Γαμψώνυχα μὴ τρέφειν, Feed not things that have sharp claws. Shun rapacity, explains Tryphon. For my part I think it agrees with the saying of
Aeschylus, which I shall give in its due place, 'The lion's cub must not be   320
fostered in the state;' that is, no admittance for 'people-devouring kings,' as
Homer has it, or for those who create factions and powerful individuals who
concentrate the wealth of the citizens in few hands, which is now the usual
practice.

Adversus solem ne loquitor   325

Πρὸς τὸν ἥλιον τετραμμένον μὴ λαλεῖν, Speak not facing towards the sun,
that is: Do not contest what is evident. For when something is established
and generally acknowledged, we say it is as clear as the sun. So it is
'speaking against the sun' to say 'Olive no kernel hath nor nut no shell.'

Gladium acutum avertas   330

Ὀξεῖαν μάχαιραν ἀποστρέφειν, Turn aside the sharp blade. I take this to
mean: Avoid dangerous matters. For there is another proverb too: A sword
in the hand of a child (we must understand Put not).

Adversus solem ne meiito

Πρὸς τὸν ἥλιον τετραμμένον μὴ ὀμιχεῖν, Do not make water facing towards   335
the sun. I think this is a recommendation to behave with modesty. However
Pliny gives a superstitious origin for this, book 8 chapter 6–I quote his actual
words: 'From the urine one may draw conclusions as to the state of health. If
it is clear in the morning and later turns reddish, this signifies on the first
occasion that digestion is taking place, then that it has taken place. It is a bad   340
sign if the urine is red, very bad if it is black; if it has bubbles in it and it is
thick, this is bad, and if the deposit is white, this indicates that there will be

* * * * *

317 *Quae uncis sunt unguibus*] Diog. Laert. 8.17
319 Tryphon] From the *De tropis* ascribed to him (see above, line 39) p 194.
320 Aeschylus] See *Adagia* II iii 77.
322 Homer] *Iliad* 1.231, a phrase which Erasmus never forgot, and added for
   instance in 1515 to *Adagia* III vii 1. The Latin version was added here in 1515,
   and the comment in 1517/8.
325 *Adversus solem ne loquitor*] This, which is not found in this form in the texts of
   Diogenes Laertius, is a duplicate of the next maxim but one, with *lalein*, speak in
   the Greek in place of *omichein*, make water.
329 Olive] *Adagia* I ix 73, citing Horace *Epistles* 2.1.31
332 another proverb] *Adagia* II v 18
337 Pliny] *Naturalis historia* 28.68–9, citing Hesiod *Works and Days* 927–32, tr C.A.
   Elton 1815

pain in the joints and in the viscera. Green urine indicates an illness of the
viscera, pale of the bile, red of the blood. It is bad when specks appear in it or
when it is cloudy, and also when watery and white; but when it is thick and   345
strong-smelling, it foretells death. Similarly in children when it is thin and
watery. Ancient sages rule against baring oneself for this purpose in front of
sun or moon, and against making water on anyone's shadow. Hesiod
recommends that this should be done against a wall, for fear of offending
some deity by nakedness.' The passage which Pliny quotes, and from which   350
the precept of Pythagoras is clearly taken, is in the poem entitled *Works and
Days*:

> Forbear to let your water flow away
> Turn'd upright towards the sun's all-seeing ray;
> E'en when his splendour sets, till morn has glowed   355
> Take heed; nor sprinkle, as you walk, the road,
> Nor the roadside; nor bare affront the sight,
> For there are gods that watch and guard the night.
> The holy man discreet sits silently,
> And to some sheep-fold's fenced wall draws nigh.   360

Hirundinem sub eodem tecto ne habeas
Ὁμωροφίους χελιδόνας μὴ ἔχειν, You shall not have swallows under the
same roof. St Jerome, following the authority of Aristotle, interprets this to
mean that we should shun the company of garrulous people and tale-
bearers. But this explanation is rejected in Plutarch, in the eighth decade of   365
his 'Table-talk'; for it would seem unjust to drive away as if bloodthirsty and
rapacious a household bird, which loves to live with man and does no harm.
As for the pretext of its garrulity, he says that it is nonsense, as we do not
refuse to admit hens, jackdaws, partridges and magpies and many other
much noisier birds to live with us; and indeed hardly anything is further   370
from the swallow than garrulity. Nor does it seem acceptable to refer the
Pythagorean precept, as some do, to the tragic story which is told about the
swallow, as if it brought an evil omen. For on that score we should have
likewise to reject the nightingale, since it is implicated in the same tragedy. It

* * * * *

363 Jerome] *Adversus Rufinum* 3.39, citing Aristotle frag 197 Rose
365 Plutarch] *Moralia* 727C–8B
372 tragic story] The familiar myth of Philomela, daughter of Pandion king of
     Athens, who was violated by her sister's husband Tereus, and eventually all
     three were changed into birds, Philomela into a nightingale, her sister Procne
     into a swallow, Tereus into a hoopoe (see eg Ovid *Metamorphoses* 6.425–674).

seems more likely that the swallow is under the same condemnation as   375
those birds which are in bad odour because they have hooked claws. It lives
in fact on flesh, and it hunts cicadas, the most vocal of creatures and sacred
to the Muses; it also preys stealthily on tiny insects, flying low along the
ground, and then it is the only bird that makes its home in roofs without
doing anything useful. The stork, for instance, even when it does not make   380
use of our roof, still makes no small return for hospitality by removing toads
and snakes, the enemies of man, from our midst. The swallow on the other
hand raises its chicks under our roof and then makes off, without returning
any thanks for the hospitality it has been given. Finally, and most important
of all, there are only two domestic creatures which never grow tame through   385
living with man, and will never allow themselves to be touched nor admit of
companionship nor share any thing or any discipline. The fly is always
afraid of being hurt, and so remains unteachable and half-wild; and the
swallow appears to have a natural hatred of man, and thus cannot be tamed,
but is always distrustful, always suspecting some harm. On this account   390
Pythagoras rightly recommended us by his precept about the swallow to
keep at a distance an ungrateful and untrustworthy companion. Plutarch
says something like this in the passage I have indicated. There seems only
one thing to add: Cicero, or whoever wrote the *Rhetorica ad Herennium*,
borrows an emblem for faithless friendship from the swallows, which come   395
with the beginning of spring and fly away at the approach of winter.

Stragula semper convoluta habeto
Τὰ στρώματα ἀεὶ συνδεδεμένα ἔχειν, Always have the bedclothes folded
up. In these days also it is considered rough and uncivilized not to make
one's bed. However I leave it to others to guess what this precept means. I   400
suspect though that it is a recommendation to modesty, even in those things
which we are obliged to do to satisfy a necessity of nature.

In anulo Dei figuram ne gestato
Ἐν δακτυλίῳ θεοῦ εἰκόνα μὴ περιφέρειν, Do not wear the image of God in a

* * * * *

394 *Rhetorica ad Herennium*] A technical treatise on rhetoric, ascribed in the Middle
    Ages to Cicero, and normally published with his works, but certainly not his.
    The first scholar to doubt the attribution was Lorenzo Valla, and in 1491
    Raffaele Regio definitively detached it from Cicero's name. The reference is
    4.48.61; for the sentiment cf Tilley s 1026 Swallows, like false friends, fly away
    on the approach of winter.
397 *Stragula*] So Diogenes Laertius 8.17; Plutarch *Moralia* 728B does not fold the
    bedclothes but shakes them up, so as to conceal the shape of the body that slept
    in them. This might be a precaution against evil influences.

ring. Perhaps this is a warning not to bandy the name of God about 405
everywhere.

Sellam oleo ne absterseris

Λαδίῳ εἰς θάκον μὴ ὀμόργνυσθαι, Do not wipe a seat with oil. There is no
explanation of this either. I think the sense is: Do not put the best things to
unworthy or unprofitable use. 410

Coronam ne carpito

Στέφανον μὴ δρέπεσθαι, Pluck not a garland for yourself. St Jerome *Against
Rufinus* interprets this to mean that the laws of cities must be observed, not
flouted or criticized, because the castellated walls of cities have the appearance of a garland. 415

Quae deciderint ne tollito

Τὰ πεσόντα μὴ ἀναιρεῖσθαι, Do not pick up what has fallen. This tells us to
become accustomed to a moderate diet. Aristophanes in the *Heroes*, according to Laertius, offers a superstitious origin for this precept; what fell from
the table was the property of the heroes, and therefore it was forbidden to 420
taste of it. Others put it thus: Taste not of what has fallen at table.

A gallo candido abstineas

Ἀλεκτρυόνος μὴ ἅπτεσθαι λευκοῦ, Do not lay hands on a white cock, because it is sacred to the Month, being the herald of the hours.

Panem ne frangito 425

Ἄρτον μὴ καταγνύειν, Do not break bread. This warns us not to break off a
friendship, because in ancient times friendship was ratified by bread. Hence
Christ our Prince by distributing bread consecrated a perpetual friendship
among His own, and so it is not seemly that that should be broken by which
friends are joined together. 430

* * * * *

407 *Sellam*] The word *ladio*, translated as oil, is in modern texts of Laertius *dadio*, a
torch or a splinter of pinewood. The sense is still not clear.
412 Jerome] *Adversus Rufinum* 3.39; 'because ... garland' added in *1517/8*
416 *Quae deciderint* This is from Diog. Laert. 8.34, and the second Greek form given
for it is Aristophanes frag 305 Kock. Erasmus added the Latin version of this in
1515, and had perhaps forgotten the source whence he had derived it, when it
1517/8 he inserted 'Others put it thus.'
427 Hence Christ] Matthew 26:26 etc; the sentence was added in *1517/8*.

Salem apponito
Τὸν ἅλα παρατίθεσθαι, Put salt on the table. This warns us that justice and
right should be part of every transaction. Whatever it has penetrated, salt
preserves; and it consists of the purest of things, water and sea.

In via ne seces ligna   435
Ἐν ὁδῷ μὴ σχίζειν ξύλα, Do not cut up logs on the road. Some explain this as
meaning: Do not torment and shorten your life with cares and anxious
thoughts.

Ne libaris diis ex vitibus non amputatis
Μὴ σπένδειν θεοῖς ἐξ ἀμπέλων ἀτμήτων, Pour no libations to the gods from   440
unpruned vines. Nothing is pleasing to the gods which is not pure and
purged. This riddle is attributed to Numa by Plutarch in his life of Numa,
and he guesses it to be a commendation of gentleness, which is part of piety;
just as the teaching of the Gospel rejects the offering of the ruthless man
who will not agree to be reconciled with his brother. Anything which is not   445
pruned is wild, and meal helps to soften anything hard; for he adds what I
shall put next.

Ne sacrificato sine farina
Μὴ θύειν ἄτερ ἀλφίτων, Make no sacrifice without meal. This enigma recommends gentleness in conduct, as has been said.   450

Adorato circumactus
Προσκυνεῖν περιφερόμενος, Turn your body as you worship. No doubt in
imitation of the perpetual wheeling of the heavens; moreover the Ancients
believed that the sky was a god. Plutarch ascribes this also to Numa as
peculiar to him. He does indeed mention the wheeling of the sky, but he also   455
adds other interpretations: as for instance when shrines face the rising sun,
and the worshipper, turning himself to the east by a movement of the body,
seems to turn himself towards God and by describing a circle to send out his
prayer to both halves of the world. He adds a third meaning, which he
seems to like the best: the turning of the body signifies the Egyptian wheels.   460

* * * * *

431 *Salem apponito*] Diog. Laert. 8.35
435 *In via*] Perhaps from Iamblichus *Protrepticus* 21
442 Plutarch] *Numa* 14.3. 'This riddle ... put next' added in 1526
444 Gospel] Matthew 5:23–4
450 as has been said] Added in 1526
454 Plutarch] *Numa* 14.3, from which the opening of the paragraph is taken.
'Plutarch ... His will' added in 1526

I take it that he is thinking of the hieroglyphics by which they signified that nothing in human affairs is stable or eternal, but that, however it shall please God to change and turn our life, it is right for us to accept His will.

Adoraturi sedeant

Καθῆσθαι προσκυνήσοντας, Let those who intend to worship be seated.   465
This signifies that we should concentrate on our prayers, and should pray steadily for what is best. This too Plutarch ascribes to Numa in his life of Numa (except that in the volume published by the Aldine press we read the word for worship in the past, not the future tense), adding that this was like a good augury that our prayers will be accepted and answered. He goes on   470
to say that some people see in this sitting quiet a way of making a break between one activity and the next, as if those who have brought their former activity to an end by sitting still in the presence of the gods are asking them at the same time to bless the action that is to follow. Others think that there is a suggestion of a different kind: that those who celebrate a religious cere-   475
mony should not do so heedlessly and as though their minds were on something else, but in singleness of heart, concentrating on the divine office. That is why, as Plutarch also relates, whenever the priest began to take the auspices or perform the rite, the heralds cried 'Attend, attend!' That cry was an admonition that those who approach sacred things should do so   480
with reverence and concentration. In his 'Antiquarian Problems' he mentions that it was customary for those who had made vows to the gods to lodge in the temples and keep a retreat, because action in this life often involves a man in troubles.

Surgens e lecto, vestigium corporis confundito.   485
'Αναστὰς ἐξ εὐνῆς συνταράττειν τὰ στρώματα, When you rise, shake up the bedclothes. This seems the same as the former, on folding the blankets.

A piscibus abstineto
'Ιχθύων μὴ γεύεσθαι, Do not taste fish. The reason why Pythagoras com-

* * * * *

461 hieroglyphics] Erasmus has added this word to his source in Plutarch, but the idea that Pythagoras was close to Egyptian 'hieroglyphics' comes from another passage, *Moralia* 354F.
467 Plutarch] *Numa* 14.3 and 5, added in *1526*; the first sentence must have been taken from the same source in *1508*.
478 Plutarch] *Numa* 14.2; perhaps a reminiscence of *Moralia* 276B, both added in *1526*
485 *Surgens*] Clement of Alexandria *Stromateis* 5.5 (PG 9.48B); the Greek in Iamblichus *Protrepticus* 21 is somewhat different.
488 *A piscibus abstineto*] Erasmus will return to this in I v 29.

manded abstinence from the *urtica marina* or sea-anemone is possibly be-   490
cause that creature is sacred to Hecate, on account of the mystery of the
number three, which they say is dedicated to this goddess; but why he
should forbid the eating of all other fish is not so easily explained. Though in
Plutarch, in his 'Table-talk,' someone produces this explanation, that fish
seem in a way to be fellow-students of the Pythagorean philosophy, owing   495
to their silence, so that As dumb as a fish has passed into a proverb. Theon
the grammarian, also in Plutarch, alleges a different reason. Fish are natives
of the sea and nourished by it, and it is an element not merely most foreign,
but most hostile, to the nature of man. For the gods gain no sustenance from
it, as for instance the Stoics believe they do from the stars; even the parent   500
and preserver of the land of Egypt, Osiris, perished by being cast into it. So
the Egyptians do not use sea-water for drinking, nor think anything which is
born in it or nourished by it either clean or useful for the purposes of man;
for they do not breathe the same air as we do, nor have we any region we can
share with them. Indeed this air of ours, which is life and nourishment to all   505
else, brings death to them, as to creatures which are born and live in
unnatural and exceptional conditions. It is no wonder, he says, if the
Egyptians abstain from creatures which are foreign to man's nature because
their element is the sea, which for the same reason are unfit to be mixed with
our breath and our blood; neither do they deign in any case to speak to   510
sailors when they meet them, because they make their living from the sea. In
the same passage Sylla advances yet another reason, that the custom of
Pythagoras was to eat only things that had been sacrificed to the gods, after
the first-fruits had been dedicated. But no fish is suitable for sacrifice.

    Plutarch himself rejects both of these interpretations, saying that the   515
apparently alien character of fish should provide all the more reason for
eating them. To live on creatures of the same sort as oneself by mutual
slaughter is monstrous and quite worthy of a Cyclops. For when, as the
story goes, Pythagoras one day bought a whole catch and let the caught fish
go, he was not scorning them as enemies and aliens but sparing them as   520
new-made friends and captives, after paying the price on their behalf. He
gives two reasons why Pythagoras did not approve of the eating of fish: it
was partly because he thought there was an element of injustice in pursuing,
killing and devouring a creature which by its very nature does no harm at all

    * * * * *

490 sea-anemone] Gellius 4.11.11–3, citing Plutarch as his authority
494 Plutarch] *Moralia* 728E
496 proverb] *Adagia* I v 29
496 Theon] He is a character in Plutarch's 'Table-talk'; the following discussion is
    all from *Moralia* 729A–30D.

to man nor ever could. Secondly, because the eating of fish is not a result of   525
necessity, but a luxury, a superfluous pleasure for the glutton. Hence, he
says, Homer represents not only the Greeks, when they were warring round
the Hellespont, as abstaining from fish, but also the Phaeacians, who were
otherwise great trenchermen. He did not set seafood even before his greedy
suitors, although both he and they were islanders. For it is among these that   530
we see a greater degree of both cruelty and luxury. The companions of
Ulysses never used hook or nets, as long as they had supplies of flour. But
when they had eaten all their stores, just before they devoured the sacred
oxen of the Sun, they began to fish, not for a more interesting diet, but to
repel hunger. There are other points about abstention from fish which are   535
mentioned in this passage of Plutarch, but these seemed sufficient for the
interpretation of the precept.

To Pythagoras is also ascribed that fine saying, as Plutarch records in
his essay 'On Exile': 'Choose the best rule of life, and custom will render it
delightful.' St Jerome also records this Pythagorean principle, in which that   540
great man seems to have comprised the whole of moral philosophy: 'These
things we must chase from us, and cut away by all means in our power –
sickness from the body, ignorance from the mind, gluttony from the belly,
sedition from the state, discord from the family, intemperance in short from
every activity of life.'   545

3   **Nemo bene imperat, nisi qui paruerit imperio**
    No one is a good commander who has not been under command

Οὐκ ἔστιν εὖ ἄρξειν μὴ ἀρχθέντα, It is impossible for one to rule well, who
has not been ruled himself. This proverb is still extant and is well known
today; no one is a good master who has not previously been a servant.   5
Aristotle quotes this in the *Politics*, book 3: 'Therefore this also is rightly said,
that no one can rule well who has not himself been ruled,' and in the same

* * * * *

530 islanders] The uncomplimentary reference ('For … luxury') was added in
   1517/8. Perhaps Erasmus was thinking of the meals he had eaten in Britain (or
   watched the British eat), and the barbarous customs-officer who had confis-
   cated all his coin on the beach at Dover when he left.
538 Plutarch] *Moralia* 602A
540 Jerome] *Adversus Rufinum* 3.39; the Greek perhaps supplied by Erasmus, as the
   original was not yet known in his day.

   3 Apparently taken straight from Aristotle. Suringar 145; Tilley s 246 He that
   has not served knows not how to command.
   6 Aristotle] *Politics* 3.4 (1277b12); 7.14 (1333a2)

book, 'For they say that it is necessary for the one who is going to rule well to be ruled first himself.' Plato expresses it in a more proverbial form, in the *Laws*, book 6: 'Now it is necessary that every man think this about all men, that the one who has not been a servant will by no means become a master worthy of praise.' Plutarch, 'To An Uneducated Ruler': 'For those who have fallen are unequal to the task of setting up others, nor is it for the ignorant to teach, or the disorderly to create order, or the undisciplined to impose discipline, or for one to rule who has not undergone rule.' The same writer gives this particular praise to Agesilaus, that he came to a position of command well trained in obeying command. Seneca, *On Anger*, book 2: 'No one can rule but the man who can also be ruled.' The proverb arose out of that famous saying of Solon, which is quoted in his Life by Diogenes Laertius: 'Rule, but after first learning to be ruled.' It can be applied either to those who by first obeying others' rule learn to rule others, or to those who exercise control over their own desires before they take control of other people. A person who is a slave to his own emotions is certainly not fit to rule over others; and he cannot be a king to others unless his own king is reason.

10

15

20

25

4 Adonidis horti
Gardens of Adonis

Ἀδώνιδος κῆποι, Gardens of Adonis, used to be applied to trivial things, which served no useful purpose and were suitable only for giving a brief

* * * * *

9 Plato] *Laws* 6.762e
12 Plutarch] *Moralia* 780B; *Agesilaus* 1, the latter added in 1535. He was a king of Sparta in the fourth century BC.
17 Seneca] *Dialogi* 4 (*De ira* 2). 15.4, added in 1533
19 Diogenes Laertius] 1.60

4 *Collectanea* no 700 had given the Greek of this from Diogenianus 1.14, followed by a passage (in Latin) from 'Pausanias the grammarian' in almost the same words as are reused here. Then came references to Pliny *Naturalis historia* 21.60 and to Plato. Pliny was drawing on Theophrastus *Historia plantarum* 6.7.3, where 'gardens of Adonis' are mentioned; but by some mistake he reproduced this in the form *adonium* as the name of a species of plant. A plant of that name would be quite irrelevant here, and so in 1508 Erasmus has dropped the Pliny-reference; but he has also missed the early reference to the 'gardens' in Theophrastus. These were pot-plants, associated with the near-eastern divine hero Adonis, and like him they had a short life; when in the ritual he was carried out for burial, they were thrown away.

passing pleasure. Pausanias tells how people used to be very fond of 5
'Adonis-gardens, well stocked particularly with lettuce and fennel; they
would plant seeds in them just as one does in pots. Thus the thing became a
proverb directed against worthless, trifling men,' born for silly pleasures –
people like singers, sophists, bawdy poets, confectioners and so on. These
gardens were sacred to Venus, on account of her darling Adonis, who was 10
snatched away in his first bloom and turned into a flower. Plato makes
mention of this in the *Phaedrus*: 'Would a sensible husbandman who has
seeds which he cares for and wants to come to fruition sometime, plant them
in gardens of Adonis in the summer and be pleased to see them become ·
beautiful in eight days, or would he do these things for the sake of sport and 15
amusement, if he does them at all?' Thus also Plutarch, in the treatise
entitled 'On the Delays of the Divine Vengeance': 'Nay, God is so particular
and concerned with trifles that although we have nothing divine in us,
nothing which in any way resembles him, nothing consistent and stable, but
rather in the manner of leaves, as Homer says, we begin to wither away and 20
shortly die, yet he has such a care for us (just like the women who cherish
and care for gardens of Adonis that bloom for a few days in earthenware
pots), that he cherishes our short-lived souls sprouting in tender flesh that is
incapable of any strong root of life, who are soon, for any chance cause, to
perish.' Theocritus recalls this in idyll 15: 'Frail gardens, in bright silver 25
baskets kept.' The proverb is also known in the form: 'more fruitless than
gardens of Adonis.'

In a metaphor not unlike this, Isaeus, according to Philostratus, calls
youthful pleasures 'gardens of Tantalus' because they are just like shadows

* * * * *

5 Pausanias] The Atticist, a lexicographer perhaps of the first half of the second
century AD. This is frag 1.27; see H. Erbse's *Untersuchungen zu den attizistischen
Lexika* in the *Abhandlungen* of the Berlin Academy (1950). The source is Suidas
A517, which suggests that Erasmus knew Suidas as early as 1500 when the
Collectanea were published, unless he drew it from some secondary source.

11 Plato] *Phaedrus* 276b, the last clause ('or would he ... at all') added in 1517/8.

16 Plutarch] *Moralia* 560B–C. An unfortunate misprint in 1508, perpetuated in all
editions of the *Adagia* down to and including LB (*foventque* for *foveatque*), made
the women cherish the souls of their pot-plants or window-boxes, instead of
God cherishing the souls of men. Erasmus would never have credited
pot-plants with souls.

25 Theocritus] 15.113–4

26 proverb] This is the form given in Zenobius 1.49.

28 Philostratus] See I iv 73 note. *Vitae sophistarum* 513 and 594–5, added in 1533.
Isaeus was a sophist of the late first century AD. For the punishment of Tantalus
(good things always tantalizingly out of reach), see II vi 14. These insubstantial
gardens form an adage in their own right, II i 46.

and dreams, and do not satisfy the soul of a man, but rather irritate it.   30
Similarly Pollux called the style of Athenodorus the sophist 'gardens of
Tantalus' because it was smooth and youthful and gave the appearance of
having something in it, when there was nothing at all.

5 Infixo aculeo fugere
To flee after planting the dart

Βαλὼν φεύξεσθαι οἴει; Do you think you can shoot and run? A proverbial
metaphor; someone has uttered an accusation or committed some misdeed,
and immediately removes himself, so as to escape being forced to uphold   5
what he has said, or having the same treatment meted out to himself.
Eryximachus the doctor, in the *Symposium* of Plato, says to Aristophanes,
who is on the point of leaving so that he may not himself have to praise
Cupid, and escaping with a few poetic jokes: 'As it seems, Aristophanes,
you think you can shoot and run. Pay attention and speak as if you were   10
going to render an account. Then perhaps if it seems good to me I'll let you
go.' He makes use of it also in the *Phaedo*, and in the *Republic*, book 1, though
in this place he changes the metaphor and speaks of the bath-attendant who
has thrown water over his client and gone away: 'Having said this Thrasy-
machus had it in mind to leave, like a bath-attendant having poured a flood 15
of words about our ears.' And soon after in the same place, 'Having cast
such a word, do you have it in mind to leave?' Plutarch thought of the
proverb in the essay 'On the Delays of the Divine Vengeance': 'But even if he
did go off after casting his weapon, it does not do to disregard the arrow that
is in the wound.' Aristotle alluded to this proverb in the third book of his   20
Lectures on Physics. Refuting the opinion of Anaxagoras, who had said that
infinity was immobile and at rest in itself, he averred that it had not been
enough to say that and then retreat, when he ought also to have stated the
reason why infinity could not be moved: 'It is not enough, having said these

* * * * *

31 Pollux] Julius Pollux, of Naucratis in Egypt, a teacher of sophistic rhetoric in the
    second half of the second century AD, and more important to us now than most
    of his type, as the compiler of an extensive dictionary of Greek antiquities, of
    which we possess an abridgement. This, the *Onomasticon* of Pollux, was first
    published by Aldus in 1502, and is extensively used in the *Adagia*.

5 Zenobius 2.71; Suidas B 87.
7 Plato] *Symposium* 189b; *Phaedo* 91c; *Republic* 1.344d, this last added in *1515*
17 Plutarch] *Moralia* 548b, added in *1515*
20 Aristotle] *Physica* 3.5 (205b8), the book-number corrected from 4 to 3 in *1526* and
    'It is not enough ... the printer's' added

things, to go away' (in passing I amend the spelling, not Aristotle's but the   25
printer's).

This will fit those people who make statements in oracular fashion,
giving others grounds for a speculation, since they do not explain why they
think in this way. It seems to be adapted from bees or wasps, which plant
their sting and immediately fly away. This is what Plato is suggesting in the   30
Phaedo. It may also be a reference to the Parthians, who cast their javelins
against the enemy and then wheel their horses and take flight, not daring to
come to close quarters. Something very like this is in Cicero, *De finibus*, book
4: 'That's a sharp stone to the departing one, but we shall see.' A sharp
pointed stone is usually troublesome to walkers. He says this more clearly in   35
his speech *Pro Flacco*: 'What did it profit Flaccus? The man was in good
health until the moment when he came forward here; he died when he had
shot his bolt and given his evidence.'

6 Nodum solvere
To undo the knot

Κάθαμμα λύειν, To undo the knot, used to be said of a person who easily
completed a job that everyone found difficult. It arose, they say, from the
tradition about Midas, who used to ride in a chariot harnessed with inextric-   5
able knots of cornel-bark. This chariot was placed in a temple, and it was
generally said among the Phrygians that anyone who could loose the bonds
that held it would become the ruler of Asia. Alexander the Great undid it by

* * * * *

30 Plato] As above
31 Parthians] Cf i ii 31.
33 Cicero] *De finibus* 4.28.80, added in 1526; *Pro L. Flacco* 17.41, added in 1536

6 From the Greek proverb-collections (Zenobius 4.46; Diogenianus 5.47, where
  the text is already corrupted; Suidas κ 31). Otto 1233; Tilley G 315 To cut the
  Gordian knot. The emphasis in Antiquity, and here, seems to lie more on the
  solution of an apparently insoluble problem than, as with us, on the use of
  illegitimate and even violent means to cut through it or bypass it. Problems
  relating to the Gordian knot are discussed with further references in an
  appendix in W.W. Tarn *Alexander the Great* (Cambridge 1948) 2.262–5.
5 Midas] A mythical king of Phrygia in Asia minor, of which Gordium, not far
  west of the modern Ankara, was one of the principal cities; he recurs in *Adagia* i
  iii 67 and i vi 24.
6 of cornel-bark] These words, and lower down 'by removing the pin which held
  the yoke to the pole,' were inserted in 1533, and come from Plutarch's *Alexander*
  18, which had been extensively used in i ix 48.

removing the pin which fixed the yoke to the pole; some say by cutting the
knot with a sword. I shall mention this story in another place, in the proverb   10
Herculaneus nodus. Cicero says in the fifth book of his *Letters to Atticus*: 'No
consideration should be paid to Caesar by the senate until this knot is
loosed,' that is, until this business is completed.

7 **Dodonaeum aes**
   Dodonean bronze

Δωδωναῖον χαλκεῖον, A cymbal, or bell, from Dodona. This is usually said of
a man whose garrulity is excessive and ill-timed. Zenodotus quotes it from
the *Ariphorus* of Menander. He relates that there were in Dodona two lofty   5
columns: on one of them was fixed a bronze basin, on the other hung the
figure of a boy holding a bronze whip in his hand, and whenever the wind
blew with any force it would often happen that the thong struck the caul-
dron which gave out a ringing sound at each blow, the reverberations of
which lasted a long time. Others think it refers to Corinthian bronze vessels,   10
which have a clearer ring than the rest. Stephanus mentions this adage
under the word 'Dodona.' Juvenal seems to have alluded to it when he says,
'You would think / As many basins or as many bells / were sounding,'

* * * * *

10 in the proverb *Herculaneus nodus*] 1 ix 48. This cross-reference (to an article in
    which our adage is confused with an unrelated one) was inserted in 1533.
11 Cicero] *Ad Atticum* 5.21.53.

 7 In the *Collectanea* (no 676), Erasmus had given the Greek form of the proverb,
    no doubt from Diogenianus 8.32, but his Latin was 'Ephyrean or Dodonean
    bronze.' Ephyra was an old name for Corinth, and Virgil had used this name to
    describe the bronze objects originating in Corinth which were keenly collected
    by Roman connoisseurs. Erasmus had found these identified, wrongly, with
    the bronze caldrons, bowls or gongs which were one of the sources of
    information at the oracle of Dodona in Epirus, and which in the descriptions
    sound highly legendary; it is Dodona, not Corinth, with which we are
    concerned here.
 4 Zenodotus] Zenobius 6.5, citing Menander frag 60. This is the most famous of
    all the writers of the New Comedy (fourth/third century BC), and although until
    recent years his work was known only in fragments, Erasmus cites it about sixty
    times (we use for the fragments the numbering of A. Körte). For the so-called
    Sententiae or *Monosticha*, a large collection of one-line moral maxims that passed
    under his name, see 1 i 30n.
11 Stephanus] Steph. Byzantius (see 1 ii 43n) p 249 Meineke.
12 Juvenal] 6.441–2

rebuking the talkativeness of women. Suidas provides a different interpretation for the proverb from Demo. He says that the oracle of Jove, formerly in   15
Dodona, was hung all round with bronze cauldrons, so that they touched
each other. In this way it was inevitable that when any one of them was
struck, all the others rang in turn, the sound running by contact from one to
another. That clanging would last for a long time, as the sound made full
circle. He thinks too that the proverb was applied to misers, and to people   20
who complain about the slightest thing. It is true that Aristotle rejects this
interpretation as fictitious, and proposes the other meaning which has been
mentioned above, the two columns and the figure of the boy.

Plutarch in his essay 'On Garrulity' declares that in Olympia there was
a certain portico which was so constructed by mathematical computation   25
that it gave back many notes in answer to one, and for this reason was called
'Seven Voices.' He compares this with immensely talkative men: you may
speak one little word to them and they immediately return such a spate of
words that there is no end to the chatter. Julius Pollux also refers to this
adage in his sixth book, in the chapter on chatterers, by the words 'the   30
bronze of Dodona.'

8   **Prora et puppis**
    Stem and stern

Πρώρα καὶ πρύμνη, Stem and stern. Cicero, in the last book of his *Letters to
Friends*, writing to his beloved Tyro, refers to this proverb in these words:
'The stem and stern (as the Greek proverb goes) of my sending you away   5
from me was that you might straighten out my financial affairs.' By 'stem
and stern' we mean to sum up our intentions; because the whole ship
depends on stem and stern, as it were on 'head and heel.' In Greek I find it

* * * * *

14 Suidas] Δ1445, citing Demo *De proverbiis* (c 300 BC), *FGrHist* 327F20; when
    Aristotle is cited, this is a slip in Erasmus' source for Aristides, another lost
    collector of proverbs.
24 Plutarch] *Moralia* 502D, added in *1515*; this was used also in Erasmus' *Parabolae*
    570B (CWE 23 156 and 224).
29 Pollux] See I i 4n; *Onomasticon* 6.120, referred to in *Adagia* IV v 51; added here in
    1515.

8   *Collectanea* no 710 gave this, with no authority except a passage from Ermolao
    Barbaro, which was dropped in the *Chiliades* of 1508. The Greek might well be a
    back-translation by Erasmus himself from Cicero's Latin. Otto 1477
3   Cicero] *Ad familiares* 16.24.1.
8   Greek] Apostolius 15.97, the last phrase ('or stem … too') added in *1517/8*

said in this form, 'they perished stem and stern,' or 'stem is lost and stern too,' that is, to complete destruction. Philostratus in the *Heroicus*: 'But it is 10 necessary to be tied to the ship like Ulysses, otherwise all perishes, stem and stern as they say.' A similar figure is used in the Apocalypse: 'I am alpha and omega,' I am the sum of all things. All things proceed from me as from a source, and all things come back to me, as to a haven of bliss. Now alpha is the first letter in Greek, omega the last. Not unlike this is the phrase of 15 Theocritus in the *Praise of Ptolemy*, 'But Ptolemy shall be celebrated among all men as the first, and last, and middle.' So Virgil's phrase: 'My first notes were inspired by you, yours shall be the last.' To this belongs the description of delivery by Demosthenes, calling it the first, second, and third, in fact the whole of eloquence. Plato in the *Laws*, book 4: 'The god himself, as the old 20 saying goes, holding the beginning and end and middle of all things.' Plutarch in the essay 'On the Education of Children': 'That the first, middle and final point in these matters is a good education and proper instruction.' Aristotle in book 3 of the *Rhetoric* quotes from a certain Alcidamas who called philosophy the 'ditch and rampart' of the laws, meaning that all safeguards 25 for law resided in philosophy. But the philosopher rejects this metaphor as harsh and insipid, as if the foregoing 'stem and stern' were not harsher still. In serious oratory, certainly, these expressions might be unsuitable; in proverbs this roughness is less offensive, because they are often of a riddling nature, and those often seem most successful which are used in a rather 30 more strained sense. Thus whenever we wish to describe the sum of the whole business, everything that is important and essential for it, we shall say stem and stern, or rampart and ditch; for instance, Piety ought to be the stem and stern of our studies. For some people the stem and stern of every consideration is money. Against the might of the Carthaginians Scipio was 35 rampart and ditch, ie the principal safeguard.

* * * * *

10 Philostratus] *Heroicus* 8.13 (ed. L. De Lannoy, Leipzig, 1977); added in 1523. The Greek, which Erasmus quotes, was first printed in the Aldine Lucian of 1503.
12 Apocalypse] 1.8 (cf 22.13)
16 Theocritus] 17.3–4
17 Virgil] *Eclogues* 8.11
19 Demosthenes] Cicero *De oratore* 3.56.243 and elsewhere
20 Plato] *Laws* 4.715e
22 Plutarch] *Moralia* 5c, added in 1533
24 Aristotle] *Rhetoric* 3.3 (1406b11)

9   **Umbrae**
    Shadows

Σκιαί, Shadows: the name given in a proverbial and humorous way to those
who came to a dinner without being invited themselves, but as companions
to those who had been invited, following them without question as the   5
shadow follows the body. Horace alluded to this proverb in the first book of
the *Epistles*, writing to Torquatus:

> Your Brutus and Septimius I'll invite,
> And if he's not engaged to better cheer
> Or a kind girl, Sabinus shall be here.   10
> Still there is room for other shades, but note –
> Too crowded feasts are scented with the goat.

In this place Acron makes no mention of the proverb, passing it over, I
imagine, as something everybody uses and knows. Cristoforo Landino, in
general a man of learning, interprets 'shadows' as places in the country   15
covered with shade, where the guests could recline at ease. And then he
interprets 'goats' as sharp-tongued jesters. Further on, he explains 'say how
many you would like to be on the day' in the following way: 'write and tell
me what kind of men, of what rank, you would wish me to invite with you;
for if you want them to be above you, you will be the last, if lower than you,   20
you will be the first.' I would not have thought of quoting this, except that it
helps to show to what lengths of absurdity a learned man can be pushed
sometimes by the ignorance of one little proverb. The meaning of Horace's
poem is as follows: he suggests to Torquatus that he should come to the
dinner accompanied by a few friends, for instance Brutus, Septimius and   25
Sabinus; not that there will not be room for more 'shadows' if he wishes to
bring them with him, but the disadvantage of being crowded together
would be that the smell of perspiration would interfere with the sweetness
of the banquet. Further, if he wishes to bring several 'shadows' or companions he should warn Horace of the number, lest the preparations should not   30
be adequate. Thus he calls Brutus, Septimius and Sabinus the 'shadows' of

* * * * *

9 Derived no doubt from Horace.
6 Horace] *Epistles* 1.5.26–30 (trans mainly Sir Philip Francis 1756). In *1508*
  Erasmus referred to both the ancient commentators on Horace, Porphyrion and
  Acron, but he struck out the former name in *1515*.
14 Landino] The Florentine scholar (1424–1504), author of the most popular
  Horace-commentary of the Renaissance, many times printed. Erasmus' stric-
  tures here are not uncalled-for.

Torquatus, if they come not as invited guests but as companions brought by
Torquatus, whom Horace has invited. In another place he says, 'Servilius,
Balatro, Vibidius were there, / brought by Maecenas as his shadows,' that is,
coming of their own accord. Plutarch in his 'Table-talk' relates what 'shad-   35
ows' are in these words: 'The question was raised as to the origin of the
custom of bringing along guests, now called shadows, these not themselves
invited, but brought to a meal by those who were invited. They thought it
began with Socrates, who persuaded Aristodemus, although he was not
invited, to accompany him to a party at Agathon's. A funny thing had   40
happened to Aristodemus. Not realizing that Socrates had been left behind
on their way, he went in first, just like a shadow going ahead of a person
who has the light at his back.' Thus far Plutarch. This story about Socrates
and Aristodemus is in the dialogue of Plato called the *Symposium*.

10 Nihil ad Parmenonis suem
Nothing like Parmeno's pig

Οὐδὲν πρὸς τὴν Παρμένοντος ὖν, Nothing like Parmeno's pig. This is said
about emulation, when it falls far short of what it was imitating. Plutarch in
his 'Table-talk,' in the second problem of the fifth decade, gives this account   5
of how the proverb came into being. Parmeno was one of those people (and
they exist also in our time) who imitate the various voices of men and of
animals so cleverly and make them sound so present, that the hearers
(though not the observers) think they hear real and not imitated voices. And
there is no lack of people who are particularly delighted with this trick.   10
Parmeno is said to have been in great favour with the people, and extremely
well known owing to this skill. When others tried to emulate him, and
everybody said 'That's all very well, but nothing like Parmeno's pig,' some-

* * * * *

33 In another place] Horace *Satires* 2.8.21–2
35 Plutarch] *Moralia* 707A
44 Plato] *Symposium* 174a–b

10 The source of this, as Erasmus tells us, is Plutarch's *Moralia* 674B–C. It is related
   to a passage in the third preface in the second volume of Erasmus' edition of
   Jerome (printed as Ep 326), where Parmeno's pig is mentioned and the Paris
   humanist Fausto Andrelini is persuaded by a trick to 'immensely admire a
   new-fangled epigram, thinking it to be ancient.' Parmeno the mimic cannot be
   identified; the *Corpus Paroemiographorum* 1.412 gives another form of the story,
   in which he is a painter, and paints a pig so lifelike that the spectators can hear
   it squeal. The sentence recording Plutarch's other allusion (*Moralia* 18c) was
   inserted in *1515*.

one came forward carrying a real piglet hidden under his arm. When the people thought the sound was an imitation and immediately cried as usual 15 'What's that to Parmeno's pig?' he proved by producing the real pig and showing it round that their judgment was wrong, and founded not on truth but imagination. The same author mentions Parmeno and this sham pig in his essay 'On How to Study Poetry.'

We can use this adage appositely whenever anyone is deceived by 20 conjecture into making a false judgment. For instance if someone should immensely admire an ignorant and new-fangled epigram, thinking it to be ancient. On the other hand, if he should dismiss as recent something which was ancient and learned. For the force of imagination is such that it can deceive the judgment of even the most erudite men. 25

11   Syncretismus
Syncretism

Συγκρητισμὸς, 'Syncretism' was the word used in a Cretan proverb whenever it happened that those who recently seemed to be most deadly enemies suddenly came into complete agreement. This often happens, 5 especially when some misfortune strikes which is common to them both. Plutarch in the essay 'On Brotherly Love' reviews the proverb and explains it in the following words: 'Furthermore it will be necessary to keep this in mind, when brothers are quarrelling, to preserve our familiarity with the brothers' friends and to associate with them especially at that time; but to 10 avoid and shun their enemies, following that example at least of the Cretans, who often fought among themselves in factions and intestine strife, but when an enemy from outside attacked them they put aside their difference and stood together; and this was called "syncretism" by them.' Thus far Plutarch. Something of the same kind is mentioned by Quintus Curtius, 15 book 9, regarding the Sudraci and Malli, 'who were otherwise accustomed to make war on each other, but were united by the common danger at the threat of Alexander's coming.' A phrase belongs here, which we shall mention elsewhere out of Aristotle: 'Troubles bring men together.' This

*****

11 Probably taken direct from Plutarch

7 Plutarch] *Moralia* 490B

15 Quintus Curtius] 9.4.15, added in *1517/8*. An edition by Erasmus of the *History of Alexander the Great* by Quintus Curtius Rufus (first century AD) was published by Matthias Schürer in Strasbourg in June 1518 (see Ep 704), and nearly all the references to his work entered the *Adagia* in *1517/8*.

19 Aristotle] See *Adagia* II i 71.

adage will also be rightly used to describe those who enter on a friendship   20
not because they sincerely love each other, but because each has need of the
other's resources; or where forces are joined to destroy a common enemy. In
our own time we see this happen over and over again, that a military pact is
made between those who are the bitterest enemies. There is such a fury for
vengeance even among Christian men. This is mentioned by a certain   25
Apostolius of Byzantium, a very recent compiler of proverbs among the
Greeks.

12 Qui circa salem et fabam
Around salt and beans

Περὶ ἅλα καὶ κύαμον, Around salt and beans, was said of those who
pretended to know what they did not know; because the soothsayers about
to make a pronouncement employed salt and beans. So those who talked   5
secrets among themselves, were called 'men concerned with salt and beans.'
It is to be found in this form in Diogenianus and in the other compilers of
Greek proverbs. Plutarch, however, in the fourth decade of his 'Problems At
Table' writes not 'beans' but 'cummin,' unless the text is corrupt: 'This
somehow has escaped you who are concerned with salt and cummin, that   10
the one is more varied but the other is sweeter.' Again in the fifth decade of
the same work: 'Florus was asking, when we were dining with him, who
these might be who are referred to in the proverb as "concerned with salt
and cummin."' But Apollophanes the grammarian solved this question by
saying that the adage signifies extreme familiarity. Those, in fact, who are   15
closely intimate with each other eat together, with either salt or cummin,
and require no elaborate preparation of dishes. Hence that jesting remark of

* * * * *

22 In our own time ... Christian men] This is an addition of 1517/8.
26 Apostolius] 15.80; the clause describing him was added in 1515. Michael
   Apostolis or Apostolius (born about the year 1422) was a refugee from
   Constantinople, whose large collection of proverbs was last printed in the
   second volume of the Corpus Paroemiographorum. Erasmus used it with
   reluctance, and his references to Apostolius are generally unflattering; see the
   section on sources in the introductory volume to this translation.

12 Treated briefly in Collectanea no 719, with no source named, but doubtless from
   the proverb-collection of Diogenianus 1.50; it is also in Zenobius 1.25. Cf
   Adagia III v 20.
 8 Plutarch] Moralia 663F; 684E (this is the Symposiaca problemata, elsewhere called
   'Table-talk' but Erasmus' use of titles is not always consistent). Apollophanes is
   a character in Plutarch's dialogue. In the Greek, kuminos, cummin, could easily
   be confused with kuamos, bean.

Octavius Caesar to someone who had invited him to a frugal repast: 'I didn't
know I was such a close friend of yours.' Here belongs another phrase which
I shall refer to in its place: 'One must not transgress salt and trencher.' That   20
is, one must not transgress against the right of friendship, which is established by these things. On the other hand, the use of salt to mean frugality of
living is often to be recognized in the poets. Horace, in the *Odes*:

> He lives well on little,
> Who keeps upon his frugal board   25
> The ancestral salt-cellar.

And again in the *Satires*: 'Give me only a three-legged table / and a shell of
pure salt.'
However it seems to be in divinations, more for religious reasons, that
salt is customarily employed. Why this honour should be particularly   30
accorded to salt, is a question asked in Plutarch, in the place I have just
quoted; for Homer also calls salt divine, and Plato wrote that salt is closely
and intimately bound up with divine things. For this reason the Egyptians
abstained from salt, out of reverence, so completely that they could not even
eat salted bread. Plutarch, however, thinks that the Egyptians were more   35
likely to have abstained for this reason, that they wished to live purely,
because it is thought especially likely to arouse desire, owing to heat. It is
also not unlikely that they renounced salt because it is the tastiest condiment
of all, so much so that it can deservedly be called the relish of relishes. For
this reason there are those who term salt 'grace,' because without it every-   40
thing seems tasteless and disagreeable. But the most divine quality of salt
seems to be that it shields dead bodies from corruption and decay, and does
not allow them to die at once, resisting death for a long time and thus as far
as it may acting like the soul – and nothing is diviner than the soul. It is the
office of the soul to protect and hold together living beings, and not to allow 45
the structure to collapse; and in the same way salt, like the soul, maintains
the harmony of bodies which are tending to decay, and preserves the

* * * * *

18 Octavius Caesar] The emperor Augustus. The anecdote is told in the *Saturnalia*
   (2.4.13) of Macrobius, an author of the first half of the fifth century AD, whose
   works were often printed from 1472 onwards, and are used in about fifty places
   in the *Adagia*. In 1508 the victim of the jest was called Maecenas, a name which
   appears in the preceding section in Macrobius, and this was not corrected till
   1526.
19 another phrase] See *Adagia* I vi 10.
23 Horace] *Odes* 2.16.13–4; *Satires* 1.3.13–4

alliance of the members among themselves. On the same grounds they
think the lightning-flash sacred and divine, because bodies struck by lightning last a long time without mouldering away.   50

Salt has another almost divine quality: it is thought to possess some
real power in connection with procreation, especially for the reason (as has
been said above) that it arouses and encourages a lusty seed. Thus people
who rear dogs feed them on salt meat and salty foods so as to make them
active breeders. One might add that a huge quantity of mice are usually bred   55
in sea-going ships. And there are some who say that if women lick salt they
can become pregnant without the help of men. It is thought too that the
poets had this in mind, and not without reason imagined Venus, the
goddess of birth, to be born from the sea, calling her 'salt-born.' Indeed they
make all the sea-gods fertile, the fathers of many children. Finally, there is   60
no creature on earth or in the air so fecund as all the sea-creatures.

Questions of this kind about salt are discussed in the pages of Plutarch,
and I chose all the more to mention them because in Christian rites also, and
especially in baptism, when we are born again and have our new birth to
salvation, salt has an important place; so that from these views of the   65
ancients about salt, even the theologian may find something suited to his
use.

13   **Duabus ancoris fultus**
     Secured by two anchors

'Eπì δυοῖν ὁρμεῖ, He sits in harbour moored by two (anchors, understood);
referring to fixed and steadfast people, who have established their affairs
well. It is taken from ships which are safely berthed in the harbour, with   5
anchors let down from both stem and stern. Aristides mentions this in his

                    * * * * *

13 The Greek of this is in Apostolius 7.61; in Latin it occurs in Propertius, Ovid
   and Seneca (Otto 586), and it is so unlike Erasmus to ignore one of the two
   languages that one might well wonder whether something in his materials
   went astray. *Adagia* IV viii 72 adds one more example, in a series of supplements
   derived from a rereading of Pindar. Tilley R 119 Good riding at two anchors.
 6 Aristides] Aelius Aristides (129–c 189 AD) was a leader of the so-called Second
   Sophistic movement, a group of orators to whom form was more important than
   matter. Erasmus had access to a manuscript of some of his works, with scholia,
   in Venice, when he was collecting material for 1508, and quotes him about sixty
   times, especially his *De quattuor* ('On the Four'), a long rhetorical essay in
   praise of the Athenian statesmen Pericles, Cimon, Miltiades, and Themistocles,
   whose names he uses as titles for the different part of the work. Here he refers
   to another piece, the *Panathenaicus* p 176 Dindorf.

Panathenaicus. Drawn from the same metaphor is the phrase used by Demosthenes against Ctesiphon: 'He does not rely on the same (we must supply, anchor) as the general run of men.'

14 Sine capite fabula
A story without a head

'Ακέφαλος μῦθος, A headless tale is used of one imperfect and incomplete. Plato in the *Laws*, book 6: 'Certainly after I took up the function of speaking, I would be most unwilling to leave our talk headless; for if anyone met it 5 wandering about like that, it would seem ugly.' Again in the *Gorgias*: 'But they say it is not right to leave stories half-finished, but one should put a head on them lest they walk about without a head.' Perhaps this is an allusion to what Plutarch relates in his dialogue 'On the Obsolescence of Oracles.' In Crete a certain festival was carried out with novel and ridiculous 10 ceremonies, which included displaying a man's dummy without a head. They said that this was the father of Homerion, who was found without a head after ravishing a nymph. This proverb is referred to by Zenodotus.

15 Inter sacrum et saxum
Between the shrine and the stone

Tyndarus, in Plautus, one of the prisoners, whose wiles had been detected and who, being thus exposed, had no skill left by which he could escape, said 'Now I am done for, now I am between the shrine and the stone, and I 5 do not know what to do.' Apuleius in the eleventh book of his *Ass*: 'And so,

　　* * * * *

7 Demosthenes] *De corona* 281. This was used again in *1520* to provide IV v 41.

14 *Collectanea* no 412, citing no authority except the first Plato-passage (in Latin). The Greek there came from Diogenianus 2.9, and it is also in Suidas A 853.
4 Plato] *Laws* 6.752a. Plato says the headless talk would be 'shapeless'; Erasmus says 'foul' or 'ugly,' perhaps taking 'without form' to mean 'without beauty of appearance.' In *1508* this was also referred to in II vii 6.
6 Again] *Gorgias* 505c10, added in *1520*
9 Plutarch] *Moralia* 417E, added in *1515*
13 Zenodotus] Zenobius 1.59

15 *Collectanea* no 28, citing the Plautus passage. Otto 1564; Tilley D 222 Between the devil and the deep sea.
3 Plautus] *Captivi* 616–7
6 Apuleius] Second century AD. *Metamorphoses* 11.28. Erasmus sometimes called this work, as we do, *Ass* or *Golden Ass*.

as the misery of poverty had come upon me, in the words of the old proverb,
I was desperately tormented between the shrine and the stone.' Apuleius
explains the allegory in the adage, clearly referring to the priestly office to
which he was to be admitted, and to poverty, harder than a stone, which   10
meant that he could not pay his way. It appears to have been taken from the
early ceremonies attending the making of a treaty, when the fetial priest
struck a pig with a stone, speaking these words at the same time: 'Whichever
people first breaks this treaty, let Jupiter strike that people just as I am now
striking this pig with a stone.' But whatever was the origin of the proverb, it   15
is clear enough that it is usually applied to those who are in confusion and
driven into the greatest danger.

16   **Inter malleum et incudem**
     Between the hammer and the anvil

Μεταξὺ τοῦ ἄκμονος καὶ σφύρας, Between the hammer and the anvil. Something like this is mentioned by the theologian Origen, in a homily on
Jeremiah, in these very words (for we lack the Greek): 'Now there is a   5
proverb often used in popular speech among the gentiles, when they say
about people who are oppressed by dread and by great misfortune, "They
are between the hammer and the anvil."'

17   **Nunc meae in arctum coguntur copiae**
     Now my forces are pressed into a narrow space

The same thing is signified by a different metaphor in Terence in the
Heautontimorumenos, when he says, 'Strictly into a narrow place are my

* * * * *

13 these words] Livy 1.24.8, from memory. Erasmus returns to the ancient Roman
    ritual of treaty-making, in which priests called *fetiales* played an important part,
    in *Adagia* II vi 33.

16 Suringar 97; Tilley H 62 Between the hammer and the anvil
 4 Origen] *Homiliae in Hieremiam* 3.1 (ed W.A. Baehrens, *GCS* 33, 1925, 304).
    Origen's Homilies on Jeremiah survive, apart from excerpts, only in one
    manuscript in the Escorial, and were not printed until 1623. Erasmus therefore
    quotes the Latin version by St Jerome, and provides a Greek form of the proverb
    (which is not in the Greek text) apparently out of his own head. The words 'for
    we lack the Greek' were added in *1517/8*.

17 From Terence *Heautontimorumenos* 669. Correctly attributed in *1517/8*; before
    that, it was given to the *Andria* by a slip of memory. It is an obvious metaphor,
    rather than a proverb.

forces pressed.' The metaphor comes from an army which is in difficulties, 5
enclosed in an unfavourable place, and surrounded on all sides by enemies
so that it can hardly escape.

18   **In acie novaculae**
     On the razor's edge

Not unlike the preceding is the saying taken from Homer, and well-known
among the greatest authors, which became an adage: Ἐπὶ ξυροῦ ἀκμῆς, On
the blade, or the edge, of the razor, meaning 'in the greatest danger.' So 5
Nestor speaks in the *Iliad*, book 10:

> For now we all stand on the razor's edge,
> Whether for the Achaeans it be life
> Or sore destruction.

Sophocles in the *Antigone*: 'Think now once again / You tread upon the 10
razor's edge of fate.' These are the words of Teiresias the seer, warning
Creon, to let him know in how great danger he stands. Again in the
Epigrams: 'Kings of Europe and Asia powerful in war, / Now both of you are
on the razor's edge.' This refers to Menelaus and Paris, deciding by single
combat which of them should gain possession of Helen. Theocritus in the 15
Dioscuri: 'Certain salvation of men standing on dagger's point.' This seems
to be taken from conjurors, who walk on the points of swords, or from
people who handle blades, as the scholia published on this author tell us.

19   **Res est in cardine**
     Things are at a turning-point

Not very different from this is the phrase 'Things are at a turning-point' or
hinge, which Servius points out as an adage, when explaining Virgil: 'In

* * * * *

18 This might easily have been taken straight from Homer *Iliad* 10.173–4.
10 Sophocles] *Antigone* 996; Erasmus gives no Latin translation, which is most
   unusual. The phrase comes again at v i 97, in a series of adages added in *1533*
   from the *Antigone*.
13 *Epigrams*] *Anthologia Palatina* 9.475
15 Theocritus] 22.6; the reference to the scholia was added in *1526*. Erasmus
   normally refers to the idylls by their ancient titles rather than by numbers.

19 *Collectanea* no 831, citing the passages from Servius and Cicero. Otto 351
 4 Servius] On *Aeneid* 1.672

such a turn of things she'll not delay,' and he thinks this is equal to saying   5
that the matter is at a turning-point. Cicero says 'the matter hinges on this,'
meaning 'on this the whole thing depends.' Quintilian, in book 12: 'Not to
speak of the careless people, to whom it matters not at all on what the hinge
of lawsuits turns.' The same, in book 5: 'For if he confesses, there might be
many reasons for the garment to be stained with blood: if he denies, he   10
places the crucial point, on which his case hinges, here, and if he should be
worsted in that, he falls down in the rest also.' This is taken from doors,
which are supported on hinges on which they turn.

20   **Novacula in cotem**
The razor against the whetstone

Ξυρὸς εἰς ἀκόνην, The razor against the whetstone. This is usually applied to
those who happen to meet the very circumstances which they least wanted
to encounter. The razor could not fall more inconveniently that in striking   5
the whetstone. Not far removed from this is that remark of Horace: 'Thinking to plunge his teeth into the crumb, / He'll break them on a stone.' This
proverb will be rightly applied to the man who is eager to hurt others,and
finally meets someone who is able in turn to hurt him, while remaining
invulnerable. Just so a razor, if it meets something soft, cuts it up, but if it   10
meets a whetstone it is blunted. It was of this that Tarquin was thinking
when he said that he had it in mind how Actius Navius the augur divided a
whetstone with a razor, meaning that the razor was powerless against the
whetstone, although Livy tells in book 1 how the augur had done what he
thought impossible.
                                                                          15

* * * * *

6 Cicero] This phrase has not been found in Cicero; perhaps Erasmus is thinking
of Jerome *Letters* 57.4.2.
7 Quintilian] *Institutio oratoria* 12.8.2; 5.12.3

20 Probably from the Greek proverb-collections (Diogenianus 6.91; Suidas Ξ 160).
But they seem to interpret it of a man who gets something that suits him, not the
thing he 'least wanted to encounter,' as Erasmus has it. The razor held skilfully
against the stone is all the better for it.
6 Horace] *Satires* 2.1.77–8
11 Tarquin] The story comes from Livy 1.36.4, but at first Erasmus seems to have
quoted it from memory: Tarquin (the Etruscan king) was *ille*, the man was
unnamed. The names, and the reference to Livy, as we have them now, were
added in *1528*.

21 Caliga Maximini
The boot of Maximinus

The boot of Maximinus is a popular saying against men of immoderate
height and awkwardness. Julius Capitolinus refers to this proverbial use in
his life of the emperor Maximinus: 'Now since, as we said, Maximinus was   5
eight and a half feet tall, or nearly so, his shoe, or rather his imperial boot,
was placed by some people in the grove which lies between Aquileia and
Arzia; and it is known to have been longer by a foot than any footprint or
measure of a man. From this is derived the popular saying about tall and
stupid men: the boot of Maximinus.' So far Julius. Thus the proverb may   10
more suitably be used if it is spoken with hatred and contempt, because that
Maximinus from whom it seems it arose was detested both by the Roman
people and the Senate, as being Thracian by race, moreover of base birth,
and lastly barbarous and savage in his conduct. Indeed even now the
common people speak ill of unusually tall men, as if they were sluggards   15
and blockheads.

22 Clematis Aegyptia
The Egyptian clematis

Close to the foregoing proverb is what Demetrius of Phalerum reports,
κληματὶς Αἰγυπτία, the Egyptian clematis, which he says is often used
jokingly about people who are unusually tall in stature and of dark com-   5
plexion. No doubt it comes from the appearance of that plant, which is

* * * * *

21 From Julius Capitolinus *Maximini duo* 28.8–9. The emperor Maximinus I was
   assassinated in AD 238 near Aquileia, which lies at the head of the Adriatic sea
   north-east of Venice. Julius was one of the authors of the so-called *Historia
   Augusta*, a collection of lives of emperors ostensibly dating from the first half of
   the fourth century AD, which Erasmus edited for Froben in 1518. Otto 1073;
   Suringar 31

22 This already provided *Collectanea* no 698, the authorities given being Demetrius
   (in Latin) and Pliny. Suidas has it (AI 76). The name seems to have been used in
   Greek of several different plants.
 3 Demetrius] of Phalerum (fourth century BC) *De elocutione* 172. This was first
   printed in the Aldine *Rhetores graeci* of 1508–9, before which it circulated in
   manuscript copies derived from Paris MS fonds grec 1741. The reference in the
   Collectanea could be secondhand.

mentioned by Dioscorides in his fourth book. Pliny, book 24 chapter 15, says: 'The Italians call it *centunculus*; it has beaked leaves in the shape of a hood, and creeps in the fields. But the Greeks call it clematis.' But though there are many forms of clematis, which Pliny lists in this passage, only one   10 seems to have given rise to the proverb, and that is the one known by the name of Egyptian clematis. It is said that this grows mostly in Egypt, that it has a long thin leaf like the bay, and is efficacious, when taken in vinegar, against snakes, particularly vipers. Some call it *daphnoides* and some *polygonoides*. Laertius in the life of Zeno writes on the authority of Apollo-   15 nius that Zeno was slender in build, tall in stature and dark of complexion; then he quotes Chrysippus as having written in the second book of his *Proverbs* that someone called Zeno an 'Egyptian clematis' for this reason.

23   **Res ad triarios rediit**
     Back to the third line

There is a Roman adage, one of the choicest and well worth commenting on: 'Things were back to the third line.' This will be suitable when we wish to convey that things have reached such a point of danger that final efforts and   5 the greatest energy have to be exerted, and recourse had to desperate measures; and if these are no good there seems nothing left to which we can look for help. For instance, in some literary discussion, when men of ordinary attainments wrangle, we may be forced to submit the matter to one man of consummate learning. Or in a transaction of uncertain outcome we   10 may be compelled to beg for help from our most powerful friends, to whom we should never have thought of appealing unless driven by the most dire necessity. Or it may be impossible to resolve things by more everyday methods, and one must have recourse to something new and really clever.

* * * * *

7 Dioscorides] *De materia medica* 4.7; he is a celebrated medical writer of the first century AD, whose text was first printed in Greek by the Aldine press in 1528. There are nearly thirty references to him in the *Adagia*, but in Latin.
7 Pliny] *Naturalis historia* 24.141
15 Laertius] Diogenes Laertius 7.1.1
17 Chrysippus] See above, Introduction, section v. This is frag 1 of his work on proverbs.

23 This must be drawn from Livy, where it is expressly stated to be a proverb; another of the same military origin is in *Adagia* I iii 94. Otto 1798. It is not far from our 'Backs to the wall.'

Thus Phormio in Terence in the play of the same name, when he meant that   15
neither Antiphon nor Phaedria nor Geta would be a defence sufficient to
blunt the old man's rage, remarks 'It's you now, Phormio – the whole thing
comes back to you.'

The adage arose from the arrangement and disposition of the Roman
army. It is mentioned and explained by Livy in the eighth book of the first   20
decade, in terms which it seems best to quote:

'Finally, the battle-line was divided into several ranks. A rank consisted of sixty soldiers' (though some read six hundred), 'two centurions,
one standard-bearer. The first line, or *hastati*, comprised fifteen maniples,
stationed a short distance apart. The maniple had twenty light-armed sol-   25
diers, and the rest of their number were "shieldmen"; those were called
"light-armed" who carried only a spear and javelins. This front line in the
battle contained the flower of the young men who were growing ripe for
service. Behind these came a line of the same number of maniples, made up
of older and stronger men; these were called the *principes*. Those who   30
followed them were all shieldmen, who were the most showily armed of all.
This body of thirty maniples they called the *antepilani*, because behind the
standards again there were stationed fifteen other ranks, each of which had
three sections, the first section in every rank being known as *primus pilus*.
The rank consisted of three *vexilla* or banners; a *vexillum* numbered a   35
hundred and eighty-three' (some say eighty-six) 'men. The first banner led
the *triarii*, veteran soldiers of proven valour; the second banner the *rorarii*,
less effective because younger and less experienced; the third the *accensi*,
who were the least dependable and were, for that reason, assigned to the
rearmost line. When an army had been marshalled in these ranks, the *hastati*   40
were the first to engage. If the *hastati* were unable to rout the enemy, they
retreated slowly and were received by the *principes* into the intervals between their ranks. The *principes* then took up the fighting, and the *hastati*
followed them. The *triarii* knelt beneath their banners, with the left leg
advanced, having their shields leaning against their shoulders and their   45
spears thrust into the ground and pointing upwards, so that their battle-line

* * * * *

15 Terence] *Phormio* 317. In 1508, citing from memory, Erasmus wrote 'Geta in
    Terence's *Phormio*' and 'nor himself' for 'nor Geta.'
20 Livy] 8.8.4–13, a well-known passage not wholly understood; the parentheses
    'though some read six hundred' and 'some say six' were inserted in 1528.
26 shieldmen] Perhaps it would be better to keep *scutati*, as it is the custom to keep
    hastati (spearmen) in this technical sense. They not only carried long shields
    but were heavily armed.

was fortified with a sort of bristling palisade. If the *principes* too were unsuccessful in their fight, they fell back slowly from the battle-line on the *triarii*. From this arose the adage "To have come back to the third line," when things are going badly. The *triarii*, rising up after they had received 50
the *principes* and *hastati* into the intervals between their ranks, would at once draw their ranks together and close the lanes, as it were; then, with no more reserves behind to count on, they would charge the enemy in one compact array. This was a thing exceedingly disheartening to the enemy who, pursuing those whom they supposed they had conquered, all at once beheld a 55
new line rising up with augmented numbers.' Thus far Livy, from whose words I think the proverb is clear enough not to need any further explanation from me.

Vegetius also in his *De re militari*, book 2, says that the *triarii* were customarily placed behind all the other lines, and armed with all kinds of 60
weapons; they took up a kneeling position, so that if it happened that the front line was beaten, they could regain the victory by reopening the battle. Modestus in his book *On Military Terms* says: 'The sixth rank, behind all the others, was selected from the most reliable men, both shieldmen and those armed with all kinds of weapons, and held the warriors whom the Ancients 65
called *triarii*. These, so as to attack the enemy the more vigorously for being fresh and fully rested, used to sit down behind the last lines, and if there had been a setback in the ranks in front of them, the entire hope hung on the strength of the *triarii* being able to make good the loss.' Flavius Vopiscus in his life of the emperor Firmus suggests that it was usual to choose the 70
stoutest of the soldiers for the *triarii*, when he tells us that he had great muscular strength on the evidence of his having even defeated a *triarius*.

* * * * *

59 Vegetius] *Epitoma rei militaris* 2.16 (he seems to have put this together in the first half of the fifth century AD); this was added in *1515*.
63 Modestus] *De vocabulis rei militaris*, quoted in the *Adagia* three times. It is an abbreviation of Vegetius ascribed to the thirteenth century, which circulated in the fifteenth as a work of Antiquity under the name of Modestus, and was printed among Cicero's works in the Juntine edition of 1516. This also was added here in *1515*.
69 Flavius Vopiscus] *Firmus* 4.2, added in *1517/8*; he is one of the authors of the *Historia Augusta* (see I i 21 note). But *triarium* in our unique manuscript of the *Historia* is a mistake for *Tritanum*, the name of a strong man well known in Antiquity.

24   Sacram ancoram solvere
     To let go the sheet-anchor

Closely similar is a well-known phrase in Greek, ἱερὰν ἄγκυραν χαλάζειν, 'to
let go the sheet-anchor,' whenever one falls back on the final defences. It is
borrowed from sailors, who call the biggest and most efficient anchor   5
'sacred' (sheet-anchor) and only let it go when they are labouring under
extreme difficulties. Lucian in his *Jupiter tragoedus*: 'Hear now the sheet-
anchor, as they say, which you cannot sever by any force.' For so he
describes an insoluble argument. Again in the *Fugitives*: 'Therefore it
seemed best for those considering the matter to lower the last anchor which   10
sailors call "sacred."' Again in the *Apology*: 'Perhaps I still have that one
anchor unbroken,' that is, there is still something left for me to take refuge
in. Euripides in the *Helena*: 'A single anchor stays my destiny,' that is, only
one hope is left me. Aristides in *Themistocles*: 'Hanging on his voice as on a
sheet-anchor.' St Chrysostom, in his fourth sermon *On Lazarus*, calls the   15
conscience a sheet-anchor, because it never allows a man to be carried away
by the force of his desires, as by a storm of wind, without making a struggle.

25   Movebo talum a sacra linea
     I will move the counter from the sacred line

The same force is given, says Diogenianus, by the following: Κινῶ τὸν ἀφ᾽
ἱερᾶς, 'I move the counter from the sacred line,' used of those who are about

* * * * *

24 This and the next were put together in the *Collectanea* no 606, having probably
   been derived solely from the Greek proverb-collections; one could not tell from
   Diogenianus, for instance, that the second proverb has nothing to do with
   anchors. With wider reading, Erasmus soon learnt to distinguish them. Tilley A
   241 To cast one's last anchor. This Greek use of 'sacred' recurs in *Adagia* IV vi
   51.
 3 Greek] Diogenianus 5.29; Suidas x 9
 7 Lucian] *Jupiter tragoedus* 51; *Fugitivi* 13; *Apologia* 10
13 Euripides] *Helena* 277
14 Aristides] *De quattuor* p 258 Dindorf (see I i 13n); in *1508* this formed part of
   Adagia I viii 37, and it was moved here in *1515*.
15 Chrysostom] Johannes Chrysostomus *De Lazaro conciones* 4.5 (PG 48.1013);
   added in *1528*, the reference in *1533*

25 The Greek for this was added in 1506 to *Collectanea* no 606, in which this and the
   preceding adage were run together. It is something like 'Playing one's last
   card.'
 3 Diogenianus] 5.41.

to resort to extreme methods. Julius Pollux explains in his ninth book that   5
this proverb comes from a certain game of counters. He says it was played
like this: each player had five counters, placed on the same number of lines
(hence Sophocles too speaks of 'five-line counters'). Between these lines,
five on each side, was one middle line which was called 'sacred'; and anyone
who moved the counter from that was said to move his man from the sacred   10
line. This was never done unless the situation demanded that the player
should fall back on his last resources. Plato makes use of this in the *Laws*,
book 5: 'As if the counters were moved from the sacred line.' Plutarch in the
essay entitled 'Whether An Old Man Should Engage in Public Affairs' says
'And finally they adduce to us old age, like a move from the sacred line,'   15
meaning 'as a very weighty reason.' The same author in the essay 'On A
Comparison Between Creatures of Land and Sea' says 'Come, making the
move from the sacred line, let us speak briefly about their divinity and
powers of divination.' Again, in the 'Against Colotes' the Epicurean: 'Colotes promptly therefore made the move from the sacred line,' that is, he   20
started in at once on the most serious point by attacking the judgment of
Apollo about Socrates. The same author, writing in his life of Martius
Coriolanus about the dismay of the city of Rome on account of the threats of
Coriolanus: 'It moved the counter from the sacred line.' For the city, in
despair at its situation, took refuge in worship of the gods by prayers,   25
sacrifices, priests, initiators, augurs and so on. Theocritus alludes to this in
his *Bucoliastae*: 'And from the line she moves the stone,' which I have also
mentioned elsewhere.

26 Nudior leberide
As bare as a snake's sloughed skin

Γυμνότερος λεβηρίδος, As bare as a snake's sloughed skin, referring to
extremely flimsy things. The *leberis* is the sloughed skin of a snake, than
which nothing could be emptier. This happens to almost all those creatures   5

* * * * *

5 Pollux] See I i 4n; *Onomasticon* 9.98, citing Sophocles frag 376 Nauck
12 Plato] *Laws* 5.739a
13 Plutarch] *Moralia* 783B; 975A (this and the next added in 1515); 1116E
22 The same author] Plutarch *Coriolanus* 32, added in 1533
26 Theocritus] 6.18 (Gow's note on the line discusses the ancient evidence).
28 elsewhere] *Adagia* I iv 30 and (with Galatea interpreted as the name of a river) I
   ix 97. This cross-reference was added in 1526.

26 Probably derived from the shorter account of the proverb in Diogenianus 3.73,
   Zenobius 2.95 being the basis of *Adagia* I iii 56.

which are protected by a covering, but of the softer sort, such as the gecko, the lizard and particularly snakes; and these shed their skins about twice a year, in spring and autumn, vipers in particular. In the snake, the skin first begins to peel away at the eyes, so that they seem to be going blind, to those who do not understand the process; and in one night and day their old age is 10 stripped off, from head to tail. Among the insect the *silpha* and gnat renew their youth, and those whose wings are covered with a case like beetles, locusts and cicadas. Among sea-creatures, the crab sheds its shell, and that more than once in the year. This also is called a slough (*syphar*) by the Greeks, and its lightness and dryness is extraordinary to feel; all the mois- 15 ture has been used to build up the new growth, as Aristotle says (in the eighth book of his *De natura animantium*). Suidas says *leberis* was the name of an extremely poor man, so that it came to be used in common parlance. Athenaeus in *Doctors at Dinner*: 'You show yourself as empty as a snakeskin.' 20

27 **Qui quae vult dicit, quae non vult audiet**
He who says what he would will hear what he would not

If you say what you like, you will hear what you don't like. St Jerome quotes this expressly as a proverb in his *Against Rufinus*: 'You will hear nothing on this subject except what is said in the street: "when you say what you like, 5 you will hear what you don't like."' Terence in the *Andria*: 'If he proceeds to say what he likes to me, he'll hear what he doesn't like.' Again in the prologue to the *Phormio*: 'If he had tried with kind words, he would have heard something kind.' He made the same allusion in the prologue to the *Andria*: 'Let them cease from bad words, in case their bad deeds come to 10 light.' It is less clear in the prologue to the *Eunuchus*: 'If there be anyone who thinks something ungentle has been said against him, let him think this, let

* * * * *

16 Aristotle] *Historia animalium* 8.17 (600b20); all this passage added in *1515*
17 Suidas] Λ 218; this also provided III ii 83.
19 Athenaeus] 8.362b; the Greek already in *1508* (which is unusual), the title of the work added in *1517/8*.

27 *Collectanea* no 511, where it was supported by three quotations from Roman comedy. Otto 205; Suringar 190; Tilley s 115 He who says what he would, hears what he would not.
3 If you say] The adage was repeated here in Jerome's wording in *1515*.
3 Jerome] *Adversus Rufinum* 3.42 (*PL* 23. 488B)
6 Terence] *Andria* 920; *Phormio* 20; *Andria* 22–3; *Eunuchus* 4–6 (this last was added in *1520*, with a suggested change in the text, which has not won acceptance).

him know no reply has been made,' for he means by a reply, an insult in
return for an insult. But this passage suggests to me that I might here discuss
the mistake made by some critics who have said in a marginal note that in   15
the following sentences I read *quia lesit* 'because he first did the injury,' and
indeed this was the reading of the commonly accepted editions. However, it
was I who first restored the true reading based on the old copies, which is as
follows: 'Such as the man (*quale sit*) who first by translating well and then
copying wrong made bad Latin plays out of good Greek ones, and has   20
recently produced the *Phasma* of Menander.' Here *quale sit* means the same
as the Greek *hoion*, in Latin 'as if' or 'of this kind' – expressions which we use
when we are going to give an example. He has remembered about the insult
which was to be returned, and then adds an instance of this, the word 'first'
corresponding to the following adverb 'recently.' He says in fact: the same   25
man who first translated many plays which you do not remember has now
recently produced a stupid play called *Phasma*, which you can certainly call
to mind.

But to return to the subject. The first begetter of this adage appears to
have been Homer, who has this line in the *Iliad*, book 20: 'The word you   30
speak is the word you will hear.' Hesiod too, in the poem called *Works and
Days*: 'If you speak evil, you will yourself soon hear worse.' Again in the
same author:

> If by yourself the first
> In word or deed some ill is said or done,   35
> Know it shall come back twofold to yourself.

Euripides in the *Alcestis*: 'If you speak evil of us / Much evil will you hear,
and that not false.' Plutarch quotes a much finer passage of Sophocles:

> The man who rashly pours out many words
> Often must hear against his will the wrong   40
> He willed to say.

* * * * *

30 Homer] *Iliad* 20.250 (more of the passage is used in III ix 16).
31 Hesiod] *Works and Days* 721; 709–11
37 Euripides] *Alcestis* 704–5
38 Sophocles] Frag 843 Nauck, cited by Plutarch *Moralia* 89B. This is followed in
the Latin text, under the heading 'There is also on record from Sophocles,' a
somewhat more accurate form of the same fragment, taken from Stobaeus
3.18.1, which was inserted in 1533 as though it were something new. It has not
seemed worth while to translate this also.

Just so in our own day people often say something of the same sort, 'the greeting you give is the greeting you will get,' that is, the reply will correspond to your own words. Plautus: 'If you speak scorn, you will hear it.' Caecilius in his *Chrysium* (quoted by Gellius) 'You'll hear ill words if you speak ill words to me.' Of the same kind is the phrase of Euripides we meet often in the authors: 'Of unchecked speech and wicked folly, the end (or reward) is disaster.' This is celebrated among the sayings of Chilon: 'There must be no evil-speaking of those with whom we have to deal; otherwise we shall hear words which bring trouble.' Here I think we should add the line quoted by Quintilian as a common saying: 'Not wrong was his reply, / For wrong was the other's question.'

28   **Sero sapiunt Phryges**
     The Phrygians learn wisdom too late

This proverb is taken from that very old tragedy of Livius Andronicus entitled *The Trojan Horse*. It is used by Cicero in his *Letters to Friends*: 'You know you are in the Trojan horse; the Phrygians learn wisdom too late.' It fits those people who repent too late of the stupidities they have committed. The Trojans, for instance, after so many disasters, only began to think of giving back Helen when nearly ten years had elapsed; whereas if they had

* * * * *

44 Plautus] *Pseudolus* 1173
45 Caecilius] Caecilius Statius (the early Roman writer of comedies) 24 (*Comicorum Romanorum fragmenta*, ed O. Ribbeck, Leipzig 1898, 45). This is cited by Gellius 6.17.13.
46 Euripides] *Bacchae* 386–8, used again in III iv 47
48 Chilon] One of the traditional Seven Sages; from Diogenes Laertius 1.69
51 Quintilian] 5.13.42, added in 1533. This is Otto 1014.

28 This, together with our nos 29 and 30, was covered in *Collectanea* no 132, with names of four ancient sources, among them Diogenianus (2.13). Otto 1410; Suringar 111; Tilley T 528 Like the Trojans, we were wise too late, E 192 To be wise after the event.
 4 Cicero] *Ad familiares* 7.16.1 cites *in extremo sero sapiunt*, 'At the last moment wisdom comes too late,' from a tragedy called *The Trojan Horse*, and a play of that name was written by Livius Andronicus, one of the early Roman tragic poets, as we know from Nonius (O. Ribbeck *Tragicorum Romanorum fragmenta*, Leipzig 1897, 3 and 271).
 8 Helen] Erasmus is thinking of an imaginary speech by the late Greek rhetorician Libanius, in which Menelaus argues that Helen should be given back to the Greeks to order to end the Trojan War, which was his own first translation from Greek, though not published till 1519.

handed her back at the very beginning when Menelaus asked for her, they
would have saved themselves from innumerable calamities. Euripides in the   10
Orestes: 'Now you are prudent late / Since then you left your house in
shame.' The words are those of Electra to Helen. This is mentioned also by
Festus Pompeius as being a proverb. According to Plutarch, Demades used
to say that the Athenians never decided to make peace until they wore
mourning; meaning that they had such an unnecessary lust for war that only   15
the destruction of their own kinsmen could warn them to think of peace. But
how much more insensate are we than the Athenians! Not even the misfortunes of so many years have taught us to hate war, nor do we even now at
long last begin to think about peace, which ought to be perpetual between
Christians.   20

29 **Piscator ictus sapiet**
    Once stung, the fisherman will be wiser

The same thought is to be found in that proverb which was very familiar in
Greek, Ἁλιεὺς πληγεὶς νόον οἴσει, The fisherman once stung will learn
sense. They say this arose from an event of this kind: when some fisherman   5
put his hand on the fish in his net and was stung by a sea-scorpion, he said 'I
shall be the wiser for being stung.' So, taught by his pain, he was careful in
the future. Pliny, book 32, explains that it is characteristic of the serpent and
sea-scorpion to wound with their spines if touched by the hand. Zenodotus
says the proverb is to be found in Sophocles.   10

                    * * * * *

10 Euripides] *Orestes* 99
13 Festus] P 460, added in *1515*. Pompeius Festus, a grammarian perhaps of the
   second century AD, made an epitome in twenty books of the dictionary of
   Verrius Flaccus, a leading teacher of the age of Augustus; but part of this
   survives itself only in an epitome made in the time of Charlemagne (late eighth
   century) by Paul the Deacon. In Erasmus' time the Festus and Paulus texts were
   not yet distinguished, and the fact that six out of seven of his numerous
   references are of *1515* or later suggests that he relied on the text published with
   Niccolò Perotti's *Cornucopia* by Aldus in Nov 1513. We refer to the pages of
   W.M. Lindsay's edition, Leipzig 1913.
13 Plutarch] Moralia 126D–E. The last reflection ('But how much more ...') was
   added in *1517/8*.

29 *Collectanea* no 132, with the preceding. Suringar 111; Tilley F 332 The fisher
   stricken will be wise, C 297 A burnt child dreads the fire, or Once bitten, twice
   shy.
 4 Greek] Diogenianus 2.31; Suidas A 1218
 8 Pliny] *Naturalis historia* 32.148, added in *1515*
 9 Zenodotus] Zenobius 2.14, citing Sophocles frag 111 Nauck

30 **Factum stultus cognoscit**
    When a thing is done, a fool can see it

Another version of the same thing: ʿΡεχθὲν δέ τε νήπιος ἔγνω, When the
thing is done, the fool understands it. This comes from Homer, who makes
use of this idea several times. So in the *Iliad*, 17 and 20:   5

> Beware of coming to challenge me
> Before suffering some harm; even a fool perceives
> A deed once done.

Euripides alludes to it in the *Bacchae*: 'For he learnt by experiencing evil.'
This refers to Pentheus, who began late, and not until he was taught by his   10
own misfortune, to revere Bacchus. This is no different from the warning of
that famous line, current among the Greek maxims: 'A man learns judgment
as he learns regret.' Virgil's phrase belongs here: 'Be warned, / Learn to deal
justly and not scorn the gods.' Demosthenes said the same thing: 'I don't
buy repentance at such a price.' And so Fabius, in Livy, very elegantly calls   15
the outcome the teacher of fools: 'It is not the outcome, the teacher of fools,
which teaches this,' he says, 'but reason.' Pliny, in the *Panegyric* he delivered
before Trajan, calls this kind of tardy and fruitless prudence 'pitiful': 'Fear,'
he says, 'and dread and that pitiful prudence gained from danger, warned
us to avert our eyes, our ears, our minds, from the State (there was practical-   20
ly no State at all).'

31 **Malo accepto stultus sapit**
    Trouble experienced makes a fool wise

Hesiod expressed the same thought, though a little differently, when he said
* * * * *
30 *Collectanea* no 132, with the two preceding. This overlaps I iii 99.
 4 Homer] *Iliad* 17.31–2; 20.197–8 (the latter reference added in *1528*).
 9 Euripides] *Bacchae* 1113
12 famous line] Menander *Sententiae* 315; a large collection of one-line moral
    maxims, ascribed to Menander (I i 7n), and some of them taken from his plays
13 Virgil] *Aeneid* 6.620
14 Demosthenes] The story is told from Gellius in *Adagia* I iv 1; Tilley R 81–2 To buy
    repentance too dear.
15 Livy] 22.39.10; Tilley E 220 Experience is the mistress of fools.
17 Pliny] *Panegyricus* 66.4

31 Suringar 111; Tilley E 220 Experience is the mistress of fools. Cf II iii 39.
 3 Hesiod] *Works and Days* 217–8

in his book entitled *Works and Days*: 'His punishment the wicked man
receives / At last, but only pain instructs the fool.' Homer too seems to allude   5
to the same saying in the *Iliad*, book 23: '... so that paying up, you'll know
the truth.' Plato in the *Symposium*: 'I am saying this to you also, Agathon, so
that you may not be deceived by this, but take warning from the knowledge
of what happened to us; and that you should not, like the fool in the
proverb, learn wisdom through the experience of evil.' Plautus' phrase in   10
the *Mercator* is to be classed with this: 'Happy is he who learns wisdom at
another's cost.' Similarly in the *Elegies* of Tibullus, book 3: 'How happy is he,
whosoe'er he be, / Who from another's woe learns woe to flee.' This is what
those speeches of the tardily-wise mean: 'Now I know what love is.' 'Now I
understand that she is wicked and that I am wretched.' 'Ah, fool that I am, I   15
have just tumbled to it at last.'

The adage seems to spring from that very old story about the two
brethren, Prometheus and Epimetheus, which is told in Hesiod, more or
less in this way. Jupiter was angry with Prometheus because he had stolen
fire from heaven and given it to men; and wishing to play a similar trick on   20
him, gave Vulcan the job of making the figure of a girl out of clay, with the
greatest possible skill. When this was done, he required each of the gods and
goddesses to endow this image with his or her gifts. This is clearly why the
name Pandora was invented for the maiden. Then, when the image had
been showered with all the endowments of beauty, accomplishment, brains   25
and speech, Jupiter sent her to Prometheus with a box, beautiful indeed, but

* * * * *

5 Homer] *Iliad* 23.487
7 Plato] *Symposium* 222b, also used in I iii 99; the Greek was added, and the Latin
   version rewritten, in *1523*.
10 Plautus] Erasmus refers to this as a line of Plautus in *Adagia* II ix 71, as Poliziano
   does in his *Miscellanea* c 9. The reference usually given is *Mercator* 4.7.40 (the
   name of the play is added here in *1520*); so Otto 61n, H. Walther *Lateinische
   Sprichwörter des Mittelalters* 2 (Göttingen 1964) no 8927. But the scene is spurious: L. Braun *Scenae suppositiciae* (*Hypomnemata* 64, Göttingen 1980) 194.
12 Tibullus] 3.6.43–4, added in *1520*. Of the elegiac poets of the first century BC,
   Tibullus only appears six times in the *Adagia*, Propertius fifteen; a strong
   contrast with Ovid.
14 speeches] Virgil *Eclogues* 8.43; Terence *Eunuchus* 70–1, *Andria* 470
18 Hesiod] *Works and Days* 47–105. The names might be translated Forewit and
   Afterwit; compare Taverner's proverb (Tilley F 595) One good forewit is worth
   two afterwits. Tilley P 40 Pandora's box
24 Pandora] Hesiod derives the name from *pan*, all and *dora*, gifts.
26 with a box] What Pandora brought was a *pithos*, a big pottery jar of the kind so
   much used in Antiquity for storage. How Erasmus came to mistranslate this as a
   box or casket (thus giving us our proverbial 'Pandora's box') and to have

concealing inside it every kind of misfortune. Prometheus refused the present, and warned his brother that if any kind of gift was brought in his absence, it must not be accepted. Back comes Pandora and, having persuaded Epimetheus, she gives him the box. As soon as he had opened it, 30 and understood, as the diseases flew out, that Jove's 'gifts were no gifts,' he began to be wise, but too late. Hesiod clearly refers to the adage when he says 'He took it, and touched by woe understood at last.' He says the same in the *Theogony*: she gave birth to Prometheus, 'the cunning one' (so he calls him) 'of many wiles / And Epimetheus, whom mistakes made wise.' Hence 35 Pindar in the *Pythians* calls him 'late-wise.' Their very names indicate this. For Prometheus means in Greek a man who takes counsel before acting, and Epimetheus one who acts first, and only then does common sense enter his head. To act like Prometheus, *prometheuesthai*, is to meet misfortunes when they threaten by taking thought. Lucian in one of his dialogues quotes from 40 some comedy-writer or other the following line, attacking Cleon on the ground that he was only wise too late when the business was all over: 'Cleon is a Prometheus after the fact.' Again, at the end of the same dialogue: 'To take counsel after the event is like Epimetheus, not Prometheus.'

The proverb is also found in the form Παρὰ τὰ δεινὰ φρονιμώτερος, 45 More prudent after hard experience, and again in this form: Ἐξ ὧν ἔπαθες, ἔμαθες, From what you suffer, you learn, or (giving the sense rather than the words) What hurts is what teaches, *Quae nocent docent*. But it is much more circumspect to learn prudence from the ills of others, according to the Greek saying: 'I learnt my lesson watching others' ills.' There is a word going 50 round among my own people: 'It is through shame and loss that mortals grow wiser.'

* * * * *

Epimetheus rather than Pandora open it, is discussed by Dora and Erwin Panofsky in chapter two of *Pandora's Box* (Bollingen series lii, 2nd ed, New York 1962). It is the same in 1 iii 35.

31 'gifts were no gifts'] A reference to Sophocles *Ajax* 665; see 1 iii 35.
32 Hesiod] *Works and Days* 89; *Theogony* 510–1. Their mother was Clymene, daughter of Oceanus and wife of Iapetus.
36 Pindar] *Pythians* 5.28, added in 1523
39 *prometheuesthai*] The verb in this form is recorded in the lexicon only from the preface to the *Problemata* of Alexander of Aphrodisias (see 1 i 40n).
40 Lucian] *Prometheus es in verbis* 2 and 7. The line he quotes is from the Old-Comedy writer Eupolis, frag 456 Kock; it reappears in 1 iii 99.
45 also found] It is a proverb in its own right in IV iii 59 and, with one word changed in the Greek, in 1 iii 99. But the correct sense is 'More prudent in the face of danger,' and it does not really belong here.
47 giving the sense] The parenthesis was inserted in 1517/8.
49 Greek saying] Menander *Sententiae* 121

32   Aliquid mali, propter vicinum malum
Something bad from a bad neighbour

Lysimachus in the *Mercator* of Plautus: 'Now I am finding out the truth of
that saying, something bad comes from a bad neighbour.' From these words
of Plautus it is abundantly clear that this remark was well known in common   5
speech. Hesiod voiced it elegantly in the book called *Works and Days*:

> When trouble falls at home the neighbours come
> Without their belts, relations gird themselves;
> An evil neighbour is a mighty woe,
> A useful one the greatest boon; to him   10
> Who lacks good neighbours there's a lack of honour,
> Nor would an ox die, were there no bad neighbour.

This saying holds good not only as between private neighbours, but experience has shown whole peoples overthrown by their neighbours. This happened to the Aetolians and Acarnanians, who destroyed each other by   15
mutual conflict, close as their borders were. So also the Carthaginians and
Byontini, whose history is told by the scholiasts on Hesiod. Virgil appears to
have made a passing allusion to this in the *Eclogues*: 'No harm will come to
them from neighbouring flocks', and 'Poor Mantua, too near to doomed
Cremona.' The proverb is a warning that we should seek out the society and   20
companionship of good men, and separate ourselves as much as possible
from bad ones. So it was clever of Themistocles in Plutarch when he was
selling an estate, to cause the auctioneer to add 'that it had also good

* * * * *

32 *Collectanea* no 221, citing Plautus; three words of the Hesiod in Greek were
   added in 1506. Otto 1893; Tilley N 108 An ill neighbour is an ill thing.
3 Plautus] *Mercator* 771–2. In *1508*, as in the *Collectanea*, this was quoted from
   memory, and ascribed to 'Dorippa in the *Miles*.' Dorippa is in fact the character
   to whom Lysimachus addresses it in the *Mercator*.
6 Hesiod] *Works and Days* 344–8, referred to again in I x 73 and the beginning of
   IV v 1. Of the peoples here given as examples of bad neighbours, Aetolia and
   Acarnania are adjacent Greek states on the north of the Gulf of Corinth; the
   other pair should be Chalcedon and Byzantium, two independent cities which
   faced each other across the Bosphorus. But Erasmus is citing the scholia of the
   Byzantine scholar Tzetzes on lines 346–8, printed in A. Pertusi's edition of the
   Scholia vetera (Milan 1955), in a corrupt text, in which these people had become
   Carthaginians (in Greek Karchedonians) and Byontini.
17 Virgil] *Eclogues* 1.50 and 9.28, the latter line added in *1523* (cf Otto 1597).
22 Plutarch] *Moralia* 185E (also *Themistocles* 18)

neighbours,' as if this recommendation would make it much more saleable. And not so very far away from this is the saying from the poem of that same   25 Hesiod: 'Oft the whole people suffers for one bad man's misdeed.'

33   Manus manum fricat
One hand rubs another

Socrates in the *Axiochus* of Plato says that Prodicus the sophist was always quoting this line of the comic poet Epicharmus: 'Hand rubs hand; give something, and you get something.' Here Socrates is poking fun at the   5 profiteering of a man who never taught anyone for nothing, and from whom he himself admitted that he had learnt what he was then about to say, and that not gratis – far from it, he had paid in coin. A notion worthy of a Sicilian, or of a 'crafty poet,' for that is what Cicero calls him. It warns us that there is almost no one to be found among mortals who is willing to bestow a benefit   10 on anyone else, without hoping that some profit will redound to himself; a favour is the result of another favour, one kindness is called forth by another kindness. The same adage exists in the form 'One hand washes the other.' The two metaphors have the same force, for it is a matter of mutual conveni- ence when one hand rubs or washes another. Among the Greek maxims this   15 couplet is in circulation: 'Town preserves town, one man likewise another; / Hand washes hand and finger washes finger.' Seneca makes use of this too in his amusing skit on the death of the emperor Claudius.

          * * * * *

26 Hesiod] *Works and Days* 240

33 *Collectanea* no 5 cited only the passage from the *Axiochus* (in Latin). Similar topics appear in I vii 95–100. Otto 1036; Tilley H 87 One hand washes another.
3 Plato] *Axiochus* (a spurious dialogue) 366c, citing the Sicilian comic poet Epicharmus (fifth century BC) frag 273 Kaibel
9 Cicero] *Ad Atticum* 1.19.8, given in full in 1533 in II i 14
13 same adage] It comes in Petronius 45 (see I ii 51 note); but as that part of Petronius' text had not yet been rediscovered, Erasmus is probably thinking of the passage in Seneca to which he will refer again in a moment.
15 Greek maxims] Menander *Sententiae* 31 and 832; why Erasmus calls these widely separated lines a distich is not yet clear.
17 Seneca] *Ludus de morte Claudii* 9. Erasmus always refers to it by a descriptive title, as though its name had not yet been settled (nowadays it is often called the *Apocolocyntosis* or Pumpkinification, a parody of the deification that awaited most Roman emperors on death, though in this lively description of the dismal Claudius' reception in the next world he is not actually turned into a pumpkin). This was added in 1517/8; most of the references in the *Adagia* are of 1515, and none earlier, because in that year the first serious edition of it was published by Beatus Rhenanus. The context of this appears in IV iv 100.

34   **Gratia gratiam parit**
     One favour begets another

The same thought is simply expressed by Sophocles in the *Oedipus Coloneus*:
'A favour favour brings.' Again in the *Ajax Mastigophoros*: 'Always one
favour begets another.' Hesiod expands on this, as it were, in the first book   5
of his *Georgics*:

> Be a friend to a friend, and frequent the one who frequents you,
> Give to the one who gives, and not to the one who gives not;
> One gives to the giver, no one gives to the giftless.

By this it is meant that a benefit is induced by a benefit, a kindness provoked   10
by a kindness. Euripides in the *Helena*: 'Let favour come in return for favour.'

35   **Par pari referre**
     To render like for like

Ἴσον ἴσῳ ἐπιφέρειν, To render like for like. Terence in the *Eunuchus* makes
use of an adage not unlike the preceding: 'Render like for like.' This teaches
us that we should behave to others as we find them behaving to us. Like the   5
Medea of Euripides we are to be friends to our friends, hostile to our
enemies, false to the false, mean to the mean, noisy with the noisy, shameless with the vile; and finally we are to return every good service with a
similar one. Thus in the prologue to the *Phormio*: 'Let him be aware that
whatever he brought will be given back to him again.' It would not be   10
inappropriate to use this when we repay words with words, flattery with
flattery, promises with promises. There is an amusing instance of this in the

* * * * *

34 Tilley T 616 One good turn deserves another.
 3 Sophocles] *Oedipus Coloneus* 779; *Ajax* 522
 5 Hesiod] *Works and Days* 353–5, the Latin version not added till 1528. The
   Virgilian title is perhaps a slip of the pen.
11 Euripides] *Helena* 1234

35 This appears in the *Collectanea* (no 561) only in the form provided by Terence's
   Phormio, with a brief reference to the commentary of Donatus. The Greek might
   be from Aristophanes *Plutus* 1132. Otto 1337; Tilley T 356 Tit for tat.
 3 Terence] *Eunuchus* 445
 6 Euripides] *Medea* 809, quoted in I iii 17
 9 *Phormio*] Terence *Phormio* 21

Ethics of Aristotle, book 9. Dionysius summoned a lute-player to play at his
wedding, and made an agreement with him on these terms, that the more
skilfully and sweetly he played, the more generous would be his fee. The   15
musician made an effort to use all his skill to play beautifully, hoping for a
really ample reward. But the next day, when the musician who had made
the bargain asked for his pay, Dionysius declared that he had already carried
out his promise: he had returned like for like, he said, he had repaid
pleasure with pleasure, and by this he meant the hope of gain, which had   20
indeed risen higher and higher the more skilfully the man played. However
the philosopher denies that this was rendering like for like; because the one
(Dionysius) got what he wanted, while the other was cheated of what he
was looking for. This seems to have been what Euripides was thinking of
when he says in the *Andromache*: 'Moderate towards us, he will find me   25
moderate; / But if he rages, he will see us rage.' The proverb may perhaps
have arisen from the habits of the ancient Greeks at drinking-parties, when
they customarily used ladles of equal size. Archippus in his second
Amphitryon, cited by Athenaeus book 10: 'Which of you, O wretch, mixed it
half and half?' Similarly Cratinus in his *Pytine*: 'But the man that brings me   30
half and half I shall pay in full.' Again in book 6: 'Not through those who sell
fish at Rome, like for like,' meaning that the fish were priced for sale
separately.

This expression 'like for like' was normal in drinking healths, as can
easily be seen from the same author. By this they meant either that the ladles   35
were the same size, or that the same amount of water was added as there
was of wine. Those other phrases are similar: 'to strike a balance' for to
recompense on equal terms, and 'level reckoning.' Pliny writes to Flaccus:
'Thank you for those magnificent thrushes, for which I fear level reckoning
is out of the question, either from my city supplies as I am now in my place at   40
Laurentum, or with anything from the sea which is now rough with all these
storms.' Cicero, in his *Orator* addressed to Brutus, reduces 'like for like' to

* * * * *

13 Aristotle] *Ethica Nicomachea* 9.1 (1164a15); the name Dionysius is supplied from
   Plutarch's *Moralia* 41D or 333F.
24 Euripides] *Andromache* 741–2
28 Archippus] Frag 2 Kock, cited by Athenaeus 10.426b, the book-reference
   added in *1517/8*. He and Cratinus are writers of the Attic Old Comedy.
30 Cratinus] Frag 184 Kock, cited in the same passage
31 Again] Athenaeus 6.224c, added in *1517/8*
35 the same author] Athen. 10.426b, the following sentence added in *1517/8*
38 Pliny] the Younger *Letters* 5.2.1, added with the preceding sentence in *1533*
42 Cicero] *Orator* 65.220, added in *1536*. The balancing and contrasting of clauses,
   and making clauses end with a similar sequence of sounds, were recognized
   devices taught in the rhetorical schools.

the level of a rhetorical figure, in which the parts of a sentence have an equal and corresponding number of syllables: 'For when like is matched with like, or unlike is contrasted with unlike, or words are set against words of similar   45 endings, whatever is elaborated in this way generally has an agreeably rhythmical cadence.'

36 Eadem mensura
By the same measure

What we have just mentioned seems to relate to the repaying of kind offices and injuries alike, but is more to be applied to the return of benefits, as Hesiod says: 'With the same measure, or better if you can,' by which he   5 means that we should repay a kindness in the same measure, or even more fully if opportunity offers; and in this way we should imitate fertile fields, which usually yield a big increase on the seed sown in them. It is quoted as a proverb by Lucian in the *Imagines*: 'With the same measure, they say, or better.' Cicero in the thirteenth book of the *Letters to Atticus*: 'I for my part   10 was making ready to pay him for his offering "in measure like, and better too" – that is, if I had been able to, for even Hesiod adds "if thou canst."' Our teacher Christ did not hesitate to use this adage in the Gospel, when he says that it shall be so, that whatever measure we have used in dealing with others will be dealt out to us again. For he speaks thus in Matthew: 'For with   15 what judgment ye judge, ye shall be judged; and with what measure ye mete, it shall be measured to you again.'

37 Crassa Minerva. Pingui Minerva. Crassiore Musa
With a stupid Minerva, a crass Minerva

Minerva, according to poets' tales, presides over the arts and the talents.

* * * * *

36 From Hesiod *Works and Days* 350
9 Lucian] *Imagines* 12
10 Cicero] *Ad Atticum* 13.12.3
15 Matthew] 7.2, the reference and the Greek text added in *1515*

37 *Pingui Minerva* (untranslatable as it stands) and *pinguiore formula* formed *Collectanea* no 402, Horace's *Satires* and two passages from Aulus Gellius being cited as authorities. In *1508* the material was much extended, and rearranged to provide our nos 37, 38 and 39. The fact that *Crassiore Musa* is still part of the heading of no 37 possibly indicates that there was an intermediate stage when 37 and 38 had not yet been divided. Otto 1119–20
3 according to poets' tales] These words were added in *1517/8*.

From this sprang the phrase 'Against Minerva's will,' as well as 'With a
crass' or 'stupid Minerva,' already in common use as a proverb in old time.   5
Columella in book 12 of his *Agriculture*, chapter 1: 'But in this science of
agriculture such minute accuracy is not called for; what they call crass
mother-wit [*pingui Minerva*] will provide the farm-bailiff with an indication
of future weather which is of great value.' Columella again, in the preface to
the first book: 'The business of farming can be carried on without great   10
subtlety of intellect, but what they call crass mother-wit [*pingui Minerva*] is
not enough.' Again in the tenth book: 'And yet the subtlety of Hipparchus is
not required for what they call the more crass education of country folk.' A
thing is said to be done *pinguiore Minerva*, by crass mother-wit, when it is
done in a way that is artless and crude and, as it were, inexpert, without   15
refined art or careful exactitude. So that old Priapus, when he asks in plain
terms for an improper privilege, which he might have asked for more
politely under a veil of words, says 'My Minerva is a bit crass.' And Horace,
describing a philosopher who was not armed with those famous close
reasonings and sophistries of the Stoics, but expressed his philosophy in his 20
way of life, as though without art, and was not eloquent but rather simple
and sincere: 'Bound to no school, a rustic sage was he, / Of homely mother-
wit.' Aulus Gellius, book 14 chapter 1: 'He gave it as his opinion that this
could certainly not be perceived and comprehended by the mind of a man,
however great, in so short and cramped a space as a lifetime, but a few   25
things might be guessed at, and to use his own words "in a rough and ready
style" [*crassius, et pingui Minerva*].'

* * * * *

4 Against Minerva's will] *Adagia* I i 42
6 Columella] (Mid first century AD) *Res rustica* 11.1.32; 1 praef 33; 9.14.12, this
   last passage added in 1528. Hipparchus was a famous astronomer, whose
   calendarial system was needlessly elaborate for agricultural use.
16 old Priapus] He was a phallic garden god, of indecent appearance and
   shameless behaviour, whose name provided a title for a collection of improper
   poems dating from the imperial period. This is *Priapeia* 3.10, and the request for
   which Priapus quite rightly apologized here was added in 1536 to I i 38.
18 Horace] *Satires* 2.2.3
23 Gellius] 14.1.5. The concluding phrase is Erasmus' equivalent for a Greek
   adverb, meaning 'somewhat coarsely.' In the *Collectanea* a different adverb had
   been given; modern texts of Gellius have exchanged this for a third, without
   much difference in the meaning.

38 Crassiore Musa
Of the more clumsy Muse

Παχυτέρᾳ Μούσῃ, Of the more clumsy Muse. The same proverb is expressed
thus by Quintilian in his *Institutiones oratoriae*, book 1: 'I should like for the
sake of those who are inexperienced or, as they say, of the more clumsy   5
Muse, to remove any doubt about the value of this.' Sometimes in writers
not without authority one finds 'To a cruder pattern,' *Pinguiore formula*, for
'clearer and more intelligible.' There is also the phrase 'to speak Latin,'
meaning 'openly and simply.' Cicero in the *Verrines*: 'I am not using the
language of a prosecutor, but speaking Latin, you must know.' And again in   10
the *Philippics*: 'As they say who speak open and plain Latin.' In the *Priapeia*:
'Simpler far to say / In good plain Latin, Let me bugger you.'

39 Rudius ac planius
More roughly and more plainly

The Greeks have a phrase which is less elegant but has the same force:
'Αμαθέστερον καὶ σαφέστερον εἰπέ, Speak more roughly and more plainly.
It is found in the same Gellius when he says 'For you know, I think, that old   5
and widespread expression, "speak more roughly and more plainly,"'
meaning 'speak in an ignorant and rough style to express yourself more
openly and clearly.' It comes apparently from a comedy of Aristophanes, the
Frogs: 'Speak thou unlearnedly and speak the clearer.' In this line Bacchus
blames Euripides for obscurity, since he has made some rather unclear   10
proposition. Suidas and the scholiast indicate that there is a proverb hidden

* * * * *

38 Included with the preceding under *Collectanea* no 402. Otto 1174
  4 Quintilian] 1.10.28. The Greek given here is perhaps a back-formation from
    Quintilian's Latin.
  6 writers] In the *Collectanea* these were 'elegant authors' (it is not clear of whom
    Erasmus was thinking), and the example given of simple expression is the
    language used by those who have to convey Aristotle to schoolboys.
  9 Cicero] *Verrines* 4.1.2; *Philippics* 7.6.17; both added in 1536. Otto 924
11 *Priapeia*] 3.8–10, added in 1536. The speaker Priapus (see 1 i 37n) is represented
    as issuing a general invitation to any boy who may enter the garden of which he
    is the tutelary deity.

39 Part of *Collectanea* no 402. Otto 863
  5 Gellius] 12.5.6
  8 Aristophanes] *Frogs* 1445
11 Suidas] A 1470

here, which circulates under the form: 'Speak to me more clearly and with
less learning.' I surmise that this proverb originated from the fact that in old
days those great sages, σοφοὶ as they are called, used to take great care to
wrap up the mysteries of wisdom in certain coverings of enigma, seemingly   15
to prevent the common herd, not yet initiated into the rites of philosophy,
from following their drift. Indeed, even today there are some who profess to
be expert in philosophy and theology who do the same: when they are
propounding something which any woman or a cobbler might say, they
have to envelop and involve it in all sorts of difficulties and extraordinary   20
language in order to appear learned. So Plato made his philosophy obscure
by his numbers and so Aristotle rendered many things still more obscure by
mathematical parallels.

40   **Sus Minervam**
The sow (teaches) Minerva

This adage is a very common one among Latin authors: Ὗς τὴν Ἀθηνᾶν,
The sow teaches or advises (understood) Minerva. This was usually said
whenever some ignorant and silly person attempts to teach the one by   5
whom he ought rather to be taught; or, to borrow the words of Festus
Pompeius, 'when one instructs another in what he himself does not know.'
The point is that the guardianship of the arts, and of the talents, is ascribed
by the poets, as I have said, to Minerva. Furthermore, there is no animal
more brutish than a pig, or more filthy, whether because it eagerly revels in   10
dung, or because of the huge size of its liver, the seat of concupiscence and
lust; or because of the grossness of its nose and dulled sense of smell, which
results in its not finding a foul stench offensive. Added to which it is so
turned towards the ground, so intent on its food, that if by any chance it is
forced to look upwards it is struck dumb with stupefaction, this being so   15

* * * * *

14 take great care to] Added in *1517/8*
17 following their drift] In *1508* this was 'understanding'; what follows was added
in *1517/8*.

40 *Collectanea* no 782, citing Jerome *Adversus Rufinum* only. The Greek proverb was
added in the revision of 1506; it seems not to occur in this form in the
proverb-collections, but might have been taken from Plutarch *Moralia* 803D.
Otto 1118; Suringar 218; Tilley s 680 A sow to teach Minerva. See also I iv 38.
6 Festus] P 408 (see I i 28n), added in *1515*.
9 as I have said] *Adagia* I i 37
10 or more filthy ... any other animal] Added in *1515*

unusual, as we are told by Alexander of Aphrodisias. Nor is there any other
animal more unmanageable, just as if it were intended by nature not for any
other purpose (as some beasts are) but solely for the pleasure of the table.
Pliny testifies to this, book 8 chapter 51: 'This is the most irrational of
animals, and it used to be thought (not unamusingly) that a soul was given it   20
only as salt.' Varro says the same in his *Agriculture*, book 2: 'They say that the
swinish tribe was provided by nature for good food, and that they were only
given a soul to act like salt and preserve the flesh.'

The meaning of these words is explained by Cicero in the fifth book of
the *De finibus*: 'For the inanimate or nearly inanimate creatures that are   25
created and preserved by nature have all of them their supreme good in the
body; hence it has been cleverly said, as I think, about the pig, that a soul has
been bestowed upon this animal to serve as salt, and keep it from going bad.
But there are some animals which possess something resembling virtue,
lions for example and dogs and horses; in these we may observe not only   30
bodily movements as in pigs, but in some degree a sort of mental activity
also.' Aristotle in his *Physiognomonica* writes that men with low foreheads
seem to be unteachable and unsuited to processes of learning, and to belong
to the swinish kind, as though utterly foreign to docility and the arts of men.
For almost all other creatures are capable, he says, of being taught; so that   35
now we commonly call swine those people who are slow-witted and seem
born for belly and stomach. Suetonius too in his list of famous grammarians
reports that Palaemon had arrogance enough to call Varro a pig, as if
literature had been born and was to die with himself. If we want to indicate
that something is uncultured and illiterate, we say it comes out of the sty, as   40

* * * * *

16 Alexander of Aphrodisias] Aristotelian scholar of the third century AD;
   Problemata (in the Latin version of Theodorus Gaza) 1.135–6, folio 265 in the
   Aldine edition of 1504. This work was also the source of the statement in the
   Parabolae (LB 1.624A) that sufferers from jaundice find honey bitter, which was
   not identified in CWE 23 274.
19 Pliny] *Naturalis historia* 8.207. 'Soul' (*anima*) means no more here than 'vital
   principle.' Cicero *De natura deorum* 2.64.160 ascribes this view to the great Stoic
   philosopher Chrysippus, and it is also found in Plutarch *Moralia* 685C, to which
   one might have expected Erasmus to refer.
21 Varro] *Res rusticae* 2.4.10, which is quoted seventeen times, mainly in the first
   two chiliads of the *Adagia*. Written in 37 BC, the work appears regularly in the
   corpus of Latin agricultural writers (*Scriptores rei rusticae*), first printed in 1472.
24 Cicero] *De finibus* 5.13.38, added in *1515*
32 Aristotle] *Physiognomica* 6 (811b28)
37 Suetonius] The second-century historian, *De grammaticis* 23.4

Cicero puts it in the *In Pisonem*: 'products of the sty, not of the school.' That is
what gave rise to this adage, 'The sow teaches Minerva.' In Cicero, in the
second book of the *De oratore*, Lucius Caesar says: 'So in the hearing of
Crassus I will speak first of humour, and play the sow teaching the great
orator, of whom Catulus said, when he heard him recently, that the other   45
speakers ought to eat hay.' Cicero again in the *Academic Questions*, book 1:
'Even if it be not a case of the proverbial sow teaching Minerva, anyway
whoever teaches Minerva is doing a silly thing.' Jerome *Against Rufinus*: 'I
leave aside the Greeks, whose wisdom you vaunt, and while you are
running after foreign things you have almost forgotten your own language,   50
in case it should seem, in the words of the old proverb, that the sow was
teaching Minerva.' He also uses it in different words in the letter to Marcellus beginning 'Charity knows no measure.' Varro and Euemerus refer the
adage to fables, or at least one may guess this from the words of Pompeius:
'This thing lies open to all as they say, yet they prefer to wrap it up in stupid   55
stories rather than quote it simply.' The jeering answer of Demosthenes is
well known, when Demades shouted at him 'Demosthenes wants to correct
me like the sow teaching Minerva,' and he replied, 'But last year this
Minerva was taken in adultery.' The saying refers to the fact that Minerva
was a virgin goddess.   60

41 **Sus cum Minerva certamen suscepit**
    A sow competed with Minerva

The same, or something extremely like it, is found in the *Wayfarers* of
Theocritus: 'Once a sow dared to enter into strife with divine Minerva.' It is

* * * * *

41 Cicero] *In L. Pisonem* 16.37, used again in IV x 81; *De oratore* 2.57.233 (Otto 649:
   the other speakers should eat hay because they now seemed no better than
   oxen and donkeys); *Academicus* 5.18 (the source was given in 1508 as his *De
   natura deorum*, and corrected in 1528).
48 Jerome] *Adversus Rufinum* 1.17 (*PL* 23 410B); *Letters* 46.1.1
53 Varro] These two ancient scholars are cited by Pompeius Festus p 408. Except
   for the last sentence, this was added in 1515.
56 Demosthenes] His opponent the orator Demades thought of himself as a
   Minerva and of Demosthenes as a sow; but he had been detected in adultery a
   year before, and Minerva the goddess was not only wise but also notoriously
   chaste, so the comparison was not a happy one. The story, which is told by
   Plutarch *Moralia* 803D, was added in 1515; the last sentence not till 1528.

41 Apostolius 17.73 took this from Theocritus; but Erasmus' source is no doubt the
   original.
 4 Theocritus] 5.23, with the ancient scholia

used whenever the ignorant and stupid, spoiling for a fight, are not afraid to   5
challenge men of the greatest expertise to a literary duel. The annotator of
Theocritus writes that this proverb is generally used in the form: 'Sow as you
are, you contend with Minerva.' Some unknown scholiast adds that those
who fight with words are said to 'contend' [*ereizein*] while another word
[*ereidein*] is used of those who fight with deeds – which makes it the more   10
ridiculous if a sow, the unteachable, contends with Minerva, who presides
over liberal studies.

42 **Invita Minerva**
    Against Minerva's will

In Latin there is another very popular saying, 'against Minerva's will,' for
something which is done against one's bent, in defiance of nature, without
the blessing of heaven. Cicero in *De officiis*: 'against Minerva's will, as they   5
say.' Again in his *Letters to Friends*, book 12: 'During the Quinquatria I
pleaded your cause before a full house, not without the blessing of Minerva.'
Also in the same work, book 3: 'As it is your wish, I may say that I shall do so
"not against Minerva's will."' Horace says, 'Naught without Minerva's aid
shall you do or say.' Seneca was alluding to this when he said 'Force a mind   10
and it will not respond.'

43 **Abiit et taurus in sylvam**
    The bull too went off into the wood

Ἔβα καὶ ταῦρος ἀν' ὕλαν, The bull too went off into the wood. A pastoral
proverb, with rather an ugly meaning, signifying divorce or neglect of an old
love. However it will be allowable to turn it into a more decent use, for   5
instance by jocularly applying it to people who seem to neglect their early

* * * * *

8 Some unknown ... liberal studies] Added in *1526*

42 Otto 1121; the sense is given by Tilley N 51 To go against nature and H 18 It goes
    against the hair.
  5 Cicero] *De officiis* 1.31.110; *Ad familiares* 12.25.1 and 3.1.1 (both these added in
     1523). The Quinquatrus were a festival held at Rome in honour of Minerva,
     which added point to Cicero's remark. The sense is 'with pleasure,' 'by no
     means against the grain.'
  9 Horace] *Ars poetica* 385
  10 Seneca] *Dialogi* 9 (*De tranquillitate animi*). 7.2

43 Taken directly from Theocritus.

friends, and to lose touch with the group of their old companions and acquaintances; or to those who desert their wonted studies and take up a different kind of life. Theocritus in the idyll entitled *Theonychus* speaks of it expressly as a proverb: 'In truth a certain tale is told, / The bull went off into the wood.' The lover is complaining in fact that he has been deserted by his lady-love, a long while back, and explains that for some time Cynisca (or Puppy-dog, for that was the girl's name) has been delighting herself with a certain Lycus and has not the slightest desire to return to their former association; any more than bulls, which also sometimes forsake the herd of cows and either seek the company of other bulls or roam alone through the glades, untouched by any desire for the female.

This departure and neglect of the cows, this divorce, as it were, is given a special name by herdsmen: they call it *atimagelein*, a word apparently composed of two words, the first meaning to neglect or despise, and the second meaning the herd. And bulls are said to do this when they are parted from the company of the females and not only take no notice of them, to the point of not desiring coition, but they do not even wish to use the same pastures. This habit of the animal and the name given to it is explained by Aristotle in the *Nature of Animals*, book 6 (I will translate the sense rather than enumerate the words): 'But the bull, when the mating season comes, then feeds with the herd and fights with the other bulls. Before that they graze by themselves, which is referred to as "straying." Often the bulls in Epirus do not appear for three months, and on the whole all wild animals, or most of them, do not graze with the females before breeding time.' It seemed to me worth remarking that in the translation by Theodorus Gaza the Greek word *atimagelein*, for which there is no Latin equivalent, is given as *coarmentari*. This term has thrown great obscurity on the passage for scholars, to such an extent that they think the text of Aristotle corrupt, and by changing that reading they extract a very different meaning, and think Theodorus to have gone considerably astray in his translation. But for my part, after close consideration of the whole thing, I seem to see that the meaning of Aristotle's words exactly fits the sense, without the alteration of any word. What he means is that the bull runs with the cows and feeds in the same pastures as mating time approaches, and does not agree with the rest

10

15

20

25

30

35

40

* * * * *

9 Theocritus] 14.43; the girl's name added in *1526*, before which Erasmus had referred to her as 'she.' The verb *atimagelein*, to forsake the herd and feed alone, comes in Theocritus 9.5 and elsewhere.

25 Aristotle] *Historia animalium* 6.18 (572b16); Gaza's was the standard translation at the time (see I i 2 line 46n), and Erasmus' criticism of the word *coarmentari* (which does not occur in classical Latin) is justified.

of the herd of males, but fights them; at other times the bulls sociably share
the pastures, not seeking out the company of the females but living together
among themselves, a thing which occurs with almost all wild animals. This
social behaviour of bulls with bulls, to the neglect of the cows, is called
atimagelein. I wonder what kind of scruple makes us think that the reading of   45
Aristotle should be changed, unless the trouble is caused by a shift in
number (plural for singular), a thing often detected in Aristotle, particularly
in this work. But the word *coarmentari* is certainly not genuine, but suppo-
sititious, either due to the negligence of copyists or rashly produced by some
person lacking learning. For I suspect the reading should be *dearmentari* or   50
abarmentari. Nor can I be brought to believe that Theodorus, a man so
perfectly versed in every kind of learned subject, should have made a
mistake, especially over a word which is not extraordinarily rare or unusual
among the Greek authors, and of which the sense is indicated by the very
etymology; particularly when it is to be found in such a well-known and   55
widely read author as Theocritus, in the *Shepherd*, or the *Oxherds*: 'And they
graze together, and in the long-tressed grasses / They wander, seeking no
separation from the herd.' Suidas shows that *atimagelos* is the name given to
the bull which neglects the herd.

I think this is what Virgil is alluding to in *Silenus*:   60

Ah, woeful maiden wandering through the hills!
He rests on hyacinth his snowy sides,
He crops pale grass beneath dark ilex-trees
Or else pursues a heifer of the herd.
'Come, Nymphs, and close the forest glades for me,   65
Close them, ye nymphs of Crete, while there is hope
That I may glimpse his wandering tracks; maybe
Some green grass tempted him, or with the herd
Some heifers led him to Gortyna's stall.'

When he says 'he rests on hyacinth his snowy sides, / He crops pale grass   70
beneath dark ilex-trees,' he is describing the bull 'straying' and also when he
speaks of the 'wandering tracks' of the bull. The poet means that bull
beloved of Pasiphae, who goes straight off alone, or goes off to such good
purpose that neglecting his own herd, he follows other cows. A mention of

* * * * *

56 Theocritus] 9.4–5, the Latin title added in *1515*
58 Suidas] A 4362
60 Virgil] *Eclogues* 6.52–60; *Georgics* 3.224–8

the fights between bulls at mating time occurs in the same Virgil in book 3 of   75
the *Georgics*:

> Nor is it their way
> To fight and stay together; one, defeated,
> Seeks distant shores for exile, and bewails
> His shame, the blows of his proud enemy,   80
> And his lost love; and leaves his fathers' halls
> With many a sad look back at his own field.

It seems to me that the term, when applied in a different sense, becomes
proverbial, just like those others *kaproun* and *hippomanein*, to want the boar
or the stallion, and it is of this term that Theocritus is thinking when he says   85
it is proverbially said 'the bull went into the wood.'

The current scholia on Theocritus have the particle *ken* instead of the
copulative conjunction *kai;* they add that the proverb is used of those who go
away never to return. When once the bull has escaped to the wood he can
never be caught again. Hence it would not be inappropriate to use this of a   90
husband who spends a long period sleeping apart from his wife, or of one
who has ceased to visit his friends, or who has long abstained from the
Muses or from living with books. A person who detests the company of
other people and lives alone can be called a 'strayer.' And it can well be
applied to someone who has wandered away from his own home and   95
abandoned it. This is not unlike the phrase used by Aristophanes in the
Lysistrata: 'At home I'll lead my life without a bull,' for so he designates the
celibate life of a woman, neglecting the bull, that is, her husband. So in
Horace: 'May Lesbia perish evilly, / who, when I was seeking a bull, showed
me an inert one – you.'   100

44 **Annus producit, non ager**
    The year, not the field, produces the yield

Ἔτος φέρει, οὐχὶ ἄρουρα, The year, not the field, produces the yield. This is a

* * * * *

84 *kaproun*] The two Greek verbs referred to mean to desire the male, to be in heat,
    of sows and mares respectively.
87 scholia] This reference was added in *1526*.
96 Aristophanes] *Lysistrata* 217; this and the next passage were added in *1523*.
99 Horace] *Epodes* 12.16–7

44 Taken from Theophrastus, Aristotle's successor, who had been printed in the
    great Aldine Aristotle of 1498

proverbial half-line referred to by Theophrastus, *On Plants*, book 8: 'Growth
and nourishment is greatly aided by the climate, and the state of the year in   5
general. For if showers, fine days and storms come at the right time,
everything will grow successfully and in profusion, even in salt soil and
infertile fields. So what the proverb says is not far from the truth, that "the
year not the field produces the yield." However the soil of the region makes
a great difference.'   10

     Here I think I ought to remark in passing that in the printed copies I
have read *ou kalôs*, that is, 'not rightly,' and this very reading itself is in my
opinion *ou kalôs*, partly because Theodorus Gaza translated it by *non perper-*
am (not incorrectly) and partly because it does not entirely square with
Theophrastus' thought. He, in fact, is asserting that the state of the weather   15
is of great importance, as the proverb also bears witness, which says not
without reason that the size of the crop can be entirely attributed to the
weather; however some difference is made by the actual nature of the soil.
Thus I surmise the true reading to be *ouk allôs*, 'not far from the truth.' All the
same I can see that the former reading, *ou kalôs* might also be defended.   20
Doubtless Theophrastus did not approve the common saying which makes
the climate responsible for everything, when the type of soil is also an
important factor. To my mind, however, the reading above is the more
attractive, and I think my opinion will be endorsed by men of learning. The
same author turns to the adage again in the third book of the *Causes of Plants*,   25
when he is discussing why wheat flourishes both in cold and warm regions;
he does not deny that the nature of the land contributes something to
fertility, but says that by far the most important thing is the surrounding air,
the mingled tempering of weather and winds, and the winds to which the
land is exposed. Plutarch too in his 'Table-talk,' decade 7 problem 2, men-   30
tions this.

     If one wishes to extend the use of this proverb, it may quite appro-
priately express this thought, that education is of far greater importance
than race in forming character, and it is of no great moment who your
ancestors were, but much more important on what lines you were brought   35
up, what principles you were taught. For it is the climate which 'educates'

          * * * * *

    4 Theophrastus] *Historia plantarum* 8.7.6; Gaza's version of this was published at
       Treviso in 1483, and often reprinted.
   19 true reading] Rightly *ou kakôs*, 'not without point'; but Erasmus' suggestion is
       on the right lines.
   24 The same author] *De causis plantarum* 3.23.4, added with the Plutarch in 1515
   30 Plutarch] *Moralia* 701A

what the earth produces. Euripides seems to have alluded to this adage in the *Hecuba*, when he makes her say:

> No new thing is it, for bad land to bear
> Good crops if heaven send good seasons; or,   40
> Lacking in that it needs, good soil may give
> Bad fruit. But as for men, let one be bad,
> Never can he be otherwise than bad;
> Worth remains worthy to the end; good minds,
> Unchanged by adverse fate, retain their goodness.   45
> Is this from parents or from nurture gained?
> Some little knowledge of the right may come
> From good upbringing.

Hecuba seems to attribute more to lineage than to teaching, and wonders why the same thing does not apply in the human character as in the   50
harvest-field. However Lycurgus gave a splendid example showing how much more powerful education is than race, by displaying to the people two dogs: one was born of a common bitch, but owing to its training it rushed valiantly after the quarry, while the other, from pedigree stock, but un-
trained, stood still at the smell of bread and food and disgracefully gave up   55
the chase.

45 **In vado**
In shallow water

A proverbial metaphor which means 'in safety,' 'out of danger,' taken from swimmers or navigators. Terence: 'Everything is in shallow water.' Plautus, *Aulularia*: 'This affair seems now to be almost in safe and shallow waters.'   5
Vadum, a ford, is the depth in which anyone who stands up has already escaped the peril of drowning.

* * * * *

37 Euripides] *Hecuba* 592–601; part of this is used again in II ii 62.
51 Lycurgus] The Spartan king and legislator; Plutarch *Moralia* 3B and 225F

45 *Collectanea* no 281, based on three citations from Roman comedy, has been divided in two and rewritten to make our 45 and 46. Otto 1843
4 Terence] *Andria* 845
4 Plautus] *Aulularia* 803

46 In portu navigare
To navigate in harbour

Similar to this is the allegorical saying, Ἐν λιμένι πλεῖν, To navigate in
harbour, by which we mean that we are now out of danger. Anyone who
steers his ship in the midst of the waves is still sailing at the mercy of winds   5
and storm, but those who are already in the harbour have nothing more to
do with winds and waves. Thus by a very well-known metaphor we call a
man in whose protection we trust our 'haven.' And those who commit
themselves to a tranquil and safe way of life are said to have come into port.
Terence in the *Andria*: 'Now the danger is his, I navigate in harbour.' Virgil   10
says it a little differently in the *Aeneid*, book 7: 'Now rest is mine, I am quite at
the harbour's mouth.'

47 Bos lassus fortius figit pedem
The tired ox treads the more firmly

St Jerome, with great elegance, makes use of this adage when writing to St
Augustine, wishing to dissuade him, being still young, from challenging an
older man. The point is that those who are already tired because of their age   5
are slower to be provoked to battle, but they are the ones who are fiercer and
more pressing when that elderly courage of theirs, aroused, grows hot
again: 'Remember,' he says, 'Dares and Entellus, and the well-known
proverb, that the tired ox treads more firmly.' It appears to be borrowed from
the old method of threshing, when the grain is shaken out by ox-waggons   10
being driven round and round over the sheaves; this is done partly by the
wheels armed for this purpose and partly by the hooves of the oxen. And the
Mosaic law, quoted by the Apostle Paul to Timothy, forbids the muzzling of

* * * * *

46 *Collectanea* no 281. Otto 1455; Tilley R 121 It is safe riding in a good harbour.
10 Terence] *Andria* 480
10 Virgil] *Aeneid* 7.598

47 This is taken largely verbatim (which is not usual) from *Collectanea* no 278; but
   the interpretation there was somewhat different, and concluded with a maxim
   from Publilius Syrus (F 13) which is now incorporated in I v 67. Otto 264; Tilley O
   108 The ox when he is weary treads surest.

3 Jerome] *Letters* 102.2.2; the name Aurelius was added to Augustine in *1517/8*.
10 threshing] This is the explanation assumed by Augustine in his *Letters* 73
   (= Jerome *Letters* 110). 4.3.
13 Paul] 1 Timothy 5.18, attributed to the epistle to the Romans in *1508* (corrected
   in *1515*)

the ox which treads out the corn. Thus the tired ox, because it stamps harder
with its hoof, is more suitable for threshing. But the tired horse is not so   15
good for running. There might also seem to be an allusion here to the fact
that young men excel in agility while old men are stronger when it comes to
a fixed battle, as Virgil shows in the fight between Dares and Entellus. Nor is
the phrase (which I find in the Greek collections) 'slowly the ox' (one must
supply 'moves its hoof') very different from this. For it moves its hoof   20
gradually, but presses harder.

48   **Tota erras via**
     You are entirely on the wrong road

Τῇ πάσῃ ὁδῷ ἀφαμαρτάνεσθαι, To stray entirely from the road. The proverb
is aimed at those who are wildly astray. Terence in the *Eunuchus*: 'You are
entirely on the wrong road.' It comes from travellers, who sometimes miss   5
their way but get to their destination in the end at some expense, or
sometimes miss it so badly that they are turned far aside and go in the
opposite direction. So people who err from the truth are said to leave the
track (*exorbitare*). Aristotle in the *Ethics*, 'They are not totally on the wrong
road.' The same author in the *Physics*, book 1, writes of those early philos-   10
ophers who examined natural causes, that 'they went off the track, and like
people thrust out of the road, utterly deviated from the truth.' This is taken
from Aristophanes' *Plutus*: 'Or have we missd the road entirely?' Just so
nowadays they say 'they are on the right road' when people start something
on a proper plan, and 'off the track' for those who tackle an affair by the   15

* * * * *

18 Virgil] *Aeneid* 5.362–484. There is a boxing match between two champions,
   Dares and Entellus, of whom the latter is the older man; and though eventually
   the referee stops the fight, it is Entellus who carries off the honours of the day.
   Erasmus made an adage of it in III i 69.
19 Greek collections] Diogenianus 3.9; Apostolius 4.24 (this parenthesis was
   added in *1517/8*).
19 slowly the ox] *Adagia* II i 3

48 *Collectanea* no 274 covered both this and the next, with the supporting
   quotations from Terence and Macrobius. Otto 1885; Suringar 225. The opposite
   is *Adagia* IV x 90.
4 Terence] *Eunuchus* 245
7 and go ... direction] Added in *1517/8*
9 Aristotle] *Ethica Nicomachea* 1.8.7 (1098b28), where Suringar notes that the
   Latin words are those used in the version by Johannes Bernardus Febrianus;
   Physica 1.8 (190a24).
13 Aristophanes] *Plutus* 961, added in *1515*, on transference from II vi 78

wrong methods. There are other metaphors, proverbial in form and most often used by scholars: 'to thrust from the road,' 'to lead back to the road,' 'to show the way,' 'to make a way,' 'to smooth the way,' 'to open the way,' 'to close the way,' 'to cut off the way.' Cicero in the first *Philippic*: 'If you think so, you are totally blind to the true way of glory.' There is also that familiar saying: 'They run well, but not on the right road.'

49   **Toto coelo errare**
     To be entirely astray (by the whole sky)

Close to this is what Macrobius uses in the *Saturnalia*, book 3: 'Did it never come into your head, Praetextatus, that Virgil was quite wrong (wrong, as they say, by the whole sky)?' This seems to be taken from Aristophanes' *Frogs*: 'Straightway he has erred sky-high.' It is said by Euripides against Aeschylus, who had been quite wrong in what he said. The metaphor is taken either from the story of Phaethon, or from that of Ceres; or from steersmen, who direct their course by observation of the sky and the stars, just as skippers who are badly astray sometimes imagine they see the Bear in quite a different part of the sky, and are totally out of their course. We might of course prefer to take 'sky' for region, as Horace does: 'Those who through the ocean range / The region, not themselves, do change.'

50   **Suo iumento sibi malum accersere**
     To fetch trouble for oneself on one's own beast

The person who is the author of his own misfortunes is said to 'fetch trouble for himself on his own beast'; it is at his own expense, by his own effort, as it

* * * * *

19 Cicero] *Philippics* 1.14.33
20 familiar saying] This is mentioned again in III i 84, but has not yet been identified.

49 *Collectanea* no 274. Otto 283
 3 Macrobius] *Saturnalia* 3.12.10 (see I i 12n); once also in I vi 36
 5 This seems ... what he said] Aristophanes *Frogs* 1135, transferred here in *1515* from I vi 36
 7 The metaphor is] So *1515*; in *1508* it was This can be thought to be. The two examples given were already in the *Collectanea*: Phaethon driving the chariot of the Sun his father, and Ceres wandering all over the world to seek her daughter Proserpine; both of them all astray.
12 Horace] *Epistles* 1.11.27, which in the *Collectanea* was treated as an independent adage (no 433), and is Otto 285

50 *Collectanea* no 237, citing Plautus. Otto 759

were in his own waggon, that he goes to fetch a pack of troubles for himself.   5
Plautus in the *Amphitryo*: 'That man brought trouble from me on his own
beast.' The metaphor comes from baggage-waggons, for the pack-animal
(*jumentum*) can mean this, according to Gellius, book 20 chapter 1; or in any
case from animals carrying burdens on their backs.

51   **Suo sibi hunc iugulo gladio, suo telo**
    I am cutting his throat with his own sword, with his own weapon

'To be killed with his own sword or weapon' is said of the man who is
refuted by his own words, or caught by a trick invented by himself; anyone,
in fact, whose word or deed can be used as a retort against himself, though   5
coming from him in the first place. Take for instance someone who follows
the example of Protagoras by taking the converse and turning a dilemma
round against the person who propounded it; or like Phalaris, taking Perillus the inventor of a torture and putting an end to him through his own
invention. Thus in the *Adelphoe* of Terence, the old man Mitio complains of   10
the harshness of his brother Demea and makes the following remark: 'This is
the particular vice which old age brings, it makes us more grasping than we
should be.' A little later Demea retorts against his brother: 'Finally I don't
take to myself that observation you, Mitio, made just now – how right and
wise you were! It is a common fault of us all to be too grasping in our old age,   15
and we ought to shun this defect.' When Mitio, compelled by this reasoning,
was forced to hand over the field for which he was being asked, Demea's
remark is 'I am cutting his throat with his own sword.' The metaphor is
borrowed from those who sometimes during a battle manage to get stabbed
with their own weapons. Plautus in the *Amphitryo*: 'And this man is to be   20
turned out of the house with his own weapon, his own wicked cunning.'
Cicero in the *Pro Caecina*: 'Your case is doomed to be destroyed, either by

* * * * *

6 Plautus] *Amphitryo* 327
8 Gellius] 20.1.26, 'in any case' added in *1517/8*, and the precise reference in *1528*

51 *Collectanea* no 53 covered our 51, 52 and 53, with references to Roman comedy
   and the Psalms. Otto 759 and 1750. Cf Tilley s 802 To be beaten with one's own
   staff.
8 Phalaris] The story is told in *Adagia* i x 86.
10 Terence] *Adelphoe* 833–4; 952–5; 958
20 Plautus] *Amphitryo* 269
22 Cicero] *Pro A. Caecina* 29.82

your own sword, as the saying is, or by mine.' Ovid alluded to this in the
Heroides: 'The oars to flee away from me, I gave them you; / I suffer from the
wounds my own darts made.' These words of Cicero's concern the same   25
thing: 'You'll have to run on your own sword's point,' and again, 'This is the
sword-point of your defence, and your speech will be obliged to run on to it.'
Nor is Livy's phrase very different, in book 2 of the *Second Punic War*:
'Hannibal knew he was being attacked by his own stratagems.' Lucian in the
Fishermen: 'The arrows which, as you admit, you took from us, you aimed   30
against us.' Plutarch relates that when Brasidas the general had a weapon
extracted from his body, he used it to stab the man who had thrown it.
Marius, one of the Thirty Tyrants, was struck down by a certain soldier, who
said as he attacked (according to Trebellius Pollio): 'This is the sword you
made yourself,' for Marius had been a blacksmith before he came to power,   35
and had employed that very soldier in his smithy. Here indeed was one who
could have been said to be killed with his own sword.

52   **Incidit in foveam quam fecit**
     He fell into the pit which he had made

The same meaning is found in that passage of the *Odes* of David, Psalm 7:
'He made a pit, and digged it, and is fallen into the ditch which he made.'
Adapted from those who dig pits or other snares and decoy wild animals   5
into them; or else from wars, in which one enemy sometimes tries to capture
another by means of underground tunnels.

          * * * * *

     23 Ovid] *Heroides* 2.47–8
     25 Cicero] *Pro A. Caecina* 29.84 (the first looks like an imperfect memory of the
        second).
     28 Livy] 22.16.5, the precise reference added in 1528 and the book-number
        corrected in 1536. *Second Punic War* is an alternative title for the third decade
        (books 21–30).
     29 Lucian] *Piscator* 7
     31 Plutarch] *Moralia* 190B, 219C and 548C; added in 1515
     34 Trebellius Pollio] *Triginta tyranni* 8.7, added in 1517/8. He is one of the authors
        of the so-called *Historia Augusta* (see I i 21n).

     52 *Collectanea* no 53 (in part). Tilley P 356 He falls into the pit he digs for another. Cf
        Otto 713.
      3 David] Psalm 7:16 (7:15 Authorised version), cited in the Greek of the
        Septuagint, as is that in the next paragraph, with a slightly variant Vulgate
        equivalent, no doubt from memory

53   **Suo ipsius laqueo captus est**
     He was caught in his own noose

Much the same is what we read in the same author, Psalm 9: 'In the net
which they hid is their own foot taken.' A well-known metaphor, taken from
those who spread out snares and lie in wait for birds or beasts.   5

54   **Hanc technam in teipsum struxisti**
     You constructed this device against yourself

The same idea is expressed in another way by Lucian: 'So you came a
cropper owing to your own invention.' This concerns a man who was
looking for an inheritance, and wrote down a rich man as his only heir and   5
showed him the will, hoping that the said rich man would do the same by
him. But suddenly the roof collapsed and crushed the testator, so that he left
everything to the very man whose wealth he had coveted. This should be
used when a trick intended for another person rebounds on to the head of its
originator, a thing which quite often happens.   10

55   **Turdus ipse sibi malum cacat**
     The thrush's droppings are its own harm

Very like these is the Greek adage: Κίχλα χέζει αὐτῆ κακὸν, The thrush's
droppings are its own harm. It is used of those who procure for themselves
the cause of their ruin. In fact, according to Pliny, birdlime is only produced 5
by being matured in the stomach and passed out through the bowels of
birds, especially of doves and thrushes. Servius mentions this in his commentary on *Aeneid* 6. Aristotle in the *Nature of Animals*, book 9, distinguishes

* * * * *

53 *Collectanea* no 53 (in part). Tilley F 626 The fowler is caught in his own snare.
 3 Psalm] 9:16 (9:15 Authorised version)

54 From Lucian *Dialogi mortuorum* 18. The second sentence was rewritten in 1536;
   before that, it ran 'and by mistake swallowed a fatal draught of the poison he
   had prepared for an old man,' referring to *Dial. mort.* 17. Perhaps Erasmus had
   forgotten that he had already used this story in 1508 in I iii 49.

55 Otto 234; Tilley T 270 The thrush limes herself with that which grew from
   her own excretion.
 5 Pliny] *Naturalis historia* 16.247
 7 Servius] The fourth-century commentator, on *Aeneid* 6.205
 8 Aristotle] *Historia animalium* 9.20 (617a18)

three sorts of thrush, the first called *ixoboron*, or as Athenaeus says
ixophagon, because it feeds on mistletoe. Since birds are caught by birdlime,   10
it is clear that their droppings are their own harm. Plautus has it a little
differently: 'the bird itself,' he says, 'creates its own death.' But I have no
doubt that Plautus really wrote *cacat* (excretes) rather than *creat* (creates),
and that the passage was then corrupted by some half-educated person who
did not know the Greek proverb, and substituted the wrong term *creat*.   15
Sophocles in *Antigone*:

> He who begets unhelpful sons,
> What would you say save troubles for himself
> He breeds, and for his foes a laughing-stock?

The proverb will fit this case, or the case of those who take to themselves   20
powerful sons-in-law, who later become their oppressors.

56 Ipse sibi mali fontem reperit
He himself discovered the source of his woe

There is also among the same people a line in frequent use as a proverb,
Αὐτὸς γὰρ εὗρε τοῦ κακοῦ τὴν πητύαν, He found himself the bond of his
misfortune, or Αὐτὸς εὗρε τοῦ κακοῦ πηγήν, He found himself the fountain of   5
his woe. So Aeschylus in the *Persae*: 'Now, it seems that a fountain of evil /
Has been discovered for all our friends.' This is a trochaic line. There are in
fact noxious springs, and to taste the water from them causes death or
insanity; it would have been better not to have discovered them.

* * * * *

9 Athenaeus] 2.65a, added in *1517/8*
11 Plautus] Frag 47, cited by Servius. Birdlime, the powerful glue used by fowlers
   to catch birds, is made from mistletoe berries; and the Ancients believed, as
   Pliny (echoing Theophrastus) has just told us, that mistletoe berries will only
   germinate if they have been eaten and digested by birds: no droppings, no
   mistletoe. Hence Erasmus' emendation, and his *cacat* is corroborated by a
   quotation of the Plautus fragment in Isidore's *Etymologiae* 12.7.71, which he
   would no doubt have mentioned had he known of it. Modern scholars seem to
   credit the correction to Pieter Burman the elder (1688–1741).
16 Sophocles] *Antigone* 645–7

56 In the *Collectanea* the Latin proverb was given, without source, as no 135; the
   line of verse which follows formed no 671, at first in Latin only, and the Greek
   was added in 1506, no doubt from the Greek proverb-collections (Diogenianus
   3.18). The adage is also in Suidas (A 4521 and II 1540).
6 Aeschylus] *Persae* 743, added in *1523*
8 noxious springs] This sentence was added in *1517/8*.

57 **Capra gladium**
    The goat (found) the sword

This belongs to the same kind, Αἴξ μάχαιραν, The goat (found, understood)
the sword. This is said of those who themselves discover what is to ruin
them. It arose from the following circumstance. Once when the Corinthians 5
were preparing to celebrate the rites of Acraean Juno (for that was the name
given to her, and it is said that a statue of this Juno was set up by Medea),
and those who had been hired to provide the sacrificial victim buried the
knife in the ground and pretended to have forgotten it, the goat scratching
with its feet uncovered the knife, dug it out and was thereupon sacrificed 10
with it. Some give the form of this adage as 'the goat supplying the knife,'
and others as 'the sheep (supplies) the knife.'

58 **Cornix scorpium**
    The crow (caught) the scorpion

Close in meaning also is this, Κορώνη τὸν σκορπίον, The crow (caught) the
scorpion. It fits those who are preparing to harm others, by whom they in
turn will suffer just as much harm. The crow seized a scorpion, but its tail 5
curved up and the crow got a fatal wound and died. There is a Greek
epigram about this by Archias, which I am not unwilling to translate:

> A scorpion had crept from the earth, and a crow
> Spied it as he sought his living in the limpid sky.
> He snatched what he saw and fled. But just as the bird   10
> Touched the ground, the scorpion struck with his sting, and killed him.
> Behold, the death the insidious bird was preparing
> For the other, the wretch achieved it for himself.

And in human affairs it often happens that the one who seems to be the

* * * * *

57 *Collectanea* no 720 gives the same story more briefly, probably from Diogenia-
    nus 1.52, as the Greek is supplied. But 'Acraean Juno' and 'Medea' must come
    from Zenobius 1.27.
    11 Some] Suidas AI 235–6, o 98
    12 others] Apostolius 12.48

58 *Collectanea* no 263 covered this adage (probably from Diogenianus 1.52) and the
    next (citing Plautus), and also our 61. Suidas κ 2107
    7 Archias] *Anthologia Palatina* 9.339, added with the following in 1515

captor is himself caught. So Horace writes: 'Thus captive Greece took her   15
rude victor captive.'

59   Calidum prandium comedisti
You have eaten a hot dinner

The following sentence of Plautus seems to refer to this: 'Today you have
eaten a hot dinner,' that is, you have done something which will cause you
great trouble. This comes from people who stuff themselves with unwhole-   5
some and deadly food and are likely to feel the pains of colic.

60   Irritare crabrones
To stir up hornets

Τὰς σφηκιὰς ἐρεθίζειν, To stir up hornets. To this saying we must refer what
Plautus has in the *Amphitryo*, 'You'll stir up the hornets.' Here the poet is
using it against the mentality of women: once they have been annoyed, you   5
will only provoke them more by having a fight and you will get the worst of
it. The hornet is a kind of insect related to the wasp; highly pertinacious and
with a most virulent sting. Pliny in the *Natural History*, book 11 chapter 21,
says that the sting of a hornet hardly ever fails to cause fever. He adds that
according to some accounts a man is killed by thrice nine stings from this   10
insect. Aristotle in book 9 of *On the Parts of Animals* remarks, among the
other things he says about hornets, that while there are some bees which
have no sting, such as drones and queens, and some stingless wasps are also
to be found, no hornet is ever discovered unarmed with a sting. But whether
the leader has a sting, he is in some doubt. St Jerome uses this adage in one   15

* * * * *

15 Horace] *Epistles* 2.1.156. This was added in the same year to I x 14.

59 *Collectanea* no 263 (in part), rewritten. From Plautus *Poenulus* 759

60 A long account of this in *Collectanea* no 54 has been used, in part verbatim. Otto
453; Tilley w 78, 79 To stir a wasps nest
4 Plautus] *Amphitryo* 707
7 related to the wasp] Added in *1515*
8 Pliny] *Naturalis historia* 11.73
11 Aristotle] *Historia* (not *De partibus*) *animalium* 9.42 (629a24–8), added in *1515*
13 queens] The original of course has 'kings,' in accordance with the ideas of the
time.
15 Jerome] The reference, taken over from the *Collectanea*, has not been identified.

of his letters. Plautus expresses the same idea with a change of metaphor:

> Oppose a bacchant in her bacchic frenzy:
> You'll make the mad madder and get hit the more;
> Yield to her then, and get off with one blow.

The custom was that those who celebrated the Bacchanalia would strike the   20
bystanders with their wands. Aristophanes in the *Lysistrata* (for that is the
name I find given to it): 'Unless someone should, as it were, rob / My wasp's
nest and provoke me'. It is to this, I think, that the writer refers who wrote
the epitaph on Archilochus the scurrilous poet: 'Stranger, on tiptoe pass,
and do not wake / The wasps for ever perched upon his tomb.' Xenophon in   25
his fourth book explains how the proverb arose, namely from efforts to drive
wasps out of their nests: 'And I see, he said, that those too who want to drive
wasps out of their nests, if they try to catch them as they are flying out, are
stung by many of them.'

61   **Leonem stimulas**
     You are goading the lion

The same force belongs to the proverb mentioned by Diogenianus, Τὸν
λέοντα νύττεις, You are pricking, or pinching, the lion. This applies to
people who provoke and goad someone powerful and fierce, to their own   5
destruction. The metaphor is too well known to need explanation.

62   **Malum bene conditum ne moveris**
     Do not disturb a well-suppressed evil

The same meaning lies in this phrase, Μὴ κινεῖν κακὸν εὖ κείμενον, Do not
disturb a well-suppressed evil, or one which is inactive. This is aimed at

*****

16 Plautus] *Amphitryo* 703–5
21 Aristophanes] *Lysistrata* 475; the Latin version was finally settled in *1528*. This
   is also quoted by Suidas Σ 1732.
24 Archilochus] The last couplet of a fictitious epitaph by one Gaetulicus on the
   Greek poet renowned for his scurrility; *Anthologia Palatina* 7.71, added in *1523*
25 Xenophon] *Hellenica* 4.2.12, added in *1523*

61 *Collectanea* no 263 (in part), from Diogenianus 1.52. Tilley L 317 Wake not a
   sleeping lion.

62 *Collectanea* no 640, probably from Diogenianus 6.54 (mentioned also in 1.52)
   4 or ... inactive] Added in *1515*

those who stir up trouble for themselves by their own stupidity, or who   5
resurrect and revive old abuses long buried. Theognis seems to have recalled the proverb in this line: 'For ofttimes it is best to hide away evil at
home.' Very like this is that other phrase, 'He rouses sleeping fires.'

63 Octipedem excitas
You are waking up Eight-feet

Cratinus in his *Thrattae*, quoted by Suidas, Ὀκτώπουν ἀνεγείρεις, You are
waking up Eight-feet, that is, the scorpion, which has eight feet and usually
lies hidden and dormant under a stone; you rouse him at your peril, because   5
of the poison he carries in his tail.

64 Movere Camarinam
To move Camarina

Κινεῖν τὴν Καμαρίνην, To move Camarina, is to bring trouble upon oneself.
Lucian in *Apophrade*: 'You see that it would have been better for you to leave
Camarina unmoved.' The origin of the adage is explained by Servius the   5
grammarian, in commenting on that passage of Virgil in *Aeneid* 3: 'And
Camarina shows up far away, / Ne'er to be moved; so have the fates
decreed.' 'Camarina,' he says, 'is a fen near the town of that name, which
once exhaled pestilence when it dried up. The people consulted the oracle to
ask whether they would be doing right to drain it altogether. The God   10
forbade them to move Camarina. But they did drain it, instead of obeying
the oracle, and the pestilence ceased; but their enemies came in across it, and
they were well punished for not attending to the oracle.' Suidas mentions

* * * * *

6 Theognis] 423, added in 1520 Theognis of Megara (sixth century BC) left us a
    collection of moral couplets, over 1200 lines, first published by Aldus in 1495/6.
8 other phrase] Virgil *Aeneid* 5.743

63 From Suidas o 130, citing Cratinus frag 77 Kock. He is a writer of the Attic Old
    Comedy.

64 Camarina was a Syracusan colony on the south coast of Sicily near its eastern
    end, destroyed in the third century BC; how it obtained fame in this way seems
    to be unknown. Otto p 67n
4 Lucian] *Pseudologista* 32. This is the only place where Erasmus refers to this
    piece by its alternative title *De apophradeô*, The unlucky day (cf III iv 64).
5 Servius] The fourth-century commentator, on Virgil *Aeneid* 3.700–1; 'for not
    attending to the oracle' was added in 1517/8.
13 Suidas] M 904; similar material is in Zenobius 5.18.

this too, with an additional explanation, that some say camarina was a shrub, whose branches gave off a foul smell if anyone disturbed or shook 15 them. But it seems to me that the former opinion comes nearer to the likeness of truth. Stephanus mentions this adage also, in a hexameter line, and reports it in this fashion: 'Move not Camarina, for it is best not moved.' But he says Camarina is a town, and a marsh of that name, in Sicily. Silius mentions it in book 14, imitating Virgil: 'And Camarina, which the fates 20 would not allow to be moved.'

65 Anagyrim commoves
You are moving Anagyrus

Very little different from the foregoing is the saying, current in Greek: Ἀνάγυρον κινεῖς, You are moving Anagyrus. It fitted those who were the authors of their own misfortunes, and who provoked another and so 5 brought about their own downfall. The origin of the proverb is related differently by the authorities. Some refer it to the nature of the shrub which is mentioned by Dioscorides in his third book, and which some call *magyrus* and others *anagyrus*, and others again *acopon*, efficacious as a medicine, but having a very strong odour, especially when rubbed by the hand; the fruit 10 when eaten produces violent vomiting. The proverb seems to arise either from the disagreeable smell which results from cutting it (since indeed the word *acopon* is evidently traceable to the same source), or else from its power of producing vomiting. Pliny also mentions this, book 27 chapter 4. There

* * * * *

17 Stephanus] Steph. Byzantius p 351 Meineke (see I ii 43n); 'in a hexameter line' was added in 1515. The line, of unknown origin, is incorporated in the Greek Anthology, *Anthologia Palatina* 9.685.

19 Silius] Silius Italicus, the epic poet of the first century AD; this is *Punica* 14.198, and was added in 1533. Erasmus had referred to him in the *Adagia* once already (I ix 1), twenty-five years before.

65 It seems that two quite distinct subjects are put together here, which are discussed by O. Crusius in his *Paroemiographica* (*Sitzungsberichte* of the Bavarian Academy for 1910) 51–5. One, the marsh-plant with a strong unpleasant smell, is mentioned in the *Collectanea* no 92, where it is said to be used as a proverb by physicians on the authority of Ermolao Barbaro; the source of this was Poliziano *Opera* Aldus 1498 sig 7 verso. The other, which formed *Collectanea* no 727, was Anagyrus, a bad-tempered rich man (in other versions a 'hero,' a local semi-divine figure in Attica), who must not be provoked. We can see Erasmus trying, not wholly without success, to organize unusually reluctant material. Zenobius 2.55 is one of his sources.

8 Dioscorides] *De materia medica* (see I i 22n) 3.150.

14 Pliny] *Naturalis historia* 27.30, added in 1515

are those who say that Anagyrus is a place in Attica, which belongs to the   15
Erechtheid tribe (my authority is Stephanus), where there is a prolific
growth of a certain bush with a heavy odour, so that we take the name
anagyrus for the shrub, just as Anticyra is used for the hellebore. Others
again think that Anagyrus is the name of a certain local deity, whose
sanctuary was violated, and who for this reason destroyed all those living in   20
his vicinity. This adage is mentioned by Aristophanes in the *Lysistrata*. And
in fact the passage in Aristophanes runs thus: 'Whence come they? From
Anagyrus, by Zeus. At least it seems we've stirred up Anagyrus.'

Suidas tells roughly the following story: Anagyrasius was a certain
tutelar deity, named so from the place just mentioned, who took revenge on   25
an old man living close by, because he had cut down his grove; and this is
how he did it. He sent a furious passion for the old man's son into the heart
of the father's concubine, who when she found that she could not entice the
young man, took the step of accusing him to his father, saying that he
continually pestered her to commit adultery. The father, persuaded by the   30
woman, threw his son down from the roof and killed him. Then, overcome
with remorse for the deed, he hanged himself. Finally the woman threw
herself into a well. As authority for this story he cites a certain Hieronymus, I
am not sure who, in a work entitled *On Writers of Tragedy*.

66 Capra contra sese cornua
The goat (turns) its own horns against itself

ʹΗ αἴξ καθ᾽ ἑαυτῆς τὰ κέρατα, The goat (turns) its horns against itself. This
belongs to the preceding group, and comes from a fable. A goat, wounded
by an arrow, looked round to see where this hurt had come from, and seeing   5
the bow made of goat's horn, it said, 'I grew those horns for my own
destruction.'

* * * * *

16 Stephanus] Steph. Byzantius p 91 Meineke (see I ii 43n); Hesychius, the
   fifth-century AD lexicographer, A 4248 may also have contributed.
21 Aristophanes] *Lysistrata* 67–8; the Greek text and its Latin version not added
   till *1523*
24 Suidas] A 1842. The hero is called 'Anagyrasian' from the place where his
   sanctuary was.
33 I am not sure who] Added in *1517/8*. The reference is to a lost author of the
   third century BC, Hieronymus of Rhodes (F. Wehrli, *Die Schule des Aristoteles*
   10, 1969, frag 32).

66 This is a variant of a familiar type of fable, in which a mortally wounded
   creature realises that it has contributed to its own execution. A bow was tipped
   with horn at either end, to take the wear of the string. Cf I vi 52.

67 Atlas coelum
    Atlas (supported) the sky

Ἄτλας τὸν οὐρανὸν, Atlas the sky (supported, understood). This is said
about people who get themselves entangled in great and grievous matters,
thus seeking out trouble for themselves. For this man received hospitality in   5
heaven; but caught in the act of laying an ambush against it, he was flung
into the Atlantic Ocean. But really there is no need to relate here the
well-known story of Atlas, supporting the sky on his head and shoulders.

68 Deus ex improviso apparens
    Unexpected appearance of a god

Θεὸς ἀπὸ μηχανῆς ἐπιφανείς, A god appearing suddenly from the machine.
This is applied to people who find, in the midst of their perplexities, some
unhoped-for person who comes to their rescue and solves the problem for   5
them. It is taken from a habitual practice in tragedies, in many of which
some god was revealed by means of certain machines, not on the stage itself,
but coming down from above so that he could finish off the play by a sudden
change in the plot. Cicero witnesses to this in book 1 of the *On the Nature of
the Gods*, as when he says this: 'You on the contrary cannot see how nature   10
can achieve all this without the aid of some intelligence, and so, like the
tragic poets, being unable to bring the plot of your drama to a dénouement,
you have recourse to a god; whose intervention you assuredly would not
require if you would but contemplate the measureless and boundless extent
of space that stretches in every direction.' There is no doubt that Cicero here   15
is imitating a passage from the *Cratylus* of Plato: 'Unless, just as the writers
of tragedy do when they are at a loss, they take refuge in machines, hoisting
up gods.' This passage of Plato has been translated quite wrongly, or at least
obscurely, by the Latin translator, because he did not know the proverb. For
he puts it like this: 'Unless like the tragic poets, whenever they are unde-   20
cided, they take refuge with the gods by means of some imaginary
machines.' The same stumbling-block seems to have got in the way of the

* * * * *

67 Presumably from Diogenianus 2.67, or Suidas A 4368

68 *Collectanea* no 144 cited the Greek proverb, no doubt from Diogenianus 2.84,
    and Cicero; the Greek is also in Suidas Θ181.
9 Cicero] *De natura deorum* 1.10.53–4
16 Plato] *Cratylus* 425d, the translator being Marsilio Ficino. This section was
    added in 1528.

writer who translated the life of Lysander from Plutarch. When Lysander decided to make changes in the state and reflected that the proposition was too difficult to tackle by the ordinary methods, he did what the poets do in   25
tragedy, he planned how to achieve what he wished by means of false oracles and reverence for the gods. The Greek is as follows: 'Just as in a tragedy, bringing a machine before the public, he composed and concocted oracular replies purporting to come from the Pythian Apollo.' The same is indicated rather vaguely, but with true elegance, by Aristotle in his   30
Metaphysics, book 1, in words which one may translate as follows: 'For Anaxagoras uses mind, like some god of tragedy suddenly shown forth as a device for the making of the world. And when he is at a loss in explaining the cause of what necessarily is, then he brings in mind. But in all other matters he ascribes the cause to anything rather than to mind.'   35

Hence there is the frequent phrase in Greek tragedy, 'Many are the forms of the gods, etc.' They work out the plot by the introduction of a god; as in Euripides' *Orestes*, where Apollo appears in the midst of the uproar and at once settles the disturbed situation. An example of this seems to be taken from Homer, when in the *Iliad*, book 1, he introduces Pallas to placate the   40
enraged Achilles; and he brings forward some divinity in various other places. But Horace, in the *Art of Poetry*, says that this should not be done in comedy, unless the situation is so difficult that it cannot be unravelled by human effort: 'Nor let a God in person be displayed / Unless the labouring plot deserve his aid.' In agreement with this, Plautus introduced Jove into   45
the *Amphitryo* and for that reason called it a tragicomedy. Lucian in *Philopseudes*: 'And I thought that this one was chosen for me by fate as a god from the machine, as the saying goes.' Again in *On Salaried Posts*: 'For these specially pertain to tragedies of this sort; or some other god from the machine, sitting on the mast-head.' Euripides thought of this in the *Iphigenia*   50
in Aulis. 'Truly I appeared to you as a great god.' Lucian in *The Sects*, 'There you stood, like that adage beloved of tragedy-writers, a god appearing from

* * * * *

23 Plutarch] *Lysander* 25.1, added in 1533
30 Aristotle] *Metaphysica* 1.4 (985a18–21); the quotation was remodelled in 1515.
36 Greek tragedy] Euripides *Alcestis* 1159 (version added in 1515), and in many of his other plays
40 Homer] *Iliad* 1.206ff
42 Horace] *Ars poetica* 191–2
45 Plautus] *Amphitryo* 59
46 Lucian] *Philopseudes* 29, used again in I ix 29; *De mercede conductis* 1
50 Euripides] *Iphigeneia Aulidensis* 973–4
51 Lucian] *Hermotimus* 86; *The Sects* (that is, of philosophy) is an alternative title.

a machine.' In Athenaeus, book 6, some poet or other makes a certain gluttonous fellow complain that the sellers of fish just show their goods and then immediately snatch them away: 'And they quickly remove the goods   55 from sight, / And sell them like gods from the machine.' Just so, whenever salvation comes from some unexpected quarter, it is usually ascribed to a god. Thus Pliny writes in book 25: 'Even in what has been discovered chance has sometimes been the finder; at other times, to speak the truth, the finder was a god.' Again, in book 27: 'Therefore this is chance, this is that god who   60 discovered most things in life.'

69 **Homo homini deus**
Man is a god to man

Not far from this is the phrase Ἄνθρωπος ἀνθρώπῳ δαιμόνιον, Man is a god to man, usually said about one who has conferred sudden and unlooked-for salvation, or who has brought help by some great benefaction. To be a god,   5 thought the ancients, was simply and solely to be of value to mortal men; thus the ancient world made gods out of the originators of grain, wine, laws, anyone who had contributed something to the betterment of life. To such an extent was this true, that they worshipped certain animals, as the Egyptians worshipped the stork, because it was believed to seek out, drive away and   10 kill the snakes which came up at a certain time of year from the marshlands of Arabia. The Romans also held the goose sacred, because its noise woke the guards and so saved the stronghold of the Capitol from the invading Gauls. This is what Cicero means when he writes in the first book of his *On the Nature of the Gods*: 'I will make my point thus: these animals are deified by   15 the barbarians for the benefits which they confer.'
    According to Prodicus of Ceos, some inanimate bodies have been held to be gods, such as the sun, the moon, water, earth, because they seemed

* * * * *

53 Athenaeus] 6.226c, added in 1517/8. He cites the New Comedy writer Alexis frag 126 Kock, but Erasmus overlooked the author's name, which had been given shortly before.
58 Pliny] *Naturalis historia* 25.17 and 27.8, both added in 1515

69 *Collectanea* no 91, from Diogenianus 1.80 (it is also in Zenobius 1.91 and Suidas A 2536), supported by the passages from Virgil and Pliny but in much shorter form. The opposite follows in I i 70. Otto 517; Tilley M 241 Man is a god to man.
14 Cicero] *De natura deorum* 1.36.101
17 Prodicus] The fifth-century philosopher Prodicus of Ceos (LB wrongly says 'of Chios'), frag 84B5 Diels-Kranz, taken perhaps from the second-century AD Sextus Empiricus *Adversus mathematicos* 9.18

conducive to life, and mortals particularly rejoiced in their benefits. The
Scythians, as Lucian tells us in *Toxaris*, swear by wind and sword as if they   20
were gods, because the one gives breath, the other death. But since, as
Cicero says, the advantages and misfortunes of men are for the most part
derived from mankind, and the special quality of God is to preserve or do
good, thus it comes about that whoever brings rescue in dire peril, or is the
means of conferring some immense benefit, performs as it were the office of   25
God, and is said to have stood as a god to the beneficiary. Agreeing with this
we have that customary expression used by Homer and by Hesiod, 'the
gods, the givers of all good things,' and what Strabo says in his tenth book,
'It is rightly said, that it is when mortals are beneficent that they most closely
imitate the gods.' The same writer says, in book 17, that for some Egyptians   30
God was twofold: immortal, the creator of all things, and mortal, of an
unknown name; and thus they gave almost divine honours to those who
conferred benefits upon them. In common parlance, too, people who are
preserved in desperate and involved situations, or in deadly peril, say that
some god had preserved them. Horace: 'Thus Apollo saved me.' Again in   35
the *Odes*, he says he was saved in war by Mercury, and once more by Faunus
from the fall of a tree. Juvenal makes the same allusion when he says,

> Would any god, or godlike man below
> Four hundred sesterces on you bestow,
> Kinder than fate ...   40

And Virgil in *Tityrus*,

* * * * *

20 Lucian] *Toxaris* 38
22 Cicero] The source of this has not been identified.
27 Homer] *Odyssey* 8.325
27 Hesiod] *Theogony* 46 and elsewhere
28 Strabo] *Geographica* 10.3.9; 17.2.3, the latter added in *1515*. Strabo, the
    invaluable geographer of the age of Augustus, was first printed in Greek by the
    Aldine press in *1516*, but a Latin version made for Nicholas v had been in print
    since 1471, and it is the Latin that Erasmus normally quotes.
35 Horace] *Satires* 1.9.78
35 Again] In *1508* Erasmus, misremembering Horace *Odes* 2.7.13–4, had Mercury
    save the poet in battle from being hit by a stone. In *1528* he removed the stone,
    which is not in Horace's text, and inserted from *Odes* 2.17.28–9 how the god
    Faunus rescued him from a falling tree.
37 Juvenal] 5.132–3
41 Virgil] *Eclogues* 1.6–10

O Meliboeus, a god gave us this respite;
To me that man for ever shall be God,
And on his altar fume a tender lamb
From our own flocks ...   45

Then he gives the reason why he will consider Caesar among the divinities,
adding the benefit conferred:

He, he it was who gave my cattle leave
To stray thus freely, and myself allowed
The play I wished for with my rustic pipe.   50

Pliny in the *Natural History*, book 2, is more clearly referring to the Greek
proverb, but speaks as irreverently about the gods as he does a little later
about the immortality of souls and foolishly about the resurrection of bodies.
For after gibing at the multiplicity of gods, and utterly refusing to attribute
the care of mortals to the one supreme divinity which he takes to be either   55
the world or some kind of Nature, he says: 'To be a god is to bring aid to a
mortal, though mortal oneself. And this is the way to eternal glory. By this
went the great men of Rome, by this now advances with divine step, with
his children, Vespasianus Augustus, the greatest ruler of all time, bringing
help in disaster. This is the oldest way of giving thanks to those who   60
deserved well, to number them with the gods. For even the names of all the
other gods, and those I have recorded above of the stars, have sprung from
the merits of men.' Thus far Pliny. Ovid says: "Tis a fitting pleasure for man
to save man; / There is no better way of seeking favour.' Plutarch in the essay
'To An Uneducated Ruler' says that the gods are not blessed because they   65
live for ever, but because they are the lords and authors of virtue. Paul,
though, places the height of virtue in charity; but charity which consists in
doing the greatest good to the greatest number. Gregory of Nazianzus
thought of this in his oration *On the Care of the Poor*: 'By imitating the mercy of

* * * * *

46 Caesar] In assuming that Virgil's unnamed benefactor is Octavius, the future
   Caesar Augustus, Erasmus follows the traditional view.
51 Pliny] *Naturalis historia* 2.18
63 Ovid] *Ex Ponto* 2.9.39–40, added in *1536*
64 Plutarch] *Moralia* 781A, added in *1515*
66 Paul] 1 Corinthians 13
68 Gregory of Nazianzus] *Oratio* 14, 26–7 (*PG* 35.892D), added in *1533*. In 1531
   Erasmus had written a dedicatory preface (Ep 2493) to a Latin version of thirty
   of his orations, made by Willibald Pirckheimer and published by Froben; he
   sometimes quotes Latin, as here, and sometimes Greek.

God you will become God to the sufferer, for man has nothing so divine as   70
kindness.'

Among Christians the name of God ought not to be given to any mortal
man even in jest, and such extraordinary and disgusting flattery must be
altogether unacceptable to our moral code; yet it can happen that this adage
finds a use, and not an immoral nor unfitting one. For instance, one might   75
say, 'At a time when I was labouring under such great misfortunes that no
mortal man either wished to help me or could do so, you alone came to my
aid – it was more than I had hoped for – and not only rescued me by your
kindness (otherwise I should have perished) but made me better fitted for
life than I had been before. Between us two, if ever, that old Greek proverb   80
can apply, man is a god to man.' Or one might speak thus: 'I owe everything
to letters, even my life; but I owe letters to you, who by your liberality
procure me leisure and support me in it. What is this, if not what the Greeks
mean when they say, "man is a god to man?"' Or in this way: 'To do a small
kindness certainly proves a man is a friend; but to spend skill and wonderful 85
care and attention so as to retain a life which is ebbing away, and restore it,
as a doctor does, what is that but what the Greeks say, man is a god to man?'
Again, 'Matters had come to such a point that not Salvation itself could bring
aid. Then you came upon me like the presence of a god, and dispersed my
troubles with marvellous speed, and set me back where I was before, not   90
expecting nor hoping for such a thing – so that I might understand that it
was no idle word of the Greeks, "man is a god to man."' Or again, 'In other
things, indeed, you have always been the greatest friend to me, but in this
juncture you were not only my greatest friend, but I might almost say, as the
Greeks do, "a man who is a god to man."'   95

70   **Homo homini lupus**
     Man is a wolf to man

"Ανθρωπος ἀνθρώπου λύκος, Man is a wolf to man. Almost the opposite of
the foregoing, and in a way derived from it apparently, is the phrase of
Plautus in the *Asinaria*, 'Man is a wolf to man.' Here we are warned not to   5
trust ourselves to an unknown person, but to beware of him as of a wolf. 'A
man is a wolf and not a man,' he says, 'to the one who knows nothing of his
character.'

* * * * *

88 Salvation] Terence *Adelphoe* 761–2
70 In *Collectanea* no 63 the line from Plautus was given anonymously, with brief
   comment. Otto 990; Tilley M 245 Man is a wolf to man.
 5 Plautus] *Asinaria* 495; the play named in *1523*, the phrase reshaped in *1528*

71 Coturnix Herculem
A quail saved Hercules

Ὄρτυξ ἔσωσεν Ἡρακλῆν τὸν καρτερόν, A quail saved Hercules, that man of
might. This is an iambic six-foot line in Greek, which is current as a proverb,
though Zenodotus says it cannot be found in any of the old writers. It was   5
usually said about people who had been preserved in danger by those from
whom they expected it least. They trace the origin of the adage to the
following fable. Hercules had a favourite quail, and when it was burnt alive,
the smell brought him back from death. Athenaeus also mentions the story
in his ninth book, where he writes that Hercules, the son of Jupiter and   10
Asteria, was slain by Typhon as he was setting out to go to Libya; but he was
restored to life by the odour of a quail which Iolaus gave him to smell, and
for this reason the Phoenicians sacrifice quails to Hercules.

72 Genius malus
An evil genius

The saying just reported, 'Man is a god to man,' seems to have its opposite in
the 'evil genius' which the Greeks call *alastor*; this is the name we give to
those whom we blame for our misfortunes, for the most part, and it remains   5
in common speech to the present day. There are some people who have such
an unlucky effect on certain others that they can really appear to be their evil
destiny, and born to destroy them. The proverb, however, seems to have

* * * * *

71 *Collectanea* no 445 gave the adage in the briefest possible form, derived from
   Diogenianus 7.10. For the *Chiliades* the line was completed and the story
   supplied from Zenobius (whom Erasmus always calls Zenodotus) 5.56. It
   might well be a line from a lost comedy.
   8 Hercules] This is the so-called Tyrian Hercules, presumably some Levantine
   deity identified with a Greek one, whom we shall meet again in I vii 41. The
   Ancients kept quails as pets and for fighting, just as we used to keep
   fighting-cocks; and the bird to which he was attached was no doubt the
   champion of many successful matches. Iolaus was his companion in many of
   his labours.
   9 Athenaeus] 9.329d–e, the book-number added in *1517/8*. Asteria was *Asterea* in
   1520 and *Astrea* in *1508*; corrected in *1528*. Both Zenobius and Athenaeus give
   as their authority Eudoxus of Cnidus, the great mathematician and astronomer
   (fourth century BC).

72 This was briefly dealt with in *Collectanea* no 256, based on Persius 4.27
   though no source is named. Otto 519

arisen from the view of the ancients that each person had two attendant
spirits whom they call *daemones* – and not people only, but also places and   10
buildings are said to have spirits – and one of these plots our destruction
while the other tries to come to our aid. Empedocles thought this, according
to Plutarch's quotation in his essay 'On Tranquillity of Mind.' There is a
connection here with what the same Plutarch says in his life of Brutus. For
when that famous day of doom was approaching for Brutus, and he was   15
watching in his tent in Asia far into the night, as his custom was, by the
dying light of a lantern, he seemed to see a figure of tragic aspect and
superhuman size. Undismayed, he asked at once who it might be, among
gods and men. In a low voice the vision muttered, 'I am your evil genius,
Brutus; you will see me at Philippi.' The same apparition came before him   20
again as he fought at Philippi, and that was his last battle. A similar story is
told by him about Mark Antony and Augustus: they were on very good
terms with each other and lived in friendship, but in the games, where they
were rivals, Octavius always used to be the winner. This was a source of
some distress for Antony. He had however in his retinue a certain Egyptian   25
soothsayer. Whether this man really knew Antony's destiny or whether he
was inventing something to please Cleopatra, he gave Antony a warning to
separate himself as much as possible from Caesar, because his own genius,
otherwise valiant, was intimidated by Caesar's genius, and the closer he
came to Caesar the more he would appear humiliated and downtrodden.   30
Plato also bears witness that Socrates had a familiar spirit, and Apuleius and
Plutarch wrote of this too. Terence seems to refer to the *genius* when he says
in the *Phormio*, 'I have found it so, I can tell you; I have in mind that I am
deserted and that my god is angry with me.' And indeed our own theologians (following the ancients, I imagine) attribute to each person from the   35
very beginning of his life two *genii* which they call angels; one is our friend,
and procures for us the things that are good, the other is evil, and he is intent
on bringing about our ruin in every possible way. The good genius is

* * * * *

12 Empedocles] Philosopher and poet of the fifth century BC, frag 31 B 122
   Diels-Kranz. The source is Plutarch *Moralia* 474B; the sentence was added in
   1515.
14 Plutarch] *Brutus* 36.3; *Antonius* 33.1–2
31 Plato] He often refers to the *daimonion* or divine sign, from which Socrates said
   he received warnings from time to time. Apuleius in the second century AD
   wrote a treatise *De deo Socratis* which is cited two or three times in the *Adagia*,
   Plutarch an essay *De genio Socratis* (see in particular *Moralia* 588B onwards). This
   last reference was added in 1515.
32 Terence] *Phormio* 73–4

expressed by Naevius in his *Stalagmus*, quoted by Donatus: 'Mine is so
favourable to me, he is my man.' Also Persius: 'with the displeasure of the   40
gods, and with an unlucky genius.' All of these expressions: with the wrath
of the gods, with the favour of the gods, have a flavour of this proverb.
Terence: 'I do not know, except that I know well enough that the gods are
angry with me for having given ear to him.' Horace in the *Satires*: 'The
blameless wall is the one to suffer, / The wall that grew in spite of gods and   45
poets.' Again, 'Born in unlucky seasons, whate'er they be.' And again in the
Odes,

>   Thou art not here, absent too long,
>   Sprung from the good gods, protector of the race
>   Of Romulus.   50

Homer, *Iliad* 5: 'Truly it is some angered god.' And Virgil: 'I think it is with
the favour of the gods and Juno's blessing.'
  These other phrases also belong here: 'Antipho, you are the only
beloved of the gods'; and 'The gods are mindful of us'; and, 'If only Jupiter is
with us'; and 'If the unpropitious deities allow anyone'; and 'May Apollo be   55
on our right hand'; and hundreds of other such passages met with in the
poets.
  This will be more attractive if you use it of a particular power: 'This man
writes his poems without the favour of the Muses one and all'; 'He sings
with Apollo against him.' 'He pleaded that cause clumsily, obviously the   60
goddess of Persuasion was angry with him.' 'We fought with Mars against
us.' 'We sailed with the favour of Neptune.' 'When I made an agreement
with that old fox, I must have had Mercury against me.' 'He is striving for
children against the will of Venus,' about someone who begets deformed
sons. 'Minerva unwilling' of someone who practises his art unskilfully.   65

                    * * * * *

39 Naevius] One of the earliest Roman poets, third century BC; com 70 (*Comicorum
     Romanorum fragmenta* ed O. Ribbeck, Leipzig 1898, 21). This is cited by
     Donatus, the ancient commentator, on Terence *Phormio* 74.
40 Persius] *Satires* 4.27
43 Terence] *Andria* 663–4
44 Horace] *Satires* 2.3.7–8; 2.7.14, used again in II ii 74; *Odes* 4.5.1–2
51 Homer] *Iliad* 5.191, which reappears in III viii 26
51 Virgil] *Aeneid* 4.45
53 other phrases] Terence *Phormio* 854 and 817; Virgil *Aeneid* 3.116; *Georgics* 4.6–7

73 **Dextro Hercule,** *aut* **amico Hercule**
With Hercules at my side, *or* **Hercules being my friend**

Of the same kind, but more obscure, is the allusion in Horace: 'Rich, by the
friendship of Hercules,' and again in Persius:

> If only   5
> A money-jar might tinkle under my mattock,
> Hercules being at my side!

The allusion fits those who are lucky in acquiring wealth. This is thought to
arise from what Hercules is supposed to have said before he died: that
anyone who would dedicate a tenth of his goods to him would become rich.   10
So many wealthy men were accustomed to do this. But Plutarch in his
'Problems' gives another reason for this custom, that Hercules himself once
sacrificed on the Palatine a tenth part of the oxen he had taken from Geryon;
or because he freed the Romans from the tenth they used to pay as tribute to
the Etruscans.   15

74 **Diis hominibusque plaudentibus**
With the applause of gods and men

That well-known hyperbole is also proverbial, 'with the applause of gods
and men,' for something done successfully and with good auspices. Cicero
to his brother Quintus: 'I annihilated Vatinius, who was openly attacking   5
him, just as the fancy took me, with the applause of gods and men.' The
same, in his *Letters to Friends*, book 1: 'I not only said so, but I do so as well, to
the delight of gods and men.' Then to his brother Quintus, book 3, he turns
the proverb round: 'Unless our friend Pompey, to the disgust of gods and

* * * * *

73 *Collectanea* no 257 cited the passages from Horace and Persius, and there is
some verbal overlap.
3 Horace] *Satires* 2.6.12–3
4 Persius] *Satires* 2.10–2
11 Plutarch] *Moralia* 267E. Geryon was a monstrous figure, a mythical king in
Spain. His oxen were carried off by Hercules, who sacrificed some of them on
his way back on what was to be later the site of Rome (Virgil *Aeneid* 7.662–3,
8.201–4).

74 Derived from Cicero. Otto 511
4 Cicero] *Ad Quintum fratrem* 2.4.1; *Ad familiares* 1.9.19; *Ad Quintum fratrem* 3.2.1
(these last two added in *1523*)

men, upsets the whole affair.' Although 'gods and men' by itself is prover-   10
bial because figurative, and often met with in the poets: 'By the faith of gods
and men!' 'Detested by gods and men.' 'Neither gods nor men does he fear.'
Homer: 'Immortal gods and mortal men,' and again: 'Parent of men and
gods.'

75   **Bonis avibus, malis avibus**
       With good or bad auspices (birds)

The phrase 'with good or bad auspices' also belongs to this class; by it we
signify success or failure in our undertakings. It is derived from the observation of the augurs. Horace says in the *Odes*: 'With evil auspices the ship sets   5
sail, / Bearing unsavoury Maevius.' And again:

> Ill-augured are you now
> Who take her homeward whom all Greece shall seek
> To take again with might.

And yet again, 'Valiant victor in war, thou shalt be sung / By Varius, that   10
winged Maeonian poet,' Homer, *Iliad* 24: 'So do not you yourself become
for me / A bird of evil omen here.' These are the words of Priam to his wife,
who was beseeching him not to go alone to the camp of Achilles to recover
the body of Hector, and foretelling many misfortunes, as women usually do.
'With the birds against him' is used by a certain Latin writer of tragedies,   15
who speaks in this way of Agamemnon setting sail against the auspices: 'He
gives orders to set sail, with rumour for him, and the birds against him.'
Cicero refers to this in book 1 of his *On Divination*. There are other phrases to
be referred to this form: 'with a fair omen,' 'well-omened,' 'with good
auspices,' 'inauspiciously,' 'with happy auguries,' and so forth; phrases   20
arising from the art of the soothsayer and taken over by popular speech.

* * * * *

13 Homer] *Odyssey* 24.64; *Iliad* 1.544

75 *Collectanea* no 236 gave the three Horace passages in reverse order. There is
    considerable overlap with *Adagia* II vii 20.
 5 Horace] *Epodes* 10.1–2; *Odes* 1.15.5–6; 1.6.1–2
11 Homer] *Iliad* 24.218–9
15 With the birds ... *Divination*] added in 1536. Cicero *De divinatione* 1.16.29 cites
    an unidentified Roman tragedy; *Tragicorum Romanorum fragmenta* ed O. Rib-
    beck, Leipzig 1897, 286, line 89.

76 **Noctua volat**
The owl flies

From that same superstition springs the Greek phrase, Γλαὺξ ἵπταται, or
ἵπτατο, The owl flies, or flew. For the early Athenians the flight of the owl
was taken as a symbol of victory, because this bird was believed to be sacred   5
to Minerva, who was said to give her blessing even to the wrong decisions of
the Athenians. On this subject we shall say more in connection with the
proverb 'Thoughtless and headstrong like Athenians.' Thus, when things
went better, and turned out according to wish, it was said 'the owl flies.'
This is in Zenodotus and Suidas. The owl may be said to have flown, quite   10
wittily, when an affair is believed to have been settled not by effort but by a
financial bargain: for the coinage of Athens bore the stamp of an owl. Hence
that other phrase, 'Lauriotic owls,' which is treated elsewhere. Plutarch, in
his life of Pericles, tells how his hero was making a speech from the upper
deck of a ship when an owl flew to his right side and perched on the mast;   15
the omen resulted in everyone agreeing with his opinion.

77 **Quarta luna nati**
Born on the fourth day of the new moon

Ἐν τετράδι γεγεννηθῆναι, To be born on the fourth. This describes people
whose birth is unlucky (see Eustathius on *Iliad* 2), because Hercules is said to
have been born at this stage of the moon, and his whole life was deprived of   5
all pleasure and filled with toil. It can be used about those who weary

* * * * *

76 *Collectanea* no 310, from the Greek proverb-collections. Tilley o 93 The owl flies.
4 or flew] The phrase was added in *1517/8* and *1523*.
8 proverb] *Adagia* I viii 44; reference added in *1517/8*
10 This is in] Zenobius ('Zenodotus') 2.89; Suidas Γ 281
13 elsewhere] *Adagia* II viii 31; reference added in *1528*
13 Plutarch] *Themistocles* (not *Pericles*) 12.1, added in *1526*

77 In *Collectanea* no 496 the only source named is Poliziano, which means his
Miscellanea c 80. This Erasmus dropped when he was able to cite Eustathius
who, although a Byzantine author, counted as a classical authority in his
Homeric commentaries. If Tilley w 28 Born in the wane of the moon derives from
this, the fourth day of the month must have been misunderstood as the fourth
quarter. Erasmus applies the saying to himself in the last sentence of III i 1, in
respect of his Herculean labours as compiler of the *Adagia*.
4 Eustathius] Archbishop of Salonica in the last quarter of the twelfth century,
but a mine of information drawn from Antiquity; on *Iliad* 24.336 (1353.5) and
Odyssey 5.262 (1534.33)

themselves by labours which bring no reward, like Hercules, who toiled to
help others and was useless to himself. Pyrrhus, in Lucius Florus, said he
thought he was born under Hercules' star, because the more victories he
won against the Romans, the more fiercely they returned to the attack   10
against him. Horace made an elegant application of this to Hannibal:
'Flourishing as fiercely as the severed Hydra / Sprouted at Hercules, chafing
in defeat.'

78   **Albae gallinae filius**
     A son of the white hen

The lucky man, on the contrary, we call 'a son of the white hen.' Juvenal:
'because you are a son of the white hen.' This is either because Latin uses
'white' for joyful and auspicious things, or because the proverb alludes to   5
that fateful hen recalled by Suetonius in his life of Galba, in these words:
'When Livia was revisiting her villa near Veii soon after her marriage to
Augustus, an eagle flying overhead dropped a white hen with a sprig of bay
in its beak on to her lap. When she had decided to feed the bird and plant the
sprig, there grew up such a flock of chickens that even today the villa is   10
called "house of hens." The bay grove was such that Caesars about to have a
triumph picked their bays from it. It was the custom for those who celebrated a triumph to plant other bay trees forthwith in the same place. And it
was observed that shortly before the death of someone, the tree set by him
drooped. So in Nero's last year the whole grove dried up by the roots and   15
whatever was left in the way of poultry died.'

* * * * *

7 like Hercules] See III i 1.
8 Florus] *Epitome bellorum omnium* 1.13.19, added in 1533. This Florus is a
  historical writer of the second century AD, and he reports a remark made by
  Pyrrhus, king of Epirus c307–272 BC, in the course of his long struggle with
  Rome. But Erasmus leaves out the point: Pyrrhus felt like Hercules, because the
  Romans were like the Lernaean hydra, and when defeated produced fresh
  troops as the hydra grew new heads. When recording the hydra as an adage
  (I x 9), he had added the remark in full in 1523, as having been put in Pyrrhus'
  mouth by Cineas, his right-hand man.
11 Horace] *Odes* 4.4.61–2, added in 1533 ; also cited in 1523 in I x 9, and with full
  context in I iii 4

78 In *Collectanea* no 817 this was supported by the first of the Juvenal quotations
  only. Otto 749; Tilley s 632 A son of the white hen
3 Juvenal] 13.141
6 Suetonius] *Galba* 1. The *De vita Caesarum* of C. Suetonius Tranquillus (first half
  of the second century AD) was edited by Erasmus for Aldus in 1518.

So the adage will fit those who experience some rare and predestined good fortune and success in their affairs. Another phrase of Juvenal's means the opposite: 'Born from unlucky eggs.' Not unlike this is what Cicero writes in the seventh book of his *Letters* to Curio: 'For after devoting myself to the   20 reception of my friends, a function more numerously attended than heretofore, because to them the sight of a fellow-citizen of sound sentiments is just as if they saw a white bird, I hide myself away in my library.' For the ancients, what they wished to be thought inauspicious they called dark or black, and the fortunate, white. Hence Asinius Pollio, quoted by Seneca: 'As   25 for the opinions of Albutius, because they were unaffected and frank, he was wont to call them white.' And in Greek the phrase 'to speak more whitely' is used of the person who explains something more clearly.

79 Laureum baculum gesto
I bear the staff of bay

Δαφνίην φορῶ βακτηρίαν, I bear the staff of bay. Suidas tells how this expression was used by people who were the victims of plotting, and luckily escaped the danger. This was because the bay tree was believed to contain a   5 cure for poison. Pliny, book 15, shows that bay was used in lustration rites; it seems that its power also avails against lightning, since this tree alone is not struck by lightning. Tiberius Caesar was so convinced of this that he never went without his wreath of bay on his head, according to his life by Suetonius.   10

80 Graviora Sambico patitur
He suffers worse tortures than Sambicus

Δεινότερα Σαμβίκου πάσχει, He suffers worse tortures than Sambicus. Of those who are tormented by exquisite pain or to whom notable evils occur.

* * * * *

18 Juvenal] 13.142
19 Cicero] *Ad familiares* 7.28.2, added in *1523*; it had already provided II ii 50.
25 Seneca] Seneca rhetor *Controversiae* 7 pr 2; added with the preceding sentence and the following in *1528*

79 From Suidas Δ 100; also in Zenobius 3.12 and Diogenianus 4.14
 6 Pliny] *Naturalis historia* 15.135, added in *1515*
 9 Suetonius] *Tiberius* 69, added in *1517/8*

80 Given in *Collectanea* no 825 in different wording, with a reference 'if I remember right, in Plutarch's *Problems*.' It is in fact from *Moralia* 302c.

Plutarch mentions this proverb in his 'Greek Questions,' and gives an origin   5
as follows: Sambicus was a man of Elis, who with a few confederates cut to
pieces a number of bronze statues at Olympia and sold them. Then with
even greater daring, he plundered the temple of Diana the protectress (there
is a temple to her in Elis which they call the Aristarcheum). But he was soon
captured, and while he refused to betray his associates, he underwent   10
searching tortures for a whole year, and under these he breathed his last.
Hence the proverb came into common speech.

81   **Foenum habet in cornu**
      He has hay on his horn

This is said of angry and abusive men: He has hay on his horn. Horace, in
the *Satires*: 'He has hay on his horn, beware.' This originates, in the view of
Acron, from the fact that in ancient times hay was attached to the horn of a   5
bull given to goring, as a sign that people who came up by chance should be
warned to take care. Plutarch indicates in his 'Problems' that this is done
because not only bulls, but horses and donkeys grow insolent and fierce
through being too well fed. This is the meaning of Sophocles' expression
about an over-weening and belligerent person: 'You seethe with insolence'   10
he says 'like a colt overfed.' That saying of Solon, in Laertius, agrees with
this: 'Satiety is begotten by wealth, but insolence by satiety.' It was sometimes said of Crassus (as the same Plutarch testifies) that he had hay on his
horn, because he never let an injury pass unavenged, being a very rich and
powerful man, and inveterate in pursuing feuds. But later on Caesar is said   15
to have pulled the hay off him, because when everyone else was fleeing from
him in fear as from a bull who uses his horns, he, Caesar, first dared to stand

* * * * *

81 *Collectanea* no 241A combined this adage and the next one, with support from
   Horace, Jerome and Plautus, and a reference to a further practice of hanging a
   bell, *tintinnabulum*, on a horse or dog given to biting, for which Acron, The
   ancient commentary on Horace (*Satires* 1.4.34), is given as the authority. Otto
   438; Tilley H 233 as above
 3 Horace] *Satires* 1.4.34, with the comment ascribed to Acron
 7 Plutarch] *Moralia* 280F, citing Sophocles frag 764 Nauck
11 Laertius] Diogenes Laertius 1.59, citing Solon (the Athenian statesman and
   poet of the sixth century BC) frag 6.3 West. His famous saying 'Satiety breeds
   insolence,' which is also found in Theognis 153, is given independent status in
   III vii 53.
13 Plutarch] *Moralia* 280F; *Crassus* 7.9. Plutarch's name was not given till 1528.

up to him. St Jerome uses this adage also, in one of his letters, when he is
threatening those by whom he might be attacked.

82 Cornutam bestiam petis
You attack a horned beast

There is a similar meaning in the phrase of Plautus, 'you attack a horned
beast,' referring to someone who assaults a person who is ready to repay the
injury, and whom one persecutes at one's own peril. Horace had this in   5
mind in the *Odes*: 'I raise my ready horns.'

83 Dionysius Corinthi
Dionysius in Corinth

Διονύσιος ἐν Κορίνθῳ, Dionysius in Corinth. An allegory with proverbial
force, by which we indicate a person reduced from the highest rank of
authority to a humble status in private life, just as Dionysius the tyrant of   5
Syracuse, after being thrust from power, became a paid teacher of letters and
music to boys at Corinth. Cicero in the *Letters to Atticus*, book 9: 'About the
optimates, let it be as you wish; but you know the saying Dionysius in
Corinth.' Quintilian *Institutions*, book 8: 'Historical instances are a source of

* * * * *

18 Jerome] *Letters* 50.5.2

82 The ascription to Plautus is found already in *Collectanea* no 241A, but the true
source appears to be Jerome *Adversus Rufinum* 1.31 (PL 23.423D), who applies
the phrase to himself. It reappears, with the same parallel from Horace, in III iii
12. Otto 439
5 Horace] *Epodes* 6.12 (often named *Odes* in the *Adagia*). This comes again in I viii
68.

83 *Collectanea* no 757, with a supporting quotation from Quintilian; the Greek
(which is not in the printed proverb-collections) perhaps from Plutarch,
though it could be a back-translation from Quintilian by Erasmus himself. Otto
559. Dionysius the younger, despot of Syracuse, when expelled in 343 BC, was
said to have opened a school in Corinth. This became a stock example of the
reversal of fortune; W.C. Helmbold in a note on our Plutarch-passage
comments 'The expression is somewhat like saying "Remember St Helena."'
Cicero in the *Tusculan Disputations* 3.12.27 gives the story a further twist: a man
used to despotic rule would rather have school-children to bully than no one
at all.
7 Cicero] *Ad Atticum* 9.9.1 (tr Shackleton Bailey)
9 Quintilian] 8.6.52

allegory, if they are not cited for some specified reason. Take the phrase   10
Dionysius in Corinth, which is so common in Greek: many similar examples
can be used.' When Cicero says 'You know the saying' and Quintilian
'which is so common in Greek,' both of course show that this was a common
expression. Plutarch explains in his essay 'On Pointless Garrulity' how the
adage arose. When he is praising terse and weighty sayings, he recalls the   15
reply of the Spartans to King Philip, who was threatening them with war
and taking a very fierce line: 'Dionysius in Corinth.' The king wrote back to
them saying that if he were ever to lead an army into Laconia, he would
destroy the Spartans; they replied in just one word 'If.' Plato made three
voyages to Sicily, not without arousing adverse comment. Hence Molon,   20
who had a great dislike of Plato, used to say that it was no surprise if
Dionysius were in Corinth, but what was surprising was to see Plato in
Sicily. The king was driven by necessity; Plato was tempted by ambition.

84 **In me haec cudetur faba**
    These beans will be pounded on me

Terence in the *Eunuchus*: 'But these beans will be pounded on me,' that is
(says Donatus' commentary) 'This trouble will recoil on me, I shall be the
one to be blamed for it.' It is transferred, it seems, from beans, which are   5
shelled and then pounded or beaten with flails, as is done on country
threshing-floors, and they do not get as much damage as the surface on
which they are pounded. Others prefer to think the proverb refers to
badly-cooked beans; if they did not soften but remained hard, the angry
master of the house would sometimes pound them with a stone on the   10
cook's head, as if wreaking vengeance on the beans and not on the cook –
but it was the cook who got the worst of it.

* * * * *

14 Plutarch] *Moralia* 511A
19 Plato] From here to the end was added, from Diogenes Laertius 3.34, in 1533.
   Laertius mentions Molon as a personal enemy of Plato.

84 This was no 532 in the *Collectanea*, also taken from Donatus, the ancient
   commentator on Terence; but the more extensive paraphrase given here shows
   that Erasmus has gone back to the original. The line referred to is *Eunuchus* 381.
   Otto 621

85 **Tute hoc intristi, omne tibi exedundum est**
You made this dish and you must eat it all up

Donatus points out a proverb not unlike the foregoing, which is to be read in
the same poet, in the *Phormio*: 'You yourself made this dish and you must eat
it all up.' The words are those of the parasite, Phormio, who since he   5
originated the plan of abducting the girl, thinks it only right that he should
finish the matter off at his own expense. It is thought to be taken from the
rustic dish pounded up with garlic. The same maxim is on people's lips in
our own day. There is also another similar saying, 'You got it ready for the
distaff and now you must spin it yourself,' ie, you began the affair and now   10
you are the one who must settle it.

86 **Faber compedes quas fecit, ipse gestet**
Let the smith who made the fetters wear them

Ausonius in his trochaics adds to the proverb from Terence something very
like it, and interprets the poet's metaphor by a different one:

> You troublesome claimant, here are some troublesome verses for you.   5
> You must eat what you have cooked: so the old proverb demands.
> The fetters he made himself the blacksmith must wear.

It fits those who are the authors of their own misfortune. But it seems to be
taken from the poet Theognis, who says 'No man, dear Cyrnus, forges
fetters for himself.' Something like this, of a humbler kind, but apt, is said in   10
common speech: 'He prepared a rod for his own back,' and that is derived
from boys or servants who are sometimes made to prepare themselves the
rods with which they are to be beaten.

* * * * *

85 *Collectanea* no 533, rewritten. Otto 869; Suringar 230. It is our 'You have made
your bed and you must lie on it.' The reference is to Donatus on Terence
Phormio 318. Not far from Tilley B 32 As you bake so shall you eat and B 189 He
that makes his bed ill lies there.

86 *Collectanea* no 758, from Ausonius. Otto 623; Suringar 75
3 Ausonius] *De bissula* (15) praefatio 4–6. 'Trochaics' was 'trimeters' in *1508*;
corrected in *1523*. Ausonius was a professor at Bordeaux in the fourth century
AD, whose skilful verses were first printed in 1472; we follow the numbering of
the text edited by S. Prete, Leipzig 1978.
9 Theognis] 539; see I i 62n.
12 or servants] Added in *1517/8*

87 **Ipsi testudines edite, qui cepistis**
Eat the turtles you caught yourselves

A proverb like this is mentioned in the Greek collections: Αὐτοὶ χελώνας
ἐσθίεσθ᾽ οἵπερ εἵλετε, You caught the turtles, now you must eat them. It is cast
at people who have thoughtlessly undertaken something and then beg the   5
help of others so as to involve them in their business. The proverb is thought
to have arisen from the following fable. Some fishermen cast their nets and
drew out some turtles. When they had shared them out among the party,
and found there were not enough people to eat them up, they invited
Mercury, who happened to come on the scene, to join the feast. But he   10
perceived that it was not out of kindness that he was invited, but so that he
could relieve them of some of their unwanted food; so he refused, and told
them they must eat up the turtles they had caught. According to Pliny, there
are tribes in Carmania who live on the flesh of turtles, and this is why they
are nicknamed *chelonophagoi* (turtle-eaters). It is said that among them turtles   15
are to be found of such a size that they roof their huts with their shells.

88 **Aderit Temessaeus genius**
The Temessaean spirit will be there

Strabo, in his *Geography*, book 6, reports that Temessa after Laus was the
chief town of Brutia, and called Tempsa in his time. It was founded by the
Ausonians, and then held by the Aetolians, companions of Thoas, and after   5
their expulsion by the Brutians it was finally completely overthrown by
Hannibal and the Romans. Near it, he says, there was a shrine hedged
round with wild olive, and dedicated to Polites, one of the companions of
Ulysses. When his shrine was violated by the barbarians, he let fly his anger
against them, so that it became a proverb, and they said, 'Beware, lest the   10

* * * * *

87 *Collectanea* no 814 has been rewritten and the Pliny-reference added.
 3 Greek collections] Zenobius 2.29; Diogenianus 1.36
13 Pliny] *Naturalis historia* 6.109; the author's name given in 1517/8

88 This was no 366 in the *Collectanea*, with a Greek equivalent not repeated here,
   which might possibly have been of Erasmus' own making. Pausanias and
   Aelian were quoted in Latin, largely in the same words as are used here. Suidas
   o 64
 3 Strabo] See 1 i 69n; *Geographica* 6.1.5, with an addition of 1528.

Temessaean spirit should threaten you.' Later, when the Epizephyrian
Locrians had obtained possession of the town, there came from Italy (so says
Aelian) a well-known pugilist of enormous strength, a certain Euthymus,
who wielded a huge stone (it is normally on show at Locri). This man had an
encounter with Polites, and came off victor in the fight; and so the neigh-   15
bouring peoples were liberated from the tribute that Polites had been accustomed to extort from them. He even compelled Polites to restore with
interest what he had taken. It is thought that the proverb is derived from
this: people who make immoral and unjust gains will find the Temessaean
spirit at hand; by which was meant that some time or other whatever had   20
been snatched by illegal means, by force or fraud, will have to be repaid with
interest.

   Pausanias, in his book on Elis, tells the story a little differently. He says
that a certain companion of Ulysses had been killed for ravishing a girl, and
for this reason his ghost used to walk and bring destruction to all ages and   25
both sexes, unless it were placated by the yearly sacrifice of a virgin. And it
was generally supposed that this was the genius of that place, whom
Euthymus the pugilist suppressed on his return to Temessa, and he set free
the maiden who had been dedicated for sacrifice and married her.

   The passage in Strabo seems to me to be not without error in the Greek   30
text. This is what we read in the Aldine edition: 'So that the dwellers in the
country round collected tribute for him in accordance with an oracle, and
there was in use a proverb referring to them … saying (*legontôn*) that the
guardian spirit of Temessa presses hard upon them.' Perhaps the reading
will be more acceptable if you eliminate the conjunction *de*, and for *legontôn*   35
read *legomenon*. However, the fact that Strabo relates the proverb before
referring to the defeat of the hero suggests that it was used against those
who attack a more powerful person than themselves. Even so, there is no
reason why the proverb should not be adapted to several uses.

                    * * * * *

13 Aelian] *Varia historia* 8.18. He is a Greek author of the second/third century AD,
   and this work, which had not yet been printed, is referred to in the *Adagia* only
   three or four times.
23 Pausanias] See I i 90 n; 6.6.7–10.
30 Strabo] This paragraph discussing the text was added in 1528. The passage is
   given of course in Greek, and one or two words in the middle of it are
   untranslatable, nor has any convincing remedy yet been found.

89   **Termeria mala**
      Termerian evils

Τερμέρια κακά, Termerian evils. In the old proverb this is used of great evils,
especially those which, when a man has forced them on others, recoil on his
own head. Plutarch recalls this adage in his life of Theseus, who used to   5
travel through the world after the manner of Hercules, making the criminals
whom he overcame undergo the same punishment as they had wreaked on
others in their fury. Hercules, for instance, threw Damascus from a high
rock; Busiris he offered up in sacrifice; Antaeus he killed, after worsting him
in wrestling; Cygnus he slew in gladiatorial style. Finally Termerus, who   10
had knocked people's heads together, he crushed in the same way with
blows. Thus the proverbial saying 'a Termerian evil' is used of people whose
misdoings recoil on their own heads. Plutarch uses it this way in his life of
Theseus. There is a type of punishment, eminently to be approved of, which
exactly fits the crime, as when we read of the man from Thurii who sold   15
smoke and was himself smoked to death; and Perillus, whom Phalaris shut
up in the bronze bull, thus destroying him by his own invention. There is a
particularly good story told in the life of the emperor Gallienus. A man had
sold false jewels for real to the empress and when the thing was found out,
he cried out for punishment. The emperor ordered the vendor to be seized   20
as if he were to be thrown to the lions, and let out a capon on him instead.
When all the spectators were amazed at so absurd a spectacle, he ordered
the herald to proclaim: 'Sham were his wares, and sham his punishment':
and so he sent the merchant away.

      Suidas offers quite a different interpretation of 'Termerian evils': he   25
says there is a place in Caria, called Termerium, which at some time or other
was used by tyrants as a prison. It was situated between Melos and Halicarnassus. Robbers used this in later times as a base for plundering, and they
could not be driven out because the place was well fortified, and so it became
a proverb. Stephanus though, places the town of Termera in Lycia, and says   30
its name is drawn from Termerus.

      * * * * *

      89 The Greek perhaps from the proverb-collections (Zenobius 6.6; Diogenianus
         8.24)
       5 Plutarch] *Theseus* 11. Erasmus repeated the reference at the end of the excerpt
         in 1533, not noticing that it had already been given.
      15 man from Thurii] *Adagia* I iii 41
      16 Perillus] I x 86
      18 Gallienus] Trebellius Pollio *Gallieni duo* 12.5 (cf I i 51 n).
      25 Suidas] τ 348
      30 Stephanus] Steph. Byzantius p 617 Meineke (see I ii 43 n).

Finally, 'Termerian evils' may be taken to mean the last extremity of
evil. For *terma* means end in Greek, and they call the last day of life *termerian*
hemeran. In Latin too the word 'extreme' is used when they wish to signify
highest or greatest: for instance extreme madness, extreme frenzy. The   35
Greeks likewise say *eschaton kakon*, 'an extreme evil,' and *eschatôn eschata*,
'the extreme of extremes,' 'greater than the greatest,' as it were.

90 Neoptolemi vindicta
The revenge of Neoptolemus

Νεοπτολέμειος τίσις, The revenge of Neoptolemus. This is exactly similar to
the preceding: when what a man has done to others, he suffers himself.
Pausanias in his book on Messene reports it and explains it as follows: 5
'Indeed in time what is called the revenge of Neoptolemus encompassed the
Lacedemonians. For it happened that Neoptolemus, the son of Achilles,
who killed Priam in the very heart of his palace, was himself slain at the altar
of Apollo, and from this to suffer what one has oneself done they call a
Neoptolomean revenge.' Euripides in the *Orestes*, where in the character of   10
Apollo it is said of Neoptolemus: 'It is his fate to die by the Delphic sword.'

91 Servire scenae
To be a slave to your theatre

Cicero said To be a slave to your theatre, meaning to serve the time, to
accommodate oneself to the present situation. This is a metaphor taken from
the actors in plays, who do not behave according to their own judgment but   5

* * * * *

33 *termerian hemeran*] This must be a confusion: the phrase of which Erasmus
   thinks (Sophocles *Antigone* 1330) and which means 'the last day' of life, has
   termian, not *termerian*.

90 The source of this must be Pausanias 4.17.4. His valuable *Description of Greece*
   was compiled in the second century AD, and Erasmus rarely cites it in the
   Greek, which was not printed till July 1516, when Marcus Musurus edited it for
   the Aldine press. Musurus was, however, a personal friend, and we are told
   that Pausanias was one of the authors to whom Erasmus had access by way of a
   manuscript in Aldus' library (Allen I p 61).
10 Euripides] *Orestes* 1656, also used in II iii 69

91 Otto 1599. Literally 'to serve the scene'; either to watch public opinion or to
   play a part in public affairs
 3 Cicero] *Epistulae ad Brutum* 17.2

think of one thing only – pleasing the eyes of the public somehow or other, otherwise they will be slow-clapped and hissed off the stage. He writes thus to Brutus: 'Now your business is to be a slave to the people and your public, as they say. For not only the eyes of your army are upon you, but those of all the citizens and almost the whole world.' This can be said of people who have undertaken some important affair, from which they must emerge either with the highest credit or the utmost shame, because so many people are watching them. To serve the time is indeed the part of the wise man, as Phocylides warns us: 'Remember, always wary, to serve the times; blow not against the wind.' However the metaphor here is taken from mariners, who once they have set out must be tossed at the will of winds and tides; it would be vain for them to strive to put up a resistance.

92 Uti foro
To take the market as you find it

Close to this is the saying Τῇ ἀγορᾷ χρῆσθαι, To take the market as you find it, meaning to make the best of the present state of affairs, and to turn one's mind wherever fortune presents itself. Terence says in the *Phormio* 'You knew how to make the best of the market.' Donatus explains that the proverb is a popular one, and the metaphor taken from merchants, 'who do not set a price for what they have brought before they reach the place of sale, but after finding out the current market prices they decide whether or not to sell their wares.' Seneca: 'Let us take the market as we find it, and what chance may bring, let us bear with equanimity.' Again in Epistle 72 he used the phrase 'to spring up under one's hand' for when the moment comes: 'The plan must be born on the day, and even this is too slow; it must spring up, as they say, under one's hand.'

* * * * *

14 Phocylides] *Sententiae* 121. Phocylides lived in the sixth century BC, but the moral maxims ascribed to him are thought to date probably from the first or second century AD. They were first printed in the Aldine Theocritus of 1495.

92 *Collectanea* no 187, not greatly altered. Otto 710. Cf Tilley T 196 Take all things as they come and be content.
5 Terence] *Phormio* 79
10 Seneca] A free quotation from the apocryphal letters of Paul and Seneca, Ep 11. Had Erasmus remembered the source from which he took this some years before, he would no doubt have warned the reader that it is spurious.
11 Again] Seneca *Letters* 71.1 (Otto 1055), added in 1533

93   **Polypi mentem obtine**
     Adopt the outlook of the polyp

There is in Greek an adage one can put in this class: Πολύποδος νόον ἴσχε,
Adopt the outlook of the polyp. This recommends us to take up for the time
being this or that kind of behaviour, this or that kind of face. Homer seems to   5
praise this in Ulysses, and calls him ' a man of many turnings,' changeful in
his ways. The adage originates from the nature of this fish, of which Pliny
speaks, book 9 chapter 29. Lucian too, in the conversation of Menelaus and
Proteus; they write that it changes colour especially in fear. When the
fishermen are out after it, it attaches itself to rocks, and its body takes the   10
colour of whatever rock it sticks to, obviously to escape being caught. In fact
St Basil reports that fish are sometimes taken in by its deceptive appearance,
and swim up, offering themselves to be caught. The proverb is taken from
Theognis, whose couplet about the polyp exists today. He is also quoted by
Plutarch in his essay 'On Having Many Friends': 'Adopt the attitude of the   15
many-coloured polyp; / Moving towards a rock, it straightway takes its hue.'
Clearchus quotes this couplet among proverbs according to Athenaeus (the
author's name is not given): 'O hero, son Amphilochus, take on the polyp's
way, / Whatever nation you shall meet, let you become as they.' Plutarch
cites the same poem out of Pindar. Thus there is a well-known proverbial   20
line: ''Tis best in season to be this, or that.'
      This advises us to suit ourselves to every contingency of life, acting the
part of Proteus, and changing ourselves into any form as the situation

* * * * *

93 *Collectanea* no 255, very much shorter. Diogenianus 1.23
 5 Homer] *Odyssey* 1.1
 7 Pliny] *Naturalis historia* 9.87
 8 Lucian] *Dialogi marini* 4.3
12 Basil] *Homiliae in hexaemeron* 7.3 (*PG* 29.153C), inserted in *1528*
14 Theognis] 215–6, in the form cited by Plutarch *Moralia* 96F; see I i 62n.
17 Clearchus] of Soli, a pupil of Aristotle who compiled a collection of proverbs;
    this is frag 75 in F. Wehrli *Die Schule des Aristoteles* 3 (1969) 130, cited by
    Athenaeus 7.317a.
19 Plutarch] In *Moralia* 916C and 978E he quotes a slightly different form of the two
    lines from Theognis which we have already been given; in the first of these
    passages the lines are preceded by two from Pindar (cited further on in this
    paragraph), and Erasmus seems to have transferred Pindar's name to this
    couplet also by inadvertence.
20 proverbial line] Zenobius 1.24; Diogenianus 1.23
23 Proteus] *Adagia* II ii 74

demands. In the same way Plutarch said, 'I turn to a different opinion.'
Aristophanes makes the same observation in the *Plutus*, telling us to live in   25
the style of the region, in local style. The saying Νόμος καὶ χώρα, Custom of
the country, points in the same direction. This means that in every region
there are certain established things, which as guests we should not condemn, but do our best to copy and act on them. Let no one think that by this
adage we are taught a disgusting type of flattery, which assents to every-   30
thing in everybody, or an improper changeability in behaviour, of the sort
which Horace elegantly castigates in the *Satires*, and which historians remark in Catiline and in the emperor Anedius Cassius, and Holy Scripture in
any bad man when it says 'the fool is as inconstant as the moon': the wise
man is like the sun, always himself.   35
    In Alcibiades one may wonder whether this changeableness is to be
taken as a vice or a virtue; he certainly had a happy and enviable dexterity of
mind and character, which made him act the polyp, so that 'in Athens he
amused himself with jokes and sallies, bred horses, and lived in pleasant
elegant style, while among the Spartans he was close-shaved, wore a cloak   40
and took cold baths. Among the Thracians he was warlike and took to
drinking. But when he came to Tisaphernes, he followed the custom of the
people and enjoyed pleasures, soft living and ostentation.' There is however
a kind of downrightness, edgy and harsh and unsmiling, among inexperienced people; they require everyone to live solely in his own way, and   45
whatever pleases others they condemn. On the contrary there is a sensible
attitude which makes good men comply on occasion with a different mode
of conduct, to avoid either being disliked or being unable to be of use, or else
for the sake of rescuing themselves or their households from great dangers.
Ulysses acted like this with Polyphemus, making a great many pretences,   50
and with the suitors, when he acted the part of a beggar. Brutus too feigned

* * * * *

24 Plutarch] *Brutus* 40.8
25 Aristophanes] *Plutus* 47
26 The saying] *Adagia* III vi 55
32 Horace] *Satires* 2.7.6–20
33 Anedius] Vulcacius Gallicanus *Avidius Cassius* 3.4. From the so-called *Historia
    Augusta* (see I i 21n).
33 Holy Scripture] Ecclesiasticus 27:12
36 Alcibiades] Most of this passage, which was added in *1515*, is translated from
    Plutarch *Moralia* 52E.
50 Ulysses] The story is told in Homer *Odyssey* 9 and 17.
51 Brutus] Lucius Junius Brutus, according to tradition the first consul to be
    elected at Rome, feigned stupidity (thereby either acquiring or explaining his
    name, for *brutus* means stupid), in order to protect himself from the tyranny of
    the house of Tarquin, whom he overthrew; so Livy 1.56.8, Ovid *Fasti* 2.717.

stupidity, David even pretended to be mad. And St Paul too congratulates himself, with a kind of saintly boasting, on having used a pious pretence, and become all things to all men, that he might win all for Christ.

There is also nothing to prevent us using the adage in a wider sense,   55
when we are observing people's faults, against the conduct of men endowed with versatile minds who take on the character of those with whom they have to do, whoever they are. Plautus aptly describes this kind of person in the *Bacchides*: 'Not a soul can be worth anything, unless he knows how to be good and bad both. He must be a rascal among rascals, rob robbers, steal   60
what he can. A chap that's worth anything, a chap with a fine intellect, has to be able to change his skin. He must be good with the good and bad with the bad; whatever the situation calls for, that he's got to be.' Eupolis in Athenaeus: 'A city man, a polyp in his manners.' Plutarch in his 'On Natural Causes' quotes these lines from Pindar: 'Adapting the mind to the colour of   65
the sea-creature, / He mingles with all cities.' And in the same place he gives the reason why this happens to the fish.

Aristotle draws a similar metaphor from the chameleon, in his *Ethics*, book 1. He says that anyone who is dependent on fortune, with its sudden changes, will be like a chameleon, continually altering, now happy, now   70
cast down; every time chance puts on a different face, this man changes his face and his mentality. Pliny mentions the chameleon, book 28 chapter 8, where he writes that this creature is about equal in size to the crocodile, but differs from it by its sharply-curved spine and breadth of tail. No creature, he says, is thought to be more easily frightened, and hence these changes of   75
colour. Plutarch, in his essay 'On Flattery,' writes that the chameleon imitates every colour except white. He also tries, in the 'Table-talk,' to explain why the polyp does not only change colour, which happens to men when they are afraid, but also matches itself to the rock, whatever colour that may be. There are some birds too which change both colour and song   80

* * * * *

52 David] From 1 Samuel 16.13
52 Paul] 1 Corinthians 9.19–22
58 Plautus] *Bacchides* 654–62 (tr Paul Nixon)
63 Eupolis] Frag 101 Kock (see I i 31n), cited by Athenaeus 7.316c.
64 Plutarch] *Moralia* 916c, citing Pindar frag 43; added in *1515*
68 Aristotle] *Ethica Nicomachea* 1.10 (1100b6); cf *Adagia* III iv 1, IV viii 35
72 Pliny] *Naturalis historia* 28.112–3
76 Plutarch] *Moralia* 53D. The second reference seems to apply to his 'On Natural Causes' (*Moralia* 916B), a passage which recurs in I ii 89. There too it was ascribed in *1508* to the 'Table-talk,' but that was set right in *1515*. On the chameleon in general, see III iv 1.

according to the season of the year; Pliny, book 10, chapter 29, is the authority, and Aristotle in book 9 on the *Nature of Animals*. This change of song is most notable in the nightingale. This is why Hecuba, in Euripides, orders Polyxena to imitate the nightingale and try all kinds of speech, so as to persuade Ulysses that she should not be killed.   85

94 **Cothurno versatilior**
    As versatile as a buskin

Εὐμεταβολώτερος κοθόρνου, As versatile as a buskin. This was used of a fickle and unreliable man, belonging to a doubtful and wavering party, by a metaphor which comes from the shoe called *kothornos* in Greek and   5
cothurnus (one letter being changed) in Latin; a footgear usually adopted by the actors in tragedy. It was 'square and suitable to either foot,' so that it could be worn on the right or on the left. Suidas adds that it was of a kind that both men and women could wear. Virgil is a witness to this: 'to bind the buskin high up on the calf.' The proverb is employed in two ways, in a   10
comparison (as versatile as a buskin) and in metonymy, when we call the man himself, who joins first one and then the other party, a buskin. This was the term used of Theramenes the Athenian rhetorician, the disciple of Prodicus of Ceos, because he sat as it were on two stools, trying to please the people and the Thirty, and seeming to be now on the side of one party and   15
now on the other, or rather on both. Plutarch in his 'Precepts of Statecraft': 'But here it is especially fitting to put on the buskin of Theramenes, conversing with both sides but joining neither.' Lucian in the *Amores*: 'So I at least would wish, if it were possible, to become Theramenes called the *cothurnus*,

* * * * *

81 Pliny] *Naturalis historia* 10.80
82 Aristotle] *Historia animalium* 9.49 (632b14)
83 Euripides] *Hecuba* 336–8

94 *Collectanea* no 353, only one sentence, probably from the Greek proverb-collections (Zenobius 3.93; Diogenianus 4.72)
 8 Suidas] E 3582
 9 Virgil] *Aeneid* 1.337
14 sat on two stools] *Adagia* I vii 2. Theramenes, the Athenian politician of the end of the fifth century BC in the days of the Thirty Tyrants, was a notorious turncoat.
16 Plutarch] *Moralia* 824B, added in 1515 (tr H.N. Fowler)
18 Lucian] *Amores* 50 used again in II ii 9; *Pseudologista* 16

in order that both of you might depart equally victorious.' Again in the   20
Pseudologista: 'And another called him *cothurnus*, likening his inconstant and
equivocal behaviour to that kind of shoe.' Plutarch remarks that Nicias the
general was commonly nicknamed the Buskin, owing to the craftiness of his
behaviour. Cicero, even, had this reproach levelled at him. Homer, if I am
not mistaken, speaks of Mars suddenly changing sides, and uses a new   25
word, *alloprosallos*.

There is no reason, however, why we should not use the proverb in a
good sense; one might call a man a *cothurnus* because he had easy ways, a
certain mobility of intellect, and a capacity for getting on with all kinds of
people. For this reason Homer calls Ulysses a 'man of many turnings'   30
because he could play any part to perfection – the general, the beggar, the
head of the house.

95 Magis varius quam hydra
As variable as the hydra

Ποικιλώτερος ὕδρας, As variable as the hydra. Spoken of the artful and wily,
because the hydra is a snake with many-coloured markings. It will be neatly
used against crafty people, clever at dissimulation, or people who are not   5
consistent with themselves. The following line is referred to in Athenaeus,
in the third book of his *Doctors at Dinner*: 'You made him more colourful than
a peacock.' This is not unlike the nickname Salpa, given to the poet Mnaseas
of Colophon as a popular jest, because he was so various in his poetry; for
this fish is wonderfully marked, with reddish gold lines drawn from head to   10
tail, and spaced along its silvery sides. But its flavour has nothing to
recommend it.

* * * * *

22 Plutarch] *Nicias* 2, added in 1533
24 Homer] *Iliad* 5.831, 889; used again in I vii 2, where the accusation that Cicero
    was a turncoat will also be found
30 Homer] *Odyssey* 1.1

95 The Greek perhaps from Diogenianus 7.69
 6 Athenaeus] 3.107c, citing the New-Comedy writer Alexis frag 110.14 Kock;
    added in 1517/8
 8 Mnaseas] Athenaeus 7.321f, the colours from 321e; added in 1533

96 Gygis anulus
The ring of Gyges

Γύγου δακτύλιος, Gyges' ring. This suits either men of fickle character, or the lucky ones who get everything they want by just wishing for it, as by the wave of a magic wand. Lucian recalls this proverb in *Wishes*, where someone   5
wishes he had several rings like that of Gyges, one so that he could get rich, one to make him attractive and lovable, another to help him to fly wherever the fancy took him. In early times superstition credited rings with great efficacy, and indeed they used to be sold as possessing various powers through enchantment, some against the bite of wild beasts, some against   10
slander, some for other purposes, either to repel bad luck or attract good luck for those who wore them. Hence in Aristophanes, in the *Plutus*, Dicaeus says to the sycophant threatening judgment, 'I take no heed of you, because I wear this ring Eudamus sold me for a drachma.' And again in the same play, 'But it has none against the sycophant's blow' (remedy, under-   15
stood). He is speaking of a ring, and the allusion is to the bite of wild beasts. The proverb is derived from a story of this sort, which Plato does not disdain to tell in his *Republic*, book 2. I likewise will not find it irksome to go over it here. A certain Gyges, the father of Lydus, was a herdsman in the service of the king who at that time ruled over the Lydians. One day a furious storm   20
arose, torrents of rain fell, finally there was lightning and even an earthquake, so that in the region where Gyges happened to be grazing his flocks the earth split open, leaving a great chasm. When he saw this (he alone, because all the other shepherds had fled in terror) he went down into the chasm, and there, among other sights marvellous to relate, he saw a huge   25
bronze horse, hollow inside. There was an aperture in the horse's flank, and looking through this he saw in its belly the corpse of a man, of more than human size. No clothing was on it nor any accoutrements, only a gold ring on one finger. This Gyges took, and turned back out of the cavern. A few days later he returned to the assembly of shepherds in which the business   30
was to elect an envoy to take the king, month by month, the proceeds of his flocks. When Gyges had taken his place among the rest, he noticed that if he happened to turn inwards the jewel set in the ring, it came about at once that

* * * * *

96 *Collectanea* no 341, no doubt from Diogenianus 3.99, and citing Plato *Republic* only. Also in Suidas г 473

5 Lucian] *Navigium* 42, for which *Wishes* is an alternative title.

12 Aristophanes] *Plutus* 883–5, the last line corrupt. The Latin verse versions were added in 1528.

17 Plato] *Republic* 2.359d

no one could see him, and they all talked about him just as if he had not been
present. Amazed at this, he turned the bezel of the ring outwards again and   35
began at once to be visible to the herdsmen. When he had tested this
carefully and often, and had ascertained that the ring had this power to
make him invisible when the jewel faced himself and visible when it faced
towards others, he contrived to get himself sent by the shepherds as their
envoy to the king. He went off, seduced the king's wife, and plotted with   40
her to murder the king. After disposing of him, and marrying the queen, he
rapidly became king from being a shepherd – and all because of the ring of
destiny. Plato mentions the same in the *Republic*, book 10. Cicero also refers
to this in the *De officiis*, book 3. Herodotus, in his first book, tells the story
very differently, without making any mention of a ring.   45

Very similar to this is the cap of Orcus, which I shall mention in
another place.

97   Virgula divina
The magic wand

There is not much difference between this and the 'magic wand': by this we
mean that whatever we desire we obtain, as if by divine aid and without the
help of man. It was thought in Antiquity that the carrying of wands, like   5
rings, held some fated and as it were, magical virtue. Cicero in his *De officiis*,
book 1: 'But if all that is essential to our wants and comfort were supplied by
some magic wand, as they say...' Varro's *Magic Wand* is also quoted sometimes in Nonius Marcellus, so that clearly this was the title of one of his

* * * * *

43 Plato] *Republic* 10.612b, added in *1536*
43 Cicero] *De officiis* 3.9.38, added in *1515*
44 Herodotus] 1.8–15, added in *1528*. The first of the great Greek historians (fifth
century BC), he had been translated into Latin by Lorenzo Valla and printed in
Greek by Aldus in September 1502, and Erasmus refers to him (rather than
quotes him) in the *Adagia* over sixty times, and afresh in almost every edition of
the book.
47 another place] *Adagia* II x 74

97 Otto 1907
 6 Cicero] *De officiis* 1.44.158
 9 Nonius Marcellus] p 7, and often; *Virgula divina* was, as Erasmus suggests, the
name of one of Varro's *Menippean Satires* (see I ii 60n). Nonius' *De compendiosa
doctrina*, a large compilation in dictionary form in twenty books made in the
early fourth century AD, is important for the nuggets of early Latin poetry
embedded in it. First printed in Rome in 1470; Erasmus used it seventy times in
the *Adagia*, adding extensively in *1533*. References are normally given by the
pages of J. Mercier, marked in modern editions.

Menippean Satires, most of which of course had proverbial titles. The adage   10
seems to be derived particularly from the wand in Homer, which he attributes to Pallas, so famous that the founder of the Cynic sect, Antisthenes,
wrote a book about it, comparing it, I imagine, with his own staff. Homer
mentions this in many places; when it changes Ulysses suddenly from a
dreary old man into a youth and makes him spruce and handsome (*Odyssey*   15
13): 'Having spoken thus Athena touched him with her wand.' Again,
turning him from a youth into an old man, *Odyssey* 16: 'Standing close by,
Pallas struck the Ithacan Ulysses / And with her rod made him an old man
again.' In the same book, again, when she turns him back into a youth and
increases his strength: 'Athena spoke, and touched him with her golden   20
wand.' In the same way he credits Mercury, as an enchanter, with a won-
drous wand which he calls a *caduceus*, *Odyssey* 24:

> And in his hands he held a wand, golden and fair;
> With it he soothes the eyes of men with sleep,
> If he so wills, or waves their sleep away.   25

He says almost the same in *Odyssey* 5 and in *Iliad* 24:

> Straight then he shod his feet with lovely sandals
> Golden, ambrosial-scented, and they bore him
> Through limpid air and over boundless lands
> Swift as the wind: with him he took the rod   30
> With which he soothes the eyes of men with sleep,
> If so he wills, or waves their sleep away.

Virgil, in imitation of this, describes his *caduceus* in the fourth *Aeneid*:

> He takes the rod: with this he calls from death
> The pallid shades, and with it others sends   35
> To the sad underworld. He gives sleep, takes it back,
> Opens the eyes in death; and on this wand
> Trusting, he drives the winds, and sails along
> Through the wild clouds.

> * * * * *

12 Antisthenes] This is from Diogenes Laertius 6.17.
13 Homer] *Odyssey* 13.429; 16.455–6; 16.172; 24.2–4; 5.44–8 (this reference added
   in *1515*); Iliad 24.340–4 (the Greek added in *1515*, and the Latin version of it in
   1528). This last passage is reused in part in *Adagia* I ii 42 and III ix 83.
33 Virgil] *Aeneid* 4.242–6

Circe was not without her wand for performing marvels, when she trans-   40
formed the companions of Ulysses: 'Striking them with a wand she drove
them to join the pigs, / And lo, they had the heads of swine.' Then a little
further on: 'When Circe strikes you with her long long wand.' A little later,
Ulysses is the only one to have drunk from Circe's cup without being
transformed into a beast: 'But when I drained the drink she gave, / She did   45
not enchant me, striking with her wand.' Finally when to please Ulysses
Circe restored his companions to their former shapes, she made use of her
wand.

Indeed, even in Hebrew literature Moses uses a rod in performing
miracles. He changed it into a snake, he restored it to its first shape, with it   50
he turned the river water into blood, killing the fish, he called forth lice, he
divided the waves of the Red Sea, he struck the rock and called out a stream
of water.

Perhaps one might add here that kings also have a wand attributed to
them, called a sceptre: hence in several places in Homer, 'sceptre-bearing   55
kings.' The same meaning is to be found in the adage we have quoted
elsewhere, 'I bear the staff of bay.'

98   **Stultus stulta loquitur**
     Fools in their folly speak

Euripides in the *Bacchae*: Μωρὰ γὰρ μωρὸς λέγει, Fools in their folly speak.
Our prophet Isaiah expresses the same thing in just the same words. Seneca
to Lucilius: 'The Greeks have a proverb that as men's life is, so is their talk.'   5
What this was like is not clear, except that there is a verse very like it current
in Greek: 'Man's character is known from what he says.' In Laertius, the
philosopher Democritus called speech 'the mirror of life,' a sort of reflection
of it, as it were. Nothing could be said more truly. For no mirror reflects the

* * * * *

41 Ulysses] Homer *Odyssey* 10.238-9, 293, 318-9
49 Hebrew literature] Exodus 4.2
55 Homer] Eg *Iliad* 1.279; Latin version added in *1517/8*
57 elsewhere] *Adagia* I i 79. In *1508* I ii 1 followed here.

98 Tilley F 459 A fool cannot speak unlike himself; F 465 A fool is known by much
   babbling; F 515 A fool's bolt is soon shot (the version given by Richard
   Taverner).
3 Euripides] *Bacchae* 369; Latin version added in *1515*
4 Isaiah] 32.6, the name added in *1517/8*
4 Seneca] *Letters* 114.1. This provides *Adagia* I vi 50.
6 verse] Menander *Sententiae* 27 (see I i 30n); also listed as frag 66 of Menander
7 Laertius] Diogenes Laertius 9.37

bodily appearance better or more definitely than speech reflects the image of   10
the heart. Men are discerned by their words just as brazen vessels are by
their resonance.

99   **Scindere penulam**
      To tear the cloak

Even today too it is a very common popular expression 'to tear the cloak,'
meaning to retain a guest with eagerness, or to invite him with urgency;
people who do this lay hands on the travelling-cloak as if trying to force   5
someone to stay. This adage springs from Antiquity, like many others.
Cicero *Letters to Atticus*, book 13, speaking of Varro, says: 'He called, and at
such an hour I had to ask him to stay. But I took care not to tear his coat (I
remember your phrase, "they were many and we were unprepared"). No
use! Soon after came C. Capito and T. Carinas. Their coats I hardly touched.   10
However they stayed.'

100   **Oculis magis habenda fides, quam auribus**
      Better trust eyes than ears

Ὠτίων πιστότεροι ὀφθαλμοί, Eyes are to be believed rather than ears. What
is seen is more certain than what is heard. So Horace: 'Wide-open ears /
Entrusted secrets ill retain.' Again in the *Art of Poetry*:   5

>   Tidings that come by ear we find
>   Less actively distress the mind,
>   Than what the looker-on espies
>   Thrust plainly 'neath his faithful eyes.

          * * * * *

99 Otto 1321; Suringar 203
 7 Cicero] *Ad Atticum* 13.33a.1 This was wrongly identified in *1508* as coming from
   the first letter of book 13, but this reference was removed in *1523*.

100 Originally it seems from Apostolius 18.71. In *1508*, when the adages were not
   yet arranged in centuries, this was very short, and stood as IV 259; it was moved
   here in the reorganization of *1515*. Otto 1272; Tilley c 815 Credit ought rather to
   be given to the eyes than to the ears; s 212 Seeing is believing.
 4 Horace] *Epistles* 1.18.70, followed by *Ars poetica* 180–2, inserted in *1523*. The
   sense has suffered a slight accident here, which the translator has thought it
   simplest to ignore; but it shows us Erasmus at work. Horace warns a friend not
   to tell secrets to an inquisitive man, because he is sure to be also a chatterbox:
   'Wide-open ears do not faithfully retain what is entrusted to them' Connection
   of wording ('trust' and 'ears') brought this up at once out of his memory, and

Though perhaps that is a little different. Closer to the meaning is Plautus'   10
phrase when he called a bawd's hands 'eyed' not 'eared,' meaning that in
the end they believe only what they see. Again, when people wish to
represent a story as actual fact, they use a word derived from *historein*, which
means 'to see.' Finally there is that fiction of Virgil's about the two gates of
the underworld, one of ivory, by which is meant what comes out of the   15
mouth, because of the ivory whiteness of the teeth, and the other of horn, by
which is meant what is seen by the eyes, because of the blackness of the
pupil. In a word, ears do more for knowing, eyes are surer in producing
confidence. And so in ordinary speech, when someone tells an unlikely
story, we usually enquire if he has seen these things. If he says no, he only   20
heard them, he gets laughed at.

The proverb is found in Julian's letter to Leontius, 'A certain Thurian

* * * * *

attached to it, unfortunately, came *Ars poetica* 181 'than what is exhibited to
eyes that can be trusted.' In the process 'faithfully' (to suit the following 'than')
became 'more faithfully;' and the result could be thought to back up the view
that eyes are more faithful than ears. It was not till *1523* that Erasmus saw that
the words from the *Ars poetica* were wrongly placed; and so he deleted them
where they were, and inserted *Ars* 180–2, which are highly relevant. But he
failed to notice that the line from the *Epistles* (still reading 'more faithfully')
had now no reason to be here at all. It is surprising that the memory of a very busy
man should not have tricked him like this more often.

10 Though perhaps ... get laughed at] Added in *1515*. The first sentence referred,
not as now to the lines from the *Ars poetica*, but to the composite quotation
which Erasmus' memory had provided. Already he was subconsciously aware
that all was not as it should be; and this sentence should have been removed
when those lines were inserted in *1523*.

10 Plautus] *Asinaria* 202, which had already been used in *1508* to make I viii 31.
The bawd's point is that she would rather handle hard cash now than listen to
promises of payment later.

14 fiction of Virgil's] He develops in *Aeneid* 6.893–6 Homer's famous image, in
book 19 of the *Odyssey*, of the two gates of Sleep or of Dreams, one of horn
through which true dreams pass and one of ivory through which pass false
dreams. The passage is intensely suggestive, but its precise meaning has been
discussed ever since; Erasmus draws his explanation from Servius the
fourth-century commentator.

22 Julian's letter] The addition of *1515* ended 'The proverb is found in the
collections of Apostolius of Byzantium.' Erasmus had a low opinion of
Apostolius, and in *1523* substituted a citation from the Emperor Julian,
Epistulae 11 (389B), ending 'it was taken from the *Clio* of Herodotus *etc*' which
means 1.8 of his *History* (he gave his books the names of Muses instead of
numbers). In *1528* came the Latin version of the Julian and the note on
'Thurian,' and the second mention of Herodotus' name was removed as
unnecessary.

saying has it, men's ears are less faithful than their eyes.' He called it
Thurian to indicate that Herodotus was the author of the saying, either
because of his divine inspiration, or because that writer lived and died at   25
Thurii; however it was taken from his *Clio*, 'For ears are less faithful to men
than eyes.'

1   **Diomedis et Glauci permutatio**
    Exchange between Diomede and Glaucus

The story told in Homer of the exchange between Diomede and Glaucus has
become a proverb, used whenever we wish to describe an unequal barter-
ing, in which something less valuable is repaid for something worth more,   5
χρύσεα χαλκείων, 'gold for bronze.' For in book 6 of the *Iliad*, the poet brings
in a certain Glaucus the son of Hippolochus, who is ruler of the Lycii, but a
braggart and a boaster rather than a fighter. Diomede, on the other hand, is
wily and clever. These two came together in a *monomachia*, that is to meet
each other in single combat. But Glaucus, when asked by Diomede who,   10
among gods and men, he might be, made a long speech in which he
expounded the line of his family and descent, and alluded to his native
country Lycia, and his city Ephyra. Then Diomede, being a Greek, perceived
the stupidity of the barbarian from the arrogance of his speech, and judged
that he was a man to make fun of rather than kill. So he replied that there had 15
been of old a friendly and familiar relationship between his forefathers and
Glaucus' progenitors, and that gifts in token of alliance (which they call
xenia) had been reciprocally exchanged between them. Now, sticking his
spear into the ground, he began to suggest that they should leave fighting
alone, and renew between themselves the old friendship of their ancestors;   20
one would entertain the other, now in Lycia, now in Argos, as soon as they
had returned, each into his own country. Meanwhile, if chance brought
them together, they were to abstain from attacking each other, but they
would preserve the oath of friendship between them – though with others
they would abide by the rules of war. 'Now,' he said, 'to make it quite clear   25
that we are maintaining our pact of friendship and this is not treachery, let
us exchange our armour, so that the rest of the army may understand that

* * * * *

1   *Collectanea* no 784 gives an unusually full treatment of the story. This, when
    amplified, stood in *1508* in front of I i 98, and was moved here in *1515*. Otto 384
3   Homer] *Iliad* 6.234–6. Erasmus gives a new twist to the Homeric story by
    emphasizing the vanity of Glaucus and his boastful swaggering. In Homer,
    Diomede does not scorn Glaucus for his lengthy description of his ancestors,
    and the inequality of the exchange is put down to Zeus, not Diomede. Perhaps
    Erasmus was influenced by his well-known hatred of war and soldiers.

we are linked in the same alliance as our forefathers.' On these words, each
leapt from his horse; they took each other by the right hand, and swore
fidelity, pledging themselves to friendship and exchanging their armour.   30
But the value of their arms was unequal: Homer says,

> Then Jove robbed foolish Glaucus of his wits,
> To change his arms with Tydeus' son, and give
> Gold for the other's bronze, a mad exchange,
> Giving a hundred oxen's worth to gain   35
> Hardly the value of nine worthless heifers.

The adage is used throughout the most celebrated authors.

Plato in the *Phaedrus* makes Socrates reply to Alcibiades in his usual
way, saying that he was greedy enough for gain to be willing to exchange
bodily beauty for the better moral beauty, 'In truth you are intending to   40
exchange bronze for gold.' (But the translator gives 'brass' instead of
'bronze.') Aristotle too, in the *Ethics*, book 5, on justice, says: 'One who gives
what is his own, as Glaucus gave to Diomede, gold for bronze, as Homer
says.' Plutarch writing 'Against the Stoics' gives this an elegant twist, when
he says that the exchange of Glaucus was not really unequal because iron   45
arms are no less useful to fighters than gold ones; but to prefer bodily
well-being to honourable living, or abandon virtue for the sake of physical
health, is truly to exchange 'gold for bronze.' Cicero in his *Letters to Atticus*,
book 6: 'Well, there is all answered, not in "gold for bronze" as you asked,
but we are giving back like for like.' Cicero indicates that each expression is a   50
proverb, 'like for like' meaning equal balance, 'gold for bronze' meaning
unequal exchange. The younger Pliny writes in a letter to Flaccus: 'You will
receive arid letters, barefacedly ungrateful ones, not even carrying out the
ingenious plan of Diomede in exchanging gifts.' Martial in the *Epigrams*:
'You, Glaucus, were never so stupid, I think, / When you gave gold for   55
bronze.' Aulus Gellius in his *Attic Nights*, book 2, when comparing and
evaluating the translation by Caecilius with Menander himself, whom he

*　*　*　*　*

38 Plato] *Symposium* (not *Phaedrus*) 218e, added in 1528; the translator referred to
   is Marsilio Ficino.
42 Aristotle] *Ethica Nicomachea* 5.9.7 (1136b9)
44 Plutarch] *Moralia* 1063F, added in 1515
48 Cicero] *Ad Atticum* 6.1.22; cf I i 35 Par pari referre.
52 Pliny] the Younger, *Letters* 5.2.2
54 Martial] 9.94.3–4
56 Gellius] 2.23.7

had translated, shows how much it fell short of the beauty of the Greek: 'On
my word, he says, there was no greater disparity between the armour of
Diomede and Glaucus.'   60

There is also a mention of this adage in the introduction to the *Pandects*
of Roman law, in these words: 'In our times a change in the laws has been
devised, like that which in Homer, father of all virtue, Glaucus and Diomede
effect between themselves, exchanging dissimilar things.' Thus far Justinian; a man, if I may speak frankly, too full of self-love and unjustifiably 65
conceited, who valued his own patchwork and uneven flights of fancy about
the laws higher than so many complete volumes by the most learned men.
As to the comment on this passage by some commentator or other, it does
not surprise me, but it fills me with shame. What wonder is there, if
ignorance is shown here by those who have the whole of antiquity in   70
contempt? But what the legal profession itself ought to be ashamed of is the
clownish impudence of one who claims to interpret the law, but is not afraid
to adduce the most foolish story, not from the authorities but from his own
fancies, in a matter completely unknown. Most of all do I find it shameful
and extraordinary to meet doctors who will teach in all seriousness, and as a 75
noble invention – and teach in our universities – a blunder so crass (I won't
say merely ignorant) and never see that this figment does not at all square
with the words of Justinian. For he means that the useless boring volumes
have been abandoned, and better and shorter writings have been adopted,
that is to say, a really unequal exchange has been effected. The commenta- 80
tor, whoever he may have been, interpreted this story as meaning that the
gifts of the exchangers were equal, but each gave what he had in superfluity
and received what he needed.

The adage may therefore be used when a good service or a gift is repaid
with a much less valuable gift, or the other way round. Or when someone   85
increases his income but with the loss of his honour; he wins his place, but at
the expense of his conscience; he gains a rich fortune, but loses his peace of
mind. He found his way into the friendship of his prince, but fell away from
the friendship of Christ.

* * * * *

61 *Pandects*] The *Constitutio 'Omnem,'* which stands at the head of Justinian's
   Digest (or *Pandects*) section 11
84 The adage] The last three sentences were added in *1515*.

2   Multae regum aures atque oculi
    Many are the eyes and ears of kings

Ὦτα καὶ ὀφθαλμοὶ βασιλέων πολλοί, Many are the eyes and ears of kings,
because they watch through their spies what each man says or does. This is
referred to by Lucian in the work called *On Salaried Posts*, and again in   5
Against An Ignoramus. Aristotle also recalls it in the *Politics*, book 3. This
kind of man is called in Greek *ôtakoustes*, and it was Darius the Younger
who first employed them, having no confidence in himself. Dionysius of
Syracuse added *prosagôgidae*, that is 'tale-bearers,' according to Plutarch.
The allegory is derived from the fact that kings have spies everywhere, and   10
they are called the king's eyes, with a number of listeners whom he uses as
ears. Nor are hands and feet lacking, plenty of them, and even bellies,
maybe. See what a monstrous creature a tyrant is, and how much to be
feared, since he is supplied with so many eyes (and prying ones too), so
many ears (and long ones too, like an ass's), so many hands and feet and   15
bellies, not to mention less decent items. Aristophanes in the *Acharnians*
calls Pseudartabas 'the king's eye,' because it was through him that he knew
what was happening. Andromache, in Euripides, speaks differently when
she calls her son the eye of her life: 'This one son was left to me, / The eye
of life,' because he was the unique delight of her life, for nothing is dearer   20
than the eye. Hence we call those we love, our eyes.

3   Longae regum manus
    Kings have long hands

What Ovid wrote, 'Do you not know that kings have long hands?' is still a
saying in common speech: 'Be wary of kings, their arms are very long,' –
        * * * * *

2 Tilley κ 87 Kings have long ears; s 795 Spies are the ears and eyes of princes.
4 because] This clause was added in *1528*.
5 Lucian] *De mercede conductis* 29; *Adversus indoctum* 23
6 Aristotle] *Politics* 3.16 (1287b29); *otakoustes* is from the same source, 5.11
   (1313b14), but was added in *1515*. The words are referred to again in I iii 67.
9 Plutarch] *Dion* 28, also added in *1515*
14 prying ones too] The phrase comes from Plautus *Aulularia* 41.
16 Aristophanes] *Acharnians* 124; Pseudartabas was an emissary from the king of
   Persia.
18 Euripides] *Andromache* 406

3 Otto 1037; Suringar 107; Tilley κ 87 Kings have long arms. An addition intended
   for this found a place in III iv 60 in *1538*.
3 Ovid] *Heroides* 16(17). 166

because of course through their servants, who are like arms to them, they 5
can do harm even to those who are at a great distance. This can also apply to
length of time, because even if kings dissimulate over a long period they
usually extract a penalty sometime or other from those with whom they are
angry, as Homer witnesses in the *Iliad*, book 1. Calchas speaks as follows:

> A king, angry with a lesser man, is a god,   10
> For though for a moment he swallows his wrath
> He still hates on, till vengeance clears his grudge.

4 Clavum clavo pellere
To drive out one nail by another

Ἥλῳ τὸν ἧλον ἐκκρούειν, To drive out one nail by another, and Πάτταλον
παττάλῳ ἐξέκρουσας, You drove out one peg with another peg, that is, you
expelled one evil by another. Lucian in *Philopseudes*: 'And as they say, you 5
are driving out one nail with another.' Again in the *Apologia*: 'I am afraid that
in addition to the accusation brought against me I might further find myself
accused of flattery, knocking out one nail with another, as they say, a
smaller with a greater.' Aristotle writes in the last chapter but one of book 5
of his *Politics*, that wicked men and flatterers are friends to tyrants, for they 10
are the ones who can be useful to them, bad people for bad ends, 'one nail
with another, as the proverb says.' Synesius to Olympius: 'Wicked for-
eigners are attacking the church; attack them. For pegs drive out pegs.' St
Jerome to Rusticus the monk: 'The philosophers of the world,' he says, 'are

* * * * *

9 Homer] *Iliad* 1.80–2. Erasmus, to suit the metre of his version, has substituted
'is a god' for the Greek phrase 'is all-powerful.' He recurs to this passage in III
vii 1.

4 *Collectanea* no 50 gave St Jerome as a source for the Latin version of this adage,
and in Greek gave only the 'peg' form, because the text of Diogenianus 5.16
which Erasmus was using (Oxford MS Grabe 30 or one derived from it) omitted
the 'nail' form; he must have added it here from Suidas H 259 or from Lucian.
Otto 396; Tilley N 17 One nail drives out another.
5 Lucian] *Philopseudes* 9; *Apologia* 9
9 Aristotle] *Politics* 5.11 (1314a4), the chapter-reference and the Greek added in
1533
12 Synesius] *Epistulae* 45.186a (*PG* 66.1373D). He was a Greek man of letters,
bishop of Ptolemais around the year 400, and his works had not yet been
printed.
14 Jerome] *Letters* 125.14.1

accustomed to drive out an old love by a new love, as one nail with another.'   15
Cicero in book 4 of the *Tusculan Questions*: 'A cure may often be effected by
change of scene, as is done with sick people who are slow in making
recovery. Some think too, that the old love can be driven out by a new, as
one nail may be driven out by another.' Julius Pollux, book 9, writes that the
adage is derived from a certain game, which is called *kindalismos*; in this a   20
peg stuck into clayey soil is driven out by another peg being struck against it.
He quotes the proverbial line: 'one nail with another, peg with peg.'

There is then a place for this adage, not only when we check one fault
with another, an evil by another evil, guile with guile, force with force,
boldness with boldness or slander with slander; but also when we overcome   25
some troublesome thing by another sort of trouble, as when we subdue the
incitements of desire by hard work, or master the anxiety of love by other
greater cares. Eusebius against Hierocles: 'He drives out demons, one de-
mon by another as they say,' surely referring to this proverb. And that moral
maxim of Publius is not unlike these allusions: 'Never is danger conquered   30
without danger.'

5   **Malo nodo malus quaerendus cuneus**
    A hard wedge must be sought for a hard knot

This alludes to the same thought: 'A hard wedge must be sought for a hard
knot.' So says St Jerome to Oceanus: 'Meanwhile, as the common proverb
says, a hard knot in the tree requires a hard wedge.' This may be used   5
whenever we blunt the power of something bad by malignity of the same
kind. It is taken from the woodmen who split oak; when they meet a

* * * * *

16 Cicero] *Tusculanae disputationes* 4.35.75, added in 1523
19 Pollux] *Onomasticon* 9.120 (see I i 4n); the version added in 1515 and revised
   later
28 Eusebius] Bishop of Caesarea, CAD 260–340; *Contra Hieroclem* 34(30) (*PG*
   22.837B), printed in the Aldine *Philostratus* of 1501–4
30 Publius] Publilius Syrus N 7, cited by Gellius 17.14; this was added in 1515.
   Publilius was a writer and actor of mimes for the Roman stage in the mid first
   century BC. Under his name (in the form Publius), and often under Seneca's,
   there circulated in the Middle Ages a collection of one-line aphorisms in verse
   (Erasmus calls them 'mimes'), much used in schools, of which the first
   competent edition was included in Erasmus' popular *Cato*, first published in
   1514.

5 *Collectanea* no 51 mentions St Jerome only. Otto 480; Tilley P 289 A knotty piece
   of timber must have sharp wedges.
4 Jerome] *Letters* 69.5.1; this replaced a more general reference in 1515.

somewhat stiffer knot in the wood they are unwilling to spoil an axe on it,
but insert some wedge, more hard than good. In agreement with this is what
is said by Sophocles in Plutarch in his essay 'On Tranquillity of Mind': 'The   10
bitter bile they purge with bitter drugs.'

6 **Malum malo medicari**
   To heal one evil with another

Tὸ κακὸν κακῷ θεραπεύειν, To heal one evil with another, is to use a second
evil to cure the first. Sophocles in the *Ajax Mastigophoros*: 'Peace, peace! Seek
not the ill to remedy / With further ill, and make fate's wound yet worse.'   5
Tecmessa warns Ajax not to add to the misfortune of his madness by yet
another and greater misfortune, his voluntary suicide. And Herodotus in
Thalia: 'Do not cure evil by evil.'

7 **Morbum morbo addere**
   To add sickness to sickness

To add sickness to sickness, that is, to double the trouble. Euripides in the
Alcestis: 'Do not thrust sickness on the sick. Misfortune weighs me down
heavily enough.' There is the same figure in Homer's *Iliad*, book 14: 'Lest   5
anyone add wound to wound.' Sophocles again: 'You added a second
ailment to the first.' Not far removed from this formula is what we find in
Homer's *Iliad*, book 7: αἰνόθεν αἰνῶς, by which we mean, to add even more
bitter things to what is already bitter. For so speaks Menelaus: 'Surely this
adds dishonour to dishonour.'   10

* * * * *

10 Sophocles] Frag 770 Nauck, cited by Plutarch *Moralia* 468B. This was added in
   1515 with the source given as 'Sophocles cited by Menander,' which was
   corrected in *1523*.

6 From Sophocles *Ajax* 362–3. Cf Tilley P 457 One poison expels another.
7 Herodotus] 3.53.4, added in *1515* (He called the books of his *History* by the
  names of the Muses.)

7 This is not in Otto as a Latin proverb, and was perhaps formulated by
  Erasmus on the basis of Euripides *Alcestis* 1047–8.
5 Homer] *Iliad* 14.130
6 Sophocles] *Oedipus Coloneus* 544, the Latin version improved in *1528*
8 Homer] *Iliad* 7.97, added in *1533*

8 **Ignem igni ne addas**
   Do not add fire to fire

Μὴ πῦρ ἐπὶ πῦρ, Do not add fire to fire. This is used by Plato. The sense is
clear. Do not join one calamity to another, lest you stir up an even greater
commotion. Diogenianus thinks this originated from some charcoalburner,   5
who as the fire burnt up caught fire himself, shouting meanwhile 'Do not
add fire to fire.' Plato in the *Laws*, book 2, forbids boys to drink wine before
the age of eighteen, for fear that, if the warmth of the wine is added to the
ardour of their age, they may seem to be piling fire on fire. Plutarch too in
'Advice to Bride and Groom': 'Let not fire be added to fire.' He makes use of   10
it in some other places, for instance in the 'Advice on Keeping Well':
'Therefore let not fire be added to fire, as the proverb says, nor repletion to
repletion, nor neat wine to wine.'

9 **Oleum camino addere**
   To pour oil on the fire

A close relation to the foregoing is, To pour oil on the fire, meaning to supply
a bad thing with nourishment and support, so that it may increase more and
more. Horace in the *Satires*: 'Add verses now, that is, add oil to fire,' ie add   5
food for greater madness. St Jerome uses it, to Eustochium: 'Wine and youth
fan the fires of pleasure twice over. Why should we add oil to the flames?'

10 **Oleo incendium restinguere**
   To quench fire with oil

Ἐλαίῳ πῦρ σβεννύεις, You quench fire with oil. This is said when remedies
are applied which exacerbate the trouble more and more. For instance,

          * * * * *

    8 *Collectanea* no 646, very briefly, from Diogenianus 6.71 (also in Zenobius 5.69
      and Suidas π 3211). Otto 844; Tilley F 785 Add fuel to the fire.
    7 Plato] *Laws* 2.666a
    9 Plutarch] *Moralia* 143F; 123E ('as the proverb says' was omitted from the Latin
      until 1526).

    9 *Collectanea* no 294 has both quotations. Otto 1283; Tilley o 30 To pour oil on the
      fire
    5 Horace] *Satires* 2.3.321, added in 1515 to III ii 54
    6 Jerome] *Letters* 22.8.2

   10 Perhaps taken direct from Lucian *Timon* 44. Otto 1283; Tilley F 287, as above

when someone tries to overcome sadness of heart by disgusting pleasures.   5
Or if a man wishes to placate someone he has offended, and does it with
quarrelling and abuse, though if he had said these things in a peaceful way
he would have no difference with his neighbour. This is what Lucian was
thinking of in *Timon*, when he says: 'As if one saw a man on fire, trying to
put himself out with pitch and oil.'   10

11   **Ululas Athenas**
     Owls to Athens

Γλαῦκας εἰς ᾿Αθήνας, Owls to Athens ('you carry' or 'send' understood).
This will fit stupid traders who transport their wares to a place where they
are more abundant anyway, as if a man were to take grain to Egypt or saffron   5
to Cilicia. It will be more attractive if the metaphor is transferred to the
things of the mind: so-and-so teaches a man wiser than himself, he sends
poems to a poet, he gives advice to a man wise in counsel. Cicero to
Torquatus: 'But again in writing thus to you I am only sending owls to
Athens.' And to his brother: 'I will send you the verses for which you ask –   10
owls to Athens.' Aristophanes in the *Birds*: 'What do you say? Who, pray,
brought an owl to Athens?' Lucian uses and explains this in his epistle to
Nigrinus. The proverb derives from the fact that there is a species of owl
peculiar to Attica, and abundant there. It is said that they live in a place
called Laureum in Attica, where there are gold-mines, and hence they are   15
also called Laureotic owls. In old times, this bird was specially beloved by
the Athenians, and held to be sacred to Minerva, owing to the grey eyes
with which it sees even in the dark, and sees what ordinary birds do not see.
Hence it is believed to be a good augury in counsel, and this is what is meant
by the proverb 'The owl flies.' It is also said of Minerva that she turned the   20
rash plans of the Athenians to a favourable outcome. However Daemon,
quoted by the annotator of Aristophanes, thinks that the phrase 'owls to

* * * * *

11   *Collectanea* no 131 gave the two quotations from Cicero. Zenobius 3.6;
     Diogenianus 3.81. Tilley o 97 You bring owls to Athens, c 466 To carry coals to
     Newcastle.
  8 Cicero] *Ad familiares* 6.3.3; *Ad Quintum fratrem* 2.16(15).4
 11 Aristophanes] *Birds* 301
 12 Lucian] *Nigrinus*, the opening words of the prefatory epistle
 15 gold-mines] The celebrated mines at Laureion in Attica were silver-mines; cf
     Adagia II viii 31.
 20 proverb] 1 i 76
 20 Minerva] See 1 viii 44.

Athens' does not only come from the fact that there are plenty of owls there, but that the owl used to be stamped on the gold and silver coins of Athens together with the head of Minerva. This coin is called a *tetradrachm*, four 25 drachmas; earlier on they used to have two-drachma pieces, the distinguishing mark of which was an ox, whence the proverb comes 'An ox on the tongue.' Some relate that there was also a *triobolus*, which they also call a half-drachma, for the drachma is worth six obols. The coin called the triobol had on one side the effigy of Jove, on the other the owl. Hence it seemed 30 absurd to take an owl to Athens, since the whole place was full of owls. Plutarch refers to the Athenian coinage in his life of Lysander, where he tells the story of the slave who made an enigmatic allusion to a theft of his master's, when he said there were 'many owls sleeping under the tiles,' giving away the fact that there was money hidden there, stamped with the 35 owl.

12   **Memorem mones, doctum doces, et similia**
     You are reminding the mindful, teaching
     the taught, etc

This is to be found in identical form in the comedies of Plautus and Terence. There is a Greek phrase with the same force: 'You are talking to the one who 5 knows all about it,' and 'You are telling the one who is informed.' Plato in the *Hippias Major*: 'O Socrates, you will speak to one who knows.' Euripides in the *Hecuba*: 'You speak no news, / But cast this in the teeth of those who know.' Homer in *Odyssey* 17 and in some other places: 'I know, I understand, you speak to one, / Who comprehends.' Again in *Iliad* 23 about 10 Nestor admonishing a son: 'He spoke with friendly heart, though knowing well, / These things himself.' Cicero in the *Letters to Atticus*, book 9: 'For our Gnaeus is marvellously anxious for despotism on Sullan lines, I speak to one who knows.'

* * * * *

27 proverb] I vii 18
28 Some ... owl] Added in *1528*
32 Plutarch] *Lysander* 16.2

12 Otto 567; 1090. 'Preaching to the converted'
 4 comedies] Plautus *Captivi* 191; *Stichus* 578; *Poenulus* 880. A similar phrase has
    not been found in Terence.
 6 Plato] *Hippias major* 301d, the Greek added in *1520*
 7 Euripides] *Hecuba* 670
 9 Homer] *Odyssey* 17.193 and 281; *Iliad* 23.305, inserted in *1533*
12 Cicero] *Ad Atticum* 9.7.3, added in *1523*

13 **Si crebro iacias, aliud alias ieceris**
    If you throw often, you'll throw this way
    and then that

Aristotle in his book on *Divination From Dreams* quotes a proverbial line as
follows: 'If you throw often enough, your luck will change.' This means that   5
we must often make an attempt, and not be immediately discouraged, if
sometimes the result is not much to our liking. It may turn out that a person
scores a success after trying over and over again. Aristotle's words are these:
'as the saying goes' and then follows the line. His subject is the dreams of the
melancholic type of person, in which he thinks there is no divination, and   10
yet it sometimes happens that some events fulfil their dreams; but since they
are prone by a weakness of nature to much and varied dreaming, there is no
wonder if coincidences arise or cases which fall out by chance exactly
according to their dream. Themistius paraphrases this passage thus (I use
the translation of Barbaro because the Greek book was not to hand): 'For   15
those who spend all day throwing sometimes aim right and take the prize.
The old adage says: If you throw often, some time you'll throw a Venus.'
    There are those who think (and it does not seem absurd to me) that the
metaphor comes from archers, not from gamblers, for *ballein* can also mean
to shoot; and that there is a subtle difference in meaning contained in this   20
word, in the first part indicating 'to shoot an arrow,' in the latter 'to strike.' It
does happen that those who throw often hit the target occasionally by

* * * * *

13 Apparently taken in the first instance from Aristotle. Otto 840; Suringar 207.
    Our 'Better luck next time'
 4 Aristotle] *De divinatione per somnum* 2 (463b20), citing a line from a lost Greek
    comedy (frag com adesp 448 Kock), whence Apostolius 2.87. The Latin version
    which Erasmus gives is an iambic line, and has been attributed to Publilius
    Syrus (see I ii 4n).
14 Themistius] a teacher of philosophy and prominent orator in Constantinople in
    the fourth century AD. A paraphrase on Aristotle's *Parva naturalia* ascribed to
    him (but really by a medieval author called Sophonias) was first published in
    Greek by Aldus in 1534, and has been edited by P. Wendland in vol 5 part 6 of
    the Berlin corpus of Greek commentators on Aristotle (1905), where our
    passage is on p 42. The Latin version by Ermolao Barbaro (1453–93) was printed
    in Venice in 1480 and often thereafter, and this is in his chapter 5.
17 Venus] The Ancients played either with three dice (*tesserae*), which were
    cubical and marked on six sides with the numbers from one to six, or with four
    knucklebones (*tali*), which had rounded ends and were marked on four sides
    with one, three, four and six. Venus was the highest throw, when all four sides
    came up with a different number; Dog lowest, when all showed one.
18–29 There are ... twice or thrice] Added in *1515*

chance. Though Cicero, in book 2 of the *On Divination*, talking about the
coincidences which I mentioned just now, refers to both metaphors: he says,
'For who is there who spends all day shooting and never hits the target? All   25
night long we dream, there is hardly ever a night when we do not sleep, and
should we be surprised when sometimes our dreams come true? What is
more uncertain than the throw of the dice? Yet there is no one who throws
often who does not sometimes throw a Venus, maybe twice or thrice.'
Venus was at one time the luckiest throw in this kind of game, as we see in   30
Suetonius (in a letter of Octavius Augustus to Tiberius): 'During the meal,'
he says, 'we played games *gerontikos*' (like old men), 'both yesterday and
today. When the dice were thrown, whoever threw a dog or a six put into
the pool one denarius for each die, and the one who threw Venus took the
lot.' Thus far Augustus. This proverb will fit also people who are trying to   35
gain their end through chance and not through skill. There is also today a
popular joke about the blind man who shot a crow with a dart.

14   **Malum consilium**
     Bad advice

Malum consilium consultori pessimum, Bad advice is worst for the adviser. This
is a proverbial line of verse about people who give wrong advice to others,
which rebounds on their own head. Indeed, as the Greeks say, Counsel is a   5
sacred thing. Just as it should be freely accepted when the situation demands it, so it should be conscientiously and honestly given if it is needed.
Otherwise there will not be lacking a Power which will exact amends from
anyone who treacherously violates a sacred and divine thing. Aulus Gellius
in his *Attic Nights*, book 4 chapter 5, thinks that this adage grew out of a   10
certain story which he tells out of the annals of Maximus and the anecdotes
of Verrius Flaccus. According to this: 'The statue of Horatius Cocles, that
valiant man, placed in the comitium at Rome, was struck by lightning. This
needed atonement by sacrifice, and augurs were summoned from Etruria,
who decided (being themselves of an unfriendly and hostile mind to the   15
Roman people) to take care of this matter by reversing the religious rites; and

* * * * *

23 Cicero] *De divinatione* 2.59.121
31 Suetonius] See I i 78n; *Divus Augustus* 71.2, added in 1517/8

14 *Collectanea* no 169 cited Gellius, but anonymously, and so briefly that the
   treatment of the adage has clearly been renewed from the materials. Otto 923;
   Tilley c 691 Ill counsel is worst to the counsellor.
5 Greeks] Zenobius 4.40. This will be found in its own right as *Adagia* II i 47.
9 Gellius] 4.5. The comitium is the place of public assembly.

they wrongly prompted the removal of the statue into a lower site, where because it was surrounded on all sides by other buildings the sun never shone. After they had gained their point that this should be done, they were denounced before the people and betrayed; and when they had admitted 20 their treachery, they were put to death. It was decided that the statue should be removed into a high place, as genuine computations later ascertained dictated, and erected in a loftier place in the square of Vulcan. This action proved favourable and prosperous for the state. So the accusation and punishment of the Etruscan augurs was vindicated, and this aptly-written 25 verse was spread through the whole town and sung by the children: "Who suffers most from bad advice, is the adviser."' Thus far Gellius. Moreover Valerius Maximus, book 7, tells a similar story about Papyrius Cursor, when he was besieging Aquilonia as consul. He wished to go into battle against the enemy, unless there were some deterring factor in the auspices, and con- 30 sulted the keeper of the chickens, who persuaded him to give battle, although the birds had given a bad augury. When Papyrius found this out he posted the keeper of the chickens in the front line, where he expiated his crime against religion by being transfixed by the first javelin. This is re- corded by Livy in his first decade, book 10. 35

Much the same story is told by Socrates in the *Tripartite History*. Eutropius the eunuch was seeking a means to punish some men who had taken refuge in a temple, and persuaded the emperor to pass a law forbid- ding the temple sanctuary to be available for evil-doers. The law was passed, and then it came about that Eutropius himself offended Caesar and took 40 refuge under the altar, from which he was dragged out and executed; his own advice had ruined him.

Virgil tacitly noted the proverb in the *Aeneid*, book 12, where he says 'Himself Tolumnius the augur fell, / The first to hurl a dart against the foe.' Varro in his *Agriculture*, book 3 chapter 1, quotes it openly in these words: 45 'In my opinion, it is not only true, as they say, that bad advice is worst for the adviser, but also that good advice is to be regarded as of value both to the one who asks for it and the one who gives it.' Sophocles in the *Electra*: 'For

* * * * *

28 Valerius Maximus] 7.2.5. His *Facta et dicta memorabilia* was a manual of historical anecdotes, compiled in the early first century AD.
35 Livy] 10.40.9–13, added in 1515
36 Socrates] Cassiodorus *Historia tripertita* 10.4 (added in 1533); the Greek historian Socrates, of the fifth century AD, was one of his sources.
43 Virgil] Aeneid 12.460–1
45 Varro] *Res rusticae* 3.2.1 (see I i 40n).
48 Sophocles] *Electra* 1047

nothing is more harmful than evil counsel.' Here he takes the harm to belong
to the one who is advised. But it is clear that this Latin line (as Gellius too   50
remarks) is a rendering of the Greek verses of Hesiod which we read in the
work entitled *Works and Days*: 'He harms himself who seeks another's
harm. / Worst is bad counsel for the counsellor.' Plutarch in his essay 'On
How to Study Poetry' thinks the notion in these lines is the same as the
teaching of Plato in the *Gorgias*, where Socrates says that it is worse to inflict   55
an injury than to suffer one, and more grievous to do harm than to receive it.
And this opinion is to be found in almost so many words in the Hebrew
writer Ecclesiasticus, chapter 27: 'The man who gives evil counsel shall have
it recoil on his own head.'

There is a Greek fable on these lines, not without charm, and not   60
altogether unworthy to be included in these notes. The lion was old and ill,
and keeping to his den. The other animals came, as in duty bound, to visit
their king – all but the fox. The wolf, seizing the opportunity, accused the
fox in the lion's presence of lèse-majesté, saying 'He thinks nothing of you,
all-powerful as you are, and it is out of scorn that he has not been to visit   65
you.' Meanwhile, the fox came in during the wolf's story and heard the last
words he spoke. When the lion saw the fox, he immediately flew into a rage
against him. The fox, however, asked for time to clear himself. 'Which of all
these animals here,' he said, 'has been as useful to you as I have? I have been
running hither and thither all over the place and I have found a remedy for   70
your illness from the doctors.' The lion eagerly ordered him to produce this
remedy, and he said: 'If you flay a wolf alive and wrap yourself in the skin,
you will recover.' The credulous lion at once leapt on the wolf and killed
him. When he had been destroyed the cunning fox laughed to see how the
evil counsel of the slanderer had recoiled on his own head. Plutarch records   75
a line to this effect: 'Ill planned for others strikes at your own heart.'

* * * * *

51 Hesiod] *Works and Days* 265–6, used again in *Adagia* IV viii 56
53 Plutarch] *Moralia* 36A; from this point to the end the paragraph is of *1515*.
55 Plato] *Gorgias* 473a onwards. This recurs in I ix 95.
58 Ecclesiasticus] 27:30
60 Greek fable] Aesop 255
75 Plutarch] *Moralia* 554A, the Latin version of the Greek line added in *1517/8*.
   Plutarch quotes the line as Hesiod's, and it is very close to *Works and Days* 265,
   which Erasmus has cited just above; but we know it from an epigram in the
   Greek Anthology by a poet called Lucillius (*Anth. Palatina* 11.183.5), and
   something very like it appears in the *Aitia* of the eminent Hellenistic poet
   Callimachus (frag 2.5 Pfeiffer).

15   **Suum cuique pulchrum**
     What is one's own is beautiful

Suum cuique pulchrum is a proverbial saying about people who prefer what is
their own, whatever it may be like, and rather out of prejudice than judgment. It arises from the usual attitude of mind among the human race, with   5
whom *philautia*, or self-love, is so deeply rooted that you will find no one
so modest, so thoughtful, or so clear-sighted that he will not be blind or
suffer from delusions, misled by some mental bias, when it comes to putting
a value on something of his own. Have we ever seen anyone born in such a
barbarous land that he does not think his home country the best of all? What   10
race is so savage, or has a tongue so uncouth, as not to consider all others
beneath it? What bodily form is so brutish as not to appear most beautiful to
itself? Aristotle wrote truly in his *Rhetoric*, book 2: 'And besides all men are
self-lovers, and whatever is their own is of necessity sweet to each, eg their
deeds and words; on this account they are as a rule fond of flatterers.' This is 15
true in general and universally (as Horace says, 'self-love is blind'), but it
particularly applies to artists, and among them specially to poets, and also to
lovers. Aristotle wrote most rightly in his *Ethics*, book 4, that every craftsman is greatly delighted by his own work, as if these were things sprung
from himself. Poets love their own poems as parents love their children. A   20
work is to the craftsman something like the offspring of the mind, and
Socrates said that the midwife was a better judge of progeny than the mother
herself. It is the way of loving husbands to vie with each other in singing the
praises each of his own bride. An outstanding example of this is found in the
youthful Tarquins. Even today there is a shrewd and common saying,   25
'there's no such thing to be found as an ugly sweetheart,' because to him

* * * * *

15 This puts together *Collectanea* no 297, which provided the two Cicero
    quotations and one from Plautus' *Stichus* which now stand near the end (with a
    cross-reference to what is now *Adagia* I ii 62), and no 601, with four lines from
    Horace, *Satires* 1.5 two of which were not taken up into the *Chiliades* at this
    point. It is Otto 1726; Suringar 219; Tilley c 812 Every creature thinks her own
    fair, M 115 Every man has his delight, M 131 Every man likes his own thing
    best.

 6 *philautia*] See *Adagia* I iii 92.
13 Aristotle] *Rhetoric* 1.11 (1371b21)
16 Horace] *Odes* 1.18.14
18 Aristotle] *Ethica Nicomachea* 4.1 (1120b13); no Greek is quoted.
22 Socrates] Possibly a reminiscence of Plato *Theaetetus* 149–51
25 Tarquins] Ovid *Fasti* 2.721ff and Livy 1.57 describe how several young Roman
    nobles on a campaign came to discuss (and praise) their wives, and set off there
    and then on an unexpected visit home to test their fidelity.

who loves them even homely things must seem very beautiful. Theocritus expressed this idea with elegance in his sixth *Eclogue*: '– for often in love, O Polyphemus, the least fair seems fair.' Plato expressed this proverb in the *Lysis*, but contrariwise: 'There is a danger lest, according to the old proverb, that should be dear which is beautiful,' as if we should not find a thing beautiful because it is dear, but dear because it is beautiful. To this belongs what Cicero writes in the fifth book of the *De finibus*: 'Everyone is most influenced by his own particular interest,' and again in book 1 of the *De officiis*: 'Each of whom, engrossed in his own profession, undervalued that of the other.'

However, it can be forgiven if that common self-love goes just so far as to make each of us tend a little to favour our own children, our own arts or business or discoveries, our own country, so long as it does not sweep us to that point of blindness which makes us libel the virtues of others and flatter our own vices, giving them the name of virtues – so that we see ourselves like Suffenus in Catullus or Maevius in Horace. In his *Epistles* Horace observes this failing: 'While my faults please me,' he says, 'or deceive me in the end.' At this place Porphyrio points out that Horace is alluding to the widespread opinion that men not only fail to be sorry for their faults but actually find them pleasing. He says there was a well-known Greek proverb on this subject, but this proverb is lacking in the texts owing to the fault of the copyists. Another remark of Horace applies to this too: 'Base vices dupe the blind, or even please: / Balbinus loves the polyp that on Agne's nose he sees.' To Balbinus, a stupid lover, even the polyp of his darling Agne seemed to smell sweet. (A polyp is an affection of the nostrils which smells strong, like the goaty smell of the armpits; so we talk about sufferers from the polyp and the goat.) Cicero to Atticus, book 14: 'My dear fellow, let me give you a general rule on matters in which I have a fair amount of experience. There was never a poet or orator yet who thought anyone better than himself. This applies even to the bad ones. How much more to one so gifted and erudite as Brutus! I actually made the experiment the other day in connection with the edict. I composed a draft at your request. I liked mine,

* * * * *

27 Theocritus] 6.18–9, cited in the *Moria* 19
29 Plato] *Lysis* 216c, inserted in *1520*. In *1533* this became an adage on its own (IV vii 81).
33 Cicero] *De finibus* 5.2.5; *De officiis* 1.1.4
42 Suffenus ... Maevius] Examples of self-satisfied poetasters from Catullus 22 and Horace *Epodes* 10
42 Horace] *Epistles* 2.2.127; *Satires* 1.3.39–40
53 Cicero] *Ad Atticum* 14.20.3 (tr Shackleton Bailey), citing the comic poet Atilius frag 1 (part reused in I vii 44)

he preferred his own. Indeed, when, at his own entreaty, I might almost say, I addressed to him an essay on the best style of oratory, he wrote not 60 only to me but to you too, that he could not agree with my preference. So pray let every man write as best suits himself. "For every man his own bride, mine for me. For every man his own love, mine for me." Not a very elegant distich. Atilius wrote it, a most clumsy versifier.' Thus far Cicero. It appears from his words that the two verses, 'For every man' etc come from some play 65 by Atilius. Again, Cicero says in the *Tusculan Questions*, book 5: 'He was, in fact, an enthusiastic musician, a tragic poet too – how good, matters little: for in this art, more than in others, it somehow happens that everyone finds that what is his own is beautiful. So far I have never known the poet (and I have been friends with Aquinius) who did not think himself the best; this is 70 the way with them: You are charmed with your work, I with mine.' The same idea is expressed by Plautus in the *Stichus*, in different words but with great elegance: 'To every queen her king is fair, to every bridegroom his bride.'

With this we can also connect that line of Theocritus: 'Nor am I so 75 unbeautiful, if truth be told.' And Virgil imitating it:

> Nor am I so ill-favoured; once of late
> I saw myself reflected on the shore
> When dying winds had left the water calm.

Horace alludes to the adage more openly in one of his epistles: 80

> You are keeping them for Jove's ears.
> Beautiful in your own eyes, you believe that you
> And you only, drip the whole honey of poetry

'Beautiful in your own eyes' means self-admiring. This phrase is little different from what St Augustine says in several places, for instance in 85 Letter 48, drawing it from a certain Tychonius: 'What we wish is sacred.' (It is a half-line from an heroic poem.) One could wish that this saying were not

* * * * *

66 Cicero] *Tusculanae disputationes* 5.22.63 (all but the proverb itself added in *1515*)
72 Plautus] *Stichus* 133 (Otto 1539)
75 Theocritus] 6.34
76 Virgil] *Eclogues* 2.25–6
80 Horace] *Epistles* 1.19.43–5, the explanation added in *1517/8*. This was partly reused in *1523* in II vi 56.
85 Augustine] *Letters* 93.43; *Contra Cresconium grammaticum* 4.37, both added with the following comment in *1520*. Cf *Adagia* IV vii 16; Otto 1854.

so applicable to the ways of some people today, who lay claim to piety more
arrogantly than ever the Pharisees did, and, while they are steeped in vices
neither to be tolerated nor mentioned, show astonishing self-satisfaction in   90
their savage criticism of the way other men live.

16   **Patriae fumus igni alieno luculentior**
     The smoke of home, brighter than others' fire

The well-turned phrase of Lucian in his *Praise of the Homeland* has the look of
a proverb, and carries on the same thought: 'And the smoke of his father-
land will seem brighter to him than fire elsewhere.' Philostratus in *Ariadne*:   5
'Theseus loves, but he loves the smoke of Athens; Ariadne he has not yet
seen, nor has he ever known her'. In Homer, Ulysses longs to see the smoke
rising from his native place, hence the proverb. So we read in the *Odyssey*,
book 1: 'Longing to see the smoke rising from his native land.'

17   Viva vox
     The living word

Viva vox, The living word, was the term used in old times for anything not
written, but taken straight from the mouth of the speaker, lifelike, as it were,
and effectual. Often the term 'living' is applied to things when they are in   5
their native condition, not artificial, as 'from the living marble,' and 'seats
cut in the living rock.' Natural things, in fact, have some quality of genuine
grace which no artistic imitation can hope to copy. Writing is indeed a kind
of voice, but as it were an artificial one, somehow mimicking the real voice.
Gesture and movement are lacking; in a word, life. Delivery, as Quintilian   10
tells us, is the life of oratory, invention of the subject-matter is its bones;

* * * * *

16 Tilley s 572 The smoke of a man's own country is better than the fire of
    another's.
 3 Lucian] *Patriae encomium* 11
 5 Philostratus] *Imagines* 317.10. He was a member of a literary family, whose
    activity extends from the second century AD into the third. The *Imagines*, which
    purport to describe a series of paintings, were first printed by Aldus in 1503.
 7 Homer] *Odyssey* 1.58–9, the Greek added in *1528*

17 *Collectanea* no 222; this mentions the passage from Jerome, and gives the Gellius
    quotation which was used in the *Chiliades* as the foundation for I ii 18. Otto
    1936.
 6 living marble *etc*] Virgil *Aeneid* 6.848; 1.167
10 Quintilian] Cf *Institutio oratoria* 11.3.1–9.

order takes the place of sinews, elocution is flesh, skin and colouring, memory stands for breath, and added to all that there is the art of speaking, *pronunciatio*, which is like the movement of life. For there is no more certain proof of life than movement. So they talk of 'living streams' and 'quicksil-   15
ver.' On the other hand things are called dead when they are torpid and inactive. Cicero says in *Tusculan Questions*, book 2, 'Certainly many examples for imitation can be obtained from reading, but fuller nourishment comes from the living voice, as they say, especially the voice of the teacher.' So in the *Letters to Atticus*, book 2: 'Where are those now who talk of the   20
living voice? How much better I see what it was all about from your letter than from his speech!' But what Cicero gives here in a mutilated and shortened form, some people extend from their own invention, as 'that greater vividness is found in the living voice.' The younger Pliny in a letter to Nepos: 'Besides, the living voice, as they say, has more power to move us.   25
For even if the things you read are more acute, yet those which are impressed on the mind by pronunciation, expression, appearance, and gesture of the speaker penetrate more deeply.' Seneca, in Letter 5: 'The living voice and the intimacy of a common life will help you more than the written word.' St Jerome in a general preface: 'The living voice has some kind of   30
hidden force, and sounds more strongly in the pupils' ears when it comes out of the mouth of the teacher.' So far Jerome. And hence the celebrated phrase of Aeschines, about Demosthenes: 'But what if you had heard the beast himself?' And that other one: 'In the writings of Demosthenes, a great part of Demosthenes is lacking.'   35

* * * * *

15 living streams] Virgil *Aeneid* 2.719; for quicksilver ('living silver' in English, as in Latin) see Pliny *Naturalis historia* 33.99.
17 Cicero] This use of 'dead' seems not to occur in the second book of his *Tusculanae disputationes*; and something seems to have gone wrong with Erasmus' notes, for the quotation which follows, unrelated to its immediate context, is from Quintilian 2.2.8.
20 So] Cicero *Ad Atticum* 2.12.2
23 some people extend] Some early editions add three words to complete Cicero's Greek phrase; the reference to this was added in *1520*.
24 Pliny] the Younger *Letters* 2.3.9
28 Seneca] *Letters* 6.5, added in *1533*
30 Jerome] *Letters* 53.2
33 Aeschines] A familiar story, told with the Greek wording by Pliny the Younger *Letters* 2.3.10

18   **Muti magistri**
     Silent teachers

What we have just mentioned is also used by Aulus Gellius, but he adds
another and opposite thought. 'Since there was a dearth of the living voice,
as they say, I learnt from what they call silent teachers.' By silent teachers he   5
meant books, which do indeed speak to us, as Socrates says in Plato, but
they are no good at answering our questions when in doubt. So good books
are not inelegantly called silent masters. This is apt, because dumb people
speak by nods and signs, not with the voice; and so books talk with us at
times by means of marks and shapes which bear a meaning. Just as spoken   10
words, according to Aristotle, are a kind of image of the meaning in the
mind, so the shapes of letters can properly be called reflections, as it were, of
the sounds of speech. Nor is it to be wondered at if that direct image of the
heart proves a better way of reproducing and communicating the soul's
intentions than that other method, writing, which imitates the imitation   15
rather than the thing itself. The question is often asked, and very sensibly,
which is the more useful in the acquisition of knowledge, to use the living
voice or silent masters. Each has its own particular advantages. What we
learn from books is often more recondite, and there is more of it; for each
reader learns as much as his quickness of mind will allow and the faithful-   20
ness of his memory retain. There is also the point that these teachers are
never tired of sharing their efforts with us. Their store is as rich as it is ready.
They are read at leisure, one can think them over in private. One can look
more closely at individual parts, go back over the ground and ponder it.

On the other hand what we learn from listening to a teacher costs us   25
less in mental effort, in eyesight, in health – particularly if the one who
speaks is someone we admire and love. What we learn in this way sinks
more deeply into the mind, stays with us longer, is recalled more promptly.
So the best plan will be to combine one type of study with the other, and
when there is ample opportunity for oral instruction prefer to listen rather   30
than read, always given that the person to whom you are listening is of
moderately sound learning. Where this is not so, you may gladly turn to
books (but they must be the best books) as to something of no less value. To
conclude, I may add that books are called silent teachers by the same

* * * * *

18 *Collectanea* no 465, citing the passage from Gellius also used in no 222 (*Chiliades* I
    ii 17). Otto 945
  3 Gellius] 14.2.1
  6 Plato] *Protagoras* 329a
 11 Aristotle] This has not been identified.

metaphor as Cicero uses when he calls the law 'a silent judge,' the judge a   35
'speaking law'; and Plutarch when he calls poetry a 'speaking picture' and a
picture 'silent poetry.'

19   **Frons occipitio prior**
     Forehead before occiput

A proverb in common use among countrymen in the old days, which
circulated like a riddle: Forehead before occiput. This is the way they
conveyed in Antiquity that a man's business is better looked after when he   5
himself is present and attending to it. 'Before' here means better, more
effective than; who could be ignorant anyhow that the forehead is the front
part of the head and the occiput the back part? Although this riddling quality
of the saying gives it a certain charm, and owing to its age it was treated like
an oracle. It can be found in Cato *On Agriculture*, chapter 4: 'If you have built   10
well, you will come more freely and frequently, and your farm will be all the
better for it. Fewer mistakes will be made, and you will get a larger return:
forehead before occiput.' Pliny too says much the same thing in his *History of
the World*, book 18 chapter 5: 'But the man who has a good house to live in
visits his property oftener, and the master's forehead does it more good than   15
his occiput – so they say, and truly.' Again in the same book, chapter 6: 'And
our forebears used to say that the master's eye is the best fertilizer for his
ground.' Aristotle in his *Economica*, book 1, seems to trace this saying to a
certain Persian, and connects with it a similar image once produced by a
Libyan. But I had better quote his words, in case anyone regrets their   20
absence: 'And what the Persian and the Libyan said to one another will be
rightly kept in mind. For one of them, asked what food best keeps a horse in
condition, replied The master's eye. And the Libyan, when asked what was
the best manure, answered The master's footsteps.' Both of them meant that
the presence of the master was the most important thing in the successful   25

* * * * *

35 Cicero] *De legibus* 3.1.2; this last sentence was added in *1515*.
36 Plutarch] *Moralia*, probably 17F rather than 346F, as in the latter passage
     Plutarch ascribes this familiar saying to Simonides, and Erasmus would
     probably have given this name had he had it in front of him.

19 Otto 719
 8 Although … oracle] Added in *1517/8*
10 Cato] *De agricultura* 4 (the chapter-number given as 1 in *1508*, and corrected in
     1528)
13 Pliny] *Naturalis historia* 18.31; 18.43 (Otto 1275)
18 Aristotle] *Oeconomica* 1.6 (1345a1–5)

conduct of affairs. Similarly Columella thinks it is a bad thing for a farm to be often let, and a worse thing when the tenant is a townsman who intends to leave the cultivation to his workpeople and not attend to it himself. This is rather like the story told by Gellius, about the fat sleek man with the lean stringy horse; when asked about it he said no one need be surprised if he   30
was in better trim than his horse, since he saw to his own meals himself and the horse was looked after by a slave. Plutarch in his essay 'On the Education of Children' says: 'Here and there one finds an elegant proverb coming from the stable: that nothing fattens the horse like the King's own eye.' The same simile is used by Aeschylus in his tragedy the *Persians*, when he calls   35
the master's presence the eye of the house: 'The eye of the house I take to be the presence of the master.' In the same vein Livy has a happy phrase: 'There is not often much success for the things you do through the eyes of others.' Terence in his *Eunuchus* has the same idea when he says 'That's what happens when the masters are away,' meaning that when the masters   40
are absent the servants are slack in their work and lax in their morals; in a word, all these add up to the same thing; if you want a thing well done, you must do it yourself, and not trust much in the diligence of others.

The person who should most take note of this is the prince, if he really has the mind of a prince and not of a pirate, that is if he has the public good at   45
heart. But in these days bishops and kings do everything through other people's hands, ears and eyes, and think the common good is what concerns them least, kept busy as they are with their own private possessions or entirely bent on pleasure.

20   **Aequalis aequalem delectat**
     Everyone loves his own age

Similarity is the mother of good will, and links people together by habit and way of life. So we see young people liking to come together and old men congregating with old men, scholars having a taste for meeting with other   5

* * * * *

26 Columella] *Res rustica* 1.1.18–20, added in *1515*
29 Gellius] 4.20.11
32 Plutarch] *Moralia* 9D
35 Aeschylus] *Persae* 169
37 Livy] 26.22.6, cited from memory
39 Terence] *Eunuchus* 600
44 The person] From here to the end was added in *1517/8*.

20 Otto 1335. Distinguished from the adage that follows by its emphasis on parity of age; but the two naturally run very close together.

scholars, ruffians getting together with other ruffians and drinkers with drinkers, sailors taking to sailors, rich men hobnobbing with other rich men, and everywhere like being attracted to like. There are a number of proverbs expressing this idea among the Ancients, such as Ἧλιξ ἥλικα τέρπει, Everyone loves his own age. Cicero uses it in the *Cato major*: 'Like readily   10 comes together with like, as the old proverb has it.' For the first beginnings of intimacy come from equality in age, in Greek *homelikia*. Homer alludes to this in *Odyssey* 15: 'Since we are of the same age.' Plato was thinking of it in the *Republic*, book 1, where Cephalus, who admits that he has reached 'the threshold of old age,' says 'For often many of us who are more or less of the   15 same age come together, keeping the old proverb.' Aristotle in his *Rhetoric*, book 2, considers what is most pleasing to whom, and writes that 'in general those who are related or similar in kind naturally take pleasure in each other, such as man and man, horse and horse, adolescent and adolescent, and that this is the sense of proverbs generally quoted, Everyone loves his own age,   20 Like will to like, Beast knows beast, Jackdaw sits by jackdaw, and others of the same kind.' Theognis says that there is close friendship between contemporaries, neighbours and old men: 'All these share mutual respect and love, neighbours, equals in strength and old men.' There is some connection between this proverb and what Empedocles says in Aristotle's *On the Soul*,   25 book 1, that the soul 'is something made by combination out of all elements'; indeed that it is in itself something of them, and recognizes each of them, for the reasons that it has some affinity with each individual element. Hence Plato says in the *Timaeus* that the soul consists of elements. The lines of Empedocles are as follows: 30

    For by earth we see earth, and by water water,

    * * * * *

  8 proverbs] Diogenianus 5.16; Suidas H 231
 10 Cicero] *De senectute* 3.7, for which *Cato major* is an alternative title
 12 Homer] *Odyssey* 15.197
 13 Plato] *Republic* 1.328e, 329a; the Greek added in *1515*. Used again in II x 46.
 16 Aristotle] *Rhetoric* 1.11 (1371b15). Against his usual custom of giving the Greek, followed by a Latin version, Erasmus here puts the Latin first and then a rather longer piece of Greek (which is what we translate), concluding with references to parallel proverbs which appear here as I ii 21, II iii 63, I ii 23.
 22 Theognis] See I i 62n; 935–6.
 25 Empedocles] Frag 31 B 109 Diels-Kranz (see I i 72n), cited by Aristotle *De anima* 1.2 (404b11). This was added in *1517/8*, with the name of Democritus instead of Empedocles (put right in *1520*).
 29 Plato] *Timaeus* 35a, in Ficino's version. This, though it is quoted by Aristotle at this point, was omitted in *1517/8*, and not inserted until *1528*. At the same time Erasmus added the discussion ('At first … written for them') which follows.

By ether we see divine ether, by fire destructive fire,
By love sweet love, and hate by baneful hate.

At first we despaired of finding any better translation of these lines than that
of Argyropoulos (although I suspect that in the first line the copyists have   35
changed *undam* into *aquam*). Later, at the request of friends I have added my
own, such as it is. (Argyropylos gives two words for one, for the sake of the
metre, and leaves out two epithets. Then he spoils the grace of repetition, by
using *aquam* and *undam*, *discordia* and *lite*, to say nothing of the harshness of
the collocation in *Terram nam*. And he added the adverb *sane* on his own. I   40
have added an epithet to 'love,' but such as the poet himself would have
added if the metre had permitted, as he added his own epithet to the
contrasting word. I am not saying this to cast aspersions on a man whose
scholarship deserves the thanks of scholars, but so that young readers may
profit by the criticism – for this is mainly written for them.)   45
     One of the philosophers, Zeno I think, relates (in Augustine) that the
soul herself is a self-moving harmony, and for this reason can be caught up
and carried away by harmonious things (this is its nature) just as children
too are affected by the modes of music through some natural affinity, even
when they have no idea what music is. Aristotle produces this definition in   50
the very place I have just quoted, without giving the author's name.

21   **Simile gaudet simili**
     Like rejoices in like

"Ομοιον ὁμοίῳ φίλον, Like rejoices in like. Aristotle in the *Ethics*, book 8:
'Like seeks like,' and in book 9: 'Like is a friend to like.' Hence that other
     * * * * *
     35 Argyropoulos] Giovanni Argiropulo (c1415–1487), one of the best-known of the
        refugees from Constantinople, who taught Greek for many years in Florence
        and later in Rome. His translation of Aristotle's *De anima*, dedicated to Cosimo
        de' Medici (d 1464) was often printed. Erasmus' Latin version of the lines and
        his are too close for the difference to appear clearly when they are turned into
        English; and this deprives Erasmus' criticisms of much of their point. Similar
        comments could be made on some of his own verse translations elsewhere in
        this work, skilful as they are.
     46 Augustine] This has not been identified. It was added in 1517/8.

     21 This and the next are represented in the *Collectanea* by no 177, which also cited
        the passages from Cicero and from Plato's *Republic* used in I ii 20. With II iii 63,
        we have a group of related phrases. Cf Tilley B 393 Birds of a feather will flock
        together, L 286 Like will to like. Otto 1335
     3 Aristotle] *Ethica Nicomachea* 8.1.2 (1155b7); 9.3.3 (1165b17). Similar material
        could have been given from Plato *Gorgias* 510b; Apostolius 12.68.

phrase: 'Similarity is the mother of affection.' So where there is absolute   5
similarity there is the most violent love, and this is the meaning of the fable
of Narcissus. Agathon in the *Symposium* of Plato: 'For the old saying is right,
that like always cleaves to like.' Plutarch in the essay called 'How To Tell A
Friend From A Flatterer,' quotes the following iambic lines:

> The speech of age is pleasant to the old,   10
> Boy suits with boy, woman with woman too,
> A sick man with the sick, and one in grief
> With one who suffers is in dear accord.

Diogenes Laertius, showing that Plato imitated some things from the writings of Epicharmus, quotes his saying that 'a bitch seems most beautiful to a   15
dog, a cow to a bull, a she-ass to an ass, a sow to a boar,' I have said
elsewhere 'To every queen her king is fair.' Plato in the eighth book of the
Laws: 'We say that like is a friend to like as far as virtue is concerned, and
equal to equal.' But the adage can rightly be transferred also to those who are
linked by a likeness in vice. Directed against those is the line of Catullus   20
'Well agreed are the abominable profligates,' and Martial's 'Worst of wives
and worst of husbands, I am surprised that you do not agree,' and Juvenal's
'Great is the concord among catamites.'

22   Semper similem ducit deus ad similem
God always leads like to like

This adage may be derived from Homer's *Odyssey*, book 17, line 217, where
Melanthius the goatherd sees Eumaeus the swineherd bringing Ulysses

* * * * *

7 Narcissus] In the myth he falls in love with his own reflection in a pool of water,
   and is drowned, a classic case of absolute similarity leading to violent and fatal
   passion. Ovid Metam. 3. 339 – 510
7 Plato] *Symposium* 195b, the Greek added in *1523*
8 Plutarch] *Moralia* 51E; the lines have been regarded as a fragment both of
   comedy (frag adesp 364 Kock) and of tragedy (adesp 1206 Nauck).
14 Diogenes Laertius] 3.16, added in *1526*
17 elsewhere] *Adagia* I ii 15, the cross-reference added in *1526*
17 Plato] *Laws* 8.837a
20 Catullus] 57.1
21 Martial] 8.35.2–3, used again in II vii 51
22 Juvenal] 2.47. This comes again in II iii 75.

22 Another form of the preceding, which appears in the Greek proverb–collections (Diogenianus 5.16); but there are no indications that they were used here.
3 Homer] *Odyssey* 17.217–8. In *1508*, having noted down or remembered the lines

with him, tattered and torn, and makes a jest about both of them, as if the   5
two of them were well matched: 'Now the worthless leads the worthless; /
Thus always God brings like to like.' Aristotle in the *Ethics*, book 8, quotes as
a proverb 'Whence they say "like will to like."'

23   **Semper graculus adsidet graculo**
     Jackdaw always sits by jackdaw

Ἀεὶ κολοιὸς πρὸς κολοιὸν ἰζάνει, Jackdaw always sits by jackdaw. This
proverb, an iambic line, is found in Diogenianus, and it is noted in the book
of Aristotle's *Rhetoric* which I have just quoted, where he calls it to mind   5
among other proverbs of the same nature, and also in book 8 of his *Ethics*:
'And jackdaw to jackdaw.' (This is a trochaic dimeter in Greek, no doubt
taken from some poet.) Gregory made use of the adage with some elegance
in a letter to Eudoxius: 'That jackdaw sits by jackdaw you hear the proverb
say.' Varro in book 3 of his *Agriculture* attests that gatherings of jackdaws   10
have long been known, whence Plutarch says, in 'On Having Many
Friends,' 'It is neither like a herd of cattle nor like a flock of daws.' The bird's
name in Greek comes from the word *kolao*, I glue together, and Varro thinks

* * * * *

and not the speaker's name, Erasmus attributed them to the suitors of
Penelope. This was a very small slip; but either he detected it somehow, or it
was pointed out to him, and he put it right in *1528*.

7 Aristotle] *Ethica Nicomachea* 8.1 (1155a34)

23 *Collectanea* no 721, derived from Diogenianus 1.61 (the adage is also in
    Zenobius 2.47 and Suidas κ 1968). Tilley L 283 The like, I say, sits with the jay.

5 Aristotle] *Rhetoric* 1.11 (1371b15), used in I ii 20; *Ethica Nicomachea* 8.1 (1155a34).
    The origin of the line seems to be unknown.

7 trochaic dimeter] In principle, two units of four syllables each, scanning
    long-short-long-short. This metrical parenthesis, which was added like many
    of the metrical comments in the *Adagia* in *1528*, refers only to the phrase as
    quoted in the second passage from Aristotle, and it is quite possible that its
    apparently metrical structure is purely accidental.

8 Gregory] of Nazianzus, *Epistulae* 178.8 (PG 37.365B), added in *1533* (see I iv
    98n).

10 Varro] *Res rusticae* 3.16.4 (see I i 40n).

11 Plutarch] *Moralia* 93E

13 Varro] *De lingua latina* 5.76, cited by Quintilian 1.6.37 (a passage to which
    Erasmus returns in I iv 37). This discussion of the origin of the word, which,
    like nearly all ancient etymology, is quite imaginary, was added in *1528*. We
    should not now expect the same man to write valuable manuals on agriculture
    and on philology, as well as satires (see I ii 60n); but Varro (116–27 BC) was a
    polymath and a ready writer.

that their Latin name too comes from their habit of flying in flocks (*graculus* from *gregatim*). Quintilian does not agree, but asserts that the name was　15 invented from the bird's call.

24　**Cicada cicadae cara, formicae formica**
　　Cicada loves cicada, ant is dear to ant

When Aristotle added (in the place I have just mentioned) 'and whatever other proverbs of this kind there are,' he was no doubt thinking of a passage in the ninth *Idyll* of Theocritus: 'The cricket is dear to the cricket, the ant to　5 the ant, the hawk to the hawk.' The social behaviour of the ant is well known, and the concert of the crickets.

25　**Figulus figulo invidet, faber fabro**
　　Potter envies potter and smith envies smith

An exception to the foregoing must be made for those who are engaged in the same trade, because with them the similarity of their occupation brings about more competition than good will. Hesiod, in his poem entitled *Works*　5 *and Days*, gave several metaphorical descriptions of this mutual envy, but without condemning competition between craftsmen – in fact, he approved and praised it. The poet had set forth two kinds of emulation, one useful and honourable for mankind, the other nasty and pernicious. The latter, he said, drove men to quarreling and warfare as they strove for wealth and honours,　10 while the former encouraged them to industry and creditable skills by putting before them examples to follow. He describes honourable emulation in the words below. I translate these very exquisite lines only to make them intelligible; for hardly anyone could achieve their beauty, and certainly not I.

* * * * *

24　From Aristotle *Ethica Nicomachea* 8.1, as above
　5　Theocritus] 9.31–2
　6　The social behaviour] This final sentence was added in 1517/8.

25　*Collectanea* no 738 gave the reference to Hesiod, and also cited an anecdote from
　　a life of Virgil, the so-called *Donatus auctus*, which Erasmus did not re-use here
　　(it seems to be a Renaissance forgery). Otto 660; Tilley P 514 The potter envies
　　the potter, the smith the smith; T 643 Two of a trade seldom agree.
　5　Hesiod] *Works and Days* 23–6; 'smith' is Erasmus' word, to help the metre of his
　　Latin version; Hesiod was probably thinking of workers in wood, carpenters.

Neighbour envies neighbour, to see him work hard and prosper –   15
Richer and richer he gets; and good is this strife for mortals.
And potter vies with potter and one smith vies with another;
Beggar is jealous of beggar and singer of singer is jealous.

These lines are often made use of by different authors, and notably by
Aristotle in the second book of his *Ethics*. Again, in book 8 of the same work   20
he quotes them as proverbial: 'They say that all such men behave like potters
to one another,' meaning that they are jealous, with an allusion of course to
the adage in Hesiod. Again in the third book of the *Rhetoric*, 'And so they
say, potter vies with potter.' He quotes there a line from some poet or other:
'And so close cousinship brought jealousy.' But there is a likeness which   25
Plutarch in his 'Table-talk' calls *machimos*, that is, quarrelsome and bellicose, –
cocks have it, and sophists, mendicants, poets, singers; and for this reason
he excludes this kind of men from meeting at feasts, for fear that quarrels
should break out. There is another sort of similarity, which he calls *epieikes*,
reasonable, like that between jackdaws. To this kind belong sailors, tillers of   30
the soil, hunters, wrestlers, who may properly recline at the same table. To
these we may add lovers, unless they happen to love the same girl.

26 **Cretensis Cretensem**
Cretan and Cretan

Ὁ Κρῆς τὸν Κρῆτα, Cretan … Cretan; one may understand whatever verb is
suitable, like Cretan incites Cretan, tries to trick him, or something of the
sort, whenever it is a matter of one rogue having dealings with another   5
rogue, or one trickster with another. The adage is taken from the ways of the
Cretans, which were severely criticized in Antiquity.

* * * * *

20 Aristotle] There seems to be some confusion in Erasmus' references: the
proverb occurs in book 2, not of the *Ethica* but of the *Rhetoric*, 2.4 (1381b16). It is
alluded to in the *Ethica Nicomachea* 8.2 (1155a35) as the converse of our I ii 22. It
comes again in two other passages of book 2 (by our reckoning) of the *Rhetoric*,
2.4 (1381b17) and 2.10 (1388a16); and in the second of these Aristotle has just
cited a line from Aeschylus (frag 305 Nauck), which Erasmus adds here.
26 Plutarch] *Moralia* 619A, added in 1515

26 Perhaps from Diogenianus 7.31. For the reputation of Cretans, see I ii 29.
Perhaps Tilley G 440 When Greek joins Greek, then is the tug of war; or our 'No
honour among thieves.'

27 **Cretensis cum Aegineta**
A Cretan with a man of Aegina

Κρὴς πρὸς Αἰγινήτην, A Cretan (acts) with a man of Aegina. This has the
same meaning, applied to two equally bad characters who hoax each other.
For the Aeginetans also had a bad reputation in old days; some think it was   5
against them that the oracle was delivered, 'Neither third nor fourth.'

28 **Vulpinari cum vulpe**
To play the fox with the fox

Ἀλωπεκίζειν πρὸς ἑτέραν ἀλώπεκα, Confronted with a fox be fox yourself.
A proverbial iambic line: be cunning with the cunning. Horace says, 'May
the designs that lie hidden in the fox never fool you.' Aristophanes in the   5
Wasps: 'It is not right to play the fox.' If I have translated the Greek word by
vulpinari, it is not to be despised as a coinage of my own or a neologism,
because Nonius Marcellus quotes it out of Varro; and Varro was bold to say
vulpinari for the Greek *alopekizein*, to play the fox, just as Horace used
iuvenari, to behave like a young fool, for *neanizein*; see the proverb   10
battarizein.

29 **Cretiza cum Cretensi**
To play Cretan with a Cretan

Πρὸς Κρῆτα κρητίζειν, To play Cretan against a Cretan, ie use lying against a
liar. Plutarch used it in the life of Lysander: 'Play Cretan against the Cretan,

* * * * *

27 This appeared briefly in *Collectanea* no 612, the source being Diogenianus 5.92.
6 oracle] See *Adagia* II i 79; the Latin translation here was added in *1515*.

28 This was in the *Collectanea*, no 416, with no ancient source named, but no doubt
from Diogenianus 2.17 (it is also in Zenobius 1.70; cf Suidas A 1388). Erasmus
also adds there that the monkey trying to deceive the fox was a common
vernacular proverb of his own day. Otto 1939
4 Horace] *Ars poetica* 437
5 Aristophanes] *Wasps* 1240, inserted in *1528*
8 Nonius] See I i 97n; p 46, citing Varro's *Menippean Satires* 327 (see I ii 60n).
9 Horace] *Ars poetica* 246
10 proverb] *Adagia* III vii 76; cross-reference added in *1528*

29 *Collectanea* no 151 gave the proverb from Diogenianus 7.65 (it is also in Suidas
II 2745), and cited Epimenides. Otto 463; Suringar 45; Tilley c 822 Use craft
against Cretans.
4 Plutarch] *Lysander* 20, added in *1520*; *Paulus Aemilius* 23, added in *1526*

as the saying is,' and again in the life of Paulus Aemilius, 'It was not at all   5
hidden from those who knew him well that he was playing Cretan with the
Cretans.' The vanity of the Cretans, as for instance about the sepulchre of
Jove which they claimed to have, with many other lies of the same sort,
became a common proverb; the line of Epimenides quoted by the Apostle
Paul testifies to this: 'Cretans are always liars, evil beasts, slow bellies.' St   10
Jerome in his commentary on this Epistle indicates that this line is to be
found in a work of Epimenides entitled *On Oracles*. Hence Paul also calls him
a prophet, either in jest or because the subject warrants it. The opening of
this poem, 'Cretans are always liars,' was used by the poet Callimachus of
Cyrene in a hymn which he wrote against the Cretans and in honour of Jove,   15
accusing them of absurdity because they boasted that they could show
Jove's tomb, although he was immortal. Thinking of this, Ovid remarks,
'Cretans do not invent everything.' Hence the verb *kretizein*, to play Cretan,
is used in Greek to mean 'tell lies.'

Suidas gives another origin for the adage, when he writes that the   20
Cretan Idomeneus, who was given the job of distributing money collected
from the spoils taken from the enemy, allocated far the best part of it to
himself. So it seems to fit those who defraud others and always consider
their own advantage more zealously. He thinks the adage is applicable to
those who try in vain to use lies against a specialist in lying. As the common   25
saying goes, it is most difficult to rob thieves, and equally difficult to get
away with lying to liars.

30   **Cum Care Carizas**
You are Carizing with a Carian

Diogenianus lists something very similar to this: Πρὸς Κάρα καρίζεις, You

* * * * *

9 Epimenides] Greek half-mythical religious poet of the sixth century BC (frag 1),
cited by St Paul, Epistle to Titus 1.12
11-17 Jerome] In his commentary on the passage in St Paul (and also in his *Letters*
70.2.2), where he picks up the quotation in Callimachus' *Hymn to Zeus* (*Hymns*
1.8 wrongly described as an attack on the Cretans). This, down to 'immortal,'
was inserted in 1515. The *Hymns* of Callimachus, a leading poet of the third
century BC, had been printed by Janus Lascaris about 1496; but Erasmus may be
using the Aldine of 1513.
17 Ovid] *Amores* 3.10.19
20 Suidas] κ 2407. In 1508 Erasmus wrote 'distributing to the Greeks the money of
the Laphyrians,' having taken *laphyra*, the Greek for 'spoils,' as a proper name;
this was set right in 1528.

30 From Diogenianus 7.65, the explanation added in 1523. Also in Suidas II 2717.
For the Carians, see *Adagia* I ii 65; I vi 14.

are Carizing with a Carian, that is to say, you are acting the rustic with a
rustic, talking barbarous language to a barbarian, or stupidly to the stupid.   5
The Carians are a people of Phrygia, whom we shall mention in another
place; their way of life gave rise to several proverbs.

31 **Cretensis mare**
    The Cretan and the sea

Ὃ Κρῆς τὴν θάλασσαν, The Cretan (supply, is ignorant or frightened of) the
sea. This proverb is quoted and explained at the same time by Strabo in his
Geography, book 10, where he writes that the Cretans took a foremost place   5
through their skill in navigation and their experience in maritime matters;
and hence a proverb grew up in ancient times, 'a Cretan knows nothing of
the sea,' applied to people who pretend to be ignorant of something they are
particularly skilled in. For how could the Cretans, island-dwellers as they
are, be ignorant of the sea which completely surrounds them? Aristides also   10
made use of this in *Pericles*, The Cretan and the sea, and Zenodotus writes
that it is to be found in Alcaeus. It is like what Horace says in his *Epistle to
Octavius*, 'Even I who say I never wrote a line am found a bigger liar than a
Parthian.' This is because the Parthians are at their fighting best when they
simulate flight.   15

                * * * * *

31 The source of this is no doubt Strabo; but since Erasmus seems to have been
    using, as he normally does, the Latin version, the Greek of his proverb
    probably comes from Zenobius. The adage is also in Suidas o 120.
4   Strabo] see I i 69n; *Geographica* 10.4.17
10 Aristides] See I i 13n; *De quattuor* p 186 Dindorf. Erasmus used Aelius Aristides
    in manuscript when he was staying with Aldus and preparing *1508*, and this is
    perhaps the only reference to him which was added in a later edition. The
    explanation may be that in *1508* I ii 31 was behind him and no longer in his mind
    when he came to the adage in Aristides, and he put it in II x 10; and it was only
    in *1517/8* that it was placed here, not from the original, to which he no longer
    had access but from the later passage.
11 Zenodotus] Zenobius 5.30, quoting the great Lesbian lyric poet (whose author-
    ship is, however, not certain) frag incert 15 in *Poetarum Lesbiorum fragmenta*
    ed E. Lobel and D.L. Page (Oxford 1955) 294
12 Horace] *Epistles* 2.1.111–2, added in *1533*. This does not seem to have been
    treated as a proverb. The Parthians, great horsemen and bowmen on Rome's
    eastern frontier, were proverbial for their tactics of galloping away and then
    turning round and discharging volleys of arrows at their pursuers, and
    Erasmus must have known this well (see his introduction, section xiii, line 181);
    the proverb which still survives, A Parthian shot, does not appear in the
    Adagia, but Tilley P 80 has The Parthians fight running away.

32 **Ad umbilicum ducere**
    To bring to the scroll's end

In a number of authors we find proverbs about bringing things to a close,
and one of these is *Ad umbilicum ducere*, To bring to the scroll-end, meaning
to complete and finish a book. The 'navels,' or scroll-ends, according to   5
Porphyrion, are those ornaments made of bone, wood or horn, in the shape
of the human navel, which were added to a finished scroll, and hence the
proverbial metaphor 'he got to the navel,' that is, to the end. Horace in the
Epodes:

> For the god, the god forbids me   10
> To bring to an end the swift measures begun,
> The song promised of yore.

Martial in the fourth book of the *Epigrams*:

> Ho there! 'tis enough, my little book.
> We have now come to the very end; you still   15
> Want to go on further and keep on going.

Again in book 5: '[a book] which, spruce with cedar oil and purple, has fully
grown with its black knobs.' Again in book 3:

> Now you may strut abroad, anointed with cedar-oil,
> And bright with the twin garnish of your brows,   20
> Run riot with your painted bosses.

Again in book 11: 'You return me my book unrolled to its very horns, /And
as if, Septitianus, you had read it through.' I am not sure whether this
proverb could be transferred to something other than a book or a poem – it
might strain the metaphor.   25

* * * * *

32 *Collectanea* no 774 gives the Horace reference. Otto 1816
 8 Horace] *Epodes* 14.6–8 (called *Odes* in *1508*, which is Erasmus' usual practice,
    but this was corrected in *1523*). Porphyrion is the scholar whose name is given
    to an ancient commentary on Horace.
13 Martial] 4.89.1–3; 5.6.14–5; 3.2.7–9; 11.107.1–2. The ancient book being in the
    form of a roll, to finish reading one meant unrolling it down to the stick on
    which it was wound; and in an expensive copy of a book this stick might be
    ornamented with a turned knob of wood or even ivory at either end, called
    umbilicus, normally the word for 'navel.' For modern books we say 'from cover
    to cover.'

33 **Summum fastigium imponere**
To put on the coping-stone

A more general metaphor is 'to put on the coping-stone,' meaning to finish
something in all its parts. You will find instances in Cicero, *De officiis*, book
3, and sometimes in the letters of Pliny. This comes from builders, who on   5
finishing a building, usually place some sign of completion on the top. Just
as the foundation is the very beginning of their work, so the coping-stone is
the last point of the finished building. So 'to lay the foundations' comes to
mean to start on something, and 'to put on the coping' means to complete
something, to add the final touch, as they call it. This is close to the Greek   10
expression, 'he set down the colophon' (full stop).

34 **Summam manum addere**
To add the final touch

To add the final touch has the same sense, and is obviously taken from
craftsmen who rough out a first attempt or mock-up of the work and call this
the first touch [*prima manus*], then shape it more exactly, and finally polish it   5
with the utmost care; and this they call the *suprema* or *summa manus*, the final
touch. Ovid says, 'No patient reading will those works receive, / Unless it's
known they lack the final touch.' Just afterwards he uses the 'file' for the
same meaning: 'Taken untimely from the anvil, that; / My writings lack the
last touch of the file.' Seneca to Lucilius: 'Devotees of wine are particularly   10
pleased by the last drink, the one which sinks them, which puts the final
touch to their intoxication.' By the same metaphor we say, nothing is lacking
but the 'extreme' touch. Instances of this are too frequent in literature for any
other references to be necessary.

* * * * *

33 This is a metaphor, which can hardly be described as proverbial.
   4 Cicero] *De officiis* 3.7.33
   5 Pliny] the Younger *Letters* 2.1.2
   10 as they call it] See the next adage.
   10 Greek expression] See *Adagia* II iii 45.

34 This was combined in *Collectanea* no 774 with our no 32. Otto 1051
   7 Ovid] *Tristia* 1.7.27–8, 29–30; added in *1536*
   10 Seneca] *Letters* 12.4, inserted in *1515*

35 **Supremum fabulae actum addere**
   To add a last act to the play

This comes in the same category: to add a last act to the play means to bring
to a termination, arising from the poets who write comedies and tragedies
and cut up their plays into acts. So Horace says, 'Five acts, no more.' They   5
usually take most care with the last act, as Cicero writes to his brother
Quintus: 'I end my letter by imploring and urging you that – after the
fashion of good poets and hard-working actors – you should take particular
pains with the last phase and finale of your office and employment; so that
this third year of your rule may, like the third act of a play, be recognized as   10
having been the most highly finished and brilliantly staged of the three.'
Again to Atticus, book 13: 'At this point the play was over, but I wanted to
fill up the page.' In his *Cato* Cicero transfers the metaphor to the end of life.
In the same way Apuleius in his *Florida*, book 3, speaking of Philemon the
playwright, says 'They announced that the poet Philemon, who was waited   15
for to finish off a fictitious plot on the stage, had already completed the true
story at home. For he had already said "Farewell, and give me your applause" to human affairs.' I think the remark of Lucilius in Nonius belongs to
this class: 'It is for a stitcher of patches to sew his last bit of patchwork best.'

36 **Catastrophe fabulae**
   The dénouement of the play

We call the outcome of anything, in proverbial language, the *catastrophe* or
dénouement. Speaking of proverbial metaphors, I have pointed out that each
discipline or type of craftmanship has its own set of terms, which are used   5
out of superstition, I might say, as is usually done in rites and ceremonies

* * * * *

35 The immediate source of this is not clear; it is an image often used by Erasmus in
   his letters referring to his own life.
   5 Horace] *Ars poetica* 189
   6 Cicero] *Ad Quintum fratrem* 1.1.46, the Latin text added in *1515*; *Ad Atticum*
     13.34; *De senectute* (often known as the *Cato major*) 23.85, added in *1523*
   14 Apuleius] See I i 15n; *Florida* 16, the full quotation given for the first time in
     1523; previously it had been loosely referred to from memory.
   18 Lucilius] The great Roman satirist of the second century BC; 747 in the edition of
     the fragments by F. Marx (Leipzig 1904), cited by Nonius (see I i 97n) p 175.
     This was added here in *1515*, and in *1533* was promoted to stand as an adage on
     its own (v i 65).

   36 From Donatus

and magical incantations; and when these are diverted to another use, they
take on the look of a proverb. For instance, from military discipline we get to
sound the retreat, to give ground, the first line, they fell back on the old
guard [*triarii*]. From music, we get prelude for preface, or for the start of   10
something; top string, lowest string, for loud or deep tone; to strike the same
wrong note, for to make the same mistake often. Every plot, as Donatus
shows, is divided into three parts, *protasis, epitasis* and *catastrophe*. The
protasis is the first excitement, swelling as it goes on. The *epitasis* is a flurry
of complications. The *catastrophe* is a sudden transformation of the whole   15
thing. So Lucian elegantly calls the outcome or result of an affair its
catastrophe in several places, and particularly in his work *On Salaried Posts*:
'And in the end of all what the *catastrophe* of the drama is' (that is, what
outcome there is to their servitude). And in *Alexander the False Prophet*: 'This
is the conclusion of the tragedy of Alexander.' And in the *Life of Peregrinus*: 'I   20
see you again, good Cronius, laughing at the *dénouement* of the play.'

37   **A capite usque ad calcem**
      From head to heel

When we mean the whole of something, we say From head to heel. There
are three ways of using this proverbial expression. It may refer to the body,
the mind, or the circumstances; the two last are the more pleasing, doubtless   5
because they are more metaphorical.
      Homer applies it to the body, *Iliad* 23: 'From head to feet,' and so does
Theocritus in the *Boukoliskos*: 'And she looked me over from head to toe.'
Plautus in the *Epidicus*, 'Look, Epidicus, from the toenail to the topmost
hair.' Horace: 'Beautiful from head to heel.' Cicero, in his *Pro Roscio comoedo*,   10
says: 'Does not his very head, and those completely shaven eyebrows, seem
to breathe out malice, and proclaim cunning? If any indication is given to

* * * * *

12 to make the same mistake often] This clause was added in *1515*.
12 Donatus] *Excerpta de comoedia* 7.1 (prefixed to his commentary on Terence)
16 Lucian] *De mercede conductis* 10, the Latin version added in *1515*; *Alexander* 60;
      De morte Peregrini 37, added in *1523* (the Latin version not till *1528*)

37 Three of these passages were cited in *Collectanea* no 82. Otto 1822; Tilley c 864
      From the crown of the head to the sole of the foot, т 436 From top to toe.
      According to Otto, this wording for the proverb is not ancient.
  7 Homer] *Iliad* 23.169
  8 Theocritus] 20.12; Erasmus often refers to the *Idylls* by title rather than number.
  9 Plautus] *Epidicus* 622–3
10 Horace] *Epistles* 2.2.4
10 Cicero] *Pro Q. Roscio comoedo* 7.20

men by the physical appearance, without words, does he not seem entirely
made up of fraud, deceit and lies, from his very toenails to the top of his
head?'   15

Aristophanes in the *Plutus* applies it to circumstances: 'Listen then,
since I shall tell you the whole thing, From the feet up to the head', though
here the comic poet amusingly transposes head and feet. St Jerome, in the
preface to the book called in Hebrew the *Book Of Days*, says: 'With his help
I collated it from the head, as they say, down to the last toenail.'   20

This can be transferred to the mind, in this way: 'I will describe his ways
and his mind, in a word the very man himself, from the topmost hair, as
they say, to the tip of his very heel'; though the instance from Cicero we
have just quoted seems to belong to the mind more than to the body. The
adage is used differently again when we speak of the 'head of the business,'   25
meaning the chief originator, just as when we speak of the fount of something. Terence says 'You are the head of this affair,' and the Greeks τὸ
κεφάλαιον, 'the gist (head) of the matter.' Lucian in the *Tyrannicide* talks
about the 'head of tyranny,' and Plato in the third book of the *Laws* said 'the
fount of sedition.' Then we have 'to arrive at the heel, in the heel of the   30
work, at the very heel of your letter'; 'to start from the very head,' 'to run
back from heel to head,' and other forms of this way of speaking, which are
to be found in all the authors. Plutarch 'Against the Stoics': 'From the
opening and beginning right to the crown.'

38   **Cursu lampada trado**
     I hand on the torch in the race

Cursu lampada tradere, To hand on the torch in the race, is a proverbial
metaphor, meaning to pass on the part you have played, as it were, to
different people in succession. Lucretius: 'Like runners they hand on the   5

* * * * *

16 Aristophanes] *Plutus* 649–50, the comment added in *1515*
18 Jerome] Praefatio in lib. Paralipomenon (*P L* 30.432)
27 Terence] *Adelphoe* 568. This is more fully developed in II i 61.
28 Lucian] *Tyrannicida* 144
29 Plato] *Laws* 3.690d
33 Plutarch] *Moralia* 1066A, added in *1515*. In *1526* this phrase was promoted to
   stand on its own, IV vi 20.

38 The passages from Varro Cicero and Persius were cited already in *Collectanea* no
   10. Otto 909
 5 Lucretius] *De rerum natura* 2.79. The great philosophical poet of the first
   century BC is cited in the *Adagia* only four times.

torch of life.' The reference is to living creatures which propagate themselves by succession, so that life is passed on from one to another turn by
turn. Varro in his *Agriculture*, book 3 chapter 15: 'But, my dear Merula, for
fear that our friend Axius may learn some natural history while listening to
this, as I have made no mention of profit, I am handing over to you the torch   10
in the race.' By these words he indicates that he is handing over the other
part of his speech to Merula, and the latter takes his turn in speaking.
Lucretius seems to have imitated Plato, who writes in the *Laws*, book 6, that
the citizens should take care in begetting and educating children, so that
they may pass on, like a burning torch, that life which they themselves   15
received from their forebears. That phrase of Persius comes in here: 'You
who are before me, why beg me to hand on the torch in the race?' Aristophanes in the *Frogs*: 'But the torch no one can carry yet, / Because of lack of
training.' He is rebuking the idleness and inertia of the citizens. The commentator adds here that the ancients used to carry torches in three sets of   20
games, those sacred to Prometheus, to Vulcan, and to Athena (the Panathe-
naia). Prometheus is believed to have been the first to institute this kind of
games, in which the runners carried lighted torches. Each runner when tired
handed the torch to the next, and he in his turn, wearied, gave it to another,
and so it was successively handed on, thus symbolically re-enacting the   25
story of Prometheus; and how, as he flew down to earth, he kept perpetually
waving the fennel-stalk in which he had taken some of the celestial fire, to
prevent its going out again. Plato mentions this in the *Republic*, book 1,
indicating that torch-processions were held in honour of Minerva too.

　　Pausanias, however, gives lengthier description of the ceremony of   30
these games in his *Attica*. Herodotus also recalls it, but briefly, in *Urania*,
where he says that this custom was established by the Persians; horses and
men were posted at intervals and one handed on the despatches to another,
like torches, so that they might be passed along more quickly. The writer of
the *Rhetorica ad Herennium* says: 'It is not the same thing as in the palaestra,   35
where the runner who receives the burning torch is swifter as he takes up
the race than the one who hands it over; if it were the same, the general who

* * * * *

8 Varro] *Res rusticae* 3.16.9 (see I i 40n). The text current in Erasmus' day does not
　make sense.
13 Plato] *Laws* 6.776b
16 Persius] *Satires* 6.61
17 Aristophanes] *Frogs* 1087–8
28 Plato] *Republic* 1.328a
30 Pausanias] 1.30.2 (see I i 90n).
31 Herodotus] 8.98 (see I i 96n); added in *1515*.
34 The writer] *Rhetorica ad Herennium* (traditionally ascribed to Cicero) 4.46.59

takes over the army would be a better general than the one who gives it up.
In the race it is the tired man who hands the torch to the fresh one; here it is
the experienced general who gives the army to a raw successor.' Thus a man   40
will be said to 'hand on the torch' when, tired out or at the end of his time, he
gives up his office to be carried on by others. And on the other hand they
also 'hand on the torch' who, in the words of Terence, 'help each other out,'
and render assistance one to the other.

39 **Principium dimidium totius**
    Well begun is half done

Ἀρχὴ ἥμισυ παντός, Well begun is half done. This adage signifies that it is in
the tackling of a task that the greatest difficulty lies. It is a half-line from
Hesiod, quoted by Lucian in *Hermotimus*. Aristotle also refers to it in the   5
Politics, book 5, and Plato in the *Laws*, book 6: 'For in proverbs it is said that
the beginning is half of a whole action, and everyone always praises a good
beginning. But, as it seems to me, it is more than half, and no one has ever
praised sufficiently a beginning well made.' Suidas quotes from a certain
Marinus: 'That was the beginning for us, and not only the beginning, nor as   10
the proverb has it half of the whole, but the complete thing itself.' Aristotle
in the *Ethics*, book 1: 'The beginning is said to be more than half of the
whole.' Horace in the *Epistles*: 'Who sets about hath half performed his deed;
/ Dare to be wise.' Ausonius: 'Begin, for half the deed is in beginning; /
Begin the other half, and you will finish.' Plutarch, in his essay 'On How to   15

* * * * *

43 Terence] *Phormio* 267. The phrase forms I vii 97.

39 *Collectanea* no 298 gave the passages from Hesiod and Horace. Otto 557; Tilley B
    254 Well begun is half done. The Greek proverb is found in Diogenianus 2.97
    and Suidas A 4097; Clearchus frag 74 (see Erasmus' Introduction section xiii line
    79) derives it from Sparta.
5   Hesiod] *Works and Days* 40, cited by Lucian *Hermotimus* 3; this and the next
    were added in 1523.
5   Aristotle] *Politics* 5.4 (1303b29)
6   Plato] *Laws* 6.753e, used again in 1528 in I ix 95 with a different Latin version.
9   Suidas] A 4091. In 1526 the quotation was added by a blundering secretary to I
    ix 95; see Erasmus' indignant rejection in Ep 3093, printed at the end of that
    edition.
11 Aristotle] *Ethica Nicomachea* 1.7 (1098b7)
13 Horace] *Epistles* 1.2.40
14 Ausonius] *Epigrammata* 15(81). He was a professor in Bordeaux in the fourth
    century AD.
15 Plutarch] *Moralia* 16A, citing Sophocles frag 747 Nauck

Study Poetry,' quotes these verses from Sophocles: 'For someone who begins well every deed, / 'Tis likely that's the way the end will be.'

40 Satius est initiis mederi quam fini
Doctoring is better first than last

Ἀρχὴν ἰᾶσθαι πολὺ λώϊον ἠὲ τελευτὴν, Doctoring is better first than last. Suidas quotes this as a proverb. Theognis says the same thing: 'Apply the treatment when disease begins.' Similarly, Persius, in the third *Satire*: 'In 5 vain you'll see them cry for hellebore, / When the sick flesh swells up; forestall the ill.' And also Ovid: 'Doctoring comes too late, / When evils have grown strong through long delay.' The adage warns us that it takes less trouble to remove an evil at the beginning, when it is still fresh, than after it has existed for a long time; that children must be sheltered from vices when 10 they are at a tender and tractable age, and animosities must be healed at once, lest they grow into strife. The smallest ills must be shunned, from which greater often spring up. Occasions must be avoided which are likely to bring to birth any kind of evil.

41 Serere ne dubites
Do not hesitate to plant

This is a country adage, but not unworthy to be included in this book: Do not hesitate to plant. It warns us not to be lazy about attempting any of those things from which a great result can come for very little outlay, if not at once, 5 at least later on; if not for ourselves, at least for posterity. Columella in the twelfth book of his *Agriculture*: 'And so that common saying about planting trees is used by countrymen, "Do not hesitate to plant."' For building often

* * * * *

40 Tilley E 202 It is good to prevent an evil at the beginning; P 569 Prevention is better than cure.
4 Suidas] A 4098
4 Theognis] See I i 62n; 1134.
5 Persius] *Satires* 3.63–4. So it finally became in *1526*. Before that, only the words 'forestall the ill' were given, and in *1508* they were ascribed to Ovid. Persius replaced him in *1515*, and was ousted by him once more in *1517/8* and the editions that followed.
7 Ovid] *Remedia amoris* 91–2

41 Otto 1631
6 Columella] *Res rustica* 11.1.29; cf I i 37.

exhausts an income, commerce depends on chance and many a man has lost
by it; similarly most things have their disadvantages or dangers, but from   10
the planting of trees the greatest advantage is to be obtained, and it is done
at little cost. Virgil expresses this figuratively when he says in the second
book of the *Georgics*: 'Do we still doubt to plant, and spend our care?'

42   **Talaria induere**
     To put wings on one's feet

There is a proverbial allegory in Cicero, 'to put on winged sandals,' meaning
to get ready to flee, and to be willing, as it were, to take flight somewhere: so
he writes to Atticus, book 14, 'That lot are scared of peace, every man of   5
them. So I had best find wings for my boots.' It comes from Homer, who
often puts wings on the heels of Mercury as he takes flight:

> Straight then he shod his feet with lovely sandals,
> Golden, ambrosial-scented and they bore him
> Through limpid air and over boundless lands   10
> Swift as the wind.

It is this passage in Homer which Virgil more or less adapts in the *Aeneid*,
book 4:

> And first he buckled on
> His golden shoes, which high o'er earth and sea   15
> Winged him along as rapid as the wind.

So we say those who prepare to run away 'put wings on their feet.' For the
very terms *avolare* and *revolare* [fly off, fly back] are often used by Cicero for
'to flee' and 'to return.'

* * * * *

12 Virgil] *Georgics* 2.433, probably from memory

42 From Cicero. Otto 1738. Literally, To put on winged sandals
 3 Cicero] *Ad Atticum* 14.21.4
 6 Homer] *Iliad* 24.340–2; *Odyssey* 1.96–8. In *1508* only one line of Latin version
   was provided; three more were added in *1517/8*, and the last was reshaped in
   1528. Already used in I i 97
12 Virgil] *Aeneid* 4.239–41

43 Tricae; apinae
Stuff and nonsense

Tricae and *apinae*, stuff and nonsense, were popular names for trifling
worthless things. Martial: 'The games I played in youth and childhood
once, / My nonsense-tricks,' and again ''Tis stuff and nonsense – worse, if   5
worse there be.' Hence they used *tricari*, which is the same metaphor, of
wasting time on nonsense. Cicero has it in several places, for instance in the
Letters to Atticus, book 15: 'He's full of nonsense of course, like the man he
is.' And again: 'Balbus is full of nonsense.' This adage arose from an actual
event. Trica and Apina were once towns in Apulia, as Pliny shows in his   10
Natural History, book 3 chapter 11, where he is speaking of the bays on the
coast of Europe: 'There Diomede wiped out tribes called Monadi and Dardi,
and two towns which proverbially have become a byword, Apina and Trica.'
Stephanus indicates that Trica was a town in Thessaly, the name being
derived from Trica, a daughter of Peneus. Nonius Marcellus takes *tricae* to   15
mean hindrances and complications, from the Greek word for hair, in which
chickens are wrapped up; hence our words 'extricate' and 'intricate.' Lucilius, whom he also quotes, has a word *tricones* for those whose nonsense
wastes people's time, and *tricinus quaestus* for late or meagre, and *tricae
Attellanae* in Varro for very complicated nonsense. I would not rule out the   20
allusion to hair, but the derivation from the town is more likely to be right.
Pliny, book 8 chapter 48, points out that sheep are valued for shortness in
the leg and well-clad underparts, and those with bare underparts he called
apicae, as rejects to be weeded out.

* * * * *

43 Built round the two quotations from Martial and one from Pliny, which formed
Collectanea no 654. Otto 127

4 Martial] 1.113.1–2; 14.1.7

7 Cicero] *Ad Atticum* 15.13a.1; the word comes again, without mention of Balbus,
in 14.19.4

10 Pliny] *Naturalis historia* 3.104

14 Stephanus] Steph. Byzantius p 635 Meineke. His geographical lexicon,
perhaps of the fifth century AD, was first printed by Aldus in 1502, and is used
mainly in the second thousand of the *Adagia* and later. The standard text is that
of A. Meineke, Berlin 1849.

15 Nonius] See I i 97n; p 8, citing Lucilius 416; see I ii 35n. The MSS of Nonius give
tricae, and Erasmus interprets this as the Greek word for hair, *triches*. The
modern editor, W.M. Lindsay, ascribes this suggestion to Joseph Mercer,
whose edition of Nonius did not appear till 1583.

19 *tricinus*] This and *tricas Attellanas* are fragments from the *Menippean Satires* of
Varro (see I ii 60n), preserved by the same Nonius in his dictionary pp 18 and 9.
From here to the end of the paragraph we have an addition of *1515*.

22 Pliny] *Naturalis historia* 8. 198; the book-number was given correctly in *1515*.

44 **Corycaeus auscultavit**
    A Corycaean was listening

Κωρυκαῖος ἠκροάζετο, A Corycaean was listening. This is used when someone has tried to conceal what he is doing but is found out by the inquisitive.
How this adage arose, I will explain from the authorities. Corycus is a   5
mountain in Pamphylia, very high and well supplied with harbours, and for
this reason it offers great opportunities for lurking pirates, who were called
Corycaeans after this mountain. These people had invented a new system of
secret attack. They scattered out among the harbours of Mount Corycus,
and mingled with the merchants on their arrival, so as to learn by eaves-   10
dropping what kind of cargo they carried, what their destination was, and at
what time they had decided to weigh anchor. As soon as they knew this,
they reported it to the pirates, with whom they were in partnership for
robbery on the high seas. And so at the right moment they attacked together
and looted the ships. When the merchants found this out they kept their   15
arrangements quiet and under cover, for fear of ambush. But even so they
did not succeed in keeping their affairs dark, as the Corycaeans smelt out
everything, and hence the proverb arose: 'A Corycaean was listening to
him.' It expresses something closely covered up and yet found out.
      Suidas says that Corycus is a promontory in Pamphylia, and the city of   20
Attalea is adjacent to it. The citizens of this town took steps not be harried

      * * * * *

44 We can see here how this book grew. In the *Collectanea* of 1500, the adage was
    illustrated by a shortened paraphrase of a passage from Strabo and a quotation
    from Cicero's *Letters to Atticus*. In the second sentence of the text of *1508*,
    Erasmus named his sources as Strabo and Zenodotus; this means Zenobius
    4.75, the presence of which we might otherwise not have detected, since he
    tells us much the same as Strabo. The *1508* text begins with a Latin paraphrase
    of the same Strabo passage at much greater length, and builds onto this out of
    Suidas and Stephanus (whose work had been published by Aldus in 1502);
    Cicero still provides the conclusion, though Erasmus has evidently gone back
    to the original, for the quotation is longer than it was in 1500. In *1528* he returns
    to the task, and gives us a much longer extract from Strabo in the original Greek
    (first published by Aldus in 1516) with a Latin version, but without cancelling
    the earlier paraphrase, as he well might have done. To this he adds two things
    which strictly are irrelevant to the proverb, a discussion of the position of
    Corycus nourished from the same sources with the addition of Mela the
    geographer, and an extract from the lexicon of Hesychius on other meanings of
    the name. His advancing knowledge crystallizes round the original theme.
  5 from the authorities] So *1528*; in *1508* 'partly from Strabo and partly from
    Zenodotus'; see above.
 20 Suidas] κ 2299; *Talaea*, from the Milan edition of 1499, became *Atalea* in *1520*,
    from Aldus' new edition of the Greek (1514).

themselves by the robbers who used the promontory as their stronghold: they spread out among the other harbours and listened to find out who had put into port and where they were going, and gave this information to the robbers. The same author quotes Ephorus as saying that the Corycaeans 25 were a mixed gang of people who founded a little town in Lydia under the peak of Corycus, which looks out to sea; they were close to Myonessus. These used to mingle with the merchants who landed at the port, as if they were also merchants, wishing to buy some commodities; and then they reported what they had come to know to the Myonessians. These latter went 30 in to the attack against the seamen and shared out with the Corycaeans either the booty taken or the ransom paid by merchants, the Greek for which is *lytra*. But according to Stephanus, Corycus is a very high mountain close to the town of Teos in Ionia, and the harbour of the same name is adjacent to it. He comments here on the stratagems of the pirates and on the proverb. 35

Strabo too gives an opinion about the Lydian Corycus; I give his words out of book 14: 'Before coming to Erythrae you come first to Eras, a small town of the Teians and then to Corycus, a lofty mountain, and to a port below it, Casystes, and to another port called Erythras and a number of others after that. They say the coastline of the mountain was frequented by 40 pirates, the Corycaeans, so-called, who had devised a new way to attack ships. Scattering themselves among the ports they would follow the merchants whose ships were anchored there, and overhear what they had on board and where they were going, and then they would come together and attack them after they were at sea and plunder the ships. Thus we call every 45 busybody who is eager to hear whatever is said in secret "a Corycaean," and say proverbially "the Corycaean was listening" whenever someone seems to himself to have acted or spoken in private and yet has not kept himself hidden, owing to the people who eavesdrop and want to know things which are no business of theirs.' So far Strabo. In these words there seems to be 50 some corruption of the text; one will be cured by reading ληστῶν for ληστήρια, the other by inserting πραττομένων καὶ before διαλεγομένων, as the translator seems to have done. As there are two cities of the same name, the authorities trace the proverb to both of them. Stephanus explains that in Cilicia also there is a city called Corycus, 'surrounded by a harbour and the 55

* * * * *

25 Ephorus] The lost fourth-century historian; *FGrHist* 70F27
26 in Lydia] These words were inserted in *1528*.
33 Stephanus] Steph. Byzantius (see I ii 43n) p 401 Meineke.
36 Strabo] See I i 69n; *Geographica* 14.1.32, added in *1528* with most of what follows.
51 corruption of the text] Neither of Erasmus' suggestions is needed.

open sea,' as Pomponius Mela says, 'and joined to the mainland by a narrow isthmus'; close by it is that famous cave celebrated in literature. Now we have been told that the Cilicians were pirates. I think this is the same city as the one which Zenodotus and Suidas place in Pamphylia, because Pamphylia borders on Cilicia, and formerly a good part of Cilicia was attributed to   60
Pamphylia. The same Stephanus indicates that there was also an island of the same name; and again that Corycia was a promontory of Crete, and that there was a harbour of that name in Ethiopia.

The writers of comedy introduce a certain Corycaeus, a god, who lends an ear and listens to what goes on: so Menander in his *Enchiridion* and   65
Dexippus in his *Thesaurus*, according to Suidas. Hesychius also had a few words about it, explaining that in Greek *corycus* means a leather bottle, a boat, or a javelin. Cicero uses this adage in the tenth book of his *Letters to Atticus*, the last letter: 'So henceforward I won't write to you what I am going to do, only what I have actually done. Every spy in the country ("all the   70
Corycaeans") seems to have an ear to catch what I say.'

45   **Fortes fortuna adiuvat**
      Fortune favours the brave

Cicero, *Tusculan Questions*, book 2: 'For it is not only Fortune which favours the brave, as the old proverb has it, but still more, reason.' This is quoted elsewhere out of Ennius. It is used in the *Aeneid* of Virgil, and pretty well   5
everywhere by everybody. Ovid in book 2 of the *Fasti*: 'Chance and God

* * * * *

56 Pomponius Mela] 1.71; he is a minor Latin geographer of the first century AD.
59 Zenodotus] Zenobius 4.75 (Erasmus always calls him Zenodotus)
59 Suidas] E 2299, already quoted
64 writers of comedy] Menander (see I i 7n) frag 137, cited by Zenobius and Suidas, and Dioxippus frag 2 Kock, cited by Suidas. This was already in *1508*.
66 Hesychius] See Erasmus' Introduction, section v n; K 4884, inserted in *1528*. The word translated by Erasmus 'javelin' (*lanceam*) seems really to mean a leathern quiver.
68 Cicero] *Ad Atticum* 10.18.1; ascribed to book 2 in *1508* (corrected in *1523*)

45 Otto 702; Tilley F 601 Fortune favours the bold.
 3 Cicero] *Tusculanae disputationes* 2.4.11
 5 Ennius] *Annals* 257, cited by Macrobius 6.1.62. For the fragments of this, the greatest of the early Roman poets, we use the line-numbering of *Ennianae poeseos reliquiae*, ed J. Vahlen, Leipzig 1903.
 5 Virgil] *Aeneid* 10.284
 6 Ovid] *Fasti* 2.782, added in *1520*. The second line, labelled Ovid in *1508*, is in fact Tibullus 1.2.16, quoted from memory.

help those who dare.' And again he alluded to it with: 'Venus herself
favours the bold.' Then Livy in the *Macedonian War*, book 4: 'They used to
say that Fortune favours the brave.' The adage advises us to make a strong
bid for Fortune; for it is for people who do this that things go well. For   10
Fortune seems to favour that kind of man, but to be inimical to those who
dare make no experiments, but for ever hide away in their shells like snails.

46   Currentem incitare
       To cheer on the runner

Τὸν τρέχοντα ὀτρύνειν, To cheer on the runner, is to encourage someone to
do the very thing he is inclined to do of his own accord. By using this
metaphor we lessen, or indeed remove, the danger of offending by exhorta-   5
tion. Cicero to Cassius: 'So as to meet Caesar in Italy (for that is what I
supposed) and to cheer on the runner as the adage has it, when after sparing
so many of our most distinguished men, he was actually returning to the
ways of peace.' Again to his brother Quintus, book 2: 'You are therefore
acting indeed like a brother in urging me (though at the present moment,   10
upon my honour, you are cheering on a willing runner).' Again to Atticus:
'When you exhort me to spend those days in the exposition of philosophy
you are urging a willing runner.' Again in the *De oratore*: 'For it is easier to
urge on the willing runner, as they say, than to stir up an inert one.' Pliny to

* * * * *

8 Livy] 37.37.4, added in 1520. *Macedonian War* is a name for the fourth decade
   (group of ten books) of his history of Rome.

46 The Greek form of this provided by the *Corpus paroemiographorum* (Apostolius
   16.100) is not identical, and it may be that Erasmus produced a Greek
   equivalent himself by a kind of cross between Homer and Cicero. There is a
   Homeric supplement in III viii 32. This and the next are very close, and are both
   covered by Otto 486; but neither quite conveys the sense in which 'to spur a
   willing horse' is often used now – to lay fresh burdens on someone who is
   cheerfully doing as much as he can already. In the *Collectanea* this was covered
   by no 254 Strenuos equos non esse opere defatigandos, Do not exhaust an
   active horse by overloading it; and one suspects that Erasmus, like many of us
   at different times, may well have felt himself often to have been in that position.
   But he describes it as 'a modern proverb among my countrymen,' *neotericum
   apud nostrates proverbium*, and perhaps that was why it was not included in the
   Adagiorum chiliades.
 6 Cicero] *Ad familiares* 15.15.3; *Ad Quintum fratrem* 2.14.2; *Ad Atticum* 13.45.2; *De
   oratore* 2.44.186
14 Pliny] the Younger *Letters* 3.7.15, added in 1515

Cannius: 'I know you have no need of the goad, but my affection for you   15
leads me to spur on the willing runner.' The metaphor is drawn from
runners who contend in a race and are usually lent speed by the cheering.
Lucian, writing to Nigrinus, quotes from Homer: 'Courage, for as Homer
says, you are urging on him who hastens willingly.' This is found in the
Iliad, book 8: 'Why do you urge me on, great son of Atreus, / Hurrying so fast   20
of my own accord?' There is an allusion to the same thing in the *Odyssey*,
book 24: 'Speaking thus he urged on Athena, / Already very eager.' Thus we
are 'cheering the willing runner' when we call a person to a task to which he
is drawn by his own desires, for which he has a bent. Dion, for instance,
recalls that Timotheus the singer often used a certain tune called 'the song of   25
Pallas' to incite the spirit of Alexander the Great to a sudden lust for war. He
did indeed incite him, but he was on the way already, being by nature
sanguinary and with a great thirst for battle. Had it not been so, he would
never have been capable of stirring up Sardanapalus, that most effeminate
of mortals, by the same music. Terence in the *Andria* turns this to a bad   30
sense, leaving out the metaphor: 'If he's not mad enough of his own accord,
give him a push.' That favourite phrase of Cicero's comes in here, 'to check
in mid-career.' At the beginning of the *Topica*: 'Your own will-power
checked you in mid-career.' Also 'to be in mid-career' and 'to interrupt in
mid-career.'   35

47   **Calcar addere currenti**
      To spur on the running horse

The same thought, in a metaphor drawn from elsewhere, is expressed by the
younger Pliny in a letter to Pompeius Saturninus: 'You begged me to send
you something I had written, when I had determined to do that very thing   5
myself. So you spurred on a horse already running with a will.' The

* * * * *

18 Lucian] *Nigrinus* 6, referring to Homer *Iliad* 8.293–4 and *Odyssey* 24.487
24 Dion] Dion of Prusa (c AD 40–120, the sophist, also called Chrysostomus, the
golden-voiced) 1.1; this is repeated in II v 93.
30 Terence] *Andria* 692
32 Cicero] *Topica* 1.1, added in 1536

47 Otto 486. Tilley H 638 Do not spur a free horse; H 688 A running horse needs no
spur.
 4 Pliny] the Younger *Letters* 1.8.1

metaphor is taken from riders, who sometimes apply the spur to a horse
when he is already running with a will, to make him run still faster. Thus a
man spurs us on who stimulates us when we are relaxed; but to spur on the
running horse, applied to us, is to increase and sharpen the desire and   10
interest we already have. Ovid has 'No need to spur the horse in full career.'
These metaphors as a class are almost always proverbial: To put spurs to, to
ply the goad, together with their opposites: To rein in, to keep on a tight
rein, to tighten the reins. Cicero to Atticus: 'He adds his support too and,
one might say, applies the spur.' Again, to the same correspondent, in book   15
6: 'But, as Isocrates said about Ephorus and Theopompus, one of them
needs the rein, the other the spur.' Plato in the ninth book of the *Laws*: 'You
did very well, Cleinias, to check me as I was almost carried away, and make
me attentive.' And Cicero's phrase: 'He recalled him in mid-career.'

48 **In trivio sum**
    I am at the crossroads

Ἐν τριόδῳ εἰμὶ λογισμῶν, I am at the crossroads of decision. This is applied
to those who are in doubt and of uncertain mind, hesitating as to which
alternative to choose, like travellers who come to a place where three roads   5
meet, and are doubtful about which way to take. 'Way' or 'path' is often
used by Greek authors to mean a choice of plan, as Euripides uses it in the
Hecuba: 'The path of your deliberations.' Theognis says 'I am standing at the
crossroads.' Plato too has a reference to this in the *Laws*, book 7: he warns us
that if some strange and unusual thing occurs, we should not rush at it with   10
open arms, but stop as if we had come to a crossroad and did not know the
way, nor should we push on until some investigation has been made to
show where each road leads; 'like,' he says, 'a man at a crossroads.'

* * * * *

11 Ovid] *Ex Ponto* 2.6.38, probably confused in memory with *Remedia amoris* 788
14 Cicero] *Ad Atticum* 6.1.5; 6.1.12
17 Plato] *Laws* 9.857c, the Greek added in 1523
19 Cicero] *De officiis* 3.33.121

48 *Collectanea* no 350 gave a very brief treatment, derived from Diogenianus 4.59
   (the adage is also in Zenobius 3.78 and Suidas ε 1489).
7 Euripides] *Hecuba* 744
8 Theognis] 911 (see I i 62n).
9 Plato] *Laws* 7.799c

49 **Bis ac ter, quod pulchrum est**
    Beauty bears repeating twice and thrice

Δὶς καὶ τρὶς τὸ καλόν, Twice and three times over what is beautiful (supply,
should be repeated). Plato makes use of this in various places, for instance in
the *Philebus*: 'I have mentioned this before; but the proverb seems to be apt,   5
that it is right to repeat what is beautiful two and three times in conversation.' And again in the *Gorgias*: 'And they say it is a beautiful thing to speak
and consider beautiful things two and three times over.' Again in the *Laws*,
book 6: 'I say again what I said just now, for there is no harm in stating what
is beautiful twice over.' Lucian in the *Dipsades* quoting the same Plato: 10
'Never too much of the beautiful.' In general, there is such a power in
excellent things that the more often and the more closely they are examined
the more they please, as Horace says: 'This, the nearer you stand, / Will
charm the more, and please you ten times over.' On the other hand, things
which are falsely coloured or commonplace sometimes have a charm to   15
begin with, through sheer novelty, but soon grow ugly on repetition. So
Pliny, book 15, chapter 14, mentions a kind of wild fruit which they call
one-bite (*unedo*) because only one can be eaten: it is 'worthless,' he says, and
hence the reason for the name.

50 **Fratrum inter se irae sunt acerbissimae**
    The bitterest quarrels are between brothers

If strife arises between brothers, it is usually more bitter than between
ordinary enemies. Many examples of this can be found in history: Cain and

* * * * *

49 This is in the Greek proverb-collections (Zenobius 3.33; Diogenianus 4.20;
    Suidas Δ 1267), but was perhaps taken originally from Plato.
 4 Plato] *Philebus* 59e; *Gorgias* 498e; *Laws* 6.754c. These three quotations were
    added in *1523*, and replaced a reference, without the Greek, to *Laws* 12.956e:
    'Plato uses it in the last book of the *Laws* in the words "Although I have already
    touched on these topics to some extent, yet (as it says in the proverb) what is
    excellent can safely be repeated two or three times."'
10 Lucian] *Dipsades* 9
13 Horace] *Ars poetica* 361–2 and 365 run together.
17 Pliny] *Naturalis historia* 15.98–9, the reference given in *1528*; he speaks of the
    strawberry-tree, Arbutus unedo. The phrase 'only one can be eaten' was twice
    revised, in *1515* and *1517/8*; it began as 'to eat one is more than enough,' and
    there was also a change in the verb meaning 'to eat' (*gustasse, mandi, edi*),
    perhaps designed to make it sound progressively more classical.

50 Tilley H 211 No hate like to brothers' if they fall at debate.

Abel, Romulus and Remus and their like, Jacob and Esau. The son of the   5
emperor Antoninus Severus had such a dire and persistent hatred of Geta
that it could not be appeased by his most terrible death, but wreaked its fury
on all his friends as well. This is the subject of our adage, which is recorded
by Aristotle in the seventh book of the *Politics*: 'For they think that these
people should be under a duty to oblige them, and therefore, over and above   10
the loss they suffer, they feel defrauded of what was owed them. Hence the
proverb "There's no hate like brothers' hate," and those who loved beyond
measure hate beyond measure too.' Thus Aristotle. Euripides had this in
mind in the *Iphigeneia in Aulis*: 'Wretched it is for brothers to come to words, /
Wrangling in speech when they fall into strife.'   15

51   **Taurum tollet qui vitulum sustulerit**
     He may bear a bull that hath borne a calf

This adage was born in the brothel, as it seems, but it can be turned to a more
modest usage, if we wish to say that a grown man will commit greater
offences if he has been used to small vices as a boy. It can be found in the   5
fragments of Petronius Arbiter, in these words: 'I was astounded, and
declared that Gito, a most bashful boy, could never be a party to this
wantonness, and that the girl was not of an age to take over the role of
womanly submission. Well, said Quartilla, is she younger than I was when I
submitted to a man? May I call down the rage of my guardian Juno, if I ever   10
remember having been a virgin. As a little child I was defiled with those of
the same age, and as the years went on I attached myself to older boys, until
I came to the age I am at now. It is from this, I think, that the proverb arose,
He can bear the bull who has already borne the calf.' There seems no

* * * * *

6 Antoninus] Aelius Spartianus *Geta* 6–7 (part of the *Historia Augusta*, see I i 21n).
9 Aristotle] *Politics* 7.7 (1328a13)
13 Euripides] *Iphigeneia Aulidensis* 376–7

51 When this appeared in the *Collectanea* (no 321), it was derived from the
   Miscellanea of Poliziano (c 89), and he provided the text of the excerpt from
   Petronius. Otto 1744; Tilley B 711 as above
6 Petronius] *Satyricon* 25.3–6. Part of what little remains to us of this famous
   novel of the mid-first century AD had been rediscovered by Poggio Bracciolini
   about 1420, and was already in print. It is referred to in the first chiliad of the
   Adagia four times; but the episode now known as 'the supper of Trimalchio,'
   which would have provided Erasmus with an exceptionally rich quarry, was
   first published in Padua in 1664.

absurdity in tracing the adage to the exploit of Milo of Croton, of whom we   15
read that he used to carry a calf for some distance every day, and when it
grew into a bull he carried it without difficulty. And thus it will fit those who
gradually become accustomed to things, however difficult.

52   **Vivorum oportet meminisse**
      One should remember the living

One should remember the living. An old adage about people who talk all the
time of the deceased; it is commonly thought unlucky to have the name of
the dead always on one's lips, and to call them as witnesses in conversation.   5
Hence Varro in the third book of his *On the Latin Language* thinks the word
lethum, death, comes from the Greek *Lethe*, the river of oblivion, as if it were
right that one who has departed this life should go into oblivion; and at
funerals it used to be the custom to announce publicly: 'That man has been
given up to death.' Cicero refers to this adage in the fifth book of his *De*   10
finibus bonorum et malorum. In this Piso and then Quintus Cicero said how
deeply they were moved by the memory of famous men, and by the
contemplation of the places where once they had dwelt when alive, and
each of them recalled those whose memory particularly delighted him. Then
Pomponius Atticus said, as if in jest: 'For my part, you are fond of attacking   15
me as a follower of Epicurus, and I do spend much of my time with
Phaedrus, who as you know is my dearest friend, in the gardens of Epicurus
which we passed just now; but I obey the old saw "I remember the living."
Still I could not forget Epicurus, even if I wanted; the members of our body
not only have pictures of him, but even have his likeness on their drinking-   20
cups and rings.' Thus far Cicero. Plautus in the *Truculentus*: 'While he lives,
you may know a man: when he is dead, you may keep silence.' But nowadays the common people do not even remember the services rendered by
their friends, though the saying of Thales is justly famous, that we should be
mindful of absent friends no less than of those who are present.   25

        * * * * *

15 Milo] Quintilian 1.9.5. Erasmus records in II iii 10 how Milo, the almost
    legendary strong man of Antiquity, lifted a four-year-old ox onto his shoulders
    and, having carried it all the way round the stadium at Olympia, then proceded
    to eat it single-handed. The horrible manner of his death is glanced at in II iv 44.

52 Otto 1930; Tilley Q 12 We must live by the quick and not by the dead. IV x 99
    adds to this.
 6 Varro] See I ii 23n; *De lingua latina* 7.42.
10 Cicero] *De finibus* 5.1.3
21 Plautus] *Truculentus* 164, added in 1523
24 Thales] This is from Diogenes Laertius 1.37; the comment was added in 1526.

53 **Cum larvis luctari**
    To wrestle with ghosts

Cum larvis luctari, Wrestling with ghosts, is said of those who heap blame on
the dead: nothing could be more unworthy of an honourable man. Suidas
quotes Aristophanes as saying: 'Stop, stop, Lord Mercury! / For his reproach   5
was against Cleon who is dead.' Lucian in *The Sects*: 'They fight a shadowy
fight against you when you are absent.' He means both the absent and the
dead. Pliny recalls this in the preface to his *History of the World* in this way:
'Plancus made a witty remark when it was said that Asinius Pollio was
preparing speeches against him which would be published either by himself   10
or by his children after the death of Plancus, so that he could not reply, and
he retorted "Only ghosts wrestle with the dead."' By this remark he dealt
them such a blow that educated opinion found them the last word in
impudence. Aristotle in his *Rhetoric* quotes Plato in the *Republic* as saying
that those who bark at the dead are like puppies which bite the stones that   15
are thrown at them, but never touch the people who have injured them.

54 **Iugulare mortuos**
    To cut a dead man's throat

Much the same seems to be *iugulare mortuos,* To cut a dead man's throat,
meaning to censure the dead and fight with those who are already no more.
It is adopted from war, in which it would be a cowardly and absurd thing to   5
cut the throat of men prostrate and already dead, just as it is brave to
contend with the living. Laertius quotes this in his life of Menedemus. He

* * * * *

53 This phrase in its shorter form is *Collectanea* no 586, and in its longer form (Otto
   1147) is no 587, with Pliny cited as the authority, as here.
4 Suidas] π 805, citing Aristophanes *Peace* 648. The second line in the Greek
   forms an iambic trimeter, and Erasmus probably took both lines to come from
   Aristophanes, which is not so, and the modern editor of Suidas gives the
   second line as a comment in prose. The Latin version is of *1515*.
6 Lucian] *Hermotimus* 33; *The Sects* is an alternative title. Mentioned in IV vi 48
8 Pliny] *Naturalis historia* praefatio 31 (Otto 1147)
14 Aristotle] *Rhetoric* 3.4 (1406b32), citing Plato *Republic* 5.469d. The dogs form
   an adage in their own right: IV ii 22.

54 The source of this may well be the Latin version of Diogenes Laertius by
   Ambrogio Traversari.
6 just as ... living] Added in *1517/8*
7 Laertius] Diogenes Laertius 2.135

says that Bion, when he was at pains to attack the soothsayers, was cutting
dead men's throats, those in fact who were already hissed off the stage and
universally rejected by public opinion. Aristophanes in the *Birds* wrote 'to   10
kill the dead.' This is a metaphor which is much pleasanter when it is farther
removed from its literal meaning: for instance if one says that it is 'cutting a
dead man's throat' to attack a book which all condemn, or to argue against
an opinion which everyone has voted down long ago, or to find fault with
something which is in itself abominated by everybody.   15

55   **Cygnea cantio**
     Swan-song

Κύκνειον ᾆσμα, Swan-song. Found among the Greek proverbs. Aelian also
mentions it in his work *On the Nature of Animals*, as a proverb. It is suitable to
those who speak with eloquence at the very end of their lives, or write with   5
great sweetness in extreme old age; this is something which usually happens to writers, their last works being the least bitter and the most honeyed,
as if their eloquence matured with age. Swans are said to break into wonderful song at the point of death, and this is celebrated in literature by everybody but no one has either verified it or believed it. Lucian declares he never   10
even saw any swans when he sailed along the Po. Aelian adds that swans
only sing when the soft west wind blows, the zephyr for which the Latin is
favonius. Martial: 'Sweet are the songs he sings with failing voice, / Makes his
own funeral music like a swan.' There are even philosophers who try to
produce a reason for this, and assert that it happens because of the efforts of   15
the breath of life to escape through that long narrow neck. St Jerome speaks

* * * * *

10 Aristophanes] *Birds* 1075

55 *Collectanea* no 603, from Diogenianus, citing only the first quotation from
   Jerome's *Letters*.Otto 497; Tilley s 1028 Like a swan he sings before his death.
3 Greek proverbs] Diogenianus 5.37
3 Aelian] *De natura animalium* 2.32; 5.34; 10.36. This is a work of entertainment
   rather than instruction, written in the early third century AD, which provided
   Erasmus with half-a-dozen items for the *Parabolae*, and is used at least sixteen
   times in the *Adagia*. Only once does he quote more than a word or two of Greek;
   the Greek text was not printed until 1556.
10 Lucian] *Electrum* 4–5, added in *1515*
11 Aelian] This reference was added in *1515*, as it was to *Adagia* I vii 22. The
   zephyr is not named in any of the passages just given, nor in Aelian's *Varia
   historia* 1.14; but it is in Philostratus *Imagines* 1.9, and becomes part of the
   tradition of the dying swan.
13 Martial] 13.77
16 Jerome] *Letters* 52.3.5; 60.1.2, the latter added in *1515*

in praise of a certain old man's eloquence, after mentioning several writers:
'All these,' he says, 'sang a kind of swan-song at the approach of death.'
And he writes in the epitaph on Nepotianus: 'Where is he, that taskmaster of
ours, a sweeter voice than any singing swan.' I used it too, in an epigram,   20
which I threw off long ago, addressed to that universal Maecenas of
studies, never to be praised enough, William, archbishop of Canterbury:

> Radiant singers thou shalt see arise,
> With voices sweet and tuneful that have power
> To fling swan's music to the distant stars,   25
> And men shall hearken in the age to come.

Athenaeus also remembers this adage in the *Doctors at Dinner*, book 14,
quoting Chrysippus, where he mentions a man who took such extraordinary delight in witty sayings that he said, just as he was about to be
executed, 'I'm ready to die when I've sung my swan-song,' meaning, I   30
imagine, that the remark had a point to it because as soon as he had spoken
he would lose his life. Cicero writes in the preface to the third book of his *De
oratore*, speaking of L. Crassus: 'The man's voice and words were divinely
beautiful, like a swan-song, and we were almost expecting to hear it when
we came into the senate-house after his burial, to look upon that very spot   35
where he last stood.'

56 Nestorea eloquentia
The eloquence of Nestor

In the same way the fluency of Nestor the leader of the Pylians became
proverbial, to indicate an old man's mellifluous speech. For Homer says he
lived through three generations, and credits him with more than honeyed   5

* * * * *

20 epigram] From the verse dedication prefixed to Erasmus' versions from
   Euripides (Paris, 13 September 1506); Reedijk *Poems* 80.22–5. The phrase
   'which I threw off' etc was added here in 1517/8.
22 William] William Warham. Beside the frequent references in Erasmus' letters to
   his encouragement, there is a memorable tribute to him in IV v 1.
27 Athenaeus] 14.616b, added in *1520*
32 Cicero] *De oratore* 3.2.6, added in *1536*

56 The ultimate origin is Homeric. Otto 1224 gives more material.
 4 Homer] *Iliad* 1.247–9

eloquence. For thus he says in *Iliad* 1. 'After them rose Nestor, the eloquent
Pylian leader, / And from his tongue flowed speech more sweet than honey.'
Theocritus copied this in the *Bucolics*, according to Plutarch: 'Because the
Muse bedewed his lips with sweet nectar.' And that phrase of Horace's
tends the same way: 'With your own beauties charmed, you surely know /   10
Your verses with a honey'd sweetness flow.'

57   **Lepos Atticus, Eloquentia Attica**
     Attic wit, Attic eloquence

Among other peoples of Greece, it is to the people of Attica that a special
native wit and humour is ascribed, to such an extent that 'Attic wit' and
'Attic eloquence' have become a proverbial way of saying 'the best.' Terence   5
in the *Eunuchus*: 'Did I not say he had Attic eloquence?' (making fun of a
bungling graceless soldier). St Jerome to Pammachius (I think he is laughing
at Jovinianus): 'This is the eloquence of Plautus, this is Attic wit, compara-
ble, as they say, to the eloquence of the Muses.' The remark about the
Muses' eloquence is a reference to Varro's well-known praise of Plautus, in   10
which he said 'the Muses themselves, if they had wished to speak Latin,
would have spoken with the lips of Plautus.' And Lucian alludes to this in
the essay *On Salaried Posts*: 'Furthermore if they have said something in a
rustic way, they wish that very thing to seem a pure Atticism and drawn
from Hymettus.' Hymettus is a mountain of Attica famed for its honey, and   15
hence we have 'Attic honey' and 'the honey of Hymettus.' These were of
special value, as Martial testifies in his *Xenia*: 'This the bee, spoiler of
Thesean Hymettus, has sent you, / Noble nectar from the woods of Pallas.'

* * * * *

8 Theocritus] 7.82; the passage of Plutarch referred to is in the spurious *De vita et
   poesi Homeri* 159.
9 Horace] *Epistles* 1.19.44–5 (tr Sir Philip Francis)

57 *Collectanea* no 277 gives *Plautina eloquentia* the status of a proverb, and cites in
   support the passages from Jerome and Varro. I viii 80 is to the same effect.
5 Terence] *Eunuchus* 1093
7 Jerome] *Letters* 57.12.3 (Otto 1177)
10 Varro] Cited by Quintilian 10.1.99
12 Lucian] *De mercede conductis* 35
17 Martial] 13.104, added in 1515. His *Xenia* ('Presents') is a book of two-line
   epigrams written to accompany gifts to friends, in this case a pot of honey from
   Attica (of which Theseus was a mythical king).

58 **Mandrabuli more res succedit**
    Things go Mandraboulus' fashion

'Επὶ Μανδραβούλου χωρεῖ τὸ πρᾶγμα, The affair goes on in Mandraboulus'
fashion – that is to say, day by day it gets worse. This comes from a certain
Mandraboulus who found a treasure, and first of all dedicated a golden   5
sheep to Juno of Samos; the following year he offered a silver one, and the
next year a bronze one. Lucian in *On Salaried Posts*: 'But you rejoice and
deceive yourself and you always think the future is going to be better. But
the opposite of what you hoped for comes about, and as the proverb says,
things go Mandraboulus' fashion, growing smaller and worse day by day so   10
to speak, and stepping backward.' Alciphron in one of his letters: 'As the
proverb says, things go in Mandraboulus' fashion.' This is appropriate for
those who change for the worse. Just as Menedemus says in Plutarch, many
people come to Athens to study; first they turn out wise men, then philosophers, then rhetoricians, and finally uneducated people. It would not be   15
out of place here to add that fine thought of Plato's, in the *Laws*, book 1: 'To
conquer oneself is the first and best of all victories. On the other hand to be
inferior to oneself is the most shameful and slothful thing that could happen.' The man conquers himself who goes forward to better things; but to
turn out inferior to oneself is to become worse.   20

59 **Mature fias senex**
    Be old early

Mature fias senex, si diu velis esse senex, Be old early, if you want to be old long,
is a Latin proverb which reminds us that while we are still unimpaired we

        * * * * *

    58 The form of the proverb is not the same in the collections (Zenobius 3.82,
       Diogenianus 4.62 Suidas ε 2659 and 2716), and Lucian seems the most likely
       source.
     7 Lucian] *De mercede conductis* 21
    11 Alciphron] *Epistulae* 1.9.1. He was a writer of fictional letters, of the fourth
       century AD, printed partly by Aldus in his *Epistolographi graeci* of 1499; we use
       the numbering of M.A.Schepers' edition, Leipzig 1905.
    13 Plutarch] *Moralia* 81F
    16 Plato] *Laws* 1.626e. The word 'slothful,' which is a possible rendering of the
       Greek though 'disgraceful' is at least equally likely, was misprinted as 'serious'
       (*gravissimum* for *ignavissimum*) in 1517/8 and later.
    19 The man] This sentence was added in *1517/8*.

    59 Otto 1626. Cicero *De senectute* 10.32, the dialogue *On Old Age* also called *Cato
       major*, is the sole source.

should cease from the exertions of youth, and begin to take care of our 5
health, if we wish to enjoy a long and vigorous old age. For the lot of old age
is leisure and rest. This is spoken by the elder Cato in Cicero: 'For I have
never given my assent to that ancient and much-praised proverb, Be old
early, if you want to be old long.' It may not win the approval of Cato, tough
character that he was, allowing himself no respite from toil even in extreme 10
old age; but we should take notice of it, especially if it is applied to the vices
of youth, such as lust, drunkenness, wild behaviour, for unless a man gives
these up in good time he will either never reach old age at all, or will have but
a short one.

60 **Senis doctor**
    A teacher of the old

Γεροντοδιδάσκαλος, A teacher of the old. This is a title quoted often by
Nonius Marcellus among the titles of Varro's plays, and there is no doubt
that like most of the others it is proverbial. It is apt for the person who 5
spends his trouble on something tardy and untimely, and spends it in vain.
Just as youth is teachable, and adaptable to any condition, so old age is
intractable, slow and forgetful. As Theognis says: 'Teach me not, age makes
me unteachable.' Euripides in the *Bacchae*: 'I, old as I am, shall guide you,
also old.' This line is found indeed in the *Philoctetes* of Sophocles, and 10
Gellius in the *Nights*, book 13, testifies that it was widely used and proverbial. Varro seems to have taken his title from the *Euthydemus* of Plato, where
Socrates relates how his teacher Connus, from whom he learnt as an old
man to play the lyre, was called mockingly by the boys 'the old man's
schoolmaster.' An alleged remark of Diogenes comes in here: 'Doctoring a 15
dead man and teaching an old one are the same thing.' However it is a
useless saying, which deters old men from learning things which it is
disgraceful not to know.

* * * * *

60 Varro] Eighteen fragments of a piece of this name are found in the dictionary of
   Nonius Marcellus (See I i 97n). Varro's *Menippean Satires* were not plays
   (Erasmus uses the word *fabulae*), but we know little of them beyond a long list of
   titles. The fragments are printed by F. Buecheler in *Petronii saturae*, Berlin 1922.
 8 Theognis] 578 (see I i 62n), the version corrected in *1517/8* and finalized in *1520*.
 9 Euripides] *Bacchae* 193
11 Gellius] 13.19.3, citing Sophocles frag 633 Nauck (from the lost play *Phthiotides*,
   not the *Philoctetes*), added in *1515*
12 Plato] *Euthydemus* 272c, added in *1523*
15 Diogenes] The source has not been identified. Added in *1523*

61   **Senis mutare linguam**
      To teach an old man a new language

Age is slow at any kind of learning, but especially at learning a language, a
faculty which is given by nature to children. It is generally well known that
children can learn to speak any tongue, while older people do not achieve it   5
or imitate it very badly. Hence the proverb 'to teach an old man a new
language,' applied to those who labour at the wrong time and in vain. St
Jerome says in the preface to the four Gospels: 'It is a worthy task, but one of
dangerous presumption, to judge others when one is open to be judged by
all, and to teach an old man a new language, and turn back a world that is   10
growing grey to its childish beginnings,' by which he means that the adult
age is less amenable in all ways than those unformed and tender years, and
Ovid puts this in an elegant metaphor:

> The tree spreading wide its shade to the walkers beneath it
> Once was a wand, when first it was planted in earth.   15
> Then a mere hand's turn could pull it from shallow ground simply,
> Now it stands firm, by its own strength grown huge.

For this reason the character must be formed while the age is malleable; the
mind accustomed to the best, while it is impressionable as wax. For later on,
by the force of years, the mind becomes rigid, and we can hardly unlearn   20
what we have learnt wrong; what we do not know can only be taught us
with infinite trouble. I am not saying this to deter older people from learning, since it is never too late to learn, but in order to urge children to study.
      We must not leave out the saying, common though it is, 'the old parrot
takes no notice of the rod.' Although the meaning of the adage is not   25
obscure, it will become clearer from the words of Apuleius, in the *Florida*,
book 2, about the parrot: 'When being trained to imitate our country speech,
it is tapped on the head with an iron key so that it really feels who is master.
This takes the place of the cane while it is learning. The young bird learns at
once, up to the age of two years, while the mouth is pliable and can be   30
moulded, and the tongue is tender and vibrates quickly. But if an old one is
caught, it is both unteachable and forgetful.' Thus far Apuleius. Pliny also

---

61 Taken from St Jerome. Suringar 206
 8 Jerome] Preface to the Vulgate version of the Gospels; *PL* 29.525 (557)
13 Ovid] *Remedia amoris* 85–8
26 Apuleius] See I i 15n; *Florida* 12
32 Pliny] *Naturalis historia* 10.119, added in *1517/8*

mentions, book 10 chapter 42, the wonderful teachableness of this bird, but only up to two years old. Close to these remarks is a common but not inelegant expression: 'it is too late to accustom old dogs to the leash.'   35

62 Cascus cascam ducit
An old man takes an old bride

Very similar is what Varro records in the third book of his *On the Latin Language*: An old man takes an old bride, used whenever like delights in like, an old fellow in an old woman, a cripple in a cripple, a barbarian in a   5
barbarian, a rogue in a rogue. For the ancients used the word *cascus* for what we call 'old'; and the authority for this is that same Varro, who says that in the Sabine tongue, which has its roots far back in the Oscan language, *casnar* is the term for an old man, and that Ennius, skilled in Oscan, wrote: 'Which first the ancient (*casci*) Latin peoples bore.' Cicero in book 1 of his *Tusculan*   10
Questions calls the ancient Latins *casci*: 'That one thing was fixed in the minds of the men of old whom Ennius styled the ancients' (*casci*). However, Varro quotes the adage as proceeding from a certain Manilius, saying 'it was no wonder if an old woman had married an old man, since he gave her such a tuneful wedding.' This seems to be a joke at the expense of the elderly bride   15
of an old man, alluding to the sound of the word *cascus* as if it came from singing (*canendo*). In the same place there is a reference to the epigram of a certain Papinius, which he wrote about a youth named Casca: 'Absurd it sounds, when your old woman calls you Casca.' I imagine the youth had married an old woman, and so it seemed ridiculous whenever the crone   20
(*casca*) called her young husband by his own name, Casca. Perhaps the jest

* * * * *

35 expression] Tilley D 500 An old dog will learn no new tricks. This was in *Collectanea* no 311 as a popular saying; see I iv 43n.

62 This appears in the *Collectanea*, no 809, and is mentioned in no 297, the source being no doubt Varro. Otto p 77 denies it proverbial status, as being an epigram made to match one particular set of circumstances.
  3 Varro] See I ii 23n; *De lingua latina* 7.28
  9 Ennius] *Annals* 24, cited by Varro
  10 Cicero] *Tusculanae disputationes* 1.12.27
  13 Manilius] A poet, probably of the early first century BC, of whom little or nothing is known. 'Tuneful' translates *canoras*, an early correction of a corrupt word, but it gives no sense; modern texts read *cariosas*, rotten with age, 'worm-eaten.' The party was mouldy, and so were the happy couple.
  18 Papinius] Another virtually unknown author; cited by Varro, from whom Erasmus gives the text in a corrupt form; the point seems to have lain in the juxtaposition of *Casca*, a Roman man's name, and *casca* meaning an old woman.

in the proverb recalls the early marriage custom mentioned by Plutarch in
his 'Problems': those who led the bride to her bridegroom's house told her
to say these words, 'Where you are Gaius, I am Gaia.'

63   **Dis dia pason**
     Double diapason

Δὶς διὰ πασῶν, Double diapason. By this proverb was signified a great
difference or very long interval; hence things which seemed most incom-
patible with each other, and totally different in kind, were said to differ *dis*   5
dia pason. Lucian in his essay *How History Should Be Written*: 'And this is,
as the musicians' proverb says, a case where they are a double diapason
apart from each other.' Again in the *Apology*: 'But realize this: there is a very
great difference between entering a rich man's house as a hireling, where
one is a slave and endures what my essay describes, and entering public   10
service, where one administers affairs as well as one can, and is paid by the
emperor for doing it. Consider every detail and examine it for yourself. You
will find the two lives a double diapason apart, to use a musical proverb, and
as like each other as lead and silver, bronze and gold, anemone and rose,
monkey and man. You are paid in the first case as in the second, and in both   15
you are under a master's orders; but there is no small discrepancy between
one position and the other.' So far Lucian. The adage, as he indicates, is
borrowed from the art of music. Macrobius, in his *Commentary On the Dream
of Scipio*, book 2, mentions five kinds of harmony: diatessaron, diapente,
diapason, diapason and diapente, and finally double diapason. The com-   20
bination of the diatessaron and the diapente constitutes the diapason, which
has been given this name because it gives complete harmony, so that there
seems to me to be a connection between this proverb and another which I
shall mention elsewhere, A full octave. Plutarch and all the ancient writers,

* * * * *

22 Plutarch] *Moralia* 271E, added in *1526*

63 A copious commentary is provided by J.-C. Margolin in *Latomus* 26 (1967)
    165–94.
6 Lucian] *Quomodo historia conscribenda sit 7*; the source was given as his
    Harmonides in *1508* and *1515*, omitted in *1517/8*, and corrected in *1526*.
8 Again] Lucian *Apologia* 11
14 bronze and gold] Added in *1515*
18 Macrobius] *Commentarii in somnium Scipionis* 2.1.24 (cf I i 12n).
23 another] *Adagia* I vii 26; in *1508* it was 'have mentioned.'
24 Plutarch] In the *De musica* attributed to him, eg *Moralia* 1138E or 1143E

Greek or Latin, who have written about musical theory, similarly fix the limit   25
of harmony at what is called the 'double diapason.' Boethius too, in the first
book of his treatise *On Music*, records that in ancient times harmonic proportion depended entirely on the heptachord, that is to say on seven strings, the
lowest being called *hypate* and the highest *nete*. Later when different people
added other strings, the number of notes was increased to the point of   30
doubling the heptachord. And this was apparently to be the end of the
development, except that harmonic theory seemed to require the *mesê* or
middle string which had occupied the place in the heptachord agreeing with
its name and which, in its relation to the furthest string in either direction,
gave the diatessaron. This string was thus added and given its due place,   35
and the result was fifteen strings, the furthest at one end being called
proslambanomenos, and at the other end *nete hyperbolaios*. So it came about
that the *mesê* in its relation to the two extremes gave the harmony diapason;
and each of the two extremes in relation to the *mesê* produced the same
harmony. Moreover the highest, taken with the lowest, gave the harmony   40
called double diapason, because the ratio I have described covered twice that
harmony which is called the diapason. So, since the harmonic ratio stopped
at this point and could not proceed any further, the expression passed into
popular speech to describe things as widely as possible different from each
other, which were said to be a double diapason apart, exactly as if one were   45
to say, so far apart that a greater separation would be impossible. An exactly
similar phrase is ἐκ διαμέτρου, diametrically opposite.

    But since I have rashly – and as it were forgetting myself – gone further
into musical matters than the nature of the work undertaken required, I
should like to add by the way some further information, which is not, I   50
think, very widely known, and will not be uninteresting to know. For at this
point, just as I was scribbling all this down in my notes, it so happened that
by great good luck along came Ambrogio Leone of Nola, an outstanding
philosopher of our time, and one endowed with incredible diligence and
expertise in exploring the intricacies of intellectual disciplines; he has also   55
had no little experience in reading and examining the works of writers in
both Latin and Greek. As he arrived just when I was writing, I read him
what I had already written, and then I said, 'I am afraid, Ambrogio, that the
general mass of musicians will make trouble over my adage "double diapa-

* * * * *

26 Boethius] *De institutione musica* 1.20. In *1508* the word *nete* was compared,
    following Boethius, with the Greek *neate*, lowest; this was cut out in *1515*.
47 similar phrase] I x 45
53 Ambrogio Leone] Of Nola; see Allen III p 352. When that was written he was
    Aldus' physician. Cf *Adagia* II iii 50 and III vii 66 for his wide-ranging interests.

son," and strongly oppose it, being "at the other end of the scale" from my   60
way of looking at it; these people do not hesitate to extend the limits of
harmony to the twentieth note of the gamut. Now you are an authority on
difficult cases and you are also experienced not only in the theory but in the
practice of music. I should like you to explain to me in a few words, if it is not
too much trouble, why the ancients were afraid of going any further, even   65
the least little bit, past the fifteenth interval, even to the extent of the thing
becoming a proverb; and why these moderns have no hesitation in pushing
the boundary out to such a wide range of consonances, setting aside the
limits of the ancients, and as the saying goes "jumping the bounds"; they are
not afraid to go on to the twentieth interval.'   70

He laughed in friendly fashion. 'What a scrupulous fellow you are,' he
said, 'to add to your worries the fear of what the singers will say about your
adage in their drinking parties! To repel the slanders of the musicians, one
shield would be enough for you: say you are repeating the old adage. It was
in any case sure to agree with the theory of the old musicians from whom it   75
came. But so as to satisfy you rather than them, here in a few words is what I
have observed, and what I think, about this subject.

'To start with, the reason which has prompted modern musicians to
exceed the limits of the ancients is something they must look to themselves.
For myself, I see two reasons why antiquity should have preferred to stop at   80
the "double diapason." First, that nature herself seems to have fixed this sort
of limit to consonances, by arranging that the human voice should not reach
beyond the fifteenth interval; if one tries to go higher the result is not a
natural voice, but forced and artificial, and seems more like a squeak than a
voice. If one strains on the contrary to push it lower, one gets out of the vocal   85
register into something like a hawking noise. Thus, since art should always
as far as possible agree with nature, it seems to me that the ancients were not
wrong in circumscribing the realm of art within the barriers which nature
had set to the human voice. This would be a sufficient reason to convince
anyone, I think, but the second is more imperative.   90

'It is this. You know that in Boethius, *On Music*, book 4, the view is
found that musical harmony should be considered not only in relation to
reason, but also in relation to the senses. For this reason Ptolemy, in the
book I have mentioned, rejects the opinion of certain Pythagoreans who
have given greater importance to the reason than to the senses when they   95
discriminate between harmonies; they say that the senses only supply the

* * * * *

69 saying goes] 1 x 93
91 Boethius] *De musica institutione* 5.3

germ, as it were, of knowledge, while the perfect understanding depends
on reason. Again, he refutes the opinion of Aristoxenus who attributed
more than their due proportion of importance to the senses, and very little to
the reason; musical harmony should be so ordered that neither the reason   100
should resist the senses nor the senses contradict the reason. Aristotle does
not disagree with Ptolemy (*Physics*, book 2) for he says that music is not
solely a mathematical science but depends partly on reason and partly on
the senses. This is impossible if the musical progression once goes beyond
the fifteenth interval, that is, the "double diapason." Now reason does not   105
in any way forbid a progression to the thousandth note, since the same
harmonies contained in the octave would recur at regular intervals. The
procedure would be no different from what it is in mathematical calculations, where the proportion of "one and a half" would be the same between
twelve thousand and eight thousand as between four and six. But musical   110
sensitivity vanishes, so to speak, beyond the fifteenth note, and it is not of
much importance to consider a rational harmony unaccepted by the senses,
because it is not perceptible to them. The reason why it is imperceptible is
because the interval is too long. The power of reason has an immense range;
but physical experience, on the contrary, is contained in very narrow limits.   115
It is the same as what happens to the sense of sight, when vision is blurred
and fails if the objects on which the power of sight is trained are far removed,
and the greater the distance the more this occurs. This is much more
pronounced with the sense of hearing, which is less acute than that of sight.
Now what happens in the use of the senses as they perceive objects which   120
come into their field, happens in the use of the mind as it judges by the
senses. If you place one colour beside another, and as the Greeks say, "put
purple to purple," does not the sense of sight immediately distinguish by
this comparison how the colours differ from each other and how like they
are to each other? In the same way, if you present to the ear one sound   125
followed by another sound, it will unhesitatingly distinguish the accord or
discord which exists between them; if they are separated by an undue
interval, the judgment soon begins to waver. Moreover, just as auditive
sensitivity is sooner dulled than ocular, so the judgment resulting from the
ear is sooner blunted than that resulting from the eye; one conclusion   130
depends on the other.

* * * * *

101 Aristotle] *Physica*, perhaps 2.2 (194a8)
122 Greeks] *Adagia* II i 74. In what follows, 'the sense of sight' and 'the hearing'
were both represented in 1508 by 'the reason'; the corrections were made in
1517/8 and 1515 respectively.

'That this is so, I have no need to confirm by further argument, as each person can immediately have proof by experiment. Strike any note on an instrument, and touch the octave at the same time, and the hearing will immediately be in accordance with the reason in recognizing a full harmony, 135 and will cast its own vote for the absoluteness of this agreement. Again, strike a note and touch another in the fifteenth position, and the hearing will at once perceive and approve the accordance found just before in "diapa-son." But if when you touch the lowest note you strike the nineteenth from that, there is no obstacle in reason against a harmony being obtained – the 140 same as came about in "diapason diapente" – but the ear receives the sounds without perceiving the rational harmony. If the sense of hearing had no definite limits, within which a certain and established judgment de-pending on it is enclosed, there would be nothing against proceeding, if one wished, to the "thousandth diapason." In fact, no number is a stumbling- 145 block to the reason, so long as it recognizes an identical relationship. But the physical senses have had their own limits prescribed for them by nature, and if they transgress these, they gradually become misty and wandering, and can no longer judge with certainty as they used to do, but through a cloud, as they say, or in a dream. It was not fitting that principles of art 150 should be drawn from an uncertainty of judgment. But since the ancients understood that beyond the fifteenth note of the scale the judgment of the ears began to fail, they decided to fix the bounds of harmony there, so that no one could have any reason to bring up that adage of yours, "unheard music is useless." And so to the moderns, who flouted the authority of the 155 ancients by introducing a "tetrachord" beyond the highest note, and equally below the lowest, would not have perpetrated such a crime if they had stopped the harmonic progression at the nineteenth note, because in this case the relation of the lowest to the highest produces for the reason, if not for the hearing, a perfect harmony. But in the twentieth there is no harmony 160 perceptible to the senses, either sensitive or abstract. So, there is no slander to be feared, Erasmus, on account of your adage.'

These observations of my friend Ambrogio seemed to me both subtly and credibly argued, and quite appropriate to the meaning of the proverb, so I was glad to extend my own remarks by this supplement, which will not, 165 I think, be unwelcome to a reader who is not excessively difficult to please.

* * * * *

150 as they say] *Adagia* I iii 63
154 adage] I vii 84

64 Ubi timor, ibi et pudor
    Where there is fear there is modesty

Ἵνα δέος, ἔνθα καὶ αἰδώς, Where there is fear there is modesty. A proverbial
saying which is still common today, and like that remark of Terence, 'We are
all made worse by licence.' The greater part of mankind abstains from   5
misdeeds 'for fear of cudgelling.' Plato in the *Laws*, book 5: 'But audacity
breeds impudence.' The word used for audacity, *adeia*, means absence of
fear. He quotes also in the *Euthyphro* from some poet or other, for it is a
half-line from a heroic poem): 'Where there is fear, there modesty is too.'
Suidas says it is from Epicharmus.   10

65 Foras Cares, non amplius anthisteria
    Out you go, slaves, the festival's over

Θύραζε Κᾶρες, οὐκ ἔτ᾽ ἀνθιστήρια, Out you go, slaves, the Anthesteria is
over. This is usually said when a person always expects to have the same
advantages, or considers that he is always free to do something which has   5
been permitted for a certain limited length of time. For instance, if one who
had once experienced a man's liberality should go on coming back to ask for
something else; or when children spin out longer the time they are allotted
for holidays and play. The origin of the proverb is said to be as follows.

* * * * *

64 The Greek is probably from the proverb-collections (Diogenianus 5.30).
    Suringar 233
4 Terence] *Heautontimorumenos* 483
6 for fear of cudgelling] A familiar tag from Horace *Epistles* 2.1.154
6 Plato] *Laws* 3 (not 5). 701a; *Euthyphro* 12b, the latter added in 1520. The half-line
   comes from one of the post-Homeric epics, the lost *Cypria* of Stasinus, frag 20
   Kinkel, 23 Allen. One might have expected Erasmus to cite it from Plutarch
   Moralia 459D, where it is quoted anonymously.
10 Epicharmus] See I i 33n. This attribution (it is frag 221 Kaibel) is found in the
    scholia on Sophocles *Ajax* 1074, but seems not to be in Suidas. The sentence was
    added in 1533.

65 This comes in part from the Greek proverb-collections (Zenobius 4.33); cf
    Suidas θ 598. The Anthesteria or Festival of Flowers (*anthe*) was a three-day
    festival of Dionysus, held in Athens in the month Anthesteriôn, which
    corresponded to the end of our February and the beginning of March. Slaves
    were then allowed greater liberty, as at the Saturnalia, a festival in honour of
    Saturn held in Rome in December; and if *Cares* means Carians (which is open to
    question), this is, as Erasmus says, a reference to their common use as
    mercenaries and slaves, which he describes in *Adagia* I vi 14.

Among the Athenians a certain month was called *anthisteriôn*, because it   10
gave birth to the most flowers. During this month there were festivals and
banquets of a freer sort, just as the custom was at the Saturnalia among the
Romans, and the slaves also were allowed to be guests at table, and take a
holiday from their work. When the holiday was over and they were recalled
to their usual tasks, the masters would speak in this fashion, 'Out you go,   15
Carians, the festival's over.' They called the slaves Carians, because that
race got its living by working for hire, and becoming the servants of anyone
who would pay them wages. Some say that the Carians once held part of
Attica. When the Athenians were conducting the ceremonies of the Anthesteria they used to allow the Carians to come into the city and into their   20
houses and to join in the feast; but once the solemnities were over, if they
found any of the Carians idling about the town, they would say jokingly,
'Out you go, Carians, the festival's over.' This Greek word has the same
meaning as the Latin *Floralia*, a festival of which the licentiousness is
commented on by many authors. Something of the same sort is said by   25
Seneca in his skit on Claudius: 'It will not always be Saturnalia.' For the
Saturnalia also gave a time of liberty to slaves.

66   **Fures clamorem**
     Thieves fear a noise

Οἱ φῶρες τὴν βοήν, Thieves (supply, fear or, have heard) a noise: This will fit
people who have a sense of guilt and are afraid of being caught, or who have
committed some crime and run away in terror. The consciousness of wrong-   5
doing, particularly of theft, has the result of making a man tremble and fear
the light. So we find among the Hebrew sayings, 'The wicked flee when no
man pursueth.' Virgil alluded to it: 'And when I shouted, Where is the
fellow running to now? / Tityrus, round up your flocks: you were lying
hidden in the rushes.'   10

* * * * *

26 Seneca] *Ludus de morte Claudii* 12.2, added in *1515*; the text was published by
   Froben with notes by Beatus Rhenanus in March of that year (see I i 33n).

66 From Diogenianus 7.36. Cf Tilley T 112 The thief does fear each bush an officer.
 7 Hebrew sayings] Proverbs 28:1
 8 Virgil] *Eclogues* 3.19–20

67 Funiculum fugiunt miniatum
They flee from the reddened cord

Τὸ σχοινίον φεύγουσι τὸ μεμιλτωμένον, They dodge the rope that's raddled with red-ochre. This can be aptly applied to a man who hastens to do his job, not because he wants to, but for fear of incurring a fine. It is a line from 5 Aristophanes, which his commentator, and Suidas too, record more or less in this form. The magistrates of Athens tried in various ways to compel the populace to make their appearance at the public assembly as often as possible; they barricaded the rest of the streets which did not lead to the market-place; they removed merchandise from the market so that there 10 should be no idling there on that excuse; and they prepared rope smeared with a red colour, which is called *miltos* (Pliny translates it by *minium*), which some call in Latin *cinnabar*. With this two officials went round roping in the people and driving them to the assembly. Everyone tried to avoid the cord, because any person who clearly bore a red mark from contact with the rope 15 was forced to pay a fine. So we may elegantly say, about anyone who is afraid of a bad mark, 'running away from the red rope.'

68 Fortunatior Strobilis Carcini
Luckier than the Strobili of Carcinus

Εὐδαιμονέστερος Καρκίνου Στροβίλων, Luckier than the Strobili of Carcinus. An ironical saying about an unlucky and wicked man. Carcinus was a poet whose sons were called Strobili by Aristophanes; he also calls them 5

* * * * *

67 From Aristophanes *Acharnians* 22 (cf *Adagia* I iii 85), with the ancient scholia.
6 Suidas] Σ 1810
12 Pliny] *Naturalis historia* 33.115. The alternative names were added in *1515*; in *1508* the only equivalent given was *sinopis* (the Middle English 'sinople'), which probably came from *Naturalis historia* 35.31.

68 Derived from Aristophanes, but with some misunderstandings and perhaps from memory. The Greek *strobílos* means something spherical (it does not seem to be applied to snails), or something that revolves, a spinning-top, a whirlwind or a whirling dance. Carcinus was a writer of tragedies of whom Aristophanes disapproved, and he makes fun of his deformed and dwarfish sons at the end of the *Wasps*; but in the *Peace*, from which this line comes, *strobíloi* describes, not the sons but the dervish-dances or 'pirouettes' introduced by their father. Similarly, this word for 'sweet-necked' does not exist in Greek; it looks like an imperfect recollection of *guliauchenes*, 'with scrawny necks,' applied to Carcinus' sons in *Peace* 789. If this is right, it should be added that Erasmus' memory rarely played him such tricks.

'*glukutrachelos*,' or sweet-necked. The joke comes in the meaning of the names, for in Greek, *carcinus* means crab, and *strobīli* snails, both misshapen and ugly creatures. The adage is listed by Suidas and Zenodotus; in Aristophanes it is in the *Peace*.

69 Festo die si quid prodegeris
Wasteful in holiday time

Plautus in the *Aulularia* puts into the mouth of the aged Euclio: 'If you are wasteful at holiday time, you may be in want at ordinary times, unless you live sparingly.' A proverbial figure, which warns us not to be so lavish at festivals that we have nothing left for everyday expenses. Days of festival were celebrated by the offering of sacrifices, by feasts in daytime, games in the honour of the gods, or public holidays; non-festal days were given to the management of public and private business. This can be suitably adapted to people who waste their substance in youth and go hungry in old age, or who squander money unseasonably and will long for it later on.

70 Feles Tartessia
A Tartessian cat

Γαλῆ Ταρτησσία, A Tartessian cat. This was a term for something huge and ridiculous. The Tartessians are in Spain, and it is said that their cats grow very large. Possibly it may be applied to the rapacious as well. Aristophanes in the *Wasps*: 'They watch me holding spits as if I were a cat who'd stolen meat.' Lucian, when he says 'as rapacious as cats,' also suggests that the greediness of cats was a general opinion.

* * * * *

8 Suidas] E 3402, added in *1517/8*

8 Zenodotus] Inserted in *1528*; the adage is not in the printed text of Zenobius, and is one of a group of over a score added in that year or in *1526* from the Aldine Aesop of 1515.

8 Aristophanes] *Peace* 864, added in *1523*; it was already used in III ii 30.

69 Taken over, largely in the same words, from *Collectanea* no 64. The source is Plautus *Aulularia* 380–1.

70 Probably from the Greek proverb-collections (Diogenianus 3.71; Suidas Γ 29). Tartessus was an early Greek colony on the south-west Atlantic coast of Spain, north of Cadiz.

5 Aristophanes] *Wasps* 363–4. It was not the speaker, but the two men watching him, who were holding the spits; whether the mistake (which involves only one letter in the Latin) is due to Erasmus or his printer, one cannot say.

7 Lucian] *Piscator* 34, the Latin version added in *1515*

71 **Ferre iugum**
To bear the yoke

Plautus in the *Curculio*: 'Does she yet bear the yoke?' Someone is enquiring
about a girl, whether she is of an age to receive a man. That this is the
meaning is sufficiently borne out by what follows: 'She is as pure, as far as   5
I'm concerned, / As if she were my sister.' Horace writes in the *Odes* of a girl
not yet ripe for a husband: 'Not yet can she bow her neck and bear the yoke,'
thus showing the transference of the metaphor from the young ox who has
not yet got the strength to do his share of work in pulling the plough. For to
sleep together demands two people on equal terms, just as it is with a pair of   10
oxen. That is why marriage is called *coniugium*, a yoking together.

72 **Feli crocoton**
A party-frock for the cat

Γαλῇ κροκωτόν (understand, You supply) a party-frock for the cat. This is
often said when an honour is bestowed on those who are unworthy of it,
and whom it does not suit at all; or else when something is given to those   5
who do not know how to use it, for instance if a most beautiful book were
given to someone entirely foreign to the Muses. The *crocoton* is a kind of
dress, of circular shape with fringes, which was worn by rich ladies. In
Nonius, under the word *richa*, the *crocoton* is included among luxury
garments. This is how I take it that the text should be read, 'a party frock, a   10
rich-embroidered *richa*.' But according to Plutarch, some used to paint
Hercules as 'wearing the *crocoton*' when he was serving Omphale. The
adage comes from a fable of Stratis, which I have related in a different place.

* * * * *

71 *Collectanea* no 65, repeated largely in the same words. Another proverbial
  expression derived from the yoking of draught-animals will be found in I vi 8.
  Plautus *Curculio* 50–1 was the original source.
  6 Horace] *Odes* 2.5.1–2

72 From the proverb-collections (Zenobius 2.93; Suidas Γ 35). In August 1535,
  when it was reported that Paul III had it in mind to create some learned men
  cardinals and that Erasmus' name had been put forward, his comment was *Feli
  aiunt crocoton*, 'A party frock for the cat, as the proverb says' (Allen Ep 3048:92).
  9 Nonius] See I i 97n; p 539, citing the comic poet Novius 71 (*Comicorum
  romanorum fragmenta*, ed O. Ribbeck, Leipzig 1898, 322). The form and meaning
  of the first word are uncertain. This was added in *1515*.
  11 Plutarch] *Moralia* 785E, added in *1515*
  13 Stratis] Properly Strattis, the author of comedies, cites (frag 71 Kock) a phrase
  close to ours in telling the story of the cat dressed in finery, who forgot her

But whether the word used in Greek, *galê*, means a cat or a weasel, or what
is vulgarly called *catus*, I leave to others to decide, since I see there is   15
an argument about it among the learned.

73   **Mustelam habes**
     You have a weasel in your house

Γαλῆν ἔχεις, You have a weasel in your house. This suits the person for
whom everything goes wrong, as if the fates and the gods were angry, as
they say. In old days this animal was thought to be inauspicious and unlucky   5
to those who had it and kept it in the house, so the saying is not very
different from those other proverbs, 'He must have Sejus' horse,' or 'He has
gold from Toulouse.' And even now in some countries, notably among the
English, it is held to be an evil omen if while they are getting ready to go out
hunting someone mentions a weasel. Even to have it running across your   10
path is now commonly accounted unlucky. The adage is mentioned by
Diogenianus.

74   **Fastuosus Maximus**
     Haughty Maximus

Κόμπος Μάξιμος, Haughty Maximus. This was said about a person who
proudly thought himself wiser than he was. It was taken from the behaviour
of a certain Maximus, an insolent fellow full of his own conceit. In some texts   5
I find a variant: *kompas Maximos*. In Greek *kompos* means arrogance and
insolence, and it gives *kompazein* (to talk big) and *kompein* (to boast). Euripides says 'insolence of tongue.' This too is found in the collections of
Diogenianus.

                    * * * * *

      new status in society when a mouse ran across the floor; Erasmus recounts it in
      Adagia I vii 11.

    73 From Diogenianus 3.84. Suringar 128
     4 as they say] *Adagia* I i 72
     7 other proverbs] *Adagia* I x 97 and 98
     9 English] Perhaps a reminiscence of Erasmus' visit to Lord Mountjoy in 1499,
        when he says he was taken hunting (Ep 103:7)

    74 From Diogenianus 5.46. *Kompos*, in Greek normally 'boasting,' is rarely used
        with a change of accent to mean 'boastful.'
     7 Euripides] *Hecuba* 627

75 **E multis paleis paulum fructus collegi**
    From a lot of chaff I got little grain

Ἐκ πολλῶν ἀχύρων ὀλίγον καρπὸν συνήγαγον, From a lot of chaff I got little
grain. That is, from a great deal of work I gained a very small advantage; or
from a wordy speech I extracted little in the way of a sound idea, or out of a   5
huge volume I gained only the least bit of learning. The metaphor is from
winnowers of wheat.

76 **Oportet remum ducere qui didicit**
    The man who has learnt to row should take the oar

Δεῖ κώπην ἐλαύνειν μαθόντα, It should be the man who has learnt, who
wields the oar. The proper person to exercise a skill is the one who has
previously learnt it. This is mentioned by Plutarch in his essay 'Can Virtue   5
Be Taught?' and Horace also in the *Art of Poetry*:

> The Man, who knows not how with Art to wield
> The sportive weapons of the martial field,
> The bounding Ball, round Quoit, or whirling Troque
> Will not the laughter of the Crowd provoke   10
> But every desperate Blockhead dares to write ...

In our own time too there is a similar proverb going round: 'Anyone who
does not know the rules of the game can keep out.'

77 **Ex ipso bove lora sumere**
    To make the leash from the bull's own hide

Ἐκ τοῦ βοὸς τοὺς ἱμάντας λαμβάνειν, Making the leash from the bull's own
hide, is what people are said to do, when for the purpose of injuring
somebody they use something received from that very person. For instance,   5

* * * * *

75 This comes from Suidas E 591; it is also in Apostolius 14.40.
    4 or from ... learning] This clause was added in *1517/8*.

76 This seems to come from Plutarch *Moralia* 440A. Close in sense to II ii 82. It is
    Suringar 162.
    6 Horace] *Ars poetica* 379–82 (tr Sir Philip Francis)

77 Another taken from Plutarch: *Moralia* 1090E–F

a man might write verse attacking the person who had taught him the rules of prosody; or a tyrant might extort money from the citizens for the support of an armed guard intended to suppress them; or someone might make an attack on rhetoric with the very weapons of rhetoric. The metaphor comes from husbandmen, who cut thongs of ox-hide with which they tie up their 10 oxen. Plutarch in his essay 'A Pleasant Life Is Impossible': 'What could anyone say? For the nature of the flesh has in itself the material of disease, and as is jokingly said, making its leash from the bull's own hide, takes its pains from the body.'

78 **Ex uno omnia specta**
From one learn all

'Eξ ἑνὸς τὰ πάνθ' ὅρα, From one learn all. So Virgil: 'From one crime learn them all.' The adage teaches that from the experience of one event we ought to learn to foresee such things next time. It is recorded by Suidas. He 5 maintains, however, that it is said of those who wrongly judge everything from a single instance; for his verb is not 'learn' but 'he learns,' as if having found one Frenchman false, one should judge them all to be so.

79 **Ex adspectu nascitur amor**
Love comes by looking

'Eκ τοῦ εἰσορᾶν γὰρ γίγνεται ἀνθρώποις ἐρᾶν, In mortals, 'tis from seeing love is born. A proverbial line of verse, telling us that love comes mainly by looking. For the unknown is not loved; mutual love is born from association. 5 And it is especially the eyes which lure one on to love, for they are particularly the seat of the soul. The poets say that in them Cupid lies in wait to send out his darts. Virgil suggested this adage when he says: 'When I saw, how I was lost, how wild delusion seized me!' And again in the *Georgics*, 'She fires him as he looks.' So in Terence, Chaerea falls helplessly in love with a girl he 10

*　*　*　*　*

8 or someone ... rhetoric] This clause was inserted in *1517/8*.

78 Tilley L 342 By the little is known the much. Derived from Suidas
  3 Virgil] *Aeneid* 2.65–6
  5 Suidas] E 1630; the discussion of the meaning was added in *1526*.

79 Tilley L 501 as above. This is largely repeated in III iv 69.
  8 Virgil] *Eclogues* 8.41; *Georgics* 3.215–6
  10 Terence] *Eunuchus* 322

has only just seen. Juvenal cites as a marvel the case of the blind lover: 'He never saw the girl for whom his passion blazed.' We read that some philosophers, and among them Democritus, put out their own eyes because they were the instigators of evil desires. And so it is for pious men to remember that it is not safe to look upon that which it is not lawful to desire. Dioge-   15
nianus records this proverb.

80   **E sublimi me derides**
    You are mocking me from your lofty height

᾿Αφ᾿ ὑψηλοῦ μοῦ καταγελᾷς, You are mocking me from your lofty height. Said of a person who laughs at another, with pride and contempt. The metaphor is taken from those who stand on a high place to speak; and   5
therefore 'look down' [*despicere*] is used in Latin for 'despise,' because whoever is in a lofty place is safer, and can disregard the person who stands in a lower spot.

81   **Extra lutum pedes habes**
    You have your feet out of the mire

᾿Εκ τοῦ πηλοῦ πόδας ἔχεις, You have your feet out of the mire. That is, you have escaped from the danger, or you are safely established out of danger. Taken from travellers. It is like that other proverb, Out of range. People are   5
said to 'stick in the mud' when they are involved in troublesome business from which they cannot extricate themselves.

82   **Ex umbra in solem**
    Out of shadow into sunlight

Ex umbra in solem educere, To bring something out of shadow into sunlight, is to bring out a thing which has been hidden and lain idle into open use by the

        * * * * *

11 Juvenal] 4.114
13 Democritus] This is from Aulus Gellius (see I i 1, line 43n) 10.17.
15 Diogenianus] 4.49

80 Another taken from Diogenianus (3.24)

81 From the Greek proverb-collections (Zenobius 3.62; Suidas E 675)
 5 other proverb] *Adagia* I iii 93; the comparison is already made by Zenobius.

82 The immediate source of this familiar expression is not clear.

public and for the common good. It is taken from athletes, whose habit it is   5
to strengthen the body's forces by endurance of sun and dust. It is the
weaklings who lie in the shade. This would be more attractive when applied
to the things of the mind: if one said, for instance, that Socrates had brought
philosophy out of the shadow into the light of the sun. There are examples
to be met with everywhere in literature.   10

83   Excubias agere in Naupacto
To keep watch in Naupactus

Φρουρῆσαι ἐν Ναυπάκτῳ, To keep watch in Naupactus. When the Achaeans
took Naupactus, they killed Pausanias, the captain of the guard and in
charge of the watch; so says Theopompus. This seems to have become a joke   5
among the people, against those who perish by their own inertia, or who
hold an office which is odious and full of danger. It is mentioned by
Zenodotus. Suidas gives it in this form, 'you shall keep watch in Naupactus.' He provides a different origin for the adage. Since those who formed
the guard for Naupactus were paid a very small wage, and bought a great   10
deal which was necessary for the purpose, it became a soldiers' jest, it
seems, at the expense of those who toiled in vain, and whose hope was not
realized. Naupactus was a town in Aetolia, which Philip held at the time; the
name is derived from ship-building, because it was there that the Heraclidae
first constructed a ship.   15

84   Devotionis templum
Temple of cursing

'Ἀρᾶς ἱερὸν, A temple of execration, was said about people who had a habit
of frequent cursing. It is a custom much to be blamed nowadays, among the

* * * * *

83 This comes from the Greek proverb-collections, and is not known from any
   literary source. Naupactus lies at the entrance to the Gulf of Corinth on the
   northern shore, and it was there that Don John of Austria routed the Ottoman
   fleet at the battle of Lepanto on 7 October 1571.
8 Zenodotus] Zenobius (always so called in the *Adagia*) 6.33, citing the lost
   historian Theopompus of the fourth century BC (*FGrHist* 115F235)
8 Suidas] Φ 742. 'Suidas … realized' was added in 1517/8.
13 Philip] King of Macedon, father of Alexander the Great. 'The name … a ship'
   was added in 1526, and comes from Stephanus Byzantius (see I ii 43n) p 470
   Meineke.

84 From Diogenianus 2.92

common people, many of whom never speak without introducing oaths and   5
curses, dreadful even to hear. In ancient times there were certain kinds of
execration, even publicly, as for instance among the Athenians against
anyone who had refused to point out the way to a person who had gone
astray. For Christians these have been replaced by what is called excom-
munication. There was also the curse laid on the enemy, mentioned by   10
Macrobius, and by Horace in the *Odes*: 'With curses I will hound you; / No
sacrifice shall purge my execration.' Hesychius states that there was a
temple of execration in Athens, of which Aristophanes makes mention in
the *Horae*, but curses were uttered only for grave calamity. Elsewhere, if I am
not mistaken, I have spoken of curses represented in tragedy, which   15
Diogenes the philosopher jokingly said had happened to him, because he
lived 'houseless and stateless, without country, without money, having no
fixed dwelling and living from day to day.' The proverb is given by Diogenianus.

85   **Expertes invidentiae Musarum fores**
     The doors of the Muses are free from envy

Ἄφθονοι Μουσῶν θύραι, The doors of the Muses are free from envy. Often
said about people who freely and frankly communicate their learning to
others, and are ready and willing to teach. It will be applicable too to those   5
who are ready to learn, like the saying we have mentioned elsewhere, 'the
doors of the Muses are open.'

* * * * *

11 Macrobius] See 1 i 12n; *Saturnalia* 3.9.15, 5.12.5–6.
11 Horace] *Epodes* (normally called by Erasmus *Odes*) 5.89–90, used again in 1 vii 61
12 Hesychius] See Erasmus' Introduction section v 35n; A 6978, citing Aristophanes frag 575 Kock; added in 1526.
16 Diogenes] This remark of Diogenes the Cynic philosopher, behind which lies a
   line from some lost tragedy (frag trag adesp 284 Nauck), is a very free quotation
   from Diogenes Laertius 6.38, added in 1526 and the Latin version of the
   fragment in 1528. It had already appeared in 1508 in 1 vii 61. The concluding
   sentence is of 1508.

85 From Diogenianus 3.23. Close to 11 vii 41, which is referred to in the last line

86 Eurybatizare
To play Eurybatus

Εὐρυβατεύεσθαι, To play Eurybatus, means to have bad morals. Eurybatus
was one of the Cercopes, a man of notable wickedness. Lucian mentions
him in his *False Prophet*: 'beyond the Cercopes, beyond Eurybatus, or Phry-   5
nondas, or Aristodemus, or Sostratus.' There was more than one person of
this name, notorious for cunning and wicked ways; for there was also an
Ephesian Eurybatus, who was sent by Croesus to raise an army, with a large
amount of money, and he defected to Cyrus, as Ephorus tells. Others think
it more likely to refer to the Eurybatus who was one of the two Cercopes, as I   10
said. Duris refers it to the Eurybatus who was a companion of Ulysses.
Nicander put on record that a Eurybatus of Aegina was by far the most
cunning and criminal. There are those who say that there was a thief of this
name, a particularly shrewd man. When he was caught and kept a prisoner,
his guards were carousing and ordered him, for their amusement, to show   15
them the methods he had used to scale houses. He refused at first, as if he
were extremely unwilling to do it, but their demands became more pressing
and in the end, with great difficulty, they persuaded him. So the fellow got
ready his sponges and stakes, and grappling-irons, which are called
engkentrides in Greek, and began to climb the wall. But as they watched, and   20
admired the originality of the technique, Eurybatus caught hold of the
fretted ceiling and escaped across the tiles before they could run round the
building. In this way he tricked his guards and got out of danger. Eustathius
mentions him in his commentary on the *Iliad*, book 1, with a reminder that
there are two ways of pronouncing the name, Eurybatus and Eurybates, and   25
that it is derived from a word meaning to go far afield. Thus it is particularly
suitable to one who is caught, but by some trick makes his escape.

* * * * *

86 This is in Diogenianus 4.76, but the principal source is Suidas E 3718, from
whence come the references to two lost fourth-century BC historians, Ephorus
and Duris (*FGrHist* 70F58c and 76F20) and to Nicander, didactic poet of the
second century BC, frag 112.
4 Cercopes] For these proverbial villains, see II vii 35.
4 Lucian] *Alexander* 4; the subject of this is Alexander of Abonuteichos a
celebrated charlatan, and *The False Prophet* is an alternative title for it, which
Erasmus always uses. One of the rascals whom Lucian mentions, Phrynondas,
stands on his own in the *Adagia* (III vii 22), and is coupled with our Eurybatus
by Plato *Protagoras* 326d. In 1528 Erasmus added that Plato-reference to III vii
22, but failed to add it here too.
23 Eustathius] See I i 77n; on *Iliad* 1.321 (110.10).

87 **Faciunt et sphaceli immunitatem**
    Aches and pains too give exemption

Καὶ σφάκελοι ποιοῦσιν ἀτέλειαν, Aches and pains too give exemption. This
is a proverb in common use in Athens, referring to people who get what
they want on any pretext whatever. It originated from the following event,   5
so they say. Peisistratus the tyrant used to exact a tithe from the Athenians
on whatever they grew in the fields. One day when he was out for a walk, he
saw an old man working among the rocks, that is to say on a stony soil, and
asked him what profit he hoped to raise from that. 'Aches and pains,' he
said, 'and Peisistratus fines us a tenth of those.' The tyrant, astonished at the   10
man's frankness, abolished the tithes on the Athenians. The thing went into
common parlance: 'even aches can gain exemption.' *Sphacelus*, however, is a
kind of illness, which usually results from excessive fatigue. Some think it is
pain in the joints, some say decay of the bone. Theophrastus in book 5 of the
Causes of Plants, explains that a defect occurs also in the roots of plants which   15
is called *sphakelismos* from the human disease. The adage is recorded by
Suidas. Hesychius points out that any severe pain is called *sphacelus*.

88 **Et meum telum cuspidem habet acuminatam**
    My weapon too has a sharpened point

A phrase with the strongest appearance of a proverb is that put into the
mouth of Hector by Homer in *Iliad* 20: 'Since my weapon too has its sharp
point.' We may properly use this whenever we admit that we are indeed the   5
weak 'r, but nevertheless do not lack the power to hurt. Similar to this is that
Virgil ɪn phrase: '– from our wound too, blood flows.' And again in Ovid: 'I
have some power too, and my darts can wound.'

* * * * *

87 This is in Zenobius 4.76, as well as Suidas (see below).
 6 Peisistratus] A notable Athenian statesman of the sixth century BC
14 Theophrastus] See I i 44n; *De causis plantarum* 5.9.1, added in *1515*
17 Suidas] κ 1206, added in *1515*
17 Hesychius] See Erasmus' Introduction section v 35n; σ 2839, added in *1526*

88 From Homer *Iliad* 20.437
 7 Virgilian phrase] *Aeneid* 12.51
 7 Ovid] *Heroides* 15.352

89 Ignavi vertitur color
The coward changes colour

Τοῦ κακοῦ τρέπεται χρώς, The coward changes colour. Plutarch in his 'On Natural Causes,' in the problem: Why does the polyp change colour? quotes as a well-known proverb 'Hence the saying that the coward's colour 5 changes.' It happens in fear that the face goes white, especially with the timid, as if all the blood were retreating to the vitals. This has more beauty if applied to the mind: as one might say, the philosopher is not at all afraid of those things which the common people have in horror, 'it is the coward who changes colour.' The proverb was born from book 13 of Homer's *Iliad*. The 10 poem goes thus:

> For the coward's colour changes and varies continually,
> Nor does his mind stay steady, but runs hither and thither
> And losing his head he shifts from one foot to another,
> His heart beats wildly as his thoughts dwell on doom,   15
> His teeth begin to chatter. Not so the brave;
> No change of colour for him, nor violent terror.

90 Ad consilium ne accesseris antequam voceris
Come not to counsel before you are called

Μὴ πρότερον εἰς βουλὴν παρέλθῃς πρὶν ἂν κληθείης, Come not to counsel before you are called. This saying, now familiar under the name of Cato, seems to have been proverbial, as Plutarch bears witness: his words in the 5 'Table-talk,' book 1, are these: 'Surely therefore it was out of place and proverbially wrong for Menelaus to become an adviser without being asked.' But some may prefer to connect this with another proverb: 'Uncalled

* * * * *

89 This seems not to be found in the printed proverb-collections, so Plutarch must be the source, as he is of the next three. Tilley c 773 A coward changes colour.
3 Plutarch] *Moralia* 916B; his *Symposiaca* or 'Table-talk' was given in *1508*, corrected in *1515*. We have had this already in I i 93.
7 This has more beauty] From here to the end we have an addition of *1517/8*.
10 Homer] *Iliad* 13.279–85

90 Tilley c 678 Come not to counsel uncalled.
4 Cato] It is no 7 among the *Breves sententiae* prefixed to the *Disticha Catonis*, the school-book of which Erasmus published an edition with notes in 1514. No connection can be traced with any historic Cato.
5 Plutarch] *Moralia* 616c

the cowards go to good men's feasts,' which I shall mention in another
place.   10

91   **Iucundissima navigatio iuxta terram, ambulatio iuxta mare**
     The most delightful sailing is by the land, and walking by the sea

Plutarch in his 'Table-talk,' book 1, records as a popular saying: 'The most
delightful sailing is by the land, and walking by the sea.' This will be rightly
adapted to carry the sense that everything is most delightful when tempered   5
by some admixture of an opposite kind; as for instance if you mingle a little
learning in your pastimes, and mix light relief with your studies. Similar to
this is the phrase quoted by the same writer from the poet Philoxenus, in the
essay which he called 'On How To Study Poetry': 'The most delicious meat is
what is not meat, and the most delicious fish what is not fish.' In the same   10
way we get more pleasure from philosophy when mingled with poetry, and
poetry with an admixture of philosophy is more attractive.

92   **Cupidinum crumena porri folio vincta est**
     The purse of desire is fastened with a leaf of leek

Πράσου φύλλῳ τὸ τῶν ἐρώτων δέδεται βαλάντιον, With a leaf of leek the
purse of the Loves is tied. This is mentioned by the same author in the book
we have just quoted, but it is best to give his own words: 'And one would   5
wonder especially at this: a man sparing and mean, once he has fallen in

* * * * *

9 in another place] *Adagia* I x 35; but there it is good men who go to feast with
  cowards.

91 From Plutarch *Moralia* 621D and 14D
 8 Philoxenus] of Leucas was one of a small band of poets in the fourth century BC
   who, in search of fresh worlds to conquer, wrote about food: see *Collectanea
   Alexandrina*, ed J.U. Powell, Oxford 1925, 251; *Poetae melici graeci*, ed D.L. Page,
   Oxford 1962, 441.

92 This was preceded in *1508* by another adage from Plutarch, *Musicam docet amor*,
   in a shorter version, which seems to be absent from the *1515* edition and became
   IV v 15 in *1517/8*; it was replaced here in *1515* with the present I ii 93, which had
   in *1508* stood near the end of the *Adagia* (IV 245). Erasmus probably derives it,
   like its neighbours, from his reading of Plutarch; but it appears in some of the
   proverb-collections, eg the Vienna Diogenianus 3.66 (*Corpus Paroemiographorum* 2.47).
 4 same author] Plutarch *Moralia* 622D, citing an anonymous fragment from the
   Greek New Comedy (frag adesp 197 Kock)

love, not unlike iron put into the fire, becomes soft and malleable, pliant and
more agreeable, so that the old humorous saying does not seem so ridiculous, that the purse of the Loves is fastened with a leaf of leek. And this is
why it is said that love is like drunkenness; it makes men hot and gay and   10
dissolute.' Plutarch thus seems to think that the proverb alludes to the
nature of the leek, which has the power to produce heat, to stimulate urine,
to rouse sexual passion, activate the menses and inflate the bowels, as we
learn from Dioscorides, book 2. Suidas explains that this adage is used of
those who go to enormous expense because they are in love, and indulge in   15
excess, like the usual lovers in comedy. Plutarch, in the essay he entitled
'Eroticus,' notes among the other commendations of Cupid or Love, that it
makes the sordid fine, the miser lavish, the churlish polite, and the timid
bold. So the pockets of Cupid are said to be tied up with a leek-leaf, because
they are easily untied, either owing to the fragile character of the leaf, or   20
because of its inherent power to relax and stimulate the body.

93 **Quem Fortuna pinxerit**
    Black-listed by Fortune

Ὃν τύχη μέλανα γράφει, τοῦτον οὐ πᾶς χρόνος δύναται λευκάναι, The man
whom Fortune writes black, can never in all time turn white: that is, if
Fortune is opposed to a man, whatever he attempts will turn out badly. The   5
allusion is to voting by black and white stones. This is found in the collections of Apostolius.

94 **Qui mori nolit ante tempus**
    Unwilling to die before his time

Athenaeus in his dinner-table talk quotes a proverb about the Sybarites: 'The

* * * * *

14 Dioscorides] See I i 22n; *De materia medica* 2.149.
14 Suidas] II 2228
16 Plutarch] *Moralia* 762B; this sentence added in *1515*

93 Removed to this place from near the end of the work in *1515*, when the
    reference to Apostolius (12.76), who must be the source, was added. The ex-
    planation from black and white voting-pebbles (*Adagia* I v 53) does not suit the
    wording of the Greek, which speaks of painting black. It also was added in
    1515.

94 Tilley τ 290 He does not desire to die before his time.
 3 Athenaeus] 12.520a. For the Greek city of Sybaris, on the Gulf of Taranto in
    Southern Italy, see *Adagia* II ii 65.

man who is unwilling to die before his appointed time in Sybaris must not
look upon the setting or the rising sun.' He writes that this was a common 5
saying, due to the fact that the city of Sybaris was situated in a low place, in a
sort of enclosed valley, so that in the summer, morning and evening alike,
they felt a terrible cold, and at midday an intolerable heat. Cicero in the *De
finibus* book 2 informs us that the same was said of certain Asoti, a race so
named for their luxurious living; for at sunset they were drunk and in the 10
morning they were snoring. Columella in the preface of his *Agriculture*
applies it to debauched fellows who spend their nights on lust and drunkenness and their days on sleep and gambling: 'And presently, then, that we
may come to our gluttonous feasts in proper fettle, we steam out our daily
indigestion in sweat-baths, and by drying out the moisture of our bodies we 15
seek to arouse a thirst: we spend our nights in licentiousness and drunkenness, our days in gaming or sleeping, and account ourselves blessed by
fortune in that we behold neither the rising of the sun nor its setting.'

95 **Barba tenus sapientes**
Bearded, therefore wise

'Εκ πώγωνος σοφοί, and ἀπὸ πώγωνος σοφισταί, and ἀπὸ πώγωνος
φιλόσοφοι, Bearded, therefore wise, and sophists and philosophers as far as
the beard goes. So they were called, who apart from beard and cloak had 5
nothing of the philosopher. Sometimes Plutarch uses this in his 'Table-talk.'
Horace alludes to it when he says: 'What time he bade me nurse my
reverend beard.' Lucian also often jokes about philosophers with 'profound
beards,' and in the *Eunuch* Bagoas says 'If we are to judge a philosopher by
his beard, the goats would carry off first prize.' Martial likewise: 'No negligi- 10
ble beard hangs from your chin.' This may rightly be turned against those
whose holiness of life consists entirely in their dress, not in mind or conduct.

* * * * *

8 Cicero] *De finibus* 2.8.23, added in *1523*; cf Otto 1662. It looks as though in a
moment of inattention Erasmus had taken the word *asotus* (a Greek adjective
meaning 'profligate') as a proper name, although it occurs in its latinized form
half a dozen times in Cicero, and he was of course familiar with it. This
happened too in the *De copia* col 36 (CWE 24.393).
11 Columella] See I i 37n; *Res rustica* 1 praef 16, added in *1523*.

95 Seemingly from Plutarch. There is more on beards in IV ii 17.
6 Plutarch] *Moralia* 709B
7 Horace] *Satires* 2.9.35
8 Lucian] *De mercede conductis* 40; *Eunuchus* 9
10 Martial] 9.47.4

96 Inter lapides pugnabant, nec lapidem tollere poterant
They fought among stones but could not pick one up

Plutarch in the fourth decade of his 'Table-talk,' problem 1: 'Seeing the young
servant who came with Philo taking bread, but wanting nothing else, he said
How strange! This is what the proverb means: The battle was among rocks   5
but not a rock could they lift.' This seems to be said about people who do not
make use of present advantages, either from laziness or from a false idea of
their condition, like those who cannot be bothered to pick up a stone off a
heap to repel an enemy. The same line is quoted in Athenaeus, book 10, and
he adds another as though it had a similar meaning: 'They died of thirst,   10
while water came up to their lips.'

97 In alio mundo
In another world

'Ὡς ἐν ἄλλῳ κόσμῳ, As if in another world. This is a form of proverb which is
still in common use, about people who are different, far and away, from the
lives of others; or to whom everything seems new; or who are far away from   5
their native land. Plutarch in his 'Table-talk': 'But the race of Greeks is completely alien and remote from us, as if they were born and lived in another
world.' Horace said in the *Odes*, with a similar metaphor: 'Why change we
our own land / For other lands warmed by a foreign sun?' And Macrobius in
the preface to the *Saturnalia*: 'Except where the true ring of the Latin tongue   10
is not allowed to us, born as we are somewhere under a different sky.' As the

* * * * *

96 From Plutarch *Moralia* 660D
   6 This seems] In *1508–20* the interpretation ran: 'Used, it seems, of a life more
     than usually laborious and frugal, the metaphor being taken either from the
     siege of some citadel set on precipitous rocks or from the cultivation of ground
     which is very stony, and therefore brings little return to the man who tills it
     except excessive labour.' Erasmus changed his view in *1523*.
   9 Athenaeus] 10.457b, added in *1523*; He is quoting a riddle as 'in general
     circulation,' which consists of three hexameter lines: 'Five men in ten ships
     landed in one place; / They fought with stones, but could not lift a stone, / And
     died of thirst, though the water was over their chins.' The solution appears to
     be lost.

97 Again from Plutarch. Suringar 88
   6 Plutarch] *Moralia* 669D; the right reading is not *Hellenôn*, Greeks but *enaliôn*,
     marine animals.
   8 Horace] *Odes* 2.16. 18–9
   9 Macrobius] See I i 12n; *Saturnalia* 1 praef. 11

sky is common to all, the phrase 'to be born under a different sky' must necessarily be a metaphor. And Virgil says regarding the Elysian Fields, 'They have their sun, and their own stars they know.' He said 'their own' meaning different from ours. So Claudian says '– we have other stars, / And   15
other orbs; purer the light you'll see.' Again Virgil, in the *Bucolics*: 'And Britons, cut off by the width of the world.' It usually happens to the generality of mortals, that when they are new arrivals in a region fairly distant from their own corner of the world, there is nothing which does not alarm them, or amaze them, or arouse their wonder, as if they had been   20
carried off into another sphere.

98   **Piscis repositus**
      A fish put by

'Αποκείμενος ἰχθύς, A fish put by, seems to have become a proverb against those who reserve nothing for a future occasion. For fish used to be a great delicacy. The prudent man always has something in the way of food put by,   5
to bring out for an unexpected guest; and it does not do to imitate Achilles in Homer, for when Priam's envoys go to him they find the house empty and starveling. The adage, it seems, should take this form: 'A fish put by should not be brought out again in front of all.' Plutarch in his 'Table-talk': 'But I smiling said, O friend, this is like dragging in the proverbial fish put by   10
along with the Pythagorean peck-measure.' This can be applied to a speech, or a story, not particularly attractive in itself, which none the less is repeated

* * * * *

13 Virgil] *Aeneid* 6.641
15 Claudian] *De raptu Proserpinae* (c AD 400) 2.282–4
16 Virgil] *Eclogues* 1.66

98 This comes in Apostolius (9.2A); but Plutarch, from whom a group of adages seems to have been taken at this point, is the more likely source.
3 against those] In *1508*, Erasmus directed his proverb 'against skinflints and those who store away even things that cannot keep'; in *1515* he replaced this by the importance of a well-stocked larder as a provision against unexpected guests. But the example he gives is surprising; for neither in *Iliad* 9.205–22, where he entertains the delegates sent by the Greek leaders, nor in 24.621–8, where Priam comes to ask for the dead body of Hector his son, does Achilles seem to suffer from any shortage of provisions.
9 Plutarch] *Moralia* 703E; what follows is quoted in *Adagia* I i 2 (line 66) in Erasmus' discussion of the maxim of Pythagoras about the peck-measure.

not without boredom. It suits the mean man, and the one who worries about the morrow.

99 Non est eiusdem et multa et opportuna dicere
Speaking much and speaking well are not the same thing

Χωρὶς τό τ᾽ εἰπεῖν πολλὰ καὶ τὰ καίρια, Different are these, to speak well and speak aptly. An iambic line in use as a proverb, which warns us to avoid verbosity: one is almost bound to fall into error if one tries to say a great deal. 5 In the Hebrew proverbs we find 'In the multitude of words there wanteth not sin.'

100 Psaphonis aves
Psapho's birds

Ψάφωνος ὄρνιθες, Psapho's birds. This is used when someone achieves fame by a new method, as when a person bribes others to praise him and as it were dictates to them speeches of praise, through which he wishes to 5 become a public figure. They tell that in Libya there was a man called Psapho, who had a mind to be considered divine; so he caught a number of birds which could be taught human speech, and trained them to say these words, 'Great God Psapho.' When he had trained them he let them go in the hills. They sang what they had been taught, and from them the rest of the 10

* * * * *

13 It suits] In this last sentence, added in 1536, Erasmus seems to return to his original view, that one should put by against a rainy day rather than for the benefit of unexpected guests.

99 Tilley M 1293 To speak much and to the matter is two men's labour. The line is from Sophocles, *Oedipus Coloneus* 808; but as Erasmus does not name the author, he probably derives it here from a proverb-collection, Suidas X 445 or Apostolius 18.47.
6 Hebrew] Proverbs 10:19

100 The story is told in the *Philosophumena* (29.4) of Maximus Tyrius, a sophist of the second century AD, and presumably this is Erasmus' source, for in a similar tale in Aelian *Varia historia* 14.30 the man's name is Anno. He refers to Maximus in 1508 in three other places, but shows no knowledge of the Greek text, which was not printed until 1557 (by Henri Estienne). There was however a Latin version by Cosimo Pacci, published in Rome in 1517 and re-edited by Beatus Rhenanus for Froben in 1519 with a dedication to Jean Grolier, and Erasmus may have used this in manuscript. He added a note that 'the proverb is recorded in' Apostolius in 1515, and changed this to 'I have found the proverb in' in 1517/8.

birds learnt to sing it too. The people of Libya, who did not know how this had been contrived, believed it to be a divine occurrence, and set about worshipping Psapho and including him among their gods. I have found the proverb in the collections of Apostolius.

1   **Aut regem aut fatuum nasci oportere**
    One ought to be born a king or a fool

Annaeus Seneca was a man, as Tacitus said, of a very pleasant wit; this is clear from that amusing skit which he wrote against Claudius Caesar, and which has recently come to light in Germany. In this short work he mentions   5
an adage, One ought to be born a king or a fool. It is best to give his very words: 'As for me,' he says, 'I know I have gained my freedom from the fact that the end has come for that man who proved the truth of the proverb, One ought to be born a king or a fool.' And again in the same book, 'He killed in one and the same house Crassus, Magnus, Scribonia, Bassionia, the   10
Assarii, although they were noble, while Crassus was such a fool that he might have reigned.' In another place, though the allusion is less clear, he refers to the same thing in his line 'He snapped the royal thread of a stupid life.' If Hesiod is right in the view that a popular saying is never meaning-less, perhaps it would not be beside the point to inquire what can have given   15
rise to this proverb, uniting as it does two such dissimilar things – a king and a fool – with the obvious intention of drawing a parallel between the two. Especially as it is the particular distinction of kings (and the only true royal one) to surpass all others in wisdom, prudence, and watchfulness.

Well, everyone agrees that those famous kings of old time were for the   20
most part well endowed with stark stupidity; one can see this in the fables of the poets on the one hand, in the writings of the historians on the other. Homer, for instance (and the writers of tragedy after him), makes his

* * * * *

1 This was written for the 1515 edition, Seneca's *Ludus de morte Claudii* (from which the adage is taken) having only just appeared, and had very slight revision later. A German version by Georgius Spalatinus (Georg Burkhard) was published in Mainz by Johann Schoeffer about 1520 (*Bibliotheca belgica* E 273), and seems to be a fairly common book.

3 Tacitus] *Annals* 13.3. Erasmus' exact phrase agrees, not with Tacitus but with Beatus Rhenanus in the preface to his notes on the *Ludus de morte Claudii*, published with the *Moria* by Froben in 1515; but it is not known which came first.

4 amusing skit] The *Ludus* aforesaid, or *Apocolocyntosis*, published as a new discovery by Erasmus in his Seneca of 1515 (see I i 33n). He refers to 1.1., 11.2 and 4.1.

14 Hesiod] *Works and Days* 763–4

Agamemnon ambitious rather than wise. What could be more stupid than to
purchase the title of commander-in-chief by the cruel slaughtering of an only   25
daughter? What could be more idiotic than to be up in arms so childishly for
the sake of a chit from a barbarous land, and then when he couldn't keep his
sweetheart, to snatch the girl belonging to Achilles, and put the whole army
in danger? And then there is Achilles himself – how foolishly he rages when
bereft of his lady-love and how childishly he goes crying to his mother! And   30
yet he is the one whom the poet sets before us as the perfect example of an
excellent prince. Look at Ajax, and his unwise anger; look at Priam, and his
senile maunderings when he embraces Helen – that shameless creature –
and calls her his daughter, and declares he has no regrets for that war which
brought him such disasters, bereaved him of so many children, plunged him   35
into such mourning so often – and all so that Paris should not fail to possess
his girl. Why say more? The whole of the *Iliad*, long as it is, has nothing in it,
as Horace says in an elegant line, but 'the passions of foolish kings and
foolish peoples.' The *Odyssey* also has its dense and stupid suitors and
characters like Alcinous. Even Hercules himself is described as sturdy and   40
spirited, but heavy and doltish in mind. Indeed Hesiod (whom some think
older than Homer) calls princes 'gift-greedy' and 'childish' – I suppose on
account of their small wisdom in government, and the way they strained
after the accumulation of riches by fair means and foul, rather than after the
public good. So they imagine old Midas, wearing his asses' ears as a mark of   45
stupidity. And I think perhaps this is the place to mention how the earliest
theologians – that is, the poets – attribute wisdom to Apollo and to Minerva,
but to Jove, the ruler of gods and men, they leave nothing but the three-
forked lightning, and that nod and that eyebrow which makes all Olympus
tremble. Moreover, what profligate, what buffoon ever fooled so foolishly,   50
or was more vilely vile, than this character whom they make ruler of the
world? He deceives his wife with tricks, turning himself into a swan, a bull, a
shower of gold; he rigs up traps for women, suborns his Ganymedes, fills
heaven with bastards. In the same way Neptune and Pluto are painted as
fierce and ruthless, but they are not credited with wisdom.   55
    But suppose we dismiss the legends and turn to more recent times, to
history: how much sense do you think Croesus King of Lydia had, if he was

*   *   *   *   *

38 Horace] *Epistles* 1.2.8. The suitors who courted Penelope while Ulysses was
   away at the siege of Troy and on his way home, were a very low-minded lot;
   but why Erasmus should have such a poor opinion of Alcinous king of the
   Phaeacians, who is presented with sympathy in the *Odyssey*, is far from clear.
41 Hesiod] *Works and Days* 39–40
45 Midas] See *Adagia* I iii 67.

truly such as Herodotus paints him, so relying on his treasure of jewels and gold that he was angry with Solon for refusing him the name of 'fortunate'? Or what could be imagined more idiotic than Xerxes, when he sent messen- 60 gers to Mount Athos, to terrify it with most scornful and threatening letters, or ordered so many lashes to be given to the Hellespont? Alexander the Great showed a no less kingly stupidity when he renounced his father and took pleasure in being greeted as the son of Jove, when he competed in drinking to excess, when he allowed himself to be worshipped as god by the 65 flatterers in his banquets, when he complained that this world was too small for his victories, and took to the ocean to find other worlds to conquer. I leave aside all the others, the Dionysiuses, the Ptolemies, the Juliuses, the Neros, the Tiberiuses, the Caligulas, the Heliogabaluses, the Commoduses, and the Domitians – among whom one arrogated to himself the name of god 70 when he was unworthy of the name of man, another exposed himself to be laughed to scorn by his very flatterers, another urged by ambition shook the whole world with meaningless wars.

But I look rather silly myself when I embark on this catalogue, and as they say, seek water in the sea. You merely have to turn over the chronicles 75 of both the ancients and the moderns, and you will find that in several centuries there have been barely one or two princes who did not by sheer stupidity bring disaster to human affairs. A prince, indeed, is either a fool to the immense detriment of the whole world, or a wise man to the immense benefit of all; although it is easier to do badly than well, and the harm he 80 does spreads or rather pervades everything more quickly than the good. But nowadays we see some princes who aspire to anything except the one thing which would make them deserve the name of prince; and stupid subjects, who admire everything in their kings except the one thing needful. 'He is young'; that would recommend him as a bridegroom to a bride, not as a 85 prince to the state. 'He is good-looking'; that is the right praise for a woman. 'He is broad-shouldered, broad-flanked'; if you were praising an athlete, that would be the way to do it. 'He is strong and can stand hard toil'; that is a testimonial for a batman or a houseboy. 'He has a large store of gold'; you are describing an active moneylender. 'He is eloquent'; that's what dazzles me 90 in a sophist. 'He sings well, he dances well'; that is the way to praise flute-players and actors, not kings. 'He has no equal in drinking' – for former princes actually delighted in this commendation! It would be fitter praise for a sponge. 'He is tall, and stands head and shoulders above the rest'; that's

* * * * *

58 Herodotus] See I i 96n; 1.30–33; 7.35.
70 Domitians] LeClerc's suggestion; the text has *Domitios*.
74 as they say] Cf *Adagia* I vii 57, I ix 75.

splendid, if one wants to reach something down from a high place. As for   95
saying 'He's a skilled dice player, he's good at chess,' that is praise shared
with the lowest idlers, and a prince should be ashamed of it. You may heap
up everything – public refinement, gold and jewels, ancestral images, a
pedigree drawn from Hercules (or from Codrus or Cecrops if you prefer),
but unless you tell me of a mind far removed from vulgar foolishness, free   100
from sordid desires for worthless things, and from the prejudices of the
herd, I have not heard any praise worthy of a king.

For it was not ill-advisedly that the divine Plato wrote that the only way
for a state to attain happiness was for the supreme command to be given to
philosophers, or else, inversely, that those who govern should themselves   105
follow philosophy. And to follow philosophy is not just to wear a mantle
and to carry a bag round, or let your beard grow. What is it then? It is to
despise those things which the common herd goggles at, and to think quite
differently from the opinions of the majority. And I don't see how it is
possible for a man who thinks he is free to do just what he likes, who   110
marvels at riches as if they were important, who thinks even a sworn oath
may be set aside for the sake of power, who is captivated by empty glory,
who is a slave to shameful lust, who is terrified of death – I just can't see how
such a man can play the part of a beneficent king.

The first requisite is to judge rightly about each matter, because opin-   115
ions are like springs from which all the actions of life flow, and when they
are contaminated everything must needs be mismanaged. The next essential is to recoil from evil and to be led towards good. For true wisdom
consists not only in the knowledge of truth, but in the love and eager
striving for what is good. You may well find among rulers one who can see   120
that it is not possible to go to war without grave disaster to human affairs,
and that an old obsolete claim to sovereignty is not very important – and yet
he will plunge everything into war merely out of ambition. There may be
one who can see that the greatest curse of a state comes from appointing as
magistrates, not those who can be of the most use to the public weal by their   125
prudence, experience and integrity, but those who can bid the highest
sums – and yet he will be impelled by avarice to look after the treasury and let
the abuse go on. And there is another who understands that the duty of a

* * * * *

99 Codrus] Codrus was the last, Cecrops according to legend the earliest king of
    Athens; both therefore are legendary figures typical of remote antiquity.
103 Plato] *Republic* 5.473c–d
106 mantle] The *pallium*, regarded in Rome as a garment typically Greek, the wallet
    to contain scraps of food obtained by begging, and the beard (*Adagia* I ii 95)
    were the trade-marks in Rome of the philosophical Greekling.

prince, who takes taxes from all, is to look after everyone's interest, to preside over trials, to stamp out crime, to watch the magistrature, to amend   130
useless laws. And yet he is called away from this business by pleasures, which do not give him the time to attend to matters worthy of a ruler. Another is conscious that he has it in his power to confer a great benefit on the human race, but at the risk of his life; and anyone who thinks it is the most terrible thing to die, will fail in duty to the state at this point. And so   135
first of all the mind of the prince must be freed from all false ideas, so that he can see what is truly good, truly glorious, truly splendid. The next thing is to instil the hatred of what is base, the love of what is good, so that he can see clearly what is becoming to a prince, and wish for nothing but what is worthy of a good and beneficent ruler. Let him recognize the good where it   140
may be found, and always measure everything by it, never varying from this aim. This is what is meant by wisdom, and it is in this that the prince must so far excel other mortals, as he excels them in dignity, in wealth, in splendour, and in power.

If only all Christian princes would copy that wisest of all kings, who   145
when he was given a free choice of a boon from Him to whom nothing is impossible, wished for wisdom alone, and that wisdom by which he might rightly govern his people! And pray what did he teach his own son, but the love and following of wisdom? It is for this reason that the Egyptians make a symbolic representation of a prince by drawing an eye and a sceptre. Indeed   150
what the eye is to the body, so is a true prince to the people; the sun is the eye of the world, the prince the eye of the multitude. As the mind is to the body, so is the prince to the state; the mind knows, the body obeys. And if the mind commands the body, it is for the body's good; it does not rule for itself like a tyrant, but for that which is in its charge. Above all, the good ruler is   155
the living portrayal of God, who rules the universe. And the closer the prince conforms to the lines of the original, the more magnificent he is. God is all-seeing, all-feeling, and swayed by no passions. He is greatest in power, but at the same time greatest in goodness. He does good to all, even the unworthy. He deals no punishments, except rarely and when he must. He   160
governs this world for us and not for himself. All the reward he asks is to do good. But the evil prince, on the contrary, seems to be the copy of the devil, and to act in his stead. Either he knows nothing, or what he knows is how to bring about public disaster. What power he has, he uses to harm the state.

* * * * *

145 wisest of all kings] Solomon; see 1 Kings 3:9.
149 Egyptians] Plutarch *Moralia* 354F, used in two other of the longest essays in the *Adagia*, II i 1 *Festina lente* and III vii 1 *Scarabaeus aquilam quaerit*

And though it is in his power to do a great deal of harm to everybody, he   165
would like to do even more than he can.

Nothing is nobler than a good king, nothing better, nothing nearer God;
equally, nothing is worse than a bad prince, nothing viler, nothing more like
the devil. There is something divine about a beneficent prince, but no wild
beast is more destructive than a tyrant. And a tyrant is whoever wields   170
power for himself, whatever name his paintings and statues give him. It is
not for us to pass judgment, as it were, upon the great ones of the earth, but
yet we are obliged – not without sorrow – to feel the lack in Christian princes
of that high wisdom of which we have spoken. All these revolutions, treaties
made and broken, frequent risings, battle and slaughter, all these threats   175
and quarrels, what do they arise from but stupidity? And I rather think that
some part of this is due to our own fault. We do not hand over the rudder of
the ship to anyone but a skilled steersman, when nothing is at stake but four
passengers or a small cargo; but we hand over the state, in which so many
thousands of people are in peril, to the first comer. If anyone is to be a   180
coachman, he learns the art, spends care and practice; but for anyone to be a
king, we think it is enough for him to be born. And yet to rule a kingdom
well, as it is the finest of all functions, is also the most difficult by far. You
choose the man who is to have charge of a ship; but you do not choose the
man to whom you are entrusting so many cities, so many human lives? But   185
there it is, the thing is so established that it is impossible to root it out. Kings
are born, and whoever may have been picked out by chance, whether he be
good or bad, stupid or wise, sane or clouded in mind, as long as he looks like
a human being, he is to be entrusted with supreme power in the state. By his
will the world is to be thrown into an uproar with wars and slaughter, all   190
things sacred and profane are to be turned upside down.

But if this is a thing which we cannot change, the next best plan would
be to improve matters by careful education; and if we may not choose a
suitable person to be our ruler, we must strive to try to make that person
suitable whom fate has given us. We see with what care and solicitude and   195
watchfulness a father brings up his son, who is the future master of one
estate. How much more care, then, should be spent on the education of one
who, if good, will be so to the immense benefit of all, and if bad, will bring
about the ruin of all – one on whose nod hangs the safety or the destruction
of the world? With what rules and precepts of philosophy must that mind be   200
fortified, not only against such great calamities as may arise in a state, but
against the favour of fortune, so often accompanied by pride and stupidity;

* * * * *

181 learns the art] Cf *Adagia* I ii 76, II ii 82.

against pleasures, which can corrupt the best natures; still more against the dangerous fawning of flatterers, and that poisonous 'Bravo!' which they chant – particularly when the prince is acting most like a madman. It seems to me that he should have attached to him, while still an infant, some skilful educator; for no one can truly be fashioned into a prince, except long before he knows that he is what he is. In the early days, I say, a preceptor should be appointed, and we should take all the more care in choosing him because we are not free to choose our prince – but we are free to educate him. Let him instil into this childish mind, as yet blank and malleable, opinions worthy of a prince; arm it with the best principles of conduct, show it the difference between a true prince and a tyrant, and lay before its very eyes what a god-like thing is a beneficent ruler, what a loathsome hateful brute is a tyrant. He will explain that a ruler who wields power for himself and not for the state is no prince, but a robber; that there is no difference between pirates and pirate-minded princes, except that the latter are more powerful and can bring so much more disaster on human affairs. He will impress on his pupil that he can be of use to so many thousands of people – nay, to the whole world, by simply behaving as one good and wise man. He will teach that among Christians supreme rule means administration of the state, and not dominion. It may bear the name of supreme rule, but he must remember that he is ruling over free men, and over Christians, that is, people who are twice free. In addition, for a person to be a prince it is not enough to be born, to have ancestral statues, the sceptre and the crown. What makes a prince is a mind distinguished for its wisdom, a mind always occupied with the safety of the state, and looking to nothing but the common good. He will warn his pupil not to judge himself by the plaudits of the stupid populace or the praise of flatterers, not to do anything on the impulsion of hatred, love, or anger, or at the urge of any passion. When he appoints magistrates, creates laws, or in his other duties, he must work for one end only, for good, and for the people's benefit. It is not enough if he himself does harm to no one – the prince is also the guarantor of the uprightness of his officials. The glory of a prince does not lie in extending his sway, in removing his neighbours by force of arms; but if he happens to acquire the sovereignty of a region, he must make it flourish by justice, by wise economy, and the other arts of peace. The teacher will recommend him to be particularly inclined to serve the cause of good men, to be ready to pardon, and with the attitude towards punishment of a friendly doctor, who amputates or cauterizes the limb which he despairs of healing; to be careful to avoid everything from which he can foresee the danger of evil to the state. Above all, he is to shun war in every way; other things give rise to this or that calamity, but war lets loose at one go a whole army of wrongs. These principles and others like them should be impressed on the child's mind, with the help of the maxims of the wise and the examples of esteemed princes.   245

What actually happens is that no kind of man is more corruptly or carelessly brought up than those whose education is of such importance to so many people. The baby who is to rule the world is handed over to the stupidest of womenkind who are so far from instilling anything in his mind worthy of a prince, that they discourage whatever the tutor rightly advises,   250 or whatever inclination to gentleness the child may have in himself – and they teach him to act like a prince, that is like a tyrant. Then no one fails to fawn and flatter. The courtiers applaud, the servants obey his every whim, even the tutor is obsequious; and he is not doing this to make the prince more beneficial to his country, but to ensure a splendid future for himself.   255 The cleric who is popularly called his confessor, is obsequious too – he has some bishopric in mind. There is flattery from the judges, flattery from playmates and companions; so that Carneades was right when he said that the only art kings could learn properly was the art of riding, because only a horse makes no distinction between prince and peasant and is unable to   260 flatter. He just tosses off the rider who is not skilful enough to stay on his back, no matter who it may be.

One of the earliest lessons is pomp and pride; he is taught that whatever he wants, he can have. He hears that the property of everyone belongs to the prince, that he is above the law; that the whole paraphernalia of govern-   265 ment, laws and policies exist stored in the prince's mind. He hears the terms *sacred majesty, serene highness, divinity, god on earth,* and other such superb titles. In short, while he is yet a boy, all he learns to play at is being a tyrant. Then he is caught up among the girls; they all allure and admire and defer to him. The effeminate crew of young friends is there, and they have no other   270 topic for jokes or conversation but girls. Next there are other diversions – gaming, dancing, feasting, lute-playing, gadding about; the best years of his life are used up like this. If he takes a fancy to beguile his leisure by reading, he reads old wives' tales, or what is worse, historical romances. His mind is not in the least equipped with any antidote, and he imbibes from them an   275 enthusiasm – what the Greeks call *zeal* – for some pernicious hero, say Julius Caesar or Xerxes or Alexander the Great. And what suits him best in them is the worst. They furnish the worst example, they foster the craziest urges. Now imagine, if you please, an intelligence not selected from among many, as should be the case, but a very ordinary mind, and an education so corrupt   280

* * * * *

258 Carneades] The leading philospher of the school called the Middle Academy (mid second century BC); this remark is recorded by Plutarch *Moralia* 58F.
268 titles] Other examples are given in *Adagia* III vi 95.

that it would corrupt the mentality of an Aristides; then imagine the poison of flattery, frolic and pleasure (which don't agree very well with wisdom), luxurious living, wealth and magnificence, the sense of power; all this at an age of ruthlessness and inclined naturally to bad courses. Add finally the tainting of the mind by false ideas. And can you wonder if, coming from this 285 early environment to the administration of a kingdom, he doesn't do it very wisely?

'But never mind,' they say, 'he's young, he'll learn by experience.' But the prince must never be young, even if he is young in years. Any prudence which is won from experience is of a sorry kind, and sorriest of all in a 290 prince. The prince's prudence will be too dearly bought by the country, if he only learns by waging war that war is the thing he must avoid at all costs; or if he fails to understand that public offices must be given to upright men, until he sees the state tottering through the audacity of evildoers. Don't tell me that those who wish to learn to sing to the lute will spoil several lutes in 295 the process, before they learn the art, as Xenophon said; that would mean that the prince would only learn to administer his state by the ruin of the state.

It is not therefore much to be wondered at, if we see things going absolutely contrary to the way they should; when instead of the passions 300 which arise from the body being controlled by the mind the disturbances in the mind spread out into the body, when the eyes see less than the rest of the body sees, when the person who is most pernicious and harmful to the public is the very person who should be beneficial to all, acting in place of God. Do we not see fine cities, created by the people, overthrown by the 305 princes? Or a state enriched by the toil of its citizens, and looted by the princes' greed? Plebeian lawyers make good laws, princes violate them; the people seek for peace, the princes stir up war.

I think these are the things which give rise to this adage, from which somehow or other we have digressed a long way; but now we return to it. So 310 it is said, One ought to be born a king or a fool, because the primitive kings were of that sort, as the ancients tell – and may the princes of our day be altogether different! For everything is permitted to fools, because of the weakness of their minds. And everything is praised in kings, because of their power. There is perhaps another way of understanding the saying, in reference to 315 the equal happiness of kings and fools; because whatever a king wants is provided by fortune, and fools are no less fortunate because of their self-

* * * * *

281 Aristides] The Athenian politician of the fifth century BC, whose integrity was so proverbial that he was nicknamed 'the just.'
296 Xenophon] *Oeconomicus* 2.13

satisfaction, it allows them to think they have no lack of good gifts. And in
fact the proverb seems to have originated among the Romans, who hated
the name of king as barbaric and tyrannous, and contrary to political free-   320
dom, of which they at that time were the most enthusiastic supporters.

2 Minutula pluvia imbrem parit
A tiny rain gives birth to a rainstorm

Ψεκάδες ὄμβρον γεννῶσαι, Tiny drops that produce a shower: suitable
whenever a thing which is small at the outset grows into something large.
As for instance in Plautus, *Menaechmi*: 'Now your leaves are falling, then the   5
trees will fall.' So it behoves us to be watchful about small things, lest we
should little by little fall into some great trouble, as the proverbial line warns
us: 'Great things you'll lose, unless you watch the small.' The Greek word
(*psekas*) means a thin drizzle, such as comes even from mist when fairly
thick.   10

3 Citra vinum temulentia
Intoxication without wine

Ἄοινος μέθη, Drunkenness without wine. Theophrastus, as Plutarch tells
us in his 'Table-talk,' called barbers' shops 'teetotal drunkenness' because as
people sat in them, doing nothing, they became so drunk with speech that   5
they poured out everything they had in their minds just as drunkards do in
their cups, pouring out words all the time in a sort of intoxication, words
which in the end will cut their throats, as Pliny says. Horace calls insolence
drunkenness, 'intoxicated with fortune's favours.' There is a common
name, 'the drunkenness of the bread-basket,' for arrogance and the moral   10
licence which often goes with prosperity, and this is much more dangerous

* * * * *

2 This could be derived from Apostolius (18.52). Tilley D 617 Many drops make a
shower.
5 Plautus] *Menaechmi* 375–6, quoted from memory; it forms II viii 68.
7 proverbial line] Menander *Sententiae* 245 (see I i 30n). The last sentence was
added in 1517/8.

3 This is in Apostolius (3.29e), but Erasmus no doubt derives it direct from
Plutarch. Suringar 41
3 Plutarch] *Moralia* 716A, citing Theophrastus frag 76 Wimmer. This recurs in I vi
70 and I x 39.
8 Pliny] *Naturalis historia* 14.141; again in I vi 70 and I vii 17
8 Horace] *Odes* 1.37.11–2

than the kind induced by wine. The heat of wine, indeed, is calmed down by a few hours, or even by sleep; but the other kind is prone to last in many cases right to the end of life.

4   **Palmam ferre**
    To bear the palm

'To bear the palm,' 'to award the palm,' 'to carry off the palm,' and suchlike expressions, even if they seem straightforward through their frequent use, are yet a proverbial figure of speech. The palm does not itself signify victory,   5
but a tree 'with leaves perpetually green,' which the Greeks call *phoinix*. Why the metaphor should be taken particularly from this tree is a question answered, I think, by what Plutarch says in his 'Table-talk,' that this tree alone was used for the crown common to all the sacred contests, whereas otherwise each game had its own tree or plant to mark the victor: such as the bay,   10
olive, myrtle or celery. Some think that this was the tree sacred to Apollo before the bay, and that the oldest sign of victory was the palm, not any other tree. Why this tree was chiefly selected by the ancients for this use, Aulus Gellius tells in *Attic Nights*, book 3 chapter 6, where he writes that the palm-tree has a peculiar quality which agrees with the natural temper of   15
brave men: 'for if,' he says, 'you place a heavy weight on the wood from this tree, and so increase the pressure that the weight of the burden cannot be borne, the palm does not break down nor bend but reacts against the weight, pushes upwards and makes a rising curve.' He quotes authorities for this amazing thing, Aristotle in *Problemata*, book 7, and Plutarch in the   20
'Table-talk,' book 8. And I found the words of Plutarch on this subject in the book cited by Gellius: 'For the wood of the palm-tree, if you subject it to great pressure under a weight, is not bent downwards, but curves the other way, just as if it were resisting the violence done to it by the weight. This very thing happens also in contests between athletes. For those who yield to their   25
opponents through weakness and lack of spirit are pushed out of the way by them. But those who persevere steadfastly in this exercise are borne forward and strengthened not only in physical force but in quality of mind.' Pliny says the same thing in his sixteenth book, chapter 42: 'Fir and larch are

* * * * *

4 This may come from Erasmus' general reading; it is scarcely proverbial.
8 Plutarch] *Moralia* 723B
14 Gellius] 3.6, citing Aristotle frag 229 Rose and Plutarch *Moralia* 724E. This recurs in the *Parabolae* 617C; cf Tilley P 37 The straighter grows the palm, the heavier the weight it bears.
28 Pliny] *Naturalis historia* 16.222; the text here does not quite make sense.

strong for bearing weight, even when placed transversely. Oak and olive   30
bend and give under a weight, but those others resist, and are not easily
broken; if they give way it is from decay rather than strain. And the palm is
the most robust of trees, for it curves the other way. But the poplar would
spread under any downward weight; the palm, on the contrary, takes the
form of an arch.' Theophrastus says the same in his fifth book on plants.   35
This virile force of mind, corresponding to the native strength of the palm-
tree, is aptly described by Virgil, when he says: 'You must not yield to
affliction, but go forth all the more daringly, / As your fortune allows you.'
And that passage of Horace is not unlike it:

> Like some tough-grained oak, lopped by the woodman   40
> On Algidus, that dark-browed, verdurous mountain:
> It bleeds, it feels the shock
> Yet draws in vigour from the very axe,
> Flourishing as fiercely as the severed Hydra
> Sprouted at chafing Hercules. Old Cadmus'   45
> Dragon-sown fields at Thebes
> Never pushed up a prodigy like this.
> Whelm it in water, it will come up brighter,
> Throw it, and it will grapple with the winner
> Again and take the applause.   50
> The wars they wage breed tales for wives to tell.

5   **Relinque quippiam et Medis**
    Leave something for the Medes too

Λεῖπέ τι καὶ Μήδοις, Leave a remnant for the Medes too, is a proverbial jest
against people who leave nothing after a banquet, or who waste their whole
substance. Plutarch in the 'Table-talk': 'This is a common saying among us   5
Boeotians, "Leave something for the Medes," from the time when the
Medes invaded Phocis and the farthest borders of Boeotia, harassing and
distressing everything with devastation.' However he adds what is still
currently said today: 'Leave something for the guests who are to come.' The

* * * * *

35 Theophrastus] *Historia plantarum* 5.6.1 (see I i 44n).
37 Virgil] *Aeneid* 6.95–6
39 Horace] *Odes* 4.4.57–68 (tr James Michie)

5   Probably taken direct from Plutarch. Suringar 194
5   Plutarch] *Moralia* 703F

proverb can be applied in various ways: ironically, as if one were to say to a   10
rich man who proposed to leave his wealth to unworthy and wasteful heirs
'Leave something for the Medes too', meaning 'You save up, and your
savings will be spent by those who bear you ill will'; or it may be said to a
wildly extravagant person, or one who talks too much out of season, as in
the *Phormio* of Terence: 'Stop, if you please, that you may have power with   15
her.'

6 Deorum manus
Hands of the Gods

Θεῶν χεῖρες, Hands of the Gods. In old days they used to say (ironically, I
suppose) that remedies were efficacious when they were made up from
various ingredients brought from far away; just the things which doctors   5
and apothecaries use today to trick the public. Plutarch in the 'Table-talk,'
fourth decade, mentions the proverb, at the same time quoting from Erasistratus, who disapproved of such doctors' mixtures: 'But much more when
they make the royal and effective mixtures which they used to call "the
hands of the gods." Erasistratus exposes the absurdity and useless inquisi-   10
tiveness of those who mixed into one potion mineral, vegetable and animal
ingredients, mingling in one whatever earth or sea produced. But he would
approve if omitting these things they had confined their art of healing to
barley-water, cupping-glasses and oil-and-water cures. But dear me, how
the mere variety of things imposes on us and stirs up longing!' Thus far   15
Plutarch. Galen recalls this adage, in his sixth tractate, quoting from Erophi-
lus. We may also add at this point in passing the words of Pliny, by which he
censures the mixtures made by the doctors. They are in the preface to book
24: 'Hence sprang the art of medicine. Such things alone had Nature decreed
should be our remedies, provided everywhere, easy to discover and costing   20
nothing – the things in fact which support our life. Later on man's usual
perfidy and the art of laying traps for human nature led to the invention of
the quack laboratories, in which each customer is provided with a new lease
of his own life at a price. At once compound prescriptions and mysterious

* * * * *

15 Terence] *Phormio* 793–4

6 Probably from Plutarch, like the last
6 Plutarch] *Moralia* 663C
16 Galen] Voluminous medical writer of the second century AD; this has not been
identified. This was added in 1515.
17 Pliny] *Naturalis historia* 24.4–5 (tr. W.H.S. Jones, adapted)

mixtures are glibly repeated, Arabia and India are valued as the storehouse   25
of remedies, and a small sore is charged with the cost of a medicine from the
Red Sea, although the genuine remedies form the daily dinner of even the
poorest. For if a plant were to be sought in the kitchen-garden, or a shrub
were to be procured thence, none of the arts would become cheaper than
medicine.' Thus far Pliny.   30

7 Quot homines, tot sententiae
So many men, so many opinions

Nothing is more widely known even today than this saying of Terence 'So
many men, so many opinions,' and in the same author there is a similar
phrase, 'every man has his own way.' Persius also: 'Men are of a thousand   5
kinds, and diverse the colour of their lives; / Each has his own desires; no two
offer the same prayer.' In the same class is that remark in an epigram that
one may find people who are willing to yield in the matter of family acres,
but not one who will give way on a matter of opinion. Horace adds an
elegant metaphor: 'Three guests I have, of wishes quite contrary; / As their   10
tastes differ, so their orders vary.' It was Horace, too, who devoted the first
ode of all to the subject of this proverb, ie that different people are led by
different interests, that some have one thing at heart and some another.
Terence, in the *Phormio*, plays upon this in jest when he says of three
advisers, 'the first says yes, the second says no, and the third says "Let's   15
think about it."' St Paul the Apostle seems to have made a reference to this
when he says that for the putting aside of strife, we should allow every man
to have his own convictions. If the general run of theologians had listened to
this advice, there would not now be such fierce contention about little
questions of no moment at all; for there certainly are some things of which   20
one may remain in ignorance without any lack of piety. The same thought is
expressed at greater length by Euripides in the *Phoenissae*:

* * * * *

7 Otto 826; Suringar 193; Tilley M 583 So many men, so many minds
3 Terence] *Phormio* 454; Erasmus, quoting no doubt from memory, seems to have
forgotten for the moment that the two phrases are parts of the same line in the
play.
5 Persius] *Satires* 5.52–3
7 epigram] Martial 8.18.9–10
9 Horace] *Epistles* 2.2.61–2 (this comes again in II vii 55); *Odes* 1.1.3–28
14 Terence] *Phormio* 449–57
16 Paul] *Romans* 14:5
18 If the general run] Added in *1517/8*
22 Euripides] *Phoenissae* 499–502; *Hippolytus* 104. Erasmus normally writes *Hippolytus crowned*, as do our medieval copies.

If what were fair and wise were so to all
Disputing strife would not exist for men,
But now for mortals naught is 'like' nor 'same,'   25
Only the words may happen to agree,
In deed and fact no likeness can be found.

Again in the *Hippolytus Crowned*: 'This man, this God, is after their own
heart / To some, not so to others.' Homer thought of this in the *Odyssey*,
book 14: 'For one man takes delight in certain things, / Another in others.'   30

8 Eum ausculta, cui quatuor sunt aures
Listen to him who has four ears

This is found among the Greek collections of proverbs: Ἄκουε τοῦ τὰ
τέσσαρα ὦτα ἔχοντος, Listen to him who has four ears. Zenodotus contributes an interpretation on these lines: a reply was given by an oracle to   5
Entimus of Crete and Antiphemus of Rhodes, saying that they should watch
the one who had four ears. He was in fact a robber named Phoenix, of whom
the oracle was warning them to beware. But why he was said to have four
ears is not easy to understand: whether he really had them, or the phrase is
to be taken allegorically as meaning that he had spies posted in four places.   10
However, as they regarded the god's reply as nonsense and paid no heed to
it, they met with the robber and were destroyed by him; and it is thought
that the proverb arose in popular speech from this event.

But an explanation which appeals more to me is the one given by the
same author out of Aristophanes the grammarian: that the Spartans used to   15
make a figure of Apollo with four ears and as many hands, either because, as
Sosibius says, Apollo was seen by them in this guise as they fought at
Amyclae, or to indicate, as I for my part conjecture, that the wise man must
hear as many things as possible, and test them out by the experience of life.
It was certainly believed by the ancients that no oracle was to be trusted   20
more than those of Apollo. Hence the current saying 'Straight from the
tripod.' And the proverb is a warning that it is necessary to listen to those
who are wiser than others because of their long and varied experience, as old

* * * * *

29 Homer] *Odyssey* 14.228

8 This appeared in the *Collectanea* as no 546, from Diogenianus 2.5, and it now
incorporates *Collectanea* no 723. Suringar 70
4 Zenodotus] Zenobius (always so called by Erasmus) 1.54
21 current saying] *Adagia* I vii 90

men usually are. It is for this reason that the speech of Nestor is praised in
Homer, as being worthy to be listened to by all, and in the *Odyssey*, book 2,   25
the poet shows the grand old man Aegyptius being first to speak: 'Bent was
he with his years, yet much he knew.' Euripides had the same idea in the
Phoenissae, and this is the passage Lucian was referring to in *Hercules
Gallicus*. I thought I should mention this in passing, because that dialogue is
one of many which I translated into Latin, and the allusion is somewhat   30
obscure. But I will give the poet's lines. These are the words of Jocasta,
already old, to Eteocles, her young son. I have translated them as follows:

> My son Eteocles, not everything is evil
> Which old age has; for through experience,
> Knowing the world, it has some power to speak   35
> Better, more prudently than untaught youth.

Our own common folk say the same thing, in less elegant terms
perhaps, but with an apt metaphor, when they say 'an old dog's bark is
worth listening to,' meaning it is best not to turn a deaf ear when old men
issue a warning of danger. For old dogs do not bark without reason, as   40
young ones do.

9   Semper feliciter cadunt Iovis taxilli
The dice always fall out well for Jove

Ἀεὶ γὰρ εὖ πίπτουσιν οἱ Διὸς κύβοι, Always the dice fall happily for Jove. A
line of poetry proverbially famous, and usually applied to people for whom
everything always falls out as they wish, by some favouritism of fortune.   5
Obviously it is taken from the throw of the dice, perhaps because it was
observed in antiquity that Jove's dice were the luckier ones; the custom
being for players to preface their throws by uttering the names of gods or

* * * * *

25 Homer] *Iliad* 1.247–9 (on Nestor, see I ii 56); *Odyssey* 2.16
27 Euripides] *Phoenissae* 528–30
28 Lucian] *Hercules* 4, citing *Phoenissae* 530
37 common folk] In the *Collectanea* no 723 'Look out when the old dog barks' had
   been given a place, as wanting none of the virtues of a proverb except ancient
   authority, and 'lest I seem to have borrowed nothing from ordinary folk and to
   have entirely despised my contemporaries.' It survives in Tilley D 484 If the old
   dog barks, he gives counsel.

 9 *Collectanea* no 488, from Diogenianus 1.58 (also in Zenobius 2.44 and Suidas A
   607), but here rewritten and sources added

men, to bring good luck. A throw dedicated to Venus was counted among
the lucky ones, as the proverb shows, 'If you throw often, you'll sometime   10
throw a Venus.' Or we may prefer to see in it a reference to the victory of
Jove and the story of discomfited Juno. Some think this applies to people
who are properly punished for their deeds, as if Jove would not suffer a fault
to go unavenged. It seems to me that it would not be improper to apply it
also to powerful and fortunate men, whose deeds are applauded even when   15
they are not quite creditable; as the proverbial verse has it, 'Great men's
concerns will always turn out well.' What is said by Euripides in the tragedy
called the *Phoenissae* is not unlike this: 'All things are easy for the gods,' and
what is often found in Homer: 'The gods can do all things.'

10 Thessalorum commentum
A trick of the Thessalians

Θεσσαλῶν σόφισμα, A trick of the Thessalians. Suidas writes that this can
be applied to various uses: to those who desert their place in the line of
battle, to those who adopt a luxurious type of dress, to those who circum-   5
vent someone else by trickery. It is thought that the source of the proverb is a
story of this kind. A certain Aratus, a Thessalian, had a reply from an oracle,
to the effect that he should take care not to be privately defeated by people
who were appealing to the oracle against him and bringing a more important
and magnificent offering. As soon as he heard this, he pronounced a vow   10
that he would sacrifice a hundred men's heads to the god. Later, when he
had completed to his satisfaction the affairs for which he had come, he put
off indefinitely the performance of his vow, under the pretext that it was not
virtuous enough, and unworthy of Apollo. The result of this, they say, was
that every year after this the people would customarily promise a hecatomb   15
to this god, but the promise was never carried out.
    Euripides in the *Phoenissae* remarks on the trickery of the Thessalians:
'Eteocles then played the Thessalian trick, / Learnt in his own experience of
that land.' And elsewhere: 'Many were present indeed, but faithless are the

* * * * *

10 proverb] *Adagia* I ii 13
16 proverbial verse] Menander *Sententiae* 862 (see I i 30n).
17 Euripides] *Phoenissae* 689
19 Homer] Eg *Odyssey* 10.306

10 This is Zenobius 4.29, but Erasmus' source seems to be Suidas.
 3 Suidas] θ 291
17 Euripides] *Phoenissae* 1407–8; frag 422 Nauck, cited by the scholiast on
    Aristophanes *Plutus* 512b

Thessalians.' So Demosthenes asserts in the *First Olynthiac*: 'Added to this,'   20
he says, 'are the affairs of the Thessalians, always mistrusted by all men by
their very nature.' This proverb is quoted by some writers in this form:
'Thessalian ways are never to be trusted.' The commentator on Aristophanes thinks that the proverb came from Jason, because he broke his
promise to Medea, and she upbraids him with this, in Ovid in his *Heroides*.   25
There is also a mention of the proverb by the writer who handed down to us
the fragments of Athenaeus.

11   **Thessalorum alae**
      The wings of the Thessalians

Θεσσαλικαὶ πτέρυγες, The wings of the Thessalians. A jesting proverbial
allusion that used to be made to the garments with sleeves (which the
Greeks call *cheirodotoi*) because these were worn by Thessalians, luxurious   5
and pleasure-loving as they were. In Virgil the Trojans are reproached by
their enemies for wearing this type of garment, as not manly enough: 'Their
tunics have sleeves, their bonnets strings to tie.' In Plautus someone in
Carthaginian dress, like an exotic bird, is ridiculed for his sleeves, hanging
and spreading out on both sides like pointed wings.   10

12   **Thessala mulier**
      A Thessalian woman

Θεσσαλικὴ γυνή, A Thessalian woman. This was said of poisoners, skilled
in evil arts; because that race was notorious above all others for this reason,
as appears clearly from the *Ass* of Apuleius and from many other writers. So   5
Horace in the *Odes*: 'What witch can rescue thee, / What wizard with

* * * * *

20 Demosthenes] *First Olynthiac* 21–2
23 Aristophanes] Scholia as above
25 Ovid] *Heroides* 12 passim
27 Athenaeus] 14.662f, added in *1517/8*

11 From the Greek proverb-collections (Diogenianus 5.20; Suidas θ 290)
 6 Virgil] *Aeneid* 9.616
 8 Plautus] *Poenulus* 975. An allusion to this was added in *1515* to III vii 11.

12 Suidas θ 289; Apostolius 8.85
 5 Apuleius] See I i 15n; *Metamorphoses* eg 2.1
 6 Horace] *Odes* 1.27.21–2

Thessalian charms, what god?' Plautus in the *Amphitryo* calls a poisoner 'the
Thessalian.' And Strepsiades, in Aristophanes' *Clouds*, consults Socrates as
to whether a Thessalian witch should be employed to pull the moon out of
the sky, so that he would not have to pay his debts at the time of the new   10
moon. It is thought that this superstition about Thessalians comes from
Medea, who when she fled that way carried through the air, dropped a little
box full of poisons and magic herbs; they were scattered abroad and
sprouted everywhere. Pliny, book 30 chapter 1, tells us that magic was
widespread among the Thessalians and was long called by their name, to   15
such an extent that 'Menander, experienced in literary refinements, called a
play *A Woman of Thessaly* which dealt with the tricks of the women who drag
down the moon.'

13   **In sinu gaudere**
     To rejoice in one's own bosom

To rejoice in one's own bosom means to feel in oneself a silent joy, without
doing as people commonly do, showing public signs of pleasure. Tibullus:
'Let the wise man keep his joy, / Hushed up within his bosom.' And   5
Propertius too: 'Keep thy joy shut within thy silent bosom.' The same: 'To
weep in one another's bosom'; this latter said of lovers, who pour out to each
other the secrets of their hearts which they conceal from everyone else.
Cicero in the *Tusculan Questions*, book 3: 'Then, as such things are not likely
to win applause, let them keep their joy in their own hearts, let them cease to   10
speak so boastfully.' Pliny the Younger, book 2 letter 1: 'For these reasons I
must pour my mourning into your bosom, as for his untimely death.' It is
sometimes found in Seneca, as in letter 106: 'If you have not boasted of your
good luck, but known how to keep your joy in your heart.' And indeed this

* * * * *

7 Plautus] *Amphitryo* 1043, added in *1523*
8 Aristophanes] *Clouds* 749–56, used also in I v 84; added here in *1523*
14 Pliny] *Naturalis historia* 30.7, added in *1517/8*. Of Menander's comedy *Thettale*,
   to which he refers, only frags 192–7 survive.

13 *Collectanea* no 485, referring to Cicero, Tibullus and Propertius. Otto 1655;
   Tilley s 535 Laugh in one's sleeve
4 Tibullus] 4.13.8
6 Propertius] 2.25.30; 1.5.30
9 Cicero] *Tusculanae disputationes* 3.21.51
11 Pliny the Younger] *Letters* 2.1.10
13 Seneca] *Letters* 105.3, added in *1533*

figure of speech seems to be taken in turn from Homer, who says in the   15
Odyssey, book 22: 'Rejoice in your bosom, old nurse, and be quiet.' 'In the
bosom' means in your breast, not on the lips or on the brow, which are the
features by which the common people usually betray what they are thinking
in the depths of their soul. Cicero says in a letter to his brother Quintus:
'Believe me, he is my bosom friend, and I never ungird myself.' By these   20
words he promises to keep silent, for he who ungirds himself lets go what
has been entrusted to his bosom. Plutarch in the life of Cato of Utica seems to
have used the term 'bosom' for intimate friendship: 'The consuls, Piso
Calpurnius, who was the father of Caesar's wife, and Gabinius Paulus, a
bosom friend of Pompey, as those people say who knew the character and   25
life of the man.' Scaevola in the *Pandects*, book 22, title *De probationibus*,
chapter 27, uses it in a somewhat different way: 'Because all the wealth
and substance which he had inherited, if any, from his mother, I had in my
bosom without security'; he says 'in my bosom' meaning 'in my power,
committed in trust to me.' What we commit to the safe-keeping of another,   30
we say we 'lay in his bosom.' So Terence: 'He gives her into my hand.'

14   **Feras non culpes, quod vitari non potest**
     What can't be cured, must be endured

Aulus Gellius writes that certain sayings of Publius the moralist, which were
couched in everyday language, were often bandied about in common
speech. This is one of them, more wholesome than any dictum of the   5
philsophers: 'What can't be cured must be endured.' These words warn us
that destined evils, when they cannot by any means be avoided nor warded
off, can at least be alleviated by resignation. The same thing, in different
words, is taught by Euripides in the *Phoenissae*, when he says 'The will of the
gods one must endure,' and again at the end of the same play, 'What the   10
gods will, mortals needs must endure.' Homer, *Odyssey*, book 9: 'A sickness

* * * * *

15 Homer] *Odyssey* 22.411
19 Cicero] *Ad Quintum fratrem* 2.11.1, added with the rest of this paragraph in *1533*
22 Plutarch] *Cato* 33. This is used again in IV ix 44.
26 Scaevola] *Digest* 22.3.27. This had been added in *1526* to II x 32.
31 Terence] *Andria* 297; cf IV v 29.

14 *Collectanea* no 283, much rewritten. Tilley A 231 What cannot be altered must be
    borne, not blamed; C 922 What cannot be cured must be endured.
 3 Gellius] 17.14.4, citing Publilius Syrus F 11 (see I ii 4n).
 9 Euripides] *Phoenissae* 382 and 1763; the Latin version amended in *1528*
11 Homer] *Odyssey* 9.411

sent from great Jove can never be avoided.' Varro's shrewd saying comes in here: 'The faults of a wife must be cured or endured,' and the proverb which I shall mention in its place, 'You shall not kick against the pricks.'

15 Sursum versus sacrorum fluminum feruntur fontes
The springs of the sacred rivers flow backwards

A proverbial allegory, which we use to signify that something is upside down, that the proper arrangement of things is reversed, as for instance if a boy should admonish an old man, or a pupil try to teach his teacher, or a 5 servant give orders to his master. The adage comes from Euripides, *Medea*:

> Upwards flow the streams of sacred rivers,
> Overturned are justice and tradition,
> The plans of men are treacherous
> And trust in the gods no longer fixed.   10

In these words the chorus is pointing out that the original order of things is reversed: men are using women's wiles and not abiding by their promises, while women are daring to do manly deeds. Lucian in *Terpsion* makes use of this proverb when the deceived legacy-hunter reproaches Pluto because he himself has been carried off by death as a mere youth, while the old man 15 whose money he had desired to inherit is still alive, against all the natural order of things. 'This is a case of Upwards flow the streams,' he says. Again in his *Apology* for the essay *On Salaried Posts in Great Houses*: 'At any rate there is a big difference between your present life and your writing; this would be, as they say, Upwards flow the streams and all things overturned, 20 and a recantation towards what is worse.' Diogenes Laertius uses this in his life of Diogenes the Cynic: he tells how Diogenes sent a message to his master, as if he were the lord and not the servant, that he should do what he had been ordered to do, and the master replied with the proverb, 'Upwards flow the streams of the sacred rivers'; 'but if you were ill,' Diogenes said, 25 'and had hired the doctor with your own money, would you follow his

*****

12 Varro] *Saturae Menippeae* 83 Buecheler (see I ii 60n), cited by Gellius 1.17.4.
13 proverb] *Adagia* I iii 46

15 A very familiar figure: Zenobius 2.56; Diogenianus 1.27; Suidas A 2596. Otto 678. Tilley s 931 Streams back to their springs do never run.
6 Euripides] *Medea* 410–3
13 Lucian] *Dialogi mortuorum* 16.2 (Terpsion is one of the characters); *Apologia* 1.
21 Diogenes Laertius] 6.36

prescription or reply in that way, "Upwards flow the streams?"' Aristotle makes use of it in his *Meteorologica*. Virgil has an allusion to it in the *Aeneid*, when he says: 'Back flows Aufidus river from Adriatic waves.' Servius remarks here that a proverb is lying concealed, suggesting unlikelihood or inconsistency. Horace expresses it thus in the *Odes*:

> Who shall deny that streams ascend
> And Tiber's currents backward bend,
> While you have all our hopes betrayed;
> You, that far other promise made,
> When all your volumes, learned store!
>
> The treasure of Socratic lore,
> Once bought at mighty price in vain,
> Are sent to purchase arms in Spain?

Porphyrion noted that this was a proverb. Ovid, too, in his *Heroides*:

> If Paris' breath shall fail not, once Oenone he doth spurn,
> The waters of the Xanthus to their fount shall backward turn.
> O Xanthus, backward haste; waters, to your springs again,
> Oenone has been deserted, and Paris feels no pain.

Propertius again, 'Rivers begin to recall their waters to their fount.'

16   Ad felicem inflectere parietem
To lean to the lucky side

Aristophanes, in his comedy entitled the *Frogs*, quotes a splendid proverb; if only it were merely a matter of literature and not a feature of the life of almost every human being:

* * * * *

27 Aristotle] *Meteorologica* (perhaps) 2.1 (353b27)
28 Virgil] *Aeneid* 11.405
31 Horace] *Odes* 1.29.10–16 (tr Sir Philip Francis); the comment of Porphyrion the ancient scholiast was added in *1533*.
40 Ovid] *Heroides* 5.29–32
45 Propertius] 2.15.33

16 Probably derived direct from Aristophanes
 3 Aristophanes] *Frogs* 534–7

This is the mark of a man
Who has mind and wit and
Has often gone to sea,
He always rolls over, cautious man,
To the snug side of the ship.   10

The proverb may be expressed more succinctly as 'to incline towards the fortunate side.' The commentator on Aristophanes thinks it comes from voyagers by boat, who when the swell forces the ship down on one side immediately rush to the other, because it rises higher out of the waves. It may be applied to those who look after their own advantage by always   15
attaching themselves to influential and wealthy friends; they are like flies, flitting to and fro round the smell of the kitchen, and what they look for in friendship is the solidest advantage, not loyalty. There are those who keep quiet while the outcome of a war is uncertain, but as soon as fortune has turned and it is clear which side is going to win, they join it at once. We read   20
that Metius in Virgil was of this mind, and Polymnestor, who 'took the winning side' rather than keep the law of hospitality; he 'slew Polydorus and secured the gold / By force.' Aristophanes again, in the *Plutus*, aptly characterizes this sort of men. When Chremylus has become rich he complains of being deafened by the greetings of people who have smelt out his   25
money: 'Hang you, be off! The nuisance these friends are, / Emerging suddenly when fortune smiles.' The phrase of Euripides in the *Medea* belongs here: 'Every friend shuns a man who's poor.' Antiphanes in the *Progoni*, cited by Athenaeus, book 6. 'Don't come near me, when things are going wrong.' The commentator remarks that there is a proverb lurking   30
here, which is often applied to those who abandon the company of their friends as soon as they get into danger, but that the poet has inverted the

* * * * *

21 Virgil] *Aeneid* 8.642; the story is told in Livy 1.27–8.
21 Polymnestor] The quotations are from *Aeneid* 3.54–6.
23 Aristophanes] *Plutus* 782–3
27 Euripides] *Medea* 561
28 Antiphanes] The line of Greek verse which follows is Aristophanes *Birds* 134, and in 1508 it was introduced correctly by the single word 'Aristophanes.' At the same time part of a fragment from the comic poet Antiphanes, cited by Athenaeus, was used in I iii 17, and attributed to 'Aristophanes in Athenaeus' by mistake. In 1523 Erasmus wished to correct this by substituting the words 'Antiphanes in the *Progoni*, cited by Athenaeus book 6' for 'Aristophanes in Athenaeus'; and unfortunately the correction was attached to Aristophanes' name here instead of in I iii 17. In both places therefore the final text, which we feel bound to translate, attributes a Greek quotation to the wrong author, thanks to a venial slip of the pen in revising.

sense and is alluding to the proverb usually expressed thus: 'Don't come near me, when things are going well.' Agreeing with this, there is the phrase of Euripides in the *Orestes*:   35

> In desperate need ought friends to help their friends.
> When Fortune gives her boons, what need of friends?
> God's help suffices, when he wills to help.

The same poet came nearer to expressing the proverb in the same tragedy, except that he is applying a general dictum exclusively to heralds: 40

> Such is the herald tribe; lightly they skip
> To Fortune's minions' side; their friend is he
> Who in a state hath power and beareth rule.

Again in the *Hercules furens*: 'When things go well, a comrade for the voyage, / Offers himself, but not to the unlucky.' Here comes in, what Aristotle   45
in the *Ethica Eudemia*, book 7, shows to be a proverb: 'Time shows who truly loves.' The passage of time proves friendship, and reveals those counterfeit friends.

17 Amico amicus
A friend to his friend

As Terence has it in the *Phormio*, 'a man is a friend only to his friend.' Donatus points out that this is a proverb, and can be found in Apollodorus, who wrote a *Phormio* in Greek: 'He alone knows how to love his friends.'   5
Aristophanes, quoted by Athenaeus:

* * * * *

35 Euripides] *Orestes* 665–8; 895–7; *Hercules furens* 1224–5 (in *1508* Juno was named instead of Hercules, and this was put right in *1523*).
45 Aristotle] *Ethica Eudemia* 7.2 (1238a15); cf Tilley T 337 Time tries friends as fire tries gold.

17 This was *Collectanea* no 566, with no support except the reference to Donatus' commentary on Terence. Otto 97
 3 Terence] *Phormio* 562; Donatus in his note cites frag 19 Kock of Apollodorus, who wrote the Greek original of the play.
 6 Aristophanes] This is the conclusion of Antiphanes frag 195 Kock, cited by Athenaeus 6.238d–f, ascribed to Aristophanes by a mistake of amanuensis or typesetter. Erasmus' attempt to correct this in *1523* misfired and hit the wrong target, as we saw in I iii 16.

But nothing care I for the common jests:
My friend's friend am I, not in words alone,
I aim to serve him both in act and deed.

The metaphor itself is proverbial on the face of it, as I showed in the   10
beginning. It will fit those who refuse no duty, as long as it is a service to
their friends. This seems close to what Euripides says in the *Medea*: 'Harsh to
a foe and kindly to a friend.' Theocritus in *Aita*:

They loved each other with an equal yoke:
Truly the men of old were golden then,   15
The loved one loved the lover in return.

Aristotle is quoted by Laertius as saying habitually: 'My friends, I have no
friend,' meaning that true friendship has perished among mortals.

18 Muneribus vel dii capiuntur
Even the gods are won over by gifts

As Ovid wrote: 'Presents, believe me, buy both gods and men: / And Jove
himself's appeased by offered gifts.' Euripides, in the *Medea*, shows that this
was well-known in common speech, when he says: 5

There is a saying that gifts bend even gods;
Surely to mortal men the yellow gold
Has weight and power more than a hundred sayings.

* * * * *

11 beginning] In Erasmus' Introduction, section xiii, line 54
12 Euripides] *Medea* 809
13 Theocritus] 12.15–6, added in *1526*. The image of the equal yoke is explored by
Erasmus in *Adagia* I vi 8.
17 Laertius] 5.21, but Erasmus uses a corrupt text, and so gives the wrong
meaning. It should run 'He who has many friends has no friend,' which is
found in Aristotle's *Ethica Eudemia* 7.12 (1245b20); cf Tilley F 698 A friend to all is
a friend to none. Added in *1526*

18 Perhaps derived from Ovid
3 Ovid] *Ars amatoria* 3.653–4. 'And Jove himself's appeased' is the text of *1523*;
before that, perhaps because Erasmus was quoting from memory, it ran 'And
angry Jove is swayed.'
4 Euripides] *Medea* 964–5

This line of poetry is also celebrated, which Plato borrowed in his *Republic*, book 3: 'Gifts move the gods and venerable kings.' Hence Seneca, quoting a 10 remark of some philosopher, says that of all things the sweetest is to receive.

19 **Manum de tabula**
Hands off the picture

Cicero says in some letter or other: 'Hands off your picture! The master is here sooner than we expected.' He seems to have been warning by this proverbial metaphor that there should be an end of writing witticisms. The 5 allusion is clearly to a saying of the famous artist Apelles. 'When he was admiring the work of Protogenes, with its immense taking of pains and over-anxious care, he said that he and Protogenes were equal in all they did, or indeed Protogenes' work was the better, but there was one thing in which he himself had the advantage: Protogenes did not know when to take his 10 hand from the picture. By this memorable precept he meant that over-diligence often does harm.' So says Pliny, book 35 chapter 10. And so, when we wish to warn someone to draw back from the work or piece of business he has in hand, we shall tell him to take his hand from the picture. This is particularly applicable to over-meticulous writers, of peevish industry, who 15 are forever poring over their writings, always adding, subtracting, altering, and whose greatest fault is that they are trying to avoid all faults.

* * * * *

9 This line] Doubtfully ascribed to Hesiod (frag 361). Perhaps Erasmus knew it first from the Greek proverb-collections, for it comes in Diogenianus 4.21 and Suidas Δ 1451, and he did not add the reference to Plato *Republic* 3.390e until 1523.
10 Seneca] Not identified

19 In *Collectanea* no 375, having at hand only the quotation from Cicero and not the familiar anecdote about Apelles (*Adagia* I iv 12), Erasmus wrongly suggested that the adage was derived from schoolboys scribbling down the piece they are to declaim to their master. Otto 1038
3 Cicero] *Ad familiares* 7.25.1
12 Pliny] *Naturalis historia* 35.80. In 1508 Ethiones, who is mentioned in the preceding section of Pliny, was given instead of Apelles; this was corrected in 1528.

20 Emere malo quam rogare
I would rather buy than beg

Cicero in the *Verrines* quotes as an adage, 'I would rather buy than beg.' The
meaning is that something bought with entreaty is not freely received;
indeed, nothing is bought more dearly than what is given to an asker. That   5
word 'I beg' is a harsh one to honourable minds, nor should it ever be
awaited between friends, as Seneca says. The saying is derived from the
custom of the ancients, by which one neighbour would beg from another
such furnishings as he himself did not happen to have in the house. We can
tell that this custom existed in old days from the *Aulularia* and *Rudens* of   10
Plautus. Apuleius in his *Florida* says: 'The man who asks is buying at a
substantial rate; the man who is asked receives no inconsiderable price; so it
is preferable for you to buy all you need rather than beg for it.' The same idea
is conveyed with more obscurity but with elegance, by a proverb well
known in Greek, which I shall give in another place: 'Pray for plenty for your   15
neighbour, but still more for your pot,' signifying that it is a desirable thing
to have a rich neighbour from whom one can borrow what one has not got of
one's own, but it is much better to possess oneself in one's own house
whatever is needful for daily life.

21 Manum non verterim. Digitum non porrexerim.
I would not turn a hand. I would not raise a finger

A proverbial hyperbole, I would not turn a hand, meaning 'it does not
trouble me,' 'it is no concern of mine.' For nothing is easier than to turn the
hand. It is found, among other places, in Apuleius, *Apology for Magic*: 'As for   5
what Mezentius thinks about me I would not turn a hand'; Cicero too, in *De*

* * * * *

20 Most of this was in *Collectanea* no 403, perhaps from Cicero. Otto 597; Tilley B
   783 Better to buy than to beg
   3 Cicero] *Verrines* 4.6.12
   7 Seneca] *De beneficiis* 2.2.1.
   11 Apuleius] See I i 15n; *Florida* 16.
   15 in another place] *Adagia* III v 6

21 *Collectanea* no 401 gave the first of these expressions, from Apuleius, coupled
   with what is now I iii 83; it is Otto 1041, Suringar 114. The second phrase, which
   is included with *Adagia* IV x 84 under Otto 548, was added in *1536*.
   5 Apuleius] See I i 15n; *Apologia* 56. 'Among other places' is an addition of *1515*,
   and the text of the quotation was added in *1523*.
   6 Cicero] *De finibus* 5.31.93 and 3.17.57, added in *1523* and *1536* respectively

finibus, book 5: 'They would not raise a hand.' Again in book 3 of the same
work: 'Chrysippus indeed and Diogenes said that apart from utility not a
hand should be raised on that account, and I heartily agree with them.' He is
there discussing glory or reputation, which is to be altogether disdained, if it   10
brings nothing useful with it, as that remark of the Satirist says: 'Glory, as
much as you like, what is it if nothing but glory?' Of the turning down of the
thumb we have spoken elsewhere. Quintilian, book 11, writes that the
movements of the hands are so important in delivery that 'it is almost
another tongue speaking, instead of any words.' 'Wonder is best conveyed   15
by the following gesture: the hand turns slightly upward and the fingers are
brought in to the palm, one after the other, beginning with the little finger;
the hand is then opened and turned over by a reversal of this motion. The
gesture which expresses interrogation is a turn of the hand, however the
fingers are arranged.' Today, we hold up the hand and turn it over to   20
express the smallest difference. In the passage from Quintilian I have just
quoted, I think it would be more correct to read not 'instead of any words'
but 'instead of any other members,' so as to indicate that the hand alone can
convey whatever might be expressed by other parts of the body. In Plutarch's life of Timoleon a messenger sent to Andromachus, after making a   25
long, cruel and barbarous speech, finally held out his hand, first palm
upwards and then palm downwards, threatening by this gesture to over-
throw their state. But Andromachus only laughed, and made the same
gesture with his hand, ordering the man to be off at once, unless he wanted
the same treatment to be given to his ship.   30

22 **Semper Leontini iuxta pocula**
    Always at their cups, the Leontini

Ἀεὶ Λεόντιοι περὶ τοὺς κρατῆρας, Always at their cups, the Leontini. This
aptly describes the luxurious, or those who are always addicted to the same

* * * * *

11 Satirist] Juvenal 7.81, added in *1536*
13 elsewhere] *Adagia* I viii 46; cross-reference added in *1526*
13 Quintilian] The first sentence is a conflation of 11.3.72 (which deals with facial
    expression, not gesture) and 85. The quotation comes from 11.3.100–1; both
    were added in *1526*, and the suggestion for a change in the text (which is
    unnecessary) in *1528*.
24 Plutarch] *Timoleon* 11.2 added in *1526*

22 *Collectanea* no 422; there is some uncertainty in the text of Diogenianus 2.50,
    which is the source, and Erasmus in his first version made Phalaris (see I x 86)
    deprive the Leontines of their drinking-cups.

studies. The Leontini are a people of Sicily, whom Phalaris defeated, and to   5
prevent them from starting a rebellion he took away their weapons and
turned them over to drinking and pleasure; hence this adage, which is
mentioned by Diogenianus.

23   **Cestreus ieiunat**
     The grey mullet is fasting

Κεστρεὺς νηστεύει, The grey mullet is fasting. This is appropriately said of
people who are both starving and voracious. Those who gape with hunger
are called *kestreis*, mullets, and there is a verb *kestreuein* which expresses an   5
accusation formerly levelled at the Athenians, Hesychius tells us. Others
prefer to apply the term to those who lead a harmless life, and refrain from
injuring others, but never reap any reward from their blameless behaviour.
The grey mullet is a kind of fish, which alone among all the rest who live by
eating each other up, abstains from the flesh of others and is therefore not   10
caught by the bait, but hides in the mud and there survives for a long time;
some think it feeds on mud. Even when caught it is not nourished by food or
any other creature, though it has sharp teeth. It is indeed easily devoured by
the pike, but for the very reason that it is not voracious, it is not very tasty.
When frightened it hides its head, thinking that thus its whole body will be   15
safe. So Aristophanes says in Athenaeus: 'Is there a colony of Kestrians
inside?' He is alluding to Cestrina, a part of Chaonia. Again Diphilus in the
same author: 'I am going to be a grey mullet, with this starvation.' Again in
book 7, he quotes out of Anaxandrides: 'He wanders about at feasts like a
starving mullet.' The adage is mentioned by Zenodotus, Diogenianus,   20

* * * * *

23   From the Greek proverb-collections, as Erasmus himself tells us
3   appropriately] So *1536*; before that, 'usually'
6   Hesychius] See Erasmus' Introduction, section v 35n; κ 2384, added in *1526*.
12   Even when ... tasty] These two sentences, derived from Aristotle's *Historia
     animalium* 8.2 (591a19, b4) partly by way of a quotation in Athenaeus, were
     added in *1517/8*.
16   Aristophanes] Frag 156 Kock, cited by Athenaeus 7.307e–f; the reference to
     Chaonia is of *1526*, and comes perhaps from Stephanus Byzantius (see I ii 43n)
     p 638 Meineke.
17   Diphilus] Frag 54 Kock
19   Anaxandrides] Frag 34 Kock; like Diphilus, he was a writer of the Attic New
     Comedy. Both this and the preceding were added from Athenaeus in *1517/8*,
     and the Latin versions revised in *1526* and *1528* respectively to make them into
     lines of verse. In *1517/8* the reference was given as book 6.
20   Zenodotus] Zenobius 4.52; the other sources named are Diogenianus 5.53 and
     Suidas κ 1429.

Suidas, Athenaeus in his *Doctors at dinner*, book 7; and this last, among other information, says that this fish is called by some the *plotes*, and is devoured by the conger-eel, as the eel is eaten by the lamprey. Theodorus Gaza translates it as 'mullet.'

24   **Ubi amici, ibi opes**
      Where there are friends, there is wealth

Plautus in the *Truculentus*: 'True is the word often quoted, Where there are friends, there is wealth.' Quintilian also quotes it as a proverb in his *Institutions* book 5. The meaning is that friends are to be preferred to money,   5
and it is more important as a protection in life to have friends without money than to have riches without friends. That is why among the Scythians (so says Lucian) that man was deemed the richest who had the best and most loyal friends. However, if anyone were to look at the ways of the world today, he would think the adage should be reversed: Where there is wealth,   10
there are friends, seeing that 'The crowd assesses friendship by its use,' and 'Friendship, that venerable name of old, / Has now turned harlot and is bought and sold.'

25   **Terra volat**
      The earth flies

Ἡ γῆ ἵπταται, The earth flies. This describes a totally incongruous thing, which cannot possibly occur. Suidas gives it as an example of the 'impossi-

* * * * *

21   Athenaeus] 7.307b–c; the book-reference and 'among other information' were added in *1517/8*.
23   Theodorus Gaza] In his version of Aristotle; see I i 2 line 46.

24   *Collectanea* no 176, coupled with *Adagia* I x 91 because Quintilian is the source of both. Otto 88; Suringar 232
 3   Plautus] *Truculentus* 885 (from *1508* through *1523* the title of the play was given as *Cruentus*).
 4   Quintilian] 5.11.41; *Institutio oratoria* (*The Education of an Orator*) is the correct title.
 8   Lucian] *Toxaris* 9
11   The crowd] Ovid *Ex Ponto* 2.3.8 (quoted, again anonymously, in II iii 86) and 19–20

25   From Suidas (A 537)

ble' [*adynaton*]. Julian, in some letter or other, mentions it under the   5
heading of a proverb, with one word changed: 'The earth is light, as the
saying goes.' This adage is of the type I have mentioned elsewhere, 'a
childless Jupiter' and 'Olive no kernel hath nor nut no shell.'

26   Ilias malorum
An Iliad of troubles

Ἰλιὰς κακῶν, An Iliad of troubles. This means the simultaneous occurrence
of the greatest catastrophes, because in Homer's *Iliad* every kind of disaster
is recounted. For this reason scholars think that the writers of tragedy drew   5
their plots from this, as the writers of comedy did from the *Odyssey*. It is a
lengthy work, hardly finished in 24 books. So a speech which is too prolix is
called 'longer than the *Iliad*,' as Aeschines against Demosthenes: 'And
saying this, he gave the decree to the scribe to read, longer than the *Iliad* and
more meaningless than the words he was accustomed to speak.' Eustathius   10
turns it round like this: 'The proverb speaks of an Iliad of evils, but this is an
Iliad of all good things.' Synesius in a letter to his brother: 'In short, an Iliad
of evils surrounded our city.' Plutarch in 'Advice to Bride and Groom': 'But

* * * * *

5 Julian] *Epistulae* 23 Hertlein (13 Wright). Erasmus has misunderstood the
  Emperor's words: referring to the Emperor Constantius, who has lately died,
  he uses the stock phrase 'May the earth, as men say, lie lightly on him,' which
  is a vague expression of good will towards the departed, not an example of
  the impossible. This was added in *1523*.
7 This adage is] So *1523*; previously the sentence began 'If this is thought worth
  listing among proverbs, it is.'
7 elsewhere] *Adagia* I ix 74 and 73 (Horace *Epistles* 2.1.31). The latter is used as an
  example of something clearly false in I i 2, line 329.

26 This adage and the next stood together in the *Collectanea* as no 193, with no
   source named, but probably taken from Diogenianus 5.26 and 6.7 (this one is
   also in Zenobius 4.43 and Suidas I 314). Otto 849; Tilley I 22 Iliads of woe
 8 Aeschines] *In Ctesiphontem* 100; the Greek was not given till *1523*, in which year
   it was used again in IV v 51. Aeschines (389–14 BC) was the principal opponent
   of Demosthenes; cf the remark quoted in I ii 17. This speech, which had been
   translated as early as 1412 by Leonardo Bruni, is quoted in Latin four times in
   1508. Aldus first printed the Greek in 1513, and nearly all Erasmus' quotations
   are additions of *1528* and *1533*.
10 Eustathius] See I i 77n; on the *Iliad*, preface (1.26).
12 Synesius] See I ii 4n; *Epistulae* 94 (or 95).233d (*PG* 66.1461A).
13 Plutarch] *Moralia* 141A, added in *1515*; the Latin version was amended and the
   explanatory sentence added in *1528*.

the marriage of these made an Iliad of evils for Greeks and barbarians.' He is
speaking of the marriage of Paris and Helen, which was the cause of   15
countless misfortunes. Cicero uses it in his *Letters to Atticus*: 'Such an Iliad of
troubles is impending.'

27 **Lerna malorum**
   A Lerna of troubles

Λέρνη κακῶν, A Lerna of troubles. Used of an accumulation of many ills all
piled up on one another. Strabo mentions this proverb in his *Geography*,
book 8, where he writes that Lerna was a lake, joining the lands of the   5
Argives and Mycenaeans, into which all the refuse from everywhere was
pitched. Hence the common proverb, 'a Lerna of evils.' The poets claim that
in this lake dwelt the famous seven-headed hydra, which Hercules destroyed with Greek fire. This hydra, as Hesiod writes, was the offspring of
Echidna and Typhaon, and nourished by Juno, doubtless in hatred of   10
Hercules. Zenodotus says that Lerna was a certain place in the Argolid into
which every kind of filth was promiscuously thrown, and from which fetid
and poisonous vapours used to rise. However he affirms that the proverb is
more likely to refer to the story of the Danaids. It is said that Danaus had
given his fifty daughters in marriage to fifty young men, the sons of Aegyp-   15
tus, whom he slaughtered all in one night; and their heads were piled up in
that place, hence the proverb. It is not unlikely, he thinks, that out of
contempt Danaus would have ordered refuse to be carried to the spot where
he had collected the heads together. Thus, when we signify a totally infamous man, stained with all kinds of baseness, or a pestilential gang of   20
men, the dregs and offscourings of the criminal classes, we shall be right in
saying 'a Lerna of evils.' In Hesychius the comedy-writer Cratinus calls the
theatre a Lerna of spectators, because it consists of the mixed and various
offscourings of humanity.

* * * * *

16 Cicero] *Ad Atticum* 8.11.3, added in *1523*

27 *Collectanea* no 193 (with the preceding), probably from Diogenianus 6.7
 4 Strabo] *Geographica* 8.6.8 (see I i 69n).
 9 Hesiod] *Theogony* 313–5
11 Zenodotus] Zenobius 4.86
22 Hesychius] See Introduction section v 35n; Λ691, citing Cratinus (see I i 35n)
   frag 347 Kock; added in *1523*.

28 **Mare malorum**
    A sea of troubles

Κακῶν θάλασσα, A sea of troubles. This is usually said of catastrophes
which are boundless and manifold, because the sea is an infinite thing, or
else because those who occupy themselves in it are subject to infinite   5
hardships. Euripides says in the *Hippolytus Crowned*: 'Wretched I see a sea of
evils, / So great that there's no hope of swimming out.' Plautus in the
Asinaria gives the name of 'sea' to harlot and bawd, because they are the
authors of so many ills: 'the sea,' he says, 'is no sea – it is you who are the
bitterest of seas.' Aeschylus in the *Suppliants*:   10

> A throng of evils bursts upon me like a river,
> Or like a deep sea, unfathomable,
> Not to be crossed without the greatest peril.

The Scriptures also, when they refer to the inexhaustible force of something,
call it an 'abyss.' And St Chrysostom says in his *De sacerdotio*, book 6, 'Look,   15
a great abyss of toil.'

29 **Mare bonorum**
    A sea of good things

The opposite is also said, Ἀγαθῶν θάλασσα, A sea of good things, with
reference to great and heaped-up benefits. This may be either because the
sea itself yields innumerable riches in the way of fish and gems; or because   5
of its tremendous width and depth, so great that it can never be exhausted,
nor does it ever overflow, though such a mass of water flows into it from the
rivers.

* * * * *

28 Perhaps taken straight from Euripides
 6 Euripides] *Hippolytus* 822–3
 7 Plautus] *Asinaria* 134
10 Aeschylus] *Supplices* 469–70
14 Scriptures] Eg Psalm 36:6 (vulgate 35:7) 'Thy judgments are a great deep';
    added in 1533.
15 Chrysostom] Johannes Chrysostomus *De sacerdotio* 6.9 (*PG* 48.686); added in
    1533. The title is given in Greek. Erasmus himself edited the Greek text for
    Froben in 1525 (Ep 1558).

29 *Collectanea* no 192, with our nos 31 and 32. From the Greek collections:
    Zenobius 1.9; Diogenianus 1.10; Suidas A 123

30 **Thesaurus malorum**
   A store of evils

Θησαυρὸς κακῶν, A store of evils. Something in the same style is found in
other places, for instance in Euripides, *Ion*: 'Alas, how great a store of evils
opens.' Among the Greek maxims there is this line: 'A wife's a store of ills if   5
she be bad.' Plautus uses this adage in the *Mercator*: 'You have indeed
brought me a store of ill.' Hence that saying so frequent in Holy Scripture,
'They treasure up evil for themselves,' that is, they collect it, seek it out,
hoard it up. But what we really mean by treasure is a mass of useful things
similarly stored away.   10

31 **Acervus bonorum**
   A heap of good things

Ἀγαθῶν σωρός, A heap of good things – referring to immense wealth.
Hence we often read of feasts or riches as 'heaped-up,' wealth as 'amassed,'
as a term for abundance, as if those things had been thrown together   5
pell-mell, poured out by mass, not by weight or counting. Aristophanes in
the *Plutus*: 'For us a heap of goods has flowed / Into our house, though we've
done nothing wrong.' Again in the same play: 'As I bring all good things to
you in crowds.' Again, in the same play, he turns it jokingly to a bad
meaning: 'You say one came bearing a pile [*soron*] of money,' the words of   10
the chorus of old men, to which the slave Carion replies jokingly: 'Nay,
rather bearing to you a pile of old men's ills.' He is alluding to the old age of
those people with 'One foot in the grave.' For the word *soros* with a short *o*
[omicron] means 'burial mound,' and *sōros* with a long *o* [omega] means
heap and mass. The slave naturally takes care to pronounce the vowel   15
wrong. These, and other phrases of the same kind, will be improved, as I
have often pointed out, if they are twisted a little from their original meaning. One might say that other orators excel in this or that quality, but Cicero

* * * * *

30 Probably from Euripides *Ion* 923–4. Otto 1777
  5 Greek maxims] Menander *Sententiae* 325 (see I i 30n).
  6 Plautus] *Mercator* 163, added in *1520*
  7 Scripture] Eg Amos 3:10; Matthew 12:35

31 *Collectanea* no 192, with our nos 29 and 32. From the Greek collections:
  Zenobius 1.10; Diogenianus 1.10; Suidas A 123
  6 Aristophanes] *Plutus* 804–5; 646; 269 and 270. In *1508* both *soros* a tomb and
  sōros a heap were spelt with an omega, and distinguished by their grammatical
  gender; this was corrected in *1526*.

is 'alone the accumulation of all good qualities.' Those phrases which come
often to Cicero have the flavour of this adage, 'to load with kindness,' 'to   20
give massive satisfaction,' 'a heap of services rendered.'

32   **Bonorum myrmecia**
     An ant-hill of good things

Ἀγαθῶν μυρμηκία, An ant-hill of good things. This describes uncounted
wealth. *Myrmecia*, the word used, is the Greek for an ant-hill or column of
ants; though this may be derived from those ants mentioned by Pliny, book   5
11 chapter 31, which he says are the colour of cats and the size of wolves in
Egypt. 'These ants dig gold out of caves in the northern territory of the
Indians, who are called Dardae. It is dug out in winter, and in the warm
summer the Indians pillage it, when the ants are hiding away in their holes
because of the heat. But sometimes, attracted by smell, they fly out and often   10
sting, even when the pilferers escape on the swiftest camels.' St Basil
appears to have been thinking of this when he writes to his nephews that
everything in excess of necessities should be despised, whether it were
Lydian nuggets or the work of gold-digging ants; and the less needed, the
more it should be despised. There is no reason, however, why he should not   15
be referring to our own ants, not only because of the immense numbers of
their marching columns but because of the natural industry of the creature in
building up its store, bringing everything it can in the mouth to add it to the
heap, as Horace wrote. It is due to this, I think, that in Antiquity an
assemblage of ants presaged wealth. Cicero testifies to this in the *On Divina-* 20
tion, book 1: 'When Midas of Phrygia was a boy, ants collected grains of
wheat in his mouth as he lay asleep. It was prophesied that he would be
extremely rich; and this happened.' Theocritus in the *Praise of Ptolemy*: 'Just
as the wealth of ever-toiling ants is piled up.' And in the *Women of Syracuse*:
'Ants unnumbered and unmeasured,' meaning a vast crowd of men. This is   25

* * * * *

19 alone *etc*] This phrase is given in Greek, and was provided with a Latin version
    in *1515*.

32 *Collectanea* no 192, with our nos 29 and 31. From the Greek collections:
    Zenobius 1.11; Diogenianus 1.10; Suidas A 123
 5 Pliny] *Naturalis historia* 11.111
11 Basil] See I i 2 line 144n; *Ad adulescentes* 9 (PG 31.586A; p 58 Boulenger).
19 Horace] *Satires* 1.1.33–5
20 Cicero] *De divinatione* 1.36.78
23 Theocritus] 17.107; 15.45, the latter added in *1515*

close to what Plato says in the *Republic*, book 9, about the 'swarm of pleasures' and Socrates in Plutarch of Chaeronea speaking of a 'swarm of virtues,' a crowd or countless number. The passage quoted by Plutarch is in Plato's *Meno*. Similar to these is the phrase used by Plato in the *Cratylus*, 'a swarm of learning.' Also what Alexis wrote in his *Pamphila*, cited by Athen-   30
aeus, book 8: 'I brought the table in, and laid thereon / A wainload of good things.'

33 Dathus bonorum
A Dathos of good things

Δάθος ἀγαθῶν, A Dathos of good things. It was customary to use this in the same sense. Dathos is a colony of the Thasians, near the Strymon; it was rich and flourishing in other ways as well as having veins of gold, so that the   5
proverb grew up 'A Dathos of good things' to suggest collected wealth. Suidas mentions this, among others; in him we read *Datos* not *Dathos*.

34 Thasos bonorum
A Thasos of good things

Θάσσος ἀγαθῶν, A Thasos of good things. This proverb grew likewise out of the fertility of a place. Thasos is an island near Thrace. Zenodotus tells a

* * * * *

26 Plato] *Republic* 9.574d, added in *1517/8*
27 Plutarch] *Moralia* 93B, added in *1517/8*
29 Plato] *Meno* 72a; *Cratylus* 401e, both added in *1520*
30 Alexis] Frag 171 Kock, cited by Athenaeus 9.380c; added in *1517/8*, as it was in I vii 74. He is a writer of the Attic New Comedy.

33 *Collectanea* no 693 began 'Eustachius, quoted by Ermolao, records that Dathos was a populous colony of the Thasians ...' This is a reference to Eustathius' commentary on the *Iliad* 11.580 (1701.6), as cited by Ermolao Barbaro in his *Castigationes Plinianae* 4.136; ed G. Pozzi 1 (Padua 1973) 247. There are other places where Erasmus omits the name of a modern authority when once he has been able to go behind him to the ancient sources; but it is unusual for him to suppress the name of Eustathius, from whom he draws without hesitation elsewhere (see I i 77n). The mention of gold-mines may be derived from Zenobius 3.11. Strabo *Geographica* 7.36 (see I i 69n) is also a source.
7 Suidas] Δ 91, added in *1526*. 'Among others' perhaps means Eustathius.

34 This was mentioned in *Collectanea* no 693 on the authority of Ermolao Barbaro (see the preceding adage). The material comes from Zenobius ('Zenodotus') 4.34; see also Suidas θ 60. The name of the island of Thasos is spelt by Erasmus here *Thassus*.

story of this sort: Callistratus the orator, on his departure from Athens, tried   5
to persuade the Athenians that they should inhabit the region opposite to
them; he gave a splendid description of its fertility, and said it had veins of
gold and the most fruitful soil. In a word, he said, it is a Thasos of good
things; and this became a popular saying about people who make
magnificent promises.   10

35 Hostium munera, non munera
Gifts of enemies are no gifts

The ancients held religiously to their belief that gifts were to be carefully
examined, as to who had sent them and with what intention; since it is well
known that anything given by those who wish us ill would usually be for our   5
destruction. It was so with the deceiving box sent to Prometheus by Jove
through Pandora; and with the garment which Medea gave to the new wife
of Jason, and the garment Deianira sent to Hercules. The commentators on
proverbs think that this proverb was derived from the story told by Homer
in the seventh book of the *Iliad*. He tells how Hector and Ajax became   10
friends and exchanged gifts: Hector gave Ajax a sword and Ajax gave Hector
a belt. Afterwards each of them came to grief through the gift he had
received. Ajax, in fact, after being defeated by Ulysses, and knowing what
he had said and done in his madness, killed himself with that same sword.
Likewise Hector was slain by Achilles before the walls of Troy, as a result of   15
that same belt. The adage is mentioned in Sophocles in the *Ajax Mastigophoros*, but the reference suggests that it was not derived from Ajax but was
already old when he used it. After his decision to kill himself, Ajax curses
the sword which he had accepted as a gift from his bitterest enemy, and
declares it was a most unlucky one for him and that thereafter nothing has   20
gone right for the Argives. He confirms his suspicions by the well-known
proverb:

> How true it is, as says the world's old saw,
> That gifts from foes are never gifts at all,
> But luckless, bringing harm.   25

* * * * *

35 Erasmus keeps us waiting for the Greek form of the proverb until we reach the
quotation from Sophocles; but he must have found it in the proverb-collections:
Zenobius 4.4; Diogenianus 4.82a; Suidas E 4028. Tilley G 109 Gifts from enemies
are dangerous.
9 Homer] *Iliad* 7.303–5
16 Sophocles] *Ajax* 664–5

There is a Greek epigram about this: 'Hector gave Ajax a sword, Ajax gave
Hector a belt; / To each his gift meant death.' Another epigram says; 'So pass
the lethal gifts from foe to foe, / Kindness apparently, but bringing doom.'
There is a hint of this in Euripides, when Medea refuses Jason's presents,
saying they will cause her destruction: 'Harm and not good must come from   30
gifts of an evil man.' Servius points out that Virgil referred to this in the
Aeneid, book 4, when he says: 'She unsheathed the blade, / The Trojan's gift,
not for these uses sought.' He is speaking of the sword left behind by
Aeneas, with which Dido stabs herself, calling Aeneas wicked, and her
enemy. We may add the warning among the proverbs in Holy Scripture, not   35
to be too sure of the enemy after reconciliation. A proverbial line runs 'Never
think friendly what is said by foe,' and another in the same vein: 'Distrust
thy foe, and thou shalt not fare ill.'

The proverb can be applied to those, poor themselves, who aim at the
favour of the rich by little presents, thus hoping to induce them to be   40
generous. This is not giving but begging. Hence Plutarch in his essay 'On
the E at Delphi' approves of what Dicaearchus thinks was said to Archelaus
by Euripides:

> I being poor do not wish to give a gift
> To a rich man, lest I be thought a fool,   45
> Or asking for a gift in return.

This will fit both those who gain the services of demons by magic arts, for
these result in the destruction of the users, and seekers after inheritances,
and those who try to please by doing a good turn, not for genuine reasons
but with another end in view. And so the proverb may be given a new   50
meaning by the alteration of a word: 'flatterers' gifts are no gifts,' 'poor
men's gifts are no gifts,' and finally 'poets' gifts are no gifts,' as I have shown
at the beginning of this work.

*****

26 Greek epigram] *Anthologia Palatina* 7.151, followed by 152.7–8
29 Euripides] *Medea* 618
31 Servius] On Virgil *Aeneid* 4.646–7
35 Scripture] Cf *Ecclesiasticus* 12:10.
36 proverbial line] Menander *Sententiae* 451 and 237 (see I i 30n); frag trag adesp
   310 Nauck.
41 Plutarch] *Moralia* 384D, citing Euripides frag 969 Nauck; the Dicaearchus
   whose opinion he quotes is a Greek historian of the late fourth century BC;
   Archelaus, the king of Macedon at whose court Euripides was a distinguished
   guest at the end of his life. The sentence referring to magic arts is an addition of
   1517/8.
53 at the beginning] In Erasmus' Introduction, section xii line 15

36 Davus sum, non Oedipus
I am Davus, not Oedipus

The ingenuity of Oedipus in cleverly proposing riddles and solving them at
the same time is famous owing to the problem of the Sphinx which he
solved: indeed his very name has become a proverb. In Terence, in the   5
Andria, the slave pretends not to understand what his master has said, and
replies, 'I am Davus, not Oedipus.' This can be made to suit anyone by
changing the name: 'I am Paul, not Oedipus'; 'I am Antony, not Oedipus.'
Since the form is proverbial in itself, it can be applied to any person or thing
well known to the public: 'How could I remember all that? I am Peter, not   10
Lucullus. How could I succeed in so many labours? I am Nicholas, not
Hercules. How can I convince you of such a difficult thing? I am Richard, not
Cicero.' Something like Terence's phrase is found in Euripides' *Hippolytus
Crowned*: 'I am no prophet to know clearly things obscure.' Again in the
Hecuba: 'I am no seer, so that hearing not, / I can search out the pathway of 15
your purposes.' Thus it can be turned against those who make a point of
speaking obscurely, and in riddles; or those who out of inexperience or a
superstitious veneration for unknown words write in such a complicated
way that they need a prophet rather than a reader. Heraclitus was of this
sort, as we learn from Plato in several places, and from Aristotle's *Rhetoric,* 20
book 3; and the latter adds that this man's obscurity arose from an ambiguous arrangement of words, since it was uncertain whether the word in
question belonged to what went before or to what followed after. Hence
Socrates said that to understand him one would need a 'Delian diver.'
Martial alludes to this when he teases Sextus, who affected obscurity: 'It's   25
not a reader your books need, but Apollo; / In your judgment Cinna's a
better poet than Virgil.' The same Heraclitus and his failing is used by
Jerome to upbraid Jovinianus. However Laertius writes that this philosopher, when he wanted to do so, used the clearest possible speech, so that

* * * * *

36 *Collectanea* no 223 (Terence only). Otto 1280
5 Terence] *Andria* 194
11 Lucullus] Roman general and statesman, proverbial for his 'more than human'
   memory; Cicero *Lucullus* 1.2
13 Euripides] *Hippolytus* 346; *Hecuba* 743–4
20 Aristotle] *Rhetoric* 3.5 (1407b14)
24 Delian diver] *Adagia* I vi 29
25 Martial] 10.21.3–4
28 Jerome] *Adversus Jovinianum* 1.1 (PL 23.211B)
28 Laertius] 9.7

it is clear this obscurity was purposely assumed, indeed he recommended   30
his disciples to practice it.

37   **Finem vitae specta**
      Look to the end of life

In Herodotus there is a famous story, of how Solon replied to Croesus that
no one can claim the name of 'fortunate' except the man who has successfully terminated the journey of life. Juvenal refers to this: ' – whom the   5
eloquent voice of Solon, / Bade to consider the last end of life.' Sophocles
extends this thought in *Oedipus Tyrannus*:

> So watch to see that final day
> And deem no mortal happy till   10
> All free from pain his life he ends.

Again, slightly differently, in the *Trachiniae*:

> There lives an ancient proverb among men,
> That none may know another good or bad
> Whoe'er he be, until his destined span
> Has run and he attains his final day.   15

Euripides has something similar in the *Andromache*: 'Never call a mortal
blessed, Until you see his day of dying.' Again in the *Troades*: 'Of those
borne on by fortune, call none happy, / Till happily he dies.' He repeats the
same in other words in the *Heraclidae*:

> Now by his fate   20
> He heralds clear to mortals all
> Not to envy him who seems to prosper,
> Until they see him die, since fates are fleeting.

* * * * *

37 Otto 1143; Suringar 80; Tilley E 125 Remember the end. It is close to our 'All's
    well that ends well.'
 3 Herodotus] 1.32 (see I i 96n).
 5 Juvenal] 10.274–5
 6 Sophocles] *Oedipus tyrannus* 1528–30; *Trachiniae* 1–3
16 Euripides] *Andromache* 100–1; *Troades* 509–10; *Heraclidae* 863–6

Ovid in the *Metamorphoses* expresses it thus:

> Yet a man's final day   25
> Is to be looked for, and no one called blessed
> Before his death and final obsequies.

Even today we often hear it said 'the affair must be judged by the outcome.'

38 Posterioribus melioribus
Better luck next time

Among the Greek proverbs we find this: Δευτέρων ἀμεινόνων, Better the
second time. This is applied to affairs which have had little success on the
first try, but sometimes turn out more favourably the second time; a mistake   5
in the first plan is corrected in the later one. Some think this arose from
religious rites: if the first victim did not give a favourable augury they
repeated the ritual, hoping for better things. This is clearly enough indicated
by the pimp in Plautus, who could not get a favourable answer after
sacrificing to Venus repeatedly. Plato in the fourth book of the *Laws* seems to   10
refer it to throwing knuckle-bones or some similar game, because it often
happens that when a player finds the game going against him, he asks to
begin it again from the outset, hoping that he will have more luck. Plato
says, 'So once again, as players are used to say, let us see whether a second
try has a better result.' It is true that the Greek word he uses, players, can   15
refer not to a game but to a more proverbial jest. However Cicero gives his
assent to the first interpretation, when he says in the second book of the *On
Divination*: 'How inconstant are the gods, who threaten with the entrails of
the first sacrifice and give good augury with the second.' Also in the twelfth
of his *Philippics*: 'Later thoughts, as they say, are wiser.' The same to this   20
brother Quintus: 'I assure you that, as for "second thoughts," I could have

* * * * *

24 Ovid] *Metamorphoses* 3.135–7

38 *Collectanea* no 315 gave the reference to Cicero *De divinatione*, and also to the
parable of the importunate man in Luke 11:5–8, which was discarded in *1508*,
probably as irrelevant. Otto 404; in part Tilley T 247 Second thoughts are best.
3 Greek proverbs] Zenobius 3.15; Diogenianus 4.15
9 Plautus] *Poenulus* 42
10 Plato] *Laws* 4.723e
16 Cicero] *De divinatione* 2.17.38; *Philippics* 12.2.5 (the number of the speech added
in *1528*); *Ad Quintum fratrem* 3.1.18

none in my relations with Caesar,' meaning 'I can find no suitable plan by which I can amend the earlier bad ones.' Davus in Terence was thinking of this when he said, 'No success here, we'll try another way.' Aristotle seems to allude to this in the first book of the *Metaphysics*, where he says, 'It is   25 necessary to end up with the opposite and the better, according to the proverb.' He is speaking of those who turn to philosophy from interest and wonder at natural causes; wishing them, once the causes are known, to cease from wonder and turn to better things. It may be that the proverb arose from the tragedy of Euripides called *Hippolytus Crowned*: 'Among   30 mortals, / Second thoughts are sometimes wiser.' The words are spoken by the nurse to Phaedra, as a recantation or palinode to what she has said earlier, now that she sees Phaedra meditating on suicide. He thought of this too in the *Supplices*:

> At home if something goes not well   35
> With later thoughts we set it right,
> But life is not the same.

The Greeks spoke of *metanoea* [hindsight] when later reflexions showed that it would have been better to act differently.

39 Actum est
All is over

We use these words proverbially even today to signify despair: 'All is over,' Greek πέπρακται. Euripides in *Hippolytus Crowned*: 'Alas, all's over, my lady's clearly lost.' Terence, in the *Eunuchus*, says *actum est, ilicet, peristi.*   5 Donatus thinks the first (it is all over) comes from the law, the second (it's finished) from the judgment, the third (you are done for) from the punish-

* * * * *

23 Terence] *Andria* 670, used again in I v 40
24 Aristotle] *Metaphysics* 1.2 (983a17)
30 Euripides] *Hippolytus* 436; *Supplices* 1082–4
38 The Greeks] This sentence was added in 1533.

39 *Collectanea* no 515 gave references to Donatus on *Eunuchus* 54 and to the *Rudens*. Suringar 1
4 Euripides] *Hippolytus* 778
5 Terence] *Eunuchus* 54–5

ment. For these three words all signify despair in an increasing degree. Since
it was not allowable to rescind the decision of the judges, and obtain a
second judgment on the same case, as Terence says, it was popularly   10
accepted that one could say of irremediable cases 'It's all over!' even if it were
to be found later that people were completely reinstated by the judge. At any
rate the phrase *actum est* is used because what is once done can never be
undone; witness the proverbial sayings to the effect that it is not permitted
even to God to undo what has been done. Plautus: 'Unless you find some   15
cover against it, the affair is finished. I am resolved to die.' We can either say
'it is over' absolutely, or with some addition of this kind, 'It is all over with
the republic.' 'It is all over with your business.' 'It is all over with human
affairs.' 'It is all over with your safety, unless you watch out.'

40 **Rem factam habere**
    To consider a thing done

Very little different is the phrase we read here and there in Martial, 'to
consider a thing done,' meaning it is certain and indubitable. Promises, to be
sure, are far from certain, but you may put your trust solely in what has been   5
kept and openly fulfilled. For instance he says to Procillus 'You thought the
whole thing was already done,' and again 'And now you take the thing as
done, Bithynicus.' He used the term 'a thing done' to show that it was not
promised, but ready and completed. Se we use 'wrought silver' of what is
not roughly made but carefully finished and chased. Perhaps he referred to a   10
legal phrase, as Terence did when he said 'all finished and concluded,' and
Cicero in the third of his speeches against Catiline 'And what first needed to
be done was finished and concluded,' used whenever reference is made in
contracts to anything which is legally agreed between the parties.

* * * * *

14 proverbial sayings] *Adagia* II iii 72
15 Plautus] *Rudens* 683–4

40 *Collectanea* no 656 quoted the two lines from Martial.
 3 Martial] 1.27.4; 2.26.3
11 Terence] *Andria* 248
12 Cicero] *In L. Catilinam* 3.6.15, added in *1533*. In the same year it was used to
    make IV x 57.

41   **Fumos vendere**
     To sell smoke

In Martial there is a particularly neat adage, 'to sell smoke,' which means to
sell the favour of the great, pretending that one can do a man the service of
recommending him because one has a certain proximity to them. Smoke, in   5
fact, begins by seeming something sizeable, but it vanishes in no time.
Martial's lines run: 'To sell about the palace no empty smoke, nor applaud
Canus, nor applaud Glaphyrus.' So it comes about that we talk of 'smoke
and clouds' when we mean a display which is all deceit, and the vain hope of
great things. St Jerome against Rufinus: 'From such a forest of books you   10
cannot produce one sprig, one bush. These are mere puffs of smoke, mere
clouds.' Rufinus had reproached Jerome with having brought the works of
the poets like smoke to the notice of nuns who were not likely to understand
them. But Jerome takes the proverb like a clumsily hurled weapon and
thrusts it back more skilfully, indicating that the word 'smoke' does not   15
mean obscurity, but vain, false ostentation. Plutarch, 'On the Divine Sign of
Socrates': 'But he sent off nonsense to the sophists, as a kind of smoke of
philosophy.'
     This kind of man, the greatest plague of kingly courts, is neatly and
excellently described by Aelius Lampridius in his life of the emperor   20
Heliogabalus. I should like to quote his very words: 'Zoticus,' he says, 'was
of such importance under him, that he was regarded by all the highest
officials of the court as if he had been the mate of their master. It was this
same Zoticus, as well, who making bad use of his familiarity used to sell for
bribes all the actions and words of Heliogabalus, hoping for enormous   25
riches from this "smoke," as he made promises to one and another and
deceived them all. Leaving the presence of Heliogabalus he interviewed

* * * * *

41 *Collectanea* no 659 in 1500 gave the couplet from Martial, and then the anecdote
   about Alexander Severus, the authority for which is given as the commentary
   on Martial by Domizio Calderini, 'who names Spartianus as his source.' This
   was compared with 'the gospel phrase *to sell oil*,' perhaps a reference to
   Matthew 25:8–10. In the revised edition of 1506 Erasmus, who had in the
   meantime read the *Scriptores historiae augustae* for himself (see I i 21n), cut out
   Domizio's name, and gave Spartianus directly as his authority. Otto 730;
   Suringar 82; Tilley s 576 To sell smoke.
   3 Martial] 4.5.7–8
  10 Jerome] *Adversus Rufinum* 3.39 (*PL* 23.484C)
  16 Plutarch] *Moralia* 580B, added in 1515. Socrates expelled humbug from the
   study of philosophy.
  20 Aelius Lampridius] *Elagabalus* 10.2–4

them one by one, saying "I said this about you," "I heard this about you,"
"This is what is going to happen to you." There are men of this kind, who if
they are admitted to too great familiarity with princes, sell the reputation not   30
only of the bad princes but of the good ones; and who live on the proceeds of
their infamous scandal-mongering, through the stupidity or innocence of
the rulers who do not perceive what is going on.' Thus far Aelius. But the
adage is given greater point by the punishment of Thurinus Verconius,
which the same Aelius recounts in his life of Alexander Severus in this   35
manner: 'When alone, in the afternoon or in the early morning, he never
saw certain people because he knew that they told lies about him, especially
Verconius Thurinus, who had been his close companion. This man had put
up everything for sale by his deceptions, with the result of dishonouring the
rule of Alexander, as if he were a stupid man whom Thurinus had in his   40
power and whom he could persuade to everything. Indeed he convinced
everybody that he could do anything by a nod. In the end Alexander caught
him by a stratagem. He sent someone to him who was asking publicly for a
favour, and approaching Thurinus for it in private, as if asking for his
support in interesting Alexander in him in secret. This was done, and   45
Thurinus promised to use his influence, and said that he had spoken to the
emperor when he had not spoken at all, but left it to be thought that the
request might yet be granted, selling the outcome for money. Alexander
ordered him to be spoken to again, and Thurinus, as if thinking of something else, assented by a nod, but still did not say anything. The request was   50
granted, and Thurinus the "seller of smoke" exacted a huge reward from the
man who had won his case. Alexander ordered him to be accused, and when
everything had been proved by witnesses, those who were present when he
had been paid and those who had heard his promises, the emperor ordered
him to be tied to a stake in the Passage Market and a fire to be made from   55
burning straw and damp wood, which killed him. Meanwhile the herald
proclaimed, "By smoke he is punished, who sold smoke." But as he did not
wish to seem cruel in even one case, he made diligent enquiries before
pronouncing sentence, and found that Thurinus had accepted bribes from
both parties in lawsuits, putting up the result for sale; and from all who had   60
received lucrative posts or provinces.' And a little further on: 'He gave no
one of these "sellers of smoke" the chance to speak ill of him, or of others to

* * * * *

35 the same Aelius] *Severus Alexander* 35.5–36.3; 67.2; 23.8
55 Passage Market] The Forum Transitorium, a landmark in the heart of ancient
   Rome, so called because it connected the Forum of Augustus with that of
   Vespasian; Erasmus' explanation of the name seems to be imaginary.

him, particularly after the death of Thurinus, who had often betrayed him as
if he were stupid and senseless.' The phrase he uses, Passage Market or
'open market,' he seems to explain himself in another part of the same Life,   65
when he says: 'The man who "sold smoke" about him, and had accepted a
hundred gold pieces from a certain soldier, he ordered to be crucified, beside
the road frequently used by his slaves on their way to the imperial estates.'
'The Emperor Avidius Cassius, we read, thought out this kind of punishment, by making a tall wooden stake a hundred and eighty feet high, and   70
tying the criminals on it from the top to the bottom, setting fire to the lowest,
so that some were burnt and others killed by the torment of the smoke and
even by fear.' Thus far the historian.

A horrible punishment, yet fitting for such heinous crimes. But I could
wish it were not true today that the Courts, not only of princes but of   75
bishops were full of this detestable kind of people, and had not only a lot of
men like Thurinus but much worse than he; who not only sell an office
falsely promised, but even sell silence itself, as it were copying Demosthenes; or indeed, what is still worse, they use the poison of the tongue to
thwart those whose bribes they have accepted for their good offices. If only   80
our princes would take care to imitate Alexander Severus. He was a pagan
moreover, and a Syrian by race, and a mere youth, and yet he was so
violently opposed to flatterers, informers, dishonest judges, sellers of
smoke and all such pests of Courts, that he was implacable towards them,
though otherwise a man of the mildest character.   85

There is a proverbial saying bandied about in our own time regarding
the splendid promises of courtiers. For they talk of 'court incense,' thinking
of that incense-vapour which is wafted in our sacred rites from a swinging
censer. That is not very different from our proverb. They speak too of the
'holy water' of courtiers, thinking of the water which is placed at the door of   90
churches, for those to sprinkle themselves with who go in or come out.

42 Columen familiae
A pillar of the household

Terence in the *Phormio*, using a proverbial phrase, I am sure, says this of
Geta, the elderly slave to whom the old man, who is setting out on a

* * * * *

69 we read] Vulcacius Gallicanus *Avidius Cassius* 4.3 (also in the *Scriptores*, I i 21n)
78 Demosthenes] He was said to have taken bribes to keep his mouth shut; see
   Adagia I vii 19.

42 Presumably taken directly from Terence *Phormio* 287, with Donatus the ancient
   commentator.

journey, had entrusted the character of his children, as their tutor and   5
guardian, and also his household affairs: 'A pillar of the household.' Donatus thinks *columen* is put for *columna* or pillar on which the rest of the house is
supported, and so in former times the older slaves were called 'props,'
columellae. Virgil's phrase agrees with this: 'On thee the whole house rests
though tottering.' So does that line of Euripides in the *Iphigenia in Tauris*:   10
'Male children are the pillars of the house.' Pindar in the *Olympians* calls
Hector the pillar of Troy: 'Who toppled Hector, Troy's unconquerable steadfast pillar.' He is speaking of Achilles. Close to this is that remark in Juvenal:
'A sorry state, to rest on borrowed fame: / Down come your rafters if the
columns crack.'
                                                                          15

43   **Ancora domus**
     The anchor of the house

With a similar metaphor Hecuba in Euripides calls Polydorus the anchor of
his family and clan: 'The one remaining anchor of my house.' We have noted
elsewhere, when we were explaining the 'sacred anchor,' how the Greeks   5
often used 'anchor' proverbially, meaning 'refuge.' Indeed, whatever we
lean on and put our trust in they call an anchor, taking the metaphor from
ships which are steadied by an anchor and so are at rest and protected from
the waves. So Aristides in the first *Panathenaic Oration*: 'All the Greeks
seemed to themselves to be in a kind of harbour, moored by two anchors' as   10
if strengthened by a double defence. I have cited this passage also a little
while back.

* * * * *

9 Virgil] *Aeneid* 12.59, quoted again in II vi 69
10 Euripides] *Iphigeneia in Tauris* 57
11 Pindar] *Olympians* 2.89–90, added in 1523 (part of this was added in 1538 to II x
     25).
13 Juvenal] 8.76–7

43 Euripides must be the source of this.
  3 Euripides] *Hecuba* 80
  5 elsewhere] *Adagia* I i 24
  9 Aristides] *Panathenaicus* p 176 Dindorf (see I i 13n).
11 a little while back] *Adagia* I i 13

44 **Nullus sum**
   I am nothing

The hyperbolic phrases of the comedy-writers are also proverbial. 'I am
nothing, I am down, I am lost'; thus we signify despair and immense
disaster. Euripides, from *Iphigenia in Tauris*: 'Cowards and idle folk are   5
nothing anywhere,' and again in *Iphigenia in Aulis*: 'You were nothing, but
ruined by fate, you were dismayed.' I think this is the very thing which
Athenaeus is quoting from Plato in his tenth book: 'For you are nothing, as
the proverb says,' although this does not refer to ruin but expresses contempt. It may seem to be taken from Homer, in whose *Odyssey*, book 9   10
Ulysses pretends that his name is Noman, suggesting that he had almost
perished. And by this invented name the Cyclops was deceived.

45 **Nolens volens**
   Willy-nilly

As has been shown earlier, and as Donatus explains, almost all figures of
this kind are proverbial – which consist largely in opposites, because they
seem to have an enigmatic quality. They are frequent among the Greek   5
poets: as in Euripides, in the *Hecuba*, 'But he not willing and yet willing,' and
in the *Iphigenia in Tauris*: 'I am in exile in a sense, not willing yet willing.' To
this form belongs what Terence says in the *Andria*, 'You were compelled of
your own free will.'

* * * * *

44 Probably also from Euripides; an addition from Sophocles was made in 1533 in v
   i 86.
5 Euripides] *Iphigeneia in Tauris* 115; *Iphigeneia Aulidensis* 351
8 Plato] (The comic poet) frag 174 Kock, cited by Athenaeus 10.441e; added in
   1517/8. This reappears in II x 8.
10 Homer] *Odyssey* 9.366

45 Otto 1852; Tilley w 40 Will he, nill he. But that means 'whether he will or no,'
   under compulsion; and much of this material means 'willing and unwilling,' in
   a state of uncertainty, and is discussed again in *Adagia* II vii 82.
3 Donatus] On Terence *Eunuchus* 1058; cf I iii 85 line 35.
6 Euripides] *Hecuba* 566; *Iphigeneia in Tauris* 512
8 Terence] *Andria* 658; the author's name was omitted in 1523 and restored in
   1526. In the *Collectanea* this formed no 756.

46 **Contra stimulum calces**
    You are kicking against the goad

Πρὸς κέντρα λακτίζεις, You are kicking up your heels against the pricks,
means to struggle in vain against those you cannot conquer, or to provoke
those who are harmful when roused. Or it may mean to rebel against   5
destiny, and by failing to bear with patience an evil you cannot avoid, not
only to fail to escape from it but to double it. For instance, a man has a
quarrelsome wife: if he is constantly disputing with her, he will achieve no
result except to make her more quarrelsome still. Terence says in the
Phormio: 'For this is ignorance – heels against the goad.' Donatus points out   10
that this is a proverb, but with an ellipse, as the word *iactare*, to kick up, is
missing, and Greek says it all in one word, *laktizein*. Plautus in the
Truculentus: 'If you fight a goad with your fists, the hands get the worst of it.'
This proverb also comes in the Acts of the Apostles: 'It is hard for thee to kick
against the pricks,' that is, to fight against God. Euripides in the *Bacchae*:   15

> I would much rather do him sacrifice
> Than hot with anger kick against the goad,
> Myself a mortal man and he a god.

Pindar in the *Pythians*: 'For this is to kick against the goad.' The metaphor
comes from oxen jabbed in the rear by ploughmen with pointed poles; hence   20
they are called *boukentai*, goaders of oxen, in the proverb 'Few men can
plough, though many ply the goad.' If the oxen fight back with their heels
against the goad, so far are they from damaging the goad that they are worse
hurt themselves. Plutarch in his essay 'On the Control of Anger' tells of a

* * * * *

46 In the *Collectanea* no 188, Erasmus gave the proverb from Terence, with
    Donatus' comment, and added the Greek equivalent from the proverb-
    collections (Zenobius 5.70; Diogenianus 7.84; Suidas π 2725). Then came
    Plautus *Truculentus* 768–9, which he dropped in 1508; but he thought of one of
    the lines later and inserted it in 1523, although it is not wholly relevant. The
    quotation from Acts, which one might have expected in 1500, was absent. Otto
    1693; Tilley F 433 Folly it is to spurn against a prick.
 9 Terence] *Phormio* 77–8, with Donatus the ancient commentator
12 Plautus] *Truculentus* 768, added in 1523
14 Acts] 9:5 and 26:14
15 Euripides] *Bacchae* 794–5
19 Pindar] *Pythians* 2.94–5, the title and some corrections added in 1523
21 proverb] *Adagia* I vii 9
24 Plutarch] *Moralia* 457A, added in 1515. The *pancratium* was an all-in contest of
    boxing and wrestling at the Greek festivals.

pancratiast Ctesiphon who was so angry with a kicking mule that he kicked   25
it in return.

47   **In aurem dicere**
     To speak in the ear

Εἰς οὖς λέγειν, To speak in the ear. This is still used nowadays, to mean a
secret and private communication. It is taken from people who come near to
whisper in someone's ear what they do not want heard by others. So   5
sometimes in Homer, 'Bringing his head near, so that the others would not
hear.' Horace in the *Satires*: 'And whisper something or other in my servant's ear.' Euripides in the *Ion*: 'Come here, for I wish to speak into your
ear.' Lucian in *Gallus*: 'Speaking a word in the ear of some Syracusans.' To
this belongs the phrase in the Gospel, 'What ye hear in the ear, that preach   10
ye upon the housetops,' that is, what you have received in private conversation, preach in public.

48   **Nec obolum habet, unde restim emat**
     He hasn't a farthing left to buy himself a rope

A proverbial hyperbole about people in the direst poverty. Lucian in *Timon*,
'Who had not an obol yesterday to buy a noose with.' The man must indeed
be poor who wants to strangle himself with a noose for very weariness of his   5
poverty; but poorer still is the man who has not a coin left to buy a rope to
hang himself with.

49   **Hinnulus leonem**
     A fawn against a lion

This is a proverbial allegory: Ὁ νέβρος τὸν λέοντα, The fawn (we must
supply) has caught, or has conquered, or is challenging, the lion (or any

* * * * *

47 Derived perhaps from general reading. Suringar 89
 6 Homer] *Odyssey* 1.157; 4.70; 17.592
 7 Horace] *Satires* 1.9.9–10
 8 Euripides] *Ion* 1521
 9 Lucian] *Gallus* 25
10 Gospel] Matthew 10:27

48 Taken from Lucian *Timon* 20

49 Probably taken, like the last, direct from Lucian, though it appears here and
   there in the Greek proverb-collections.

other verb which gives the gist of the saying); used whenever a far weaker 5
antagonist defeats a stronger, thus turning things upside down. Lucian, of
the legacy-hunter who, young as he is, is caught out by an old man, the
pursuer outdone by his quarry: 'This is just what the proverb says, the fawn
has caught the lion.' This was in the mind of whoever wrote *Megara the Wife
of Hercules*: 'Is it because your glorious son suffers boundless woes at the 10
hands of a worthless man, as a fierce lion might from a fawn?' It can also be
suitably extended to the case where a much weaker person attacks a stronger, or one who is far less learned disputes with an accomplished scholar.

50 **Iungere vulpes**
To yoke foxes

Said of a palpably ridiculous thing, Ζευγνύειν τὰς ἀλώπεκας, To yoke foxes
together. Virgil in *Palaemon*: 'Who hates not Bavius, let him like your songs,
Maevius, / Let him yoke foxes to the plough and milk he-goats.' The fox is an 5
animal utterly foreign to the plough.

51 **Mulgere hircum**
To milk a he-goat

Τράγον ἀμέλγειν, To milk a he-goat. This has the same sense. Lucian, in his
Life of Demonax, recalls among the many witty sayings of this man the
following: when he saw a pair of philosophers, each as ignorant as the other, 5

* * * * *

6 Lucian] *Dialogi mortuorum* 18(8), the opening words. The speaker (now in the
nether world) had left his property to a rich old man, and showed him the
will, hoping that in gratitude he would leave his young benefactor a fat legacy
and then predecease him. But it was the young man who died first and the old
man who got the legacy, thus (as Erasmus puts it) 'turning things upside
down.' This was reused in 1536 in a rewriting of I i 54.
9 *Megara*] A poem by an unknown hand (lines 4–5), printed (sometimes under
the name of Moschus, a poet of the second century BC) after Theocritus in the
corpus of the Greek bucolic poets. This sentence was added in 1526, the Latin
version in 1528.

50 Our nos 50 and 51 together formed *Collectanea* no 379, the source being Virgil's
Eclogue. Otto 1942; Tilley F 661 as above
4 Virgil] *Eclogues* 3.90–1

51 *Collectanea* no 379, with the preceding, from Virgil. Otto 812; Tilley B 714 To milk
a he-goat; cf R 27 While one milks the he-goat, the other holds the sieve.
3 Lucian] *Demonax* 28. This is referred to again in II iv 33.

disputing together, one propounding absurd questions and the other giving crazy answers, entirely off the point: 'Why, friends,' said he, 'is not one of these fellows milking a he-goat and the other putting a sieve under it?' Diogenianus gives it in these words, 'Which is the stupider, the one who milks the he-goat or the one who holds the sieve?' Both are equally absurd.   10
Not unlike this is that other proverb Like lips, like lettuce, and The cover is worthy of such a cup.

52 **De asini umbra**
About an ass's shadow

ʿΥπὲρ ὄνου σκιᾶς, About an ass's shadow. That is, about a thing of no moment. Sophocles in the *Cedalion*, cited by Suidas: 'All things are the shadow of an ass,' that is, nonsense, rubbish. Also cited by him, Aris-   5
tophanes in the *Daedalus*: 'Concerning what are you now at war? Concerning the shadow of an ass.' The same author quotes Aristotle, in the *Didaskaliai*, as saying that there was a play with the title *Shadow of An Ass*; it was a comedy of Archippus, I think, that he meant, of which Zenodotus makes mention. Lucian, in *The Sects*, 'All philosophers, or almost all, are   10
fighting over the shadow of an ass.' Aristophanes in the *Wasps*: 'What are we fighting about? About an ass's shadow.' Demosthenes in one of his *Philippics* says: 'Going to war with the whole world now about that shadow in Delphi.'
    There are some who think that this adage was first derived from   15
Demosthenes as its author, and they tell this story: Once when Demosthenes was defending someone on a capital charge, and he had judges who

* * * * *

9 Diogenianus] 7.95
11 proverb] *Adagia* I x 71 and 72

52 *Collectanea* no 649, from Diogenianus 7.1, reinforced with a reference to Apuleius, part of which has found a more appropriate home in I iii 64. The story was given also in Zenobius 6.28 and Suidas O 400, Y 327, and provided an Aesopic fable (339 Halm). Otto 187 (including I iii 64)
4 Sophocles] Frag 308 Nauck, cited by Suidas O 400
4 Aristophanes] Frag 192 Kock, from the same source
7 Aristotle] Frag 625 Rose
9 Archippus] A writer of the Attic Old Comedy; frags 33 and 34 Kock come from a play of this name, which is mentioned by Zenobius 6.28.
10 Lucian] *Hermotimus* 71 (for which *The Sects* is an alternative title)
11 Aristophanes] *Wasps* 191
12 Demosthenes] Not one of his *Philippics*, but the *De pace* 25
16 Demosthenes] This anecdote could all be taken from Zenobius 6.28.

were inattentive but interrupted constantly, he said, 'Lend me your ears for
a little while, and I will tell something new and amusing, and merry to hear.'
At these words they pricked up their ears to listen to him. 'A certain young   20
man, ' he said, 'had hired an ass to carry goods from Athens to Megara. On
the way, as the midday heat grew stronger, and he could not find a tiny bit of
shade to shelter him from the sun, he took off the pack-saddle and sat under
the ass, protecting himself with its shade. However the owner would not
allow this, and dragged the man out, shouting that he rented the ass but not   25
the ass's shadow. The other held the opposite view, and declared that he
had paid for the ass's shadow too. The quarrel between them dragged on
until they came to blows, the one stoutly asserting that the ass's shadow had
not been paid for, the other declaring on the contrary that he had hired it as
well. Finally they went to law.' Having got thus far, when he knew the   30
judges were listening carefully, Demosthenes suddenly began to leave the
rostrum. The judges called him back and asked him to go on with the rest of
the story. 'Do you mean to say,' he said, 'that you will listen to something
about an ass's shadow, but you can't bother to hear the cause of a man in
peril of his life?'   35

    Plutarch tells the story a little differently in his life of Demosthenes, as
follows: 'When the Athenians interrupted him in a speech in the assembly,
he said he would like to tell them a short story. When there was silence he
said: A young man hired an ass one summer to go from the city to Megara.
At midday when the sun was burning fiercely, he and the owner wanted to   40
lie down in the shadow of the ass. But each prevented the other from doing
so. The owner said he had rented the ass, not the shadow, and the other
who had hired it replied that he had full rights over the ass. And after saying
this he was preparing to depart. But the Athenians detained him, asking
him to tell the rest of the story of the ass. He said, "Are you willing to listen   45
when I speak of the shadow of an ass, but not willing to listen when I speak
of serious matters?"' Some say that the ass was hired in Athens to go not to
Megara but to Delphi, and this appears from the words of Demosthenes
who mentions the 'Delphic shadow' at the end of his speech *On the Peace*: 'Is
it not stupid, is it not truly lamentable, that we, who are already at odds with   50
one another about our own concerns, many of them of the greatest importance, should be going to war with the whole world now about that shadow

* * * * *

36 Plutarch] *Moralia* 848A–B, in his (spurious) *Lives of the Ten Orators*
48 Demosthenes] *De pace* 25, as before; the Greek inserted in 1515 with its Latin
    version. The 'shadow in Delphi' was the Amphictyonic League, now,
    according to some, a mere shadow of its former self.

in Delphi?' Apuleius in the *Ass* claims jokingly that it came from him. Menander in the *Enchiridion* and Plato in the *Phaedrus* make use of this adage, Plato saying that inexperienced politicians act impudently and dangerously when, speaking to a public equally inexperienced, they praise, not the shadow of an ass, which would be something frivolous and unimportant, but evil as though it were good: 'not so much exalting the ass's shadow as if it were the shadow of a horse, but praising evil instead of good.' Procopius says in one of his letters: 'I myself believe that, holding as you do the opposite view of the art, my clever friend, you are starting a quarrel on the proverbial ass's shadow, for the pleasure, I suppose, of the scurrilities.' Origen used it in the preface to his third book *Against Celsus*. 55

60

But it was time long ago for me to abandon the ass's shadow, before anyone laughs at me legitimately for fussing over the shadow of an ass. 65

53 De lana caprina
About goat's wool

A very similar adage is found in Latin, about goat's wool, which seems to have arisen from some event of the same kind, when two people were disputing as to whether a goat has wool or hair; or else from a discussion on goats' hair as a useless and unimportant subject, just as there is a proverb about asses' wool. Horace in the *Epistles*, to Lollius: 5

> Another, with devotion fervent,
> Is more than your obsequious servant;
> Admitted as a humbler guest
> Where men of money break their jest,
> He waits the nod, with awe profound, 10

* * * * *

53 Apuleius] See I i 15n. *Metamorphoses* 9.42; the story is quoted in I iii 64.
54 Menander] Frag 141, cited by Zenobius 6.28
54 Plato] *Phaedrus* 260c
60 Procopius] Of Gaza, a rhetorician of the fifth/sixth century AD, cited from the Aldine *Epistolographi Graeci* of 1499. This is *Epistula* 3 in Hercher's edition of 1873.
63 Origen] *Contra Celsum* 3.1 (*PG* 11.921A), added in *1517/8*. The concluding sentence is of *1515*.

53 *Collectanea* no 154, citing Horace only. Otto 340; Tilley G 170 You go to a goat to buy wool.
7 asses' wool] *Adagia* I iv 79
7 Horace] *Epistles* 1.18.10–11 and 13–16 (version adapted from Sir Philip Francis)

And catches, ere it reach the ground,
The falling joke, and echoes back the sound.
A schoolboy thus with humbler air   15
Repeats to pedagogue severe;
His players act an under-part,
And fear to put out all their art.
Another in disputes engages,
With nonsense armed for goat's wool rages.   20

He is talking about people who are bad-tempered with their friends, and start a quarrel with a friend on the slightest pretext.

54 **De fumo disceptare**
    To dispute about smoke

Similar to this is what we read in Aristophanes' *Clouds*: 'Already he seeks to quibble and speak subtly of smoke, περὶ καπνοῦ στενολεσχεῖν.' It is a dig at philosophers, who discuss with great earnestness about smoke, that is,   5
things of no importance. There is a spice of comic wit in the very words he uses for the joke, *leptologein, stenoleschein,* one meaning to discuss silly and frivolous things, the other to be tormented with care and anxiety about sheeer nonsense. So the school of Socrates was called a *phrontisterion,* a thinking-shop.   10

55 **Talpa caecior**
    As blind as a mole

Τυφλότερος ἀσπάλακος, As blind as a mole. Suidas and Diogenianus record this, referring to people whose sight is exceptionally poor, or who have no judgment, for the metaphor will be more pleasing if it is transferred to the   5
mind. Pliny, book 11, writes that among quadrupeds, 'the mole is without

* * * * *

54 No doubt derived directly from Aristophanes *Clouds* (320 and 94)

55 *Collectanea* no 675, a very brief entry derived from Diogenianus. Otto 1739;
    Tilley M 1034 As blind as a mole. Erasmus might have been expected to quote
    for this use of 'mole' the passage from Jerome's *Letters* which provided him with
    Adagia III i 7.
    3 Suidas] T 1216
    3 Diogenianus] 8.25
    6 Pliny] *Naturalis historia* 11.139

sight, and yet the shape of the eyes is there, if the covering membrane is drawn back.' From this arose the adage.

56   **Caecior leberide**
     As blind as a sloughed skin

Τυφλότερος λεβηρίδος, As blind as a sloughed skin. This phrase belongs to the same order of ideas. It is quoted from Aristophanes. The *leberis*, as I have shown elsewhere, is that dry skin which snakes, crickets and other kinds of   5
creature slough off, whenever they renew their youth. In this there is at least the appearance of eyes, and that extremely thin membrane which protects the eyes of snakes. Some say that this, so well known in snakes and crickets, happens to fish also. Lycophron calls this skin *syphar*, in his iambic poem: 'A *syphar* he will die, fleeing the covering of the sea.' *Syphar* is used symbolical-   10
ly; it is his way of speaking of an old man, either because that age brings blindness, or because it is worn out and dried up, deprived of sap and strength. Sophron in the *Mimes*: 'What is Xysilus, what Syphar, for a man?' He gives the name Xysilus to a dry and scabby old man, from the Greek for scraping, or Syphar, as if he were now no man at all, but a dry and empty   15
skin. This too has a hint of the proverb in it. It is said however that *leberis* properly signifies the outer membrane which protects the foetus of cows, and in which there are merely vestiges of the eyes. There are three forms of the adage: 'As blind as a sloughed skin', 'As bare' or 'As empty.'

* * * * *

56 Taken from the Greek proverb-collections (Zenobius 2.95; Diogenianus 3.73; Suidas τ 1217)
 4 Aristophanes] Frag 35 Kock, cited by Zenobius and by Hesychius Γ 1003
 5 elsewhere] *Adagia* I i 26
 9 Lycophron] *Alexandra* 793. Lycophron of Chalcis, a scholar and writer of tragedies of the early third century BC, survives in the *Alexandra*, a poem of 1474 iambic lines, which is reputed the most obscure work in all Greek literature. Erasmus cites it half-a-dozen times; and as it was not printed until 1513, in the Aldine Pindar that contained also Callimachus, the quotations in *1508* must come from a manuscript source.
13 Sophron] A lost comic writer of the fifth century BC; this is frag 55 Kaibel, cited by the *Etymologicum magnum* (see I v 52n) 737.1, with the Latin version added in *1515*.
18 three forms] The first is that given by the collections already mentioned; the other two will be found in I i 26. 'As empty' (*kenôteros*) replaced in *1523* the false reading 'as young' (*neôteros*), which was given in some current texts of Zenobius.

57 Tiresia caecior
As blind as Tiresias

Τυφλότερος Τειρεσίου, As blind as Tiresias. Taken from a well-known story.
Juvenal: 'Neither a deaf man nor a Tiresias, / Is one of the gods.' He used
Tiresias for a proverbial way of saying 'blind,' as Horace says 'Irus' for   5
'poor': 'It differs much if wealth or Irus speak.'

58 Hypsea caecior
As blind as Hypsea

Horace used a similar metaphor in the *Satires*: 'Not with Lynceus' eye her
charms inspect, / While blind as Hypsea to her plain defect.' It is clear that
the proverb comes from a certain woman of ill fame named Hypsea, well   5
known for her blindness.

59 Sine sacris haereditas
Inheritance without rites

When something advantageous is thrown in a person's way unexpectedly
and at no cost, the ancients called this An inheritance without rites. Everything in fact in the way of profit which might have accrued from any source   5
without our effort they styled, as though proverbially 'an inheritance,'
particularly because what comes freely, while we are asleep, as it were,
seems to be the gift of Fortune. So Ergasilus the parasite says in Plautus, in
the *Captivi duo*: 'I have acquired an ample inheritance without rites.' And in
another place: 'At the present price it is an inheritance without rites.' For it 10
was the custom for the heir to celebrate certain rites at his own cost, either

* * * * *

57 In *Collectanea* no 653 this, with the Juvenal reference, was joined to its
opposite, which became II i 54 Lynceo perspicacior.
4 Juvenal] 13.249. Tiresias, one of the most famous seers of antiquity, was blind.
5 Horace] *Ars poetica* 114; this reading (*divesne loquatur an Irus*) seems to be an
emendation of the more colourless transmitted text 'if god or hero speak'
(*divusne loquatur an heros*). For Irus, the proverbial beggar, see *Adagia* I vi 76.

58 Taken direct from Horace (*Satires* 1.2.90–2). For Lynceus see *Adagia* II i 54;
of *Hypsaea* (as she should be spelt) nothing seems to be known.

59 Perhaps taken direct from Plautus. Otto 806
8 Plautus] *Captivi* 775; *Trinummus* 484 (Erasmus quotes an incomplete sentence,
and it is not clear what sense he found in the Latin); *Curculio* 125.

for the welfare of the dying or as offerings for the departed. Plautus again elsewhere: 'Such legacies do not often come my way.' Cicero against Verres, in the fifth speech: 'Verres seemed to himself to have come into a legacy, when he saw come into his dominions, and under his power, that man.' 15 Andrea Alciati in his *Praetermissa*, book 1, prefers to trace the origin of the adage to a practice in ancient law. The code of the Twelve Tables says: 'Private rites shall be maintained in perpetuity.' These words are interpreted by Cicero, in the second book of the *De legibus*, as meaning that anyone to whom the estate of the head of household might pass was under an obliga- 20 tion to celebrate these rites. He also quotes the interpretation of Scaevola the pontifex to the effect that an inheritance is subject to five kinds of sacrificial rites. Those who inherited by right of kinship were bound by partnership in rites which they shared. But it is normally more agreeable when some advantage befalls one unexpectedly like an inheritance without rites. These 25 and other matters are discussed most learnedly by my friend Alciati, and I willingly give my vote in favour of his interpretation, albeit slightly different from mine. Moreover I think the phrase of Plautus contains an allusion to the well-known Greek proverb 'To devour the sacrifice before it has been offered,' and also to that passage in Hesiod, 'From unhallowed vessels to 30 take aught to eat.'

60 **Inter caesa et porrecta**
Between the slaying and the offering

A particularly choice adage is to be found in Cicero, in his *Letters to Atticus*:

* * * * *

13 Cicero] *Verrines* 4.27.62
16 Alciati] Andrea Alciati of Milan (1492–1550), celebrated humanist and teacher, known for his law studies but above all for his famous *Emblemata*, first published in 1531. See Allen Ep 1250 introduction, and his correspondence with Erasmus in 1521–2 (Epp 1250, 1261, 1278, 1288). His works are cited as authoritative in *Adagia* I v 45, I vii 34, IV ix 36. The present passage was added in 1526. This reference to Alciati's *Praetermissa* reports his opinion accurately. In a later edition (Lyons 1543, p. 235B) Alciati refers to this adage and says he is aware that Erasmus, 'incomparable in every way,' deduces the adage from the stage, but that he prefers his own explanation.
17 Twelve Tables] The oldest code of Roman law, surviving in fragments; this one is preserved by Cicero *De legibus* 2.9.22, and discussed in 2.29.47–8.
29 Greek proverb] See *Adagia* II iii 87.
30 Hesiod] *Works and Days* 748–9; cf *Adagia* I vi 27. The Latin version was put into verse in 1526.

60 Taken probably direct from Cicero. Otto 293
3 Cicero] *Ad Atticum* 5.18.1

'Many other points, all other points in fact, but first and foremost that
nothing be added to my responsibilities or my tenure between slaying and   5
offering as the saying is.' He seems to mean delay and wavering hesitation,
an interval as it were between laying aside something begun, and beginning
something which has to be renewed. This is taken from the old method of
augury, when the priest carried out certain ceremonies 'between the slaying
and the offering,' as Varro explains in his *On the Latin Language* book 2: 'For   10
the *Flamen Dialis*,' he says, 'solemnly inaugurates the vintage, and when he
has ordered the grapes to be picked he makes a sacrifice to Jove of a ewe
lamb; between the slaying and the offering of entrails, precisely, the priest
picks the grapes.' That 'entrails slaughtered' among the ancients meant an
extension of time, Cicero makes clear in his *On Divination*, book 2: 'What has   15
the diviner in mind, why does the cutting up of the lung, even when the
entrails are favourable, interrupt the time and postpone the day?'

61 Pensum persolvere
To complete one's task

Pensum persolvere means to fulfil one's part, to do the duty expected of one. It
is adapted from the way women worked at the wool: each of them had a
definite weight of it distributed to her for her to work up. Plautus in the   5
Persa: 'I have finished the task I was given.' Also in the *Bacchides*: 'I will make
a nice job of my allotted task.' And Cicero, in the third book of the *De oratore*:
'Now I will go on to the rest, and recall myself to my duty and allotted task.'
Varro in his *Agriculture*: 'We have fulfilled our allotted task.' Jerome writing
to Rusticus: 'And you may complete your allotted task.' But the further the   10
metaphor is twisted to new uses, the more attractive the adage will be: if, for
instance, it is applied to speech, to study, to moral obligations or other
mental activities.

* * * * *

10 Varro] *De lingua Latina* 6.16 (See I ii 23n).
15 Cicero] *De divinatione* 1 (not 2). 39. 85

61 Perhaps derived originally from Jerome's *Letters*, where the exact phrase
   occurs. The *pensum* is basically the quantity of wool 'weighed out' for each
   woman in a Roman household for carding or spinning.
 5 Plautus] *Persa* 272, added in *1520*; *Bacchides* 1152, added in *1523*
 7 Cicero] *De oratore* 3.30.119, added in *1523*
 9 Varro] *Res rusticae* 2.2.1 (see I i 40n).
 9 Jerome] *Letters* 125.15.2

62   **Ne per somnium quidem**
      Not even in a dream

Οὐδ' ὄναρ, Not even in a dream. In Greek, this is a proverbial way of
saying 'by no means, at no time.' No one was ever so utterly deprived of
happiness that he did not occasionally, at a quiet moment, dream of happier   5
things. Lucian *On Salaried Posts*: 'Not even in a dream did he ever have his fill
of white bread.' He makes use of it also in *Gallus*, when he says that kings
cannot enjoy any pleasant thing, even in a dream: 'because of which not
even a dream of some pleasure is possible.' Again in *Electrum*: 'As for the
sweet singing, such as you tell of, we haven't heard it even in our dreams.'   10
Theocritus made a charming allusion to this in the *Boukoliskos*, when he
described Eunica, a well brought-up girl, thrusting aside a boor who tried to
kiss her; she was so far from giving him a kiss, she said, that he need not
hope for it even in a dream. The poem runs thus:

> Take yourself off, and good riddance!   15
> Do you want to kiss me, you boor?
> I never learnt to kiss the country folk,
> But city lips to press, nor shall you ever
> Touch with your filthy lips my shining mouth
> Even in a dream.   20

Cicero uses the same thing in *Letters to Atticus*: 'Not one statesman is to be
found, even in a dream.' Theocritus in *Megara, Wife of Hercules*: 'This happened to no one else, even in a dream.' Galen *On the Natural Faculties*, book
2: 'And these things should not have been unknown to Erasistratus, if even
in dreams he had ever happened to be familiar with the Peripatetics.' Even   25
men of the humblest sort may have magnificent dreams, like the Micyllus of
Lucian, who was the richest of men in his dreams, but when he woke up he
was a cobbler almost poorer than Irus. For to dream is a kind of hoping. So
Virgil in the *Eclogues* calls the vain hopes of lovers 'dreams': 'Those who

---

62 Perhaps taken direct from Lucian, but it is a very familiar phrase.
 6 Lucian] *De mercede conductis* 17; *Gallus* 25; *Electrum* 5, this last added in *1520*
11 Theocritus] 20.2–5
21 Cicero] *Ad Atticum* 1.18.6, the actual words of the quotation added in *1523*
23 Theocritus] Preserved and at first printed among the works of Theocritus, this
   is now doubtfully assigned to Moschus (4.18); cf I iii 49.
23 Galen] *De naturalibus facultatibus* 2.8 (Kuehn 2.107) added in *1528*
27 Lucian] *Gallus* 1. For Irus, see above, no 57 and I vi 76.
29 Virgil] *Eclogues* 8.108

love, do they shape their own dreams?' Horace was thinking of this in the   30
Satires, when he says:

> When he shall free you from your servile fear
> And tedious toil; when broad awake, you hear
> 'To good Ulysses, my right trusty slave,
> A fourth division of my lands I leave.'   35

So to say 'not even in a dream' is equivalent to saying 'you do not even dare
to hope.' Plutarch, in the essay he wrote 'Against the Stoics,' expresses the
adage in a slightly different way: 'One cannot even take their dreams
beyond ordinary thoughts.' St Chrysostom in his third sermon against the
Jews expresses it thus, 'not even as a dream.'   40

63   Per nebulam, per caliginem, per somnium
Through cloud, through darkness, as in a dream

Our memory or grasp of some things may be doubtful, vague or even
fading, and then we say proverbially that we register them through a mist,
we remember them as in a dream, we see them darkly. What we saw as   5
children, we recall as old men as if in a dream, as if faint images of those
things were clinging to our minds; this is the form memory takes of ordinary
dreams. When we gaze at something through an intervening mist, we see
only its confused image, like a wavering shadow; so it is with things seen in
darkness, through the obscurity, and hence the metaphor. These turns of   10
speech are frequently found among writers. Plautus in the *Pseudolus*, 'There
are things we particularly want to ask you, which we know and have heard
ourselves as if through a cloud.' Again in the *Captivi duo*: 'I go back in
memory, seeming to have heard myself as if through a cloud.' Cicero in book

* * * * *

30 Horace] *Satires* 2.5.99–101, added in *1517/8*
37 Plutarch] *Moralia* 1074A, added in *1515*
39 Chrysostom] Johannes Chrysostomus *Adversus Judaeos crationes* 1.4 (*PG*
48.848), added in *1528*. These appeared in Erasmus' translation in *Joh.
Chrysostomi lucubrationes aliquot*, Froben, March 1527; he derived the Greek text
no doubt from Hieronymus Froben's copy, now Oxford Bodleian MS misc gr
27.

63 *Collectanea* no 279, with vague references to Plautus and Jerome. Otto 1210
11 Plautus] *Pseudolus* 462–3, added with all the rest of the paragraph in *1523*;
Captivi 1023–4
14 Cicero] *De finibus* 5.15.43

5 of the *De finibus*: 'In the years of immaturity and intellectual weakness the   15
powers of our nature are discerned as through a mist.' Plato in the seventh
book of the *Laws*: 'But I must try to make what I am saying clear, with
examples brought out into the light. For they appear now like things which
are said in some kind of darkness.' In the same book we read 'through sleep'
or 'in sleep.'   20

64   **De asini prospectu**
     About the ass that poked its head in

Ὄνου παρακύψεως, About the ass that poked its head in. This old adage
used to be said of those who speak ill of someone for an absurd reason, or
take someone to court for a trifling cause. The event which gave rise to the   5
story is variously told by different authors. Some tell it as follows: a certain
potter had created various shapes of birds and displayed them in his shop.
But a donkey, followed by its driver, who was not looking, poked its head
through the shop window and knocked over the birds and the rest of the
pots and smashed them to pieces. The owner of the shop took the driver to   10
law. When asked by everybody what he was going to law about, he said:
'About the ass that poked its head in.' Others say that the birds were not
made of clay, but real birds, which the ass disturbed by thrusting its head in
as aforesaid, so that they broke their perch and upset the other pots. The rest
of the story is the same. Lucian in his *Ass* claims to have given rise to this   15
proverb; when, being an ass, he tried to turn his head sideways to see
through the window what was happening, he gave both himself and his
masters away. This was greeted by all with a mighty laugh and became a
proverb. However for Lucian the phrase is more applicable to people who
try to keep up a foolish pretence but are betrayed by their own stupidity.   20
Apuleius copies the passage of Lucian in the ninth book of the
Metamorphoses, where he writes as follows: 'When I heard the noise and
uproar of the quarrel, being an ass of a most curious disposition and endued
with the most restless indiscretion, I poked my head out slantwise through a
small window and sought to discover what the tumult might mean. But one   25

* * * * *

16 Plato] *Laws* 7.788c and 800a

64 Zenobius 5.39 provides the first section of this. Otto 187
15 Lucian] *Asinus* 45. His Lucius, like Apuleius' hero, was turned by mistake into
an ass.
21 Apuleius] See I i 15n; *Metamorphoses* 9.42 (tr H.E. Butler, adapted).

of the soldiers chanced to see me out of the corner of his eye, and espied my shadow. Whereupon he called all the others to bear witness. A great uproar arose, they rushed upstairs, laid hands on me, and dragged me downstairs as a prisoner. Then without a moment's delay they searched everything even more carefully than before. Among other things they opened the chest, 30 found the wretched gardener, dragged him out and showed him to the magistrates. Then they led him away to the public jail to be punished for this offence. As for me, they never tired of laughing and jesting about the way I had poked my head out. And from this the well-known proverb has arisen about the ass that poked its head out and the ass's shadow.' Thus far 35 Apuleius.

65 **Suo ipsius indicio periit sorex**
The shrew-mouse gave itself away

Terence in the *Eunuchus* says much the same thing: 'Today, alas, I perished by giving myself away like the shrew.' It is Parmeno speaking, when the deceit of Pythia has led him to betray himself to the old man. Donatus 5 explains that the proverb is directed against people who give themselves away by their own talk. He thinks the metaphor comes from the fact that shrews typically squeak louder than mice, or make more noise when they are gnawing at bits and pieces; and people often notice this squeak and pin them down even in the darkness of night. St Augustine uses this adage in 10 the first book of the *De ordine*, about his friend Licentius, who frightened a shrew by hitting his writing tablet and making a noise, thereby letting Augustine know that he was awake. Origen has the same allusion in his third homily on Genesis: 'But I shall seem to have been caught by the hints I gave myself.' 15

* * * * *

35 ass's shadow] see Adagia I iii 52.

65 *Collectanea* no 572, with quotations from Terence and from Jerome (*Letters* 133.11.6), of which the latter was discarded in the *Chiliades*. Otto 1676
3 Terence] *Eunuchus* 1024
10 Augustine] *De ordine* 1.3.9 (PL 32.981)
13 Origen] *Homiliae in Genesim* 5.3 (ed W.A.Baehrens GCS 29.44), added in 1536. These are known only in the Latin version of Rufinus, of which the first edition was published by Aldus in 1503, and another edited by Erasmus in that same year 1536. He made a similar addition at the end of III i 95.

66 Induitis me leonis exuvium
You are dressing me up in the lionskin

Ἐνδύετέ μοι τὴν λεοντῆν, You are dressing me up in the lionskin. Said of those who undertake a work beyond their means, and who bear themselves with more pride than their rank warrants. Some think this comes from 5 Hercules, whose accoutrement was this: he wore a lionskin, held in one hand a club and in the other a bow, and thus equipped he went down into the underworld to bring out Cerberus. Aristophanes, alluding to this in the *Frogs*, pretends that Bacchus, like Hercules equipped with lionskin and club, proposed to descend to the underworld to hear Euripides and Aeschy- 10 lus having a dispute. However, Hercules makes fun of him, on the grounds that such accoutrements are not in the least suitable to a weak effeminate character like his. Similarly, the famous Menippus of Lucian feigns to have returned from the underworld in the same array. But there is no reason why the proverb should not refer to the story told by Lucian in the *Fisherman*. In 15 Cumae there was a certain donkey who got tired of servitude, broke his leash and ran away into the woods. There he happened to find a lionskin, and put it on himself. He then behaved like a lion, frightening men and wild beasts with his noise and his tail (for the good people of Cumae know nothing of lions). So the masquerading donkey had it all his own way for 20 some time, and was taken for a fierce lion, and feared. This went on until a visitor came to Cumae who had often seen both lions and donkeys, and thus it was not difficult to discern – he recognized the donkey by its long sticking-out ears and some other indications, and after giving it a good beating led it back to the owner who claimed it. The unmasking of the 25 donkey roused a general laugh at the expense of the population of Cumae, who had been almost terrified out of their wits for so long by an imaginary lion. The people of Cumae of whom he speaks, are not, however, those in Italy but those who live in Aeolis above Lesbos. The people of both Lesbos and Cumae are famous for their stupidity, as Stephanus remarks. 30

* * * * *

66 *Collectanea* no 792, referred only to the passage from Plato's *Cratylus* (in Latin), but probably derived the Greek form of the adage from Diogenianus 4.54 (it is also in Zenobius 3.75 and Suidas E 1190).
8 Aristophanes] *Frogs* 46–7
13 Lucian] *Nekyomanteia* 1; *Piscator* 32. The story of the ass at Cumae recurs in *Adagia* I vii 12 Asinus apud Cumanos.
30 Stephanus] Steph. Byzantius p 392 Meineke (see I ii 43n); this was added here in *1528*, as it was at the same time to I v 61 Cumani sero sapiunt.

The Socrates of Plato uses this adage in the *Cratylus*, declaring that he
need not be frightened at the importance of the discussion embarked upon,
once he had put on the lionskin. Lucian in *Pseudologista*: 'There is no need of
anyone to strip away your lion's skin that you may be revealed as a donkey,
unless perhaps someone has just come to us from the Hyperboreans, or has   35
spent so much time in Cumae as not to know, as soon as he sees you, that
you are the most unbridled of all asses, without waiting to hear you bray.'
Eusebius of Caesarea against Hierocles: 'Indeed he will depart from us as a
philosopher, but he is an ass covered with a lionskin.' Lucian altered the
proverb a little in *Philopseudes*, where he says, 'I had failed, in all these years,   40
to notice that his lion's skin covered a silly ape.'

67 Midas auriculas asini
Midas has ass's ears

Μίδας ὄνου ὦτα, Midas has ass's ears. Recorded by Diogenianus. It is taken
from the well-known story about Midas, king of Phrygia; when he had
stupidly judged Pan's singing to be superior to Apollo's, the god fixed a pair   5
of ass's ears to his head. For a long time he managed to hide them under a
turban, but his barber saw them and told the tale abroad. The adage will be
properly applied to stupid people, with dense ears and doltish wits; or to
tyrants, who have ears as long as asses' and hear from a long way off, since
they have eavesdroppers sent out to bring back news of what they hear.   10
Plutarch in his essay 'On Being a Busybody' has special Greek words for
'listeners' and 'tale-bearers.' Lucian, in his essay on *Not Believing Slanderers*,
draws a portrait of Calumny and gives her Midas's ears, because of her
eagerness to eavesdrop and catch what other people are doing: 'On the right
sits a certain man with very large ears, almost like those of Midas.'   15
    Aristophanes in the *Plutus*: 'Midas indeed, if you put on the ears of an

* * * * *

31 Plato] *Cratylus* 411a
33 Lucian] *Pseudologista* 3, much altered in *1523*
38 Eusebius] See I ii 4n. This is *Adversus Hieroclem* 5 (PG 22.804C); the Latin version
   was added in *1515*.
39 Lucian] *Philopseudes* 5

67 *Collectanea* no 645 gave the Greek from Diogenianus 6.73, and cited Persius
   only. Otto 1111
11 Plutarch] *Moralia* 522F, added in *1515*; the words, which are given in Greek, are
   already recorded in I ii 2.
12 Lucian] *Calumniae non temere credendum* 5
16 Aristophanes] *Plutus* 287, with the Scholia

ass.' The commentator on this passage notes the proverb about asses' ears and gives several reasons for the fabrication. He says that according to some authorities Midas was turned into an ass for having at one time scorned and disparaged the divinity of Bacchus. Others tell a story about his having one 20 day passed the asses of this god and insulted them, so Bacchus in anger gave him asses' ears. Some say that he had ears that were overlong by nature and stuck out like asses' ears, and hence this jesting tale arose. Most of them, however, prefer to take the meaning of this allegory to be that Midas, being a despot, used to send out spies and eavesdroppers, whom he used as ears, to 25 let him know whatever was being said or done all over the country. Hence, as there was general astonishment at the way in which he had news even of things which were done in secret and far away, these gave rise to the proverb, that Midas was said to have asses' ears. Perhaps it was because no other animal has more acute hearing than the donkey, except the mouse; or 30 because it has the longest ears of any. Persius: 'Who has not the ears of an ass?' Some say that the poet first wrote: 'King Midas has the ears of an ass,' and changed it into a question, 'Who has not' for fear of the emperor.

68   **Hinc illae lachrymae**
     Hence those tears

In the *Andria* of Terence there is a phrase which seems a proverbial allusion borrowed by Horace, 'hence those tears.' Cicero made use of it in his speech in defence of Marcus Caelius: 'Hence those tears, indeed, and this is the 5 cause of all those offences and criminal charges.' It may be said, when the reason for something has remained long concealed and at last the truth is discovered. For instance, suppose someone said that the barbarians despise Greek learning for fear, of course, they themselves should appear unedu- cated; he could usefully add 'hence those tears' that is, because it makes 10 them uncomfortable. This sort of allusion often appears in good authors; and it takes on a proverbial function even if there is no proverbial metaphor

* * * * *

25 spies] The word used is 'Corycaeans,' explained in *Adagia* I ii 44.
31 Persius] *Satires* 1.121; the anecdote is provided by the Scholia on the passage, and by the life of Persius ascribed to Valerius Probus.

68 Taken directly from Terence. Otto 904; Tilley T 82 From thence came these tears.
 3 Terence] *Andria* 126
 4 Horace] *Epistles* 1.19.41
 4 Cicero] *Pro M. Caelio* 25.61, added in *1520*

present. Of this kind is the often-repeated Homeric phrase in Cicero's *Letters to Atticus*: 'I fear the Trojans.'

69 Haec Helena
This is the Helen

Something of the same kind is said by Lucian in the *Eunuch*: 'This, Pamphilus, was that very Helen, αὔτη Ἑλένη, for whom the champions fought so
fiercely.' He speaks of two Peripatetic philosophers, contending dis-   5
gracefully in court about fees and filthy lucre. The allusion is to the fight in
single combat between Menelaus and Paris, which Homer describes in the
Iliad, book 3.

70 Ebur atramento candefacere
To whiten ivory with ink

To whiten ivory with ink is to apply external refinement and decoration to
something naturally beautiful, so as to obscure rather than enhance its
native charm. The bawd in Plautus says to the naturally pretty girl who is   5
asking for white pigment to smear on her cheeks: 'You might as well ask for
ink to whiten ivory.' Every attempt to add allurement to things which are
beautiful by nature results in disfiguring them, not beautifying. It would be
the same if one were to use the face-paint of rhetoric to prettify truth, the
most beautiful of all things. White-lead used to be used to produce a white   10
complexion, and similarly rouge to redden the cheeks. On the same lines
Plautus says in the *Mostellaria*, 'It's a lovely piece of work and you want to
furbish it up with a new look.'

* * * * *

13 Homeric phrase] *Iliad* 6.442; it was with Cicero a favourite way of referring to
public opinion, and he cites it *Ad Atticum* 2.5.1 and in five other letters, spread
over fifteen years.

69 Taken from Lucian *Eunuchus* 3. The Homeric allusion is to *Iliad* 3.340–82. This is
not really proverbial.

70 Rewritten from *Collectanea* no 220, which quoted the first Plautus line with no
author's name
5 Plautus] *Mostellaria* 259 and 262, the latter added in *1523*

71 **Sincerum vas incrustare**
To daub a sound vessel

To this class belongs the metaphor in Horace which we read in the first book
of the *Satires*, poem 3: 'But we distort their virtues to a crime, / And joy
th'untainted vessel to begrime.' That is, we corrupt and mask things which   5
are right in themselves, by applying to them unsuitable names. It would
however be neatly matched with the previous saying: we apply a covering to
things which are in themselves seemly, and this masks their native comeli-
ness instead of increasing it.

72 **Pulchrorum etiam autumnus pulcher est**
Even the autumn of beauty is beautiful

Τῶν καλῶν καὶ ὀπώρη καλή, Even the autumn of beauty is beautiful. The
proverbial metaphor comes from an observation of Archelaus, made by him,
according to Plutarch, about Euripides, who was showering kisses at a   5
banquet on Agathon, already a young man and grown up. It is not far from
that Homeric phrase I shall comment on elsewhere, 'to judge by the husk.'
In the spring months everything is tender and shining, since all is in flower
or leaf. But in the autumn when all things have turned to straw and bare
branches, they seem harsh and wild. This can be applied to naturally   10
excellent things which do not seem wearisome even when they grow old.
Nothing, indeed, is so ugly that it has not a time of attractiveness. This can
be suitably said also of those who carry their age well.

73 **Magnorum fluminum navigabiles fontes**
Great rivers have navigable springs

There seems to be a similar metaphor in the saying quoted by Quintilian in

* * * * *

71 Wrongly associated by Otto under his number 1849 with the precept quoted
from Horace in *Adagia* I i 2 (line 246) that what is put into a sour vessel will itself
soon turn sour. Here a vessel which is sound is coated with a slip to conceal
non-existent flaws. The source is Horace *Satires* 1.3.55–6 (tr Sir Philip Francis,
who misunderstood it in a different way).

72 Given very briefly, and with no Greek, in *Collectanea* no 548; probably taken
direct from Plutarch
5 Plutarch] *Moralia* 177B Agathon was a boy celebrated for his good looks.
7 elsewhere] *Adagia* I x 41; IV ii 3

73 Taken from Quintilian *Institutio oratoria* 8.3.76. Otto 681

the *Institutions*, book 8: 'Great rivers have navigable springs.' He says this
was often repeated everywhere when he was young. Its meaning is that   5
things belonging to the great, however tiny, have more power than all the
possessions of the small. But Quintilian gives a bad mark to maxims of this
kind, on the ground that they may be clearly seen to be false.

74 **Generosioris arboris statim planta cum fructu est**
    The slip of a noble tree bears fruit at once

He adds this similar saying in the same place. It seems to mean that excellent
and well-endowed minds mature early and come to fruition. Quintilian
criticizes this kind of saying. It seemed right to me, however, to include   5
these in the list of adages, because he testifies to their having been in general
use, and the shameless exaggeration (as has been said earlier) does not
exclude them from this class.

75 **Cornicum oculos configere**
    To pierce crows' eyes

Cicero in his speech in defence of Murena writes thus: 'In the second place,
if any awe attached to that profession in the time of our ancestors, it fell into
utter contempt and was destroyed by the publication of your mysteries. In   5
former times very few knew whether or not an action at law could be
brought; for the calendar was not publicly known. Those who gave legal
decisions had great power; they were asked to indicate the day on which a
suit could be brought, as if they were Chaldean astronomers. A clerk by

* * * * *

74 Likewise from Quintilian: 8.3.77. Otto 153

75 This was treated at some length in *Collectanea* no 16, first with a vague reference
    to Cicero ('although the passage is not to hand just at the moment') followed by
    the passage from Jerome *Adversus Rufinum*. Erasmus then admits that he has
    not yet been able to find any authority for the precise meaning of the adage,
    and conjectures that it may be used of those who wish to reject what has been
    approved since Antiquity, because crows are famous for their longevity; some
    of the wording is incorporated here verbatim. The sense seems to be something
    like our 'paying a man out in his own coin,' 'giving a man a taste of his own
    medicine,' because crows were themselves keen-sighted, and pecked out the
    eyes of other birds. In Ep 1479 of 31 August 1524 Erasmus speaks of the trouble
    this caused him, and says he consulted two or three friends and still got no
    satisfactory solution. Otto 435–6; Tilley c 856 One crow never pecks out
    another's eyes, seems based on a different interpretation.
    3 Cicero] *Pro L. Murena* 11.25; *Pro L. Flacco* 20.46

name Gnaeus Flavius was found who pierced the crows' eyes and published   10
the calendar, enabling the people to learn up which were court days, and
plucked their wisdom from the learned counsel themselves. And so these
men, enraged because they were afraid that lawsuits could be conducted
without their assistance, once the proper days were published and made a
matter of general knowledge, invented certain legal formulae that they   15
might still have a part in every transaction.' Again in the speech for the
defence of Lucius Flaccus: 'Here, by Hercules, is a case of the proverbial
crow's eye. For he swindled Hermippus here, a learned man, his own
fellow-citizen, who should have been thoroughly acquainted with him.'

Whether the proverb comes from some fable, or event, or is taken from   20
a metaphor, is not quite clear. Wherever it came from, the meaning of 'to
pierce crows' eyes' seems to be: to put the learning of older generations in
the shade with some new discovery, and make it appear that earlier people
knew nothing, have seen nothing. It is uttered in irony. Jerome, in his
second apologetic against Rufinus, used it in the same way: 'Now, indeed,   25
owing to the diversity of the regions, different copies are in circulation, and
the genuine old translation has been corrupted and spoilt; and so you may
think it within our province either to judge between several as to which is
authentic, or to found a new work on the old one, and when the Jews laugh
at us, as they say, to pierce their crows-eyes.' Jerome means by this to   30
suggest that his examination of texts might seem to impute ignorance to the
Jews, to whom at that time one had to go to get the truth of the Old
Testament. Macrobius uses it in much the same way in the seventh book of
his *Saturnalia*: 'And since we confess ourselves unable to cope with this
labyrinth of words, come, Vettius, let us urge Eustathius to maintain the   35
contrary opinion and be good enough to give us all the arguments for a
mixed diet. In this way the language of violence will be the victim of its own
weapons and just like one crow pecking at another's eyes, one Greek will
steal the applause from another.' Thus far Macrobius. It would not be
inappropriate to suggest to the reader that he should consider very carefully 40
whether crows have given rise to this proverb through their long life and
peaceful cohabitation. Indeed the crow was the symbol of concord in Antiquity; and its length of life is celebrated in a Greek proverb. So that anyone

* * * * *

24 Jerome] *Adversus Rufinum* 2.27 (PL 23.450D). In the *Collectanea*, 'which is
   authentic' was 'what was translated' (*versum* for *verum*).
33 Macrobius] *Saturnalia* 7.5.2 (see I i 12n).
43 Greek proverb] *Adagia* I vi 64

who tried to bring into contempt, cancel or remove the things which antiquity approved with one accord, may be said to wish to 'pierce the crows'   45
eyes.' This is not so absurd, if one takes 'piercing the eyes' to mean removing the sight from those who have it at the clearest and best, so letting the
darkness flood in; or to mean touching the very thing with the point, as they
say, so skilfully that not only the target or the bird is pierced by the dart, but
its very eyes.   50

76 Gladiatorio animo
With a gladiator's spirit

The phrase we read in the *Phormio* of Terence has the look of a proverb:
'Why, they are on their way to me in a gladiatorial spirit.' This means with
the intention of wreaking harm on another even if it were to one's own peril, 5
steadfastly resolved and ready to destroy or be destroyed. For a gladiator, all
set for the fight, has the gamble of battle before him, either to kill if he should
gain the upper hand, or to fall dying if he yields. Aristotle calls this kind of
bravery, carrying with it scorn for one's own safety, 'Celtic.'

77 Frusto panis
For a crust of bread

'For a crust of bread' is still used in our own day by the common people to
mean something quite insignificant and worthless. Marcus Cato, charging
Marcus Coelius in a speech with cowardice, not only in what he said but in   5
what he did not say, observes that 'he can be bribed with a crust of bread
either to keep silence or to talk.' This is quoted by Aulus Gellius in his *Attic
Nights.* The hyperbole seems to be taken either from dogs which we tempt
with a piece of bread or from beggars.

     * * * * *

48 as they say] *Adagia* II iv 93

76 Taken no doubt from Terence. The idea recurs in III viii 73 and IV vii 26.
  3 Terence] *Phormio* 964
  8 Aristotle] *Ethica Nicomachea* 3.7 (1115b28)

77 From Gellius 1.15.10, citing frag 112 of the elder Cato (234–149 BC). Otto 1333;
  Suringar 81. Tilley H 820 Hunger makes a man leap at a crust overlaps this.

78 **Quem mater amictum dedit observare**
    To keep to the clothes one's mother gave one

To keep to the clothes one's mother gave one. This means to live like a child,
following the dictates of others; we read it in Quintilian, book 5: 'For what
could be more pitiful than that law; it is like following up letters traced   5
beforehand for infants, and (as the Greeks say) carefully keeping to the dress
prescribed by mother?' From these words of Quintilian it is clear that this
was a proverb in Greek, and it is adopted, and indicated as a proverb, by
Lucian in *Nigrinus*: 'And whence comes this peacock? Perhaps it is his
mother's clothing.' These jeers are addressed to one who arrives in a gaudy   10
garment. Plutarch in his essay 'On the Fortune of Alexander': 'Preserving
like a small child the dress which the custom of his country, like a nurse, had
prescribed for him.' The very phrase 'to live according to prescription' seems
to be a proverbial metaphor (nothing could be more commonplace): it is
apparently taken from children, who (as Plato says) have writing-copies   15
given them by their teacher as a model, so that they can imitate them and
learn to form the letters. This is the kind of imitation made fun of by Horace,
imposed and servile: 'O servile herd of mimics, all your fuss / Has roused so
oft my laughter and my jest.' And Quintilian thinks nothing less conducive
to good oratory than the practice of following the rules of the art in such a   20
way that one dares not diverge from them by a finger's breadth, when the
nature of the case calls for it.

79 **Quid distent aera lupinis**
    What a difference between bronze coins and lupins!

Horace's phrase in the *Epistles* has the appearance of a proverb: 'Yet he
knows well enough / How far bronze coins are from lupins.' That is, he

* * * * *

78 As this does not start with a Greek equivalent, Quintilian is no doubt the
   source. Otto 86; Suringar 184
4 Quintilian] 5.14.31
9 Lucian] *Nigrinus* 13
11 Plutarch] *Moralia* 330B, added in *1515*
15 Plato] *Protagoras* 326d
17 Horace] *Epistles* 1.19.19–20, perhaps quoted from memory, as 'laughter' (*risum*)
   should be 'indignation' or 'spleen' (*bilem*).
19 Quintilian] Identified by Suringar as a reminiscence of 4.2.85

79 *Collectanea* no 427 gave the line from Horace, with no author's name. Otto 978
3 Horace] *Epistles* 1.7.23. The pods or seeds of lupin (which was grown as a
   fodder crop) were used conventionally for money on the Roman comic stage.

knows the difference between what is cheap and what is precious. Horace is   5
speaking about people who do not confer benefits on anybody and everybody, as it were throwing them away, but place them so as to correspond to
the merit and dignity of the recipient, and the value of the gift which is
given. Juvenal too mentions, as a proverb, the worthlessness of the lupin:
'I'd rather keep my pea-pods to myself / Than have the praise of the whole   10
countryside.' Lucian in *On Salaried Posts* mentions it, when he asks if there
were such a famine of lupins and spring-water, that he should give himself
up to such slavery.

80   **Me mortuo terra misceatur incendio**
     When I am dead the earth can burn up

There is a Greek iambic line of a proverbial kind in Suetonius Tranquillus'
life of Nero: 'When I am dead, the earth may burn with fire.' When this was
quoted by someone as a common saying, Nero replied 'Even while I live,'   5
alluding to the burning of the city, which he brought about soon after. This
proverb is mentioned by Cicero in the third book of the *De finibus*: 'And as
we feel it wicked and inhuman for men to declare (the saying is usually
expressed in a familiar Greek line) that they care not if, when they themselves are dead, the universal conflagration ensues.' Similarly, Seneca in the   10
De clementia, book 2, when he says that 'many powerful but detestable
sayings touch human life, and become popular, such as that famous "Let
them hate, so long as they fear." There is a Greek line similar to this, which
calls for fire on the earth as soon as the speaker is dead.' This same saying
still exists among mortals to this day: 'When I die,' they say, 'the whole   15
world dies.' They mean that it does not matter to them what happens to
future generations, whether it be good or bad, when they themselves,
removed from life, will feel nothing at all.

* * * * *

9 Juvenal] 14.153–4; used again in II ix 62
11 Lucian] *De mercede conductis* 24

80 Suetonius seems to be the source. Suringar 116
  3 Suetonius] See I i 78n; *Nero* 38. The line comes from an unidentified Greek
    tragedy (frag adesp 513 Nauck).
  7 Cicero] *De finibus* 3.19.64, added in *1515*
  10 Seneca] *De clementia* 2.2.2; this is used again in II ix 62.

81 **Mare coelo miscere**
To mingle sea and sky

To mingle sea and sky, is a proverbial hyperbole, meaning to throw everything into confusion, to leave nothing undone. Livy: 'Why do they mingle
earth and heaven?' Again in another place, 'Finally what are they doing,   5
why do they mingle heaven and earth?' Juvenal: 'You may confound sea and
sky with your bellowing, / I am a man after all.' Lucian in the dialogue
between Prometheus and Mercury: 'Was it necessary on account of this to
mix earth and sky, as the saying goes?' Virgil in book 5, speaking of Juno
trying everything: 'All the seas and sky / She mingled.' The same author, a   10
little differently in book 12:

> Not though in deluge it confound the earth,
> And plunge it in the waves, shatter the sky,
> And cast it down to Hell.

Aristophanes in the *Lysistrata* said with a similar metaphor, 'Zeus the   15
Lord-Thunderer shall turn high to low.' Plutarch in the life of Romulus
makes use of it to equate people who 'mix earth and heaven' with those who
turn gods into men and men into gods, and tell very human stories about
divinities: 'Total denial of the divinity of virtue is impious and ignoble, and
to mix earth and heaven is utter stupidity.'   20

82 **Miscebis sacra profanis**
You will mix sacred and profane

In a similar way Horace says: 'You will mix the sacred with the profane'
meaning 'there is nothing you will not do.' Also 'confounding right and

* * * * *

81 *Collectanea* no 458; the use of *confundere* there as the verb suggests that Juvenal
was the original source, and with that were associated *suque* (sic) *deque*, which
became no 83 below, and no 85. For the *Chiliades* Erasmus in effect began again.
Otto 280

4 Livy] This looks like 4.2.6 quoted from memory, and then repeated in its correct
form in 1520.

6 Juvenal] 6.283–4

7 Lucian] *Prometheus* 9

9 Virgil] *Aeneid* 5.790–1; 12.204–5

15 Aristophanes] *Lysistrata* 772–3

16 Plutarch] *Romulus* 28.6, added in 1533

82 The source here is Horace *Epistles* 1.16.54.

4 Also] Perhaps a reminiscence of Ovid *Metamorphoses* 6.585–6

wrong.' Among the ancients a great difference was made between what   5
belonged to man and what to the gods, so that Homer even distinguishes
the names used customarily by the gods from any human words. And
Pythagoras ordered abstinence from some things because they were consecrated to the divine powers; hence those who have no scruples, who dare
anything, mix sacred with profane.   10

83   **Susque deque**
      Neither here nor there

In Plautus and other authors a proverbial phrase is found 'To me it's neither
here nor there, I reckon it's neither here nor there,' meaning 'I have no
concern with it, I am entirely indifferent.' Plautus in the *Amphitryo*: 'He   5
accuses me of things that were never done and which I never thought of
doing, and he thinks I shall take it as neither here nor there.' Aulus Gellius in
book 16 of the *Nights* says that to take something as neither here nor there is
equivalent to 'being composed in mind and indifferent to what happens,
and sometimes to ignoring and despising it,' on the lines of 'the Greek verb   10
adiaphorein, to be indifferent.' He quotes Laberius in his *Compitalia*: 'Now
you are unconcerned; now you reckon it neither here nor there.' Marcus
Varro too in his *Sisenna*: 'Even if the beginnings of all these were not the
same, it would be neither here nor there.' Finally he cites these lines out of
Lucilius: 'All this is but a game, which neither here nor there is – / Neither   15
here nor there, but all is a game and jesting.' This is imitated from the familar
Greek phrase Ἄνω καὶ κάτω, Up and down, by which we convey that there
is no order and no distinguishing feature between things.

      * * * * *
      6 Homer] *Iliad* 1.403–4
      8 Pythagoras] Cf *Adagia* I i 2 (lines 423, 489).

      83 The Latin phrase means literally 'Upwards downwards,' two adverbs. 'Neither
         here nor there' renders adequately the sense of indifference ('all's one for
         that'), but does not convey the slightly archaic flavour that the Romans seem to
         have felt in the Latin. *Collectanea* no 401 combined it with our I iii 21, and no 458
         with I iii 81 and 85. Otto 1723
      5 Plautus] *Amphitryo* 885–6, added in *1528*
      7 Gellius] *Noctes Atticae* 16.9.3 (added in *1515*), citing three poets of the Roman
         republic
      11 Laberius] Writer of mimes, first century BC; 29 (*Comicorum Romanorum
         fragmenta*, ed O. Ribbeck, Leipzig 1898, 344)
      13 Varro] *Saturarum Menippearum reliquiae*, ed A. Riese (Leipzig 1865) 256.
      15 Lucilius] I ii 35n; 110–1 Marx. Repeated in IV iv 39. The jingle parodies a certain
         type of repetition found in Homer.
      16 This is imitated] With this sentence we are back in the text of *1508*.

84 **Ultro citroque**
To and fro

To and fro is used as a proverbial phrase, and is equivalent to saying 'now on this side, now on that,' or 'on both sides.' The metaphor is more attractive if applied to disputes, altercation, discussion or quarrels. Cicero uses it like 5 this in the *De republica*: 'We spent the whole of that day in much talk to and fro.' Again in the *De officiis*: 'By kind services given and received, to and fro.' Seneca in the *De beneficiis*, book 5: 'Kindness and gratitude ought to pass to and fro.' Using the same phrase we say 'The question was tossed to and fro,' 'Damage was inflicted and received to and fro,' 'There was a competition in 10 insults to and fro.'

85 **Sursum ac deorsum**
Up and down

This is very like the previous phrase, and comes from Terence's *Eunuchus*: 'I will give you peace for all these six months, Parmeno, so that you don't run up and down,' that is, here and there, or at any rate beteeen Thais and your 5 master and your master and Thais, after the manner of lovers' servants. A little more style is given to it by widening the meaning, and speaking for instance of lawyers turning rapidly from volume to volume, from statute to statute, from commentator to commentator, switching from time to time and ranging up and down. This metaphor seems to be borrowed from the 10 Sisyphus of legend, rolling his stone in the underworld. The Greek phrase for 'up and down,' ἄνω καὶ κάτω, which I have just mentioned, is so close

* * * * *

84 This perhaps owes its original selection to Donatus on Terence *Eunuchus* 1058, where it is described as proverbial. Otto 1814
3 'now on this side, now on that' or 'on both sides'] The wording is of *1523*; in *1508* it was 'hither and thither.'
5 Cicero] *De republica* 6.9.9 (= *Somnium Scipionis* 1.1); *De officiis* 1.17.56, added in *1523*
8 Seneca] *De beneficiis* 5.11, added in *1528*

85 Combined in *Collectanea* no 458 with our no 81, above. Otto 1716
3 Terence] *Eunuchus* 277–8
11 Sisyphus] See *Adagia* II iv 40.
12 just mentioned] In *1508*, Erasmus had the Greek phrase *ano kai kato*, 'up and down' (which had been in *Coll.* no 458) in the heading of this paragraph. In *1515* he cut it out and replaced it with this cross-reference, because it had come shortly before in no 83.

that it seems the same. Demosthenes in the first *Philippic*: 'Even though news has come that Philip is somewhere else, you run up and down just the same.' Aristophanes in the *Acharnians*: 'They chatter in the market-place and up and down they run, / Fleeing the ruddled rope.' Euripides in the *Bacchae*: 'Confusing all things together, up and down.' Plato in the *Phaedrus*: 'One ought to turn all the arguments over, up and down, and consider them.' Again in the *Theaetetus*: 'It might be, as the proverb says, that all is up and down.' He also used it in the *Parmenides*. Aristides the rhetorician uses the same phrase in several places, notably in *Cimon*: 'Really I cannot see how everything could be more completely jumbled up and down.' Menander, quoted by Plutarch: 'Nor would they fuss up and down and say O me!' For 'up and down' Euripides used 'back and forth': 'The gods are tumbling these things back and forth.' The line has been corrupted by copyists, and will run better if we omit the definite article. In Athenaeus, book 6: 'But each of them shifts these things up and down.' He is speaking of the poets, who make no new discoveries themselves but mix up the inventions of others and make them their own by a fresh treatment.

And so the proverb can be applied either to the man who tries everything or to the one who confuses everything, or to the acuteness of one who looks at a subject from all sides. This is very like a phrase in Terence, in the *Hecyra*: 'Running *rursum prorsum*, back and forth,' for hither and thither. For *rursum* properly means 'backwards' and *prorsum* 'forwards.' That this form is proverbial was also remarked by Donatus. Of the same sort are those others, *sursum deorsum, intro foras, hac illac*, and two Greek examples ἄνω καὶ κάτω, πρόσσω καὶ ὀπίσσω. The further the adage is removed from the physical world, the pleasanter it will be. Of this kind is Julianus' saying to

* * * * *

13 Demosthenes] *First Philippic* 41
15 Aristophanes] *Acharnians* 21–2; the Latin verse version (which is not that used for the second line of the quotation in Adagia I ii 67) was added in *1528*.
16 Euripides] *Bacchae* 349
17 Plato] *Phaedrus* 272b; *Theaetetus* 153d; added in *1520*; *Parmenides* 129c, added in *1533*
20 Aristides] See I i 13n; *De quattuor* p 204 Dindorf.
22 Menander] *Citharista* frag 1, cited by Plutarch *Moralia* 466b; added in *1515*
24 Euripides] *Hecuba* 958; the emendation (which cannot be far from the truth and was not difficult) was added in *1533*.
26 Athenaeus] 6.225c, citing Xenarchus the New Comedy writer, frag 7 Kock, added in *1528*
32 Terence] *Hecyra* 315, added, with the mention of Donatus' commentary, in *1517/8*. The explanatory phrase, and the other words of similar meaning, come from Donatus, but were not added till *1528*.

Galen, in the book Galen wrote to confute him: 'Nor could they persuade
either us or themselves truly that they know what nature is, about which   40
they chatter up and down, declaiming on all sides.' So anyone who thinks
out for himself the various aspects of a thing can be said to have thought it
out up and down.

86   **Omnium horarum homo**
     A man for all hours

The man who suits himself to seriousness and jesting alike, and whose
company is always delightful – that is the man the ancients called 'a man for
all hours.' Quintilian tells us that Asinius Pollio was called so. In Suetonius,   5
Tiberius used to call two of his boon companions the merriest of men, and
friends for all hours, even in his imperial orders. A friend of this kind is
depicted, with vividness and grace, by Ennius, in the person of Geminus
Servilius. Although the poem is preserved in the *Attic Nights* of Aulus
Gellius, book 12 chapter 4, I have pleasure in transcribing it here: 10

> When he had spoken thus, he called the man
> Who shared with him his table and his talk,
> And all he had; with whom at close of day,
> Wearied with counsel and affairs of state,
> He might with jesting tell things great and small   15
> And pour out all he thought and know it safe;
> A mind to which he turned with full delight
> In public and in private, never swayed
> By others' views to doing wrong, but light
> Of heart, and without malice; learned and loyal;   20

* * * * *

39 Galen] See I iii 6n. *Adversus Julianum* 5.1 (Kuehn 18A, 264), added in *1528*; the
   first edition of this work had been published by Aldus in 1525.

86 *Collectanea* no 760, citing Quintilian as the source. Otto 830
  5 Quintilian] 6.3.110; Pollio was a prominent figure in the political and literary
    world of the first century BC.
  5 Suetonius] See I i 78n; *Tiberius* 42.
  8 Ennius] See I ii 45n; *Annals* 234–50, cited by Aulus Gellius 12.4.4. The version
    corrects some corruptions in Erasmus' Latin text. It is easy to suppose that
    when he wrote out this long passage for the first edition, *1508*, he was thinking
    of Thomas More, in whose company he had been staying in London not long
    before, and to whom he applies our adage directly in the preface to the *Moria*
    (Ep 222), written a few years later.The rendering 'A man for all seasons'
    appears in Robert Whittinton's *Vulgaria*, which was first published in 1520.

A man of pleasant ways and power of speech,
Happy, contented with his own, and shrewd,
Speaking a word in season, ready with help,
Sparing with talk, retentive; prizing high
The value of the buried years of old,   25
Keeping old ways but not despising new,
Wise in the ancient laws of gods and men,
Able to speak but also hold his peace.

Such a one among philosophers is said to have been Aristippus, who did not
refuse to obey the command of Dionysius and dance with the rest in the   30
purple worn by women, though Plato objected, adding that even in the
Bacchanalia one should behave with modesty. Hence Horace says: 'Every
colour became Aristippus.' Those on the other hand who have their own
code of behaviour and do not find it easy to live with anyone else, are said to
be 'men of few men,' as Terence says. In Horace: 'He lacks, we say, the   35
common feelings of a man.'

87 Pecuniae obediunt omnia
Everything bows to money

It seems as if this was as popular a saying among all peoples as it is now in
general use: Everything bows to money. It is mentioned among Hebrew
proverbs in Ecclesiastes, chapter 10, and is well known in the same form in   5
Greek and Latin alike. Euripides in the *Phoenissae*: 'Nothing is dearer to
mortals than money, / Among men it has the greatest power.' Again Aristophanes in the *Plutus*: 'Nowhere will you find anything sound, / But all
alike bow to the love of gain.' Demosthenes alludes to this in the *First
Olynthiac*: 'In a word, money is needed, and without this nothing can be   10

* * * * *

29 Aristippus] The Cyrenaic philosopher (fifth/fourth century BC). This anecdote
   is taken from Diogenes Laertius 2.78, and was added in 1526.
32 Horace] *Epistles* 1.17.23, added in 1526
35 Terence] *Eunuchus* 409. This is the text of 1508 again.
35 Horace] *Satires* 1.3.66

87 Suringar 168; Tilley M 1084 Money will do anything, T 163 All things are
   obedient to money.
5 Ecclesiastes] 10:19, the precise reference added in 1515
6 Euripides] *Phoenissae* 439–40
7 Aristophanes] *Plutus* 362–3
9 Demosthenes] *First Olynthiac* 20

done that needs to be done.' Aristophanes again in the *Plutus* explains in humorous vein how everything which is done among mortals, good or bad, is done on account of money, and even the worship of the gods themselves in performed for no other reason. Among many other remarks he quotes this all-embracing thought: 15

> If aught be fine, magnificent or fair,
> It comes to men from thee alone; to wealth
> All things together are obedient.

Horace calls money a queen: 'Queen Money gives us all; well-dowered wife, / Loyalty, friends, beauty, and lineage.' But no one more clearly describes   20 the tyranny of money than Euripides when he makes Bellerophon speak in this way. Seneca quotes a few lines in his volume of *Letters*, no 115, for the play itself is lost; as these lines are exceptionally amusing and charming, I will transcribe them with pleasure (but emended in some places, since in Sencea these are corrupt):   25

> Call me the worst of men, but call me rich.
> None asks if a man's good, but is he rich?
> Not whence or why they ask, but what have you got?
> A man's prestige hung everywhere on pelf.
> What (do you ask) is shameful to have? Naught.   30
> We ask if he is rich, not if he's good.
> I wish to live rich, but if poor, to die.
> It's a good death, to die while making profits.
> Money, that blessing to the race of men,
> Cannot be matched by mother's love, or lisp   35
> Of children, or the honour due one's sire.
>   * * * * *

11 Aristophanes] *Plutus* 144–6
19 Horace] *Epistles* 1.6.36–7
21 Euripides] Frag 324 Nauck, cited in Latin by Seneca *Letters* 115.14–5 (Erasmus gave the reference originally as 'in the twenty-first book of his *Letters*'). All this was added in *1515*, except the sixth line of the quotation, which did not appear till *1528*. After *1517/8* but before *1520*, he recognized part of the Greek original, as he tells us, in Athenaeus 4.159b; and so he appended it, followed by a sentence recording that with the aid of this Greek he had restored *Veneris* for *venerit* in the last line but one of the Latin. In *1528* he struck out this sentence, and added in its place a new Latin version of the Greek lines, without cancelling Seneca's version which he had incorporated in *1515*. Then he launched into the reflections which fill the remainder of the paragraph from *1528* onwards.

And if the sweetness of the lover's glance
Be half so charming, Love will rightly stir
The hearts of gods and men to adoration.

'When these last lines in the play were spoken,' he writes, 'the whole   40
populace rose up as one man to throw out the actor and the poem, until
Euripides himself jumped up in the audience and begged them to wait and
see what a bad end was reserved for the worshipper of gold. Bellerophon
paid the same penalty in that play as each man does in his own.'

But from these lines quoted in Latin by Seneca, I found some later Greek   45
ones in the *Doctors at Dinner* of Athenaeus, book 4, with no author's name,
and I will add them here:

O gain of gold, most honoured among men,
So that no mother, father, children bring
Such pleasure to the house as you confer   50
On those who hold you in their home; if Love
Has eyes that shine so bright, it is no wonder
If loves be numberless.

It comes into one's mind to wonder at the perversity and unreasonableness
of the human mind. A vile opinion spoken by a vile character in a fictitious   55
play, recited by an actor on the stage – they can't bear this, and they riot to
have him thrown out; but every man of them makes light of it in his own
house. How many of them do not declare in their wishes, in their life, just
what that actor was declaiming? Are they shocked at words in the theatre,
and not at the thing itself in everyone's life? What is there more infamous,   60
more generally detested than that word 'lie,' and what more common than
the thing itself in the conduct of men? What is there more hateful than
perjury? Examine the lives of men, and you will find perjury everywhere.
Look at the vows which princes swear to their people, and bishops and
abbots too – nay, look at the vows all Christians take at baptism. Compare   65
their actual behaviour, see what a mass of perjuries you will find. How we
execrate the name of 'thief'! But in real life you will find nothing else. Unless
it is not theft, to accept a loan with no intention of paying it back, to deny
that a thing was entrusted to you when you have it packed safely away, to
usurp an inheritance or someone else's property, to hoodwink a purchaser,   70
to filch part of the goods you have in your charge, to offer glass for gems, to
sell one kind of wine as another. In short, to lose no opportunity of defraud-
ing your neighbour. But I return to the *Adages*.

88 Veritatis simplex oratio
The plain speech of truth

This adage is found in the collections of Diogenianus. It stands however in
the *Phoenissae* of Euripides, thus:

> The tale of truth is simple   5
> And it needs no fancy explanations.
> For it has its own proportion, but the unjust word
> Being diseased, has need of clever drugs.

It is quoted by Seneca, letter 49: 'For as that writer of tragedy says, the
language of truth is simple.' The proverb can be taken up against orators and   10
poets, who usually trick out their lying words with decorative touches. Or
against those who speak fair, and since they do not speak from the heart, are
all the more careful to adorn their speech, and make their words imitate true
feelings just because those feelings are lacking, 'as those who are paid to
weep at funerals / Say and do more than the truly sorrowful.' Meanwhile   15
old-fashioned rustic truth is plain, and knows nothing of this kind of
pretence in speech, calling a fig a fig, a spade a spade. Or it may be used
against soothsayers, who produce their prognostications in ambiguous
terms, for fear they may be caught out; there is always a chink through
which they can slink away. Finally it hits at those who talk in riddles to hide   20
the truth. Often this is the sign which gives the falsehood away, as in the
Eunuchus of Terence:

> Are you going on talking roguery with me in riddles?
> I know, I don't know, he went, I heard, I wasn't there.
> Will you not speak to me openly, and tell me the truth?   25

* * * * *

88 *Collectanea* no 145 gave the adage, no doubt from Diogenianus, and added
  'Poliziano points out that this must come from some writer of tragedies.' The
  reference is to his *Miscellanea* c 23, and it was naturally discarded in the
  Chiliades of *1508*, when the line had been identified as coming from Euripides.
  Otto 1873; Tilley τ 593 Truth's tale is simple.
  3 Diogenianus] 2.85
  4 Euripides] *Phoenissae* 469–72. Aeschylus frag 176 Nauck is very like this.
  9 Seneca] *Letters* 49.12, added in *1515*
  14 as those] Horace *Ars poetica* 431–2
  17 calling a fig a fig] *Adagia* II iii 5
  22 Terence] *Eunuchus* 817–9

89 Tunica pallio propior est
The tunic is nearer than the cloak

In the *Trinummus* of Plautus we read a proverbial allegory in these words:
The tunic is nearer than the cloak. It means that among our friends there are
some who are more closely linked with us than others, and not all are to be   5
considered on the same footing. Among the ancients the first obligation was
towards parents, the next to wards committed to our care, the third to clients
[dependants], the fourth to guests, the fifth to kinsmen and relatives, as
Gellius says, book 5 chapter 13. Besides, some affairs are more our concern
than others. The cloak was the outer garment of the Greeks, like the toga   10
worn by the Romans. The tunic was covered by the toga, and frequently as
in Homer both are mentioned together.

90 Genu sura propius
The knee is closer than the calf

Γόνυ κνήμης ἔγγυον, The knee is closer than the calf. The collectors of Greek
proverbs say that this adage arose from an event. When in battle, a man saw
two friends both in peril of their lives, one his brother and the other his   5
cousin, and was not able to help them both, he left the cousin and defended
his brother, saying these words meanwhile, which turned into a proverb:
'the knee is closer than the calf.' It is mentioned by Aristotle in the *Ethics*
book 9: 'Widely-known proverbs touch on the same thing, like "one soul,"
"among friends all things are common," "friendship is equality," and "the   10
knee is nearer than the shin-bone."' Theocritus in the idyll entitled *The
Graces*, applied this proverb to the grasping man who lives for himself, and
wishes to give nothing to his friends:

* * * * *

89 *Collectanea* no 282 covered this and 91 (but not 90), with references to Plautus
and Terence. Otto 1324; Tilley P 250 Near is my petticoat but nearer is my smock;
c 251 Charity begins at home is close to 89, 90 and 91.
3 Plautus] *Trinummus* 1154, the name of the play added in *1523*
9 Gellius] 5.13.2. This sentence was added in *1515*, when the reference given
was 5.12 (corrected in *1520*).
12 Homer] Eg *Iliad* 2.262

90 A pendant to the preceding, added from the Greek proverb-collections.
3 collectors] Zenobius 3.2; Diogenianus 3.78; Suidas Γ 383
8 Aristotle] *Ethica Nicomachea* 9.8.2 (1168b8)
11 Theocritus] 16.16–9

Every one keeping his right hand close to his chest
Asks only whence his money will increase,   15
Nor would he give a friend the rust therefrom,
But straightway says: knee nearer is than shin,
I would prefer a profit for myself.

Athenaeus book 9 seems to have applied it differently, as if speaking of
those things which belong more nearly to the matter in hand. Plautus seems   20
to have invented from this his own 'The tunic is nearer than the cloak.' The
saying of Hesiod is close to this adage: 'Do not equate a friend with a
brother.' We must establish an order among those we love. But there is
nothing to prevent a different application, for instance, if one were to say
that life is worth more than money, the body than clothes, the soul than the 25
body, he would be right to adduce this proverb.

91 **Omnes sibi melius esse malunt, quam alteri**
    Everyone wants things to go better for himself than for others

The same idea is expressed simply by Terence in the *Andria*: 'True is the
word oft spoken far and wide, / I want the best myself, whate'er to you
betide.' Again in the same play he twists it to suit a character: 'The nearest 5
person to myself is me.' Aristotle in the *Ethica Eudemia*, book 7: 'For it seems
to some that each man is his own best friend.' Plato again in the fifth book of
the *Laws*: 'This is what they say, that each man by nature is a friend to
himself, and that is right.' Even today there is a proverb in vogue among
theologians, that charity begins from oneself, derived apparently from the   10
words of the mystic Song of Songs: 'ordain charity towards me.' But I will
explain more carefully what I think about this when opportunity arises.

* * * * *

19 Athenaeus] 9.383b, added in *1517/8*
20 Plautus] See I iii 89.
22 Hesiod] *Works and Days* 707

91 Part of *Collectanea* no 282, with our no 89 which is very close; both, as Erasmus
    there tells us, are to be taken, not as instruction how we should behave but as
    criticisms of the way men do behave in practice. Otto 1479; Suringar 160
 3 Terence] *Andria* 426–7 and 636; Tilley N57 I am nearest to myself. Then followed
    in *1508* a reference in Latin to Plato *Laws* 5.731e which Erasmus cut out in *1523*
    when he noticed that he had quoted the same passage in Greek a few lines
    lower down.
 6 Aristotle] *Ethica Eudemia* 7.6 (1240a9)
 7 Plato] *Laws* 5.731e
11 Song of Songs] 2:4

Euripides expressed the thought of Terence in the *Medea*: 'That each one loves himself more than his friend.' Again in the collections of Greek maxims: 'None loves another man more than himself.'   15

92 Philautoi
Self-lovers

People who are in great favour with themselves, and who diligently study their own advantage, even to the neglect and detriment of the affairs of others, are gracefully called *philautoi* (self-lovers) in Greek. The vice itself is   5
called self-love or *philautia*. Horace paraphrases it neatly: 'Blind love of self.' This is the vice which Plato names the fount of all evils. Aristotle, in the *Ethics*, book 9, makes it clear that this shameful term of self-love was commonly bandied about as a proverb, when he says that men who are over-fond of themselves are publicly reproached with the base and disgrace-   10
ful name of self-lovers. Those of the opposite sort who dislike themselves are called pedantic: Martial, 'One is rank and the other pedantic.' It is a deeply rooted fault which makes people approve of everything belonging to themselves, rather than what belongs to others; it seems to have been especially so in Africans. It is a sickness never more incurable than in matters   15
of doctrine, once we have been imbued with them. Galen notes this neatly, in the first book of his *On the Natural Faculties*: 'Contention on matters of conviction is such an evil, that it is hard to shake off, quite indelible, more incurable than any scabby disease.'

93 Extra telorum iactum
Out of range

Ἔξω βελῶν, Out of range. This means in safety, out of danger. It is a

* * * * *

13 Euripides] *Medea* 86
14 Greek maxims] Menander *Sententiae* 528 (see I i 30n).

92 Tilley s 218 Self-love is a mote in every man's eye.
6 Horace] *Odes* 1.18.14, already used in I ii 15
7 Plato] *Laws* 5.731e
7 Aristotle] *Ethica Nicomachea* 9.7 (1168a29)
12 Martial] 4.20.4 added in *1528*. The word *putidus* is very difficult to render, ranging as it does from 'pedantic' to 'stinking.'
16 Galen] *De naturalibus facultatibus* 1.13 (Kuehn 2.34), added in *1528*

93 From the Greek proverb-collections (Zenobius 3.89; Diogenianus 4.71; Suidas E 1822).

metaphor from battles, in which those who do not want to be hit by missiles
remove themselves to a spot too far away to be within reach of a weapon, or   5
else take shelter in a place protected against missiles. Hence that frequent
phrase in historians: 'They had now come within range.' Quintus Curtius,
book 3: 'The battle-lines were now in sight of each other, but out of range.'
Again in book 4: 'So that they were out of range.' And again: 'They had not
yet come within range, the Greek for which is ἐντὸς βελῶν. But 'out of range'   10
is applied not only to those who are futher away than a javelin's cast could
reach but to those also who are safe in any respect. Seneca in book 7 of the *De
beneficiis* used a similar metaphor, 'Out of harm's way': 'The blasphemer
indeed cannot injure God, whose divinity places him out of harm's way.'
Lucian in *Wishes*: 'To look down from on high, hovering out of range;'   15
someone is wishing for wings, so that he might observe the fighting from
above, safe himself from being hit. Again: 'And he was outside the range of
missiles.' So Polyphemus of Ulysses, who had already escaped, so that the
Cyclops could not reach him with a missile. *Odyssey* 10, near the end. Again
the same author: 'Why not strike the Muses, who are safe from your darts?'   20
He alludes to this again in *Nigrinus*: 'And as they say Zeus rescued Hector, I
withdrew myself "out from the javelins, / The slaughter and the tumult and
the blood," planning to spend the rest of my life at home.' This is in Homer's
Iliad, book 14: 'Out from the javelins, lest anyone add wound to wound.'
Conversely, when we wish it to appear that someone is in danger, we shall   25
say that he is 'within range.' Lucian in *Bacchus*: 'Not waiting even for a
moment to be within range.' Virgil in book 11: 'Now both had come within a
spearcast's range.'

* * * * *

7 Quintus Curtius] 3.10.1; 4.2.23; 4.13.36 (see I i 11n). The second and third of
   these were added, with an introductory sentence, in *1517/8*. and the first
   inserted in *1533*.
12 Seneca] *De beneficiis* 7.7.3, added with the two preceding sentences in *1528*
15 Lucian] *Navigium* 44 (*Wishes* is an alternative title); *Quomodo historia conscribenda
   sit* 4
18 Polyphemus] Homer *Odyssey* 9 (not 10). 539–40. The *Odyssey* was first named
   in *1528*, and Erasmus did not notice that the two following quotations, introduced by 'Again the same author,' are thus ascribed to Homer instead of
   Lucian, as they rightly were at first.
19 Again the same] Lucian *Dialogi deorum* 19.2; *Nigrinus* 18 (added in *1515*), citing
   Homer *Iliad* 11.163–4 (the name Hector added in *1520*)
23 Homer] *Iliad* 14.130, already used in I ii 7
26 Lucian] *Bacchus* 4
27 Virgil] *Aeneid* 11.608

94   **Post principia**
      Behind the front rank

This has much the same meaning: 'Behind the front rank.' It also comes from
war, in which the safest place is behind the front rank. In the front line stood
the spearmen, in the second the van (*principes*), a sturdier age-group; these   5
were followed by the shield-bearers, the most remarkable for feats of arms,
and after them came the *triarii* and *rorarii* (skirmishers) in the manner
described by Livy in the first decade, book 8, so there is no place safer than
behind the van. Terence in the *Eunuchus*: 'You draw these men up, I will be
behind the front line, / Thus I shall give the signal to all.' This place was   10
suitable to a cowardly wretch, as Gnatho mockingly says: 'That's real
shrewdness,' he says, 'to draw up others in battle array and take care to find
a spot for himself.' It was the usual practice of Pyrrhus. Donatus points out
that this is a military term, and Vegetius in the second book of his *De re
militari*, bears witness that the important soldiers in the line (*principales*) are   15
properly called *principia*. He says as follows: 'Now that I have explained the
old-time formation of the legion, I will now indicate the names and dignities
(according to present arrangements) of the *principales*, or to use the right
word, *principia*.' Axius, in Varro: 'I should like you to start behind the front
rank, as they say in the camp.' You will find more about this in the proverb   20
'Back to the third line.'

95   *Procul a pedibus equinis*
      Far from the horses' hooves

'Εκ τῶν ποδῶν ἱππείων, Far from the horses' hooves. Even today this is
commonly said, to mean that one must fly from danger. By this expression

* * * * *

94 Derived originally from Terence. Our 'Behind the firing-line.'
  8 Livy] 8.8.8. This replaced in *1528* a sentence running 'in which those who are in
      the front rank are in the greatest danger, whence those who bear themselves
      valiantly in battle are said *promachesthai*, and called *promachoi*,' Homeric words
      for front-line fighters, champions.
  9 Terence] *Eunuchus* 781–2; Donatus, the ancient commentator was added in
      1515.
 14 Vegetius] *De re militari* 2.7 (see 1 i 23n) added in *1515*
 19 Varro] *Res rusticae* 3.4.1 (see 1 i 40n); Axius is a character in the dialogue-
      setting of the book.
 20 proverb] *Adagia* 1 i 23; cross-reference added in *1528*

95 Suringar 178; Tilley H 711 Trust not a horse's heel.

they usually conveyed the warning that everyone must take care in cavalry   5
contests to keep away from the horses' hooves. This was later taken up by
the public as a proverb.

96   Porro a Iove atque fulmine
      Away from Jove and from the thunderbolt

Πόῤῥω Διός τε καὶ κεραυνοῦ, Away from Jove and from the thunderbolt. This
is found in Diogenianus. It is a warning to have nothing to do with great
men, who can destroy you with a nod if they feel like it; especially avoiding   5
kings and tyrants. They have their thunderbolt, when they are roused. The
thunderbolt is an attribute of Jove, according to the poets, and some kings
wished to have their colossal statues made in this image; so says Plutarch.
He gives a very neat comparison: just as when a man is struck the blood is
seen before the wound, and just as the lightning is seen before the thunder   10
is heard, so it is with tyrants (and this means almost all princes), the
condemnation comes before trial and the accused perishes before his crime
is proved. Suidas quotes this hemistich: 'Steer clear of the strong.' And
Diogenianus gives this too among the adages. He warns that it is not safe to
have to do with princes, for whom their liking is their licence; you might   15
apply to this the Greek saying: 'There is great danger that the man who can
have everything he wants may want something he ought not to.' This
matches the warning that Aristotle gave to Calisthenes, that his talk with
Alexander should be either infrequent or such as would give pleasure.
Plutarch makes the same point in his life of Solon. Croesus had scorned   20
Solon for replying too freely to a question about happiness, and when as a
result Aesop the writer of fables warned him that one should have either the
least possible, or the most agreeable possible, conversation with kings,
Solon rephrased the saying: 'Indeed not! but rather either the least possible

* * * * *

96 From Diogenianus. Tilley J 81 Far from Jove, far from lightning
 4 Diogenianus] 7.77b (it is also in Suidas Π 2086).
 8 Plutarch] *Moralia* 779F, added in *1515*
13 Suidas] A 1149. See III iv 60.
14 Diogenianus] 2.56
16 Greek saying] This has not been traced.
18 Calisthenes] The story is told in Valerius Maximus (see I ii 14n) 7.2.ext. 11; this
    and the next were added in *1526*.
20 Plutarch] *Solon* 28.1. Aesop became 'the writer of fables' in *1528*; in *1526* he was
    'an historian' (*historicus*).

or the best.' Ovid alluded to the proverb, when he had felt the touch of this   25
thunderbolt: 'Live to thyself; as far as thou may'st, shun worldly grandeur; /
From the height of grandeur the fierce thunderbolt falls.'

97   **Septem convivium, novem convicium**
      Seven make a feast, nine make a fray

Seven make a feast, nine make a fray. A neat saying, with a neat pun in it,
meaning that there should be few invited to a dinner, otherwise it will be
noisy and unpleasant. Horace means this when he says, 'Still there is room   5
for other shades, but note – / Too crowded feasts are scented with the goat.'
There were laws in old days which prescribed both that the number of
guests should be moderate and the expenses kept down. In Gellius, Marcus
Terentius Varro judges that the number of guests should stand between the
Muses and the Graces – at the most seven, at the least three. But this adage   10
forbids that it should rise to the number of the Muses. Pliny, book 28 chapter
2, writes that Servius Sulpitius suggested that the reason why it was unlucky
to leave the table was because at that time the number of guests was still not
more than five. Chaerephon in Athenaeus, book 6, seems to permit up to
thirty guests, but only at weddings. Those who had the task of counting the   15
guests were called *gunaikonomoi*. He tells there an amusing story: a hanger-
on who had attended a wedding uninvited and had taken the end place at
table, was ordered by the *gunaikonomoi* to leave, after they had counted the
guests, because he had followed on after number thirty, and this was against
the law. 'Count again,' he said, 'and begin with me.' In this way he would   20
not be the extra one. There is a mention by Julius Capitolinus in the life of the
emperor Lucius Verus: 'And it is well known that he gave a banquet in

* * * * *

25 Ovid] *Tristia* 3.4.5–6, added in *1536*. He had been exiled after displeasing the
   emperor Augustus.

97 The source must be the *Historiae Augustae scriptores* (Julius Capitolinus); see
   below. Otto 429; Tilley s 257 Seven at a feast, nine at a fray
 5 Horace] *Epistles* 1.5.28–9
 8 Gellius] 13.11.2 (the author's name was changed to Celsus in *1540*); 'seven' is a
   mistaken correction introduced in *1528* for 'nine,' which is the correct number
   for the Muses, and Varros' maximum for a dinner-party.
11 Pliny] *Naturalis historia* 28.26, added in *1515*; the last word was at first 'three,'
   and became 'five' in *1528*.
14 Athenaeus] 6.245a, added in *1528*.
21 Julius Capitolinus] *Verus* 5.1. The two final sentences were added in *1526*. This
   is part of the *Historia Augusta* (see I i 21n).

which he took twelfth place, for the first time, although there is a well-known saying about the number of guests, seven to a feast, nine to a fray.' By 'fray,' *convicium*, he means noise, as though the word were *convocium*. This can be applied to a multiplicity of friends, or a mass of arguments in discussion, or of examples in proving a point, or even to versatility in skills. In everything, overcrowding leads to confusion and trouble.

98 De gradu deiicere
To upset, disconcert

A proverbial image, 'to push someone off the step,' to throw him into consternation, to disturb the balance of his mind. Cicero *De officiis*, book 1: 'But it takes a brave and resolute spirit not to be perturbed in times of difficulty and thrown off the step, as the saying is, in agitation, but to keep one's presence of mind and act with deliberation.' There is the same image in the phrase *in gradum reponere*, to settle someone back again, as it were to restore him to his previous place. Quintilian, *Institutions*, book 4: 'Or if they should falter at all they may be restored to their place, as it were, by the opportune questioning of the person who has introduced them.' To the same class belong *movere loco*, 'to move from its place,' *deturbare gradu*, 'to disturb from its position,' *restituere in locum*, 'to restore to its place.'

99 Post mala prudentior
Sadder and wiser

Μετὰ τὰ δεινὰ φρονιμώτερος, Sadder and wiser. Said when someone becomes more cautious through a sad experience, like people who have tasted poison and only know it to be poison when they begin to feel its effects. It is close to the proverb quoted elsewhere: 'The fool is wise after the event.' Or

* * * * *

25 *convocium*] A word invented by ancient grammarians in an attempt to connect *convicium*, noisy abuse, with *vox*, the voice

98 Otto 767. *Adagia* v i 43 is close to this.
  4 Cicero] *De officiis* 1.23.80
  9 Quintilian] 5 (not 4). 7.11

99 This was rewritten and placed here in *1515*; in *1508* it was very brief, and stood as IV 251. It is a doublet of *Adagia* IV iii 59, with *meta* for *para* in the text of Apostolius, who is named as the source. Tilley A 42 Adversity makes men wise.
  6 elsewhere] *Adagia* I i 30; Homer *Iliad* 17.32 and 20.198. For the second quotation see I i 31 (end).

to this: 'Cleon is a Prometheus after the fact.' The adage occurs in the collections of Apostolius, an author whom I would not quote except for the lack of anyone better.

100 **Ex ovo prodiit**
He came out of an egg

Ἐξ ᾠοῦ ἐξῆλθεν, He came out of an egg. They say this remark used to be made about people of great beauty and brightness, as if to say that they were not born in the ordinary way of men but out of an egg, like Castor and 5
Pollux. In the stories of the poets, Leda the daughter of Tyndarus lay with Jove and gave birth to two eggs: from one came the twins Castor and Pollux, boys of exceeding beauty, and from the other was born Helen, whose beauty is celebrated in all literature.

1 **Non est cuiuslibet Corinthum appellere**
It is not given to everyone to land at Corinth

Οὐ παντὸς ἀνδρὸς ἐς Κόρινθόν ἐσθ᾽ ὁ πλοῦς, It is not given to everyone to land at Corinth. A proverb as fine as it is old, regarding things which are dangerous and difficult to approach, and not to be attempted by all and 5
sundry. It originated, according to Suidas, from the fact that the approach to the harbour of Corinth is neither easy nor without danger to sailors. Strabo, in the eighth book of his *Geography*, gives another origin for the proverb, deriving it from the luxury of Corinth and its courtesans. He shows that Corinth, being on the Isthmus, had two harbours, one looking towards Asia 10
and one facing Italy, and was thus extremely rich owing to the crowds of traders. In this city, he says, there was a temple dedicated to Venus, so rich

* * * * *

8 Apostolius] 13.90. Erasmus had a low opinion of Apostolius (Michael Apostolides), who was not much older than himself, but he could not get on without him; there are similar remarks, for instance, in III iii 31, 42 and 66.

100 Like the last, this was rewritten to fill a gap here, having made a very brief appearance near the end in *1508* as IV 258.

1 *Collectanea* no 124 cited Horace and (anonymously) Gellius, and no doubt derived the Greek form of the proverb from Diogenianus 7.16 (it is also in Zenobius 5.37). Otto 431; Tilley M 202 It is not given to every man to go to Corinth.
6 Suidas] o 924
7 Strabo] *Geographica* 8.6.20 (see I i 69n).

that it had over a thousand girls whom the Corinthians had consecrated to
Venus as prostitutes in her honour. And so for their sake a large multitude
crowded into the city, with the result that the public funds became enriched   15
on a vast scale; but the traders, visitors and sailors were drained of resources
by the extravagance to which the city's luxury and voluptuousness led
them. Hence the proverb got abroad, 'it is not for everyone to land at
Corinth.'

Horace and Aulus Gellius refer the proverb to the distinguished cour-   20
tesan Lais. The former writes in his *Epistles*:

> To have pleased great men is not the finest praise,
> 'Tis not for every man to go to Corinth –
> He stayed at home, who feared lest he should fail.

He is apparently alluding to Aristippus, who is known to have been intimate   25
with Lais, and so intimate that his boast was that he alone possessed Lais,
and the others were possessed by her. The latter, Gellius, contributes this
story, book 1 chapter 8, from Phocion the Peripatetic: 'Lais, the Corinthian
woman, earned vast sums by her elegance and beauty. It was notorious that
the richest men of all Greece went to see her but no one was admitted unless   30
he gave whatever she had asked. And that girl asked far too much, hence
the oft-quoted proverb in Greek 'Not every man can go to Corinth,' because
it would be in vain to go there to see Lais if one could not give what she
asked. The great Demosthenes went to her in private, and asked for her
bounty. But Lais demanded ten thousand drachmas. Demosthenes, much   35
struck and alarmed by the woman's impudence and the amount of money,
withdrew, and said as he departed, 'I'm not spending ten thousand drachmas on something I should be sorry for.'

Others prefer to relate this proverb to all the harlots of Corinth in
general; their rapacity was also commented on in the Old Comedy. Aris-   40
tophanes says in the *Plutus*:

> And they say Corinthian courtesans,
> When a poor man approaches them by chance

* * * * *

20 Horace] *Epistles* 1.17.35–7. We have met the philosopher Aristippus already in
   I iii 86.
27 Gellius] 1.8.3–6 (see I i 1n); the anecdote about Demosthenes, which is
   apocryphal,is alluded to in I i 30.
40 Aristophanes] *Plutus* 149–52; no Latin version was provided, which is quite
   exceptional.

They ignore him, but if a rich man does
They straightway turn their *prôktos* to him ...   45

I would not hesitate to translate these lines into Latin if they were as decent
as they are elegant. Strabo records the remark of a certain prostitute, which
gives an illustration of their greed. When a married lady taxed one of this
order with shameful idleness, because she did not work and spent no time
on her weaving, the girl said 'Indeed I do; I may be what I am, but I have   50
worked off three pieces of cloth in no time at all.'
    However, it seems to me that there is no absurdity in taking the
proverb to refer to the dangerous navigational approach to Corinth, which
Strabo mentions in the same book. From this meaning it would later be
turned to other uses. The hanger-on in the comedy twisted it in a neat way: 55
'It isn't everyone who can get near the table.' Stobaeus quotes it from
Nicolaus, a comic poet, and Eustathius too recalls and explains it in his
commentary on the Catalogue of Ships, adding that it is an imitation from a
line of Sophocles: 'The sailing's not this way for prudent mortals.' This line
of Sophocles which Eustathius quotes is from the *Philoctetes*.   60
    There are thus two ways of using the proverb: either when we are
describing something too big for the powers of the person who is attempting
it (for instance, a person may aim at becoming a scholar without having the
natural endowments or the necessary funds, or one who is weakly in body
might try to emulate a Paul or an Antony); or else when someone is   65
preparing to tackle a dangerous business, which is not likely to have a happy
outcome, for instance if he should begin a never-ending lawsuit before
gift-eating judges, or should give himself up to Court life or undertake a
war. None of these usually has so good an outcome that there is no occasion
to repent of the course of action.   70

        * * * * *

47 Strabo] As above. The prostitute's retort contains a *double entendre* for which
   Erasmus could not contrive a Latin equivalent, nor can we one in English.
56 Stobaeus] 3.14.7, citing Nicolaus (a writer of the New Comedy) frag 1.26 Kock.
   Johannes Stobaeus compiled an important florilegium from Greek poetry about
   the year 500 AD.
60 Eustathius] see I i 77n; on *Iliad* 2.570 (290.36), citing Sophocles *Philoctetes* 304.
   The Latin version of the line was added in *1515*, and the sentence identifying
   the play in *1523*.
61 There are thus] The rest of the paragraph was added in *1515*. Paul and Antony
   are two famous hermits who lived in the Libyan desert.
68 gift-eating] The word is a reminiscence of Hesiod *Works and Days* 221, 264.

2 Satis quercus
Acorns have had their day

Ἅλις δρυός, Acorns have had their day [literally, enough of the oak]. An old adage, aimed at those who have left behind a squalid way of life and proceeded to a more polished and wealthier one. It comes from the fact that   5
early men, rough and wild as they were, abandoned the habit of living on acorns as soon as Ceres showed them the use of grain. Pliny testifies, however, in book 16 that in his time many races lived on acorns, and among the Spanish they were a great delicacy, so much so that they were brought in after dinner as a dessert. A sweetmeat like that was eminently suitable to a   10
people who used urine to clean their teeth. The proverb is not inapplicable to those who leave behind the fine old-fashioned virtues and take up with the behaviour and outlook of their times, beginning to copy the ways of modern folk. Cicero seems to have used it like this, when he writes to Atticus, book 2 (in the letter which begins, 'I have many things on my mind ...'): 'The   15
combats with Clodius which I have to expect give me only moderate concern, for I think I can either face them with all honour or decline them without embarrassment. Perhaps you will say "Like acorns, these have had their day. Think of safety if you love me." Oh dear, why are you not here?' The passage reads thus in all the texts, but I think learned readers will agree   20
with me when I say it should run: 'Perhaps you will say that honour, like acorns, has had its day. Think of safety if you love me,' by which you may understand that all thought for honour (like acorns) and the old-fashioned striving for virtue are to be left behind, and henceforward safety is to be considered rather than reputation. He writes elsewhere that this is in his   25
mind (*Letters to Atticus*, book 4): 'Recantation had a look of pettiness to me; but farewell true, upright, honest counsels.' The proverb is rather more clearly explained in book 2 of the same: 'What will you say? Are we to consider those people to have been bribed? What shall we do, if there is no other possibility? Are we to serve freedmen, even slaves? But as you say,   30
zeal has had its day' – explaining in fact what the acorns mean, that is, probity and principle. There is no reason why we should not use this in general as a proverb, whenever some old-established interest or principle is given up.

* * * * *

2 *Collectanea* no 486, from Diogenianus 1.62 (it is also in Zenobius 2.40). Otto 762; Tilley A 21 Acorns were good till bread was found.

7 Pliny] *Naturalis historia* 16.15; the way the Spaniards clean their teeth is from Catullus 37.20. Both references were added in *1515*.

14 Cicero] *Ad Atticum* 2.19.1 (where Erasmus' correction is now printed on the authority of MSS); 4.5.1; 2.1.8

3 Fenestram aperire, et similes metaphorae
To open a window, and similar metaphors

'To open a window' is to give an opportunity, or, so to speak, a handle.
Terence in the *Heautontimorumenos*: 'Ha, what a window onto wickedness
you will have opened!' This is always used in a bad sense, but 'to open the   5
door' also in a good one. Pliny to Suetonius Tranquillus: 'And indeed that
speech of mine opened the ears of men, and the door of fame.' Plutarch in
the essay 'On Osiris': 'Opening great gates for the godless people.' On the
same lines is that remark of Cicero's when defending Plancus: 'Since I have
entered into the case by a door by which I was reluctant to enter it.' Then   10
those others, 'to open the way,' 'to make ready the way,' 'to bar the way,' 'to
lay the foundations,' which we have mentioned elsewhere. A certain Cynic
philosopher was called 'the gate-crasher,' in a different sense, because he
used to burst into anyone's house to voice his objections to anything he
disliked; but the same expression can be used for those who show the way to   15
others.

4 Ansam quaerere, et consimiles metaphorae
To look for a handle, and similar metaphors

A handle is what enables something to be seized and held. The metaphor
from this supplies various kinds of adage. Plautus in the *Persa*: 'Do you not
see how this man is looking for a handle?' – that is, on the watch for an   5
opportunity to go back on an agreement and invalidate it. This is taken from
the Greek metaphor, as it is common for them to say 'to look for a handle, to

* * * * *

3 *Collectanea* no 484 cites the passages from Terence and Cicero.
4 Terence] *Heautontimorumenos* 481
6 Pliny] the Younger, *Letters* 1.18.4
7 Plutarch] *Moralia* 360A, added in *1515*
9 Cicero] *Pro L. Plancio* 3.8
12 elsewhere] Eg *Adagia* III vi 70, the phrase added in *1515*
13 'gate-crasher'] Plutarch *Moralia* 632E; Diogenes Laertius 6.86. This is an
   addition of *1526*.

4 *Collectanea* no 482, citing Plautus only. No 483 was the very similar expression
   Occasionem arripere, To seize the opportunity (Otto 1262), which followed here
   in the *Chiliades* of *1508*, and was abolished in *1515*, probably because it so
   closely overlapped I vii 70 *Nosce tempus*.
4 Plautus] *Persa* 670–1, the title of the play added in *1515*

supply a handle.' Aristophanes in the *Lysistrata*: 'For if one of us gives them a handle however small, / These women will not forego their comfortable crafts.' Plato, *Laws*, book 3: 'And the word itself gives us a handle.' Aristides in *Pericles*: 'To give a handle that he might seem to be envious.' The same author said in *Timon*, using a similar metaphor, 'Nor does he give room for false accusation,' and Plato again in the *Laws*, book 7: 'That they might furnish many with handles for disagreement.' Again in book 8 of the *Republic*, he points out that the metaphor is taken from wrestlers, whose greatest skill is to arrange the body so that it cannot be seized: 'Again like a wrestler offer the same hold.'

The same applies to 'chancing upon the same handles' or opportunities, 'to grasp a handle,' 'to let a handle slip,' 'to neglect a handle,' and possibly others. Epictetus in his *Enchiridion* wrote that everything has two handles: by one it can be held, but not by the other. Therefore it is important to grasp everything by the handle by which it can be held: that is, to choose the good everywhere and bear with the evil. A certain philosopher refused to admit young people without instruction in mathematics, because he said they were without a handle to philosophy. But Plutarch wrote beautifully in his essay 'On How to Study Poetry,' that there are many parts of the body by which vices can creep in, but there is one approach or handle to virtue and one only – the ears of the young if they have been pure, not taken up by the talk of men who flatter and corrupt them.

* * * * *

8 Aristophanes] *Lysistrata* 671–2; Latin version added in *1515* and rewritten in *1520*.

10 Plato] *Laws* 3.682e.

10 Aristides] *De quattuor* pp 159 and 214 Dindorf (see I i 13n). 'Timon' should be 'Cimon.'

13 Plato] In *1508 Laws* 3.682e, and the passage ascribed to book 7 (which has not been found there) stood here in the Latin only, having been taken over from the *Collectanea* of 1500. The former of the two was removed in *1523*, when it was seen to be a duplicate of what had just been given above in Greek.

14 Again] *Republic* 8.544b, added in *1517/8*

20 Epictetus] *Enchiridion* 23. This compilation by Arrian of the teaching of the famous Stoic moralist (first/second century AD) is referred to in Latin. The Greek text was not yet in print, but a Latin version by Angelo Poliziano had been printed in Bologna in May 1497.

23 philosopher] Plato, who inscribed over his door 'No admittance without a knowledge of geometry' (*Adagia* III iii 60); added in *1533*

25 Plutarch *Moralia* 38A–B, added in *1533*

5   Cyclopis donum
The gift of the Cyclops

Κύκλωπος δωρεά, A present from the Cyclops. This means 'a useless gift.'
The favours of tyrants and brigands are of this sort: if they do no harm, or
only do it later, they claim this as a great benefaction in itself. Cicero writes   5
to this effect in the second *Philippic*: 'How are brigands benefactors, except to
be able to maintain that they have granted life to those from whom they have
not taken it?' Lucian in *Cataplus*: 'That gift of the Cyclops delights me not at
all – his promise "I shall eat Noman last."' The words are those of Micyllus
the cobbler: when he had complained that he was not received at once with   10
the others into Charon's boat, and Clotho, one of the Fates, expected him to
be grateful for it as a favour, that he should be granted a short delay before
going down to the underworld, he replied in this fashion. There is no doubt
that Lucian was recalling the passage in Homer, in the ninth book of the
Odyssey, where the Cyclops Polyphemus, delighted with the sweet wine   15
Ulysses had given him, promises a present which would make Ulysses
vastly happy – so that he would offer the Cyclops another draught from his
flagon. Ulysses gave him more, and more again, in the hope of this present.
Then when he thought the Cyclops well softened up with wine and likely to
reply gently, Ulysses asked for the promised gift. The Cyclops replied: 'First   20
I'll devour your friends, then you, Outis. The others first: that's your present
from me.' *Outis* in Greek means No man, and this was the name Ulysses had
invented for himself to delude Polyphemus.

6   Tuis te pingam coloribus
I'll paint you in your own colours

I will paint you in your own colours, that is, I'll describe you as you really
are. Taken from painters, who sometimes portray and exhibit a man's face as
it really is, and sometimes beautify it with false colours. Or perhaps the   5
allusion is to the crow in Aesop, who passed himself off in colours not his

* * * * *

5 This is in Apostolius (10.20a), but could well have been derived directly from
Lucian.
5 Cicero] *Philippics* 2.3.5, added in *1528*
8 Lucian] *Cataplus* 14
14 Homer] *Odyssey* 9.369–70

6 *Collectanea* no 821, citing the two passages from Jerome *Adversus Rufinum*. Otto
64
6 Aesop] Phaedrus 1.3 dresses his jackdaw in peacock's feathers.

own. St Jerome against Rufinus: 'I might also paint you in your own colours,
and rave against a raving man.' In the same work again: 'You boast that you
know of crimes which I have confessed to you alone as to my best friend,
and you say you will declare these publicly and that I must be painted with   10
my true colours.' Pliny in the preface to the *History of the World*: 'And lest I
should seem to be speaking altogether ill of the Greeks, I would wish us to
be understood through them, and to be painted in those colours which you
will find in these books.' And Cicero in *Letters to His Brother Quintus*, book 2,
the last letter: 'in your colours, but with my own brush.' This, however, is   15
slightly different.

7 Ornatus ex tuis virtutibus
Adorned according to your virtues

Terence's ironic remark comes close to this in meaning; it occurs in the
Adelphoe: 'If I were king, you should be adorned according to your virtues,'
that is, you should have rewards fitting your deeds. For in old times kings   5
used to pay great honour to those who had perpetrated some famous deed.

8 Domi Milesia
Leave (Milesian) luxury at home

Οἴκοι τὰ Μιλήσια, Leave Milesian things at home. This is usually said about
people who parade their domestic luxury in a place where it is least acceptable; for everyone is free to live in his own way in his own house. However,   5
it is the duty of a guest to praise the dress and customs of those with whom
he is staying, and to imitate them as far as he can, but in any case not to
vaunt his own way of life and scorn any other. This is what some inexperienced people are apt to do; wherever they go in the world they pour scorn

* * * * *

7 Jerome] *Adversus Rufinum* 3.42 and 41 (*PL* 23. 488A and 487C)
11 Pliny] *Naturalis historia* praef 26 (Erasmus' Latin text was defective.)
14 Cicero] *Ad Quintum fratrem* 2.14.2; the reference added in *1528*, before which
the text ran 'Cicero somewhere or other'

7 Taken from Terence *Adelphoe* 176. It is not proverbial.

8 *Collectanea* no 480 consisted of a quotation from Poliziano (who cites 'Zenodotus'), repeated with very little change (and no mention of 'Zenodotus'), to
which Erasmus added 'the authority is Apostolus of Byzantium' (in our printed
Apostolius it is 12.37). This is rewritten here from a wide range of new
materials. Milesian luxury comes again in I ix 49.

on everyone and everything, praising what is their own to the skies, even   10
extolling vices as the highest virtues.

The adage is mentioned by Angelo Poliziano in his *Miscellanea,* and he
adds that it comes from the story of a certain Milesian who was once a guest
of the Spartans, and boasted of the delights of his own country. The reply
came: 'Your Milesian things are at home, not here.' He quotes as the author   15
of this proverb a certain Zenodotus, a collector of adages. There are indeed
extant the collections of one Zenobius, but whether he is the man whom
Poliziano calls Zenodotus, I cannot say. However in these collections I find a
story of this sort which Suidas also records. One Aristagoras, a Milesian,
went to Sparta to ask for help for the Ionians, who were being harried by the   20
Persians. But when he appeared before the assembly, dressed with an
elegance unusual among the Spartans, and overflowing with other luxuries
from Ionia, one of the ephors is said to have warned him, 'Leave Milesian
delights at home.' An ephor is one of the Spartan magistrates, whose duty is
to investigate questions of contract, as Aristotle affirms in the third book of   25
his *Politics*; the very form of the word indicates that it means 'overseer.'

Athenaeus, however, gives a different reason for the proverb in book
12: he says that the Milesians had imitated the luxury of the people of
Colophon and had infected the regions round about with this disease.
Finding themselves unpopular on this account, they took warning that their   30
refinements should be enjoyed in the home, not exhibited abroad. He
quotes the proverb in the form: 'Milesian things at home, strictly domestic,
not in public view.' Just as the austerity of the Spartans is famous in
literature, so the luxury of the Milesians became a byword, so much so that
when people want to describe anything soft and effeminate they call it   35
Milesian. Thus a certain Aristides entitled his book which was full of improper stories, *Milesian Tales.* And Lucian in the *Amores* calls the lascivious

* * * * *

12 Poliziano] *Miscellanea* c 17
16 Zenodotus] The name provided by some late manuscripts, and normally used
   by Erasmus, for the abbreviated collection of proverbs that passed under the
   name of Zenobius; Erasmus has already touched on this question of name in
   section v of his Introduction to the *Adagia,* and more will be found in our
   Prolegomena (CWE 30). The reference is Zenobius 5.57; Suidas o 91.
25 Aristotle] *Politics* 3.1 (1275b9)
27 Athenaeus] 12.524b, added in *1517/18*
36 Aristides] Mentioned by Julius Capitolinus; see below. His *Tales* (c 100 BC)
   might be important for the early history of the novel, had they survived.
   Erasmus met the name first in Poliziano's *Miscellanea* c 16.
37 Lucian] *Amores* 1

talk of lovers 'Milesian.' Martianus Capella speaks of the 'Milesian delights
of all the different myths found in the poets.' Apuleius, too, in the iambic
poem with which he chose to inaugurate his *Ass*, calls his enticing and   40
wanton stories 'Milesian talk.' Julius Capitolinus in the Life of Clodius
Albinus: 'Some people speak of his Milesian tales, which enjoy a not undis-
tinguished reputation, although they are poorly written.' And that this was
also said of the stories of Apuleius, appears from what Julius Capitolinus
quotes a little later on from a letter of Severus: 'It was a matter for greater   45
regret that you should have thought him deserving of praise as a writer,
since he spent his time on some nonsensical old-wives' tales, and grew old
between the Punic Milesian tales of his dear Apuleius and literary frivolity.'
Thus far Capitolinus. He speaks of 'his dear Apuleius' because Albinus
himself like Apuleius was an African.   50

The luxury of the Milesians, however, was mainly in dress, because
they produced the softest of all textiles. Hence Maximus Tyrius calls the
Milesians *euhimatotatoi* [superbly cloaked] on account of the elegance of their
costume. And Virgil in the *Georgics* calls the softest fleeces Milesian. Horace
too: 'Another shuns the Milesian-woven cloak / Worse than a dog or snake,'   55
meaning a cosy garment, not austere enough. Aristophanes in the *Frogs*
says 'bundled up in Milesian bedclothes,' and Theocritus too and many
other writers speak of these. But this is more than enough for the understanding of the proverb. Euripides alludes to it in the *Helena*, 'Revered you
may have been out there, not here.' And Antiphanes in Athenaeus, book 4,   60
alludes to it in these lines:

> When you go to Sparta,
> You must do as Sparta does;

* * * * *

38 Martianus Capella] 2.100. He is an encyclopaedic Latin writer of the first half of
   the fifth century AD, who is cited only twice in the *Adagia*.
39 Apuleius] *Metamorphoses* 1.1 (see I i 15n); the description of his words as verse
   is perhaps a slip of memory.
41 Julius Capitolinus] *Clodius Albinus* 11.8 and 12.12; this is part of the *Historia
   Augusta* (see I i 21n).
52 Maximus Tyrius] *Philosophumena* 32.10 (see I ii 100n); the Greek word should be
   eueimenôtatoi.
54 Virgil] *Georgics* 3.306; 4.334
54 Horace] *Epistles* 1.17.30–1
56 Aristophanes] *Frogs* 542–3
57 Theocritus] 15.126–7
59 Euripides] *Helena* 454
60 Antiphanes] Frag 44 Kock, cited by Athenaeus 4.143a, added in 1517/8; he is a
   writer of the Attic New Comedy.

Go to their mess to dine,
And their black broth enjoy;   65
Wear a moustache and be careful
To scorn nothing, to ask for nothing better.

9 Mense maio nubunt malae
Bad women marry in May

This old Roman adage is to be found in Ovid: Bad women marry in May. It
can be said about women who choose the wrong time to be voluptuous, or
about people who do something at an inopportune moment, or who make a   5
beginning without good auspices. For in old days it was thought inauspicious for women to marry in May, perhaps because it was in that month that
the ghost of Remus, killed by his brother's guard, is believed to have
appeared to his foster-father Faustulus and to Acca Laurentia, and to have
commanded that due honours be paid to his shade. So the festival estab-   10
lished by Romulus and called 'Remuria' began to be called by later generations 'Lemuria' (one letter being changed) as if it came from *lemures*, or
spectres. It was the custom to pay service at this time to the shades of
ancestors, and so those days were observed as part of the festival of the
dead, and thought unlucky for weddings.   15
    Ovid in the *Fasti*:

> The times are unsuitable for marriage, both of widow and maid;
> She who marries then will not live long.
> For the same reason, if you give weight to proverbs,
> Common folk say bad women wed in May.   20

    Plutarch in the 'Problems' gives other reasons why people should
abstain from marrying in this month. For one thing, it comes between April
(sacred to Venus) and June (dedicated to Juno) and both these goddesses
preside over weddings; so to gain the favour of the goddess the people who
were rather in a hurry married in April, and those who wanted to put it off a   25
little married in June. Another reason was connected with certain mournful
rites which the Romans used to observe at that time, by throwing human
effigies from the bridge into the Tiber, as they had formerly been used to

* * * * *

9 Taken apparently from Ovid. Otto 1011
16 Ovid] *Fasti* 5.487–90 (tr Sir James Frazer)
21 Plutarch] *Moralia* 284F. For the casting of men, or their effigies, into the Tiber,
   see *Adagia* I v 37.

throw Greeks. On this account the priestess of Juno spent these days as it
were in mourning, and did not perform any solemn rite. A further reason   30
was that May seems to take its name from 'elder' [*maiores*] and June from
'younger' (*juniores*) and a more advanced age is unseasonable and unlucky
for marriage. Thus Euripides wrote: 'But old age bids the Cyprian farewell /
And Venus is the enemy of old men.'

10   **Ovem lupo commisisti**
     You have handed the sheep over to the wolf

Τῷ λύκῳ τὴν ὄϊν, The sheep to the wolf. Terence says in the *Eunuchus*, 'You
wicked woman, you have handed the sheep over to the wolf,' speaking of
the young man Chaerea, to whom alone the maiden has been entrusted   5
under the belief that he is a eunuch. Donatus picks this out as a proverb,
which contains respect for women combined with a lascivious idea. We can
use it appropriately whenever something is committed to the care of a
person, whose presence would be a better justification for placing it under
guard. Cicero in the third *Philippic*: 'For he had declared in a speech that he   10
would be the city's guardian, and would keep his army near the city till the
first of May. What an excellent guardian of sheep, say they, is a wolf! Would
Antonius be the guardian of the city, or rather its plunderer and harasser?'
Hence it seems to fit the case, when an affair is handed over to an enemy,
one who has the worst intentions towards us; because the wolf and the lamb   15
have a natural antipathy for each other. Homer also shows this in the *Iliad*,
book 22:

> Between lions and men there are no faithful oaths,
> Nor do wolves and lambs agree,
> But always they have evil intentions and hate each other.   20

And Horace in the *Odes*: 'Great is the enmity 'twixt wolf and lamb / By nature
fixed – and between me and you.' To this we may add the saying quoted by

* * * * *

33 Euripides] Frag 23 Nauck, cited by Plutarch as above

10 *Collectanea* no 540 cites Terence and Cicero, and also gives a Greek form of the
    proverb. Otto 983; Tilley w 602 Give not the wolf the wether to keep. *Adagia* III
    vii 36 and VI vi 42 are related.
 3 Terence] *Eunuchus* 832, with the comment of Donatus
10 Cicero] *Philippics* 3.11.27
16 Homer] *Iliad* 22.262–4, the book-number added in *1520*
21 Horace] *Epodes* 4.1–2

Suidas, 'sooner the wolf will pasture the lamb,' to mean anything entirely unlikely. Plautus has something like it in the *Miles*: 'The pantry is in the care of a good butler's boy,' but he gets nearer still in the *Truculentus*: 'His sheep   25
are not far from the wolves.'

11   **Mustelae sevum**
     Suet for the weasel

Γαλῇ στέαρ, Fat for the weasel. The sense is, you give or hand over (understood) 'fat to the weasel,' when what is given is the very thing the recipient
has a natural appetite for; this animal is particularly fond of fat. Thus it may   5
happen that one praises a man who is specially avid for praise, or one incites
a naturally bibulous person to drink, or invites people to play at dice who
have a passion for the game. The adage is found in Diogenianus.

12   **Nullam hodie lineam duxi**
     I haven't done a stroke today

Τήμερον οὐδεμίαν γραμμὴν ἤγαγον, I haven't done a stroke today. The
adage takes its origin from the painter Apelles. It applies to those who have
taken an idle moment from their study or their art. This is recorded by Pliny,   5
book 35 chapter 10, and it is a pleasure to me to quote his words in these
notes: 'It is well known what occurred between Protogenes and Apelles.
Protogenes lived in Rhodes, and when Apelles sailed there, he was eager to
examine the work of a man whom he knew only by his reputation. He
looked for the workshop at once. Protogenes was not there, but a large   10
picture stood on the easel, and only one old woman was in charge. She said
that Protogenes was out, and asked who she should say had enquired for
him. "This man," said Apelles, and taking the brush, he drew a line in

* * * * *

23 Suidas] π 2291
24 Plautus] *Miles gloriosus* 837 (the name of the play added in 1523); *Truculentus*
657, added in 1523

11 *Collectanea* no 308, which combined this with our III vi 16 *Ranae aquam*, derived
it no doubt from Diogenianus 3.83

12 *Collectanea* no 152, giving as the source a much shorter quotation from the same
passage of Pliny. Otto 957; Tilley D 93 No day without a line. A rare example of
overlapping with the *Parabolae* (601C), where the anecdote is also told. For an
interpretation with a coloured plate, see E.H. Gombrich, *The Heritage of
Apelles* (Oxford 1976) 14–18.
5 Pliny] *Naturalis historia* 35.81–4

colour, of the greatest thinness, across the picture. When Protogenes returned, the old woman showed him what had been done. They say that as   15
soon as he saw the delicacy of the line, he said "Apelles has been here." So
perfect a piece of work could not belong to anyone else. Then he himself
drew with another colour a still thinner line along the first one, and went
away, directing that if the other returned, she should show it to him and say
that this was the man he was looking for. So it fell out. Apelles did come   20
back, and blushing at the thought of being defeated, cut across the lines with
a third colour, leaving no room for further minuteness. Protogenes admitted
himself vanquished, and rushed to the harbour to find his guest. It was
resolved to hand the picture down to posterity as it was, as a wonder to all
but especially to artists. It is known that it was burnt in the first fire in   25
Caesar's house on the Palatine, but before that we had eagerly examined it.
Though of large size, it contained nothing but lines vanishing from sight,
and among the excellent work of many other painters it seemed empty, but
for that very reason full of attractiveness, and finer than any other work. It
was the constant habit of Apelles never to pass a day, however fully   30
occupied, without practising his art by drawing a line, and so the proverb
arose from him.' Thus far Pliny. It was moreover to this line, by which he
was immediately recognized by Protogenes, that Statius referred in *Hercules
Vindex on the Dinner-Table*, when he says 'The line which speaks afar the old
Apelles.'   35

13   **Neque natare, neque literas**
     Neither swim nor read

Μήτε νεῖν μήτε γράμματα, He can (which must be supplied) neither swim
nor read. This is said about people who are unusually ignorant and have
learnt absolutely nothing in childhood in the way of useful knowledge. For   5
these two skills were the first things learnt by the boys in Athens. And in
Rome too, as Suetonius asserts plainly enough in his *Augustus*: 'He himself,
for the most part, taught his nephews letters, and swimming, and the other
rudiments.' The same author reveals that Caligula, although very quick to
learn other things, did not know how to swim – as if this were the very last   10

* * * * *

33 Statius] *Silvae* 4.6.29. This is a volume of occasional verse from the very end of
    the first century AD, cited four or five times in the *Adagia*.

13 *Collectanea* no 641, citing Plato's *Laws* in Latin, and the Greek proverb from
    Diogenianus 6.56 (it is also in Suidas M 989).
7   Suetonius] See I i 78n; *Divus Augustus* 64.3; *Caligula* 54.2, both added in 1517/8.

thing anybody would not know. Plato in the *Laws*, book 3: 'Those who take the contrary part are to be called wise, even if they know neither how to read nor how to swim, as the saying goes.' Aristides also in the *Joint Defence of Four Orators*: 'But as the saying goes, deeming it right to reject him as one who knows neither how to read nor how to swim.'

15

14 Mordere frenum
To bite on the bit

Decimus Brutus in book 11 of the *Letters to Friends*, seems to use To bite on the bit in the sense of rebelling even lightly against servitude: 'If you bite on the bit, I'll stake my life that not one of the whole lot will be able to face you if   5
you attempt to speak,' that is, if you indicate in any way that you resent servitude. This is borne out by Cicero's reply: 'Even if I were timorous, that letter of yours would have wiped away all fear from my heart. But, as you advise, I have bitten on the bit. Indeed, seeing that during your confinement I rested all my hopes upon you, what do you imagine I am doing now?' But   10
Papinius in the *Wedding Hymn of Stella and Violantilla* takes it in a different sense, doubtless meaning 'to accept servitude,' to receive the bit: 'Silence, rumour: he has taken his orders and bitten on the bit,' that is, he has accepted the fetters of marriage. However, I leave to the learned the question whether the words of Cicero can be understood in this sense. The   15
proverb seems to be taken from the play of Aeschylus called *Prometheus*, where Mercury speaks as follows:

> For you are not touched or softened by my prayers;
> Biting the bit like a newly-yoked colt,
> You rage and strive against the reins.

20

* * * * *

11 Plato] *Laws* 3.689d
13 Aristides] See I i 13n; *De quattuor* p 368 Dindorf. Erasmus gives his excerpts from this work various titles; he never saw it in print.

14 *Collectanea* no 296 gives Brutus' letter as the source and compares what is now *Adagia* III vii 78. Otto 715; Tilley B 670 To bite upon the bridle. To be distinguished from our 'To take the bit between one's teeth' (Tilley B 424), which means to assert one's independence.
3 Brutus] Cicero *Ad familiares* 11.23.2; 11.24.1
11 Papinius] Statius *Silvae* 1.2.28 (cf I iv 12n).
16 Aeschylus] *Prometheus vinctus* 1008–10, added in 1523. The proverb is derived, not from Aeschylus, but from experience.

15 **Manibus pedibusque**
    With hands and feet

To express the greatest effort we say 'with hands and feet,' because hands
indicate diligence in bringing something to a conclusion, feet indicate swift-
ness in getting it done. Davus in the *Andria* of Terence: 'I am obliged,   5
Pamphilus, in service to you, to strive with hands and feet.' Aeschines uses
this adage more than once in his speech against Demosthenes. Homer, *Iliad*
20: 'But whatever I can do with hands and feet.'

16 **Omnibus nervis**
    With every sinew

This has much the same sense: with all one's force, with all one's concentration. For strength lies in the sinews, so say the philosophers. Hence we say
'to stretch the sinews,' 'to prepare the sinews,' and we call those things   5
'sinewy' which are lively and vigorous, not in the least sluggish. Cicero to
his brother Quintus: 'So strive with every sinew and all your capacity.'
Again in the *Letters to Friends*, book 15: 'You may strive towards this with
every sinew,' and again in the second *Verrine*: 'Such that my manhood and
determination may fitly strain every sinew to bear it.'   10

17 **Velis equisque**
    With sail and horse

The same sense of endeavour is in this saying 'with sail and horse,' more for

               * * * * *

     15 *Collectanea* no 40 combined our 15, 16 and 24, quoting Terence and Quintus
         Cicero. Otto 1034; Suringar 113; Tilley T 422 Tooth and nail; M 923 With might
         and main. A passage from Pindar which came to hand after this paragraph was
         already in type was added to III ix 68.
      5 Terence] *Andria* 675–6
      6 Aeschines] *In Ctesiphontem* 109; see I iii 26n.
      7 Homer] *Iliad* 20.360

     16 Included at first in *Collectanea* no 40. Further material, from Greek sources, is in
         III ix 68.
      6 Cicero] Quintus Cicero *Commentariolum petitionis* 14.56
      8 Again] Cicero *Ad Familiares* 15.14.5; *Verrines* 1.12.35, both added in *1523*

     17 Erasmus seems to have been misled by defects in his text of Cicero into setting
         up a proverb, 'With sail and horse,' 'Full sail full gallop,' which does not exist,
         though it is found already in 1506 incorporated in *Collectanea* no 41. In the first

flight or pursuit than achievement. Cicero, *Letters to His Brother Quintus*,
book 2: 'So I, who have been asleep so long over the matter of paying court to   5
your friend (though you, heaven knows, repeatedly tried to rouse me) shall
make up for my slowness by galloping, with horses and sails too.' However
in this place the ordinary texts have men [*viris*] for sails [*velis*]. Again, in
De officiis, book 3: 'Now that these schools are out of date, Epicurus has come
into vogue—an advocate and supporter of practically the same doctrine.   10
Against such a philosophy we must fight it out with horse and sail as the
saying is, if our purpose is to defend and maintain what is right.' In these
examples he used the metaphor in a slightly different way, first with reference to speed and then to two different kinds of warfare, with cavalry or at
sea.   15

18   **Remis velisque**
     With oars and sails

With oars and sails is very similar, and comes from the fact that when the
ship is driven onwards by rowers and sails both together, the greatest effort
of the sailors is being put forth. Cicero, *Tusculan Questions*, book 3: 'For it is a   5
loathsome thing, wretched and execrable, and ought to be avoided (so to
speak) with all power of sails and oars.' Again, in the first *Philippic*: 'Then
indeed I was fired with such eagerness to return, that no oars, no winds
were swift enough for me.' Plautus in the *Asinaria*: 'As fast as you can, with
oar and sail, hurry away and flee.' When the ship is propelled by oarsmen,   10

* * * * *

Cicero-passage the manuscripts offer, as he says himself, *tum equis tum viris*,
'horse and foot'; in the second, *viris equisque, ut dicitur*, 'foot and horse, as they
say'; and his *velis*, 'sails,' introduces an idea alien to the context. *Equi viri* or
virique is commonly used in its literal sense (Otto 609).
4 Cicero] *Ad Quintum fratrem* 2.14.2; *De officiis* 3.33.116

18 *Collectanea* no 41, which had included the preceding and cited only the line of
   Plautus as the authority. An addition was made in *1528* in IV vi 72. Otto 1521.
   The second paragraph provides a different adage, Ἀμεταστρεπτί, Without
   looking back, and it is not clear why Erasmus put the two together.
5 Cicero] *Tusculanae disputationes* 3.11.25; *Philippics* 1.4.9 (this was added in *1533*
   to III iv 71).
9 Plautus] *Asinaria* 157
10 When the ship] *Deuteros plous*, literally 'second sailing,' when the wind drops
   and you have to row (IV v 79), is a standard Greek phrase for a second-best
   course of action, and stands as an adage on its own in III iv 71. For the other
   Greek words cited, there are several possible sources. The whole sentence was
   added in *1533*.

the Greeks call this Δεύτερος πλοῦς, the 'secondary mode of travel': when it is carried along by sail, they use the word 'sail-borne,' but when it runs before a following wind, they have a word 'breeze-borne.' The metaphor is reversed by Aristophanes, to mean tardiness, in the *Ecclesiazusae*: 'Now we neither run nor are otherwise driven along,' and the commentator explains,   15
'we are travelling neither with sails nor oars.' However there is nothing to prevent the proverb being used for horse-racing. Virgil expresses it simply in the third *Aeneid*: 'Then all our company made to port with oars and sails.'

In this category falls the phrase of Plato in the ninth book of the *Laws*: 'From the society of evil men you must flee *irreversim*,' that is, not even   20
looking back. He referred to the story of Eurydice, who was commanded never to look back. So in Genesis, Lot is ordered to flee from Sodom 'without turning round' and Virgil says, 'Cast them over your head; do not look back.'

19   **Navibus atque quadrigis**
      With ships and chariots

Horace used 'With ships and chariots' to mean 'with the greatest eagerness, the greatest haste,' in his *Epistles*:

> A stenuous inactivity drives us on.   5
> With ship and chariot the good life pursue–
> But what you seek is here.

Plutarch in his attack on usury: 'So do not wait for splendid horses or

* * * * *

13 breeze-borne] The Greek adjective is compounded with a word meaning 'following breeze,' and this cannot be rendered in English.

14 Aristophanes] *Ecclesiazusae* 109. In 1533 this was added to III iv 71, and also made into an independent adage in IV viii 47.

17 Virgil] *Aeneid* 3.563

19 Plato] *Laws* 9.854c

21 Eurydice] Wife of Orpheus, who was allowed to bring her back from the world of the dead on condition that he did not look behind him on the way; Virgil *Georgics* 4.485–91, Ovid *Metamorphoses* 10.50–2. Eurydice in Erasmus' sentence should strictly be Orpheus.

22 Genesis] 19:17

23 Virgil] *Eclogues* 8.102. At a sacrifice it is often very dangerous to look behind you; see, for instance, J.G. Frazer's note on Ovid *Fasti* 6.164.

19 Taken from Horace. Otto 1207

3 Horace] *Epistles* 1.11.28–9

8 Plutarch] *Moralia* 828E

chariots veneered with horn, plated with silver, which borrowing rapidly overtakes and outruns; rather make use of the first donkey or sorry hack that 10 offers and escape that enemy and tyrant, the moneylender.'

20 Citis quadrigis; Iovis quadrigis
With swift chariots; with the chariots of Jove

To flee 'with swift chariots, with Jove's chariots,' that is, as rapidly as possible, is found in Plautus, borrowed from Homer, who credits the gods with chariots which carry them off at once wherever they wish to be from 5 Olympus to earth, and from earth to heaven. Cicero alludes to this, writing to his brother Quintus: 'Since you write that my poem meets with his approval on the car of poesy, only you must give me Britain for a subject, so that I may paint it in your colours, but with my own brush.' Plautus in the *Aulularia*: 'Let him hasten to obey these orders with swift chariots.' Livy, in 10 the first decade, book 5, tells how Camillus, after taking Veii, made a triumphal entry into the town in a chariot drawn by white horses, and for this reason the triumph achieved more notoriety than popularity, because he was attempting to vie with the chariots of the Sun and of Jove.

21 Equis albis praecedere
To lead the way with white horses

When they wished to say that someone was far superior to others in some particular way, surpassing them by a great distance, they would say that he 'led the way with white horses,' either because in ancient times white horses 5 were considered the best, or because victors were usually drawn by white horses in a triumph, or because white horses were believed to be lucky and

* * * * *

20 Otto 1498

4 Plautus] *Aulularia* 600, quoted below, and *Amphitryo* 450. In Homer, the chariot of Poseidon (*Iliad* 13.23ff) is an example.

6 Cicero] *Ad Quintum fratrem* 2.14.2. This is continuous with the words quoted in I iv 17, but faulty punctuation has allowed Erasmus to divide the sentence in two, so that the fanciful words 'on the car of poesy,' which belong with the first half of the sentence, make very little sense here. The last phrase is reused in its own right in I iv 6.

9 Plautus] See above; this was quoted in *Collectanea* no 275.

10 Livy] 5.23.5–6, added in *1515*

21 Most of this is taken almost verbatim (which is unusual) from *Collectanea* no 275. Otto 1498

likely to prosper, if we apply the metaphor to equestrian contests. Apuleius
indicates this when he says 'After I got clear of the steep hills, the dewy
meadows, and the muddy fields, riding on a pure white native horse, and   10
one already fairly tired.' It is not without reason that he adds 'native' (that is,
from Thessaly) and 'white,' for both contribute to the idea of fleetness.
Horace in the *Satires*, on a certain Persius:

> Presumptuous, vain and obstinate was he,
> Able in hatred to defeat a king,   15
> In bitterness of speech so far outstripping
> Sisenna, Barrus and their kind, as if
> He led the way with white horses.

Sisennna and Barrus were great slanderers; although Acron reads *barros* as if
it were an adjective. The phrase of Plautus in the *Asinaria* is similar: 'For if 20
this chance is let slide, he'll never catch it again, by Jove, not with a chariot
and four white horses.' Greek simply says 'to ride ahead' for 'to surpass by
far,' because travel by horses is the swiftest.

22   **Mordicus tenere**
     To hold fast with one's teeth

To hold fast with one's teeth is to guard with the utmost pertinacity, ὀδάξ in
Greek. Cicero in the first book of his *Academic Questions*: 'We shall declare
that all presentations of this nature are devoid of perspicuity, to which we   5
are bound to cling with clenched teeth.' St Augustine in one of his letters to
St Jerome: 'Those disturb me more who, though their versions were more
recent and though they held on with clenched teeth, as the saying is, to the
method and the rules of Hebrew in both words and idioms, not only did not
agree among themselves, but even left many things out.' In the same way   10
Seneca says in book 7 of his *De beneficiis* 'With both hands': 'Our good

* * * * *

8 Apuleius] *Metamorphoses* 1.2 (see I i 15n).
13 Horace] *Satires* 1.7.6–8, with the ancient commentary ascribed to Acron
20 Plautus] *Asinaria* 278–9
22 Greek] Added in *1533*, from Suidas II 654

22 Otto 1139
 4 Cicero] *Lucullus* 16.51
 6 Augustine] *Letters* 28.2 (= Jerome *Letters* 56.2.3)
11 Seneca] *De beneficiis* 7.2.1; cf Otto 1054 and *Adagia* I ix 16. The citation was
    added in*1515*, and the precise reference in *1528*.

Demetrius recommends the learner to hold on to these things with both hands, and never let go of them.'

23 **Toto corpore, omnibus unguiculis**
    With the whole body, with all one's nails (claws)

With one's whole body, and With every claw, have the same sense of pertinacity. The metaphor is taken from wild animals, who hold on with teeth and claws and their whole body to anything that they refuse to have   5
wrenched away. Lucian in the dialogue of Diogenes and Crates: 'But the gold they safeguarded with their teeth and claws and any device they had.' Cicero in his *Tusculan Questions*, book 2: 'With the whole force of the body, with all their nails, as the saying is, they second the straining of the voice.'

24 **Noctes diesque**
    By night and day

Ceaseless and tireless industry is often expressed by this figure, By night and day. Horace, in the *Art of Poetry*: 'Turn them over by night and by day.' Hesiod: 'Nights and days,' and elsewhere: 'Both when he goes to bed and   5
when returns/The golden sun.' It is often found in Homer also: 'All the nights and days.'

25 **Terra marique**
    By land and sea

By land and sea also has the look of a proverb, used whenever we describe great effort and eager desire. Theognis: 'For over land and sea, Cyrnus,/

* * * * *

23 The Cicero-passage must be the source of this, although the text of the quotation is a late addition. Otto 1828; Tilley T 422 Tooth and nail. I iv 15 is close in sense.
 6 Lucian] *Dialogi mortuorum* 21(11).4
 8 Cicero] *Tusculanae disputationes* 2.24.56, added in 1526

24 Included in *Collectanea* no 40 with I iv 15 and 16
 4 Horace] *Ars poetica* 269
 5 Hesiod] *Theogony* 724; *Works and Days* 385, 562; ibid 339
 6 Homer] *Odyssey* passim, the Greek and its Latin version added in 1515

25 This familiar phrase, so summarily treated here, is dealt with more fully in *Adagia* IV x 26. Otto 1762
 4 Theognis] 179–80 (see I i 62n).

Some freedom must be sought from wretched poverty.' And Horace: 5
'Fleeing from poverty through sea, through rocks, through fire.'

26   **Toto pectore**
     With the whole heart

When we describe sincere and perfect love, we say 'whole-hearted' or 'with
all one's soul,' παντὶ στήθει καὶ παντὶ θύμῳ. Cicero in the first book of the *De
legibus*: 'What becomes of that sacred thing, friendship, if the friend himself   5
is not loved for his own sake with the whole heart, as people say?' Aristotle
too in the *Ethics* quotes, and quotes as a proverb, 'with the whole soul.'
'With the whole heart' however can also refer to earnest study and diligence.
Cicero uses it in this way in his *Letters to Friends*, book 13 epistle 1: 'Let us
whole-heartedly consider Scapula's house and gardens.' Again in book 12:   10
'Give yourself up whole-heartedly to this thought.' Seneca, letter 3: 'Ponder
for a long time whether you should admit a given person to your friendship;
but when you have decided to admit him, welcome him with your whole
heart.' Cornelius Tacitus in the *Dialogue on Orators*: 'And this singleness of
mind and strict upbringing pointed to one result: each of them had a   15
single-minded integrity, not warped by any vicious habits, which could
absorb the liberal arts at once with the whole heart.' St Augustine has
somewhere 'with the whole vitals, as they say,' as though the image was
made less coarse by popular usage. 'With the whole heart' is the phrase in
Hebrew.   20

* * * * *

5 Horace] *Epistles* 1.1.46, added in *1515*. This recurs in II iii 55.

26 This seems to be a common Latin expression (Otto 1368), provided by Erasmus
   with a Greek equivalent in order that it may be married with a similar, but much
   rarer phrase in Greek.
4 Cicero] *De legibus* 1.18.49
6 Aristotle] *Ethics*; this has not been traced. The Greek phrase was added in *1533*.
9 Cicero] *Ad Atticum* (not *Ad familiares*) 13.12.4; 12.35, added in *1523*
11 Seneca] *Letters* 3.2, inserted in *1533*
14 Tacitus] *Dialogus de oratoribus* 28.7, inserted in *1533*. The *Dialogus* had been in
   print since about 1470; the fact that Erasmus' seven references to it in the *Adagia*
   are all additions of *1533* may not be unconnected with the publication in that
   year by Froben in Basel of a text edited by Beatus Rhenanus.
17 Augustine] Untraced
20 Hebrew] Eg Deuteronomy 4:29; added in *1528*. We have lost a small distinction
   here by using so freely the English idiom 'heart.' Erasmus used *pectus*, 'breast'
   for the Latin; *animus*, 'soul' for the Greek; and *cor*, 'heart' to represent the
   Hebrew.

27 **Molli brachio, levi brachio**
With a gentle touch, a light touch

Almost the opposite of these are With a gentle touch, With a light touch
[literally 'arm'], by which we signify work not taken seriously. Cicero in the
second book of the *Letters to Atticus*: 'As you take me to task with a gentle   5
touch, as it were, for my friendly relations with Pompey, I should not wish
you to think thus.' To the same, book 4: 'The consuls, who handled the
business with a light touch, referred the position to the senate.'

28 **Omni telorum genere oppugnare**
To fight with every kind of weapon

This is found among the appropriate writers to mean 'to pursue in every
possible way.' The metaphor may seem to be taken from that Homeric line:
'With spear and sword and immense stones they press.' Close to this is 'with   5
cut and thrust,' these being the two ways by which we assail the enemy.

29 **Cominus atque eminus**
At close quarters and at long range

Ἐγγύθεν καὶ πόρρωθεν, At close quarters and at long range, belongs to the
same form and is also from war, in which the fighting is now hand-to-hand
with swords, now with machines which hurl missiles at the enemy from a   5
distance. If this is transferred to the things of the mind, it will be more
attractive: peace must be kept between men, but with vices we must fight,
both at close quarters and at long range. Hand-to-hand fighting in Greek is
συστάδην μάχεσθαι, spear-fighting is διὰ δοράτων μάχεσθαι.

       * * * * *

27 Otto 270 and 271. From Cicero *Ad Atticum* 2.1.6; 4.17.3

28 Derived perhaps from Livy; an obvious metaphor, rather than a proverbial
    expression
 4 Homeric line] *Iliad* 11.265
 6 cut and thrust] Livy 22.46.5

29 Another common metaphor from warfare. The second sentence is of 1517/8 and
    the third of 1533.

30 Omnem movere lapidem
To leave no stone unturned

Πάντα λίθον κίνει, Leave no stone unturned: that is, try everything, leave
nothing unattempted. Many writers say that this adage arose in the following way. When Xerxes made war on the Greeks, and was vanquished at   5
Salamis, he himself moved away from there but left Mardonius behind to
carry on the war in his name. When the latter had also been worsted in the
fight at Plataeae, and had taken flight, a rumour got about that Mardonius
had left an immense treasure buried in the ground near his tent. Incited by
this prospect, Polycrates, a Theban, bought that piece of ground. However, 10
when he had looked for the treasure long and thoroughly, and had made no
progress, he consulted the oracle of Delphi, as to how he could find that
money. Apollo replied in these words 'Leave no stone unturned.' As soon as
he had done this, he found, they say, a great hoard of gold. Others think the
metaphor comes from those who hunt for crabs along the seashore; for the   15
crabs usually lie hidden under rocks which the people looking for them
move.
      The adage is also found with the word rock *petra* instead of stone *lapis*,
Πάντα κινήσω πέτρον, meaning 'I'll risk everything.' Euripides in the
Heraclidae, where the phrase means 'to leave nothing undone.' Pliny the   20
Younger in one of his letters: 'I make straight for the throat and concentrate
on that. He certainly concentrates on his chosen target, but he often makes a
bad choice. I pointed out that it might be the knee or shin or ankle when he
thought he had the throat. I can't see the throat, I said, so my method is to
feel my way and try everything – in fact I leave no stone unturned.' St Basil   25
to his nephews: 'For the preparations for our journey, we must, as they say,
leave no stone unturned.'
      Perhaps Theocritus is alluding to this in his *Boucoliastae*: 'And from the
line she moves the stone.' He is speaking of Galatea wantonly trying every-

* * * * *

30 *Collectanea* no 449 gave this briefly, from the Greek proverb-collections, to
   which Erasmus himself refers here. Tilley s 890 To leave no stone unturned.
4 Many writers] Zenobius 3.63; Suidas II 223. See also Diogenianus 5.41.
18 also found] Diogenianus 7.42
19 Euripides] *Heraclidae* 1002
20 Pliny the Younger] *Letters* 1.20.14–5 (tr Betty Radice). Pliny uses the proverb in
   Greek; and familiar as it is to us, it seems not to have become naturalized in
   classical Latin.
25 St Basil] See I i 2 line 144n; *Ad adulescentes* 10 (PG 31.588C; p 60 Boulenger).
28 Theocritus] 6.18, the title of the idyll added in 1526. This metaphor from moving
   'men' or pieces on a board (which recurs in I v 55) is something quite different.

thing to make Polyphemus angry with her; I have mentioned this else-   30
where. The commentator points out that this is a proverb and means the
same as 'to shake out every rope.' He adds that the metaphor comes from
some sort of game in which a player who cannot vanquish his opponent by
any other means moves from the back line a piece called the 'king.' However, what he says about the stone statue which Galatea could move by her   35
beauty is more far-fetched, in my opinion.

31   **Omnem rudentem movere**
     To move every rope

Πάντα κάλων σείειν, To shake out every rope. This has a different figurative
origin but the same meaning. Aristophanes in the *Knights*: 'Now you must
let out every rope, And keep your spirit high and words ineluctable.' Lucian   5
in his *False Prophet*: 'And I began to move every rope wishing to get revenge.'
Apollonius in the *Epistle to Euphrates*: 'They say that a merchant ought to
move every rope.' Plato in the dialogue entitled *Sisyphus*: 'Let us therefore
reflect carefully, by heaven! letting out, as they say, every rope, and uttering
all sounds.' Julius Pollux in his *Vocabulary*, book 1: 'We sailed letting out   10
every rope,' and 'with all our cordage.' In this way he describes a difficult
voyage, in which everything must be tried.

* * * * *

30   elsewhere] *Adagia* I i 25 and I ix 97, the cross-reference added in *1515*
31   commentator] The ancient scholia on the Theocritus-passage; added in *1526*.
     The proverb quoted by the scholiast follows immediately here, I iv 31.

31   From the Greek proverb-collections (Zenobius 5.62; Suidas π 221)
 4   Aristophanes] *Knights* 756–7; one might have expected a reference to Euripides
     Medea 278, where the same phrase occurs. For 'spirit' in *1508* Erasmus rightly
     had the Greek *lêma*; this was changed in *1515* to *lemma*, and it is not clear
     what he thought the meaning to be.
 5   Lucian] *Alexander* 57, for which *False Prophet* is an alternative title
 7   Apollonius] A vegetarian miracle-working sage or charlatan of the first century
     AD, from Tyana in Asia Minor. The letters ascribed to him are accessible as
     printed by F.C. Conybeare (Loeb Classical Library) in the second volume of
     Philostratus' life of Apollonius, a work which will be used later in the *Adagia*.
     This is from Ep 7 (2.412 of the print).
 8   Plato] *Sisyphus* (a spurious dialogue) 389c, added in *1528*
10   Pollux] *Onomasticon* 1.107, added in *1515* (see I i 4n).
11   In this way] It is not evident that Erasmus understood this adage. The ropes of
     which it speaks are said to be the brails, the small ropes attached to the sails of a
     ship with which they can be reefed or partially furled, in order to control the
     area of sail exposed to the wind; and to shake out or let out these would have
     the effect of increasing the ship's speed. The difficulty of the voyage is not in
     issue.

32 Omnem iacere aleam
To cast all the dice

To cast all the dice means to risk everything, to commit all to the will of
fortune. Dice, in fact, is a game of chance rather than skill. So in a figurative
way, when we describe a thing of uncertain outcome, as if it depended not 5
on the will of the thrower but on luck, we say 'the die is cast.' Thus Terence
in the *Adelphoe* said that 'the life of man is like playing the dice – what does
not fall right in the throw you must correct by skill.' Lucian in the dialogue
entitled *For the Images*: 'I shall dare to cast the dice.' Euripides in the *Rhesus*:
'He should receive a reward worthy of his toil / Who risks his life on 10
Fortune's dice!' Aristides in *Pericles*: 'And a single die was cast on behalf of
everything, life, money, reputation, political leadership.' When Caesar
came to the Rubicon, the river which divides Italy from Gaul, he hesitated
privately and considered in his mind what a difficult thing he was proposing
to do; when his spirits were revived by a sign, he said, 'Let us go whither we 15
are called by the portents of the gods and the wickedness of our enemies; let
the die be cast.' Plutarch in the *Apophthegmata* recalls that a phrase like this
was used, 'let every die be cast.' Lucan has an allusion to this. 'Let the die of
fate be cast, / Which will sink one or the other.' Plutarch in the *Life of
Coriolanus* seems to have used the term 'last dice' in the same sense, 'throw- 20
ing, as it were, the last dice.' And so Petronius Arbiter: 'The die is cast, let
Fortune be the judge.' Cicero in his *On Divination*, book 2: 'Do you fail to see
in choosing the victim it is almost like a throw of the dice, especially as facts

* * * * *

32 *Collectanea* no 771 cited several authorities of doubtful relevance (but Suetonius
was included), and for the *Chiliades* Erasmus virtually made a fresh start. The
Greek proverb-collections (Apostolius 2.93; Suidas A 2310) give the phrase in
the form 'Let the die be cast,' 'The die is cast,' so his prime source was very
likely Plutarch, who has 'all the dice.' Otto 55 and 1768; Tilley D 326 The die is
cast.
6 Terence] *Adelphoe* 739–41, referred to in 1533 in IV ix 75
8 Lucian] *Pro imaginibus* 16
9 Euripides] *Rhesus* 182–3
11 Aristides] *De quattuor* p 190 Dindorf (see I i 13n).
12 Caesar] Suetonius *Divus Julius* 32 (see I i 78n).
17 Plutarch] *Moralia* 206C
18 Lucan] 6.7–8. This most brilliant of all Latin epics is used in the *Adagia* only four
times.
19 Plutarch] *Coriolanus* 3, added in 1526
21 Petronius] *Satyricon* 122, line 174 (see I ii 51n).
22 Cicero] *De divinatione* 2.15.36, added in 1536

prove it? For when the entrails of the first victim are disastrous and have
been without a head, which is the most fatal of all signs, it often happens   25
that the sacrifice of the next victim is altogether favourable.' Here Cicero is
using 'dice' for chance.

It seems as if the adage were derived from Menander; for Athenaeus,
book 13, gives some lines from a comedy of his called *Arrhephorus*, or the
Flute-Player: 'If you are wise you will not marry, leaving this life behind. I   30
myself did marry, therefore I urge you not to marry.' To this the other
replies: 'The matter's settled, let this die be cast.' The Greek lines in Athenaeus are rather deformed by the ignorance of the scribes. But they can be
restored with very little trouble. I think they were first written like this
[*second version follows*]. According to Plutarch, Plato said that life is like a   35
game of dice; one must throw properly, and whatever falls to one's lot, one
must use it rightly. What falls, is in the hand of fortune; but to apportion
rightly what has fallen to us by chance, is for us to do. This is the comparison
which Terence seems to have imitated in the *Adelphoe*.

33   **Vela ventis permittere**
     To spread the sails to the winds

Quintilian uses a similar figure in the preface to his *Institutiones Oratoriae*:
'Let us spread our sails to the winds, and wish good luck to those who leave
the shore,' that is, let us try out the uncertain fate of publishing, whatever   5
may befall. Seneca in the *Agamemnon* has a very similar saying, 'I gave my
craft to the waves,' that is, I committed my all to the will of fortune.
Theognis: 'Wherefore now we are borne on, unfurling to the winds our
white sails.' The Greeks beautifully say 'to be carried along by swelling
white sails' for someone who is urged towards some goal with all his heart   10
and all his efforts. So Plutarch on Scipio, in the 'Elder Cato.' Cato rebuked

* * * * *

28 Menander] Frag 59.1–4, cited by Athenaeus 13.559d–e; added in 1523, the
   Latin version in 1526, and the textual comment (which is mistaken) in 1528
35 Plato] *Republic* 10.604c, referred to by Plutarch *Moralia* 112F and 467A
39 Terence] *Adelphoe* 739, as above

33 *Collectanea* no 776. *Adagia* IV vi 1 is similar, V i 32 is the opposite.
 3 Quintilian] In his letter to Trypho, which precedes the *Institutio oratoria*
 6 Seneca] *Agamemnon* 143
 8 Theognis] 671 (see I i 62n).
 9 The Greeks] In Greek 'by swelling white sails' is one compound word, which
   originally was applied to the wind and meant 'filling the sails.' This sentence,
   with the illustration from Plutarch which follows, is an addition of 1526.
11 Plutarch] *Marcus Cato* 3.6, added in 1526

Scipio for using bribes for corruption. Scipio replied that he had no need of an over-diligent treasurer since he himself was carried on 'with swelling sails' towards war. Ovid: 'And because I am carried along on the great sea and have spread full sails to the winds.'   15

34   Sub omni lapide scorpius dormit
Under every stone sleeps a scorpion

Ὑπὸ παντὶ λίθῳ σκορπίος εὕδει, Under every stone sleeps a scorpion, or to keep the metre (an anapaestic dimeter), *est sub lapide scorpius omni*. The adage warns us that a man should beware of speaking heedlessly in the   5
presence of fault-finders and slanderers; for whatever he touches, there is a risk that he will be stung. Scorpions do normally hide under stones, and if a rash person dislodges them he will get himself stung and be wounded. This aptly fits ill-tempered people who will argue about anything, or lazy ones, who will use the most trivial excuses to escape doing a job of work. Aris-   10
tophanes in the *Thesmophoriazusae*:

> I praise the ancient proverb,
> One must look beneath every stone
> Lest a politician bite you.

The commentator on Nicander cites the following line from the *Captives* of   15
Sophocles: 'For under every stone a scorpion keeps watch.' That is, nothing is safe, everything demands caution.

35   Asinus ad lyram
An ass to the lyre

Ὄνος λύρας, An ass [we must supply, listening] to the lyre. This is a hit at people who lack judgment through their ignorance, people who have dull

* * * * *

14 Ovid] *Metamorphoses* 15.176–7, added in 1536

34 *Collectanea* no 687, very briefly, from Diogenianus 8.59 (also in Zenobius 6.20 and Suidas γ 534). Tilley s 894 Under every stone sleeps a scorpion.
4 metre] This suggestion was added in 1517/8.
10 Aristophanes] *Thesmophoriazusae* 528–30
16 Sophocles] Frag 34 Nauck, cited by the scholiast on Nicander *Theriaca* 18 (see I ii 86n).

35 *Collectanea* no 125, citing Gellius and Jerome *Letter* 61. It is also in the Greek proverb-collections (Diogenianus 7.33; Suidas o 391), but these need not have been used. Otto 184; Tilley A 366 To see an ass play on a harp

ears. Varro gave this proverbial title to one of his *Satires*. In Gellius are to be 5
found these words of his, extracted from the Satire entitled *The Will*: 'If an
only son, or more than one, is born to me in ten months, and if they turn out
to be asses at the lyre, they shall be disinherited'; meaning by this phrase
unteachable, as far as good learning is concerned, and unmanageable. St
Jerome to Marcella: 'Although I could justifiably set these people aside, since 10
it is useless for the lyre to play to the ass, yet lest they accuse us of pride, as
they usually do ...' and again against Vigilantius: 'Although it is a stupid
thing that I am doing, to seek masters for the master of all, and to place a
restraint on him, who does not know how to speak and cannot keep silent.
There is a true proverb in Greek, An ass to the lyre.' Lucian *On Salaried Posts*: 15
'For what communication can there be, as they say, between the ass and the
lyre?' And *Against An Ignoramus*: 'But you are an ass listening to the lyre and
wagging your ears.' Hence the adage is used in this form, 'the ass twitching
its ears,' or again, 'Someone told a story to an ass, and it twitched its ears.'
This is turned against those people who understand nothing, and yet make 20
play with nods and smiles to those who are talking, as if there were nothing
they did not understand. It is natural to the donkey to twitch its ears as if to
convey that it has understood, when it has not even heard.

Sometimes applied to the ass not listening to the lyre, but trying to play
itself. Lucian: 'Especially when he plays, he wants to appear merry and 25
charming, an ass, as they say, himself playing on the lyre.' Again in
Pseudologista: 'As the popular saying goes, an ass seeing the lyre and trying
to play.' This line is also quoted: 'The donkey listened to the lyre, the porker
to the trumpet.' This can be applied to people who make an unseemly
attempt to follow a craft of which they have no experience, having rather a 30
natural unfitness for it. Stratonicus turns it round amusingly in Athenaeus,
Doctors at Dinner, book 8: There was a certain Cleon, nicknamed the Bull,
who sang well, but had not an equal knowledge of the lyre. When Stratonicus heard him play, he said, 'There was an old saying about an ass at the
lyre, but now it's the bull at the lyre.' 35

* * * * *

5 Varro] *Menippean Satires* 543 (see I ii 60n), cited by Gellius 3.16.13.
10 Jerome] *Letters* 27.1.2; 61.4.1
15 Lucian] *De mercede conductis* 25; *Adversus indoctum* 4
18 in this form] Zenobius 5.42, Diogenianus 7.30, Suidas o 393; Otto 183. The
   second of these alternative forms reappears, with more material, in IV vii 36.
25 Lucian] *Dialogi meretricii* 14.4; *Pseudologista* 7
28 This line] Cited by Suidas o 391. When this was added here in *1533*, Erasmus
   must have overlooked that it already followed immediately afterwards; he also
   made for it a new, and in details slightly different, Latin version.
31 Athenaeus] 8.349 c–d, added in *1517/8*

36 Sus tubam audivit
The pig heard the trumpet

Σάλπιγγος ὗς ἤκουε, The pig heard the trumpet. This will fit people who
hear good talk but neither understand nor admire it; or those who are
neither pleased nor moved by what they hear. Horses are incited to war by   5
the sound of the trumpet, but it drives the pig away rather than inspiring it
to fight. Suidas gives an iambic line of this kind: 'Unmoved the donkey hears
the lyre, the pig the trumpet.'

37 Nihil graculo cum fidibus
A jackdaw has no business with a lute

A jackdaw has no business with a lute. That is, stupid and ignorant people
have nothing to do with good learning. For the jackdaw is a silly troublesome chatterbox, and a noisy one, so much so that it is thought the name   5
comes from the chatter, according to Quintilian in the first book of the
Institutions: 'Then it loves to congregate with its kind, so as to make the noise
more tedious by general chattering.' But the lute requires silence and attentive ears. At the end of the preface of the Attic Nights of Aulus Gellius, this
adage is neatly turned against certain dull-witted fellows endowed with   10
stupid loquacity, profane, amousoi (that is, averse to the rites of the Muses),
people who can either laugh at polished literature and refined knowledge or
even despise it, but never understand it; people who only appreciate what
they themselves have learnt, of course – squalid, wordless, ignorant stuff.
These people are equally insistent on disturbing the teaching of others and 15
advertising their own ignorance and forcing it on everybody; they despise
anyone except themselves. This is the kind of man Gellius is taking a stick to
in his collections, the most polished and erudite possible. 'There is an old
adage,' says he, 'a jackdaw has no business with a lute.'

* * * * *

36 From Suidas o 391; compare the preceding adage.

37 *Collectanea* no 3 combined this with the adage that follows here, citing the
passage from Gellius' preface. The sense is not far from I vii 22 Graculus inter
Musas. Otto 766; Tilley J 38 The jay is unmeet for a fiddle. But Tilley also quotes
a much closer version from Sir Thomas Elyot's *Dictionary* (1538) 'The daw hath
nothing to do with the lute, nor the sow with marjoram.'
6 Quintilian] 1.6.37, added in *1528* to I ii 23
9 Gellius] Praefatio 19

38   Nihil cum amaracino sui
     A pig has nothing to do with marjoram

He (Gellius) immediately adds another similar phrase: 'A pig has nothing to
do with marjoram,' meaning that to stupid people the very best things are
stinking and unpleasant. Marjoram is a kind of plant named in the Sicilian   5
tongue after a son of Cynaras, king of Cyprus, called Amaracus who is said
in legend to have been changed into this plant. But Servius, on book 1 of the
Aeneid, writes that Amaracus was the king's page in charge of perfumes,
who accidentally fell while carrying them and created a supreme scent by
the mixture; hence the best perfumes began to be called *amaracina*, and he   10
was later changed into this plant. It is also called *samsucum*, and has many
other names, as Dioscorides asserts in his third book, where he says it has a
most delightful perfume, and every part of it is scented. Pliny, book 13
chapter 1, mentions *amaracinum* among the finest perfumes, and tells how in
Cos it was once highly praised; later *melinum* was preferred there. Then he   15
shows that *samsucum* is mixed with various other perfumes, such as *telinum*,
though a splendid ointment can be made from the juice of the *amaracus*
itself. Pliny also writes, book 21 chapter 22, that the most highly prized and
scented *samsucum* comes from Cyprus, and he explores various uses of it as
remedies. An oil is also made from it, called *amaracinum* or *samsucinum*.   20
         This, then, is what *amaracinum* is like, and on the contrary there is
nothing dirtier than the pig, and nothing that likes dirt more. For this reason
Virgil says, 'Foul pigs remember,' and Horace, 'or else mud-loving swine,'
and 'Gallops the miry pig.' Nothing is less suited to a pig's snout than
refinements of perfume; what smells sweet to it is what smells of filth. This is   25
particularly true of marjoram, among all the scents; it is inimical to the
swinish tribe through some particular property of its own, and virtually

                * * * * *

38 Combined in *Collectanea* no 3 with the preceding, while the passage from
    Cicero used here towards the end provided *Coll.* no 706. Otto 1720. For a
    version in Tudor English, see the headnote to I iv 37. There was perhaps
    another. The Latin for marjoram is *origanum*. Anyone who saw this proverb in
    Latin paired, as it often is, with our no 35 *Asinus ad lyram* might expect the pig,
    like the ass, to be confronted with some inappropriate musical instrument. If he
    did not know the word *origanum*, he might well confuse it with *organum*; and
    the result in English would be Tilley P 306 A pig plays on the organs.
3   Gellius] *Noctes Atticae*, praefatio 19
7   Servius] The fourth-century commentator on Virgil *Aeneid* 1.693
12 Dioscorides] *De materia medica* 3.39 (see I i 22n).
13 Pliny] *Naturalis historia* 13.1.5 (also 10 and 13); 21.163
23 Virgil] *Georgics* 1.400
23 Horace] *Epistles* 1.2.26; 2.2.75

poisonous to them, if we are to believe Lucretius, who has these lines in his
sixth book: 'In fact the pig flees marjoram, and fears / All scent, stark poison
to the bristly swine.'   30

The Egyptians of old considered the pig such a disgusting animal that
if anyone had happened to touch one in passing he would at once run to the
river to wash himself and his clothes. Swineherds, even native to the
country, they held in such detestation that they were not admitted into the
temples, and marriage and relationships arising from marriage were forbid-   35
den to them, according to Herodotus, book 2.

Cicero appears to have been thinking of this proverb when he says 'to
so-and-so an alabaster vase full of scent smells bad,' meaning that the best
things are as distasteful to him as the worst. Something of the same sort can
be said of the dung-beetle; to him perfume is dung and filth is perfume.   40
Plutarch suggests that this was currently said in common speech, when he
says in his essay comparing the doctrines of the Stoics with the words of the
poets: 'They say that beetles flee from perfume but pursue a foul smell.'

39 Quid cani et balneo?
What has a dog to do with a bath?

Τί κοινὸν κυνὶ καὶ βαλανείῳ; What has a dog to do with a bath? I quote this
adage with all the more pleasure because it refreshes and renews my
memory, and my affection, for Rodolphus Agricola of Friesland, whom I   5
name as the man in all Germany and Italy most worthy of the highest public
honour: in Germany, because she gave him birth, in Italy, because she made
him a great scholar. No one was ever born this side of the Alps more
completely endowed with all literary gifts; let this be said without prejudice.

* * * * *

28 Lucretius] *De rerum natura* 6.973–4 (see I ii 38n).
36 Herodotus] 2.47, added in 1515 (see I i 96n).
37 Cicero] *Academica* 2 frag 11, cited by Nonius (see I i 97n) p 545.
41 Plutarch] *Moralia* 1058A

39 Much of this material, including a rather shorter panegyric on Rodolphus
   Agricola, with Barbaro's epitaph and the mention of Alexander Hegius, was
   given already in 1500 in the *Collectanea* no 25. The Greek proverb could be from
   Suidas τ 584.
 5 Rodolphus Agricola] Otherwise Huisman (1444–85), from Baflo in Friesland,
   one of the greatest of the early northern humanists. Erasmus had already
   written a glowing tribute to him, and to his pupil Hegius, in 1489(?) in Ep 23;
   see the notes in Allen Ep 23:57n and in CWE Ep 23:58n. He tells us in *Adagia*
   III iii 62 (in an addition of 1515) that Agricola owed his death to his doctor's
   delay in coming to see him.

There was no branch of fine learning in which that great man could not vie   10
with the most eminent masters. Among the Greeks he was the best Greek of
them all, among the Latins the best Latin. As a poet you would have said he
was a second Virgil; as a writer of prose he had the charm of a Poliziano, but
more dignity. His style, even extempore, had such purity, such naturalness,
that you would maintain it was not a Frisian who spoke, but a native of   15
ancient Rome herself. Such perfect eloquence was paired with the same
degree of learning. He had delved into all the mysteries of philosophy.
There was no part of music in which he was not accurately versed. At the
very end of his life he had bent his whole mind on the study of Hebrew and
the Holy Scripture. In the midst of these efforts he was snatched from this   20
world by the envy of the fates, not yet forty years old, as I am told. There are
a few literary remains of his work, some letters, poems of various kinds; the
Axiochus of Plato translated into Latin, and a version of Isocrates' *To Demon-
icus*. Then there are a couple of lectures given in public session in the
University of Ferrara, for it was there he both learnt and gave open lectures.   25
There were lying hidden in some people's possession his treatises on dialectic, and they have recently appeared, but in a mutilated state. He had also
translated some of Lucian's dialogues. But since he himself cared little for
glory, and most mortals are, to say the least of it, careless in looking after the
work of others, none of these have yet seen the light. But the works which   30
are extant, even if not published by himself, give plain proof of something
divine about the man.

Let it not be thought that I as a German am blinded by patriotic feeling;
to avoid this I will transcribe the epitaph written for him by Ermolao Barbaro
of Venice. It is superb, and one might find it difficult to decide whether it   35
was more worthy of the man who wrote it or the man it was written about.
Here it is:

> Under this stone, the jealous Fates decreed
> The Frisian hope, his country's light, should come,
> Rudolph Agricola; in life, indeed,   40
> He brought such praise to Germany his home
> As ever Greece could have, or ever Rome.

* * * * *

21 as I am told] Added in *1517/8*
26 were lying hidden] In *1508–23* this was 'are lying hidden'; but in *1521*
   Agricola's *De inventione dialectica* was published by J. Knoblouch at Strasbourg,
   so the phrase was altered in *1526*, and 'they have recently appeared' etc was
   added.
34 Ermolao Barbaro] The eminent Italian humanist (1454–95), often referred to by
   Erasmus, and praised in *Adagia* IV vi 18

What ampler or more magnificent tribute could be paid to our dear Rodolphus than this splendid testimony, so complete, and offered not to a living
man but to one already dead – so there is no question of its proceeding from   45
affection rather than from judgment? and to a German, so there is no
possibility that love for a country they both shared should diminish the
weight of the testimony? And it came from that man who had brought glory
not only to his native Italy, but to this whole age of ours; whose authority is
such among all learned men that it would be most impertinent to disagree   50
with him; whose work in restoring literature is so outstandingly valuable
that anyone would have to be utterly impervious to culture, or at least
utterly ungrateful, who did not hold the memory of Ermolao as sacrosanct.

Such full and ungrudging praise of this man has, I confess, a singular
charm for me, because I happened while yet a boy to have his disciple   55
Alexander Hegius as my teacher. He was headmaster of the once famous
school of the town of Deventer, where I learned the rudiments of both
languages when I was almost a child. To put it in a few words, he was a man
just like his master: as upright in his life as he was serious in his teaching.
Momus himself could have found no fault in him except one, that he cared   60
less for fame than he need have done, and took no heed of posterity. If he
wrote anything, he wrote as if he were playing a game rather than doing
something serious. And yet these writings, so written, are of the sort which
the learned world votes worthy of immortality.

So it was not without thought that I plunged into this digression; not to   65
boast of the glory of Germany, but to perform the duty of a grateful pupil,
and acquit myself of the debt I owe to the memory of both these men,
because I owe to one the loving respect of a son, and to the other the
affection of a grandson.

Now to turn to the adage, which I remember having learnt from a   70
certain very learned letter of my beloved Rodolphus, at a time when I was a
mere child and as yet ignorant of Greek. In this letter he is trying to persuade
the town council of Antwerp, with conviction and eloquence, that they
should appoint as master of their school someone proficient in liberal
studies, and not (as they usually do) entrust this office to an inarticulate   75
theologian or naturalist, the sort of man who is sure he has something to say
about everything but has no notion of what it is to speak. 'What good would
he be in a school? As much good, to use the Greek repartee, as a dog in a
bath.'

* * * * *

56 Alexander Hegius] Rector of the school at Deventer 1483–98, referred to again
in *Adagia* II ii 81; see CWE Ep 23n.
58 when I was almost a child] This clause was added in *1515*.

Lucian *Against an Ignoramus*: 'And each one of the onlookers im-   80
mediately voices that very handy proverb: what do a dog and a bath have in
common?' Again in the *Parasite*: 'But to my way of thinking, a philosopher at
a drinking-party is just like a dog in a bath.' So this is to be applied to those
who are totally useless for certain purposes, just as there is no use for dogs in
a bath.   85

40   **Asinum sub freno currere doces**
     You teach a donkey to race with a bit

You teach a donkey to race with a bit. That is, you are teaching the unteachable. For a horse is suitable for racing but a donkey is useless in a horse race.
Horace: 'You waste your labour, as if one should try / To make an ass run   5
docile to the curb.' Acron indicates that this is a proverbial saying about
donkeys. There is another one different from this, which we have quoted
elsewhere: 'The horse to the plain.'

41   **Alienam metis messem**
     You are reaping another's harvest

'Αλλότριον ἀμᾷς θέρος, You are reaping another's harvest. There are two
ways of using this adage: it fits equally well when applied to people who
take over advantages gained by the labour of others, and to those who are   5
not diligent enough about their own affairs. The metaphor arises from the
old custom among neighbouring farmers of lending each other aid in reaping their crops. It is the way of men to be much more attentive to their own
business than to that of others. This is neatly expressed by that old fable
about the crested lark, which I would readily tell, if it were not easy for   10
anyone to read it in Aulus Gellius. It can also refer to a thing which

* * * * *

80 Lucian] *Adversus indoctum* 5; *De parasito* 51, the latter added in 1520

40 *Collectanea* no 555, from Horace, in very similar wording. Otto 181
 5 Horace] *Satires* 1.1.90–1, with the ancient commentary ascribed to Acron
 8 elsewhere] *Adagia* I viii 82

41 *Collectanea* no 141 (no 749, which is a doublet in different wording, seems to
   have been neglected); this is used in part almost verbatim. The Greek comes no
   doubt from Diogenianus 2.75 (it is also in Suidas A 1344). Otto 152. See I v 32.
11 Gellius] 2.29.2–16. The fable is Aesop 210 Halm, and also in Babrius' collection
   in Greek verse (no 88). A crested lark has nested in a field of grain; and as long
   as she hears the farmer arranging for neighbours and kinsmen to come and help
   harvest the field, she does not trouble to move. When they fail to appear, and

sometimes happens, when those who have done the sowing are thrown out
and others take their place, and enjoy the fruits of others' toil with no trouble
to themselves. Hence Virgil's phrase, 'for whom did we sow our fields?'
Aristophanes in the *Knights*: 'reaping someone else's harvest.' This is   15
against Cleon, who came when everything was ready and the result had
been prepared with great efforts by Demosthenes, captured Pylos, and took
over all the glory of the victory for himself, leaving Demosthenes nothing
but unpopularity. Homer says something like this in the *Odyssey*, book 1:
'Since with impunity they eat another's sustenance.' And Aristophanes in   20
the play just mentioned expresses the same idea: 'Walking about, I stole
from a shop / The prepared pot cooked by another.'

42 **Penelopes telam retexere**
    To unravel Penelope's web

To unravel Penelope's web. That is, to take up a useless task, and then undo
what one has done. It comes from Homer, who in the second book of the
Odyssey makes Penelope, the wife of Ulysses, hoodwink the suitors who are   5
already pressing her urgently, by making this condition, that she will marry
when she has finished the piece of weaving she has in hand. They agreed to
the condition, and the clever woman began every night to unravel what she
had woven during the day: 'Every day she kept weaving a large web, / But in
the night, with torches placed beside her, she unravelled it.' Plato takes over   10
this adage in the *Phaedo*. So does Cicero in the *Academic Questions*, book 2:
'What of the fact that this same science destroys at the end the steps that
came before, like Penelope unweaving her web?' He is thinking of dialectic,
which by the same reasoning which has been used to make an assertion

* * * * *

she hears him say 'To-morrow we'll do it ourselves,' she gathers her nestlings
and quits forthwith. Gellius' version was reprinted at the beginning of the
Aldine Aesop of October 1502; it is used again in IV i 42.
14 Virgil] *Eclogues* 1.72
15 Aristophanes] *Knights* 392
19 Homer] *Odyssey* 1.160
20 Aristophanes] *Knights* 744–5

42 *Collectanea* no 399, beginning 'I remember reading in Plato.' Otto 1379; Tilley P
186 Penelope's web. With this begins a series of over fifty adages indicating
labour misdirected, to which others might be added, eg II viii 37 Calvum vellis,
You pluck the hair of a bald man.
 4 Homer] *Odyssey* 2.104–5
10 Plato] *Phaedo* 84a
11 Cicero] *Lucullus* 29.95

subsequently weakens and destroys it, so that nothing seems to have been   15
settled. Seneca, *De beneficiis*, book 5: 'For what is the good of laboriously
untying knots which you yourself have made in order that you might untie
them?' Aristides in the *Defence of Four Orators*: 'And unravelling I know not
what web; for whatever wisdom they have gained, they lose as much by
turning out so arrogant.' Since he joins this to other proverbs which we shall   20
mention later, he indicates clearly that this too is a proverb.

43   **Annosam arborem transplantare**
      To transplant an aged tree

Γεράνδρυον μεταφυτεύειν, To transplant an aged tree, is said about people
who at a late time of life, already past their prime, try to unlearn the customs
they have been long used to as young men. Or it may be simply applied to   5
those things which we attempt in vain. A tree must not be moved from its
place when the roots have already struck deep, but while it is still a small
plant. The ancients declared that a tree should not be transplanted at less
than two years old or more than three, so says Pliny. The proverb appears to
apply particularly to the oak, which of all trees strikes its roots deepest (thus   10
the word used in Greek for 'aged tree' derives from the word for oak); or
perhaps it is because this is thought to have been the first of all trees. For this
reason it was sacred to Jove, and the wood of Dodona was an oak wood,
from which the first of all the oracles are believed to have proceeded.
      Seneca made elegant use of this proverb in his book of *Letters*, Letter   15
86: 'If what I am saying shall seem to you too pessimistic, charge it up against
the country-house where I have learned a lesson from Aegialus, a most
careful householder and now the owner of this estate; he taught me that a
tree can be transplanted, no matter how far gone in years. We old men must

* * * * *

16 Seneca] *De beneficiis* 5.12.2, added in 1528
18 Aristides] See I i 13n; *De quattuor* p 405 Dindorf. Cf I iv 78.
21 later] *Adagia* I iv 77 and 78

43 *Collectanea* no 311, no doubt from Diogenianus 3.77 (it is also in Zenobius 3.1
    and Suidas Γ 180). Tilley T 491 Remove an old tree, and it will wither to death.
    Erasmus continued in 1500 'It is commonly said nowadays that an old dog
    never gets used to the leash' (or perhaps 'to the whip'; *vetulum canem vix loris*
    assuescere), 'in which field I have wasted much labour and lamp-oil in days
    gone by.' This was dropped in 1508, perhaps because his attention had turned
    away from proverbs drawn from common speech. But the two proverbs re-
    appear in I ii 61 and I iv 62. Philemon, the comic poet, frag 147 Kock
  9 Pliny] *Naturalis historia* 17.83, added in 1515
 15 Seneca] *Letters* 86.14, added in 1536

learn this precept; for there is none of us who is not planting an olive-grove   20
for his successor.'

44   Arenam metiris
You are measuring the sands

Ἄμμον μετρεῖς, You are seeking the measure of the sands, or counting
them. This is a way of saying: you are taking on something which involves
infinite toil, which you can never bring to an end; or else you are attempting   5
something in vain, which you can never achieve. Athenaeus, book 6, gives
the instance of a certain Alexis, who used the expression 'sand-hundred' for
innumerable as if equal to the sand: 'using sand-numbered names' if I am to
imitate the invented Greek word. Plato in the *Theaetetus*, 'Is more hidden
from him than, as they say, the sands of the sea.'   10

45   Undas numeras
You are counting the waves

Κύματα μετρεῖς, You are counting the waves. This has the same meaning as
the previous one, and both are elegantly touched on by Virgil in the second
book of his *Georgics*:   5

> If you wish to know their number, go and tot up the grains
> Of sand that are whirled around by a sand-storm in the Sahara,
> Or count the waves that break along Adriatic coasts
> When an easterly gale comes down in gusts upon the shipping.

Theocritus in *The Graces*: 'But it is like the toil of measuring the waves on the   10
beach/As many as the wind drives shoreward from the sea.' This seems to

* * * * *

44 *Collectanea* no 138, from Diogenianus 2.27 (also in Zenobius 1.80 and Suidas A
  1621). Otto 786; Tilley s 91 As difficult as to number the sands of the sea
6 Athenaeus] 6.230d, added in 1517/8. Alexis the comic poet uses *psammakosioi*,
  formed from *psammos*, sand, on the analogy of *diakosioi, triakosioi* etc, the normal
  words for two hundred, three hundred and so on; Erasmus coins *arenaginta*,
  arena being sand, like *triginta* and the other Roman numerals up to ninety.
9 Plato] *Theaetetus* 173c, added in 1533. The sand is imported by Erasmus: Plato
  wrote 'than how many gallons of water there are in the sea.'

45 The Greek phrase might be taken direct from Theocritus.
4 Virgil] *Georgics* 2.105–8 (tr C. Day Lewis)
10 Theocritus] 16.60–1. The first line has already been used as an example of the
  impossible as a figure of speech in section xiii of Erasmus' Introduction.

have come from an Aesopic fable recounted by Lucian in his *Sects*. Once a
man sat by the seashore, trying to count the waves one by one; but he was
defeated by waves following close on other waves, and distressed in his
mind because he could not number them. Then a crafty fox encouraged him   15
with a timely piece of advice. 'Why are you distressed,' it said, 'about the
waves which pass? You should begin counting from here, and consider the
rest as finished with.'

46 Surdo oppedere
To break wind in front of a deaf man

Παρὰ κωφῷ ἀποπαρδεῖν, To break wind in the presence of the deaf, is said
when an action is useless, or when some fault is committed against stupid
people who cannot perceive it, or reproaches are heaped on a person who   5
takes no notice, just as if he had not heard. It is mentioned by Diogenianus
and Suidas.

47 Aranearum telas texere
To spin spiders' webs

Τὰ ἀράχνια ὑφαίνειν, To spin spiders' webs. This means to spend infinite
and anxious efforts on some futile thing that is worth nothing. It is mentioned as a proverb by St Basil at the beginning of his exposition of the   5
Hexameron. So also in the life of Zeno by Diogenes Laertius, a certain
philosopher used to say that dialectical reasoning is like spiders' webs,
which look like something constructed with care and accuracy, but are really
trifling and fragile. Someone else compared the laws to webs spun by
spiders, which are easily torn apart by big birds and only trap flies.   10

* * * * *

12 Lucian] *Hermotimus* 84; cf Aesop 60 Halm.

46 Taken, as Erasmus tells us, from the Greek proverb-collections, Diogenianus
   7.43 and Suidas π 371

47 The first sentence is taken over verbatim from *Collectanea* no 596, where St Basil
   was given as the source.
   5 Basil] *Homiliae in Hexaemeron* 1.2 (PG 29.8B)
   6 Diogenes Laertius] Perhaps a confused recollection of a passage in his *Zeno*
   (7.18), where precise and careless language are compared to certain coins well
   and ill struck. The spiders' webs are found, compared with laws, in his life of
   Solon (1.58), a comparison used shortly afterwards by Erasmus in his *Parabolae*
   (616c), and in Tudor England in Tilley L 116 Laws catch little flies, but let great
   flies go free.

48 **Laterem lavas**
    You are washing a brick

There are several proverbs of this kind used in Greek, by which we signify
unprofitable work; as for example Πλίνθον πλύνεις, You are washing a brick,
which is used by Terence in the *Phormio*, 'Shall I speak? I shall rouse anger.   5
Shall I be silent? I shall provoke him. Shall I try to clear myself? I shall be
washing a brick.' Theocritus in *The Graces*: 'And to have washed a black
stone in clear water.'

49 **Lapidem elixas**
    You are boiling a stone

Something very like this is quoted by Aristophanes in a comedy entitled
Wasps: Λίθον ἕψεις, You are cooking a stone, in the sense of 'you are toiling
in vain': 'But when anyone entreated, lowering his head thus, he used to   5
say: "You cook a stone."' For a stone never softens, however long it is
boiled. This will suit in general any vain effort, particularly directed against a
hard man whom no prayers can mollify.

50 **Aethiopem lavas; Aethiopem dealbas**
    You are washing, or whitening, an Ethiopian

These expressions have the same meaning: Αἰθίοπα σμήχεις, You are
washing an Ethiopian, and Αἰθίοπα λευκαίνεις, You are whitening an Ethiopian. Lucian, *Against An Ignoramus*: 'And according to the proverb I am   5

* * * * *

48 This is included in *Collectanea* no 408 in a list of similar phrases, 'by which we
     indicate that a task is hopeless'; the Greek equivalent is probably taken from
     Diogenianus 7.50 (also in Zenobius 6.48 and Suidas II 1776). Otto 922; Tilley
     T 289 To wash a tile.
  5 Terence] *Phormio* 186
  7 Theocritus] 16.62

49 Probably taken direct from Aristophanes *Wasps* 279–80 (which in the original is
     in a lyric metre, and is rendered by Erasmus as prose), though it is found in
     Apostolius 10.68. Another example, from the spurious Platonic *Eryxias* 405b,
     has found its way into III v 84, and there is one in I iv 55.

50 *Collectanea* nos 407 and 414, probably from Diogenianus 1.45 (it is also in
     Zenobius 1.46 and Suidas AI 125). Perhaps a list of these proverbially
     impossible actions in the scholia on Aristophanes *Wasps* 284 also contributed.
     Otto 32; Tilley E 186 To wash an Ethiop white.
  5 Lucian] *Adversus indoctum* 28

trying to wash an Ethiopian.' That inborn blackness of the Ethiopian, which
Pliny thinks to be a result of heat from the nearness of the sun, cannot be
washed away with water nor whitened by any means whatever. This will be
particularly apposite when a matter of doubtful morality is decorated by a
gloss of words, or when praise is given to one who does not deserve praise,   10
or an unteachable person is being taught. The adage, it seems, comes from a
fable of Aesop. A man bought an Ethiopian, and thinking his colour was not
natural, but the result of a former master's negligence, he tried everything
which is used to whiten clothes, and so tormented the poor creature with
perpetual washing that he made the man ill – but still he stayed the colour he   15
had always been.

51   **Arare littus**
To plough the seashore

Αἰγιαλὸν ἀροῦν, To plough the seashore. This means to take fruitless pains.
Ausonius to Theon: 'What are you labouring on, there at the world's end,/O
poet tiller of sands, fated to plough the shore?' meaning that he was   5
labouring in vain. There will be a special appropriateness in using this when
a kindness is bestowed on one from whom you will never see any return; for
instance if one were to teach the donkey to play the lyre, or were to do a
favour to an ungrateful person. For the salt causes the seashore to remain
almost sterile, and there is even a proverb about this: 'a brackish neighbour-   10
hood' meaning infertile. And sea-water is so sterile that it will not even grow
trees. Various causes for this are adduced by Plutarch in his essay 'On
Natural Causes,' in the very first problem.

52   **Arenae mandas semina**
You are sowing seed in the sand

Εἰς ψάμμον σπείρεις, You are sowing seed in the sand. Sands being sterile,

* * * * *

7 Pliny] *Naturalis historia* 2.189, added in *1515*
12 Aesop] 13 Halm, added in *1515*; it was already in III x 88.

51 One of the list of phrases expressing fruitless labour in *Collectanea* no 408. Otto
   789; Tilley s 89 To plough the sand.
4 Ausonius] See I i 86n; *Epistulae* 12.3–4
8 donkey] *Adagia* I iv 35
10 proverb] *Adagia* I vi 37
12 Plutarch] *Moralia* 911C, added in *1515*

52 Otto 789; Tilley s 87 He sows the sand.

especially along the shore, they are unsuitable for sowing. Oenone to Paris, in Ovid: 'What are you doing, Oenone, why sow your seeds in the sand?/ 5 You plough the sea-shore with oxen that will bring no harvest.' But in my native Brabant there are husbandmen so industrious that they force the thirstiest sands to bear, and to bear wheat.

53 In aqua sementem facis
You are sowing seed in water

Εἰς ὕδωρ σπείρεις, You are sowing seed in water. Theognis: 'Just as if one should throw seed into the grey salt sea.' He is speaking of those who confer a benefit on ungrateful and wicked men: it is as entirely lost as if one were 5 sowing seeds in the waves of the sea. The scholiast on Aristophanes quotes this proverb also (using *thalassa* instead of *hydor*): 'You are sowing the sea.'

54 In saxis seminas
You are sowing among the rocks

Κατὰ πετρῶν σπείρεις, You are sowing among the rocks. It is quite possible that the parable in the Gospel about the seed which fell on stony ground is an allusion to this proverb. For soil of this kind is usually sterile, either 5 because it cannot be broken up by the plough, or because what is sown can find nowhere to put down its roots.

55 Ignem dissecare
To cleave fire

Εἰς τὸ πῦρ ξαίνειν, To belabour fire, belongs to the same category, though we have included it with the precepts of Pythagoras. Aristides in the *Joint*

* * * * *
5 Ovid] *Heroides* 5.115–6, the author's name added in *1515*
7 Brabant] This sentence was added in *1526*.

53 Probably from the Greek proverb-collections (Zenobius 3.55; Suidas EI 326)
3 Theognis] 106 (see I i 62n).
6 scholiast] On Aristophanes *Wasps* 284, added in *1528*

54 Probably from Suidas EI 313, with the next adage; also in Apostolius 9.45
4 Gospel] Matthew 13:5
5 For soil] Sentence added in *1526*

55 The Greek verb *xainein* is used of combing or carding wool, and the purport of this adage is to card your wool into the fire, instead of into the big basket out of

Defence of Four Orators: 'Didn't you realise that you were exposed to all the   5
proverbs: belabouring a fire, boiling a stone, and sowing the rocks?' He is
reproaching Plato for not doing anything worthwhile at the court of Dionysius the tyrant.

56   **In aqua scribis**
     You write in water

Καθ' ὕδατος γράφεις, or εἰς ὕδωρ γράφεις, You write in water, that is, you are
wasting your time. Lucian in *The Tyrant*: 'Are you joking, Charon, or are
you, as they say, writing in water, if you expect anything in the way of an   5
obol from Micyllus?' Plato in the *Phaedrus*: 'Will he not then write these
things carefully in black water, sowing with his pen?' There is a line of verse
to this effect among the Greek maxims: 'The oaths of wicked men are writ in
water.' Xenarchus misquotes this in his *Pentathlon*, cited by Athenaeus in his
tenth book: 'To me, a woman's oath is writ in wine.' And then Catullus: 10
'What a woman says to her ardent lover should be written in wind and in
running water.'

* * * * *

which you will draw it when you come to spin it into thread; which is indeed an
example of labour wasted. Erasmus seems not to have known the word in this
sense, and confuses this adage with the Pythagorean precept against using a
sword to poke the fire (see I i 2, line 135), which looks like a survival of ancient
folklore. He did however know that *xainein* could be used of flogging; and
hence this phrase about 'belabouring' the fire (*diverberare*), which as the child of
confusion cannot be expected to make sense. The same trouble recurs in III v 84.
The Greek of the adage might have been found by him in Zenobius 5.27 or
Suidas EI 313. The example from Aristides (see I i 13n) is from the *De quatuor*
p 302 Dindorf.

56 *Collectanea* no 610 gave the first of the two forms of the adage, no doubt from
   Diogenianus 5.83; the second is that of Suidas EI 327, but might have been
   taken direct from Lucian. Tilley W 114 To write in water.
4 Lucian] *Cataplus* 21 (*Tyrant* is an alternative title).
6 Plato] *Phaedrus* 276c
7 line of verse] Menander *Sententiae* 26 (see I i 30n).
9 Xenarchus] A writer of the Attic New Comedy, frag 6 Kock, cited by Athenaeus
   10.441e. This, which found a place in *1508* in I vii 1, was added here in *1517/8*,
   with 'wine' for 'water' in both Greek quotation and Latin version. Erasmus, or
   his printer, changed this to 'water' in *1533*, but omitted to alter the version;
   'wine' is clearly right.
10 Catullus] 70.3–4, added in *1520*

57   In arena aedificas
     You are building on the sand

Εἰς ψάμμον οἰκοδομεῖς, You are building on the sand. The parable in the
Gospel seems to allude to this. What one has built on the sand does not
remain firm. This can be appropriately applied when someone has under-   5
taken a piece of work which is bound to be useless, because the foundations
have not been properly laid.

58   Ventos colis
     You are tilling the winds

᾿Ανέμους γεωργεῖς, You are tilling the winds. (I am using *colis*, you are
tilling, to mean 'bringing into cultivation.') This is found in Zenodotus. It is
said of people who reap no profit from their labours.   5

59   Ferrum natare doces
     You are teaching iron to swim

Σίδηρον πλεῖν διδάσκεις, You are teaching iron to swim. This refers to
people who try to do something against nature, something which can never
be done.   5

60   Cribro aquam haurire
     To draw water in a sieve

Κοσκίνῳ ὕδωρ ἀντλεῖ ἤ ἐπιφέρει, He draws water in a sieve. This can be

      * * * * *

   57 Presumably from Matthew 7:26. Tilley s 88 To build on sand

   58 Briefly recorded in *Collectanea* no 417 from Diogenianus 1.88. 'Zenodotus'
      means Zenobius 1.99, and it is also in Suidas A 2261. The parenthesis, which
      brings out more fully the meaning of the verb, was added in 1526. Tilley w 451
      To plow the winds

   59 Apostolius 15.46 is perhaps the source.

   60 *Collectanea* no 230, citing Plautus as the source, and without the Greek, which is
      available in Apostolius 9.91 and Suidas κ 2136. There was a cross-reference to
      the grand-daughters of Belus (Danaus' father), who carry water in jars full of
      holes; they appear in their own right in *Coll.* no 368, which became our I x 33.
      Otto 466; Suringar 91; Tilley w 111 To draw water in a sieve

applied, not unsuitably, to forgetful people. Plautus in the *Pseudolus*: 'It is as
profitless as to catch a shower of rain in a sieve.' That this was formerly   5
included among the *adunatōtata* [impossible things] is shown by the fact that
when Tucia, a Vestal virgin, carried water in a sieve, this was counted
among wonders; it was in the year 609 from the foundation of the city,
according to Pliny, book 28 chapter 2. Dionysius of Halicarnassus recalls it
too in his *Roman Antiquities*, book 2. It is derived from the story of the   10
Danaids, whom Plato described as undergoing this kind of punishment in
the underworld; they had to carry water continually in leaky jars to a leaky
tub. Alciphron in a letter from Galen to Cyrto: 'And, as the saying goes, we
are emptying pitchers into the jars of the Danaids.' Lucian in *Timon*: 'As if
from a basket with holes in it.' It is also found in the form, 'You are carrying   15
water to a leaky tub.' Plautus in the *Pseudolus*: 'We are pouring our words
into a leaky tub, labouring in vain.'

61 Apud fimum odorum vaporem spargis
You are sprinkling scent on manure

Εἰς κόπρον θυμιᾷς, You are sprinkling scent on manure. All scent vanishes
and is overcome by the smell of manure. Suidas has this. It is suitable for
those who offer something excellent to unworthy people. A similar phrase is   5
Perfume on the lentils.

* * * * *

4 Plautus] *Pseudolus* 102 (in the *Collectanea* and the 1508 edition of the *Chiliades* the
  source was given as his *Mercator*); cited from memory, and set right in 1520.
8 year 609] Reckoned from the foundation of Rome; our 144 BC.
9 Pliny] *Naturalis historia* 28.12, added in 1515
9 Dionysius] 2.69. added in 1533. The *Roman History* of Dionysius, who wrote
  under Augustus, was not printed in Greek till 1547; but a Latin version made in
  the fifteenth century by Lapo Birago and first printed in 1480 had been revised
  by H. Glareanus and published by Froben in 1532.
11 Plato] *Republic* 2.363d (this was given in Latin in *Collectanea* no 368); *Gorgias*
   493b. See *Adagia* I x 33.
13 Alciphron] *Epistulae* 1.2.1 (see I ii 58n).
14 Lucian] *Timon* 18
15 the form] Apostolius 6.79; Suidas EI 321
16 Plautus] *Pseudolus* 369, added in 1533. It recurs in I x 33.

61 Suidas EI 284; the cross-reference to *Adagia* I vii 23 was added in 1526.

62   **Oleum et operam perdidi**
     I have wasted both oil and toil

To this class belongs the saying of Plautus in the *Poenulus*: 'Heavens, I have
wasted both oil and toil,' meaning that whatever I spent, whether money or
labour, was spent in vain. The metaphor comes from the contests of gla-   5
diators and athletes: when about to compete they anoint themselves with
oily unguents. Cicero in his *Letters*: 'As to the athletes, why should I
suppose that you miss them – you, who treated the gladiators so contemp-
tuously? And on them Pompey himself admits that he wasted both oil and
toil.' It can however refer to the lamps of writers; and Cicero seems to have   10
meant this when writing to Atticus, book 13: 'When I was writing against the
Epicureans, before daybreak, I jotted down something to you using the
same oil and toil, and despatched it before dawn.' To the same, in another
place, he says: 'Let us not lament, in case we lose the oil and toil of our study,
but let us discuss with a quiet mind.' This is all the pleasanter here because it   15
is transferred to the realm of the mind. The oil, here, refers to expense, and
the adage has also this form, as in Plautus in the *Rudentes*: 'They lose both
work and outlay.'

    Here belongs that phrase which the talking raven learned to say, 'Care
and cost lost.' Macrobius tells this story in book 2 of the *Saturnalia*. As the   20
tale seems worth the telling, I will readily write it down here, and in his own
words. 'Octavius was returning in high triumph from his victory at Actium.
Among those who hurried to congratulate him was a man carrying a raven,
which he had taught to say "Hail, victorious Caesar, hail, emperor." Caesar
was amazed at the obliging bird, and bought it for twenty thousand *nummi*.   25
A partner of the successful trainer's, who had not laid hands on any of the
cash, had informed Caesar that the man also had another raven, and asked
that he might be commanded to bring it. When he brought it, the words he
had taught it to say were "Hail, victorious Antony, emperor." Good-
humouredly, Octavius thought it sufficient to order him to share the present   30
made to his mate. When he was similarly greeted by a parrot, he ordered
that to be bought. A magpie which astonished him by the same trick was

* * * * *

62 *Collectanea* no 201, citing Plautus and Cicero, with a bare reference to
   Macrobius. Otto 1284
 3 Plautus] *Poenulus* 332
 7 Cicero] *Ad familiares* 7.1.3; *Ad Atticum* 13.38.1; 2.17.1 (comment added in 1523)
17 Plautus] *Rudens* 24
20 Macrobius] See I i 12n; *Saturnalia* 2.4.29–30. Octavius is the future emperor
   Augustus, who finally defeated his rival Mark Antony at the battle of Actium
   in 31BC.

bought too. These events prompted a certain poor cobbler to teach a raven a similar salutation; at the end of his resources, he often used to say to the unresponsive bird, "Care and cost lost." Finally, however, the raven did 35 begin to say the oft-repeated greeting. Augustus heard it as he passed, and replied, "I have enough of these compliment-mongers in my house." A memory came to the raven which moved it to add what it had heard its scolding master say so often: "Care and cost lost." The emperor laughed at this, and had the bird bought at a higher price than any he had paid before.' 40 Thus far I have quoted the words of Macrobius.

Writing to Pammachius, St Jerome seems to have subjoined another proverb to this one: 'he loses oil and expense, who sends an ox to the wrestling-ring' [ceroma]. This phrase about the ox and the wrestling-ring sounds like a proverb, meaning to teach the unteachable or to appoint 45 somebody to an office for which he is least fitted, and which is foreign to his whole character. For ceroma is the name of the ointment with which athletes formerly used to anoint themselves, made out of oil and certain kinds of earth. For contests, the ox is quite useless.

63 Reti ventos venaris
You are chasing the winds with a net

Δικτύῳ ἄνεμον θηρᾷς, You are trying to catch the wind in a net. Used of people who toil in vain, or who chase foolishly after things they have no hope of catching, or who snatch in a futile way after futility. The wind can be 5 contained in a bladder but never in a net.

64 Tranquillum aethera remigas
You are plying windless air

Αἰθέρα νήνεμον ἐρέσσεις, You are rowing in still air. In Zenodotus this is used of people who work in vain, as if one said 'You are cleaving the air, as rowers do.' 5

* * * * *

42 Jerome] *Letters* 57.12.3, the final sentence added in 1515. This stood by itself in the *Collectanea* as no 202, and is Otto 263; and one may wonder why Erasmus, who was always on the lookout for material with which to increase the total sum of his collection, did not give it independent status.

63 From the Greek proverb-collections (Zenobius 3.17; Diogenianus 4.29; Suidas Δ 1115). Tilley w 416 He catches the wind in a net.

64 From Zenobius ('Zenodotus') 1.39

65 **Mortuum flagellas**
You are flogging a dead body

Νεκρὸν μαστίζεις, You flog a dead man. Said of people who scold others, who are not to be moved in the least by scolding; or who attack and outrage the dead.   5

66 **Ollam exornas**
You are decorating a cooking-pot

Χύτραν ποικίλλεις, You are adorning or decorating a cooking-pot, is said of people who make great and useless efforts for quite ridiculous reasons. It is lost labour to paint designs on a kitchen pot, a despised object meant for   5 cooking. There is another common saying something like this, To apply gold-leaf to walnut-shells.

67 **Ovum adglutinas**
You are sticking an egg together

Ὠὸν κολλήεις, You are sticking an egg together. This is mentioned by Diogenianus. It is a ridiculous task to piece together a broken eggshell and mend it with glue.   5

68 **Utrem caedis**
You are beating a wineskin

Ἀσκὸν δέρεις, You are beating a wineskin, or, skinning a leather bottle; it is

* * * * *

65 Printed from a Paris manuscript (fonds grec 2720) in the *Corpus Paroemiographorum* 1.344

66 From the Greek collections (Diogenianus 1.45; Suidas x 610). Suringar 158

67 Perhaps from Diogenianus 1.45; but the verb there is *tilleis,* 'you are shaving,' not *kolleeis,* which is no true Greek form for 'you are sticking together.' Tilley E 76 It is very hard to shave an egg. Erasmus seems to have been misled by a corruption in his text of the Greek.

68 *Collectanea* no 424 (coupled with our I vi 39, the sense of which is quite different), probably from Diogenianus 3.3. Erasmus seems to have gone astray here: the meaning is probably 'to flay (a man until he becomes no better than) a wineskin,' and the passage in Apuleius is quite irrelevant.

to be found in Aristophanes in the *Clouds*. Apuleius seems to have alluded
to this in the *Ass*, when he recalls the three leather bottles which he struck   5
and wounded. This may be taken from the rites of Bacchus, or from those
who make an empty noise by banging on skins.

69   **Utrem vellis**
      You are plucking a wineskin

Very similar to this is Ἀσκὸν τίλλεις, You are plucking a wineskin, either
because it has no feeling, or because it has no hairs.

70   **Actum agere**
      To reopen a closed subject

Terence in the *Phormio*: 'Here! Don't reopen a closed subject, as they say.'
This is taken from the practice of the lawcourts, under which it is not
permitted to reopen a case once judgment has been given. Plautus: 'You are   5
pleading a case already finished,' that is, you are working to no purpose.
Quintus Fabius in Livy, decade 3 book 8: 'I know that to many of you,
senators, it seems to-day that we are reopening a closed subject, and that he
will speak to no purpose who expresses an opinion about the province of
Africa as though the question were not yet settled.' Cicero in his little book   10
on friendship suggests that this was customarily used of a piece of business
conducted in the wrong order: 'But we suffer from carelessness in many of
our undertakings; in none more than in selecting and cultivating our
friends. We put things back to front, and go over things already settled, in
defiance of the old proverb.'   15

      * * * * *

      4 Aristophanes] *Clouds* 442, added in 1523
      4 Apuleius] *Metamorphoses* 3.9 (see I i 15n). The hero there was set upon in the
        night by three bandits, whom he fought and wounded; next morning, he
        found they were wineskins, which had taken human shape at the orders of
        some local magician.

      69 From Suidas A 4176

      70 This appears in *Collectanea* no 408 (with our I vi 39) in a list of expressions
        signifying waste of labour, supported by two citations from Terence and
        Plautus; though sometimes in the negative it has a colouring of Tilley W 260 Let
        well alone. Otto 42
      3 Terence] *Phormio* 419. Erasmus adds a Greek version of the Latin phrase.
      5 Plautus] *Pseudolus* 260
      7 Livy] 28.40.3, added in 1533
      10 Cicero] *De amicitia* 22.85

71 **Cotem alis**
You are feeding a whetstone

'Ακόνην σιτίζεις, You are feeding a whetstone. This is said about gluttonous
people, who eat a lot and are in no better condition for that. There is a
common proverb going about today which refers to the leanness of whet-   5
stones: they say 'as fat as a whetstone' when they mean 'emaciated.' Ermolao Barbaro, in a letter to Pico, explains this proverb as meaning 'to bestow a
kindness wrongly and get no thanks for it'; so that it would be close to the
other one which will be recorded elsewhere, Feed the wolf's cubs, when
poor thanks are returned for a benefit.   10

72 **Hylam inclamas**
You are calling for Hylas

Ὕλαν κραυγάζεις, You are calling for Hylas. Said about people who shout
with no result, or generally about those who make no progress. The proverb
was derived from the following event. Hylas, the son of Theodamas, was   5
one of the Argonauts, a beautiful youth beloved by Hercules. When he was
in Mysia, he went out to fetch water, fell into the spring and was drowned. It
is said that the Nymphs fell in love with him and carried him away.
Polyphemus was sent to find him, and went calling his name 'Hylas!' with
great shouts, but he had no success. Hence the proverb arose. Virgil seems   10
to relate it to the shouts of the sailors, when he says:

> He joins to these Hylas, left by the sailors beside a spring,
> Shouting for him, till the whole coast rang with the name
> Hylas, Hylas.

Theocritus too remembers it in idyll 13:   15

* * * * *

71 From the Greek proverb-collections (Zenobius 1.58; Diogenianus 2.8; Suidas A
   922). Suringar 44
 6 Ermolao Barbaro] See I iv 39n; *Epistolae* ed V. Branca, Florence 1943, i p 108,
   added in *1528*
 9 elsewhere] *Adagia* II i 86

72 *Collectanea* no 678, citing Virgil's lines; the Greek from Diogenianus 8.33 (also in
   Zenobius 6.21 and Suidas Y 90)
10 Virgil] *Eclogues* 6.43–4
15 Theocritus] 13.58–9

Thrice he called 'Hylas' with the loudest shout he could muster
From his deep throat; and thrice the lad heard,
But faintly his voice struck the ear.

There is no reason why it should not refer to the sacred rites instituted in
memory of the snatching away of Hylas; his name was shouted during these   20
rites. It would be more elegant and apt to use it for someone longing for
something he lacks, weeping for it or wishing for it. So a man reduced to
poverty might long for the hundred talents he used to possess. Aristophanes seems to have thought of this proverb in the *Plutus*: 'You long for
one not present and you call in vain.' This is said of Mercury, lamenting for   25
the cakes which he had once been accustomed to eat during the ceremonies.

73 **Inaniter aquam consumis**
    You are wasting water (time)

῎Αλλως ἀναλίσκεις ὕδωρ, You are wasting water (time). This will be suitable
for people who try to persuade others, but in vain. It comes from the ancient
custom of judicial trials, when a time-limit was set by the water-clock.   5
Aeschines, speaking against Demosthenes, explains that the first measure
of water was poured in for the plaintiffs, the second for the defence, the
third for the judges to decide on the penalty, unless the accused had been
acquitted by the first votes. And Demosthenes challenges Aeschines to say if
he can, in his own water-time if need be, what decree had ever been passed   10
on a proposal moved by him: 'Let him get up and speak – yes, he can have
my own water-time.' Lucian, playing with the idea in *On Salaried Posts In
Great Houses*, jokes about a professional rhetorician who made speeches at
drinking-parties among the barbarians measured not by water but by the
wine-jar. Again in *Twice Accused*: 'For the water that is running now is hers.'   15
Plato seems to suggest this in the *Theaetetus*, when he says that some people
can report what has been done in the least possible water-time. Again, in the
same work, 'The running water urges on,' because the orator's business is to

* * * * *

23 Aristophanes] *Plutus* 1127

73 *Collectanea* no 423, naming no source, but presumably from the proverb-
   collections (Diogenianus 2.61; Suidas A 1400)
 6 Aeschines] *In Ctesiphontem* 197 (see I iii 26n).
 9 Demosthenes] *De corona* 139, The Greek phrase added in 1528
12 Lucian] *De mercede conductis* 35; *Bis accusatus* 16
16 Plato] *Theaetetus* 201b and 172e, both added in 1520, and the Greek of 201b
   added in 1533

speak by the periods allowed him on the clock. Apuleius in the *Golden Ass*:
'Again, when summoned by the herald with a great roar, an older prosecu-   20
tor rose and for a set space of time (there was a vessel with a sort of thin pipe
by way of a neck, through which water poured into it came slowly drop by
drop) he made an appeal to the people, as follows.' Pliny the Younger,
writing to Falco: 'And anyone who can order someone else to be quiet,
should have silence imposed on him by the clock.' The same to Arrianus   25
again: 'I spoke for nearly five hours. For my twenty periods by the clock,
which I had supposed ample when I accepted them, were increased by
four.' Quintilian, book 12: 'And if you make an assumption, you have to
prove it, and there is not enough water-time for the speech you have worked
on and built up with days and nights of study.'   30

Cicero at the end of the second book of his *Tusculan Questions*: 'To-
morrow then by the water-clock; for that is how we speak.' Cicero again in
the *De oratore*, book 3, speaking of Pericles: 'But this man had not been
taught by some noisy declaimer to rant by the water-clock, but (as we
understand) his teacher was the great Anaxagoras of Clazomenae, a man   35
with a supreme grasp of the most important subjects.' Philetas, in Athenaeus, book 2: 'I have said so much, like orators who talk by the clock'; for
his speech had actually been about water. In this lies the charm of the
allusion. Demades used to joke about Demosthenes 'the water-drinker,'
saying that others timed their speeches by water but Demosthenes timed his 40
writing by it. Philostratus in his life of Adrian the sophist calls sophists
'water-clock men,' because they practised against the clock. In early times
lines and shadows were used to tell the hours. The first to invent a water-
clock was Publius Scipio Nasica, and then one could tell the time even on a

* * * * *

19 Apuleius] *Metamorphoses* 3.3
23 Pliny the Younger] *Letters* 1.23.2; 2.11.14
28 Quintilian] 12.6.5, cited again in I iv 100
31 Cicero] *Tusculanae disputationes* 2.27.67, added in *1526*; *De oratore* 3.34.138,
   added in *1528*
36 Athenaeus] 2.43f gives the Greek words; they are his own, and the name
   Philetas has come in from elsewhere.
39 Demades] Athenian politician of the 4th century BC; Lucian *Demosthenis*
   encomium 15, added in *1526*
41 Philostratus] *Vitae sophistarum* 58b, added in *1533*. He is a sophist of the second
   or third century AD, or more probably several writers under that name whom
   we cannot separate with certainty; the *Vitae* were first printed in Greek in the
   Aldine Lucian of 1503.
42 In early times] From here to the end is an addition of *1515*, except the refence to
   hour-glasses (filled with sand), which was added in *1528*. Scipio's invention
   comes from Pliny *Naturalis historia* 7.215.

cloudy day or at night. Now they use instead of water-clocks hourglasses   45
and automatic clocks.

74 In aere piscari, venari in mari
To fish in the air, to hunt in the sea

Of the same sort are the phrases Plautus makes use of in the *Asinaria*: 'to fish
in the air, to hunt with a spear in the sea.' These will directly fit those people
who try in vain to achieve the impossible, or who look in the wrong place for   5
something they can never hope to find there. For instance, a man might seek
a quiet life in magisterial office, or a blessed one in the midst of pleasure, or a
happy one in the midst of wealth. So Libanus the slave, ordered by his
master Demaenetus to get money away by fraud from the latter's own wife,
indicates by his reply that there is no way of taking anything away from a   10
really close-fisted woman: 'Order me at one and the same time to go fishing
in the air, and hunting with a javelin in the midst of the sea.'

75 Aquam e pumice postulas
You are asking for water out of a pumice stone

We find in the same poet something not very different from the above: 'to
look for water from a pumice-stone,' meaning to seek in vain to obtain
something from a person who is in great need of it himself. For nothing is   5
dryer than a pumice-stone, or more thirsty for water; it is just as if we were to
ask for teaching from the most untaught, to expect advice from the most
ill-advised, or a present from a pauper, protection from the helpless, money
from a close-fisted miser. Plautus: 'For you are asking now for water from a
pumice-stone, which is thirsty itself.' 'The pumice-stone,' says the same   10
author, 'is not as dry as this old man.' The pumice is a stone full of holes,
which is used to polish books; so dry in its nature that if you put it into a

* * * * *

74 *Collectanea* no 56, taken directly from Plautus *Asinaria* 99–100. Otto 27. In *Coll.*
there was a brief reference, without text, to Boethius *Consolatio philosophiae*
metrum 8.5–8, not used in the *Chiliades*.

75 *Collectanea* no 249, with the two citations from Plautus. Otto 1487, 1487a; Tilley
w 107 To fetch water out of a stone
9 Plautus] *Persa* 41–2; *Aulularia* 297
11 pumice] The use of pumice-stone to smooth the surface of papyrus or
parchment before writing on it or to give a neat finish is often referred to; eg
Catullus 1.2; Pliny *Naturalis historia* 36.154–6. All this section was added in
1515.

boiling pot, it will stop the boiling, not only for a time but altogether. There is no other cause for this, thinks Theophrastus, than that because of its extreme dryness it strives to draw all the froth into itself. He recalls the case   15
of a certain Eudemus of Chios, who habitually provided himself with a pumice stone sprinkled with vinegar, so that after the seventh draught of hellebore he could not be provoked to vomit either by baths or by drinking wine.

76 Nudo vestimenta detrahere
To drag the clothes off a naked man

This also belongs to the same line of thought, and is used by the same poet: To drag the clothes off a naked man, meaning to hope for gain from a person who has nothing that can be taken away. Thus the aforesaid Libanus, in the   5
Asinaria of Plautus, is ordered by his master to steal from himself, by a trick, the money to buy a girl for his son, and he says: 'You're joking – you want me to get the clothes off a naked man.' St Chrysostom also quotes a popular proverb, to the effect that 'a hundred men cannot despoil one naked man.' Apuleius, in the first book of the *Ass*, wrote that 'a naked man cannot be   10
robbed by ten wrestlers.'

77 Anthericum metere
To reap asphodel-stalks

Τὸν ἀνθέρικον θερίζειν, To reap asphodel-stalks, was said of those who take on useless and fruitless work. Asphodel is a kind of plant which cannot be mown, but must be pulled up by hand like flax. The word *antherices* means   5
the tips of ears of grain, or awns. Herodotus calls the stalks of asphodel

* * * * *

14 Theophrastus] *Historia plantarum* 9.17.3 (see I i 44n).

76 *Collectanea* no 57, citing Plautus. Otto 1249; Tilley R 7a To take clothes from a naked man; B 650 It is ill to take breeks off a bare arse.
6 Plautus] *Asinaria* 91–2
8 Chrysostom] Johannes Chrysostomus *In Matthaeum homiliae* 83.2 (PG 58.748), added in 1517/8
10 Apuleius] *Metamorphoses* 1.15, added in 1533

77 From Aristides; see next adage.
6 or awns] The beard or bristles of an ear of grain; Erasmus uses the Greek word (in Latin letters), which he would have learnt from his reading of Lucian. This was an addition of 1526.
6 Herodotus] 4.190 (see I i 96n), cited by Suidas A 2497.

antherices, according to Suidas, and he says they are too tough to be broken. Pliny, book 21 chapter 17, mentions asphodel-stalks: 'In the Greek compilations I find *antherices* and *atherices* used indifferently.'

78 **Ex arena funiculum nectis**
    You are twisting a rope of sand

'Εκ τῆς ψάμμου σχοινίον πλέκειν, To twist a rope of sand. This means trying in vain to do what can by no means be done. What could be sillier than to want to twist a rope out of sand, which cannot stick together? Both proverbs,   5
this and the one just quoted, are used by Aristides in his *Joint Defence of Four Orators*: 'But hiding themselves in holes, and there inventing their marvellous wisdom, they draw together words in shadow, as you say, O Sophocles, reaping asphodel, weaving rope from sand, unravelling I know not what web.' By these adages he indicated that the private study of the   10
philosophers bears no fruit at all. Columella in the preface of his poem on gardening: 'For although there are many parts of this of which we could speak, they are so tiny that, as the Greeks say, from their incomprehensible smallness one cannot make a rope of sand.' The proverb can be particularly adapted to use as follows: if one should try to bring into agreement people   15
who are far apart in way of life, with nothing whatever in common; or if one should put together a speech woven out of discordant arguments, creating a kind of chimaera or a monster like that described by Horace, with a man's head on a horse's neck and with the rest of the limbs collected from different kinds of animal, 'making a woman beautiful from the waist up end miser-   20
ably in a black fish.'

* * * * *

8 Pliny] *Naturalis historia* 21.109, added in *1526*

78 For the source of this, see below. Suidas E 1536. Otto 790; Tilley R 174 To twist a rope of sand. II vi 51 is a doublet of this.
6 Aristides] *De quattuor* p 405 Dindorf (see I i 13n). It can hardly be a coincidence that in that passage our no 77 (a rare adage) and 78 stand one after the other as they do here: both adages were taken direct from Aristides for incorporation in the *Chiliades*. In *1508* another clause followed about losing what you have gained in wisdom through arrogance; and this was cut out in *1515*, perhaps because it had already been used in I iv 42.
11 Columella *Res rustica* 10 praef 4, added in *1515*. Though he wrote a very valuable treatise on agriculture (in the middle of the first century AD), his tenth book, on gardening, was composed in verse as a complement to Virgil's *Georgics*.
18 Horace] *Ars poetica* 1 and 3–4. Homer's chimera was a composite animal, made up of lion, she-goat and serpent.

79 **Ab asino lanam**
    Wool from a donkey

Very nearly the same is this phrase, about people who stupidly search for
what does not exist: Ὄνου πόκας ζητεῖς, You are looking for wool from a
donkey. The proverb is also found in the form 'donkey's wool.' Aris-   5
tophanes: 'Who's for the plain of Lethe? Who for donkey's wool?' Meaning
by ass's wool something empty and non-existent. The phrase makes a Greek
trimeter if you leave out the second *tis*.

80 **Asinum tondes**
    You are shearing a donkey

Τὸν ὄνον κείρεις, You are shearing the donkey. This has the same sense, and
is used of people who attempt something ridiculous and useless, because
you can neither comb a donkey, with its shaggy hair, nor shear it, because it 5
has no wool. Aristophanes recalls it in the *Frogs*.

81 **Lupi alas quaeris**
    You are looking for the wolf's wings

Λύκου πτερὰ ζητεῖς, You are looking for the wolf's wings. Used of people
who seek something which does not exist, or when someone produces
alarm merely by words, making a threat he will never carry out. It is quite 5
impossible that a wolf should ever turn up with wings. The proverb is listed
by Suidas.

                    * * * * *

79 *Collectanea* no 355, presumably from Diogenianus 4.85 or 6.99 (see also
    Zenobius 5.38 and Suidas o 399). 'Goat's wool' has already appeared in I iii 53.
    Apparently not in Tilley, but the *Oxford Dictionary of English Proverbs* (1970) 307
    cites from T. Elyot's *Bibliotheca* (1548) Thou shearest an asse.
  5 Aristophanes] *Frogs* 186; his 'Donkey's wool' is an imaginary place in Hades.
    The metrical comment was added in *1528*.

80 From the scholiast on Aristophanes *Frogs* 186, cited on the preceding adage, of
    which this is a variant

81 *Collectanea* no 626, very briefly, from Diogenianus 6.4. The reference to suidas ʌ
    822 was added in *1517/8*.

82 **Quae apud inferos**
    The things in Hades

In the same place the commentator mentions this proverb also, as if it had
the same meaning: Τὰ ἐν ῞Αδου, The things in Hades, and he quotes
Aristarchus as his authority, and thinks it arose from the story in Cratinus of   5
a man in the underworld twisting a rope while a donkey chewed off the part
he had already twisted, so that the twister's work was quite in vain. This
phrase 'the things in Hades' relates however in general to everything that
the poets' stories tell us, not to be believed except by children; so when we
describe empty dreams or the like we can appropriately say 'the things in   10
Hades.' Athenaeus relates in book 4 of his *Doctors at Dinner* that Democritus
wrote a book with this title, *About What Is In Hades*, probably stuffed with
monstrous fables, and it may be from this that the proverb arose.

83 **Contorquet piger funiculum**
    The sluggard twists the rope

So similar as to seem almost the same, is what Pausanias tells in his *Phocica*,
about Ocnus the ass, or the 'lazy ass,' well known, he says, among the
Ionians: Συνάγει ῎Οκνος τὴν θώμιγγα, The sluggard twists the rope. I will   5
give his own words: 'Beyond these there is a man sitting, and the inscription
indicates that he is Ocnus [sloth]. He is portrayed in this way: he is twisting a

* * * * *

82 From the scholia on Aristophanes *Frogs* 186 like no 80; but the reference to
    Aristarchus is from Suidas o 399.
  5 Cratinus] A leader of the Attic Old Comedy. Frag 348 Kock, cited by Suidas. See
    also the adage which follows.
 11 Athenaeus] 4.168b, added in *1523*

83 *Collectanea* no 27 dealt with this at some length. It began with a Greek word
    schoinotroges, rope-eaters, which Erasmus could have got only from Suidas σ
    1793; this he dropped in *1508*, having perhaps discovered that it was really
    schinotroges, men who chew mastich to clean their teeth (i viii 33). Ocnus (the
    name means 'hesitation' in Greek, not 'lazy') is industrious in Pausanias,
    though to no effect; it is Pliny who, probably by mistake, makes him lazy, and
    confuses Erasmus, who produces a phrase 'the lazy ass' which has no warrant
    in the Greek. As an example of the industrious maker of ropes whose product is
    maltreated he then gives St Jerome, showing that already before 1500 he was
    concerned over the corruption of the Vulgate by scribes and interpreters,
    which was to call forth his own work on the New Testament. Most of this
    material he reuses in the *Chiliades*. Cf Suidas o 399.
  3 Pausanias] 10.29 (i i 90n), the book-reference added in *1523*

rope, and a she-ass standing near by is continually gnawing away at what he
has twisted. They say that this Ocnus is an industrious man bent on his
work, but he has an extravagant and spendthrift wife, so that whatever he   10
gets together by working is soon wasted by her. I can testify that if the
Ionians see someone labouring away at something which brings in no profit,
they habitually say, "this man is twisting the rope of Ocnus." ' The subject of
the picture seems to have been taken from a word with a double meaning.
The Greeks say 'to get together a living' for 'to procure one's livelihood.' The   15
one who increases his substance gets together; the one who squanders
scatters it. And this subject seems to have been illustrated in old days by the
work of many artists. Pliny, in his *History of the World,* describes among the
themes of the famous painter Socrates the picture of an ass gnawing a rope.
'And the sluggard' he says 'called Ocnus, twisting the rope which the ass   20
chews off.' It is said that the same picture was at Delphi, dedicated by
Polygnotus the Thasian. However, they deny that it means an idle and
indolent man, as Varro thought, but much more a diligent and industrious
one with an extravagant wife. So Pausanias says that the donkey in the
picture was a female and not a male. Ermolao Barbaro testifies that a carving   25
illustrating the same subject is on show at two places in Rome, namely on
the Capitol and in the gardens of the Vatican. Propertius also made use of
this proverb: 'Worthier' he says,

> To twist the rope for Ocnus sideways sitting,
> And feed for aye the ass that's always eating.   30

It is curious, by the way, that Pliny should say the man who twisted the rope
was called Ocnus, which means lazy, and not rather the gnawing ass,
especially as Propertius does not give the name Ocnus, lazy, to the man who

* * * * *

18 Pliny] *Naturalis historia* 35.137
21 It is said] From here to 'the Vatican' is taken over from the *Collectanea,*
   incorporating a reference to Varro (not yet identified) which came at the
   beginning of the earlier account.
25 Barbaro] See *Adagia* I iv 39n. This is from his *Castigationes Plinianae* xxxv.11 (ed
   Rome 1492, sig I 2).
27 Propertius] 4.3.21–2; he says that someone is 'worthier than Ocnus to twist a
   rope' which is to be eaten by a donkey to all eternity, but the Latin could
   equally mean 'worthier to twist a rope for Ocnus,' and that is how Erasmus has
   taken it, thus adding to the haze of misunderstanding that hangs (so
   uncharacteristically) over his treatment of this adage.

twists, but says that the rope is being twisted for him; so that one would
think 'lazy' was applicable to the ass rather than the rope-maker. Plutarch   35
recalls this adage in his essay 'On Tranquillity of Mind': 'But it is just like the
man in the picture of the underworld who is twisting a rope, and close to
him stands one who eats away what he has made.'

84 **Littori loqueris**
You are talking to the seashore

Αἰγιαλῷ λαλεῖς, You are talking to the seashore. This is quoted in the Greek
collections. It is said of people who advise or pray in vain, as if they spoke to
the deaf. For the seashores are called deaf because of the continual noise of   5
the waves. Ovid: 'Deafer to me than the sea as I shrieked out the name of
Orestes, /He dragged me with hair all disarrayed into his palace.'

85 **Vento loqueris**
You are talking to the wind

Suidas adds this one: Ἀνέμῳ διαλέγῃ, You are talking to the wind. It means
'in vain' because the wind blows everything away and makes it disappear.
Virgil spoke of 'commands scattered on the breezes' which had vanished in   5
oblivion. Plautus, *Mostellaria*: 'The only word he knows to cry to the wind is
"interest."' In Athenaeus we read, with a similar metaphor, 'to call on
heaven and earth.'

* * * * *

35 Plutarch] *Moralia* 473C

84 Taken, as Erasmus says, from the Greek proverb-collections (Zenobius 1.38;
   Diogenianus 1.37; Suidas AI 41)
6 Ovid] *Heroides* 8.9–10, added in 1536

85 This might come, like the last, from Zenobius 1.38. Otto 1864. *Adagia* III iv 46 is
   similar. Tilley w 438 To talk to the wind
3 Suidas] A 2263
5 Virgil] *Aeneid* 9.312–3
6 Plautus] *Mostellaria* 605–7, added in 1523 (but the manuscripts are corrupt, and
   vento, to the wind, is not now accepted as a correction).
7 Athenaeus] 3.104c; this became an adage in its own right (I v 75) in 1523.

86 Mortuo verba facit
He addresses the dead

Νεκρῷ λέγουσα μύθους εἰς οὖς, Telling a story to a dead man's ear. Plautus says 'Now I am talking to the dead.' Terence: 'Words are spoken to the dead.' Plautus again: 'It makes no more difference than if a joke were told to 5 a dead man in his tomb.' Apposite here is what is said by Aeschylus in the *Agamemnon*: 'Alive, I wail in vain to the tomb of the dead.' The proverb arises from the foolish custom of the ancients, of calling three times the name of the deceased. For this reason they are called 'the lamented' [*conclamati*] especially at funerals were there is much bewailing of the dead man. This 10 custom is derided by Lucian in his essay on *Mourning*, which I have translated into Latin.

87 Surdo canis, surdo fabulam narras
You are singing, or telling a story to the deaf

This has the same force: Κωφῷ ᾄδεις, You sing to a deaf man. Virgil in the *Bucolics*: 'We are not singing to the deaf; the woods echo it all.' Horace: 'He'd think a tale were told / To a deaf ass.' Terence in the *Heautontimorumenos*: 5 'Truly he hardly knows what a story he is telling to my deaf ears.' Livy in the *Macedonian War*, book 10: 'I am afraid they were singing to empty ears.' Aeschylus in the *Seven Against Thebes*: 'Did you hear, or did you not? Am I talking to the deaf?' Ovid alludes to this in the *Amores*, book 3: 'If Phemius

* * * * *

86 This and the next provided *Collectanea* no 199, and it was referred to in no 172. It comes from the Greek proverb-collections (Diogenianus 6.82; Suidas N 142). Otto 1145–6

3 Plautus] A recollection, perhaps of *Poenulus* 840
4 Terence] *Phormio* 1015
5 Plautus] *Bacchides* 518–9
6 Aeschylus] *Choephoroe* (not *Agamemnon*) 926, added in 1523
11 Lucian] *De luctu* 19; Erasmus' version was first printed in Paris (Bade) 1 June 1514, and the reference to it was added here in 1515.

87 This was joined with the preceding in *Collectanea* no 199. Otto 1715; Tilley T 51 You tell a tale to a deaf man.
3 Virgil] *Eclogues* 10.8
4 Horace] *Epistles* 2.1.199–200
5 Terence] *Heautontimorumenos* 222
6 Livy] 40.8.10, added in 1520
8 Aeschylus] *Septem contra Thebas* 202, added in 1523 (the Latin version in 1528)
9 Ovid] *Amores* 3.7.61–2, added in 1523. Phemius is a singer in Homer; Thamyras the ancient seer was blind.

sings to deaf ears, what's the use? What use is a picture to poor Thamyras?'   10
This seems to have arisen from a ridiculous situation, when it often happens
that a stranger chances upon a deaf man and asks him many questions, to
the amusement of those who know him to be deaf.

88   **Frustra canis**
     You sing in vain

Ἄλλως ᾅδεις, Πρὸς κενὴν ψάλλεις, You sing or play in vain. Said of those
who urge to no purpose. Derived from singers, who when they are unpleas-
ing to their audience 'sing in vain' because no one listens, or those who sing   5
at their own expense and carry away no reward. The Greeks often use the
proverbial metaphor of singing to describe a speech. Hence the phrase in the
Hecuba of Euripides: 'Some song will come.' And 'you are singing the same
song,' and 'croaking in one's ears' and 'going beyond the song.' The poet
Lycophron used and at the same time explained this saying: 'Thus you will   10
rouse the idle notes of the lyre, / Playing your foodless unrewarded songs.'
The commentator adds that the proverb is sometimes found in this form,
'you are touching the lute-strings in vain.' But this is from lute-players, who
sing without being paid anything, and get their food at home, that is at their
own expense and cost, as Plautus says, 'they sing for others.' Perhaps one   15
might see here a reference to the fable of Aesop, about the flute-player who
tried in vain to charm the fishes by his music. For he had heard the story of
Arion.

89   **Lapidi loqueris**
     You are speaking to a stone

Λίθῳ διαλέγῃ, You are speaking to a stone. This has the same meaning. In
          * * * * *

     88 *Collectanea* no 451, probably from the Greek proverb-collections (Zenobius 1.72;
         Diogenianus 2.19; Suidas A 1399)
      8 Euripides] *Hecuba* 84, used again in II v 76
     10 Lycophron] *Alexandra* 139–40 (see I iii 56n).
     15 Plautus] There are several phrases similar to this in the comedies; *Menaechmi*
         905 is perhaps the closest.
     16 Aesop] Fable 27 Halm; the musician tries in vain to charm the fish by his music,
         as Arion the famous Greek lyric poet had charmed the dolphin who brought
         him safe to shore. Added in *1515*.

     89 Our 89 and 90 were briefly mentioned in *Collectanea* no 199. This came
         presumably from some Greek collection. It recalls the Irish 'whistling jigs to a
         milestone.'

Terence in the *Heautontimorumenos* 'stone' is several times used for a stupid,
dull sort of man. There was good sense in the reply quoted by Laertius to the   5
person who asked Aristippus what improvement education would bring to
his son: 'If nothing else,' said Aristippus, 'he won't sit in the theatre like one
stone sitting on another'.

90 **Parieti loqueris**
    You are talking to the wall

Πρὸς τὸν τοῖχον λαλεῖς, You are talking to a wall. This also is found in the
Greek collections, and also in the form 'to talk through the wall.' It used to be
said about anyone who did something particularly absurd. Perhaps it came   5
from lovers, who sometimes talk to the doors and windows, or even the
walls of their sweethearts, as if there were understanding in them. Plautus
in the *Truculentus* adopts it in the sense of speaking to one who will keep
quiet: 'I will be a wall; you go ahead and talk.'

91 **Nugas agere**
    To play the fool

A proverb familiar in Greek and Latin alike, To play the fool, meaning to do
something trivial and silly, or to make efforts in vain. A phrase familiar in
Attic Greek is 'to fool with foolery,' λῆρον ληρεῖς. Aristophanes in the *Clouds*   5
calls Socrates the high-priest of subtle foolery, the originator, so to speak, of
witty frivolities: 'You, the high priest of most subtle foolery.' Galen said in
his *On the Natural Faculties*, book 2: 'Thus every hypothesis of ducts as an
explanation for natural functioning is complete foolery.' It is more amusing
when applied to an individual, as in Athenaeus, book 6: 'But, he says, poets   10

* * * * *

4 Terence] *Heautontimorumenos* 831 and 917
5 Laertius] Diogenes Laertius 2.72, added in *1526*

90 From the same source as the preceding; the variant form is from Diogenianus
    4.31 or Suidas Δ 795.
7 Plautus] *Truculentus* 788, added in *1523*

91 One of a list of expressions for waste of time in *Collectanea* no 408
4 familiar] Aristophanes *Plutus* 517
5 Aristophanes] *Clouds* 359
7 Galen] See I iii 6n; *De naturalibus facultatibus* 2.3 (Kuehn 2.80), added in *1528*
10 Athenaeus] 6.225c, citing Xenarchus (a writer of the Attic New Comedy) frag
    7.1 Kock; added in *1528*

are foolery.' They also say 'you are crazy,' 'you are being nonsensical,' taking this over from old women who are beginning to get weak in the head with age and usually babble foolish nonsense. Ausonius to Paulus:

Phoebus demands that we should speak the truth.
He may let the Pierian sisters rave, 15
But he himself will never twist the furrow.

In these lines the allusion is rather obscure, I might almost say out of place. Bilingual as he was, the man had in mind both languages and a double meaning of the word. In Greek *lêros* means nonsense and in Latin *lirae* or *porcae* are words for furrow. Ploughmen first open up the ground, then 20 break up the clods, then plough a furrow [*lirant*]. Then he adds 'never does he twist a furrow.' Formerly ploughmen were said *delirare* when they deviated from the straight line of the furrow. And so it is transferred to people who are doting.

92 **In coelum iacularis**
You are shooting at heaven

Ἐς τὸν οὐρανὸν τοξεύεις, You are aiming your arrow at the sky. This is found in Zenodotus and Suidas; it refers to people who toil in vain, or who dare to attack those whom they cannot harm. For the man who shoots at the skies 5 can never hit anything; he only seems to be attacking the gods. It often happens that his missile falls back on himself. There is something like this in the proverbs of the Hebrews too, namely in *Ecclesiasticus* chapter 27: 'Whoever throws a stone straight up, it shall fall on his own head; and a treacherous blow opens up wounds for the treacherous. He who digs a pit will fall 10 into it, and he who has set up a stone for his neighbour will fall over it, and he who sets a snare for another will perish in it.'

* * * * *

13 Ausonius] *Epistulae* 4.8–10 (see I i 86n).

92 *Collectanea* no 373, with Francesco Filelfo cited, as though Erasmus had taken it from him before he found it in the Greek proverb-collections (Zenobius 3.46; Suidas EI 300). Tilley S 889 The stone you throw will fall on your own head; H 356 Who spits against heaven, it falls in his face.
8 of the Hebrews too] So *1515*, with all that follows; in *1508* it was 'of the Christians too: "Whoso casteth a stone on high, it shall fall back on his own head."' The reference is Ecclesiasticus 27:28–9 Vulgate (25–6 AV).

93 **Delphinum cauda ligas**
You are tying a dolphin by the tail

Δελφῖνα πρὸς τὸν οὐραῖον δεῖς, You are tying a dolphin by the tail. This refers
to people who try to do something in vain; because the dolphin has a
slippery tail and cannot be held by that part, or else because the tail is so   5
strong that ships are sometimes overturned by its thrashing, so that there is
no catching it at that end. This is also applicable to those who make an attack
on someone using means by which he cannot possibly be overcome.

94 **Cauda tenes anguillam**
You are holding an eel by the tail

᾿Απ᾽ οὐρᾶς τὴν ἔγχελυν ἔχεις, You are holding the eel by the tail. This comes
in appropriately when people have to do with untrustworthy and treacherous men, or have possessions of a fleeting and uncertain kind which they   5
cannot retain for long.

95 **Folio ficulno tenes anguillam**
You are holding an eel in a fig-leaf

Τῷ θρίῳ τὴν ἔγχελυν, (we must supply, You are holding) the eel in the
fig-leaf. This is a little different: used when an otherwise evasive, slippery
person is held by a grip too tight for him to escape. A fig-leaf has a rough   5
surface, so much so that Plutarch wrote that its name was synonymous with
harshness; and for that reason perfectly adapted for keeping hold of a
slippery eel.

* * * * *

93 *Collectanea* no 331, derived presumably from Diogenianus 4.38 (also in
Zenobius 3.38 and Suidas Δ 212)

94 Apparently of vernacular origin, for it is introduced in *Collectanea* no 331 (see
the preceding entry) with 'To-day too there is a common saying.' If so, the
source of the Greek equivalent is not clear. Suringar 54; Tilley E 61 He holds a
wet eel by the tail; cf H 508 There is as much hold to be taken of his word as of a
wet eel by the tail, W 640 Who has a woman has an eel by the tail.

95 *Collectanea* no 686, probably from Diogenianus 8.55. Tilley E 62 Hold fast an eel
with a fig-leaf.
6 Plutarch] *Moralia* 684B ('so much so ... harshness' was added in 1515); why
thrion, the Greek word for a fig-leaf, should connote roughness, is not clear.

96   Medius teneris
      You are gripped by the middle

Close to the previous saying is the remark of Aristophanes in the *Frogs*: Νῦν
ἔχῃ μέσος, Now you are held by the middle, of someone held in such a way
that he cannot possibly extricate himself. It comes from wrestlers and   5
athletes, who have an easy victory if they have seized someone by the
middle. These are the words of Aeacus to Bacchus: 'But now you are held by
the middle.' To the same belongs the phrase of Terence, 'I'd catch him round
the waist and lift him up.'

97   **Delphinum natare doces**
      You teach a dolphin to swim

Δελφῖνα νήχεσθαι διδάσκεις, You teach a dolphin to swim. This fits those
who try to give advice to another person on a subject of which he has great
experience, and so needs no teacher. The dolphin has the swiftest impetuos-   5
ity in swimming, so that it not only exceeds in speed every kind of swimming creature, but all land animals too; see Aelianus, book 12. It even leaps
over ships, and holding its breath propels itself forward like a missile.

98   **Aquilam volare doces**
      You teach an eagle to fly

Ἀετὸν ἵπτασθαι διδάσκεις, You teach an eagle to fly. The same sense comes
out of a different metaphor. As the dolphin among fish, so is the eagle
among birds. They have one thing in common, that it is said each has a love   5
for boys. Gregory seems to have been hinting at this in a letter to Eudoxus

            * * * * *

96 From Aristophanes *Frogs* 469
 8 Terence] *Adelphoe* 316 (tr J. Sargeaunt)

97 Included with the following adage in *Collectanea* no 499, from Diogenianus 4.33
   (also in Zenobius 3.30 and Suidas Δ 212). Erasmus returns to the dolphin in the
   sixth paragraph of II i 1.
 7 Aelianus] *De natura animalium* 12.12 (see I ii 55n).

98 In the *Collectanea* no 499 this was joined with what precedes here. The source
   was Diogenianus 1.65; it is also in Zenobius 2.49 and Suidas A 573.
 6 Gregory] Gregory of Nazianzus (see I i 69n) *Epistulae* 33.6 (PG 37.73B), added in
   1533. This letter was not addressed to Eudoxus, but he was the recipient of *Ep*
   178, in which the eagle and the jackdaw provide another adage, used in III ii 65.

the Rhetor: 'Say farewell to the common herd, consider those to be jackdaws who test the flight of eagles.'

99 In eodem haesitas luto
You are sticking in the same mud

Terence says in the *Phormio*: 'You are sticking in the same mud.' It applies to those who are so involved in some affair that they cannot extricate themselves. It comes from travellers, when they fall into the mire and try to pull   5
one foot out and the other sinks deeper in; and then to pull this one out, the one they had freed has to be stuck again. Horace says about this: 'Wishing in vain to pluck your foot out of the mire.'

Similar to this is 'to stick in the same track': Quintus Curtius, book 4: 'On the third day, livid with fear, weighed down by their arms, they stuck in   10
the same track.'

100 In aqua haeret
He is stuck in the water

A proverb something like this is quoted by Cicero in *De officiis*, book 3: 'In many passages he has much to say, but he sticks in the water, as the phrase is.' He is describing Epicurus, too little consistent in disputation and getting   5
himself mixed up, so that what he says in one place contradicts what he said in another, and so he floats about, as it were, and never reaches solid ground. This happens to people who wander from the truth and wrap the matter up in deceitful words. It seems to be taken from people floating, who

* * * * *

99 Coupled in *Collectanea* no 44, which cites Terence only, with *Adagis* IV iii 70. Otto 994
3 Terence] *Phormio* 780
7 Horace] *Satires* 2.7.27
9 Curtius] 4.14.2 (see I i 11n), added in 1533.

100 Erasmus here seems to have gone slightly astray. Under the influence of the preceding adage, to stick in the mud, he supposed there was another, to stick in the water. But the phrase is not, for example, 'ille in aqua haeret,' he sticks in the water, but 'illi aqua haeret,' for him the water sticks, he is (to use a colloquial phrase) stuck, or bogged down; and what water this was that refused to flow, we have no means of knowing, but it was clearly not the well-disciplined fluid in a water-clock. Most of what Erasmus says therefore is off the point, though the general effect is right. This was *Collectanea* no 45, citing Cicero *De officiis* only. Otto 142
3 Cicero] *De officiis* 3.33.117; *Ad Quintum fratrem* 2.6.2

have lost touch with the bottom and are thrown hither and thither; the more   10
they struggle, the greater danger they are in. Or else from the water-clocks
of orators, which we have mentioned elsewhere; we say a man 'sticks in the
water' when he cannot extricate himself from the case for the defence even
when the water has all run out. Cicero to his brother Quintus, book 2: 'What
had been said should be done on the ides and the next day about the land in   15
Campania, has not been done. In this case the water sticks for me.' It is
uncertain whether he means that the whole lawsuit was left to him, or that
the case was incapable of resolution. Here we may place what we quoted
previously out of Quintilian: 'There is not enough water for the speech you
have worked on and built up with days and nights of study.' What I shall say   20
later about the proverb 'He is sticking in shallow water' is not dissimilar.

1   **Multa cadunt inter calicem supremaque labra**
    There's many a slip 'twixt the cup and the lip

In the *Attic Nights* of Aulus Gellius, book 13 chapter 17, the grammarian
Sulpitius Apollinaris records two proverbs, one Greek and one Latin, both
with the same meaning. The Greek is a hexameter of proverbial form, he   5
says: 'Many things happen between the cup and the final touch of the lip.' It
is a warning to us that nothing we hope for is so certain, and nothing so
close, that it cannot be suddenly upset by some turn of chance. So little is it
safe to trust in things to come, that we are scarcely certain of what we hold in
our hands.   10
      The origin of the proverb is traced in some quarters to the following
story. Ancaeus, the son of Neptune and Astypalea, daughter of Phoenix,
planted a vineyard; and he vehemently harassed and urged on his workers.
One of them tired of the work and turned against his master; he swore that
his master would never taste any wine from those vines. Later on, when the   15
vines had grown well and the grapes had ripened, the master exulted in
      * * * * *
19 Quintilian] 12.6.5, cited above in I iv 73
21 later] *Adagia* IV iii 70, which stood next after this one in *1508*. The cross-
   reference was added here in *1528*.

1 This proverb and the following, which belongs with it, were placed here in
  1515; in the first edition of *1508* they stood before what is now I v 29. In the
  Collectanea they had shared a paragraph (no 128), which is reused, partly
  verbatim, here. The material was no doubt taken originally from Gellius and
  from Diogenianus 7.46 (it is also in Zenobius 5.71 and Suidas II 1869). *Adagia* IV
  viii 30 is very close. Tilley T 191 Many things fall between the cup and the lip.
3 Gellius] 13.18.3 (see I i 1n). In *1508* the reference was given as book 12 chapter
  16.

triumph and sent for that servant, and ordered him to pour his master a cup
of wine. As he was just about to raise the cup to his lips, he reminded the
slave of what he had said, and pointed out how vain his prophecy had been.
But the slave answered his master with this saying: 'Between the cup and   20
the lips much may befall.' The event justified the slave's saying. For as they
were talking, before the master had drunk the wine, another servant came in
and announced that the vineyard was being wrecked by a huge boar.
Hearing this, Ancaeus put down the cup and rushed off at once after the
boar, which gored and killed him during the hunt.   25
    Lycophron takes this over in his *Iambics*:

> Learning the truth, poor wretch, at my own expense
> That Fate, directing the affairs of mortals,
> Tosses many things between the lip and the drinking-cup.

The commentator gives Aristotle as the authority, who also told the story of   30
Ancaeus, with a certain variant. Ancaeus was planting the vineyard, when a
seer who had been summoned prophesied to him that he would never taste
the wine from it. He poured out some wine into a cup and taunted the seer
as a 'false prophet.' The rest agrees with what we have related from the
collections of others. Festus Pompeius says it was an augur from the neigh-   35
bourhood, passing by, who made the prophecy. Lycophron alters it in
another way, bringing in the father Agapenor, and making Ancaeus the son
of Actor and Eurythemistis, and the boar the Calydonian boar. Dionysius, in
Zenodotus, prefers to connect the proverb with Antinous, mentioned by
Homer in *Odyssey* 22. This Antinous was one of the suitors of Penelope, and   40
was holding a cup, just about to drink, when Ulysses shot an arrow which
transfixed him by the throat. The cup fell from his hands and he collapsed
and died. It would not be out of place to transcribe Homer's lines:

> He spoke, and aimed the bitter arrow at Antinous.
> He was about to lift the fair cup,   45

        * * * * *

26 Lycophron] *Alexandra* 488–90 (see I iii 56n); the first line appeared in *1508* in
    I v 61.
30 Aristotle] Frag 571 Rose, cited by the Byzantine scholars John and Isaac Tzetzes
    in their commentary on the passage in Lycophron.
35 Festus] P 132 (see I i 28n), added in *1515*.
39 Zenodotus] Zenobius 5.71 (Erasmus always calls him Zenodotus).
40 Homer] *Odyssey* 22.8–19

Golden, two-handled, taking it in his hands
To drink the wine; murder was not in his thoughts;
Who would think that at a crowded banquet   50
There was one among many, strong though he be,
To bring him evil death and dark destruction?
But Ulysses aiming at his throat struck him with his arrow
And the point pierced his tender neck straight through.
He swerved to one side, and the cup fell from his hand,   55
And immediately the thick stream of the man's blood
Issued from his nostrils.

I think it is not inappropriate at this point to recall the reply which
Julius Caesar received when he reproached the soothsayer with talking
nonsense: 'The Calends of March have come but not gone.'

2 Inter os et offam
Between mouth and morsel

The Latin proverb runs thus, and is taken from eating as the Greek one that   5
precedes is taken from drinking. In old days the Romans lived on *offae*
[morsels, bits and pieces] as Valerius Maximus bears witness. 'Between
mouth and morsel' is as if you said 'between the mouth and the food.' In
Gellius the proverb is quoted from some speech or other of Cato's, about
improper appointment of magistrates, in these words: 'Now they say, there

* * * * *

57 Julius Caesar] Suetonius *Divus Julius* 81.4 (see 1 i 78n). Caesar had been warned
   by a soothsayer against a great danger that would not last beyond the Ides of
   March (March 15), and when that day had arrived without incident, he mocked
   the prophet for his mistake, and received this reply. Later that day he was
   assassinated. 'Calends' (first of the month) is a curious slip for 'Ides.'

2 This adage was joined with the preceding in *Collectanea* no 128. Just what
   Erasmus thought *offa* meant, is hard to say; it seems to have been applied to any
   object of no particular shape, usually edible, and often farinaceous (an English
   'dumpling' would be an *offa*, but not every *offa* would be a dumpling), a 'lump'
   of dough or fat or meat. Otto 1311. III vi 73 *Ollarius deus* preceded this in *1515*
   and *1517/8*, and followed it in *1520* and *1523*, before being moved to its present
   position in *1526*.
5 Valerius Maximus] See 1 ii 14n; Erasmus is thinking perhaps of 2.5.5.
7 Gellius] 13.18.1 (Gellius' name put here in *1515*), citing Cato's *Orationes* frag 217
   (*Oratorum Romanorum fragmenta*, ed H. Malcovati, Turin 1955, 88)

is good grain both in the ear and in the blade. Do not be too hopeful about
that. I have often heard it said that between the mouth and the morsel much   10
can intervene. There is certainly a wide interval between the morsel of food
and the blade.' Festus records the adage as 'between the hand and the chin.'

3 **Ita fugias, ne praeter casam**
   Run away, but not beyond the house

In the *Phormio* of Terence there is one of the most charming proverbs: 'Run
away, but not beyond the house,' which warns us not to avoid one fault in
such a way that we imprudently fall into a worse one. 'It is by our own fault,'   5
he says, 'that it is profitable to be bad, when we are trying too hard to be
called good and kind. Run away, but not beyond the house, as they say.'
The words are those of old Demophon, reproaching himself with having
striven too eagerly to avoid the reputation of being a miser, and so incurring
the blame of being a fool. Donatus explains the metaphor of the adage in the   10
following way (always supposing this comment is by Donatus): 'Run away,
but not overlooking your own house, which can be your safest place of
refuge.' Or, 'Run away, but not beyond the house, where a thief can better
be guarded against and caught and punished with a good flogging. Or,' he
says, 'the word is that of a man shouting at a thief and taking care that he   15
should not pass in front of the house, and in passing steal something from
there too.' Who would put up with this kind of guesswork, with its variable
and uncertain conjectures, if we did not see this to be the very method of
commentators on the law and on the Greek adages? The first interpretation
suits me best. Some people, in the urgency of their flight, run past the very   20
place where they could comfortably stay quiet. The Greeks have one word
for this, *parapheresthai*, meaning to rush past or be carried past by mistake,
away from the thing which was to be grasped. I think Lucian had this adage
in mind when he writes in *Nigrinus*: 'And as the saying goes in the tragedies
and comedies, swiftly running past the house.'   25

* * * * *

12 Festus] P 132, added in 1515; cf *Adagia* IV viii 30, Otto 1035. In 1508 the last
   sentence was 'So Gellius.'

3 *Collectanea* no 166, much of which is taken over verbatim. Otto 353
3 Terence] *Phormio* 766–8, with Donatus' comment on the passage; used again in
   III vii 4
23 Lucian] *Nigrinus* 31, added in 1515. Erasmus' text of Lucian is incorrect here;
   and even so, the phrase seems to bear no relation to the adage he is discussing.

4 Evitata Charybdi in Scyllam incidi
Having escaped Charybdis I fell into Scylla

Τὴν Χάρυβδιν ἐκφυγὼν τῇ Σκύλλῃ περιέπεσον, I escaped Charybdis but fell into Scylla. These are iambic dimeters, *akephaloi* [without a beginning] whether produced by chance or created by art is uncertain. The meaning is 5 this: 'While I was avoiding a more serious evil I fell into a different one'. The adage comes from the story in Homer, which tells how Ulysses sailed too close to Scylla for fear of Charybdis, and lost six of his crew. Some say that Scylla was the daughter of Nisus king of the Megarians, who for stealing her father's golden lock of hair was changed into this sea-monster, as Pausanias 10 tells in his book on Corinth. Virgil seems to agree with this in the *Bucolics*, when he says

> Or what shall I say of Scylla, Nisus' child,
> Whom story pictures as a lovely woman
> Ringed round with howling monsters to her waist, 15
> Her sea-dogs' fangs tearing the trembling sailors?

Servius states that Scylla was the daughter of Phorcus and the nymph Crateis. When Glaucus fell in love with her, Circe, who had a passion for him, saw that he was fonder of Scylla than of herself, and mixed magic poison in the spring where the nymph was accustomed to bathe. When she 20 stepped down into it, she was changed from the waist downwards into a variety of shapes. For this was the special quality of Circe, to change human beings into the shape of beasts. Hating her deformity she flung herself into the sea, and became the subject of the legend.

Where the truth lies, opinion differs among writers. Sallust thinks 25 there was a rock jutting out into the sea, which looked like the shape of a woman to anyone who saw it from a distance, and the waves dashing against it seemed to imitate the sound of wolves howling and dogs barking,

* * * * *

4 *Collectanea* no 378, rewritten at much greater length. Otto 382. Tilley s 169 Between Scylla and Charybdis

4 akephaloi] 'headless'; Erasmus uses the Greek term denoting a metrical line in which the first syllable is deliberately omitted. He may have found the Greek, which is normally regarded as prose, in Apostolius 16.49.

7 Homer] *Odyssey* 12.235–46

10 Pausanias] 2.34.7 (see I i 90n).

11 Virgil] *Eclogues* 6.74–5 and 77, with Servius' commentary on the passage

25 Sallust] Frag 4.27 of his lost *Histories* (first century BC), cited by Servius on *Aeneid* 3.414

so it was imagined that she was girdled from the waist down with such wild
animals. In the Greek collections I find that there was a trireme, a particular- 30
ly fleet one, called *Scylla*, from *skyleuein*, to despoil, because the pirates who
lurked in her infested the Tyrrhenian and Sicilian seas and whenever they
overtook other ships, despoiled them: hence the story arose. As to Charybdis, the fables of the poets tell that she was a ravenous woman who stole
the oxen of Hercules and was struck by Jove's thunderbolt, and flung into 35
the sea, there to become a monster which retains its previous nature to this
day. For it swallows up everything, and what it has swallowed is driven
towards the shore round Taormina, according to Sallust. Thus Horace gives
the proverbial name Charybdis to a greedy courtesan of insatiable covetous-
ness: 40

> Wretched youth,
> In what a great Charybdis art thou caught,
> Lad worthy of a better flame.

Servius says Scylla is in Italy, Charybdis in Sicily. In the *Aeneid* Book 3, Virgil
has a beautiful description of the narrow strait between the two perils: 45

> Once on a time, they say, these two lands were a single
> Country; then there came a convulsion of nature which tore them
> Hugely asunder – the ages can bring such immense geological
> Change – and the sea rushed violently in between them, dividing
> Italy from Sicily, severing their coasts and washing 50
> Cities and fields on either side with a narrow strait.
> Scylla guards the right shore, insatiable Charybdis
> The left.

and the same elsewhere: '– not to attempt the passage, there being on either
side / So narrow a margin of safety.' In the *Odyssey* Book 12, Homer 55
describes the double danger at great length, and makes Circe warn Ulysses
to keep his course nearer to Scylla than to Charybdis, because it would be
better to lose six of his crew than have them all perish; she assures him that
Charybdis is more hazardous than Scylla:

> Heaven keep you from being there when she sucks the waves in her jaws, 60
> * * * * *

30 Greek] Apostolius, as above
38 Horace] *Odes* 1.27.18–20
44 Virgil] *Aeneid* 3.414–21; 685–6 (tr C. Day Lewis)
55 Homer] *Odyssey* 12.106–10

For not even Neptune could save you from such disaster.
No; you must hug Scylla's rock and speedily drive your ship by;
It is better you should have to mourn the loss of six
Of your company, than that of your whole crew.

The adage can be used in three ways. First, when we give a warning 65
that if a point is reached where we are in such straits that there is no escape
without cost, we must choose the lesser of the two evils, following the
example of Ulysses, and tend to the side where the loss is slighter. For
instance, if someone is in danger of losing his money or his safety, he
chooses to have his money in danger rather than his life, because the loss of 70
possessions can be repaired in one way or another, but life once lost can
never be restored. Secondly, we may use it to point out that a transaction is
double-sided and dangerous, and that it needs the utmost prudence to keep
from erring on either side. In this case there will be no question of deciding
which is the greater risk; but this at least is clear, that on each side there is 75
great danger. An example of the first would be, 'Remember it is far better to
incur expense through Scylla than to lose health in Charybdis.' It is preferable to have a financial loss, to run into Scylla as it were, than to fall into the
Charybdis of dishonour. Of the second: 'Take care to please the people in
such a way that you do not offend the ruler. Do your business with caution 80
and circumspection, remembering that you are steering a course between
Scylla and Charybdis.' Thirdly, you could turn it the other way, like this: 'By
being afraid to seem not very learned, you have brought on yourself the
reputation of arrogance; that is exactly what is meant by avoiding Scylla and
falling into Charybdis.' In Latin this line is famous, whoever was the author 85
(at present it does not come to mind): 'Into Scylla he fell, in hopes of
avoiding Charybdis.'

5 **Fumum fugiens, in ignem incidi**
   Fleeing from the smoke I fell into the fire

Κάπνον γε φεύγων εἰς τὸ πῦρ περιέπεσον, From smoke I fled, into the fire I
fell; an iambic line very close to the previous saying. Lucian in *Necyomantia*:

* * * * *

85 In Latin] A familiar proverbial line, identified by von Leutsch as Gauthier de
   Châtillon *Alexandreis* 5.301 (c 1180 AD)

 5 *Collectanea* no 683, very briefly, probably from Diogenianus 8.45. Tilley s 570
   Shunning the smoke he fell into the fire; F 784 Out of the frying-pan into the
   fire. IV vii 40 belongs here.
 4 Lucian] *Necyomantia* 4

'It had escaped my notice, that, as they say, I was forcing myself out of the   5
smoke into the fire.' Plato also uses it in the *Republic*, book 8, when he says
that a people which refuses to obey free men is avoiding the smoke and
running into the fire – meaning that they will be forced to obey slaves.
Horace alludes to this when he says in the *Satires*, 'For all in vain one fault
you may avoid, / If by the other you are warped.' And in the *Art of Poetry*:   10
'Shunning a fault leads to another failing, / If without skill.' Plutarch 'On
False Shame': 'But it invariably happens that foolish shame fleeing the
smoke of disgrace throws itself into the fire,' that is, into something worse.

6 Latum unguem, ac similes hyperbolae proverbiales
A nail's breadth, and other similar proverbial hyperbolae

To swerve by a finger's breadth, or a nail's breadth, is a common saying in
Cicero, meaning 'by the least distance.' The metaphor is pleasanter when
we use these words to convey perfect imitation and full agreement, as in the   5
Academic Questions, book 2: 'From this rule I may not swerve, as they say, by
a nail's breadth.' And again, 'For where does he follow Xenocrates, whose
books on method in speaking are many and much approved by many, or
Aristotle himself, than whom nothing has more acuteness or polish? Never
does he stir a foot from Chrysippus.' He is speaking of Antiochus, who   10
despised all others and followed Chrysippus in everything. Again in
Academic Questions book 2, 'Once these are conceded, not a finger's breadth
of progress can be made.' Again *Letters to Atticus*: 'I am determined not to
stray a finger's breadth from the path of strict honour.' Again in the same
work, book 13: 'One must take care, and this in every kind of life, each one of   15
us, not to swerve one nail's breadth from our conscience.' Again in the
Letters to Friends: 'Urge him therefore to stray a nail's breadth, as they say,
from his writing.' Less metaphorical, but still proverbial, are the words of

* * * * *

6 Plato] *Republic* 8.569b (the reference added in 1523)
9 Horace] *Satires* 2.2.54–5; *Ars poetica* 31
11 Plutarch] *Moralia* 532D. 'False shame' is the Greek *dysôpia*, for which there is no
   name either in Latin (Erasmus tries several equivalents) or in English — the
   Loeb Classical Library uses 'compliancy.' It is the mistaken wish not to give
   offence, that makes one say yes to a request when the right answer clearly
   would be no.

6 *Collectanea* no 377, from Cicero. Otto 1825; Suringar 104; Tilley N 7 Not to stir a
   nail's breadth, H 28 Not to stir a hair's breadth
4 Cicero] *Academica* 2.18.58; 2.36.116 (added in 1528); *Ad Atticum* 7.3.11; 13.20.4;
   Ad familiares 7.25.2

Euclio in Plautus' *Aulularia*: 'By Hercules, if you move out of this place by a
finger or the breadth of a nail ... .' And Cicero in the *Verrines*, 'They did not   20
yield a finger's breadth.' The same, *Letters to Atticus*, book 13, the first letter:
'We have not yet set foot outside the villa, such heavy and continuous
rainstorms we have had.' The same in *Academic Questions* book 2: 'I am not
seeking from them those first principles of mathematics, which must be
conceded, or else not a finger's breadth of progress can be made.' And St   25
Jerome in imitation of this: 'And following in the footsteps of the apostolic
will, let us not depart by one point, as they say, by the breadth of a nail, from
his opinions.'

The metaphor appears partly to be derived from those who measure a
plank or a piece of stone, or something of the kind, by fingers' breadth,   30
whenever a precise measurement is required, for we are used to measure
other things by cubits. A fingerbreadth is the smallest possible measurement. Partly it comes from land-surveyors, who measure the ground by
stadia, paces, or for the smallest measurement, feet. Even now the people
say 'a straw's breadth' using the same sort of figure of speech, to mean 'not   35
in the very least.'

7 **Pedem ubi ponat non habet**
   He has no place to set his foot

This proverbial hyperbole often used by Cicero seems to come from the
same source: He has no place to set his foot, meaning he does not possess
the least scrap of land. *Letters to Atticus*, book 13: 'The son of Ariobarzanes is   5
coming to Rome. I imagine he wants to buy a kingdom from Caesar, for as
things now stand he has not a place of his own to set his foot.' Again in the
second *Philippic*: 'What place in the world was there, where you could set
foot on your own ground?' Again *Letters to Atticus*, book 7: 'Clearly there is
not a foot of soil in Italy which is not in that man's grasp.' Again in *De finibus*,   10
book 4: 'What was to become of wisdom? She had not a place to set her foot,
when all her functions were taken away.' It applies to a particularly poor and

* * * * *

19 Plautus] *Aulularia* 56–7
20 Cicero] *Verrines* 4.15.33; *Ad Atticum* 13.16.1; *Academica* 2.36.116 (added for the
   second time in *1536*)
26 Jerome] *Letters* 120.10.3, added in *1515*

7 Taken direct from Cicero. In *1533* an apt quotation which had appeared too late
   to be included found a separate home as IV x 50. Otto 1394
3 Cicero] *Ad Atticum* 13.2.2, added with the next two in *1523*; *Philippics* 2.19.48,
   used again in IV viii 7; *Ad Atticum* 7.22.1; *De finibus* 4.25.69, added in *1536*

needy man, who has not as much ownership of land as the sole of his foot.
The same writer has a joke about a farm 'which can be shot from a sling.'

8 Iterum eundem ad lapidem offendere
To stumble twice over the same stone

Δὶς πρὸς τὸν αὐτὸν αἰσχρὸν εἰσκρούειν λίθον, It is shameful to stumble twice
on the same stone. A neat and proverbial iambic line which is quoted by
Zenodotus in his collection of adages. Cicero, *Letters to Friends*, book 10: 'The   5
error of "twice against the same stone" is held up to reproach in a familiar
proverb.' Ovid, *Tristia*, book 2: 'But as it is – such madness accompanying
my disease – I strike my foot again on those remembered rocks.' Ausonius
uses this in one of his letters: 'Truly, you made your request, so that you
should twice fall over the same stone in your letter, but I, whatever fortune   10
should befall, would only blush once.' 'To fall over the same stone twice' is
to go wrong twice in the same matter. For the first mistake, as in the Greek
adage, deserves forgiveness; but for one who repeats the offence there is no
excuse. Among the Greek maxims this one is also famous: 'It is not for a wise
man to take the same tumble twice.' There is a Greek epigram also, of   15
uncertain authorship: 'He, married once, who takes another wife, / Seeks
the wild ocean with a shipwrecked craft.' A proverbial maxim current under
the name of Publius has something not unlike this expression: 'He wrongly
rails at Neptune, who suffers shipwreck twice.' But Scipio does not allow the
wise man to err even once, or to say 'I never expected this.'   20

* * * * *

14 The same writer] Quintilian 8.6.73 cites a distich by Cicero (frag poet 4 Morel),
   mocking a man who called a bit of earth his country estate (*fundus*) when it was
   so small that it might have been shot from a sling (*funda*).

8 This and the next were coupled together in *Collectanea* no 398. Tilley s 882 He
   that stumbles twice at the same stone deserves to have his shins broke. Close to
   IV v 62
5 Zenodotus] Zenobius 3.29 (also in Diogenianus 4.19 and Suidas Δ 1267)
5 Cicero] *Ad familiares* 10.20.2, added in 1523
7 Ovid] *Tristia* 2.15–6, added in 1523
8 Ausonius] *Epistula* 11 (see I i 86n).
14 Greek maxims] Menander *Sententiae* 183 (see I i 30n).
15 Greek epigram] *Anthologia Palatina* 9.133, added in 1515
18 Publius] Publilius Syrus I 63 (see I ii 4n); it is one of the Publilian lines quoted in
   Gellius 17.14.4 (Publius was the current spelling of the name in Erasmus' day).
19 Scipio] The anecdote is preserved by Valerius Maximus (I ii 14n) 7.2.2. The
   expression *Non putavi* or *Non putaram*, 'I never thought of that,' used by people
   who are surprised by events which they ought to have foreseen, has as much

9　**Eadem oberrare chorda**
To strike the same wrong note

Horace expresses the same idea in the *Art of Poetry*, with a different metaphor: 'The lute-player is mocked who is forever playing the same wrong note.' Adopted from musicians, for whom it is a terrible thing to play　5
a wrong note more than once on the same string. It can well be said of those who frequently go wrong in the same matter, or commit the same fault over and over again. The first lapse may be ascribed to chance or rashness, but to do it again argues stupidity or inexperience.

10　**Non tam ovum ovo simile**
As like as one egg to another

Several adages about resemblance are found in the authors, among them 'as like as one egg to another,' of things indistinguishably alike. Cicero, *Academic Questions*, book 4: 'Do you see how the proverb speaks of the　5
likeness of one egg to another? Yet we have been told that in Delos at the time of its prosperity, a number of people were in the habit of keeping hens for profit. These men, when they had inspected an egg, used to say which hen had laid it. Nor is this against us. For it is enough for us to tell the eggs apart.' Quintilian also quoted this proverb. It is made use of by Seneca as　10
well, in the skit he wrote to make fun of the Emperor Claudius.

　　　* * * * *

　　proverbial status as many phrases which are admitted by Erasmus; cf Tilley P 77
　　It is the part of a fool to say 'I had not thought.'

　9　Taken from Horace *Ars poetica* 355–6, and rightly included in *Collectanea* with
　　the preceding. Tilley s 936 identifies it with To harp upon one string; but that
　　means to bore one's hearers by saying the same thing over and over again,
　　and our adage means to make the same mistake, always to play the same
　　wrong note.

　10　This and the next two appear together in a brief list of 'Adages of similitude' in
　　Collectanea under no 396. With them was *Eiusdem farinae* Of the same kidney
　　(literally, dough); and one might have expected this too to have been taken
　　over at this point into the *Chiliades*, since it is a phrase not unfamiliar in
　　Erasmus' own letters. But he had no warrant for it except Poliziano (in a letter to
　　Bartolommeo della Scala, *Opera* Aldus July 1498, sig q vi verso); when he had
　　secured classical backing for it, it was incorporated as III v 54. Otto 1318; Tilley E
　　66 As like as one egg is to another
　4　Cicero] *Lucullus* 18.57
　10　Quintilian] 5.11.30
　10　Seneca] *Ludus de morte Claudii* 11.5 (see I i 33n); this was added in *1515*.

11 Non tam lac lacti simile
    As like as milk to milk

This has the same force, and is used by Plautus in the *Amphitryo*: 'Milk is not
more like milk, than that "I" is like myself.' This is said by Sosia about
Mercury, who had assumed his shape. Again in the *Miles*: 'As like as milk to   5
milk.'

12 Non tam aqua similis aquae
    As like as water to water

Another phrase of Plautus, in the *Menaechmi*, has the same force: 'Not water
to water, nor milk to milk, believe me, was ever more exactly resembling
than he to you, and you to him.' Like this is the phrase from the same scene,   5
'He's so like you that he might be your mirror.' Again in the *Miles*: 'For never
could water be drawn from the top of a well as like water as this.'

13 Quam apes apum similes
    As like as bees to bees

Cicero adds to these another, in *Academic Questions*, 'as like as eggs to eggs,
and bees to bees,' when he is joking about the worlds of Democritus, each
one just like the other. They say likewise, 'as like as one sheep to another.'   5

14 Acanthia cicada
    The grasshopper of Acanthus

Ἀκάνθιος τέττιξ, The grasshopper of Acanthus. Used as a proverb against

* * * * *

11 Joined in *Collectanea* with the preceding, and derived from Plautus *Amphitryo*
    601 and *Miles gloriosus* 240 (added in *1523*). Otto 899 gives two other instances
    from him, which Erasmus does not quote.

12 Part of *Collectanea* no 396; from Plautus *Menaechmi* 1089–90 and *Miles gloriosus*
    551–2 (added in *1523*). Otto 132

13 From Cicero *Lucullus* 17.54; the last sentence was added in *1528*. This was
    followed in *1508* by *Penelopes telam retexere*, which after that became I iv 42. The
    reference is to the cosmology of Democritus, the early Greek philosopher.

14 *Collectanea* no 307, where Stephanus is named as the authority and the Greek is
    given, presumably, from Diogenianus 1.49 (it is also in Zenobius 1.51 and
    Suidas A 798).

people who are ignorant, inarticulate or unskilled in music. It is Stephanus
Byzantius who tells us that it was near the town of Acanthus, in Aetolia, that   5
grasshoppers are mute, though they chirp elsewhere; hence this proverb.
He quotes as his authority Simonides. Pliny, in his *Natural History*, book 11
chapter 27, writes that in the territory of Rhegium all the cicadas are silent,
while across the river in the Locrian territory they sing. Pausanias says the
same in his second book on Elis. Strabo *Geography*, book 6, reports that the   10
territory of Rhegium is separated from the Locrian by a river named the
Alex. The cicadas which live on the Locrian side chirp loudly, while those of
Rhegium are silent. He thinks the cause of this is that the district of Rhegium
is shady and dark, and makes the wing-cases of the cicadas heavy with
moisture, while in the Locrian country, which is sunny, they are dried by the   15
heat of the sun and are readier to emit their noise. The very fact that there is a
well-known story about the vocal powers of their neighbours increases the
mystery about the cicadas of Rhegium. For the aforesaid Strabo quotes
Timaeus as his authority for the story that Eunomus the Locrian and Ariston
of Rhegium competed with each other in song in the Pythian games. Ariston   20
invoked the Delphic Apollo to his aid as a singer, because the people of
Rhegium formerly came from Delphi. Eunomus replied that it was not for
the people of Rhegium to enter into any musical contest at all, since in their
country that most vocal of creatures, the cicada, lacked a voice. As they were
competing, one of the strings of Eunomus' lyre snapped, and a cicada flying   25
overhead hopped down and supplied by its chirp the note which would
otherwise have been missing. He was therefore proclaimed the victor, and
he put up a statue of a lyre-player with a cicada perched on his instrument.
This is more or less what Strabo relates.

15   **Eadem pensari trutina**
     To be weighed on the same scales

To be weighed on the same scales, that is, under the same conditions.
   * * * * *
   4 Stephanus] Steph. Byzantius p 57 Meineke (see I ii 43n); the name Aetolia and
     the reference to the early Greek poet Simonides (frag 105 Page) were added in
     1526, perhaps from Stephanus.
   7 Pliny] *Naturalis historia* 11.95
   9 Pausanias] 6.6.4 (see I i 90n).
   10 Strabo] *Geographica* 6.1.9 (see I i 69n), citing the lost historian Timaeus of
     Tauromenium (fourth/third century BC), *FGrHist* 566 F 43b.

   15 *Collectanea* no 316 cited both passages from Horace and the Persius, and also
     Matthew 7:2 'With what measure ye mete, it shall be measured to you again,'
     which was not taken into the *Chiliades*.

Horace in the *Satires*: 'This granted, he'll be placed on the same scales.' And
again in the *Epistles*: 'On the same scales Rome's writers must be weighed.'   5
This agrees with the well-known rule of the lawyers: 'You must suffer the
law you have yourself laid down.' You must let the same treatment be given
to you as you have given to others. Persius: 'In that great scale the lying
tongue set straight.' A very similar saying is 'To assess by the same yard-
stick, ἴσῳ σταθμῷ, by equal weight, that is, with level scale or balance.   10
Plutarch: 'But with equal weight the vice that hangs about all men drags
them down, "as leaden weights pull down a fishing-net."'

16   **Zonam perdidit**
     He's lost his belt

A soldier's proverb meaning 'he hasn't a penny,' taken, says Acron, from
some Greek fable. Porphyrion derives it from the soldiers' habit of carrying
whatever they posses in their belts. Lucilius, as quoted by Nonius, has a fine   5
description of such a man:

> He has no mount, no servant, no companion,
> But always with him has his money-bag;
> With money-bag he eats, and sleeps, and washes,
> The man's one hope is in his bag, and all   10
> The rest of life's devoted to it.

Bulga is the word used by Lucilius for a purse or pouch, a small bag hanging
from the arm. So Horace says 'With copy-book and satchel on their arm';
though Festus indicates that *bulga* is a Gaulish word. In Aulus Gellius,

* * * * *

4 Horace] *Satires* 1.3.72; *Epistles* 2.1.29–30
6 rule of the lawyers] *Digest* 2.2
8 Persius] *Satires* 1.6–7, used again in II v 37. The 'great scale' is the balance of
   public opinion.
11 Plutarch] *Moralia* 75B, citing Sophocles frag 796 Nauck, which Erasmus does
   not seem to have detected.

16 *Collectanea* no 320, citing Horace *Epistles* only. Otto 1950
 3 Acron] He and Porphyrion are ancient scholars whose names are attached to
   extant commentaries on Horace (here *Epistles* 2.2.40).
 5 Lucilius] 243–6 (see I ii 35n), cited by Nonius (see I i 97n) p 78; added in *1515*.
13 Horace] *Satires* 1.6.74, added in *1515*
14 Festus] P 31 (see I i 28n), added in *1515*
14 Gellius] 15.12.4, added in *1515*. He cites Gaius Gracchus' defence of his
   administration in Sardinia in 124 BC (*Oratorum Romanorum fragmenta*, ed H.
   Malcovati, Turin 1955, 182, frag 28).

Gracchus talks in the same way: 'When I set out for Rome, those full belts of   15
silver I took out with me, were empty when I brought them back from the
province.' Horace in the *Epistles*: 'He will go where you will, who's lost his
belt.' Plautus in the *Poenulus*: 'You who have no belt-bag, how did you come
to this town? What are you looking for?' In these words of Plautus there is a
double allusion to the garment worn in the Carthaginian fashion without a   20
girdle, and to the money carried in the belt, indispensable for living in a
costly city. Pescennius Niger, according to Spartianus, forbade the soldiers
to carry their belts with them into war, but if they had any money they were
to hand it over to the care of the State, and it would be returned to them after
the battle. Thus at one and the same time he took away from them the means   25
of spendthrift living, and from the enemy their booty in case of any disaster.
In Lampridius, writing about Alexander, we find: 'A soldier is not afraid,
except when clothed, shod, armed, and with something in his belt.'

17 **Cocta numerabimus exta**
    We shall count the entrails when cooked

Diomedes the grammarian, defining a proverb, adds this as an example. He
gives the meaning as 'we shall know from the outcome.' In the same vein is
the argument in the comedy: 'the facts will show.' For as Ovid says, 'The   5
event justifies the deed.' And in Greek αὐτὸ δείξει, The thing itself will
show.

18 **Multa novit vulpes, verum echinus unum magnum**
    The fox knows many things, but the hedgehog one big thing

Πόλλ᾽ οἶδ᾽ ἀλώπηξ ἀλλ᾽ ἐχῖνος ἕν μέγα, Many-sided the skill of the fox: the

* * * * *

17 Horace] *Epistles* 2.2.40

18 Plautus] *Poenulus* 1008–9

22 Spartianus] *Pescennius Niger* 10.7, added in *1517/8*. This and the next are from
   the *Historia Augusta* (see I i 21n).

27 Lampridius] *Severus Alexander* 52–3, added in *1528*

17 *Collectanea* no 333, citing Diomedes; the wording is partly re-used. Otto 618;
   Tilley P 608 The proof of the pudding is in the eating.

3 Diomedes] p 462 Keil (*Grammatici latini* 1, Leipzig 1857)

5 comedy] Terence *Eunuchus* 469; this forms *Adagia* III iv 49.

5 Ovid] *Heroides* 2.85

6 in Greek] Suidas A 4490

18 Taken from Zenobius (it is also in Suidas II 1931). Tilley F 636 The fox knows
   many tricks but the hedgehog one great one.

hedgehog has one great gift. Zenodotus quotes this line from Archilochus. It
is said about cunning people who are involved in various plots, or rather   5
when we want to show how some people manage to do more with one piece
of astuteness than others with their different schemes. The fox protects itself
against the hunters by many and various wiles, and yet is often caught. The
echinus, by which I take it he means the hedgehog (for in this place he is
talking of the land-animal, not the sea-urchin) by its one skill alone is safe   10
from the bites of dogs; it rolls itself up with its spines into a ball, and cannot
be snapped up with a bite from any side. In the same Zenodotus these lines
are quoted from Ion of Chios, a tragic poet; and Athenaeus quotes the same
from the same in his *Table-talk*, from a tragedy entitled *Phoenicia*:

> But on land a lion's way I praise,   15
> But even more the hedgehog's wretched arts:
> When he perceives another creature's smell
> Rolling his spiny self into a ball
> He lies impregnable to touch and bite.

Plutarch refers to the proverb and to the poem in his essay entitled 'Whether   20
Land or Sea Animals Are Cleverer.' I will give his words: 'The defending and
guarding of their own safety by hedgehogs has provided the proverb: "The
fox knows many things, but the hedgehog one big thing." For when the fox
approaches, they say, "Rolling his spiny self into a ball, / He lies impreg-
nable to touch and bite."' Plutarch, or whoever was the author of this work,   25
mingled with the lines some words of his own; I say this so that no one will
suspect me of the error. But it is Pliny who described most fully the intelligence and astuteness of this animal (book 8 chapter 37): 'Hedgehogs also',
he says, 'prepare their food, and by rolling over the apples lying on the
ground spike them on their spines; they take just one in their mouths and   30

* * * * *

4 Zenodotus] Zenobius 5.68, citing the early Greek poet Archilochus frag 201
   West
9 hedgehog] In *1508* Erasmus used the word *ericius*, which occurs in a fragment
   of Varro cited by Nonius p 106; in *1515* he changed this to the more usual
   herinaceus, and added the point that the *echinus* of the Greek proverb is the
   hedgehog and not the sea-urchin. The same word is used for both, as 'urchin'
   used to be in English.
13 Athenaeus] 3.91d–e, citing Ion of Chios frag 38 Nauck (fifth century BC)
20 Plutarch] *Moralia* 971E–F, citing the last two lines of the same fragment of Ion of
   Chios, though this is concealed by an error in Erasmus' text of Plutarch which
   obliterates Ion's name, and he provides two quite different Latin versions. The
   comment which follows was added in *1528*.
27 Pliny] *Naturalis historia* 8.133–4; 9.100, both added in *1515*

carry them into hollow trees. By retreating into their holes they foretell the
change of wind from north to south. But when they know the presence of a
hunter, they contract snout, feet and the whole of their underpart, which is
covered with sparse and harmless hair, and they roll up into the shape of a
ball, so that nothing can be taken hold of that is not spikes. When driven to   35
desperation they void urine which corrodes their hinder parts and damages
their spines.' Anyone who wishes to learn more about this must consult the
reference I have given. This is the part which touches most closely on the
sense of the proverb.

The sea-urchin also is famous for intelligence; foreseeing the raging of   40
the sea, it collects stones and weighs itself down with them, so that the
weight will keep it from being easily shifted, and its spines will not be worn
out with too much rolling. When sailors see this, they make fast their boats
with several anchors. This is what Pliny says in book 9 chapter 31.

The fox is crafty, and knows a great many tricks, as many fables relate,   45
especially this one, which is told by Plutarch in his *Moralia*. Once, when the
leopard was making a scornful comparison between himself and the fox,
claiming that he had a coat of varying and many-coloured spots, the fox
replied that while the leopard's ornamentation was on his skin, his own was
in the mind. And truly it was much better to be endowed with cunning   50
brains than with a party-coloured skin. The Greeks call a clever and guileful
person *poikilophron* and *poikilometis*; the Latin words are *vafer* and *versipellis*.

Another story is told, not unlike this proverb: once the fox was talking
to the cat, and boasting that he had so many skills at his disposal that one
might say he had a bag of tricks; the cat replied that she had only one, to   55
which she trusted in danger. While they were discussing this there was
suddenly a noise of approaching hounds. The cat lept up into a high tree,
while the fox was encircled and caught by the pack of hounds. The moral of
this story is that it is sometimes worth more to have one plan, if it is realistic
and efficacious, than several wiles and trivial schemes. For instance, a poor   60
man might court a girl with manifold devices, but a rich man would have
one only, the one described by Ovid: 'Say "take what you like," you will say
well.' The fox knows many things, but the hedgehog one big thing.

* * * * *

46 Plutarch] *Moralia* 155B and 500C, referring to Aesop, fable 42 Halm
51 The Greeks] Erasmus' point is that in Greek, words that mean mental agility are
   compounds of the normal word for 'many-coloured' (*poikilos*); in Latin, a clever
   man can be described as one who changes his skin. The analogy between
   versatility of mind and variegation of colour has been built into the language.
53 Another story] Not classical, it seems; Stith Thompson's *Motif-index of Folk
   Literature* (1955) J 1662; La Fontaine's *Fables* 9.14
62 Ovid] This has not yet been identified.

19 **Simulare cupressum**
    To paint a cypress

Horace in the *Art of Poetry*: 'Perhaps you can paint a cypress tree; / But that's
no use, if shipwrecks earn your fee.' Acron points out that this is a proverb,
derived from an inexperienced painter who could not paint anything but a   5
cypress. A man who had been in a shipwreck asked him to paint his portrait
and show the shipwreck, whereupon the painter asked if he wanted anything added in the way of a cypress? The thing first became a joke and then
an adage. It can aptly be used to describe people who are always obtruding
what they have learnt at inopportune moments, and when it has no bearing   10
on anything.

20 **Flamma fumo est proxima**
    Fire follows smoke

This is found in the *Curculio* of Plautus. The adage warns us to make an early
retreat from danger; whoever wishes to avoid a calamity should avoid what
gives rise to it. Thus whoever wishes not to be corrupted should avoid bad   5
company; if one does not wish to lie with a girl one should not kiss her. The
poet adds at once, 'Smoke can burn nothing, but fire can.' Smoke is the sign
of fire about to break out.

21 **Ad restim res rediit**
    It all comes back to the rope

Terence in the *Phormio*: 'By your doing my situation is obviously getting back
to the rope.' This proverb expresses an utterly desperate situation; for at this

* * * * *

19 Horace *Ars poetica* 19–21 with the note of Acron the ancient commentator; taken
   over from *Collectanea* no 489, where it was followed by a jibe against those
   preachers who have learnt just two or three sermons by rote. The man who had
   escaped from shipwreck had a votive picture made of this moving scene. If he
   could afford to, he hung it in a temple; if he had to beg his living, he kept it to
   touch the hearts of passers-by. In *1508*, *Adagia* I iv 44–6 stood in front of this.

20 *Collectanea* no 66 is partly reused. Otto 666. Not to be confused with our
   'There's no smoke without fire.'
   3 Plautus] *Curculio* 53–4, the name of the play added in *1523*. Erasmus used the
   phrase again in IV vii 40.

21 *Collectanea* no 165, from Terence. Otto 1528
   3 Terence] *Phormio* 685–6

point some frantic people are apt to turn to the noose. Juvenal: 'Can you bear   5
a mistress when ropes are to be had?' That other phrase belongs here:
'Choose your tree and hang yourself.'

22 **Paupertas sapientiam sortita est**
    Poverty has drawn wisdom as her lot

Πενία δὲ τὴν σοφίαν ἔλαχε, Poverty has drawn wisdom as her lot. Zenodotus quotes this from Euripides; others attribute it to Ariston. Wealth is idle,
but Need is the discoverer of many arts. Aristophanes in the *Plutus* makes   5
her boast of this, claiming the invention of all the arts for herself. Virgil: 'Toil
conquers all, / Persistent toil, and need in hardships dire.' Ovid: 'Ills often
cause the mind to stir.' Persius: 'The belly's a great teacher of craftsmanship, /
Bestower of brains.' This line is also quoted in Greek, 'Harsh hunger is the
teacher of many men.' Xenophon called poverty 'wisdom learnt without a   10
teacher: what wisdom persuades us to by speaking, poverty drives us to by
the very thing itself.' Theocritus in the *Fishers*: 'Poverty alone, Diophantus,
awakens the arts, / She is the teacher of toil, the mistress of studies.' This
explains why Jupiter withdrew the readily available plenty of the Golden
Age, 'That many arts should be hammered out / By thought and practice.'   15
And so the familiar proverbial maxim says not inelegantly, 'By poverty's
command, a man learns much.'

* * * * *

5 Juvenal] 6.30, added in *1526* to I x 21
6 other phrase] *Adagia* I x 21

22 From Zenobius ('Zenodotus') 5.72, who cites Euripides frag 641 Nauck (cited
   again in IV vii 55); it is also in Suidas II 967. There is some overlap with II vi 55
   and III ix 99. Tilley P 527 Poverty is the mother of all arts.
5 Aristophanes] *Plutus* 510–6
6 Virgil] *Georgics* 1.145–6, used again in II ii 53
7 Ovid] *Ars amatoria* 2.43. This and the following quotation compose *Adagia* IV ii
   48.
8 Persius] *Satires* prologus 10–11
9 This line] Menander *Sententiae* 630 (the standard text has 'Time' or 'Opportunity,' not 'Hunger'); see I i 30n.
10 Xenophon] This has not been identified.
12 Theocritus] 21.1–2, added in *1526*; 'mistress of studies' was supplied by
   Erasmus to fill out his line, and is not in the Greek.
15 That many arts] Virgil *Georgics* 1.133
16 maxim] Publilius Syrus H 8 (see I ii 4n).

The proverb may also refer to something we see happening, inexplic-
ably: wealth goes to Midas and to the wicked, while the learned and the
good are usually poor. On this subject there are two problems attributed to   20
Aristotle. In one he asks why poverty usually elects to dwell with good men.
He gives various reasons for this: one is that the wicked prefer to amass
riches by hook or by crook rather than to have a long acquaintance with
poverty, and so she flees from those who might take her as an excuse for
great crimes, and turns towards the people who (she thinks) will use her   25
with uprightness and moderation. Another reason he gives is that poverty
lacks both strength and counsel, and thus being a woman hopes to find
better support among the 'men of many tears' as the proverb has it. Or else,
being bad herself, she avoids bad people, lest she should 'add fire to fire' as
the saying is, that is, evil on evil, and become unbearable and incurable.   30
      The other question he asks is why do bad men usually have money,
which is not true of good men. Is wealth blind, he asks, and thus misguided
in its choice? These questions seem more those of a poet and sophist than of
a philosopher, especially a serious one, and I think it is hardly likely that
they come from Aristotle. However, what is said about 'blind riches' is   35
mostly taken from the *Plutus* of Aristophanes. Here Plutus, the god of
wealth, is asked how he came to incur the evil of blindness? He replies as
follows:

> 'Twas Jove that caused it, jealous of mankind;
> For when a little chap, I used to brag   40
> I'd visit none except the wise and good
> And orderly: he therefore made me blind,
> That I might ne'er distinguish which was which,
> So jealous is he always of the good!

Lucian in *Timon* relates much the same sort of thing about Plutus, whom he   45
makes not only blind but lame; always blind, but only lame when sent to
good men – otherwise remarkably fleet-footed.

                * * * * *

21 Aristotle] *Problemata* 29.4 and 8 (950b9 and 36)
28 proverb] *Adagia* II vii 64. For 'fire on fire' see I ii 8.
36 Aristophanes] *Plutus* 87–92
45 Lucian] Timon 20

23 Ollae amicitia
Cupboard love

Χύτρης φιλία, Cupboard love. This applies to that widespread kind of friend
who is attracted by the stewpot, not drawn by affection. On these, see
Juvenal: 'He thinks you have been caught by the smell of his kitchen. And he   5
isn't far wrong.' The Scriptures call these 'table-friends.' Plutarch in his book
'How to Tell a Flatterer From a Friend' says that such people were commonly
called 'oil-flask and trencher-carriers' because they love from the stomach
and not from the heart; those who are always on the spot when they hear
'water for the hands.' For Aristophanes the grammarian, in Athenaeus,   10
book 9, tells how the washing of the hands which preceded a meal was
called *kata cheiros* [on the hands], and after the meal *nipsasthai* [to wash]. If I
am not mistaken, it is against them that the saying of Menander the comic
poet is aimed, as quoted by Athenaeus: 'once hands are washed [for dinner]
friends stick closely.' There is a proverb like this, 'The pot boils, friendship   15
thrives.'

24 Antiquiora diphthera loqueris
You are talking of things older than the diphthera

Ἀρχαιότερα διφθέρας λαλεῖς, You are talking of things older than the
diphthera. This applies to people who tell nonsensical stories, or speak of

* * * * *

23 *Collectanea* no 359 cited Ecclesiasticus (disguised as 'a certain wise man'), and
    derived a Greek form of the phrase from Diogenianus 4.96. Otto 1286; Tilley c
    912 Cupboard love, F 762 Trencher friendship. Erasmus returns to the topic
    with fresh material in *Adagia* IV iv 53.
5 Juvenal] 5.162–3 (from memory)
6 Scriptures] Ecclesiasticus 6:10
6 Plutarch] *Moralia* 50c
10 water for hands] An invitation to wash (slaves perhaps bringing water) seems
    to have been an ancient equivalent of our dinner-bell.
10 Athenaeus] 9.408f, citing Menander frag 405; added in 1517/8
15 proverb] Zenobius 4.12; Diogenianus 4.96; Suidas z 48. The proverb gets much
    of its point from the close resemblance of the Greek verbs for boiling and for
    living and thriving.

24 In the *Chiliades* of 1508, this adage was preceded by what are now I iv 47–91 and
    followed by I iv 92–6. It is a fragment of an unidentified Greek comedy (frag
    adesp 546 Kock), and was probably derived from the proverb-collections
    (Diogenianus 3.2; Suidas A 4076). For the goat which suckled the infant Jupiter,
    see I vi 2.

things that are far in the past and out of date. A *diphthera* or tanned hide was   5
some relic of the early concoctions of legend. They say that a diphthera was
the skin of that goat which suckled Jove, on which (or so said the ancients)
he wrote everything which happened. So the events which neither survive
in the chronicles of the historians nor are preserved in the memory of men
were said to be fetched from Jove's goatskin. Indeed you will often read in   10
Aristophanes words like 'primitive, ancient' for 'nonsense,' I imagine because antiquity is so full of fables; and 'archaically' to mean crazily and
foolishly. It is in the same style that we call old, obsolete, finished things
kronika. So in Athenaeus, book 7, someone, Arrianus I think, says 'Those are
victuals dating from Saturn's time, my friend.' The poets pretend that   15
Saturn was ousted from his kingdom and Jove reigned in his stead.

25   Auribus lupum teneo
I hold the wolf by the ears

This is in the *Phormio* of Terence: a young man, Antiphon, had a wife at
home whom he could not throw out, either because he did not wish to,
being desperately in love with her, or because it would not have been   5
upright to do so, since she had been adjudged to him by the pronouncement
of the magistrates; but neither could he keep her, because of the violent
resentment of his father. And when his cousin called him happy, because he
possessed in his house what he loved, he answered 'It's all very well, I am
holding the wolf by the ears, as they say. For I cannot see how I can send her   10
away, nor do I know how to keep her.' Later the pander asserts (as if
referring to the proverb) that he has the same experience with Phaedria,
whom he can neither keep on, because he pays nothing, nor reject, because
he is terribly charming and promises mountains of gold. Donatus adds the
Greek proverb in Greek words: 'I hold the wolf by the ears, and can neither   15

* * * * *

10 Jove's goatskin] This comes again in I x 58.
14 *kronika*] derived from Kronos, the Greek deity (in Latin, Saturn) who was
    displaced by Zeus (Jupiter), and became the symbol for antiquated ways of life;
    eg II i 75, viii 40.
14 Athenaeus] 3 (not 7). 113a; Arrianus, the speaker, is a character in the fictitious
    dialogue which forms the core of the work. All this final section on *kronika* was
    added in *1528*.

25 *Collectanea* no 164, which was based on Donatus and Gellius, is partly reused.
    The Terence was also quoted in *Collectanea* no 357. Otto 987; Tilley w 603 He
    holds a wolf by the ears.
 3 Terence] *Phormio* 506–7
14 Donatus] The ancient commentator, on *Phormio* 506

keep him nor let him go.' Suetonius in his life of Tiberius: 'The reason for
delay was fear of the risks threatening on all sides, so that often he said he
was holding the wolf by the ears.' Plutarch in 'Precepts of Statecraft': 'A
wolf, they say, cannot be held by the ears,' while men are particularly led by
this part, that is by persuasion.   20
     This is said about people who become involved in some affair which it
would not be honest to abandon, and yet cannot be borne. It seems to have
been derived from some event, like many other proverbs; or at any rate it
springs from the fact that while the hare has very long ears and can easily be
held by them, the wolf has ears which are short for its size, and there is no 25
holding it in that way, but on the other hand it is most dangerous to let it
escape from one's hands, since the beast has such a bite. Caecilius in Aulus
Gellius, book 15 chapter 9, has the same idea but without the metaphor: 'For
these are the worst friends, cheerful of face, / Dismal at heart, whom you can
neither clasp nor let go.' Theognis alludes to it, even more distantly: 'My 30
heart's so strangely moved by love for you / That I can neither love nor can I
hate.' An imitation of this, it seems, is the line 'Not with thee can I live nor
yet without thee.' Varro also give as an example of an adage: I hold a wolf by
the ears.

26 Necessarium malum
A necessary evil

Very close to this is the saying Ἀναγκαῖον κακόν, A necessary evil. There are
people whom you cannot throw over because their help is needed in some
way, but you can hardly tolerate them because of their immorality. This   5
seems to come from the remark of a certain Hybraeas, recalled by Strabo,

                    * * * * *

16 Suetonius] *Tiberius* 25.1, added in *1517/8*, as often (Erasmus published the text
    in 1518).
18 Plutarch] *Moralia* 802D; 'while men ... persuasion' was added in *1533*.
27 Caecilius] Caec. Statius (see I i 27n) 79–80, cited by Gellius 15.9.1; the exact
    reference added in *1528*.
30 Theognis] 1091–2 (see I i 62n).
32 line] Martial 12.46.2, used again in II ix 92
33 Varro] *De lingua latina* 7.31 (see I ii 23n).

26 Otto 1023 cites several parallels from Greek comedy, which Erasmus does not
    use. Tilley W 703 Women are necessary evils; W 386 Wives must be had, be they
    good or bad.
6 Strabo] *Geographica* 14.2.24 (see I i 69n). He tells us that in his time (first century
    BC) Mylasa in Caria had had two prominent politicians, Hybreas and
    Euthydamus; and this was said by one about the other.

book 14. Euthydamus was a man with a certain overbearing quality, but in many ways useful to the state, so that his vices and virtues seemed to break equal. The orator Hybraeas in some speech spoke of him thus, 'You are a necessary evil to the state; we can neither live with you nor without you.'   10 The emperor Alexander Severus decreed the abolition of the public account-ants, but when he reflected that they could not be abolished without damage to the state, he called them 'a necessary evil.' Publius Cornelius Ruffinus was another of this type, thievish and miserly but all the same an excellent commander; Fabricius Luscinus preferred to be plundered by him rather   15 than be sold into slavery, as Gellius tells us in book 4, and Cicero in the *De oratore*, book 2. It can be turned round to apply to wives, who are uncomfort-able to live with, yet without them the commonwealth cannot exist. It can also be applied to things, as when one may say that a medicine is a trouble-some thing, but a necessary one. Euripides in the *Orestes*: 'A possession   20 painful, but necessary.' Not unlike this in form is the response of an oracle recorded by Pliny, book 18 chapter 6: 'By what methods should the fields be cultivated? Saith the oracle, by bad, by good: this means, in its riddling way, that the fields should be cultivated with the least possible expense.'

27 **Non absque Theseo**
    Not without Theseus

Οὐκ ἄνευ Θησέως, Not without Theseus. Here we mean that something is achieved with outside help, or we use it to mean that there is association and partnership in all things. For Zenodotus writes that Theseus was of assist-   5 ance to many of the strongest men in their contests; for instance he was with Meleager in destroying the Calydonian boar, and he assisted Perithous in

* * * * *

11 Alexander] Lampridius *Severus Alexander* 46.5. This forms part of the so-called *Historia Augusta*, on which see I i 21n.
16 Gellius] *Noctes Atticae* 4.8.1–6; the anecdote was added in 1515. Luscinus made great efforts to get his enemy Rufinus elected to command the army: better win the war and be fleeced by him, than lose it and lose everything.
16 Cicero] *De oratore* 2.66.268, added in 1523
17 It can ... exist] This is of 1515.
20 Euripides] *Orestes* 230
22 Pliny] *Naturalis historia* 18.39, added in 1515

27 The first half of this is taken from Zenobius.
 5 Zenodotus] Zenobius 5.33 (also Suidas o 849)

the battle against the Centaurs, and Hercules in his fight with the Amazons. The story of the boar is as follows: Oeneus the father of Meleager made offerings to the gods of the firstfruits of the year, but he left out Artemis. She, in her anger, sent a huge boar into the Calydonian country, which laid everything waste. Oeneus called for all the most valiant men to destroy it, promising rewards. Among those who competed was Meleager, who slew the beast, but after summoning Theseus to his aid. The rest of the story has nothing to do with the meaning of the proverb.

As to Perithous, the tale runs as follows: Perithous, the suitor of Hippodamia, made a banquet and invited the Centaurs, because they were kinsmen of his bride. As soon as they had warmed up with their wine, they began to try to take the bride by force, and a fight started. Theseus came to the help of Perithous and slaughtered many Centaurs.

About Hercules, they tell this tale: Eurystheus had laid on Hercules the task of stealing the girdle of Hippolyta queen of the Amazons. Hercules set out to fulfil this promise, but Juno, who was always hostile to him, took the form of an Amazon and spread abroad everywhere the news that a stranger, or rather an enemy, was coming to violate the queen and carry off by force the girdle which she wore as part of her royal insignia. When they heard this, the Amazons took up arms against Hercules. He, realising that this was no mistake, but the result of craft, killed Hippolyta and took the belt. Then, to take further vengeance on the Amazons, he went to war with them and defeated them, but with the help of Theseus.

Plutarch too mentions this adage in his life of Theseus, and he indicates that Theseus, as I have said, came to the help of many, but from his frequent contests he reaped no reward; and he quotes Herodotus as authority for this. Aristides recalls the proverb in his speech to the Thebans about military aid: 'When Hercules himself, however, was in need of a friend, Theseus conducted him to Athens and restored and revived him.'

Thus whenever some deed is celebrated under a borrowed name, which has been achieved by the work of another, for instance if someone were to publish a book in his own name after using the work of a more learned man, this adage will be found apt: Not without Theseus. Or someone might say that no joyous chance can come his way 'without a Theseus.'

* * * * *

31 Plutarch] *Theseus* 29.3, citing one Herodorus, not Herodotus
34 Aristides] *Symmachicus* p 723 Dindorf (see I i 13n).

28 **Sphaera per praecipitium**
    A ball runs downhill

A proverb of this kind is reported by Eustathius on the second book of the
Iliad of Homer, Ἡ σφαῖρα κατὰ πρανοῦς, A ball on a steep slope (rolls or
moves along, is understood). It is just like saying 'To cheer on the runner.'   5
The ball easily runs down a steep slope of its own accord. This fits those who
have taken up some way of life for which they seem naturally inclined; it
agrees with that other phrase, 'the horse to the plain.'

29 **Magis mutus quam pisces**
    As dumb as the fishes

Ἀφωνότερος τῶν ἰχθύων, As dumb as the very fishes; a proverbial metaphor
about quite inarticulate people, who have no gift of speech. It will also suit a
man of extraordinary taciturnity. Horace in the *Odes*: 'Thou that couldst lend   5
the swan's song to dumb fish / If it pleased thee.' For fish make no sound,
except for a very few, among them the dog-fish. Lucian *Against An
Ignoramus*: 'Truly you are as dumb as a fish.' Again in *Gallus*: 'I shall be much
more silent than fish.' Hence Plutarch in his 'Table-talk' thinks that the
Pythagoreans abstained from fish because they recognised them as follow-   10
ers of their rule of life, owing to their silence, a thing peculiar to fish among
all living creatures. All the rest have their own voices. Birds are for the most
part songful; some of them even imitate human speech. So, among animals,
does the manticore in Egypt, if we are to believe Pliny. Fish alone have no

* * * * *

28 In the *1508* edition of the *Chiliades* this was preceded by what are now I iv 97–98,
    and followed by I iv 99–100, IV iii 70 and I v 1–2.
    3 Eustathius] On *Iliad* 2.414 (249.1); see I i 71n.
    5 To cheer on] *Adagia* I ii 46
    8 other phrase] I viii 82; cross-reference added in *1515*

29 This seems not to be in the proverb-collections, and was probably taken direct
    from Lucian. Tilley F 300 As mute as a fish.
    5 Horace] *Odes* 4.3.19–20
    7 Lucian] *Adversus indoctum* 16; *Gallus* 1, added in *1523*
    9 Plutarch] *Moralia* 728D, the title of the work given in *1515*. For the Pythagorean
      taboo, see I i 2 line 488; it was repeated at the end of this in *1528*.
    11 a thing ... voiceless] A long addition of *1515*
    14 Pliny] *Naturalis historia* 8.75 (cf 73 and 107). The manticore is thought to be a
      fabulous version of the tiger.

voice. Aristotle gives as a reason that they have no lungs, no windpipe, no   15
gullet. There are a few which give out some sound or noise; among these are
the dolphin, the gurnard, the maigre, the voca (which seems to be so called
because it gives out a voice; that it is sacred to Mercury is revealed by
Athenaeus, book 7), and the scallop. But he thinks this sound is not produced by the natural organ of the voice, but by the rubbing together of the   20
gills, or from the internal organs round the belly. Plutarch thinks the fish is
called *ichthys* by the Greeks because it has a compressed voice. And Lucian
in *Halcyon* says, 'For the creatures which live in the water are voiceless.'

Athenaeus in book 8 of his *Doctors at Dinner* quotes an author, Mnaseas
of Patrae, who asserted that in the Clitorius, a river of Arcadia, there were   25
speaking fish. He also cites Philostephanus, who wrote that in the river
Aornus, which flows through the town of Pheneus, there was a fish called
the *poecilias* which had a voice rather like that of the thrush. Aristotle,
however, denies a voice to all fish, except the scapher and the porpoise. The
ancients called any fish *ellops*, because it could not make a sound (from   30
illesthai, the same as *eirgesthai*, to be confined or compressed, and *ops*, the
voice). So in Theocritus we have *ellopieuein* for 'fishing.' Athenaeus adds
that the disciples of Pythagoras do not abstain altogether from other animals, but some of them they use for food and some even for sacrifice; but
fish alone they do not taste, holding them sacred on account of the 'silence'   35
taught by Pythagoras.

* * * * *

15 Aristotle] *Historia animalium* 4.9 (535b14)
19 Athenaeus] 7.287a; this parenthesis was inserted in *1517/8*.
21 Plutarch] *Moralia* 728E. Plutarch said, not that the fish was called *ichthus*, but
     that the fish (*ichthus*) was called *ellops*; but this word had fallen out of the
     traditional text of Plutarch, on which Erasmus depended. This passage did
     however provide him with the derivation of *ellops* which he will give us lower
     down. The word is still a puzzle.
22 Lucian] *Halcyon* 1. This ends the addition of *1515*.
24 Athenaeus] 8.331d, citing Mnaseas of Patara (*Fragmenta historicorum graecorum*,
     ed C. Mueller, 3, Paris 1849, 150) and Philostephanus of Cyrene (ibid 3.32).
     This, down to 'the thrush,' was added in *1517/8*. Pausanias 8.21.2 says he
     himself stayed by the river till sundown in hopes of hearing this fish sing, but
     without success.
28 Aristotle] Frag 300 Rose, cited in the same passage of Athenaeus. This, with
     what follows, was added in *1528*.
32 Theocritus] 1.42
32 Athenaeus] 7.308c

30 **Turture loquacior**
    As garrulous as a turtle-dove

Τρυγόνος λαλίστερος, As garrulous as a turtle-dove. This is said about
chattering and extremely talkative people. The metaphor is taken from the
nature of the bird, which makes a noise not only with its beak but with the   5
hind part of the body, so they say; I imagine because when it coos it seems to
wag that part too. This is quoted in Zenodotus from the *Plocium* of Menander. Aelian, book 12 chapter 10, recalls this proverb, and the bird speaking
with both parts of the body. Theocritus in the *Women of Syracuse* calls
talkative women 'turtle-doves': 'Like turtle-doves they will wear me out   10
with their endless broad vowels.'

31 **Rana Seriphia**
    A Seriphian frog

Βάτραχος ἐκ Σερίφου, A frog from Seriphos; used about silent men, and
those who are quite unskilled in speaking or singing. Seriphian frogs, when
transferred to Scyros, ceased to croak – hence the proverb. The collections of   5
Greek proverbs taken from the books of Didymus, Tarrhaeus and others
have it in this form. Suidas has it in the same words. It is said that in the isle
of Seriphos there were mute frogs; Pliny recalls this, in book 8 chapter 58: 'In
Cyrene,' he says, 'the frogs were mute, although vocal frogs were imported
from the mainland and their kind still exists. They are mute at the present   10

* * * * *

30 *Collectanea* no 679 gives the proverb from Diogenianus 8.34 (it is also in
    Zenobius 6.8 and in Suidas τ 1094), and adds that 'to chatter worse than a
    magpie' is in contemporary use. Suringar 229
7   Zenodotus] Zenobius 6.8, citing Menander frag 346.
8   Aelian] *De naturis animalium* 12.10 (see I ii 55n).
9   Theocritus] 15.88, added in *1515*

31 In *Collectanea* no 303, the authority for this is given as Stephanus (which means
    Steph. Byzantius p 561 Meineke) quoted by Ermolao on Pliny 8.227. The Greek
    proverb-collections do not appear to have been used, and in fact their evidence
    was not added until *1528*. It is a little surprising that the name of Ermolao is not
    given here until *1528*, and that Stephanus, whom Erasmus uses quite often
    elsewhere (see I ii 43n), is not mentioned at all. The autograph of the *1528*
    additions to this paragraph still exists in the Stads- en Athenaeumbibliotheek,
    Deventer (33 D 24); see Allen 5. p xxi; B. Berkenvelder-Helfferich and A.C.F.
    Koch in *Scrinium Erasmianum* (Louvain 1969) 253–61.
5   collections] Diogenianus 3.44; Suidas β 190; both these references added in
    1528
8   Pliny] *Naturalis historia* 8.227

time on the island of Seriphos. The same frogs transferred elsewhere sing;
this happened, as they say, in Sicendum, a lake in Thessaly.' Though in the
common texts it is 'Seriphian cicadas' which are mentioned, not frogs, but
Ermolao restored the right reading, relying on old manuscripts. Seriphus is
one of the islands which the Greeks call the Sporades. But the words of Pliny   15
do not seem to agree very well with the Greek compilations. He says the
frogs were silent in Seriphos; while they declare the frogs stopped making
any sound when transferred to Scyros, as if they were vocal in Seriphos and
went mute in Scyros. However if you look more closely at the matter there is
no absurdity here. Seriphus had mute frogs. These were taken to Scyros as a   20
curiosity, and the Scyrians marvelled at their being mute, unlike their own
frogs, and so they talked about Seriphian frogs and this became a proverb.

32   **Alii sementem faciunt, alii metent**
     Some sow, others will reap

Ἄλλοι μὲν σπείρουσιν, ἄλλοι δὲ ἀμήσονται, Some sow, others will reap.
This also recurs as follows, without the metaphor Ἄλλοι κάμον, ἄλλοι
ὤνηντο, Some laboured, others gained the reward. Similar to this is what   5
Fabius says in Livy, in the tenth book of his *Rome From the Foundation*: 'When
one has planted a tree, for another to collect the fruit under it is intolerable.'
Hesiod alludes to this when he writes in his *Theogony*: 'They draw another's
toil into their own belly.' Theognis too: 'Give not to another the fruit of the
work you have already done.' The same figure of speech is that used by   10
Diocletian when he was not yet emperor: 'I kill the boars, but another enjoys
the meat.' This is related in his life more or less to this effect. When

* * * * *

14   Ermolao] Barbaro *Castigationes Plinianae* ad loc, added in *1528* with Erasmus'
     own comments as far as the end

32   *Collectanea* no 413 gave what is here the first form of the adage from
     Diogenianus 2.62, where it has the one-word explanation 'obvious.' Some of
     the material which might have been used to supplement this has been taken by I
     iv 41. Otto 125; Tilley s 691 One sows, another reaps.
4   also recurs] In Zenobius 1.65; Diogenianus 2.13; Suidas A 144
6   Livy] 10.24.5, under a title which Erasmus sometimes uses to distinguish the
     first decade (books 1–10). This was added in *1528*, in which year the phrase
     also provided IV vii 37.
8   Hesiod] *Theogony* 599
9   Theognis] 925 (see I i 62n).
11   Diocletian] Flavius Vopiscus *Carus* etc 14.2–3, one of the works in the *Historia
     Augusta* (see I i 21n). He cites Virgil *Aeneid* 10.830, which reappears in II ii 8.
     Aper, not uncommon as a personal name, is the Latin for wild boar.

Diocletian was among the Tungri in Gaul, as yet campaigning in small places, he spent some time in a certain tavern and became familiarly acquainted with a female druid. She scolded him for meanness, and he is said to have replied, not seriously but in jest, 'that he would be liberal when he became emperor.' To this the woman said, 'Do not jest, Diocletian, you will truly be emperor, once you have killed the boar.' Taking the woman's words as an omen, he began to hunt the boar with passion, but that was because he did not understand the riddle, which the outcome later made clear. For the emperor Numerianus had been slain by the conspiracy of Arrius Aper [boar] his son-in-law. When this was known, the soldiers elected Diocletian as their claimant and saluted him as Augustus. Then, so as to fulfil the Druid's saying, he stabbed Aper in public with his own hand, adding Virgil's phrase: 'By the right hand of great Aeneas you fall.' But while he was still an unknown man and had killed many boars without the slightest hope of empire, it is said that he used to say 'I kill the boars but another enjoys the meat.'

33 Aliena iacis
You are making a bad throw

Ἀλλότρια βάλλεις, You are making a bad throw. Said whenever things fall out against one's wishes. Taken from dice-players, when the results as they throw are as far as possible from winning. So when hope deceives us we aptly say 'It's a bad throw.' The adage is found in Diogenianus.

34 Aliam quercum excute
Go and shake another oak-tree

Ἄλλην δρῦν βαλάνιζε, Go and shake another oak-tree. This aptly fits those who are endlessly asking for something, or who beg for a loan over and over again from the same person. With this adage we may send those people away to din their requests into other ears and leave us alone. It is thought that the proverb arose because in old times human beings lived on acorns, the use of cereals not having yet been discovered. The people who shook the oaks and collected the acorns, and were hired to do so, were called *balanistae*, which means acorn-gatherers, or *glandiarii*. When these were

* * * * *

33 From Diogenianus 2.60 (also in Suidas A 1343)

34 *Collectanea* no 253, partly reused and the application somewhat enlarged. Taken from the Greek proverb-colllections (Zenobius 2.41; Diogenianus 1.19; Suidas A 1194)

taking a look round to see if a few acorns still remained on the tree, the passers-by would shout jestingly 'Go and shake another oak.' This cry was taken over by the public and turned into a proverb. It may well be applied to a business transaction which should be abandoned, since no profit can now be made out of it, or a friend who is to be forsaken because he has now ceased to be useful, or a teacher to be changed because there is nothing more you can learn from him.

35 Nuces relinquere
To leave the nuts behind

To leave the nuts behind means to give up the interests and games of childhood and turn towards weightier and more serious matters. Persius: 'Our record, since we left the nuts behind, / And like wise uncles try to teach mankind.' The metaphor is adapted perhaps from the old wedding ceremonies, in which the bridegroom who was marrying a wife used to scatter nuts around, as if now renouncing his boyhood. So Catullus in his marriage song: 'Give nuts, boy, quickly, / Give nuts, beloved slave.' Virgil, *Bucolics* 8: 'Scatter the nuts, bridegroom.' However Pliny, in book 15 chapter 22, gives other reasons why nuts used to play a part in old nuptial rites. But it is best to quote his own words: 'The walnut, though it also accompanies the Fescennine songs sung at weddings, is considerably smaller than a pine-cone taken as a whole, but the kernel is longer in the same proportion. Moreover the walnut has a distinction of structure that is peculiar to it, in that it is protected by a double covering consisting first of a cushion-shaped cup and then of a woody shell. This is the reason why walnuts have become emblems consecrated to weddings, because their progeny is protected in so many ways; a more likely explanation of the custom than that it is due to the rattling rebound which it makes when it falls on the floor.' Festus also notes that it was customary at weddings for children to scatter nuts, as a good omen for the bride when she entered the house of her new husband. Servius adds that the boy catamites when they were retiring from their disgraceful

* * * * *

35 *Collectanea* no 225 gave four of these passages in a different order, with Servius first. Otto 1257
4 Persius] *Satires* 1.10–11
8 Catullus] 61.124 and 128
9 Virgil] *Eclogues* 8.30, the reference added in *1533*
10 Pliny] *Historia naturalis* 15.86 (tr H. Rackham, adapted)
20 Festus] P 179 (see I i 28n), added in *1515*
22 Servius] On Virgil *Eclogues* 8.29

servitude used to throw nuts as a sign that they were casting away all
childish things.   25

It may be from this, or at any rate from children's games in which nuts
play a part, that the proverb takes its origin. For boys used to play with nuts
and knucklebones, as Horace is witness: '– Your knucklebones and nuts,
Aulus.' To this form of the proverb can be attached the rest of these figures:
'Never to leave the nuts behind,' 'To return to the nuts,' 'To throw away the   30
nuts,' 'To give the nuts a respite,' 'To indulge in, or go back to, the nuts,' and
others like them.

36 Bis pueri senes
Old men are children twice over

Δὶς παῖδες οἱ γέροντες, Old men are children twice over. This is one of those
proverbial titles of the *Satires* of Varro. It will suit those people who in
advanced age cling to some childish occupations, unseemly and inoppor-   5
tune though they may be, or old men doddering with senility, turning back
again as it were to childhood. Seneca says, 'We are not children twice, as is
commonly said, but always; the only difference is that we play with bigger
toys.' Plato in the *Republic*, book 1: 'Not only will the old man, as it seems, be
a child twice over, but so will the drunkard.' Aristophanes in the *Clouds*:   10
'You will say you think this is the work of a child, / But I retort that old men
are children twice over.' Sophocles in the *Peleus*:

> I, the only guardian of the house,
> Guide Peleus, aged son of Aeacus;
> An aging man becomes a boy again.   15

* * * * *

28 Horace] *Satires* 2.3.171

36 *Collectanea* no 290, giving Varro and Seneca as the authorities; also in the
   proverb-collections (Diogenianus 4.18; Suidas Δ 1267). Otto 1625. Tilley M 570
   Old men are twice children. The topic recurs in II iii 48.
4 Varro] The title of one of his *Menippean Satires* (see I ii 60n), cited by Gellius
   7.5.10
7 Seneca] Frag 121, cited by Lactantius (early fourth century AD) *Divinae
   institutiones* 2.4.14
9 Plato] *Laws* (*Republic* is a slip of memory) 1.646a, the Greek added in 1520
10 Aristophanes] *Clouds* 1416–7, the Latin version versified in 1528. The scholiast
   there cites Sophocles frag 447 Nauck and Theopompus (a lost poet of the Old
   Comedy) frag 69 Kock.

Theopompus: 'It is rightly said that old men are children twice over.' Plato: 'The puerile old man seems like an old man twice.' Antiphon: 'To take care of an old man is like taking care of a child.' Lucian in the dialogue called *Saturnalia*: 'For thus I would prove true the proverb which says that old men become children again.'   20

Here comes in the remark of Varro in his *On the Latin Language*, book 3, where he says that sometimes in the Attellane farces the words *pupum senem* mean what the Oscans in their language call *casnar* [an old man]; for the ancients called a boy *pupus*. The proverb means not merely that old men turn silly by reason of their age, but that in all ways, as though they had   25 finished their life, the old seem to go back to the beginning, as Aristotle shrewdly said in one of his *Problems*, where he asks how it may be decided which things are called first and which last. To begin with, there returns the whiteness and thinness of the hair, both usual in children, and then the lisp, as in a second infancy. The gums lose their teeth, or very few remain and   30 those are loose, which again is a thing shared with babies. Indeed, the whole body, in old men, shrinks to a childish size, and there is a parallel loss of strength. Even the food they eat suits both ages. Finally there is their silliness of behaviour and triviality of mind, and the fact that they have no sense seems to suggest infancy in the old. In the *Politics*, Aristotle avers that   35 after the age of forty-eight the mental powers decline. Hence, Euripides in the *Bacchae*: 'When I see your old age lacking sense.' So it comes about that old men delight in children, as if drawn by the love of like to like.

* * * * *

16 Plato] A spurious line, invented according to Meineke by Marcus Musurus, who edited the Aldine Aristophanes of 1498. He seems to have found in Clement of Alexandria the quotation from Plato's *Laws* which we have just read, supposed it to be from Plato the comic poet, altered it slightly to make a line of verse, and inserted it in the scholia on *Clouds* 1417 (see Plato comicus frag 269 Kock). Erasmus had it before him in a corrupt form, which he bravely rendered in Latin verse, but he could not make sense of it, nor can we.
17 Antiphon] Antiphon the sophist frag 87B66 Diels-Kranz, cited by Clement of Alexandria *Stromateis* 6.2 (*PG* 9.233A)
18 Lucian] *Saturnalia* 9
21 Varro] *De lingua latina* 7.29 (see I ii 23n). The Atellane farces were a traditional Italian entertainment, of which we know very little.
26 Aristotle] *Problemata* 17.3 (916a21–2)
35 Aristotle] *Politics* 7.16 (1335b32); but *Rhetoric* 2.14 (1390b9) is closer.
36 Euripides] *Bacchae* 252
38 like to like] *Adagia* I ii 22

37 **Sexagenarios de ponte deicere**
    To throw the sexagenarians off the bridge

To throw old men of sixty off the bridge means to consign older people to
idleness, as if they were doting and useless in all walks of life, and to cut
them off from the exercise of all occupations. It originates from the fact that   5
in old times people over sixty had no right to vote, their age incapacitating
them from public functions; or it may be that the youth of Rome, wishing to
be the only ones to cast a vote, drove the helpless old men headlong off the
bridges. It had already begun to be the custom to vote from the bridge; and
this opinion is accepted by Sisinnius Capito in Festus Pompeius as more   10
likely than the widespread notion that after the city was liberated from the
Gauls there was such dearth of food that they began throwing sexagenarians
off the bridge into the Tiber.

      Varro (*On the Life of Our Fathers*, book 2) explains that there was an
honourable and religious reason: when they came to the fifth stage and were   15
fifty years old, they were free at last from public business, relieved from
care, at leisure. Thus some think that the phrase became a proverb, 'sexagenarians must be thrown off the bridge,' because they did not cast the
votes, which was done by crossing the bridge. Nonius Marcellus: 'It was
generally understood that "throwing the sexagenarians off the bridge" was   20
a bad expression.' Macrobius in the *Saturnalia*, book 1: 'Do you wish to take
away from learned men the right of voting in the *comitia*, and so to speak,
throw the sexagenarian elders off the bridge?' Ovid in the *Fasti*: 'Some think
the weak old men were thrown from the bridge so that the young alone
might cast their vote.' Old men are thus called *depontani*, unbridged, which   25
is to say *emeriti*, relegated to leisure from civil administration. Plato, *Laws*,
book 6, speaking of the function of his 'guardians of the laws,' does not
admit to this office anyone under fifty years of age, nor does he allow them
to continue in it after seventy; so that if a man of fifty became a magistrate, he
would have twenty years in office; if he were sixty, only ten.   30

      The proverb may be used to express aversion for old age, as useless for
anything, and needing to be cut off from all the activities of life; or simply

                        * * * * *

      37 *Collectanea* no 19, with the evidence from Ovid and Macrobius. Otto 1638
      10 Festus] P 452 (see I i 28n); this sentence was added in *1515*.
      14 Varro] Cited by Nonius p 523 (see I i 97n).
      21 Macrobius] *Saturnalia* 1.5.10 (see I i 12n).
      23 Ovid] *Fasti* 5.333–4
      25 *depontani*] The source of the word is probably Festus p 66.
      26 Plato] *Laws* 6.755a

applied to those who owing to the weakness of old age have sought retirement, and accepted exemption from ordinary duties.

38   Crambe bis posita mors
Twice-served cabbage is death

Δὶς κράμβη θάνατος, Twice-served cabbage is death. Pliny, book 20 chapter
9, lists *crambe* third among the species of *brassica*. Dioscorides, book 2, gives
three kinds of *crambe*. The first of these, besides being efficacious otherwise   5
in a number of remedies, even takes away the troublesome results of
drunkenness and intoxication, if you eat it raw with vinegar before the meal,
as Marcus Cato indicated. Aristotle thinks that the reason for this is that
being cold, and having a juice which is mild and dispersive, it draws the
vinous liquor into the bowels and the thinner liquor slides into the bladder;   10
the cabbage itself remains in the stomach and cools the body. Thus the
humours are drawn off in both ways and the cooled body allows the
tipsiness to wear off. There is however a special quality in cabbage, which
resists wine, and if it is planted in a vineyard the wine is weaker. Thus it was
an accepted custom with the Egyptians and Sybarites to eat cooked cabbage   15
before everything else; the custom of some men was to take cabbage-seed
from an amethystine goblet before drinking, so as to be able to indulge in
wine without fear of intoxication.

Athenaeus, book 1 says something like this, adding that in early times
the cabbage and the radish were held to be the same thing. Theophrastus   20
asserts that the grape-vine, even when growing, shuns the smell of
radishes. But to return to the proverb.

* * * * *

33 have sought retirement] Erasmus uses the phrase 'have been presented with
   the *rudis*,' some kind of wooden weapon given to gladiators as a badge of
   honourable retirement; this is a familiar metaphor, which provided him with
   Adagia I ix 24.

38 *Collectanea* no 20, much enlarged. Otto 454; Tilley c 511 Cabbage twice sodden.
 3 Pliny] *Naturalis historia* 20.74
 4 Dioscorides] *De materia medica* 2.120–2 (see I i 22n).
 8 Cato] *De agri cultura* 156.1, added in *1515*
 8 Aristotle] *Problemata* 3.17 (873a37), added in *1515*
13 There is] The information in these two sentences, which were added in *1517/8*,
   comes from Athenaeus, although in that edition he was not named.
19 Athenaeus] 1,34c–e, citing Theophrastus (see I i 44n) *Historia plantarum* 4.16.6;
   this was added in *1528*.

Suidas writes that cabbage used to be served at banquets in antiquity, but when recooked it produced such nausea that it became proverbial in Greek for aversion. Whenever they were describing something disagreeable repeated over and over again, not without disgust, they said 'twice cabbage is death' (that is, recooked). Poliziano thinks that Juvenal was referring to this adage in his seventh Satire:

> You teach rhetoric, O iron-hearted Vettius,
> When your troop of many scholars slays the cruel tyrants.
> For what each has just learnt in his seat
> He stands and declaims, reciting the self-same things
> In the self-same verses; served up again and again
> The cabbage is the death of the unhappy masters.

He means by 'cabbage served up again' an utterly boring speech which has to be listened to over and over again. This is close to the phrase we quoted in another place 'Corinthus son of Jove,' and it is the opposite of that other one, 'Beauty bears repeating twice and thrice.' Something lovely in itself still pleases, as Horace says, even if repeated ten times. A foolish thing is tolerated at the first taste for the sake of novelty, but when repeated is hardly bearable and causes disgust.

Yet this plant was highly celebrated in early times, so much so that it was not without veneration, and for this reason was called *mantis*, a prophet. It was the custom to swear by it, especially among the Ionians, 'so help me, cabbage!' and this also might be seen as an origin for the proverb in the sense of aversion, as Athenaeus says in *Doctors at Dinner*, book 9.

* * * * *

23 Suidas] K 2318
27 Poliziano] *Miscellanea* c 33, citing Juvenal 7.150–4
37 another place] *Adagia* II i 50; I ii 49
39 Horace] *Ars poetica* 365. After 'novelty' followed in *1508* a brief comparison with *unedo*, the fruit of the strawberry-tree, which it is said that no one eats more than once; but this was cut out in *1515*, probably because it had been used in I ii 49.
46 Athenaeus] 9.370b. Why the word 'prophet' (*mantis*) should be applied to cabbage evidently puzzled Athenaeus as much as it might a modern reader; but in the fragment of Nicander (I ii 86n) from which he gets the phrase, it is 'a prophet for vegetables,' and this may mean no more than that if your cabbage-crop does well, your other vegetables will follow suit.

39 Ne Hercules quidem adversus duos
Not even Hercules can take on two

Μηδ' Ἡρακλῆς πρὸς δύο, Not even Hercules can take on two. The meaning
is that no one so far excels in strength that he alone can be equal to a number
of others. There is no disgrace in yielding to a multitude. The metaphor will   5
be pleasanter, however, if we use it to say that no one, however learned, can
stand up to two people in debate, or that one man is not equal to handling
several business affairs at the same time, or that there is no resisting the
prayers of two people begging for the same thing. The proverb might be
turned into another form, in this way: if they say that Hercules is not   10
sufficient against two opponents, how shall I, weak as I am, stand up to two
Hercules? But I have explained shortly the way to use this proverb at the
beginning of the book.

   Plato in the *Laws*, book 11: 'It is true, and well-known in old times as a
proverb, that it is hard to fight against two opposite things, as in illness or at 15
many other times.' He indicates that we have a double battle to fight, against
wealth and against poverty. He adapted the same in the *Phaedo*, where
Socrates jokingly urges Phaedo to confute Cebes and Symmias in argument,
and Phaedo replies, 'But it is said that even Hercules was not strong enough
against two.' Catullus alludes to it in a marriage song, when he says 'Do not   20
contend with two.' This thought, though not in the same words, is sometimes found in Homer, as in the *Odyssey*, book 20: 'It is difficult for one to
hold off many.' Telemachus says this about himself and the suitors. Also in
the *Iliad*, book 5: 'Aeneas did not wait, nimble warrior though he was, /
When he saw the two men standing together.'   25

   The origin of the adage is recounted in different ways. Some say that
the Molionids once laid an ambush for Hercules, and he, alarmed by their
numbers, did not dare to make a stand against them, but sought safety in
flight, and so it came into everyday speech. More probable is what Suidas
relates, that Hercules, having founded the Olympic contest, dared at first,   30
relying on his strength, to contend with two adversaries and defeated them

   * * * * *

39 *Collectanea* no 21, with no source named, but said to be a Greek proverb, and
   therefore presumably from Diogenianus 7.2. It is also Zenobius 5.49, and
   Synesius uses it in *Encomium Calvitii* 2 (PG 66.1169B). Otto 584; Tilley H 436
   Hercules himself cannot deal with two.
13 beginning] In Erasmus' Introduction, section xii
14 Plato] *Laws* 11.919b; *Phaedo* 89c
20 Catullus] 62.64, used again in 1533 in v ii 30
22 Homer] *Odyssey* 20.313; *Iliad* 5.571–2
29 Suidas] O 794. The 'Some say' which follows is an allusion to Zenobius.

both. These, they say, were Creatos and Eurytus, whose father was Neptune and their mother Moliona. Then at the next Olympiad he met with two
opponents again, and was overcome by them. Some say, however, that
these were Laeus and Pherandrus, and it was these who defeated Hercules,   35
not losing the fight to him. But Plato in the *Euthydemus* tells a very different
story: he supposes that Hercules fought with the hydra at the same time as
with a huge crab which came out of the sea, and Hercules gave way as the
weaker, and for this reason begged the help of his nephew Iolaus. But I will
willingly transcribe his own words. In the dialogue I mentioned, Socrates is   40
disputing with two brothers, sophists, and as usual, insolent fellows; he
was, in fact, facing two monsters alone. Dionysodorus reproached him with
running away, and not replying to their questions, and this was his answer.
'It is reasonable of me to take flight. For since I am unequal to either, why
should I not flee from both? Certainly I am much weaker than Hercules, and   45
he was not equal to sustaining this sort of fight, both against a sophistical
hydra, so clever that when one head of speech was cut off many others
sprang up, and against a sophistical crab of some kind coming out of the sea,
and recently, as I think, arrived here. When Hercules was close pressed on
the left by this creature and sharply bitten by its words, he called on his   50
nephew Iolaus for help, and he gave liberal assistance. If my Iolaus Patroclus
were to come, he would keep up the other side of the contest.' By this biting
allegory Socrates is calling the two brother sophists hydra and crab respectively, himself Hercules, and Ctesippus Iolaus.

40   **Unus vir, nullus vir**
      One man, no man

Εἷς ἀνήρ, οὐδεὶς ἀνήρ, One man indeed is no man. The meaning is that
nothing excellent can be achieved by one man, bereft of any help. To this
belongs what Euripides says in the *Heraclidae*, 'The single-handed man is   5
weak in fight,' and from the same author, 'One man does not see all.' The
proverb can be turned to various uses: 'life has no sweetness without a

        * * * * *

   36 Plato] *Euthydemus* 297b–c, the Greek added in *1517/8*. The name 'Patroclus'
      makes no sense, and should be removed.

   40 In *1508* this began, like no 71 below, with 'It is on record in the collections of
      Greek adages'; and this was cut out both here and there in *1515*. The words
      themselves are thought to be a fragment from an unidentified comedy (frag
      adesp 679 Kock); they are in Suidas ε 1229 as well as Zenobius. Tilley M 353
      One man is no man; o 52 One is as good as none.
   5 Euripides] *Heraclidae* 274; *Phoenissae* 745. Both these were reused in II iii 95.

friend to live with'; 'it is better not to trust to the judgment of one person'; in
literary studies, if there is no companionship or rivalry as they say in the
service of the Muses, it is cold and uninspired; or finally, about whatever   10
business has to be conducted, which cannot be brought off properly without
the assistance of someone else. Zenodotus mentions this proverb.

41 Asinus inter simias
A donkey among apes

Ὄνος ἐν πιθήκοις, A donkey among apes. This occurs when a person finds
himself among satirical and insolent people, himself being a dull fellow
whom they mock with impunity. It comes in Aulus Gellius, book 2 chapter   5
23, where Menander the comedy-writer introduces into the plot of his play
entitled *Plocium* a husband complaining of the insulting behaviour of his
wife: 'This man's an ass among apes, as the saying goes.' The ape, as is well
known, is a most impudent creature; it is not even afraid to tease a lion by
clinging playfully to its rump. In our own day too there is a similar saying in   10
common parlance, 'an owl among the crows,' when some doltish person
happens to fall among impudent and sarcastic people. There is nothing to
prevent it being used as a general phrase when someone finds himself
involved in troublesome business or in a misfortune from which he cannot
extricate himself.   15

42 Asinus inter apes
A donkey among bees

Ὄνος ἐν μελίτταις, A donkey among bees. This has the same sense as the
previous one, and is said when someone has the bad luck to fall among
worthless and unmannerly people. The metaphor is clear enough. The   5
adage, however, seems to have arisen from some occurrence. Suidas mentions it.

* * * * *

12 Zenodotus] Zenobius 3.51 (Erasmus always calls him Zenodotus).

41 *Collectanea* no 30, the wording of which is partly reused here. Derived, it seems,
   from Gellius. Suringar 20
 5 Gellius] 2.23.9, citing Menander frag 333 in the Greek original

42 *Collectanea* no 448, very briefly; taken no doubt from Diogenianus 7.32 (it is also
   Suidas o 388).

43   Asinus in unguento
     A donkey wearing perfume

Ὄνος ἐν μύρῳ, A donkey wearing perfume. Used when delicacies are put
before people for whom they are not fitting, and who do not know either
how to use them or how to enjoy them. A donkey, indeed, prefers straw and   5
hay to gold, or scented ointment, which he actually dislikes. There would be
a place for this adage if an uneducated person should happen to meet with
the best authors, which he would either neglect out of ignorance, or even
distort; or if a man who is a stranger to the Muses should come to live among
learned people, and could neither profit by their company nor even be   10
happy in it. The proverb occurs in Diogenianus.

44   Neque coelum neque terram attingit
     It touches neither heaven nor earth

Οὔτε γῆς οὔτε οὐρανοῦ ἅπτεται, It touches neither earth nor heaven. Said of a
thing which is wildly absurd and out of place, and has no connection at all
with the matter in hand. Lucian in his *False Prophet*: 'He sent me eight   5
oracular responses pertaining neither to earth nor heaven, as they say.'
Aristides in *Cimon* alludes jokingly to the proverb, and indicates that the
metaphor comes from those who hang in mid-air, unattached on all sides.

45   Nihil ad versum
     Nothing to do with the verse

Οὐδὲν πρὸς ἔπος, Nothing to do with the verse. This applies to things which
are far different from what was intended. It seems to come from the stage,
where the actor expresses by his movements and gestures the kind of   5
dramatic poem he is representing. Possibly one recited the verses and

* * * * *

43   This is not in Scheidewin's edition of Diogenianus (the form of text used by
     Erasmus for the *Collectanea*), but he prints it as Appendix 4.23 from his Coislin
     manuscript, which also contains the proverbs that precede and follow it here. It
     is also in Suidas o 388.

44   *Collectanea* no 836 gives Lucian as the authority.
 5   Lucian] *Alexander* 54
 7   Aristides] *De quattuor* p 205 Dindorf (see I i 13n).

45   Probably taken from Lucian, like those which immediately precede and follow
     it.

another acted the part. For there appears to have been one reciter, whose name is seen at the end of comedies: 'I, Calliopius, went through this.' Otherwise I cannot see the force of what Cicero says about the actor selecting a play for which he would be naturally fitted; the actor who speaks the 10 prologue of a comedy of Terence complains that noisy plots have been allocated to him and less troublesome ones to the others. If the acting did not correspond to the metre of the poem, they would say 'Nothing to do with the verse.' Lucian in *Philopseudes*: 'These things have nothing to do with the verse, as they say, nor was I inquiring about these.' If anyone in the dances 15 did not fit in with the rhythm of the dance, they called him *akrotêtos*, and he was said *akrotein*, to miss the beat.

Andrea Alciati, a luminary of our age not only in Roman law but in all kinds of learning, is no less to be admired for the rare sincerity of his mind than for his accurate grasp of all liberal disciplines. In the second book of his 20 *Dispunctiones* he agrees with me about the meaning and use of the proverb, but differs somewhat on the question of its origin. He prefers to think that it was derived from the oracles, which used to be delivered in verse, preferably heroic verse, the inventor of which was said to be the Pythian Apollo. This was called in Greek *epos*, because the facts follow [*hepetai*] the oracle. 25 This etymology is contributed by Eustathius at the beginning of the *Iliad* of Homer; and my friend Alciati thinks for this reason that more probably this phrase, 'nothing to do with the verse,' was used whenever events occurred which did not bear out what was promised or proposed.

Ulpian made use of it in the *Pandects*, book 11, title *De interrogatoriis* 30 *actionibus*, chapter 12: 'With regard to the Praetor's expression "declines to answer at all," later authorities took his words in the following sense: a man,

* * * * *

8 Calliopius] Erasmus is on the wrong lines here with his suggestion that the speaking and miming in Roman comedy were allotted to different people. Calliopius was not an actor, so far as we know, but an unknown individual who corrected a text of Terence in late Antiquity, and whose name is preserved at the end of plays in many manuscripts. The discussion of this problem ('Possibly ... with the verse') was added in *1517/8*.

9 Cicero] *De officiis* 1.31.114

11 Terence] *Heautontimorumenos* 35–45

14 Lucian] *Philopseudes* 1

16 *akrotêtos*] This sentence was added in *1533*; the word is found in Hesychius' lexicon (A2625).

18 Alciati] See on *Adagia* I iii 59; this reference to his *Dispunctiones* 2.10 was added in *1526*, and applies to a collection of legal works, first published in Milan in 1518, of which there was a copy in Erasmus' library.

26 Eustathius] Prologue to the *Iliad* 4.4 (see I i 77n).

30 Ulpian] In the *Digest* 11.1.11.5, added in *1533*

they said, is held to decline to answer who does not answer the precise
question he is asked, that is nothing to do with the verse.'

Suidas affirms that this phrase is sometimes used to mean 'rashly,   35
without reason' or 'not to the point.' He quotes these lines from some
unidentified poet: 'Should I speak so far from the verse, so senselessly, /
Before I know the whole thing as it stands?' The first line in the Greek will
stand, if for οὕτως you read Χ᾽ οὕτως. Aristophanes also made use of it in his
Ecclesiazusae, a reference I have given in the proverb 'Out of tune.'   40

46   **Nihil ad fides**
     Nothing to do with the lyre

Οὐδὲν πρὸς τὴν χορδήν, Nothing to do with the lutestring; aimed at those
whose life is inconsistent, or whose behaviour is different from their words.
Lucian, *On Dancing*: 'And nothing, as they say, to do with the lyre-string,   5
for the foot says one thing and the rhythm something else.' Again in
Dialogues of Courtesans: 'And because her foot answered truly to the lyre.'
Plutarch in his essay 'On False Shame': 'And yet it is not because the foot is
not attuned to the lyre as Plato says, that cities in conflict with cities, and
friends with friends, inflict and suffer such disasters, but because the laws   10
and justice are sinned against.' The passage Plutarch is quoting is in the
Laws, book 7: 'Giving back tones in accord with the sound of the lyre. Then
[it makes] a discordance and conflict every time the strings produce notes in
a different rhythm from the one chosen by the composer of the song, and so
on.' It seems to have been to this proverb that St Augustine alluded in a   15
certain letter to Licentius: 'But if I play and you dance to another tune, even
so I am not sorry.' Singing has its own delight, even when the person to
whom the song is sung with the tender tones of love does not move a limb in
response.

                    * * * * *

35 Suidas] o 804–5, citing Aristophanes *Ecclesiazusae* 751–2; added in 1526. The
   textual correction is unnecessary. It was added in 1528, with the cross-
   reference to *Adagia* II ii 47, where lines 750–1 of the same play are quoted;
   Erasmus has not realized that what he adds from Suidas here is the same as
   what he had used, from his own reading of Aristophanes, in 1508 in the later
   passage.

46 *Collectanea* no 837, naming no source, but probably from Lucian; here entirely
   rewritten
 5 Lucian] *De saltatione* 80; *Dialogi meretricii* 3.2
 8 Plutarch] *Moralia* 534E; he cites Plato *Clitopho* 407c–d, and not *Laws* 7.812d, as
   Erasmus says. This 'false shame' is *dysôpia*; see I v 5n.
15 Augustine] *Letters* 26.3, added in 1520

47 Formica camelus
Ant or camel

Μύρμηξ ἤ κάμηλος, Ant or camel. Referring to things which are violently
unequal, and now tiny, now huge, just as if a camel were to be turned all at
once into an ant. Lucian, in the *Saturnalia*, letter 1: 'But as we now live, "ant   5
or camel,"' as the proverb says.' He is speaking of the unequal distribution of
wealth among mortals, so that one has more than enough and another is in
dire need. It can aptly be used too of persons who are inconsistent, and go to
extremes in either way. Euripides describes this kind of man in the *Troades*:
'Why do you jump from one mood to another? You hate and love excessively   10
whomsoever you chance upon.'

48 Os sublinere
To smear someone's face

To smear someone's face is to give him empty words and make a fool of him
by some form of trickery; it is found several times in good authors. Nonius
Marcellus thinks it is taken from some silly kind of game, in which a person's   5
face is smeared while he is asleep. Plautus in the *Aulularia*: 'I thought Faith
was the one god one could have faith in, but she's smeared my face
dreadfully.' Again elsewhere: 'I've got my face smeared all right.' Again in
the *Epidicus*: 'If I'd deputed a less intelligent man to this business, one less
clever at the job, I should have had my face smeared.' Marcus Varro in his   10
Mysteria, cited by Nonius: 'To have defrauded the innkeeper of his money,
to have smeared the goodwife's face with mud, while their cash softened up
the customs men.' Sophocles in the *Antigone*: 'These also see, but they are

* * * * *

47 From Lucian *Saturnalia* 19. The lines from Euripides are *Troades* 67–8.

48 *Collectanea* no 409 had combined this with the next two, citing passages from
   Plautus as the source. Otto 1312. We know no English equivalent.
 4 Nonius] P 45 (see I i 97n).
 6 Plautus] *Aulularia* 667–8; *Epidicus* 491, slightly confused in memory with *Captivi*
   783 or *Curculio* 589; *Epidicus* 427–9 (the text used in Erasmus' day ran 'deputed
   one who was less a man than intelligent': it was corrected later by his friend
   Joachim Camerarius).
11 Nonius] P 24–5, citing Varro *Mysteria* (from his *Menippean Satires* 329; see I ii
   60n); added in 1515.
13 Sophocles] *Antigone* 509 (the Greek means, not 'they smear your face,' ie
   deceive you, but 'they keep their mouths shut in front of you,' tell you
   nothing).

smearing your face.' Virgil too in one of his *Bucolics* describes boys playing a
trick on Silenus by smearing his face with mulberry-juice: 15

> She stained his brow and temples
> With mulberry-juice, and he, awake by now,
> Smiled at their ruse, and said 'Fetters? What for?'

49 Dare verba
To give empty words

This occurs everywhere throughout the authors, with the meaning of cheat-
ing. Persius, fourth *Satire*: 'Well, just as you please, give empty words and
fool your sinews.' Terence: 'It is difficult to give him empty words.' Ovid: 5
'Every lover gives empty words.' The last-named finely applies it to
attempts to allay one's own anxieties: 'With study I engage my mind, and
beguile my sufferings, / I try to see how I can give empty words to my cares.'
But examples are so frequent and so clear that it would be waste of effort to
track them down. I would only suggest that more pleasure is to be derived 10
from the proverb if it is turned away from a simple matter of speech and
used to express the fraud and imposture which are effective even without
the colouring of words. For instance one could say that this world 'gives
empty words' to its worshippers; that what they call the art of alchemy 'gives
empty words' to those who study it, and that people who promise them- 15
selves something they can hardly hope for are 'giving empty words' to
themselves.

50 Addere manum
To make sport of someone

To make sport of someone. There is a phrase in Plautus, *Persa*, which is less
usual: *addere manum*, 'to put a hand to,' to make a laughing-stock of some-

* * * * *

14 Virgil] *Eclogues* 6.21–3. A merry nymph helps the two shepherd-boys to play a
trick on the old demigod Silenus, whom they have caught asleep.

49 *Collectanea* no 409 (part)
4 Persius] *Satires* 4.45
5 Terence] *Andria* 211
5 Ovid] *Remedia amoris* 95; *Tristia* 5.7.39–40, added in *1536*

50 *Collectanea* no 409 (part). Otto 1057
3 Plautus] *Persa* 795–6; *Poenulus* 457, 460–2; *Aulularia* 378; *Casina* 935. In the
Collectanea Erasmus had recognized *adierit* as a possible alternative for *addiderit*

one. I think it comes from people who put a hand to their ear and waggle it,   5
to make fun of someone else. The words of Plautus are these: 'What do you
say, you gallows, you wearer-away of the whip? How have you imposed on
me today? Into what embarrassments have you led me? How have I been
baulked [*manus mihi addita est*] about that Persian?' Again in the *Poenulus*:
'By these means I fairly played a trick [*adii manum*] on the greedy Venus.'   10
Again in the same scene: 'I'll make the other gods and goddesses henceforth
more contented, and less greedy, when they know how the procurer put a
trick [*addiderit manum*] upon Venus.' Again in the *Aulularia*: 'Thus did I
baulk [*adii manum*] all those rascals.' Again in the *Casina*: 'Were you two
tripped up [*addita manus*] neatly enough?' Although I find it written in   15
different ways, now *adii* and now *addita*. The more correct reading seems to
me *addidi*, taking the metaphor, as I said, from a gesture of mockery; Persius
recalls this: 'Nor a hand that can imitate by its motion a donkey's white ears.'

51   **Circumtondere comam**
     To cut the hair all round

Περικείρειν τοὺς πλοκάμους, To cut the hair all round. This is a proverb in
Greek, and means to make a butt of someone. For this is a joke usually
played on stupid people: their hair is cut all round without their being aware   5
of it. Lucian in the *Misanthrope*: 'You sat while they cut your locks.' He uses it
again in his *False Prophet*.

52   **Fucum facere**
     To play a trick

Fucum facere, originally 'to apply a dye,' in the sense of practising an imposture and deceiving by skilful pretence, is frequent among good authors.
        * * * * *
        in the second passage from the *Poenulus*; modern texts derive the verb in all
        these places from *adeo* and not *addo*, but why *adire manum* should carry this
        meaning is apparently not known. Erasmus' explanation is thus all at sea. 'As
        I said' was added in 1515.
     17 Persius] *Satires* 1.59; this is the gesture conveying a low opinion of a person's
        intelligence by imitating a donkey's ears, of which Erasmus has spoken.

     51 This seems not to be in the Greek proverb-collections, and is no doubt taken
        from Lucian *Timon* 4, which was added in 1528 to II iv 69. The other passage is
        Alexander 6, where two charlatans go about shearing their victims.

     52 *Collectanea* no 37, citing Terence and Quintus Cicero. Erasmus gives correctly
        what seems to be the evolution of the meaning of *fucus*, from seaweed to an

Terence in the *Eunuchus*: 'Came secretly across another's roof, in order to   5
play a trick on a woman,' *fucum factum mulieri*, where *factum* is a supine not a
participle. Quintus his brother writes to Cicero: 'If you perceive that a man
who has made you a promise wishes to play a trick on you, as they say, you
must conceal the fact that you have heard this and know all about it.' For
fucus is a species of plant, in Greek *phykos*, used for dying woollen cloth.   10
Thus *fucus* may be found meaning simply 'dye,' and *fucare* 'to colour';
Horace in the Odes: 'coloured with crocodile dung.' Especially if we mean to
say that the colour is not natural or original, but artificial or falsely applied,
as in Horace again: 'Wool purple-dyed / Never regains the hue it once has
lost.' So the cosmetic which women apply to their skin to hide blemishes to   15
their beauty, as if they were putting on a mask, is called *fucus*; Plautus: 'They
hide the body's faults with rouge,' *fucus*. And just as the *fucus* is colour
added by art, so a mask is not a true face but an applied one. Seneca says
wittily 'so that he likes the mask better than the face,' that is, he prefers to
seem rather than to be. Lucretius too in book 3: 'Now from the inmost heart   20
true voices come; / The mask is snatched away, the real is left.' Cornelius
Tacitus in the *Dialogue on Orators*: 'Thus there was not lacking an excellent
teacher, a man of real distinction, to show the true face of eloquence and not
its image.' Thus we say people are 'wearing a mask' when their appearance
belies what they really are. And things are called 'eye-wash,' *offucias*, when   25
they are empty appearances, which trick the eyes of the spectator like sleight
of hand. In Greek there is a single word for this kind of imposture,
phenakizein, and the noun *phenakismos*; the contriver of the disguise is
phenax. The compiler of the *Etymologicum graecum* – and a dishonest and

* * * * *

inferior red dye made from it; thence to cosmetics, especially those such as
rouge which can be smeared on, and so to pretences and to artificial ornament
of any kind, especially in literary style. Otto 723
5 Terence] *Eunuchus* 588–9
7 Cicero] Quintus Cicero *Commentariolum petitionis* 9.35 (normally printed with
Marcus Cicero's letters to his brother Quintus)
12 Horace] *Epodes* 12.11 (Erasmus usually calls them *Odes*); *Odes* 3.5.27–8
16 Plautus] *Mostellaria* 275
18 Seneca] *De beneficiis* 2.13.2; used also in *Collectanea* no 405 and in *Adagia* I VII 7
AND III vii 6
20 Lucretius] *De rerum natura* 3.57–8 (see I ii 38n).
22 Tacitus] *Dialogus de oratoribus* 34.5 (see I iv 26n); added in 1533
29 *Etymologicum*] The *Etymologicum magnum*, a Greek dictionary compiled
perhaps in the early twelfth century, of which the first edition, by Marcus
Musurus, was published in Venice in 1499 by Zacharias Callierges; this is
790.18. 'In Greek ... false hair' was added in 1515.

corrupt writer he was – thinks the term came from *pênêkê*, a Greek word for 30
false hair, which is *galericulum* in Latin.

  Julianus, quoted by Ulpian in the *Pandects*, book 14 title *Ad senatus-consultum Macedonicum* chapter 9, used *color* in the sense of *fucus*: 'But
Julianus adds' he says 'that if any *color*, any line of defence has been thought
up to the effect that the son of the family who was proposing to accept the 35
loan should give a surety.' Experts in forensic rhetoric also use the word
'colour' for a line of argument likely to carry conviction which they have
invented for the defence. Juvenal: 'Quick quick, Quintilian, please give us
some colour.' And when that great expert is in difficulties, the wife caught in
the act defends herself with the most impudent of 'colours': ' 'Twas agreed 40
of old / You should do what you like, and also I / Should please myself.'

53 Album calculum addere, et similes figurae
To add a white stone, and similar metaphors

Λευκὴν ψῆφον προσθεῖναι, To add a white stone. This means to vote approval, and we often find it among learned authors. It comes from the custom in
Antiquity of placing pebbles in an urn to signify the opinions of the judges: 5
white stones meant acquittal, black condemnation. If it happened that they
were equal in number, the accused was dismissed. Aristotle treats the
reason for this at length in his *Problems*. Ovid recalls the custom of voting by
pebbles in the *Metamorphoses*, book 15:

* * * * *

31 *galericulum*] A wig, from Suetonius *Otho* 12.1, added here in *1533*
32 *Pandects*] Justinian's *Digest* 14.6.7; Ulpian, the great jurist, is one of the
  principal sources from which it is compiled. This 'title,' the name for the larger
  subdivisions of books of the *Digest*, deals with the situation when a son who is
  not yet his own master but subject to the *paterfamilias* has unlawfully pledged
  his credit for a loan. Added, with what follows, in *1533*
38 Juvenal] 6.280 and 281–3. A 'colour' in this sense is 'the favourable light in
  which a speaker endeavours to place an action which he is defending' (J. D.
  Duff). Eminent counsel are not so clever at this as women.

53 *Collectanea* no 622 must have originated in Diogenianus 6.9, since it stands in a
  long series of proverbs arranged by Greek and not Latin alphabetical order,
  which come from him. Erasmus added a vague reference to Pliny's *Letters*, and
  also a phrase with 'black stone' instead of white, which he ascribes perhaps
  from memory to Plautus, and does not reuse here. The whole thing is now
  rebuilt with fresh materials. Otto 299–300
 7 Aristotle] *Problemata* 29.13 (951a20), repeated in III vi 76
 8 Ovid] *Metamorphoses* 15.41–6 (tr A. E. Watts)

With pebbles, black and white, in olden time,   10
'Twas custom to convict, or clear, of crime;
And thus the fatal vote was cast: each stone
Was black, that in the unfeeling urn was thrown.
But when, upturned, it poured them back to light
For counting, all the blacks had changed to white.   15

The younger Pliny says in one of his letters: 'To sharpen your critical powers
I must confess that my friends and I are thinking of publishing it, if only you
cast your vote' [your white pebble] 'for the proposal, mistaken though it
may be,' meaning, if you confirm our error with your judgment. Lucian in
the *Apologia*, 'Not considering it a matter of little importance for me to be   20
given a white vote by you.' Plato, *Laws* book 2: 'I would not have given this
vote.' To this may be added what Alcibiades says about not wishing to
submit to the sentence of the judges: he says that he would not trust his own
mother in such a dangerous situation, but would suspect her of being
capable of putting in a black stone instead of a white. Aristides in *Pericles*   25
puts it in one word, *epipsephizein*, meaning 'to assent,' and adopts this term
as Platonic.

54   **Creta notare, carbone notare**
     To mark with chalk, with coal

These belong to the same category: to mark with chalk for to approve, and to
mark with coal for to condemn. This is because of what Pythagoras says, that
white belongs to the nature of good, and what is black to that of evil. Thus   5
we call happy things 'white' and villains 'black.' Cicero in his speech *Pro
Caecina*, speaking of the witness Sextus Clodius Phormio: 'No less black and
no less brazen than Phormio in Terence.' Also Horace: 'This man is black;
beware of him, thou Roman!' and again in the *Satires*: 'Are they sane, to be

* * * * *

16 Pliny] the Younger, *Letters* 1.2.5 (tr Betty Radice)
19 Lucian] *Apologia* 15
21 Plato] *Laws* 2.674a
22 Alcibiades] From Plutarch *Alcibiades* 22.2
25 Aristides] See I i 13n; *De quattuor* p 165 Dindorf (*psêphos* is a voting-pebble).

54 *Collectanea* nos 272 (from Horace and Persius) and 664. Otto 299
 4 Pythagoras] Philosopher of the sixth century BC; Diogenes Laertius 8.34
 6 Cicero] *Pro A. Caecina* 10.27
 8 Horace] *Satires* 1.4.85; 2.3.246

marked with chalk, or coal?' Persius, imitating him, says in his fifth *Satire*:   10
'What to follow and what to avoid / You first marked, the one with chalk, the
other with coal.' Horace again in the *Odes*: 'Let this fair day not lack a Cretan
mark.' He calls the white stone a Cretan mark, because the ancients used to
mark in this way days of good omen. It is true that some read *Thressa*,
Thracian for *Cressa*, Cretan in this place, because the custom is said to have   15
existed among the Thracians.

To this class belongs that other expression, 'to mark with a pearl,'
which often occurs in literature, meaning to count something fortunate and
prosperous. It arises from the superstition of the ancients, who used to mark
every day in the year by means of the exact number of pebbles placed in an   20
urn, or (among the Scythians) in a quiver, and by these pebbles they
indicated which day they considered to have been prosperous, with a white
stone, or chalk; which had been particularly lucky, with a pearl; on the other
hand, the unlucky one was marked with a black stone. Persius: 'This day,
Macrinus, mark with a finer stone.' Pliny recalls this superstition in book 7   25
chapter 40: 'Vain mortality, so ingenious in circumscribing itself, counts by
the method of the people of Thrace, who put into an urn pebbles of different
colour according to the experience of each day, and on the last day counts
them all out separately, and thus decides about each one. What if that
much-praised day with the white stone had in it the origin of evil?' Thus far   30
Pliny. Plutarch in the life of Pericles tells a story not without relevance to
this, which it would perhaps be appropriate to transcribe in his own words:
'Dividing the whole group into eight parts he had them draw lots, and he
allowed those who got the white bean to feast and relax, while the others
fought. Therefore those to whom something good happens call it a "white   35
day" from the white bean.'

This is close to our way of calling important things 'matters of higher

* * * * *

10 Persius] *Satires* 5.107–8
12 Horace] *Odes* 1.36.10. The Romans identified the words *creta*, chalk and *Creta*,
   the island of Crete, and could therefore call a white mark 'Cretan.' But Pliny
   Naturalis historia 7.131 tells us that it was a Thracian custom to mark lucky and
   unlucky days by putting a white or a black pebble into an urn; and hence the
   idea that 'Cretan' here should be 'Thracian.' This suggestion, inserted here in
   1523, was finally refuted in 1711 by Richard Bentley. The chalk or white stone
   became a pearl in the poets of the Empire, eg Martial.
21 Scythians] This detail is from Zenobius 6.13.
24 Persius] *Satires* 2.1; ascribed to Juvenal, apparently by a slip of memory, from
   1536 onwards
25 Pliny] *Naturalis historia* 7.131, already referred to
31 Plutarch] *Pericles* 27.2, added in *1520*

note' just as Cicero sends someone 'greetings of a superior brand.' Livy,
decade 1 book 4, uses the phrase 'a sinister mark': 'Postumius had no sinister
mark against him,' that is to say, he was not sullied by an imputation of   40
cruelty.

55   **Calculum reducere**
     To take back a move (or counter)

To take back a move (or counter). This means to change an action for which
one is sorry, or to alter the plan of some badly-arranged affair. Nonius quotes
Cicero in the *Hortensius*: 'So I allow you, as in the twelve stones of old, to   5
change your move [*calculum*] if you repent of any given proposition.' It
appears to be adapted from people who make calculations, or more likely
from the game of *laterunculi* (chess). In short, whatever metaphors are
created out of counters or markers [*calculi*] take the form of a proverb. Thus
to 'call to a reckoning' [*ad calculos*] means to initiate an audit or valuation.   10
Cicero in his dialogue *On Friendship*: 'But such a view reduces friendship to a
question of figures [*ad calculos revocare*] in a spirit far too narrow and illiberal,
as though the object were to have an exact balance in a debtor and creditor
account.' Valerius Maximus, book 4, the chapter on liberality: 'If one esti-

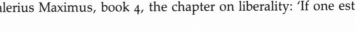

38 Cicero] *Ad familiares* 7.29.1; Erasmus' point is that for things of the highest
   'note' (highly noteworthy) Latin uses the same word, *nota*, as for a chalk-mark.
   This was added, both here and in II i 79, in 1533 from memory; the letter is
   written to Cicero by his friend Curius, not by him.
38 Livy] 4.29.6, added in 1533

55 *Collectanea* no 38 is partly reused, but Erasmus drops a quotation from Poliziano
   in which he had used the phrase, being now able to provide more evidence
   from classical authors. This is not a very easy article to translate, because the
   underlying imagery (of 'pebbles') covers not only the 'men' or pieces in a
   board-game but also the counters on an abacus or counting-board; and thus we
   may have metaphors from the way in which the Romans kept their accounts, on
   which we are none too well informed.
 5 Cicero] *Hortensius* frag 60, cited by Nonius (see I i 97n) p 170. This refers to a
   board game; it should read 'twelve lines,' not 'stones.'
11 Cicero] *De amicitia* 16.58. We are now keeping accounts.
14 Valerius Maximus] 4.8.1 (see I ii 14n). In 1508 this was attributed to the
   previous chapter, on friendship; that Erasmus should have corrected this,
   shows what an eye he sometimes had for detail. Valerius recalls how in the war
   against Hannibal, Fabius Maximus had secured the return of some prisoners of
   war, and when the senate refused to find the money he had promised for their
   ransom, he sold all his own property and paid it himself, rather than be a party

mates the amount [*ad calculos revocatur*], it was small, coming from a piece of   15
land of seven acres and that hidden away in Pupinia; if one regards the
motive of the man who made the advance, it was more than any amount of
money.' And 'to go back to the counters [*calculi*]' means to return to the
argument, the consideration, the scheme. Cicero to Atticus: 'So let me now
at all events return to the standards [*calculos*] I then rejected, and adopt   20
counsels of safety (in some degree) as well as of glory.' And in Pliny's *Letters*
'to move the counters' means to put forward arguments. And he says 'to set
out the counters on each side' when he means to weigh up the arguments
each way; and 'let this counter be added' means 'this matter of importance is
also to be considered.' There is no reason why one should not say 'a counter   25
drops out' or 'to take a counter away.'

56   **Theta praefigere**
     To prefix a theta

To prefix a *theta*. This means to condemn. Persius: 'And you may prefix a
theta to the error.' Ausonius, in a choliambic poem against a gormandizing
schoolmaster: 'Wretched pedant, *ou* to your obscenity, / May a cleft *theta*   5
mark your name.' Some say this refers to the shape of the Greek letter,
because it has somewhat the appearance of a human heart pierced through.
I do not know if we are to believe Isidore, who writes in the first book of the
Etymologies that it was a military custom to use the mark Θ for the slain, T for
the survivors. Certainly there is a reference to the sign T in the Apocalypse,   10
which bears the name of St John the Evangelist. But more likely to be true is

* * * * *

to such a breach of public faith. ('The man who made the advance,' if that is
what the Latin means, can hardly be what Valerius wrote.)

19 Cicero] *Ad Atticum* 8.12.5. If 'standards' is right, there is another change of
meaning: the phrase used (*ad illos calculos revertamur*) would normally mean 'do
my sums over again,' think things out afresh.

21 Pliny] the Younger *Letters* 2.19.9; cf 1.14.9.

56 *Collectanea* no 261, from Persius. Our last sentence is partly taken from *Coll.*, but
the distinguishing letters were given there as θ, κ and λ.

3 Persius] *Satires* 4.13

4 Ausonius] See 1 i 86n; *Epigrammata* 87.12–3; an indecent poem full of what
appear to be alphabetical symbols, the purport of which is not clear.

8 Isidore] Bishop of Seville 600–36, *Etymologiae* 1.3.8. This, a standard encyclo-
pedia of the Middle Ages, is referred to in the *Adagia* twice.

10 Apocalypse] There are many references in that book to such a seal or mark, eg
13.16, but its identification as a *theta* or T comes from Ezekiel 9:4; 'the
evangelist' was added in 1517/8.

what Asconius Paedianus writes, that in old times there were three marks
on the lots cast into the urns in legal cases. Of these, Θ was indeed the sign of
condemnation, T of absolution, while Δ stood for deferment, when they
indicated that it was not sufficiently clear to them as yet, and the case should   15
be tried again.

57   **Stellis signare. Obelo notare**
     To mark with stars. To brand with an obelus

Ἄστροις σημειοῦσθαι or τεκμαίρεσθαι, To mark with stars or to tell by the
stars. Eustathius on the fifth book of the *Odyssey* suggests that the saying
concerns travellers on a long and deserted road, needing to mark their   5
regional position by observation of the stars; and that the metaphor comes
from seafarers, who when they are far enough out from land to have nothing
but 'sky all around and all around them sea,' regulate their course by the
indications of the stars, especially the Little Bear and the Great Bear. Thus
Aratus in the *Phaenomena*; I will copy the translation of his verses out of the   10
version of Germanicus Caesar.

> Here the Great Bear, and lesser Cynosure,
> Jove's nurses, shine; one guides the Greeks, great-starred;
> Pure white, the other rules Phoenician ways.
> The Great Bear shines unmatched in liquid splendour,   15
>
>   * * * * *

12 Asconius] He was a valuable commentator on Cicero's speeches, of the first
   century AD; but the comment on the *Verrines*, the only one to which Erasmus
   refers in the *Adagia*, is by a much later hand, now known as Pseudo-Asconius.
   What he quotes here is on pp 193 and 231 of *Ciceronis orationum scholiastae*, ed
   T. Stangl, Vienna/Leipzig 1912. In *Adagia* IV x 85 the three letters are given, 'if
   the manuscripts are free from error,' as *theta*, *T* and *NL* (for *non liquet*, not clear).

57 From the Greek proverb-collections (Diogenianus 2.66; Suidas A 4257). The
   forced association of the stars as guides to navigation and the stars (asterisks)
   and other signs used by scholars seems to be Erasmus' own.
 4 Eustathius] See I i 77n; on *Odyssey* 5.276 (1535.56).
 8 sky all around] Virgil *Aeneid* 3.193
 9 Great Bear] In *1508* the text went on 'as Ovid bears witness,' and then the two
   lines quoted below. This was replaced in *1515* by the lines from Aratus and
   Germanicus, and then came the title of Ovid's poem.
10 Aratus] *Phaenomena* 36–44. His didactic poem on constellations and weather-
   signs (first half of the third century BC) was first printed in the Aldine *Astronomi
   veteres* of October 1499, and with it a version in Latin verse by Germanicus
   Caesar, who died in AD 19. Our version must do duty both for Aratus' Greek
   and for Germanicus' Latin (*Aratea* 39–47).

When Sun in Ocean's plunged his dazzling face,
Where with seven fires glitters the Cretan star;
More certain for the ploughers of the sea
Is Cynosure, whose short course turns itself
On steady hinge, and never once deceived   20
The craft from Sidon which had sight of her.

And Ovid imitating Aratus, in the fourth book of the *Tristia*:

Ye two beasts, great and small, one the guide
Of Grecian, the other of Sidonian ships.
Ye never-setting.   25

Virgil mentions the same thing in Book 5, speaking of Palinurus: 'While he
spoke, he kept a good grip on the tiller – / By no means would he release it –
and a steadfast gaze on the stars,' and elsewhere, 'All the stars he scanned as
they slid through the quiet sky.' Likewise Homer in several places, as in the
Odyssey, book 5:   30

And taking his seat artfully with the steering oar he held her
On her course, nor did sleep ever descend on his eyelids
As he kept his eye on the Pleiades and late-setting Bootes,
And the Bear, to whom men also give the name of the Wagon,
Who turns about fixed ever in the same place,   35
And she alone is never plunged in the wash of the Ocean.

Thus those people seem to 'tell the way by the stars' who use signs and
conjectures skilfully worked out to inquire into or follow up a subject which
would otherwise be difficult to investigate; or who by means of certain signs
reckon up far in advance what is going to happen. Later on the meaning   40
changed, so that people were said to 'note down the stars' when they
pointed out something particularly worthy of notice.
　　To mark with an obelus is different: it means to affix a marginal sign
shaped like a spit for confutation and condemnation. It is taken from
Aristarchus, who gathered together the poems of Homer and arranged   45

* * * * *

22　Ovid] *Tristia* 4.3.1–2
26　Virgil] *Aeneid* 5.852–3; 3.515
29　Homer] *Odyssey* 5.270–5 (tr Richmond Lattimore), used again in III v 42, where
　　further material on navigation by the stars is added
45　Aristarchus] The greatest of ancient Homeric scholars (second century BC),
　　used as a type of the severe literary critic by Erasmus in his own letters

them in books, rejecting by means of 'obeli' or small dagger-signs prefixed to them the spurious lines, that is to say the counterfeit and substituted lines which did not seem to have the true feeling of the Homeric vein. Those, on the other hand, which seemed outstanding and genuine he marked with asterisks, little stars. Both Origen and St Jerome followed this method in   50
Holy Scripture.

The very name of Aristarchus became a proverb, since he was the person who invented this system of approving or rejecting by means of critical marks. Cicero to Atticus: 'In short, he worked up most impressively the whole theme which in aristocratic style I am in the habit of embroidering   55
in my speeches (you are their Aristarchus) all about fire and sword (you know my colour-box).' He calls Atticus the Aristarchus of his speeches, that is, the censor and emendator, because it was his custom to mark with red pencil anything which did not meet with his approval in the writings of Cicero. Cicero makes this clear in another place, *Letters to Atticus*, book 16:   60
'Your good opinion makes them sparkle the brighter in my eyes. I was terrified of those little red wafers of yours.' The same to Dolabella: 'The latter brings forward, I take it, record in two little lines of money advanced, and the other, a regular Aristarchus, obelizes them, while I, like an ancient critic, have to decide the matter.' Varro, also in his *On the Latin Language*, calls the   65
grammarians who criticize books 'Aristarchs.' And Horace: 'He will become an Aristarchus,' that is, a censor and critic of others' writings. St Jerome often calls someone 'the Aristarchus of his time' because he condemns some things and approves others at his own sweet will.

58 Notari ungui et similia
To be marked with the finger-nail, etc

Another which belongs to the same group is *Notare ungui*, to mark with the finger-nail, because it was the custom to make a mark with the nail against anything unsatisfactory. Horace spoke of drawing a cross-stroke with the   5
pen, when he meant 'to condemn.' In the same way, the phrase 'critical

* * * * *

50 Origen] Probably a reminiscence of Jerome's preface to the Pentateuch
54 Cicero] *Ad Atticum* 1.14.3; 16.11.1; *Ad familiares* 9.10.1
65 Varro] He refers several times in his *De lingua latina* (see I ii 23n) to Aristarchus and his school, the *Aristarchei*.
66 Horace] *Ars poetica* 450
67 Jerome] *Adversus Rufinum* 1.17 (PL 23.410B)

58 This is partly covered, very briefly, by *Collectanea* no 774.
 5 Horace] *Ars poetica* 447

mark,' *censoria virgula*, is found several times in St Jerome to express the
power of correcting something and branding it as spurious. Again, in
Quintilian, *Institutions* book 1, 'And this the ancient grammarians used so
severely that they mark with some sort of critical sign not only single lines'   10
and what follows. This is derived from the censors in Rome, whose duty it
was to pick on anything in the behaviour of the citizens which needed
correction, and to impose a fine. Here belong the sponge, the file and the
chisel, which have become proverbial as instruments of emendation. A
sponge wipes out what is unsatisfactory. A file removes excess and polishes   15
crudity. A chisel shapes and fashions what is still unfinished. So Augustus
said of his *Ajax*, which he had wiped out, that 'he had fallen upon his
sponge.' A polished piece of writing is said to have been under the file, and
the word 'sculpture' is used of well-chiselled prose.

59 Stilum vertere
To reverse the pen

To reverse the pen is to change what you have written. Horace in the *Satires*:
'Often reverse the pen.' In Antiquity they used to write on wax tablets with a
writing-stylus, using one end, very sharp, to trace the letters in the soft wax,   5
and the other broader end to rub out what they had written. Jerome *Against
Rufinus*: 'As long as I did not refuse your praise, you followed me like a

* * * * *

7 Jerome] *Letters* 61.2.5; see also *Adagia* IV vii 26.
9 Quintilian] 1.4.3, added in 1523
16 Augustus] Suetonius (see I i 78n) *Divus Augustus* 85.2 Ajax in the story lost his
reason, and on recovery killed himself by the standard heroic method of falling
on his sword. The emperor Augustus is said to have begun a tragedy on this
theme, using for his rough draft, it would seem, not the more usual wax-
covered tablets, but a slate, which could be wiped clean with a sponge for
future use. After he had abandoned the attempt, he told friends who enquired
how Ajax was getting on that he had come to this untimely (but for a rough
draft not inappropriate) end.
19 sculpture] The description of a carefully-wrought speech as 'sculpted' is
ascribed to Demosthenes by Quintilian 12.9.16. This was followed in *1508* by
what purported to be another metaphor for polished writing, 'smoothed with
pumice-stone, for books were polished with pumice to make them more
elegant'; but this was cut out in *1515*, no doubt because it referred not to the
style of the writing but to the physical exterior of a book (which would be
written on papyrus in the form of a roll).

59 *Collectanea* no 770 (partly reused), with the quotation from Jerome. Otto 1692
3 Horace] *Satires* 1.10.72
6 Jerome] *Adversus Rufinum* 1.31 (PL 23.424 A)

master, calling me brother and colleague, and declaring that I was orthodox
in all things. But since I have not accepted your praises, and judged myself
unworthy of being publicly commended by such a great man, you reverse   10
your pen and you are showering blame on everything you praised before,
producing both sweet and sour from the same mouth.' Jerome copied
Cicero, who writes as follows in the fourth of his *Verrines*: 'He was at last
thoroughly frightened and upset; and then he reversed the pen on his
records, thereby making an end of all his chances of acquittal.' One also   15
finds 'to stick in the stylus,' 'to attack with the stylus,' meaning to upbraid
and reproach in one's writings.

60 **Omne tulit punctum; Omnium calculis**
   He obtained every point; With everyone's votes

He obtained every point; With everyone's votes. We read these phrases as a
way of saying 'with everyone's agreement and assent.' The first is adapted
from the custom of carrying round in election meetings a wax tablet on   5
which people indicated by a dot, *punctum*, which of the candidates they
were voting for; and the other from the system of voting by the judges,
which we have just mentioned. Horace: 'All votes [*punctum*] he won, who
mingled use with pleasure.' For those who write nothing but agreeable
things please only the readers who seek for pleasure, and those who pro-   10
duce useful writings only win the approval of the readers in search of the
useful. But the one who has combined pleasure with usefulness will win the
approval of all. Horace again in his *Epistles*: 'Alcaeus I in his opinion
[*punctum*] shine, He soars a new Callimachus in mine.' And again in the
choliambic epigram quoted by Porphyrion: 15

> This Rufus, noted maker of stork-pie,
> This man's more elegant than both the Planci.
> He didn't carry seven votes.

Aristides in *Themistocles* uses the phrase 'the common voting-pebble of the

* * * * *

13 Cicero] *Verrines* 2.41.101, added in 1523

60 *Collectanea* no 492 gave the two quotations from Horace, with an explanation,
   which is partly reused here.
 8 Horace] *Ars poetica* 343; *Epistles* 2.2.99–100, used again in I vii 96
15 epigram] Anonymous lines (*Fragmenta poetarum latinorum* ed W. Morel, Leipzig
   1927, incert 21), cited by Porphyrion on Horace *Satires* 2.2.50
19 Aristides] *De quattuor* p 262 Dindorf (see I i 13n).

Greeks' to mean the consensus of all Greece. Cicero, *Tusculan Questions,*   20
book 2, 'What fire have these men not been through who once used to
gather in these things vote by vote?' He is speaking of the magistracies,
which were allotted by the votes of single citizens. Apuleius in his *Ass,* book
6, says 'death in some form or other had been allotted to him by the general
pebble' meaning the votes and opinions of all.   25

61 Cumani sero sapiunt
The people of Cumae learn wisdom late

'Οψὲ αἰσθάνονται οἱ Κουμαῖοι, The people of Cumae learn wisdom late. This
adage is mentioned by Strabo, *Geography,* book 13. He thinks these people
were generally decried as foolish and absurd, because after two hundred   5
years of exacting taxes at the port for the purpose of building the town, they
did not stop paying them when the town was built. He adds another story:
that the Cumaeans had built a colonnade with borrowed money, and then
when they failed to repay the money on the appointed day, they were
forbidden to walk there. Some time later there was a heavy rain, and the   10
creditors sent out a crier in jest, to publish an edict that the Cumaeans must
come under the colonnade. Thus admonished by the voice of the crier, they
did so; and hence the origin of the proverb 'the people of Cumae learn
wisdom late,' because it was only after receiving advice that they learned
they should come in out of the rain. Stephanus remarks that Cumae and   15
Lesbos both had a bad name for stupidity. The proverb does not apply to
Cumae in Italy but to Cumae in Aeolis, which had been called Amazonium,
and Phriconitis, or as Herodotus says in his Book 1, Phriconis. It resembles
that other phrase, 'The Phrygians learn wisdom late.' There is no reason
why it should not also be used with regard to people who only follow good   20
advice when taught by their misfortunes.
            * * * * *
20 Cicero] *Tusculanae disputationes* 2.26.62, used again in II iii 55
23 Apuleius] *Metamorphoses* 6.31

61 Taken direct from Strabo *Geographica* 13.3.6 (see I i 69n).
15 Stephanus] Steph. Byzantius (see I ii 43n) p 392 Meineke; this was added both
   here and to *Adagia* I iii 66 in *1528.*
18 Herodotus] See I i 96n; 1.149, added in *1528.*
19 other phrase] I i 28 (in *1508* the paragraph began with this sentence).
21 misfortunes] In *1508* the text continued: 'This class of men is picked out by
   Lycophron (*Alexandra* 488) "Learning the truth, poor wretch, at my own
   expense." Aristides alluded to this in his *Themistocles* [*De quattuor* p 245
   Dindorf; I i 13n)] "And yet the wisdom that comes after the event, and the
   reproof that is offered with no fear of reprisals, have, it is said, nothing brilliant

62 Mala attrahens ad sese, ut caecias nubes
Attracting trouble as the north-easter draws clouds

Κακ' ἐφ' αὑτὸν ἕλκων ὥστε καικίας νέφος, Attracting trouble as the north-
easter draws clouds. This is an iambic line, in common use as a proverb
against those who are the very begetters and purveyors of their own trou-   5
bles, in the way of lawsuits and affairs. The comparison comes from the
nature of the wind called *caecias*, which as Pliny writes, 'blows between
north and east,' and unlike any other of the northerly winds does not drive
the clouds away but attracts them. I will give his own words: 'The coldest of
the winds are those which blow, as we said, from the north. The north-west   10
wind, *corus*, is close to these. These hold the others in check, and drive away
rainstorms. The south wind and the south-west wind (*auster* and *africus*) are
wet, especially the former in Italy. They say that in Pontus the *caecias* draws
the clouds to itself.' Thus far Pliny. Aristotle in his *De mundo* thinks that the
north-east wind blows roughly from the sun's point of rising in summer,   15
and adds that some people identify it with the wind others call *thraskias*,
which blows nearest to the *argestes*. Why it should be that this wind does
not, like the others, drive the clouds away, but calls them to it, Aristotle
attempts to explain in the *Meteorologica*: 'Either because another wind is
blowing the other way at the same time; or because this one blowing from   20
the highest part of heaven (say from the east) is not carried across the land,
but makes a curving back on itself and turns towards the place from whence
it came. And so it happens that it draws the clouds to itself.' So in his *De
mundo* he counts the north-easter among what are called 'regressive winds.'
In the *Problemata*, section 26, he gives two causes for this. One, he thinks, is 25
that another wind is blowing contrary to the north-east wind at the same
time. The other is in agreement with what I have said; that the north-easter

* * * * *

about them." These belong to the flock of adages which I have put forward
elsewhere, *Piscator ictus sapiet* [I i 29] and others like it.' This was removed in
1515; the line from Lycophron had already appeared in I v i, but the Aristides
never found another home.

62 *Collectanea* no 122 cited the passages from Pliny and Gellius, of which the latter
    is reduced here to a mere mention, perhaps because it has little new to add. The
    Greek is a line from an unidentified tragedy (frag adesp 75 Nauck) or comedy,
    or from an iambic poet (*Anthologia lyrica graeca*, ed E. Diehl, Leipzig 1925, 1.263),
    and is recorded also by Diogenianus (4.66). Tilley E 197 Drawing evil about one
    as the north-east wind does clouds
  7 Pliny] *Naturalis historia* 2.120 and 126
 14 Aristotle] *De mundo* 4 (394b22 and 30); *Meteorologica* 2.6 (364b13); *De mundo* 4
    (394b36); *Problemata* 26.29 (943a32), this last reference added in 1515

blows from a higher region of the sky, namely that which lies towards the
east; that this is loftier than the west, he deduces from the size and depth of
the western sea. Thus it comes about that the north-easter, blowing into the   30
western regions, collects the clouds together, and draws them towards itself
by a spiral movement. Plutarch mentions this in his life of Sertorius; he
writes that this general observed the nature of the north-east wind at a time
when it happened to be blowing, and forced his adversaries the Cacitani (or
as the Greek copies have it, Characitani) to surrender, in the following way.   35
In front of the caves where they were keeping close, he threw up mounds of
ashes. When these were disturbed by the onrush of the cavalry, the north-
east wind sent so much dust into the mouth of the caves that the enemy
could not endure it, and gave themselves up to Sertorius.

The adage is mentioned by Aulus Gellius, book 2 chapter 22, out of   40
Aristotle, and also by Theophrastus in his book on the nature of winds. But
both he and Aristotle mention it in such a way that it appears it can be used
in a good sense; for he says 'attracting riches to himself as the north-easter
attracts clouds.' Plutarch in his essay entitled 'How to Profit by One's
Enemies': 'Just as the north-easter attracts the clouds, so a wicked life   45
attracts disgrace.' In the 'Precepts of Statecraft' he makes use of it in a good
sense.

So it seems that it can be used about anything in either a good sense or
a bad. 'This man gathers a swarm of learned men about him, as the north-
easter attracts the clouds.' 'This man attracts money to himself, from every-   50
where, as the north-easter the clouds.' 'Every kind of good fortune follows
that man, as the clouds the north-easter.' 'Wherever this man is there are
disputes – he collects lawsuits as the north-easter collects clouds.' Similarly
it may be used of things: 'Ambition is a turbulent thing, attracting to itself, as
the north-easter attracts clouds, envy, strife, extravagance, and other trou-   55
bles of the same kind.' 'Modesty attracts to itself the goodwill of all men, as
the north-easter attracts clouds.'

* * * * *

32 Plutarch] *Sertorius* 17, used again in *Adagia* II ix 43; the variant in the Greek text
   was added in *1528*.
40 Gellius] 2.22.24
41 Theophrastus] *De ventis* 7.37. In *1508* there followed 'He (Aristotle) mentions
   this in his *Problems* too'; but this was cut out in *1515* when the text of the
   passage had been inserted just above.
44 Plutarch] *Moralia* 88E; 823B, the latter added in *1515*

63 Oleum in auricula ferre
To carry oil in the ear

To carry oil in the ear. This is in Martial. In this passage the commentator
Domizio Calderini does not satisfy me, though otherwise he is a learned
man enough. For the poet seems to be twitting a man with an inflexible,   5
up-turned ear, a distinction made also in Greek ('having a proud and lofty
ear'). Martial's poem is as follows: ''Tis said he made a witty jest, Marullus, /
Who said you carry oil in your ear.' Aristotle wrote in the *Problemata*: 'The
ears are disturbed by water poured into them, but it is not so with oil. If by
chance water gets into the ear, we relieve this by pouring in oil, for when the   10
ear becomes slippery the water flows away. Thus divers have formed the
habit of dropping oil in their ears, so that the water may do them less harm.'
The adage seems to have originated from this, that is from the gesture of
those who have some liquid injected and bend the ear upwards so that it will
not flow out, which gives them the appearance of averting their ears and   15
being unwilling to listen. I would think it could also refer to flatterers, who
instil something like oil in the ear when they speak what is pleasant rather
than what is wholesome. A different idea comes out of the phrase in Persius:
'Grating on delicate ears with the harsh truth.' To this meaning belongs the
allusion in the Gospel to the sellers of oil. But if one chooses this latter sense,   20
one must read the accusative case, *in auriculam* [into the ear]. But I did not
think it right to omit the version which appears to have a proverbial meaning
and which Martial's mention shows to have been commonly used.

64 Quid si coelum ruat?
What if the sky should fall?

Τί εἰ οὐρανὸς ἐμπέσοι; What if the sky should fall? An ironically proverbial
dig against people who in the safest of situations have absurd fears. Its

* * * * *

63 *Collectanea* no 661 cited Martial, with Domizio Calderini, the standard
    fifteenth-century commentary (1447–78). The meaning of the phrase seems to
    be still uncertain. Otto 210
 3 Martial] 5.77
 6 Greek] Suidas A 2574
 8 Aristotle] *Problemata* 32.10–11 (961a18)
18 Persius] *Satires* 1.107 and 108 run together, as in II ix 53
20 Gospel] Matthew 25:9

64 *Collectanea* no 558, giving Terence as the source. Otto 286; Tilley s 516 What if
    the sky fall? The Greek equivalent, which was not in *Coll.*, is perhaps a
    reconstruction based on Theognis (see below).

origin is indicated by Aristotle in the fifth book of his *Metaphysics*, where he 5
writes that early primitive men were convinced that the sky which they saw
overhead was held up on the shoulders of Atlas. If he were to withdraw
from under it, the result would be that it would fall from its height on to the
earth. And this was not only a product of the poets' fancy, but asserted by
some natural philosophers. Plutarch in his essay 'On the Face which 10
Appears in the Orb of the Moon' quotes a certain Phenaces, who was afraid
that the moon would fall upon the earth, and grieved for the fate of those
who would be beneath it, like the Ethiopians and Taprobani, if such a weight
should fall upon them; he was in fear too about the earth and the sky, if not
held up by the pillars of Hercules. Theognis: 'Then on my head may fall vast 15
brazen Olympus, / The thing so feared by men of olden time.' Terence in the
Heautontimorumenos: 'What if I go back to the people who say, what if the sky
should fall now?' Horace alludes to this in the *Odes*:

> Were the vault of heaven
> To break and fall upon him, yet its ruins 20
> Would smite him undismayed.

65 **Umbram suam metuere**
To be afraid of one's own shadow

Τὴν αὑτοῦ σκιὰν φοβεῖσθαι, To be afraid of one's own shadow. This is said of
people who tremble like children when there is no danger at all. It comes
either from those who catch sight of their own shadow and are suddenly 5
frightened, or from the melancholics of whom Aristotle speaks, who on
account of weak spirits in the eye see something like an image of themselves
in the surrounding air, and then they think they see their own ghosts.
Socrates says in the *Phaedo* of Plato, 'But you, afraid of your shadow, as they

* * * * *

5 Aristotle] *Metaphysica* 4.23 (1023a20), freely paraphrased
10 Plutarch] *Moralia* 923c, added in *1515*; Pharnaces is a speaker in his imaginary
dialogue.
15 Theognis] 869-70 (see I i 62n).
16 Terence] *Heautontimorumenos* 719
18 Horace] *Odes* 3.3.7–8

65 *Collectanea* no 262 and 400, citing Plato and Cicero. Otto 1817; Tilley s 261 To be
afraid of his own shadow
9 Plato] *Phaedo* 101d

say,' that is, mistrusting yourself. Quintus to Cicero on seeking the con-   10
sulship: 'The other indeed, in heaven's name, of what distinction is he?
First, of the same aristocracy as Catiline. Of greater? No, but in his valour.
For this reason, Manius, the man who feared his own shadow, you will
indeed despise.' This passage, however, was corrupted in the manuscripts
in more ways than one. Plutarch, decade 7 of the 'Table-talk,' 'The one who   15
refuses and resents the name of "shadow" seems truly to be afraid of a
shadow.' He is speaking of 'shadows' so called because they themselves
were not invited by the host but followed an invited guest to the feast.

66   **Vel muscas metuit praetervolitantes**
     He is afraid of the very flies fluttering past

This seems to be a proverbial hyperbole, quoted by Aristotle in his seventh
book on the state: ἀλλὰ δεδιότα μὲν τὰς παραπετομένας μυίας, 'but fearing
even flies flitting by,' meaning that he is afraid from some trivial cause.   5
Much the same thing is recalled in the *Ethics*, book 7, speaking of people
who are so unnaturally timid that even if a shrew squeaks they nearly die of
fear.

67   **Funem abrumpere nimium tendendo**
     To stretch the rope till it breaks

Ἀπορραγήσεται τεινόμενον τὸ καλώδιον, The taut rope will break. Said of
people who make extreme efforts and in doing so estrange those they are
dealing with; thus they incur an entire loss because they are immoderately   5
intent on gain. Lucian in one of his dialogues makes a bawd scold her

          * * * * *

10   Cicero] Quintus Cicero *Commentariolum petitionis* 2.9. The textual comment was
     added in 1536, and is justified; several words in the passage are corrupt, and
     have never been finally corrected.
15   Plutarch] *Moralia* 709C. The final sentence was added in 1515; for 'shadows' as
     uninvited guests, see *Adagia* I i 9.

66   This seems to be taken directly from Aristotle *Politics* 7.1 (1323a29); *Ethica
     Nicomachea* 7.6 (1149a7). The latter passage is quoted again in III iv 4.

67   *Collectanea* no 147, where the first text quoted is Lucian, and one would
     suppose the adage to have been taken direct from him; but the source is
     Diogenianus 2.89, who quotes the Lucian-passage, for it comes in a series of
     adages arranged by the alphabetical order of the Greek form, all of which are in
     Diogenianus.
   6 Lucian] *Dialogi meretricii* 3.3, cited by Diogenianus 2.89

daughter because she has shown scorn for her lover in too spirited a way at a banquet; the danger is, says she, that the young man in his annoyance and irritation will take his love and his money elsewhere. 'Look out,' she says, 'in case we snap the rope by pulling on it too much, as the proverb says.' Pindar, in Plutarch: 'to one loosing the rope of unbearable cares.' Although there is some difference here from the proverb, and it is more in agreement with the phrase in Seneca, *Letters to Lucilius*, about the need to undo the chains of business, and break them if they cannot be undone. The proverb can be applied in general to any attempt of the immoderate kind, which ends in trouble through excessiveness. Near this is the Hebrew saying, shrewd and not unpicturesque: 'Blow your nose too hard and you'll make it bleed.' And so says Publius' well-known maxim: 'Oft-wounded patience will to madness turn.' And the other similar saying, by the same author, I think, even if it bears the name of Seneca: 'A kind heart wounded makes for deeper rage.'

68 In matellam immeiere
To make water in a chamber-pot

'Εϲ τὴν ἀμίδα ἐνουρεῖν, To make water in the chamber-pot. When people are treated basely, or are appointed to some dishonourable function, who can be seen to be not unworthy of it, being dishonest and knavish themselves, as if they were made for disgrace. Lucian, *On Salaried Posts*: 'Therefore those would not suffer anything dreadful or unworthy, nor would these be considered insolent for, as they say "pissing into the chamber-pot."' The chamber-pot, after all, was made for that. On the other hand Martial twits a certain Bassus with using a golden vessel for his excretions and drinking out of glass: 'You catch your belly's burden, unrepentantly, in gold (poor gold!); / But you drink from glasses, Bassus: dearer cost your stools.'

* * * * *

11 Pindar] Frag 248, cited by Plutarch *Moralia* 68D
13 Seneca] *Epistulae* 22.3, from memory; a more remote allusion was added in 1515 to I x 9.
16 Hebrew saying] *Proverbs* 30:33
18 well-known maxim] Publilius Syrus F 13 and B10 (see I ii 4n). The moral maxims that circulated under his name, and were called *Mimi Publiani* in Erasmus' edition of them (Ep 298 of 1 August 1514), passed also as the 'Proverbs of Seneca.' The first of these is Tilley P 113 Patience provoked turns to fury.

68 Probably taken direct from Lucian *De mercede conductis* 4
9 Martial] 1.37

69 Risus Ionicus
An Ionian laugh

Γέλως Ἰωνικός, An Ionian laugh. Said of the luxurious and pleasure-loving.
For the voluptuousness of the Ionians, like the extravagance of the Sybarites, became proverbial, the first being the most luxurious of the Greeks, the   5
second, of the barbarians. Athenaeus, in book 12 of *Doctors at Dinner*,
speaking of Ionian luxury, says there is a golden proverb which testifies to
the way of life of that race, and I think he means this one. He also asserts in
book 14 that there was a wanton, lascivious dance which was called Ionic.
Valerius Maximus, in *Memorabilia*, book 2, tells how the Ionians were the   10
first to invent the custom of handing out scent and garlands at banquets, and
having dessert, both notable incitements to luxury. Maximus Tyrius in his
dissertation entitled *The Aim of Philosophy*: 'A man of Crotona loves the wild
olive of Olympus, the Spartan loves weapons of war, the Cretan hunting,
the Sybarite luxury, the Ionian dancing.' So Horace in the *Odes*: 'The maiden   15
early takes delight / In learning Ionian dances,' meaning lascivious steps and
less than decorous gestures. In Aristophanes too we have *ionikôs*, in Ionian
fashion, for *habrôs*, meaning softly and delicately.

70 Risus Megaricus
A Megarian laugh

Γέλως Μεγαρικός, A Megarian laugh. Said of those who make jokes at the
wrong time, and – a thing Quintilian advises against – would sometimes

* * * * *

69 In the *Collectanea* no 833 this was coupled with two other types of luxury in the
   ancient world, Miletus (*Adagia* I ix 49) and Sybaris (II ii 65), and the source was
   no doubt Diogenianus 3.87.
 4 Sybarites] Sybaris was a Greek colony in South Italy, and one would not expect
   Erasmus to describe it as barbarian.
 6 Athenaeus] 12.526d, the precise reference inserted in 1517/8; 14.629e, added in
   1517/8
10 Valerius Maximus] 2.6.1 (see I ii 14n).
12 Maximus Tyrius] *Philosophumena* 29.1 (see I ii 100n). In 1508 he was 'Maximus of
   Thurii,' and this was corrected to 'of Tyre' in 1523.
15 Horace] *Odes* 3.6.21–2
17 Aristophanes] *Thesmophoriazusae* 163

70 From the Greek proverb-collections (Diogenianus 3.88; Suidas Γ 115)
 4 Quintilian] 6.3.28

rather lose a friend than a witticism; or whose arts have now become   5
despised and put in the shade by better craftsmen following them. It can be
fairly applied to old men who eagerly pursue indecorous games and the
pleasures of youth, at a time of life when this is indecent. Ionian comedy had
a vogue in its time, then came into disrepute and was mocked by the
Athenians. This line of poetry on inopportune laughter is well known: 'It's a   10
serious thing to laugh in the wrong place.'

71 **Risus Chius**
    The laugh of Chios

Γέλως Χῖος, The laugh of Chios. This refers to a wanton, lascivious game, for
the Old Comedy rebuked the Chian way of life. The adage is mentioned by
Diogenianus.
                                                                            5

72 **Quicquid in buccam venerit**
    Whatever came into his mouth

Whatever came into his mouth. Used whenever we speak of people talking
freely and in security, without premeditation, saying whatever comes into
their heads. This is what we do in the company of our loyal friends, with   5
whom we can joke and chat with confidence. Cicero to Atticus, book 14: 'If
there is nothing special, write to me whatever comes into your mouth.'
Again in book 12, 'When we are together, and chatter away with whatever
comes into our mouths.' This is applicable to those who talk rashly and
without forethought, just as if their words were born not in their hearts but   10
in their throats.

               * * * * *

10 This line] Menander *Sententiae* 144 (see I i 30n).

71 Like I v 40, this began in 1508 'This too is found in the collections of Greek
    adages,' and the words were cut out in 1515. The source is Diogenianus 3.87.

72 Taken, it seems, directly from Cicero *Ad Atticum* 14.7.2; 12.1.2. Otto 273 gives
    many more examples from Greek as well as Latin. We are more likely to say
    'whatever comes into our heads.'

73 Quicquid in linguam venerit
    Whatever may come on the tongue

Clearly akin to this is a saying used by Lucian in his essay on 'How History
Should be Written': 'Devising and inventing whatever comes in a rash
moment to the tongue, as the saying goes.' Plato quotes this expression in   5
the *Republic*, book 8, out of Aeschylus the tragic poet. Athenaeus in *Doctors
at Dinner*, book 5, also used it: 'As the poet says, whatever comes in a rash
moment to the tongue.' Isocrates in his *Panathenaic Oration* gives what is
virtually an interpretation of it: 'I shall seem like those who talk rashly, in an
arrogant and vulgar way, saying whatever comes into their heads.'   10

74 Momo satisfacere, et similia
    To satisify Momus, and the like

Τῷ Μώμῳ ἀρέσκειν, To satisfy Momus, This is a proverbial hyperbole.
Hesiod in his *Theogony* mentions a certain Momus, whose mother (he says)
was Night, and his father Sleep. This god has the habit of producing nothing   5
of his own, but staring at the works of the other gods with inquisitive eyes,
and if anything is lacking or wrongly done he criticizes it with the utmost
freedom. Momus, in fact, means 'reproof' in Greek. Aristotle *On the Parts of
Animals*, book 3, speaks of him as one who reproached nature for having

* * * * *

73 Derived from Lucian. This and the preceding are combined under Otto 273.
 3 Lucian] *Quomodo historia conscribenda sit* 32. The second half of the quotation is a
   fragment of lyric poetry by an unknown author (*frag adespota* 102 Page), in
   which the reading was uncertain. As first printed by Erasmus, he thought it
   meant 'whatever comes to the unguarded tongue.' By 1517 he had seen the
   same fragment in a better text in Athenaeus; so in *1520* he improved the reading
   in Lucian out of that new source, and in *1523* he altered his Latin version of it to
   read as it does now. The point is of no interest in itself, but it is a good example
   of his unceasing concern for details in the *Adagia* over the years.
 5 Plato] *Republic* 8.563c, citing Aeschylus frag 350 Nauck. The Plato-reference
   became 'somewhere' in *1517/8*, and was restored to its present form in *1520*.
 6 Athenaeus] 5.217c, citing the same lyric fragment; this was added in *1517/8*,
   and the Latin version in *1523*.
 8 Isocrates] *Panathenaicus* 24, added in *1523*. He is an eminent Attic orator of the
   fifth/fourth centuries BC, first published in Milan in 1493.

74 *Collectanea* no 34 cited Plato's *Republic* and gave very briefly the story of Venus'
   sandal, but no Greek. Cf Suidas M 1331. Otto 1129
 4 Hesiod] *Theogony* 214
 8 Aristotle] *De partibus animalium* 3.2 (663a38)

given oxen horns on their heads rather than on their shoulder-blades, no   10
doubt so as to strike harder. Lucian was apparently making an allusion to
this when he writes (*Verae historiae*, book 2) that he has seen some oxen
whose horns were not on the forehead as they usually are, but under the
eyes. That was the idea of Momus. The same Lucian recalls him in several
other places, especially in the dialogue about philosophical schools, where 15
he tells this story about him. Minerva, Neptune and Vulcan were competing
with each other for the prize of the best craftsmanship. Each produced an
outstanding specimen of his art: Neptune created a bull, Minerva planned a
house, Vulcan put together a man. Momus was chosen a judge of the contest
and assessor of the workmanship. He inspected the work of each one; apart   20
from the deficiencies he had noticed in the works of the others, he particularly complained that in the making of the man the craftsman had not added
some windows or openings in the breast, to allow an insight into what was
hidden in the heart, which he had made full of caverns and winding
sinuosities. Plato mentions this fable too. Philostratus in a letter to his wife 25
writes about Momus in the following strain: he says that Momus could find
nothing in Venus to carp at, except that he blamed her sandal for being
squeaky, making too much of a chatter and a troublesome noise. If Venus
had walked without the sandal, naked as when she came up out of the sea,
Momus would have seen nothing at all to find fault with. This god is not as   30
popular as the others, because few people freely accept true criticism, yet I
do not know if any of the crowd of gods in the poets is more useful.
Nowadays, however, our Joves shut out Momus and only listen to Euterpe,
preferring flattery to wholesome truth.

   This Momus supplies various forms of adage, whether in Plato who   35
writes in the *Republic*, book 6, that the study of philosophy is such that not
even Momus could reprove it; or when the Venus of Lucian, about to face
judgment, says she has no misgivings even if Momus is to be the judge; or
when Cicero writes to Atticus, book 5; 'So far as concerns the capital object of
your exhortations, the most important point of all, in which you are anxious   40
that I should satisfy even that Momus Ligurinus, well, confound me if

* * * * *

11 Lucian] *Verae historiae* 2.3; *Hermotimus* 20 (often called by Erasmus *The Sects*)
25 Plato] The passage is referred to below.
25 Philostratus] Cf 1 iv 73n; *Epistulae* 37(21); this was addressed, not to his wife,
   but to a lady of his acquaintance.
33 Euterpe] One of the Muses, whose name is easily interpreted as 'the
   Well-pleasing.'
35 Plato] *Republic* 6.487a, the book number added in *1536*
37 Lucian] *Dearum iudicium* 2
39 Cicero] *Ad Atticum* 5.20.6

anything could be done more elegantly!' Therefore all these types of formula
will have the appearance of a proverb; 'I would not hesitate to fight it out
with you even if Momus were the judge.' 'That man's life is so free from
faults that Momus himself could not carp at him.' 'This face is one with   45
which Momus himself could not find fault.' 'I would not refuse the judgment of Momus.' 'These things may satisfy Momus himself.' And so on,
whatever of the kind can be made up. Ovid's expression about the beauty of
Adonis comes in here: 'Envy itself would praise so fair a face.'

In short, all hyperbole of this kind takes on the look of a proverb, as   50
when Terence says of a miserable family 'Salvation itself could not save this
house if willing.' Again, on a strongly fortified place, 'Mars himself would
never have made it yield.' On an inflexible and pertinacious man, 'Not even
Vertumnus himself could bend his mind.' On a man-mad woman, 'This
woman's appetite would not be sated by Priapus in person.' On something   55
highly improbable, 'Peitho herself could not persuade one of this.' On
something hard to conceal, 'Neither Harpocrates himself nor Angerona
could hold this in.' 'In the middle of such a din Sleep himself could not
manage to sleep.' On a suspicous and diffident man, 'That man could not
have any faith in Faith itself.' 'This one would deceive Argus himself,' on a   60
very clever person. 'This man is so much to be pitied, that Envy itself could
not envy him.'

But we have written an account of this form of speech at the beginning
of this book.

75 **Coelo ac terrae loqui**
    To call on heaven and earth

To call on heaven and earth. This is what people are said to do who call out in
vain; for those who despair of help from mankind usually cry out 'O

* * * * *

48 Ovid] *Metamorphoses* 10.515
51 Terence] *Adelphoe* 761–2, from memory
52 Mars] The god of war; Vertumnus of the changing year, able himself to change
   his shape (*Adagia* II ii 74); Priapus of sexual licence; Peitho the Greek for
   persuasion, often personified; Harpocrates the Egyptian god, and Angerona
   the Roman goddess, of silence (IV i 52); Argus the mythical watchman with a
   hundred eyes (Ovid *Metam.* 1.625).
63 beginning] See Erasmus' Introduction section xiii.

75 In *1508* this did not exist, and nothing stood in its place. Erasmus then made up
   Corinthiari, and in *1515* he placed it here. In *1523* he moved it to its present place
   as IV iii 68, and replaced it here with another short new piece, derived from
   Athenaeus, already used in I iv 85.

Heaven! O Earth!' Theognetus in Athenaeus, book 3, and again in book 5:   5
'You have philosophized babbling to earth and heaven, / Who pay no
attention to your words.' This is close to the phrase we have quoted elsewhere, 'You are speaking to the wind.'

76 In portu impingere
To be shipwrecked in the harbour

To be shipwrecked in the harbour. This is in Quintilian, in the *Insitutions*: it
means, to make a mistake at the very outset of a work. St Jerome adopts it in
his second apologia *Against Rufinus*: 'As soon as I left the harbour I wrecked   5
the boat.' Again to Pammachius: 'Leaving the harbour we immediately were
wrecked.' It is taken from seamen, for whom it is a disgrace to dash the boat
to pieces before they have left the harbour. Papyrius Fabianus takes it in a
different sense, as reported by Seneca in his *Controversies*: 'You are sinking
the boat in harbour,' referring to an old man who had begun to live lux-   10
uriously at the wrong age. It can well be said of all who have a final collapse
after having almost finished their affairs with credit. The Greeks have the
same saying: ἐν τῷ λιμένι προσκρούειν. A certain Nilus, a Greek author,
quotes it thus: 'Do not be too elated lest you should come to shipwreck in
harbour.'   15

* * * * *

5 Theognetus] Frag 1 Kock, cited by Athenaeus 3.104c, 15.671c. he is a writer of
   the late New Comedy.
7 elsewhere] *Adagia* I iv 85

76 In *Collectanea* no 287, Quintilian and Jerome are mentioned, but not quoted.
   Otto 1454; Tilley H 219 To shipwreck in the haven. 'Shipwreck' is literally 'run
   aground.'
3 Quintilian] 4.1.61
4 Jerome] *Adversus Rufinum* 2.15 (PL 23.437c); *Letters* 57.12.2, both quotations
   were added in *1515*.
9 Seneca] the Elder *Controversiae* 2.6.4, added in *1515*
12 The Greeks] In *1508* this Greek was in the title.
13 Nilus] A late fourth century ascetic, whose works (printed in PG 79) include
   Sententiae morales, of which Willibald Pirckheimer published a Latin translation
   at Nuremberg in 1516. We have not found this in the printed text. It was added
   here in *1533*.

77 **In limine deficere aut offendere**
    To fail or stumble on the threshold

To stumble or fail on the threshold is very close to the previous one. It is
taken from people who are just going out of the house and immediately
catch their foot on the threshold, before they have begun to do anything.   5
Virgil: 'Why·fail we on the threshold in disgrace?' – that is, immediately and
when the battle has scarcely begun. Quintus Curtius, book 6, said less
poetically: 'We stand on the very threshold of victory,' meaning, a victory is
at hand. This is the opposite of what Seneca writes in his *Letters to Lucilius*:
'He fails at the top of the slope,' the metaphor being adapted from those who   10
have almost climbed a mountain, and then give in from weariness when
they are close to the summit.

78 **Cantherius in porta**
    The gelding at the gate

The gelding at the gate. This is close to the foregoing ones. It is derived from
a certain Sulpitius Galba, who was about to leave for his province when his
gelding fell down at the gate. 'It makes me laugh,' said he, 'that you, my   5
gelding, should be tired already, with such a long journey ahead of you,
when you have just set out.' This remark turned into a proverb. The adage is
mentioned by Festus Pompeius under the word *Ridiculus*, and he indicates
that it is usable when someone loses heart at the outset of a thing scarcely
begun. He explains clearly what a *cantherius* is, a castrated horse, differing   10
from the *equus* [horse] as a barrow hog differs from a boar, a capon from a
cock, a wether from a ram.

* * * * *

77 Apparently from Virgil. Otto 952; Tilley T 259 To stumble at the threshold
  6 Virgil] *Aeneid* 11.423–4
  7 Quintus Curtius] 16.3.16 (see I i 11n), added in *1517/8*.
  9 Seneca] *Letters* 92.15, added in *1515*

78 Derived, perhaps not in the first instance directly, from Festus. Otto 337.
    Festus p 356 (see I i 28n) gives the whole story, though the second half of the
    paragraph with his name was not added till *1515*. Maybe Erasmus had been
    reading the new text published by Aldus in 1513, for he also went over the first
    half, added the name Sulpicius, and wrote 'was setting out for his province' (as
    a governor) instead of 'was leaving on a journey.' The lemma under which
    Festus gives all this was changed in *1528* from *Rideo* to *Ridiculus*.

79 **Citra pulverem**
    Without dust

'Ακονιτί, Without dust. The Greeks say this when someone reaches his
objective easily, with no trouble, taking it either from the *aphe*, the handful
of powder with which a man about to enter the wrestling-ring sprinkled   5
himself, or at least from that not inglorious dust, as Horace wrote, which
soils the contestants at Olympia, or those who wage war. Pliny, book 35:
'Alcimachus made a statue of Dioxippus, who carried off the prize in the
pancratium at Olympia without touching the dust, or as they say *akoniti*.'
Aulus Gellius, book 5: 'It is a cause of rejoicing that a surrender was quickly   10
made and a bloodless victory ensued, without dust, as they say.' Horace in
the *Epistles*:

> What strolling gladiator would engage
> For vile applause to mount a country stage,
> Who at th'Olympic games could gain renown   15
> And without danger bear away the crown?

One also finds ἀνιδρωτί, 'without sweat,' and ἀναιματί, 'without blood.'

80 **Deserta causa**
    Case undefended

'Ερήμη δίκη, An undefended case, when there is no opposition. Taken from
lawsuits in which sometimes one party withdraws and abandons the case to
his opponent. So 'to win an undefended case' is to win against no resistance.   5
Lucian in *Jupiter tragoedus*: 'What else then shall we seem to be doing than
winning by default?' Again in *Toxaris*: 'And so many cities taken by you by

* * * * *

79 Perhaps from Suidas A 923. Otto 1484
 6 Horace] *Odes* 1.1.3; 1.6.14
 7 Pliny] *Naturalis historia* 35.139
10 Gellius] 5.6.21
11 Horace] *Epistles* 1.1.49–51, the first line added in 1523. This version by Sir
   Philip Francis has turned 'without dust' into 'without danger.'
17 without blood] Added in 1515. Cf Tilley v 52 It is a great victory that comes
   without blood.

80 From the Greek proverb-collections (Zenobius 3.84; Diogenianus 4.67; Suidas E
   2961). Erasmus returns to the topic in II ii 17 and x 92.
 6 Lucian] *Jupiter tragoedus* 25; *Toxaris* 11

default.' Socrates makes use of it in his defence in Plato: 'Bringing a charge
against no opponent, the case being undefended.' Lawyers use for judgments by default a compound noun, *eremodikia*. So Paulus in the *Pandects*,   10
book 4, title *De minoribus*, chapter *Et si sine dolo*: 'He also gets some relief in
cases where judgment has gone by default. It is established that men of any
age ought to be restored to the list after judgment by default, if they show
that they had just cause for their absence.' Again in book 46, title *Iudicatum
solvi*, chapter *Quum quaerebatur*: 'When security has been given for payment   15
of any sum adjudicated, if the party does not defend the case and afterwards
allows judgment to go by default, would he be committed by the clause
having reference to the sum adjudicated, etc.' Again in the *Code*, book 3, title
De iudiciis, chapter *Properandum*: 'But if a defendant should be absent, and a
similar search go forward for him to the one we have ordered for the person   20
of the plaintiff, even in the absence of the defendant judgment would go by
default.' So Justinian. It is an *eremodikion* therefore, a judgment by default,
when a case is decided in the absence of one of the parties.

81   **Citra arationem citraque sementem**
     Without ploughing and without sowing

Things that fall to our lot by chance, without our own doing are called in
Greek ἄσπαρτα καὶ ἀνήροτα: they happen 'without sowing and without
ploughing.' Lucian in *The Parasite*: 'He alone, according to wise Homer, does   5
not plant with his hands or plough, but without sowing or ploughing he
enjoys everything.' The same in the *Teacher of Public Speaking*: 'But to you
everything may come without the toil of sowing and ploughing,' that is,
without exertion. The adage seems to have arisen from the legend of the
Fortunate Isles, of which Horace writes in the *Odes*: 'Where every year the   10
land unploughed yields corn, / And ever blooms the vine unpruned.' But I
think it comes from Homer, who describes the land of the Cyclops in this
way, in the *Odyssey*, book 9:

               * * * * *

     8 Plato] *Apology* 18c, added in 1523
    10 Paulus] *Digest* 4.4.7.12; 46.7.13 (these are both Ulpian, not Paulus; possibly
       another quotation has fallen out).
    18 *Code*] 3.1.13.3. These three legal texts were added in 1528.

    81 Perhaps from Diogenianus 1.18
     5 Lucian] *De parasito* 24; *Rhetorum praeceptor* 8
    10 Horace] *Epodes* 16.43–4
    12 Homer] *Odyssey* 9.106–11

We came to the land of the Cyclops, proud and lawless,
Who relying on the immortal gods   15
Neither sow with their hands, nor plough,
But all things grow wild without sowing and without ploughing,
Wheat and barley and vines which give good wine
And the rain of Jove makes them increase.

82 Dormienti rete trahit
The sleeper's net makes a catch

Εὔδοντι κύρτος αἱρεῖ, The sleeper's net makes a catch. This refers to people
who get what they want without trying. It comes from an event which
sometimes happens, when fish are caught entangled in the nets when the   5
fishermen are asleep. Some attribute it to Timotheus the Athenian general,
who had great success more from the favour of fortune than from his own
effort, and was nicknamed Lucky. Some people who begrudged him this,
depicted Fortune driving cities into the net while he lay sleeping near by. He
gave them a mocking answer, according to Plutarch: 'If I capture such cities   10
when I am asleep, what do you think I will do if I am awake?' Terence
alludes to this when he says in the *Adelphoe*: 'What? Did you think the gods
were going to do this for you as you slept? And the girl would be led home to
your bedroom without any effort of yours?' There is a saying of the same
kind in Livy, in book 7 of *Rome From the Foundation*: 'The one and only   15
general in the war, who thinks that victory will fly down from heaven to
light on him, without his doing anything.' Cicero in the *Verrines*, in his last
speech: 'But I have not the same privileges as men of noble birth, who while
they are asleep have all the honours the Roman people can bestow laid at
their feet.' Today too it is commonly said of such people 'He does it more by   20
good luck than good management.' And in Athenaeus, Eupolis the comedy-
writer: 'O city, city, / How fortunate you are rather than wise.' This agrees

* * * * *

82 *Collectanea* no 352, in a series of adages arranged by alphabetical order of their
   Greek equivalents, the source of which is Diogenianus (this is 4.65). Otto 579;
   Suringar 61; Tilley N 128 The net of the sleeper catches fish.
10 Plutarch] *Moralia* 187B
11 Terence] *Adelphoe* 693–4
15 Livy] 7.12.13, added in *1528*. This title means the first decade of his *History*
   (books 1–10).
17 Cicero] *Verrines* 5.70.180, added in *1533*
20 commonly said] The same phrase is given in I viii 44.
21 Eupolis] Frag 205 Kock (see I i 31n), cited by Athenaeus 10.425b.

with the comments I shall make on the proverb 'The rashness of the Athenians.'

83 · Cum mula pepererit
When the mule foals

When the mule foals. A very old adage, used when we signify that something will never happen, or happens so rarely that it seems wicked and foolish to hope for it. It may seem to arise from what Herodotus says in   5
Thalia: when the city of the Babylonians was besieged by Darius, a certain Babylonian shouted insults at Darius and his army, saying, 'What are you sitting here for, you Persians? Much better take yourselves off, you will only take our town "When mules give birth,"' obviously meaning that the time would never come, as mules are sterile by nature. But it came about soon   10
after that a mule belonging to Zopyrus did have a foal, and by this marvel he was encouraged in the hope of taking Babylon, and took it. A similar thing is reported by Suetonius in his life of the emperor Galba. When this emperor's grandfather was making a sacrifice to avert the lightning, an eagle snatched the entrails from his hands and carried them off to an oak covered with   15
acorns. This was interpreted to him as meaning that his family would attain imperial rank, but late. Laughing, he said, 'Yes when a mule foals.' Galba was so struck by this omen, that when later on he was planning revolution, nothing encouraged him so much as the foaling of a mule, and while others shuddered at this unlucky marvel, he alone accepted it as most propitious,   20
remembering his grandfather's sacrifice and his remark. Pliny, book 8 chapter 44, writes as follows about sterility in mules: 'It has been observed that the offspring of two different species is a third species, and unlike either parent. Also that they themselves, which are born in this way, do not bring forth young in any kind of animal, and therefore mules do not foal.' Alexan-   25
der of Aphrodisias alleges as a cause of this that when seeds of different nature and character are mixed together, they produce a third creature unlike either, and henceforth lose the force of the simple strains; just as when you mix black and white, both colours disappear and you have grey,

* * * * *

23 proverb] *Adagia* I viii 44; this sentence was added in *1528*.

83 This looks like a product of general reading. Otto 1161
 5 Herodotus] 3.153 (see I i 96n).
13 Suetonius] *Galba* 9.2 (see I i 78n).
21 Pliny] *Naturalis historia* 8.173
25 Alexander of Aphrodisias] *Problemata* 1.132 (see I i 40n), in the Latin version of Theodorus Gaza (Aldus 1504), added in *1515*.

neither the one nor the other, which is called *leukophaion* in Greek. But   30
Aristotle is much more precise on this in his work *On the Generation of
Animals*, book 2 chapter 6, where he refutes Democritus and Empedocles.
However, it is recorded in the annals of Rome that mules often foaled, but
this was regarded as a portent, as Pliny testifies in the passage just quoted.
Theophrastus states that they commonly foal in Cappadocia. Aristotle *On*   35
the Nature of Animals, book 1 chapter 6, states that mules mate and give birth
in Syria above Phoenicia, but there the animal is of a special kind, even if
similar.

84   **Ad Graecas calendas**
     At the Greek calends

At the Greek calends has much the same sense: that is, never. The Greeks
did not have calends in the Roman manner, but 'new moons' and they
settled their debts at the return of the moon; hence Strepsiades in Aris-   5
tophanes' *Clouds* longs for a sorceress to cause the moon not to rise, by her
spells, so that he will not have to pay his debts, seeing that the bankers give
loans at the new moon, and interest increases moon by moon. Augustus
was thinking of this when he said that some people 'would settle at the
Greek calends,' meaning that they were never going to pay back a loan.   10
Suetonius Tranquillus writes thus in his life of Augustus: 'Some of his

* * * * *

30 *leukophaion*] This Greek equivalent was added in *1517/8*. The word was used as
   a classical equivalent for the name of Erasmus' English friend Thomas Grey
   (Epp 66 and 221).
31 Aristotle] *De generatione animalium* 2.8 (767a24–769a6). This and the reference
   to Alexander were inserted in *1515* into the middle of a direct quotation from
   Pliny, of which the second half, following this, was then adjusted to read as it
   does now. Theophrastus' statement is taken from Pliny, as above.
35 Aristotle] *Historia animalium* 1.6 (491a2); this final sentence is a mosaic of *1508*,
   1515 and *1533*, this last year providing the precise reference. Other ancient
   references to the sterility of mules are collected by A.S. Pease in his commentary
   on Cicero *De divinatione* 1.18.36.

84 *Collectanea* no 139; the ultimate source must be Suetonius. The second sentence,
   about the Greek *noumenia*, is repeated almost verbatim from *Coll.*, to which it
   had been added only two years before, in the revision of 1506. Otto 301;
   Suringar 4; Tilley G 441 At the Greek Calends. The division of the month into
   three unequal parts, of which the first days were called respectively calends,
   nones and ides, was an exclusively Roman practice.
5 Aristophanes] *Clouds* 749–56
11 Suetonius] *Divus Augustus* 87.1

letters, written with his own hand, show that he made frequent and prominent use of certain words in his everyday speech. In the same letters, when he means to say that some men will never repay, he says they will pay at the Greek calends.' A similar expression is used now by the learned when they   15
say 'in the great year of Plato' which they think will never be.

85   Acessaei luna
The moon of Acessaeus

'Ακεσσαίου σελήνη, The moon of Acessaeus. This is said of procrastinators, who often find yet another reason to put off a piece of business. It comes from the behaviour of a certain seaman called Acessaeus. He was a lazy   5
fellow, who used to postpone sailing because he said he was waiting for a more propitious moon. The Greeks, especially the Spartans, observed the moon with superstitious care when they were looking for omens to start something. Euripides hints at this in the *Iphigenia in Aulis*, when Agamemnon makes the reply that his daughter will be wedded when the   10
right-hand curve of the moon comes in sight, meaning at full moon. Lucian in his essay *On Astrology* openly states that Lycurgus laid down a law for the Spartans, that they should not go into battle before the full moon. Aristophanes makes fun of this superstition; he says that 'at full moon' means late or never. And indeed when Datis and Artaphernes, generals of the king   15
of Persia, had invaded Marathon, they were waiting for the full moon as the time to go into battle. Thus it was that before they came the Athenians took the initiative. Herodotus recalls this in book 6 of his *History*. Hence 'at full moon' is a proverbial way of referring to dilatory people and those who take any excuse for putting a thing off. The adage is mentioned by Diogenianus. I   20
shall say something about 'Spartan moons' elsewhere.

* * * * *

16 Plato] His name was commonly attached to the doctrine of a great cycle of many thousand years (variously estimated), at the end of which the heavenly bodies, which change their relative positions from year to year, will have returned to the stationa they occupied at the beginning. Erasmus mentions it again in III v 58. This sentence was added here in *1533*.

85 *Collectanea* no 527, from Diogenianus (also in Suidas T 512); the first three sentences here are repeated thence almost verbatim.
 9 Euripides] *Iphigeneia Aulidensis* 717
11 Lucian] *De astrologia* 25, added in *1515*. This comes again in II v 25.
13 Aristophanes] Cf *Acharnians* 84.
18 Herodotus] 6.106, added in *1528*
20 Diogenianus] 1.57
21 elsewhere] *Adagia* II v 25, added in *1528*

86 Ubi per Harma fulgurarit
When lightning strikes through Harma

'Οπότε δι' "Αρματος ἀστράπτει, When lightning strikes through Harma.
Referring to things which are done slowly and late, or not often enough; or
when the opportune moment for carrying something through is waited for   5
too anxiously and with superstitious fervour. Strabo in his *Geography*, book
9, explains how the adage originated. He writes that there is a certain village
near Mycaletus in Boeotia (or Mycalessus, in the territory of Tanagra) called
Harma or 'chariot.' It is abandoned and deserted. There is also another
different one with this name in Attica, where the population was part of   10
Attica but similar to that of Tanagra, and on account of this resemblance they
shared the same name. The Harma in Boeotia was so called because the
empty chariot from which Amphiaraus had been thrown was conveyed to
that place, where there is now a shrine to him. Others say that when
Adrastus was in flight, his chariot was smashed in pieces at this place, but he   15
himself was saved by the help of Arion. The proverb 'when the lightning
flashes through Harma' arises from the action of the Pythian seers, who kept
watch for a special sort of lightning that came from that place, and as soon as
they had seen it sent offerings to Delphi. They used to keep watch every
three months for three days in the month, and as many nights; and also from   20
the hearth-altar of Jove the Thunderer, which is in the wall between
Pythium and Olympium. Thus far Strabo. Plutarch clearly indicates the use
of the proverb in his 'Table-talk': 'For those who give dinner-parties as
infrequently as lightning flashes "over Harma," as they say, are forced to list
every acquaintance and suitable person.' So it seems to be used of infrequent   25
and uncertain things. It could also be applied in jest to things which we
think will never happen, as they say 'at the Greek calends.'

87 Lydius lapis, sive Heraclius lapis
The Lydian, or Heraclian, stone

Λίθος Ἡρακλεία, ἢ λίθος Λυδή, The Lydian, or Heraclian, stone. This is said
of people whose judgment is particularly sharp and precise. It is mentioned

*   *   *   *   *

86 Apparently from Strabo; also in Suidas A 3963
   6 Strabo] *Geographica* 9.2.11 (see I i 69n).
  22 Plutarch] *Moralia* 679C.
  24 as they say] *Adagia* I v 84

87 This could be from the Greek proverb-collections (Zenobius 4.22; Diogenianus
   5.2; Suidas H 459), or from Theophrastus. It overlaps I vii 56.

by Theophrastus in his book *On the Nature of Stones*. He says there is a stone   5
called Lydian or Heraclian, which when rubbed will tell the quality of gold or
silver. Some think that this is a kind of magnet, like the stone of Hercules,
which attracts iron to itself, hence also called *siderites*, loadstone; but from
the words of Theophrastus it is clear that the *basanos* or touchstone is meant,
which in Latin is *index*. It was into this that the shepherd Battus was   10
transformed, in Ovid, keeping even as a stone his tendency to betrayal. It is
not called Heraclian from Hercules, but from Heraclea, a city in Lydia. Pliny
recalls this, book 33 chapter 8: 'A description of gold and silver is necessarily
accompanied by that of the stone known as *coticula*. In former times, according to Theophrastus, this stone was nowhere to be found, except in the river   15
Tmolus, but at the present day it is found in numerous places. By some
persons it is known as the "Heraclian," and by others as the "Lydian" stone.
It is found in pieces of moderate size, and never exceeding four inches in
length by two in breadth. With these stones persons of experience in these
matters, when they have scraped a particle off the ore with a file for testing,   20
can tell in a moment the proportion of gold there is in it, how much silver, or
how much copper; and this to a scruple, their accuracy being so marvellous
that they are never mistaken.' Theocritus alludes to this in *Aites*: 'That I may
have a mouth like a Lydian stone,' suggesting that by this he might judge
best between various kisses and tell whose they were – for such is the   25
foolishness of lovers. The scholiast thinks these stones are found in Lydia,
and hence the origin of the proverb. So that you should not doubt that he is
speaking of the touchstone, there follows the 'gold-test': 'From whose
influence the money-changer tries / The gold, if it be good.' The adage can be
applied either to persons or things. To persons, in this way: 'You are the best   30
judge of my writings, the very Heraclian stone, as they say.' Or like this:
'With the most brilliant flair for weighing up and judging mental quality, a
very Lydian stone, as they say.' Or applied to things in this way: 'Freedom
opens the minds of the young, but to grown men, to be given authority is the
Lydian stone.'   35

* * * * *

5 Theophrastus] *De lapidibus* 1.4 (see 1 i 44n).
11 Ovid] *Metamorphoses* 2.687–707
12 Pliny] *Naturalis historia* 33.126
23 Theocritus] 12,36–7, added in *1515*; the reference to the scholiast added in
   1526

88 Amussis alba
An unmarked rule

Λευκῇ στάθμῃ, An unmarked rule. This means 'without selection, making no distinctions.' Aulus Gellius in the *Attic Nights*: 'For all those people, and among them especially the Greeks, read eagerly and widely and swept 5 together everything they came across without discrimination, using a "blank ruler" as they say, simply intent on quantity alone.' Plutarch, in his essay 'On Garrulity,' says, 'The garrulous person is absolutely an unmarked rule as far as conversation goes,' because he talks nonsense with no discrimination about anything whatever. The adage is found in an expanded form 10 in some writers: 'a white line against a white stone.' It is used for those who have no judgment, or for the stupid, or for people who base proof or exposition of doubtful things on doubtful facts. Sophocles in the *Cidalion*, in Suidas: 'Your words tell me no more, / Than a white line on a white stone.' Nonius Marcellus quotes Lucilius, book 30 – but in a corrupt form, in my 15 opinion. Many of his sayings are like this: '– and he loved all, / For a white line marks nothing, makes no distinction.' Plato adopts it in his dialogue entitled *Charmides*, where Socrates says his attitude to beautiful boys can be described as 'a white rule against a white stone,' because he did not distinguish clearly between types of beauty, and loved them all alike. That 20 well-known rope was smeared with red-lead so as to show up a difference, so Persius called it 'red-ochre': 'if he should set the red-ochre straight with one shut eye.'

* * * * *

88 *Collectanea* no 23, citing Gellius, and 24, citing the *Charmides* in Latin at greater length, run together. The first part is in Diogenianus 6.8. Otto 51
   4 Gellius] Praefatio 11
   7 Plutarch] *Moralia* 513F, added in *1515*
  11 some writers] Zenobius 4.89; Suidas Λ 325
  13 Sophocles] Frag 307 Nauck, cited by Suidas
  15 Nonius] See I i 97n; pp 282 and 405, citing Lucilius 830–1 (see I ii 35n).
  17 Plato] *Charmides* 154b
  21 well-known rope] *Adagia* I ii 67
  22 Persius] *Satires* 1.66; this appears again in III v 12.

89 Eadem per eadem
Over and over again

Αὐτὰ δι᾿ αὐτῶν, Over and over again. This occurs in the collections of
Diogenianus, about people who always teach the same things, or con-
tinuously repeat the same actions. It is not unlike that other which I have   5
mentioned in another place, 'Corinthus Son of Jove.' It can also be applied to
those who treat frivolities frivolously, for example a man who writes ignorant notes on an ignorant author, or obscenities about an obscene person.

90 Ad amussim
By rule

In the best authors we often find *Ad amussim*, By rule (with *examussim*,
examussatim, *amussatim*) put for 'with the utmost diligence,' 'with the most
precise care.' Gellius, book 1 chapter 4: 'He inspected all these ancient   5
writings with such care, weighing their merits and investigating their short-
comings, that you would say his judgment was made exactly by rule.' And
we find *amussitata* for 'examined' in Nonius. This is taken from stone-cutters
or carpenters, who test the evenness of their work with the familiar measur-
ing-line. Festus however records, under the word *examussim*, that for some   10
people the *amussis* is not a line or a rule but an iron tool used by blacksmiths
for polishing. Persius, describing a poet composing finished verses, as I
quoted above: 'Expert to stretch his verse, as if he should / Set the red-ochre
straight with one shut eye.' Also in the *Vir bonus*, a poem on the good man
which is ascribed to Virgil: 'That nothing gape, no corner jutting out / But all   15

* * * * *

89 From Diogenianus 3.21, with a cross-reference to *Adagia* II i 50. The last
sentence was added in *1515*. The natural sense of the Greek would seem to be
something like 'Things by themselves.' It cannot carry the sense Erasmus found
in it.

90 *Collectanea* no 773 deals with this at some length, and mentions two other ways
of conveying the same meaning, *pensiculate* or *pensiculatim*, which must come
from Gellius, and *ad filum*, on the line, which is said to be 'now in current use.'
Otto 102
5 Gellius] 1.4.1, added in *1515*
8 Nonius] P 9 (see I i 97n), added in *1515*.
10 Festus] P 70 (see I i 28n), added in *1515* (the precise reference is of *1528*; before
that, it was 'somewhere or other').
12 Persius] *Satires* 1.65–6
15 Virgil] an anonymous poem ascribed to him, the *De viro bono* 10–11

parts equal, by the unfaltering line.' Basil too uses it when writing to his
nephews, recommending them to consider every branch of learning in its
relationship with the final aim of felicity, just as stones, according to the
Doric proverb, are 'marked out against the rule.' It may be thought to come
from Homer's *Odyssey*, book 5, where he speaks of Ulysses building his   20
ship: 'Trimmed with great skill and trued them to the line.' Again in the
Iliad, book 15:

> But as the line sets a ship's timber straight
> For the skilled shipwright, master of his trade,
> Taught by Minerva all that cunning art.   25

It also occurs in several other places in the same author.

91   Ad unguem
To the finger-nail

To the finger-nail has the same meaning. The metaphor is taken from
workers in marble, who draw the nail over the surface to test the joins in the
stone. Horace: 'Fonteius, finished to the finger-nail,' that is, a really   5
polished person. Again, in the *Art of Poetry*:

> That poem you should blame,
> Where time and tenfold proving has not shaped
> The finished work, and smoothed it to the nail.

Virgil in the second book of the *Georgics*:   10

> Let every alley, when your trees are set,
> Square to the nail where'er it cuts the path.

* * * * *

16 Basil] See I i 2 line 144n; *Ad adulescentes* 4 (*PG* 31.570D; p 46 Boulenger).
20 Homer] *Odyssey* 5.245; *Iliad* 15.410–2. The first of these was ascribed to the *Iliad*
   in *1508* (set right in *1520*).

91 *Collectanea* no 772 gave the two Horace passages and the Persius, with no
   Greek. Otto 1827; Tilley F 245 To have it at his fingers' ends, conveys a different
   sense.
 5 Horace] *Satires* 1.5.32–3; *Ars poetica* 292–4. In the first of these passages the
   name was given from *1500* to *1520* as Cocceius (who is mentioned earlier in the
   same line), in *1523* as Fronteius; it was corrected in *1533*.
10 Virgil] *Georgics* 2.277–8.

Persius: 'So that each joint may let the searching nail / Glide o'er it smooth-
ly.' Macrobius *Saturnalia* book 1 chapter 16: 'Nor could any other man's
judgment be so misguided as not to admire the arrangement of the Roman   15
year, thus refined as it is to the nail.' In the same way Greek has a word
dionychos for something exact and precisely finished. Plutarch 'Precepts of
Good Health: 'The very precise rule of life observed, as they say, to the nail'
[*dionychos*].And *exonychizein* for 'to examine carefully.' Athenaeus uses this
expression in book 3: 'You run your nail over everything that suits those   20
who indulge in thorny discussions with you.'

92   **Incudi reddere**
     To put back on the anvil

Horace uses this phrase, To put back on the anvil, elegantly, for remaking,
altering, correcting: 'Back to the anvil with your ill-turned verse.' In the
same way they say 'to recook.' Quintilian, book 12: 'But particularly to   5
Apollonius Molo, whom he had heard at Rome, he went to be improved and
as it were recooked, in Rhodes.' So Horace: 'A quinquevir rehashed into a
clerk.'

* * * * *

13 Persius] *Satires* 1.64–5
14 Macrobius] *Saturnalia* 1.16.38, added in *1528* (see I i 12n).
16 In the same way] added in *1520*. Erasmus seems to have taken as a single word
    in his Plutarch (*Moralia* 128E) what is really two words *di' onuchôn*, to the nail, or
    (as we might say) to a hair's breadth. The verb *exonuchizein* he added, no doubt
    from Athenaeus, in *1517/8*.
19 Athenaeus] 3.97d, added in the Greek in *1523*. The Greek, as Henri Estienne
    points out in a note reprinted in LB, does not really make sense.

92 This seems taken direct from Horace, and to give a lively metaphor (or
    metaphors) rather than anything proverbial.
 3 Horace] *Ars poetica* 441. The verses are like a metal bar which has been so
    misshapen by incompetence on the lathe that it has to be reheated and beaten
    out afresh.
 4 In the same way] This clause was introduced in *1515*, to make it clear that the
    two following quotations (which were already in place) employ a different
    metaphor.
 5 Quintilian] 12.6.7; Cicero puts himself in the hands of Molo, a famous teacher
    of rhetoric.
 7 Horace] *Satires* 2.5.55–6; the sense is not clear, but a *quinquevir* seems to have
    been a very low grade of official.

93 **Lesbia regula**
   By the Lesbian rule

By the Lesbian rule. This is said when things are done the wrong way round,
when theory is accommodated to fact and not fact to theory, when law is
suited to conduct, not conduct corrected by law; or when the ruler adapts   5
himself to the behaviour of the populace, though it would be more fitting for
common people to conduct their lives according to the will of the prince; if
only the prince himself has right conduct before his eyes as his rule and aim.
Aristotle mentions this adage in his *Ethics*, book 5: 'For the rule of what is
indefinite is also indefinite, like the leaden rule used in Lesbian architecture;   10
the rule changes to fit the shape of the stone and does not remain a rule.'

94 **Indignus qui illi matellam porrigat**
   Unworthy to hold out a chamber-pot to him

Unworthy to hold out a chamber-pot to him. A proverbial hyperbole,
describing total inequality, where there is no comparison on any grounds.
Martial: 'May I die, if you are fit to hold a chamber-pot to Pylades, / Or be a   5
swineherd to Pirithous.' It is indeed the most squalid service to present the
chamber-pot for a man to piss into, and anyone unfit for this is obviously the
lowest of the low. Hence St Jerome in a letter to Nepotianus lists this also
among the sordid services of legacy-hunters: 'they themselves,' he says,
'bring the chamber-pot and lay siege to the bedside.' Plutarch in his 'Sayings   10
of Spartans' recalls that a Spartan boy captured and sold by Antigonus
obeyed the master who had bought him, in everything which was not
dishonourable to the free-born. But when ordered to bring the chamber-pot,
he refused this service, adding 'I will not be a slave.' The master got up, and
the boy said 'You shall know whom you have bought!' Rushing up im-   15
mediately to the roof, he threw himself down.

                 * * * * *

   93 Taken, it seems, directly from Aristotle
    6 though it would be] This clause is of *1515*, and what follows is of *1517/8*.
      Erasmus had been meditating on these subjects for his *Institutio principis
      christiani*, 1516.
    9 Aristotle] *Ethica Nicomachea* 5.14 (1137b29–32). This is of *1508* again.

   94 Probably taken direct from Martial. Otto 1069; Suringar 90
    5 Martial] 10.11.3–4
    8 Jerome] *Letters* 52.6.4, added in *1515*
   10 Plutarch] *Moralia* 234C, added in *1526*

There is a very common saying used in our own day: 'He is not fit to take off that man's shoes.' This adage is used in the Gospel by John the Baptist. People even say 'not to be named in the same day' when they want to describe utter inequality.   20

95 Scopae dissolutae; Scopas dissolvere
Loose broom-twigs; To untie a broom

Cicero calls worthless men, entirely without forethought, 'loose broom-twigs.' Writing to Atticus, in book 7 of the *Letters*, he uses these words: 'Early on 25 January, I saw Caesar at Minturnae with the most absurd   5 instructions, directed not to men but to a set of loose brooms, if ever there was one. Indeed it looks to me as though Caesar were deliberately making a mock of us.' Also in the *Perfect Orator*, disputing with those who despise rhythm in a speech, he uses this phrase 'to untie a broom' to mean doing a totally useless thing. For brushwood twigs bound together have a look of   10 being something, and are useful for sweeping the floor. But if you untie them, nothing could be more useless or untidy. Cicero's words are these: 'If, however, anyone likes a loose style let him by all means use it, but in the manner of one who should take apart the shield of Phidias: if anyone ever takes it apart, he destroys the beauty of the composition but not the charm of   15 the several pieces. In Thucydides, for example, I miss only the poetic structure, the ornaments are there. But when these people take a speech to pieces in which there is neither matter nor words which are not mean, they seem to me not to be taking apart a shield, but as the proverb has it – and if the expression is somewhat vulgar yet it is apt – to be untying a broom.'   20

96 Apertis tibiis
Using all the holes (With all the stops out)

Using all the holes (With all the stops out) means 'with a loud sound.' It is taken from flute-players: when they play with the holes in the instrument

* * * * *

18 Gospel] Mark 1:7; John 1:27. 'By John the Baptist' was added in *1515*. Tilley has L 84 Not worthy to loose the latchet of his shoes, and s 378 Not worthy to wipe his shoes.

95 From Cicero *Ad Atticum* 7.13a.2; *Orator* 71.234–5. Otto 1609

96 *Collectanea* no 175 offered the Quintilian-reference; but in compiling the *Chiliades* Erasmus obviously went back to the original, for the quotation is now much longer. Otto 1784

closed, the notes are subdued, but with all the holes open the sound is   5
piercing. Quintilian, *Institutions* book 11: 'And then those words in which he
opens almost every stop, as the saying is: "who, wherever they turn, look in
vain for the familiar environment of the courts and the traditional procedure
of the law."' The metaphor would be more graceful if a person were to
inveigh against another 'with all the holes open,' that is, not opposing him   10
privately but assailing him publicly and tearing him to pieces with accusa-
tions; or it might be to sing someone's praises 'with all the holes open,' that
is, openly and splendidly. Perhaps there is a reference to this in that line of
Greek poetry which Cicero quotes in his *Letters to Atticus*, book 2, from some
poet or other: 'What our friend Gnaeus is up to now, I simply do not know.   15
On tiny pipes he now no longer blows.' He seems to be suggesting that
Pompey was promising great things from his agrarian law, and setting on
foot great events. Athenaeus, book 4, speaks of a kind of flute which
Anacreon calls 'half-holed,' smaller than the others and giving a less clear
note, as the name itself shows.   20

97 **Quid opus erat longis canere tibiis?**
    What need was there to play on the long pipes?

Dion, book 1, quotes an adage of this sort: Τὶ γάρ με ἔδει μακροῖς αὐλοῖς
αὐλεῖν; Of what avail was it for me to play on the long pipes? They say that
this fits people who have expended futile labour or expense. It comes from   5
Otho, who had performed sacrificial rites after the slaying of Galba, and in
these the entrails foretold an inauspicious outcome. He was sorry for the
cost and trouble spent for no result, and is said to have spoken thus, 'Of
what avail was it for me to play on the long pipes?' and his words turned into
a common proverb. It was formerly the custom to play long pipes in   10
religious rites, a custom later discontinued, according to Plutarch. Suetonius

*****

6 Quintilian] 11.3.50; he is illustrating a point from the celebrated opening of
  Cicero's *Pro Milone* (1.1).
14 Cicero] *Ad Atticum* 2.16.2, citing Sophocles frag 701
18 Athenaeus] 4.177a, citing the lyric poet Anacreon frag 375 Page; added in 1536

97 Probably taken from Dio Cassius 63.7.1, he wrote a history of Rome in Greek
  (second/third century AD).
11 Plutarch] This has not been identified.
11 Suetonius] *Otho* 7.2 (see I i 78n). The commentator referred to is not Filippo
  Beroaldo.

also recalls this in his life of Otho: 'The next day too,' he says, 'when a storm arose as he was taking the auguries, he fell down heavily and was heard to mutter over and over again, What have I to do with long pipes?' On this passage, I wonder what caused a certain person (a commentator of no   15 obscure reputation) to reject the words of Suetonius as spurious and to prefer to substitute those of Dion; as if it were not permissible for authors to express the same thought in different words, or as if Suetonius has not phrased it more elegantly than Dion.

98 **Utinam mihi contingant ea, quae sunt inter Corinthum et Sicyonem**
    If only I had what lies between Corinth and Sicyon!

Eustathius, commenting on the *Iliad*, book 2, says that this line was cele-brated as a proverb in old times: Εἴη μοι τὰ μεταξὺ Κορίνθου καὶ Σικυῶνος, 'What lies between Sicyon and Corinth, would it were mine!' This became a   5 proverb because each of these towns was very wealthy and the intervening land of the utmost fertility. Aristophanes in the *Birds* says it arose from an oracle: 'But when wolves and gray crows dwell / In the space that lies between Corinth and Sicyon.' The commentator ascribes it to Aesop, who asked the advice of the oracle on amassing wealth and received this reply: 'If   10 you possess what lies between Corinth and Sicyon.' Zenodotus quotes it, and Athenaeus in his *Doctors at Dinner*, book 5. It is apt when a person wishes for great things. It can also be applied in jest to one who goes on wishing and dreaming about something he cannot obtain. A similar metaphor is used by Theocritus in the *Ergatinae*: 'Would I possessed what   15 they say Croesus had.'

* * * * *

98 Apparently collected from Eustathius, but it also occurs in Suidas EI 337.
 3 Eustathius] See I i 77n; on *Iliad* 2.572 (291.30); the Latin version improved in 1526.
 7 Aristophanes] *Birds* 967–8; a Latin version added in prose in *1515* and in verse in *1526*
 11 Zenodotus] Zenobius 3.57
 12 Athenaeus] 5.219a, added in *1517/8*
 15 Theocritus] 10.32, added in *1526*

99 **Deum esse. Deum facere**
To be a god. To make a god of someone

These are proverbial hyperboles about people who deserve high praise.
Cicero in his *De oratore* book 2: 'In which you seem to me to be a god,' that is,
outstanding and supreme. Terence in the *Adelphoe*: 'I make a god of you,'   5
meaning I exalt you with the highest praise. It derives from the fact that early
men, when they looked up to someone for his excellent and unusual virtues,
called him a god, or a son of the gods. This happened to Alexander the
Great, Scipio Africanus, Octavius Augustus, and many others. Aristotle
falls in with this in his *Ethics*, book 7: 'This heroic virtue they call more than   10
human, and close to divinity. Hence Homer makes Priam speak of Hector in
this way.' *Iliad* 24: 'He did not seem, / To be a child of mortal man, but of a
god.' It was a particular way of the Spartans (as the same author says) to call
someone whom they strongly admired 'a godlike man.' Socrates recalls this
in Plato's *Meno*: 'And the Spartans, when they praise some good man, say   15
"This man is divine."' Hence those customary phrases in Homer, 'like to
god,' 'of divine nature,' 'equal to a god,' 'absolutely divine.' On the other
hand, men of extreme wickedness we call wild beasts, and that also is the
commonest of terms in ordinary speech. St Jerome, writing to Augustine,
turns this round in irony, and applies it to people who are not content with   20
the ordinary judgment of men, but want something new – he calls them
'gods.' Quintilian, *Institutions*, book 1, tells us that a man of consummate
perfection used to be called in common speech 'a mortal god': 'For the sages
who are forming a person to be completely perfect, and as the phrase goes "a
mortal god," think he should be taught with not only divine but human   25
wisdom,' etc.

* * * * *

99 *Collectanea* no 762 gave only the brief quotation from Terence. Otto 515.
Suringar 58. It bears some relation to I i 69.
4 Cicero] *Do oratore* 2.42.179
5 Terence] *Adelphoe* 535
9 Aristotle] *Ethica Nicomachea* 7.1 (1145a20 citing Homer and 1145a28 referring to
the Spartans). The Homer is *Iliad* 24.258–9, and at first Erasmus gave it in Latin
verse only, having taken it from Aristotle. In *1526* he followed his usual
practice with Homeric quotations and added the book-number and the Greek
text; with the result that the words 'as the same author says' appear to refer to
Homer instead of Aristotle.
15 Plato] *Meno* 99d, added in *1523*
19 Jerome] Unidentified; the last clause added in *1515*
22 Quintilian] 1.10.5, added in *1528*

100 **In coelo esse**
     To be in heaven

To be in heaven is close to the foregoing; it means to be extraordinarily
fortunate and renowned. Cicero to Atticus, book 2: 'Bibulus is in heaven, I
don't know why, but they praise him as if "One man by his delay had saved   5
our all."' The same elsewhere to the same: 'If however the bargain as
respects myself is not observed, I am in heaven.' Elsewhere again: 'It is not
incongruous that the tyrannicides should be lauded to the skies.' Horace
alludes to this when he says, 'They link me with the gods above,' that is,
they call me blessed and famous. And Theocritus in the *Wayfarers*, 'I shall   10
rise to heaven before your eyes.' On the other hand, those who suddenly fall
from the height of felicity are said to have 'fallen from the stars.' Cicero to
Atticus, book 2, speaking of Pompey: 'What a sight! Only Crassus could
enjoy it, not so others. He was a fallen star, one looked upon him as a man
who had slid rather than moved of his own volition.' But consider, reader,   15
whether this saying does not rather belong more to the one we have quoted
elsewhere: 'Here's a third Cato, fallen from the skies!' This is related to the
phrase 'to laud to the skies,' meaning to give the highest praise. Livy,
decade 1 book 2: 'The talk runs through all the town: they laud the Fabii to
the skies.'   20

                    * * * * *

    100 This was *Collectanea* no 761, very short, with no authority given except the
         second of our citations from Cicero's *Letters to Atticus*. For *1508* it was rewritten;
         it was then followed by the related *Caelum digito attingere*, but this was removed
         in *1515* to stand as IV iii 67. Otto 288; Tilley H 350 To be in heaven. We speak
         more often of 'the seventh heaven.'
       4 Cicero] *Ad Atticum* 2.19.2 (the quotation lengthened in *1523*); 2.9.1; 14.6.2, the
         text somewhat corrupt
       8 Horace] *Odes* 1.1.30
      10 Theocritus] 5.144, added here in *1515* and to IV iii 67 in *1526*
      11 On the other hand … from the skies] added in *1523*. The Cicero passage comes
         from *Ad Att.* 2.21.4
      17 a third Cato] Juvenal 2.40, also in I viii 86 and 89
      18 Livy] 2.49.1, added (from 'This is related') in *1533*

WORKS FREQUENTLY CITED

This list provides bibliographical information for works referred to in short-title form in this volume.

ASD	*Opera omnia Desiderii Erasmi Roterodami* (Amsterdam 1969–)
Collectanea	Desiderius Erasmus *Adagiorum Collectanea* (Paris 1500); we use the numbering of the revised edition of 1506/7
CWE	*Collected Works of Erasmus* (Toronto 1974–)
Diels-Kranz	H. Diels and W. Kranz eds *Die Fragmente der Vorsokratiker* (Berlin 1951–2) 3 vols
FGrHist	F. Jacoby ed *Die Fragmente der griechischen Historiker* (Berlin/ Leiden 1926–)
Kaibel	G. Kaibel ed *Comicorum Graecorum fragmenta* (Berlin 1899)
Kock	T. Kock ed *Comicorum Atticorum fragmenta* (Leipzig 1880–8) 3 vols
LB	J. Leclerc ed *Desiderii Erasmi Roterodami opera omnia* (Leiden 1703–6) 10 vols
Nauck	A. Nauck ed *Tragicorum Graecorum fragmenta* (Leipzig 1889)
Otto	A. Otto *Die Sprichwörter ... Der Römer* (Leipzig 1890)
PG	J.P. Migne ed *Patrologia graeca*
PL	J.P. Migne ed *Patrologia latina*
Reedijk	C. Reedijk ed *The Poems of Desiderius Erasmus* (Leiden 1956)
Suringar	W.H.D. Suringar *Erasmus over nederlandsche spreekwoorden ...* (Utrecht 1873)
Tilley	M.P. Tilley *Dictionary of Proverbs in English in the Sixteenth and Seventeenth Centuries* (Ann Arbor, Michigan 1950)

The name 'Suidas' has been retained for the great Byzantine lexicon, now known to be properly called 'the Suda' (ed A. Adler, Leipzig 1928–38), since Erasmus supposed Suidas to be the compiler's name.

TABLE OF ADAGES

This book

was designed by

ANTJE LINGNER

based on the series design by

ALLAN FLEMING

and was printed by

University

of Toronto

Press